P9-EDE-799

—

The Science of Economic Development and Growth

The Science of Economic Development and Growth

The Theory of Factor Proportions

Clement C. Onyemelukwe

M.E. Sharpe
Armonk, New York
London, England

Library of Congress Cataloging-in-Publication Data

Onyemelukwe, C. C. (Clement Chukwukadibia)
 The science of economic development : the theory of factor proportions / Clement C.
Onyemelukwe.
  p. cm.
 Includes bibliographical references and index.
 ISBN 0-7656-0604-6 (hc. : alk. paper)
  1. Economic development. 2. International economic relations. 3. Factor proportions—
Developing countries. I. Title.

HD75 .O596 2002
338.9—dc21   2001054677

Printed in the United States of America

To my wife Catherine on our 40th wedding anniversary

Contents

List of Tables and Figures

Preface

This book has been long coming. I have experienced a gradual but dramatic change in my economic beliefs over the past forty-four years. I graduated as an electrical/mechanical engineer from the University of Leeds in the United Kingdom in 1956. Shortly after, I obtained a degree in economics from London University. I also qualified as a member of the prestigious British Institute of Management and other specialist international professional institutions. After working in the electricity industry in the United Kingdom, I became the first Nigerian chief electrical engineer of the then Electricity Corporation of Nigeria in 1961, a position I took over from the British chief electrical engineer following Nigeria's independence from Britain in 1960. In my new position, I immediately became intimately involved with development projects, as many of these involved the provision and supply of electricity. I also managed a staff of over 10,000 throughout the country.

As an engineer and economist, I was well equipped to write my first book, *Industrial Planning and Management in Nigeria*, in 1966. In its prescriptions for what was needed to develop a Third World country like Nigeria, the book was very much like many books in development in circulation today, espousing conventional concepts like the need to embrace globalization, build infrastructure, promote international trade, attract foreign investment, establish good governance, and so on.

As time went on, I began to feel disillusioned with the management content of my book. I soon realized that I was not getting the results I expected even though I was employing the best of Western management practices and theories. Following further research conducted with my wife in twenty-four businesses in Nigeria, I revised my views on management in the next book I published in 1973, *Men and Management in Contemporary Africa*. In the book, I concluded that management is culturally dependent, and that the Western-style management I had learned at the British Institute of Management was not in itself adequate in a non-Western culture such as Nigeria.

My disillusionment also turned on the conventional development economics I espoused in my 1966 book. It soon became clear to me that despite the foreign investment that was at the time flowing into Nigeria, and the buoyant trade in Nigerian exports of cocoa, groundnut, palm oil, and petroleum, and the successful building of new infrastructure in which I had executive responsibilities—there was a growing wealth gap, a population drift to urban areas, growing urban slums, and consequent denuding of what were previously stable rural areas. I noticed that small craft and "native" industrial activities in the country began to disappear in the face of new imports. These adverse economic trends have gained momentum ever since. My disillusionment crystallized in my 1974 book, *Underdevelopment: An Inside View,* which repudiates much of the conventional development economics in my 1966 book. The 1974 book, as its title implies, was based on an inside view of underdevelopment by a local resident researching and learning, not the typical Western outsider visiting the Third World believing that he or she already knows the answers to problems of underdevelopment.

In 1976, I moved back to the United Kingdom where I set up the company, Colechurch International Ltd., which later also became a U.S. company. I now live in the United States with my American wife. Colechurch International Ltd. is a successful international project management company. Since 1976, I have therefore focused my profession as an engineer and an economist on the practical assessment and management of "development" projects of all types, both in the advanced economies and in Third World countries.

My resultant research and studies expanded my disillusionment with the whole field of conventional economics. Advanced economies have problems that have defied conventional economic solutions: the environment, waste inflation, job creation, economic cycles, and economic inequalities are only a few. To date, there is not a single Third World country that has achieved sustainable economic growth despite almost half a century of World Bank/IMF governance. On the global level, the gap between poor and rich countries is not shrinking. It is not static. It is increasing almost by the hour. Contrary to what some would claim, world poverty is on the rise. A global economy has been proposed as the instrument to spread growth to poor countries. Our detailed analysis shows that the economic theories on which a global economy is justified cannot provide poor countries the economic growth they need. These economic failures are adding to a world that is increasingly unstable and insecure and are putting the fate of millions of poor people into heightened jeopardy.

Controversy, not often disciplined, is the stock in trade of conventional economics in which protagonists, at will, pull in psychology, sociology, politics, advanced mathematics, and even common sense to win a point. Ironically, it is this controversy that adds to the influence of conventional economics. Economics dominates political debate such that it is scarcely possible to have a serious political career in most countries of the world without the ability to espouse an aspect of the controversy with some flair. Politics provides excitement because each side in the political debate has its ardent supporting economists. To its true believers within the profession and among policymakers in most parts of the world, the ability of conventional economics to understand the world and its problems has never been greater. Conventional economics is not about to die, as one author claimed in the late nineties. I liken conventional economics, instead, to the emperor without clothes.

As I studied the structural economic problems of advanced economies over the years after I left Nigeria, it began to occur to me, as a scientist, that many of the concepts I evolved in my 1974 book on underdevelopment also applied to advanced economies. I discovered that there was a structural science linking all economies.

Many conventional economists like to claim that conventional economics is a science. Over the years, there have been real attempts to justify this claim. For example, there has been great, but unsuccessful, effort to achieve mathematical precision of economics so that it will enjoy the status and prestige of science. The claim that conventional economics is a science is no different from the claim of students of politics that they are studying political science. The fact that a researcher uses scientific methods to study a subject does not make the subject a science.

Conventional economic concepts and theories are essentially intellectual reconstructions and interpretations of what their proponents have observed. The problem is that what is observed differs from place to place and differs with time. Theoretical models were intended to ensure that economics was firmly rooted in reality. But not all reality is economically desirable. Empiricism can only have validity if it has a sound enveloping scientific economic theory to back it, which conventional economics lacks.

Conventional economics is focused on money and finance at a time when the world is increasingly being shaped by science and technology. The focus on money and finance is important in everyday economic life as the medium of exchange and storage of value. Prices are assigned to goods, materials, capital and labor to facilitate this exchange and storage. But value itself has no physical existence. Value is in our imagination. It is not science. Therefore conventional economics cannot be science because science deals only with real things (materials, capital equipment and labor) which themselves drive economic activity. It is the real things that give rise to values. One cannot "create" science from something that is not "of" science. Composed of intellectual, but nonetheless non-scientific concepts, conventional economics contains many contradictions and ambiguities as will be evident in the chapters that follow. Because conventional economics is not rooted in science and technology, it has no tools with which to evaluate new science and changing technology. It often reaches wrong conclusions when confronted with new technologies and at other times it cannot explain them, as will be particularly evident in the chapter "New Economy: The Third Industrial Divide."

The fact that there are many unsolved economic development and growth problems facing both the advanced and non-advanced countries and the world at large should make the most ardent conventional economist ask the questions, for the sake of a safer and more stable world: Suppose we are wrong? Are there alternative solutions? I believe that this book at least provides new insight. The theory of factor proportions, proposed here, is a new economic formulation for ensuring the sustainable economic development and growth of all economies. Its adoption will bring far-reaching changes in the way national and international affairs are conducted. Even though the theory is new, it is simple and easy to understand. It gives a new meaning to balanced growth, whose definition has so far eluded conventional economists.

In conclusion, I wish to acknowledge the cooperation and support of my wife, Catherine, in what is, in effect, the result of over forty years of research. She still does not agree with everything I have said in this book!

Clement Onyemelukwe

The Science of Economic Development and Growth

1

Taking Stock

Robert Berg, chairman of the International Development Conference (a coalition of leaders of 125 U.S. associations and organizations concerned with U.S.–Third World development policy—the largest and oldest forum on development in the United States) declared at a private lecture in March 1999 that economic development was suffering a clinical depression. He should have said that economic development was clinically dead but on life support.

The 1998 edition of the UN publication *World Economic and Social Survey* makes sober reading. It concludes that "it is no longer clear that all the conventional [economic] growth policy measures and prescriptions remain valid" because "the world economy seemed to be on the cusp of a transition that was neither sought nor foreseen."[1] This is a very serious indictment of economists and policy makers, for it is they who are responsible for a seeming failure of economic theory and practice.

After more than fifty years of economic development programs in developing countries, poverty is still very much with us. The gap between rich and poor nations has widened. Over 23 billion people earn less than $1 a day. Africa, for example, with a population in 1990 of about 500 million (a figure that is expected to double by 2010 and reach 2.8 billion by 2150) had an economic growth rate less than its rate of population increase, which means that living standards are falling. A rate of growth of output that raises per capita GDP by 3 percent a year in developing countries can be considered the absolute minimum needed over a sustained period to achieve even moderate levels of income per capita. According to the *World Economic and Social Survey,* only thirty-five countries managed this growth rate in 1997. Africa and Western Asia averaged 1.7 and 2.6 percent, respectively.[2]

In Latin America and the Caribbean, the prospects for sustained economic development are no better. In a 1996 World Bank paper titled "Dismantling the Populist State—The Unfinished Revolution in Latin America and the Caribbean," S. J. Burke and Sebastian Edwards (then respectively the World Bank's regional vice president for Latin America and the Caribbean and the Henry Ford II chair in international management at the University of California, Los Angeles) stated that although Latin America overcame the most pessimistic post-Mexican-crisis forecasts, "economic growth [i.e., for the region] was too anemic to prevent poverty from increasing. . . . An increasing number of people [in the region] are disillusioned and beginning to look at alternative policies." They were of the view that disenchantment with economic performance was slowly generating "reform skepticism," with a concomitant danger of antireform activism.[3] After a brief decline in the late 1970s, the number of poor have increased steadily in the region since 1975; in 1996 approximately 165 million people in the region lived in poverty, and the figure is still rising.

As if this were not bad enough, 1997 witnessed the economic collapse of several East Asian newly industrializing countries (NICs), after decades of stunning growth rates. The bursting of this huge economic bubble returned millions of people to near destitution and poverty. The Asian "tigers" had been regarded by many economists as evidence that economic development strategies in developing countries can work. The World Bank and IMF lavished praise on these countries. There was no shortage of books and publications that have sought to provide theoretical and empirical reasons why the Asian tigers succeeded. But now the economists who endorsed the original strategies have sought to make everyone else, including fund investors, leaders of the Asian countries, and the countries' institutions, the scapegoat.

On the heels of the Asian debacle, the international financial system nearly collapsed in October 1998. President Clinton at the time described the situation as the greatest economic crisis the world had witnessed in fifty years. It was the third major currency crisis in five years. According to the *World Economic and Social Survey,* the 1998 crisis showed that a major international financial market could fail in a major way. Yet just a year before this crisis, there was not only official optimism about the prospects of world growth but also a high degree of official confidence that the globalization-fostering economic policies of the preceding decade were beginning to have a positive effect.

The failure of development efforts in the developing countries, the East Asian crisis, and the economic problems in Latin America—all of which basically were the result of attempts by economists to reproduce the success of the so-called advanced economies, along with the 1998 currency crisis— are worrying because it means that economists do not have a full understanding of the basic processes through which the present advanced economies got to where they are.

Economic development, as a field of study (sometimes called development economics), is concerned with the problems, processes, and policies in poor countries (sometimes called underdeveloped, developing, or Third World countries) in connection with their possible transition into developed economies. There has been a tendency to regard development economics as a distinct field of economics. Srinivasan has, for example, stated that "as long as there are countries that have not made the transition to the status of developed countries, development economics will continue to exist."[4] Some universities have created subdivisions in their economics departments specializing in development economics.[5]

There is a degree of uncertainty among economists as to what the relationship between development economics and the economics of advanced economies should be. Meier said of this relationship, "Although it cannot be gainsaid that the problems of underdevelopment are different in degree . . . and to some extent in kind . . . from those encountered in developed countries, nevertheless, it would be overreaching to conclude that entirely different tools and principles are needed to analyze these problems." He asserted that progress made in development economics has been within "the framework of traditional economic analysis."[6] On the other hand, Myint claimed that early development economists believed that a great deal of existing Western economic theory was so "bound up with the special conditions of problems and preconceptions of industrially advanced countries that large portions of it have to be abandoned before we can come to grips with the problems of underdeveloped countries." Myint preferred to "improve the applicability of existing theory to underdeveloped countries."[7] Neither is particularly clear what the relationship between development economics and the economics of advanced economies should be. The issue of which tools to use in analyzing an underdeveloped economy as distinct from an advanced economy becomes important only after we are clear what the relationship between the two types of economics should be.

The closest analogy to the relationship between a developing economy and an advanced economy involves the development of a human being. A human is conceived in the womb as an undeveloped being, is born, and grows to an advanced age. At each stage we are dealing with the same individual, with the same basic personality, if you will. One cannot fully understand the outward features of this individual without understanding the process of conception and growth process.

It is clear, therefore, that those who treat development economics as separate from the study of advanced economies are wrong. Growth theory has unfortunately been seen as dealing more with advanced economies and has been faulted because it does not address "origins." Growth from a state of underdevelopment to advanced development is one process. Economic development theory and growth theory therefore are different names for the same process, which encompasses both the maturation of poor economies and the challenges that face advanced economies. Economic development can be understood only as part of a comprehensive growth theory, and there is no separate economics of underdevelopment.

The basic idea of the continuity of the economic development/growth process is the essence of Rostow's stages of development in his book *Stages of Economic Growth.* In this historical analysis, Rostow concluded that "it is possible to identify all societies, in their economic dimensions, as lying within one of five stages." He said that "these stages have an inner logic and continuity. . . . They constitute, in the end, both a theory of economic growth and a more general, if still highly partial, theory about modern history as a whole."[8]

Barro and Sala-i-Martin have observed that growth theory "died as an active research field by the early 70s" and that "the fields of economic development and economic growth have [since] drifted apart and the two areas became almost separated."[9] This separation is precisely why much that has gone on under the rubric "economic development theory" is defective.

The weaknesses in existing development theory and growth theory have their origins in earlier times. Krugman observed that "once upon a time there was a field called development economics . . . [which] attracted creative minds and was marked by a great deal of intellectual excitement. . . . [T]hat field no longer exists." Krugman concluded that "between 1960 and 1980 high development theory was virtually buried, essentially because the founders of development economics failed to make their points with sufficient analytical clarity to communicate their essence to other economists, perhaps even to each other. Only recently have theorists in economics made it possible to reconsider what the development theories said, and to regain the valuable ideas that have been lost."[10]

The same pessimism about the state of development theory is highlighted in a 1996 book aptly titled *The Rise and Fall of Development Theory,* by Colin Leys (a man who has been intimately involved in development theory for over three decades).[11] Leys is of the opinion that development theory is now at an impasse. According to him, development theory basically held that governments of underdeveloped countries could initiate and implement economic plans in order to catch up with advanced countries, but recent changes toward globalization of the world economy, in which capital can flow where it wants, have curtailed the ability of these governments to manage their economies and tackle poverty. As early as the end of the 1950s, Leys says, "the original optimism that this approach [development theory] would yield rapid results had begun to evaporate and the limitations of development economics as a theory of development were beginning to be exposed."[12]

Given the widespread disenchantment with development theory, some people have advocated the abandonment of the concept of development. Others have denounced the idea of development as a Western concept meant to impose Western ideas of progress on others as ideologies of social control dressed up as a doctrine of improvement. As Leys writes, "The thinking seems to be to stop wanting development," and we should rather "devote ourselves to deconstructing the meaning buried in its subtexts, and expose the masculinist, linear, repressive project hidden beneath its surface."[13] There has been a turn away generally from what often have been called "grand narratives." This has left the field of development studies at something of an impasse.[14]

Others have been so taken by the diversity among poor countries that they are sure successful economic strategies cannot be the same in different countries. Todaro concluded, for example, that "economic policies will naturally be different for countries with large public sectors and ones with sizable private sectors. In economies dominated by the public sector, direct government investments and large rural works programs will take precedence whereas in private-oriented economies, special tax allowances designed to induce private businesses to employ more workers might be more common."[15] Griffin stated, "It is clear that there are many paths to development although some no doubt are more circuitous than others." "Enough time," he claims, "has elapsed and enough data are available to make it possible to test the strength and limitations of most widely advocated strategies of economic development against actual practice." He identified and discussed in some great detail what he called six broad strategies of economic development.[16]

Works such as Griffin's have encouraged empirical studies in development economics. In 1991 Booth declared that empirical research had begun to show potential for fresh theoretical initiative and allowed theory to be sensitive to the great diversity of situations in the Third World. He was of the view that empirical work is more relevant than general theory to the concerns of people engaged in practical development work.[17] However, it was a mistake for Griffin, Booth, and other economists like them to regard empirical work as a substitute for general development theory. Empirical studies need a general theory to inform them.

In the remainder of the chapter we will discuss postwar trends in development theory, which can be grouped broadly into five categories: the positivist orthodoxy of the 1940s and 1950s (Harrod, Domar, Lewis, Rosenstein-Rodan, Nurske, Hirschmann, etc.), the modernization/rational choice schools of the 1960s and 1970s (Apter, Huntington, Almond, North, etc.), the dependency school of the early 1970s (Frank, Cardoso, Sunkel, Beckman, etc.), the neoliberal school of the 1980s (Bauer, Belassa, Little, etc.), and the endogenous growth theory of the 1990s (still in vogue).[18]

Much of the poor circumstances of present-day Third World countries and their present relationship with the industrialized nations today are due to these theories. We will show in what ways they are deficient and demonstrate that none of them is based on scientific reasoning. In particular, we will show that the lack of progress in economic development theory is not due just to globalization, as Leys claims; that these theories derive either from assumptions that are not backed up or from reasons that are not economic, and in some cases the theorists were simply reacting to prevailing economic problems of the time; that there has been a rush to adopt quick-fix solutions, in which theorists seek to reproduce outwardly observable features of advanced economies in poor countries; and that although earlier theories may seem to be discarded in favor of newer ones, in fact basic concepts are often recycled and presented as new ideas. So one is compelled to conclude, despite appearances to the contrary, that not much has really changed in the theorizing on growth and development. It is hoped that the following review of these theories will set out the theoretical challenges facing us in the next chapters.

Positivist Orthodoxy

Lewis's 1954 seminal article on the labor surplus economy in poor countries was aimed at the goal of raising rural productivity and transferring underutilized labor out of agriculture into industry.[19] Economists had noted that as development proceeded over the decades, employment in agriculture tended to decline while employment in industry rose. Development economists used this empirical observation to support the Lewis strategy even in the short run.[20]

Lewis's approach was reinforced by two observations about agriculture: that productivity is substantially lower in agriculture than in industry,[21] and that agriculture provided fewer linkages to other sectors than industry.[22] So the shift of workers to industry, along with increased capital investment, was supposed to provide a big boost to overall growth. This kind of thinking encouraged planners who wanted to quicken the pace at which resources were moved from agriculture to industry—a justification for government intervention and leadership.

Lewis was writing at a time when a number of factors were at work. The roots of market pessimism go back to the immediate postwar period. The Depression had destroyed confidence in market capitalism. Keynesianism was a growing force in economics during this period, and it too suggested government intervention to maintain strong economies. The Marshall Plan and the recovery of Europe following the war required reconstruction planning by the recipient governments. At the time, the example of the Soviet Union's industrialization under communism added to the appeal of planned economies. All in all, the era produced a growing impatience with the traditional gradual, almost unplanned approach that characterized the early development of Europe. To the group of economists active in this period, a frontal attack on development was required.

There were, naturally, differences among the contributing economists about how this attack could be launched. The basic contention was the same, namely, that development is a series of discontinuous jumps. It is as if the functional relationships among the causal factors in economic development are full of "lumps" or discontinuities, and so an initial effort or big "push" was required to overcome this inertia and start the development process. In his presentation of these views, Rosenstein-Rodan argued that there were three kinds of "indivisibilities" in development process—indivisibility in the production function, lumpiness of capital (for example, one cannot operate half a railway track), indivisibility of demand, and indivisibility in the supply of savings. For each of these indivisibilities, there is a minimum level of activity required to operate the system.[23] Nurske later emphasized the second indivisibility, pointing out that any investment is risky when other kinds of investments are not available to provide the required complement.[24] Similar ideas were also put forward by Leibenstein, who made an attempt to estimate the critical minimum effort required by calculating an incremental cost-output ratio (ICOR) of between 3:1 and 5:1.[25] Nelson, using the same concept of minimum effort, argued that an economy can be indefinitely "trapped" at a low level of income.[26] Nurske was to add his own voice by specifying in great detail how the big push was to be carried out. He remarked, "Most industries catering for mass production are complementary in the cause that they provide a market." For any individual entrepreneur, he maintained, the investment of capital in underdeveloped countries is inhibited by the extensive risk arising from the small size of the market. He added that any solution to this vicious circle has to be found at a level higher than that of the individual investor.[27] A strategy of more or less synchronized application of capital to a wide range of complementary industries should be initiated, providing a big boost to the development process.

Opponents of a balanced pattern attacked it on several fronts. Singer argued that if the concept of a big push is extended to agriculture, then the notion of balanced growth, if accepted, sounds like orthodox economic theory that "structural changes must rest on a foundation of raising productivity within the existing structure . . . until incomes have risen to a level which justifies structural change."[28] Singer argued that the resources required to pursue a policy of investment in both industry and agriculture are of such an order of magnitude that a country disposing of such resources would in fact not be underdeveloped. Enke added that "the balanced growth doctrine would involve the superimposition of a modern public sector upon a private subsistence economy with almost no exchange between them and hence little penetration of the substance economy by the market economy."[29]

These views were considerably reinforced by Hirschmann, who contended that a policy of deliberate unbalancing of the economy in accordance with some predetermined strategy was the best approach to economic development of poor countries. In his view, if the economy is to be kept moving ahead, the task of development policy is to maintain tensions, disproportions, and disequilibria, as chronic imbalances set up "incentives and pressures" that increase the rate of growth.[30] Hirschmann's views seem to have carried the day, with the result that the first phase of development in most underdeveloped countries has been marked by large public investments in roads, electricity, communication, and health (social overhead capital), which Hirschmann argued will set up imbalances that act as an incentive to industry and other productive investments. Hirschmann favored the establishment of industries in cities (rather than in smaller towns, to economize on outlay of capital) because it compels additional or complementary capital formation. He opposed a policy of establishing small industries outside cities because "it economizes on capital formation rather than on capital."[31]

Schultz completed the picture when he sought to reverse Lewis's image of agriculture as a traditional, stagnant industry.[32] He demonstrated that farmers were rational decision makers who, over years of experimentation, weighed economic costs and benefits to evolve an efficient farming system, given resource constraints and risks of crop failure. If farmers had evolved efficient techniques, then new technology, he believed, was essential to increase agricultural productivity.

The proponents of positivist orthodoxy had no scientific basis for their theories. A cornerstone of their theories is that capital is the main springboard of economic development. This is an assumption with no scientific foundation. From this assumption, some of them treated the issue of economic development as one of balance versus imbalance, as if it were just a matter of whether capital investment was to be made either in an "ordered" form or in a "planned disordered" form.

If one were to question the advocates of positivist orthodoxy as to why they prescribed capital and capital formation as the best approach to rapid development in poor countries, they would probably say that it is because the industrialized societies got where they are through capital formation and continue to forge further growth in the same way. They mistakenly believed that, as Myint put it, poverty in underdeveloped countries was "bound up with the special conditions and preconceptions of industrially advanced countries." Myint was of the view that large portions of such a belief have to be abandoned before "we can come to grips with the problems of the underdeveloped countries."[33]

The positivist orthodoxists, in effect, fell into the trap of concentrating on the outward, visible difference between the underdeveloped economy and an industrialized economy—lack of capital facilities and so on—and thinking that the answer to poverty was to introduce capital formation as soon as possible. The economists were confusing effects with causes. Unfortunately, the assumption that capital accumulation is the seed of economic development continues to be recycled and has become the foundation of latter theories.

As late as 1994, the World Bank stated in its World Development Report for that year that "infrastructure represents, if not the engine, then the wheels of economic activity"—a script that could have suited Hirschmann very well.[34] In the period 1975 to 1990 developing countries invested the staggering sum of $200 billion a year in infrastructure (what Hirschmann would call social overhead capital). In their standard text, *Economics*, Paul Samuelson and William Nordhaus declared, "In many developing countries, the single most pressing problem is too little saving. . . . The result is often too little investment in the productive capital so necessary for rapid development."[35]

As noted, proponents of positivist orthodoxy often cite a positive historical correlation between growth and capital formation. But, as we shall see, this correlation is not always there; history does not vindicate the claim that industrialization was triggered by capital formation.

Coman in *Industrial History of the United States* estimated that per capita income in the United States increased from $780 in 1876 to $1,235 in 1900. In the United States, she stated, concentration of capital in the hands of successful entrepreneurs had been a significant tendency only since the 1930s. In 1890, she estimated, there were only about 4,000 millionaires and multimillionaires in the nation. "The equalizing influence of the pioneer period in the U.S. passed around 1900 by which time the massing of capital and concentration of industry consequent on the introduction of machinery was evident."[36]

In regard to Europe, Landes in his *Wealth and Poverty of Nations* said of the industrial revolution: "In the eighteenth century, a series of inventions transformed the British cotton manufacture and gave

birth to a new mode of production—the factory system. At the same time, other branches of industry made comparable and often related advances and altogether, mutually reinforcing, drive further gains on an ever-widening front."[37] Unfortunately, this type of description can give the impression that industrialization in Europe started with the industrial revolution. Heaton has correctly stated that "the industrial innovations of the 18th century did not come suddenly out of a clear sky."[38] There was instead before the eighteenth century a buildup of industrial capacity and know-how (a theme that will be taken up in later chapters) through small activities.[39] As Heaton put it, "The great majority of industrial workers [up to about 1750] laboured in their homes, in town cellars or garrets or in village cottages."[40] Science was already at work making some of the initial discoveries that were later to be further exploited in the eighteenth century. In regard to capital accumulation, Heaton observed that the accumulation of spare funds in the pockets of the middle class, the rich, and insurance companies was a development of the nineteenth century that was accompanied by the growth of the vast capital market.

Daunton observed that the level of capital accumulation in Britain did not rise significantly until after the railway age. Up till then, industrialization required only low investment.[41] Nef reached a similar conclusion. He traced the process of industrialization in Britain back to the sixteenth century and concluded that "as for capital formation, the sense that emerged was that it was not until capital hungry railways after 1830 that the rate rose to the level asserted by Rostow."[42]

If capital accumulation had the importance that positivist orthodoxy economists ascribe to it, Spain and Portugal should have led the industrial growth that marked eighteenth-century Europe. Landes remarked that "Spain . . . became (or stayed) poor because it had too much money. The nations [of Europe] that did the work, learned and kept good habits, while seeking new ways to do the jobs faster and better. . . . By the time the great bullion inflow ended in the mid 17th century, the Spanish crown was deep in debt."[43]

It seems, therefore, that any claim that the early economic growth of the United States or Europe was rooted in capital accumulation is misleading. Gerschenkron has correctly concluded that "most economists of an empirical or historical bent have argued all along that capital formation is at best only a part of the growth story and probably not the most important, particularly for developing countries."[44] After sitting around watching as the top role of capital was beginning to be challenged, the World Bank in 1991 concluded that intangible investment in knowledge accumulation was decisive for development, rather than physical investment, "as was once believed." This theme was to be later reinforced in the 1990s, as for example when the *World Development Report 1998/99* said that knowledge had become the most important factor determining the standard of living.[45]

The Modernization and Rational-Choice Schools

Few theories in development economics remain unchallenged for long, either by events or by other new theories. The modernization and rational-choice schools had one thing in common: They were the first attempts to introduce noneconomic factors into development theory. They were a reaction and answer to the question why positivist orthodoxy did not work in poor societies. Instead of seeking economic answers, sociologists and political scientists came up with the idea that the problem of underdevelopment arose not from capital but from unfavorable social and cultural factors.[46] They argue that in the transition from traditional to modern forms of social organization (as had already occurred in the industrialized West), the necessary interrelation-

ship between economic factors and politics and social factors work to promote economic development. Apter represented this as a three-dimensional matrix of norms (values and interests), structures (roles, role networks, and classes) and behaviors (motivation and perception), and believed that these interactions could be studied with some precision using structural-functional analysis.[47] The three constitute a system in which a change in one will result in changes in the others.[48]

Modernization theory was in essence an American response at the time when the U.S. government was beginning to fund research as part of its international policy agenda. The result is that many of the exponents of the theory were closely connected with the American State Department.[49] Hobsbawm has declared that in framing modernization strategy, it was widely supposed in the United States that it was the business of Americans to reconstruct the world in its own image. The theory equated (1) the interests of the United States, (2) the functioning of liberal market economies, (3) resistance to communism, and (4) the future prosperity of the world.[50] Here were the origins of the United States' need to spread the theme of democracy in new countries and to make this theme part of an economic development package.

A later development of modernization theory focused attention on what to do to raise the capitalist class in poor countries, inspired in a way by the influence of Max Weber. Some modernization theorists were concerned with what they regarded as the persistence of precapitalist social and cultural practices in the poor countries.

The reasoning went as follows: Development must involve the accumulation of capital. In any developing society, someone must see to it that production is organized so as to yield the necessary surplus and to see to it also that surplus is set aside and invested. In capitalist societies this task is undertaken by capitalists supported in varying degrees by the state. It is therefore argued that for development to occur there must be local capitalists in the underdeveloped countries.

Modernization theory has therefore regarded it as crucial that we understand what determines the relative strengths and weaknesses of each underdeveloped country's domestic capitalist class. Kennedy, discussing the African situation, was of the view that the prospects for encouraging African capitalists were good despite what may appear to be factors against this development.[51] Specifically, traditional society is supposed to be nonindividualistic, particularistic (instead of universalistic), role-diffused (instead of role-specific), otherworldly, and emphasizing age and birth (not achievement or ability). These attributes are supposed to negate initiative and problem-solving attitudes in those societies.

Kennedy gave many suggestions that he thought should guide further research on how to develop the African capitalist class. In addition, proponents of modernization theory thought that what was required in underdeveloped societies was a greater number of candidates to play the elite roles necessary to enable a capitalist economy to develop. They felt that the traditional system in these societies inhibited the emergence of these elites.[52] McClelland even developed the thesis that the level of "achievement orientation" in any culture can be scientifically measured and could be accelerated by inculcating businesspeople with the "achievement factor" that may be missing in their culture.[53] (Indeed, the United States sponsored training programs based on McClelland's concepts.) Other people have explored the ways in which societies undergoing change resisted the application or absorption of capitalist rationality[54]—the kind of studies that Leys claimed were very much akin to the World Bank's attempted recycling of the same theme in the late 1980s.

Very much in tune with modernization theory was rational-choice, which was another reaction to the apparent failure of development theory. Rational-choice theory sought to explain the failure in terms of institutions in the society. The central theme of rational-choice theory, which is a kind of political economy, was that an efficient economy requires a set of institutions that will benefit the individuals in the society in such a way as to encourage them to do those things that serve the material interest of the total society. Hinged on this is the belief of rational-choice theorists that the institutions in any society are the underlying determinant of the long-run performance of its economy.[55]

This rational-choice-based kind of political economy was applied by Bates, a political scientist, in his analysis of the crisis in African agriculture.[56] In 1981 the Nobel-prize-winning economic historian North argued that this "new institutionalism" raised the possibility that a general theory of development could cover the span from early times to the present.[57] The World Bank drew much of its micro policy in the late 1980s and early 1990s from the work of a network of new institutionalists.[58]

The underlying belief of the exponents of modernization and rational choice is that by changing the sociocultural and political framework of societies, the route to economic development can be cleared. This belief is in part supported by the fact that human experience all over the world seems to be converging and not diverging.[59] European culture's promise of material success seems seductive and compelling. The Western ideas of progress as limitless material improvement, of the right of each individual to assert himself, and of nationalism as the proper basis for political organization have all produced consequences going far beyond what was expected by those in the West who so confidently passed on to others the recipes that they believed underlay their own success. The introduction of new machines, railways, mines, computers, banks, newspapers, and much else has transformed social (and political) life in other cultures in ways no one willed or envisaged.[60]

The error comes when Western political and social scientists think that they can control these processes and that they can devise theories on how to change other societies to meet prescribed modernization and rational-choice standards. They fall prey to what Landes called "self congratulatory analysis."[61] The well-known anthropologist Margaret Mead stressed diversity as the basis of nature's sociocultural matrix; what may, for example, seem to be a wholesale adoption of the Western sociocultural matrix may in fact be so only in form, not in spirit. Conscious rejection of some elements in a foreign sociocultural package and the inertia of well-established cultural patterns explain why modernizing change is sometimes superficial. At times, there is organic, selective absorption from an incoming culture, resulting in something new that is neither the pure old culture nor the pure new culture. Hence Tu notes in his book *Confucian Ethics Today* that in East Asian countries, traditional Confucian ethics have been combined with and modified by Western ethics to form what he called "New Confucian ethics."[62] Christopher Lingle, who lived in Singapore for many years, concluded that he did not see why clashes of civilization need be played out along cultural rather than economic or political lines. He was of the view that what will increasingly emerge is a competitive process whereby individuals choose parts or entire aspects of various culture arrangements from a global menu.[63]

Modernization and rational-choice theories in general are earnest attempts to explain the economic dominance of the West and how to install the systems in other societies in order that they can achieve economic development. Huntington, who played a key role in initiating what could be termed "new" modernization theory in the late 1960s and early 1970s, seemed to have changed course in 1993, when he predicted that the international economic order of the twenty-first century will feature a "clash of civilizations" and various forms of cultural

protectionism.[64] More specifically, his view is that at least three (and as many as seven or eight) great civilizations are likely to become embroiled in a troubling and unstable struggle for dominance. It seems that as each civilization achieves economic success, it will claim its values are responsible for that success. Patten had this to say about the success of the East Asians at its height when it was being confidently forecast that the Asian economies will overtake the West in about the year 2010: "Economic success, the applause of international financiers, the headlines in business magazines, the soaring stock markets, the visiting dignitaries—all encouraged a growing confidence in Asia, and in some countries [i.e., in East Asia] a feistiness, even a cockiness, about their commendable record of achievement. They had put up with being patronized and pushed around by Westerners for long enough. Now it was time for Americans and Europeans to listen."[65]

One unanswered central question still remains: whether the transition from traditional to modern society in whatever context is the cause or effect of economic development. We know, for example, that the introduction of the steam engine radically changed habits and attitudes. So has the arrival of electricity and the computer. These technologies have affected entire economic systems and have led to far-reaching changes in social factors. For example, one cannot speak of a society as "modern" if it does not have widespread access to electricity. With this matrix of cause and effect, it seems risky to assume that "modern" principles of social organization are the prerequisite for economic development. Instead, in the economic explanation of culture, favored by Karl Marx, culture is regarded as superstructural and having a derivative relationship to economic development. The economy is said to set the conditions for culture, and when economy changes, culture changes to accommodate it.

It is also not clear whether democracy is the cause or effect of economic development. Democracy as we know it thrives with the emergence of a middle class. Yet it is economic development that to date has produced a middle class.

Democracy in Western societies is rooted in individualism. Landes has declared that nations can reconcile social purpose with individual aspirations and initiatives and enhance performance through their collective synergy.[66] Contrast this well-established Western view of the relationship between the state and the individual with the example of Japan, the world's second-largest economy, where individual initiative is discouraged. It is incontrovertible that this group approach served Japan well in its emergence as a world economic power; whether these particularly Japanese values will be eroded as Japan faces a more difficult future may all be part of the possible convergence of experience referred to earlier.

How does one evaluate these views? First, the general view of traditional societies held by modernization theorists is wrong. Traditional societies in Africa, for example, exhibit wide differences. Whereas some traditional societies, such as among the Ibos in Nigeria, were highly egalitarian, others, such as among the Yorubas, were hierarchical. In both these societies, however, the prestige of a man rests on how many cattle he has and how big his barn is at the end of the harvesting season. Indeed, he might acquire a title because of his bravery and wealth.

The assumption that no traditional societies possess technological skills is not true. The explorer Georg Schweinfurth in the late nineteenth century trekked from what now is northeast Congo to Sudan and was reported to have been amazed at the sophistication of the Mangbetu court there. According to him, Mangbetu King Munza kept a huge retinue of craftsmen employed in carving furniture, producing weapons, and creating ornaments of ivory and copper. The kingdom of Benin became known for bronzes produced with the lost-wax method of casting after King Oba invited a Yoruba smith from Ife to teach his trade there; this technique is known to have originated in the Middle East and was brought to Africa through trans-Sahara trade. With the decline of the Benin empire (invaded and defeated by the British), increasing quantities of European brass and copper were brought to coastal West Africa and were traded further inland. In effect, the colonizing power destroyed the basis of that region's industrial beginning.

To take another example, in the seventeenth century, according to Landes, "India produced the world's finest cotton yarns and textile, and the English were quick to seize the opportunity."[67] Cotton was, according to Landes, a commodity of such broad and elastic demand that it drove the industrial revolution in England. As Kennedy noted, "Because the Indian states had been unable to resist Britain's East India Company military, their subjects could do little when British machine-made textiles—not only cheaper but of better quality than native cloth—poured into the country, driving out traditional domestic producers in the process."[68] Kennedy went on:

> The awful result, according to one calculation, was that whereas the British and Indian peoples had roughly similar per capita levels of industrialization at the onset of Industrial Revolution (1750), India's level was only one-hundredth of the United Kingdom by 1900. India imported one million yards of cotton fabric in 1814 but the figure had risen to 51 million yards by 1830 and a staggering 995 million yards by 1870. A textile exhibition in the History Museum in 1988 in London brought into display samples of native West African textiles with African colors and imprinted images sent to England by English traders in West Africa to be copied and machine produced in the U.K. and exported back to West Africa at cheaper prices and of higher quality than indigenous industrial hand-woven equivalents. The colonial powers in West Africa banned the production of

fire arms, "beer" production, and related technology on the false premise that such activities threatened security and order.[69]

As yet another example, Kennedy pointed out that centuries before the Reformation, Islam led the world in mathematics, cartography, medicine, and many other aspects of science and industry, and the Islamic world contained libraries, universities, and observatories when Japan and America possessed none and Europe only a few.

It is therefore possible to understand what Latouche meant when he said that "Westernization is nothing more than a cultural cladding for industrialization. Westernization of the Third World is first and foremost a deculturalization; that is purely and simply the destruction of all traditional structures economic, social and mental."[70]

Another factor is the slave trade. Traditional societies in Africa affected by the slave trade suffered serious dislocation, as it disrupted their social, cultural, and political fabric. Speaking of its effects in the Congo, for example, Ihle in 1929 said, "Gradually the last social links were broken and the whole [economic and social] structure utterly destroyed."[71] Landes has commented that most writers—and we presume economists as well—prefer to say nothing on the subject of slavery.[72] This means that we pass over the effects of slavery and the slave trade on societies around the world. In fact, societies accumulate knowledge and pass it on to coming generations. When the social fabric of a society is disrupted by external causes such as war, colonization, or slave trade, accumulated knowledge, whether of art or technology, is lost. What follows may be a society without base. We have argued that no country can develop without indigenous technology.[73]

The scientific strength of modernization and rational-choice theory has been questioned by many people. Leys described Huntington's ideas on modernization as "vague, tautologous and circular."[74]

Much of Huntington's work was based on assumptions or concepts (e.g., participation, institutionalization, adaptability, coherence, complexity, autonomy) that were poorly defined. Many of the correlations on which he built his ideas did not stand up.

Bates' ideas on rational choice did not fare well when put to the test on African agriculture. In particular, data from Berry suggest that Bates' claim that rural people in Africa give priority to their immediate material interest cannot be supported.[75] With regard to North, his promised general theory of development never materialized; it seems that the defects in his theorization became all too apparent to him. For example, North attempted to offer a rational-choice-based interpretation of world history in which he sought to claim that rises in productivity have always occurred in the context of strong property rights. It is not true, for example, that property rights are essential for ensuring economic growth. Most of North's theory as a theory of development arise from illustrations in the early period of industrialization in the West, and this can account for his wrongly placing such importance on property rights. Leys called North's theory "a series of illustrations of the alleged explanatory power of institutions and especially property rights. . . . It is a matter of speculation." Gustafsson retorted that the prevalent view is that "economic progress is supposed to be dependent upon the activity of innovators, entrepreneurs and other deviant agents, who break rules and want to modify or even abolish existing institutions."[76]

We have undertaken this detailed appraisal of the work of U.S. and European social and political scientists in the area of economic development to show that at best their prescriptions are culturally specific and manifest a certain cultural homogeneity. In effect, these theories held that the observed social, cultural, and political differences between advanced economies and traditional underdeveloped economies required the installation of the socio/

cultural/political matrix of the former within the latter. Such theories have serious limitations and in many instances are misleading; at times their authors had pure political motives. This is why they were abandoned as the search for a general theory of development continued.

It is clear that political and sociocultural analysis is not a suitable tool for framing a general theory of economic development. Leys said, "The construction of a new theory of development is necessarily a political task, involving political choices about whom (what social forces) the theory is for, to accomplish what ends and in what context."[77] In a subsequent lecture Leys gave to the Royal African Society in London in February 1996, he correctly said that "what made the debates [i.e., on economic theory] of the sixties and seventies exciting was just this—they turned ultimately on political issues, beliefs, and commitments that were fundamentally opposed to each other."[78] The fact that Leys said that these factors were often fundamentally opposed is itself an acknowledgment by him that they cannot provide the basis for evolving a development theory.

The work of modernization and rational-choice theorists was essentially to determine which social and political conditions were conducive to economic development and growth. By implication, they also wished to identify those conditions that are inimical to economic development and growth. Yet identifying conditions conducive or inimical to economic development is not in and of itself economic development. A conducive environment cannot guarantee economic development. North himself seems to accept this when he says: "The major source of changes in an economy over time is *structural change in the parameters* held constant by the economist—technology, population, property right and government control over resources."[79]

Even though the original modernization and rational-choice theories have largely been discarded, much of their basic content has been recycled for use today. In the last few years, the World Bank, via the Education Program of its Economic Development Institute, has focused on what it calls the creation of civil societies in the Third World countries. The program is intended to increase education levels and establish a participatory and interactive culture aimed at laying the base for democracy and acting as a counterweight to undemocratic and often corrupt central governments in these countries. Much of the World Bank's aid money is being channeled into "village immersion programs" and to NGOs engaged in various "modernizing" activities in the Third World. James Wolfensohn, the president of the World Bank, summarized the essence of this approach:

> Our role . . . is to assist countries in trying to get the mechanisms in place—to get a justice system, to get a legal system, to have a system of property rights, to have roads, to have education, to have health, to stop street crime, to enable people to invest and to develop these countries. . . . So we brought in the best educators and we also put them together with the people in the villages under the guidance of the Indian government and regional authorities and we also brought in NGOs to assist and in the case of some villages we brought in local business. . . . We are now focusing at the level of women, at the level of the family, at the level of people and trying to make sure that development starts at the root.[80]

In a recently published report, *Assessing Aid— What Works, What Doesn't and Why,* the World Bank makes a renewed case for aid, defined as what it calls "sound management." Sound management, according to the bank, consists of the institutions and policies that if installed will lead to rapid economic development in an underdeveloped country. Such institutions and policies include the rule of law, property rights, open trade, social safety nets, efficient public bureaucracies, and institution building.[81]

Such are the complexities of the social and cultural matrix, however, that modernizing policies may sometimes have the opposite effect, killing off the local initiatives they set out to install. Among a sizable group of Africans (sometimes including the Western-educated elite), there is a feeling that technology is whites' exclusive endowment. It is probably this kind of state of affairs that the Peruvian Salamaar Bondy had in mind when he defined underdevelopment as "a state of mind—a way of expression, a form of outlook and a collective personality marked by chronic infirmities and forms of maladjustment."[82]

With regard to the recycling of rational-choice ideas, it is noteworthy that rational choice has permeated much of present-day economic thinking. Krugman has recently asserted that "the central ideas of economic theory are very simple: they boil down to little more than the proposition that people will usually take opportunities plus the observation that my opportunities often depend on your actions and vice versa."[83] Some students of the subject have wondered why rational-choice theory gained the considerable influence it did despite its weak theoretical base. Leys has ventured that North's reputation as a Nobel-prize-winning scholar helped to foster a somewhat uncritical respect for rational-choice ideas in the United States.[84]

Dependency Theory

Dependency theory emerged in the early 1970s in response to structuralist theories. It refused to accept that underdevelopment was the result of the "wrong" sociocultural pattern in poor countries. Rather, dependency theory held that external forces contrived to keep some countries underdeveloped.

It is not surprising that the leading exponents of dependency at the time were from Latin America, where many countries had achieved formal independence a century before and where social and cultural norms among the elites were not so very different from those in Europe, yet where sustainable economic development had not occurred. Dependency theory soon gained popularity in international circles, especially in Third World countries.

There was surprise and disappointment in Latin America that despite a program of import substitution industrialization, the region was still economically backward. The program itself arose from ECLA's 1948 posture that conventional economic theory as expounded in developed capitalist countries was inadequate for dealing with problems of underdevelopment. The ECLA argued that the Latin American engine of growth was faced with a long-term structural decline in South American countries' terms of trade and that the advanced countries' income elasticity of demand for traditional exports from the region (the periphery) was declining while the region's income elasticity of demand from the advanced countries (the center) was increasing. The result was a chronic structural balance-of-payments crisis. In addition, it argued that there is an unequal distribution of productivity gains. In the center, productivity gains led to higher wages and other factor prices, while in the periphery, they led to a decline in commodity prices and stagnant wages. Hence the ECLA proposed a program of import substitutions in a sharp departure from the prevailing outward-oriented development path, called *desarrollo hacia afuera*—a reference to the proposition that exports were the engine of growth of Latin American economies. The new import substitution strategy led to a proliferation of industries producing final consumer goods, especially consumer durables. Later on the ECLA proposed the establishment of a Latin American Common Market to achieve economies of scale.

By 1960, it had become obvious that the import substitution model was in crisis. It had not lessened dependence. The unequal income distribution it hoped to cure was growing, and a large segment of the population remained marginal. National policies for industrialization seemed to have succumbed to the multinational corporation.

There were different formulations of dependence theory, including some that were particularly Marxist in their origin. The differences between these formulations is clearest when it comes to perspectives of political action. They have in common their focus on what they consider the many forms of acute dependence of underdeveloped countries on the powerful international economic interests and states that dominate the financial and commodity markets. The basic hypothesis of the theory of dependency is that development and underdevelopment are partial, interdependent structures of one global system. Dos Santos summarized it as follows: Dependence is a conditioning situation in which the economies of one group of countries are conditioned by the development and expansion of others. A relationship of interdependence between these two or more economies or between such economies and the world trading system becomes a dependent relationship when such countries can expand through self-impulsion while others, being in a dependent relationship, can only expand as a reflection of the expansion of the dominant countries, which may have a positive or negative effect on their immediate development.[85]

In the case of Latin America, each author emphasized different aspects as to why international economy and its changes conditioned changes in Latin America. Cardoso was primarily interested in the economic process as a social process.[86] He and Faletto emphasized that dependency is not an external variable but part of a system of social relations between different classes within the same broad ambit of dependency. In their view, the dominant economic groups in a dependent economy are those clustering around the interchanges with the metropolitan country; these groups develop an interest in maintaining or only slightly modifying these interchanges. Others, such as Sunkel, analyze dependency from a historical perspective in which underdevelopment is the result of the two great polarizations—that between the industrial, advanced, developed, metropolitan countries and the underdeveloped, backward, poor, peripheral, and dependent countries. Sunkel and his Latin American compatriots chafed at what they regarded as the subordination of the interests of Latin America to the interests of the United States and international companies in their domestic politics.[87] In Dos Santos' view, the development of capitalism led and continues to lead to unequal development of its constituent parts. It is the compromises and collisions among the various international and national elements that create dependency.[88]

As could be expected in the long-running battle on development theory, dependency theory was attacked. The main criticism of interest in this book is that dependency theory did not specify what it meant by economic development or what alternative development route it would substitute. Its proponents were said not to be clear about what they meant by dependency and how it can be evaluated. On the other hand, dependency theorists undoubtedly accurately identified many of the forces that explain the pattern of modern African development. Case studies in virtually every African country testify to the reality of the structures to which the theory points.

O'Brien thought that theories of dependency "may seem at best trivial or irrelevant and at worst political slogans wrapped up as a theory."[89] Leys referred to "the existence of fundamental problems of analysis which UDT [i.e., dependency] cannot solve or even formulate and the central problem of development strategy which are linked with these and about which UDT is either silent or ambiguous."[90] Lall said, "One sometimes gets the impression on reading the literature [on dependency] that 'dependence' is defined by circular manner." This is because some dependency literature argues that poverty is caused by dependency, while others argue that dependency is caused by poverty. Lall is of the view that in order for dependency to be a useful theory, (1) it must specify certain characteristics of an economy that are not found in a nondependent economy, and (2) these characteristics must be shown to adversely affect the course of development of dependent countries. He found that, for example, Canada and Belgium, which are advanced economies, depended more on foreign investment than Indian or Pakistan. He said that dominance and dependence exist and that they are as commonplace in the center as in the periphery.[91]

Kay concluded, "This concept [dependence] fails to grasp the real nature of the process of underdevelopment."[92] Larraín added, "There is little doubt that if one examines the theory of dependency . . . as a testable theory with precisely defined variables and concepts whose characteristics are exclusive and apply only to dependent countries and one requiring measurable empirical evidence which substantiates the hypotheses then the theory of dependence does not pass the test."[93]

While critics of dependency theory castigate its proponents for having no viable theory of economic development, they do not offer one, either. In addition, they, like the proponents of dependency theory, have fallen into the same mistaken notion that economic development, whether at the periphery or in the center, must be capitalist-led. Leys, for example, wrote: "The most important shortcoming of dependency theory is that it implies that there is an alternative, and preferable, kind of development of which dependent economies are capable—when this alternative does not exist."[94] He argued that while the economic link between one group of countries and another, dependent group may block the latter's growth, that blockage is not absolute. He maintained that some Third World countries, including African countries, have experienced "some growth," and while it may be painful, wasteful, and ruthless, like early capitalism everywhere, it is development nonetheless: "Just as capitalism developed unevenly in today's industrial economies, marginalizing and pauperizing whole regions while concentrating production and wealth in others, so on a world scale whole countries and regions seem likely to become chronically and for all practical purposes permanently marginal with the added problem that their labor power is not even required elsewhere."[95] But in this book we are concerned with *sustainable* growth.

Leys' comments are misleading in many ways. Earlier in his book he regretted that the breakdown of the Bretton Woods arrangements had given unfettered freedom to the flow of private capital into former colonial countries and made it difficult for governments in those countries to undertake development strategies of their liking, in accordance with development theories which he and others were just evolving. Later he seems to be saying that dependent development is the only viable choice for poor countries. What happened to the evolving development theories whose raison d'être was, according to him, supposedly ended by the collapse of Bretton Woods? The truth is that there were no viable scientific development theories on offer from Leys. Second, we are saying not that no development can occur under dependency, but that what growth occurs may be unsustainable; the waste, inequality, and other socioeconomic problems it causes can be seen in such Latin American countries as Brazil. Third, Leys is wrong to compare the imbalances in the world capitalist economy with those internal to an advanced country, because despite what may appear to an ordinary observer as similarities, these are due to very different scientific (economic) factors.

It should be pointed out that in the strong and sustained criticism of dependency during the 1970s, there was quite a body of scholars (mainly non-Marxist) who did not bother to attack the theory because they believed the dependency growth experience of the East Asian NICs was sufficient evidence of the fallacy of dependence. The recent economic crisis suffered by these countries seems to put into question such an assumption.

It is true that dependency theory focused attention on the issue of why economic and commercial links between advanced countries and underdeveloped countries have not resulted, as was expected, in the sustained economic growth of the latter. Dependency theorists saw metropolitan policy as maleficent, not beneficent, inasmuch as the inflow of foreign investment was considered to result in even greater outflows of profit. Sunkel saw multinational companies as the most powerful economic agents of the developed countries in the penetration of the underdeveloped countries.[96] These constitute what has been called the "external orientation" of many Third World economies.

After all the political rhetoric of Latin American dependency has been cast aside, the basic views are germane. Even with the best of intentions, transfer of resources from the center to the periphery in order to assist the periphery cannot advance the economy of the latter, as we will show. Such an idea runs counter to the science of development. Cardoso asserted that national development—sovereignty, internal cohesion, and progressive social integration —should be posed as an alternative to dependent capitalist development.[97] Despite Cardoso's lack of knowledge of how this strategy might be put into practice, it is noteworthy that a scientific theory of development, which will ensure sustained economic development in the periphery, embodies autonomous national development strategy.

Frank more than once staked his reputation on the assertion that so long as Latin America (and the rest of the Third World) remains integrated into the world capitalist system, it will not undergo development. It will only experience what he called the "development of underdevelopment." The World Bank's assessment of Latin America cited at the

beginning of this chapter seems to lend some credence to Frank's assertion.

Despite dependency theory's loss of influence, some things in it have been recycled. Dependency has been described as a new "philosophy of poverty" based on a preoccupation with the "bad side" of periphery capitalism.[98] Dependency theorists draw attention to the socioeconomic consequences of dependency in the periphery—poverty and low incomes for the majority, and highly unequal income distribution. From these considerations emerged the relatively recent idea that development meant something closer to the alleviation of poverty than to mere achievement of aggregate economic growth. It became the view in academic circles and within the international community that the latter will not necessarily deliver the former.

By the mid-1970s, the World Bank under Robert McNamara had announced that development should be judged not by economic growth but by the extent to which poverty was reduced. Indeed, many of McNamara's speeches in this period incorporated much of the main thesis of dependency theory, though with the rhetoric removed. The World Bank and other Western governments reoriented their aid policies so as to focus explicitly on the poorest people and countries—the basic needs approach, as it was called.[99] Moreover, the introduction of policies in the South aimed at alleviating poverty while maintaining growth became the orthodoxy of development theory and practice as preached by governments and institutions of the North during the second half of the decade, and ever since.

The distinction between growth and poverty alleviation is unfortunate and undesirable. It shows the low level to which knowledge of economic development has sunk. The lack of a viable theory of development and its usurpation by the orthodoxy of capitalist-led development have forced practitioners such as the World Bank into this distinction, since it is relatively easy to provide money and basic facilities in the poor rural areas of the Third World and to see what appears to be immediate, tangible evidence of poverty alleviation, leaving the more problematic issue of economic development unsolved. It is almost as if the practitioners are saying to themselves, "Let us at least be seen to be doing something."

The *dependencistas* of Latin America could not, however, be accused of quick-fix solutions, an accusation that can be made of proponents of all other theories so far discussed. In general, their main preoccupation was to define what they considered to be the problem.

Neoliberal Theory

As expected, the "structuralists," as they were called, soon came under attack. The basic building blocks of the dependency approach—an emphasis on the importance of initial conditions, of national resources, of the size of the country and its relationship with the international economy, and so on—are variables that were thought to influence the appropriate balance and composition of policies aimed at higher growth rates and better income distribution. There was therefore an agreement among most of its proponents about the need for government to intervene and about the need to bring poverty alleviation to the center of the stage.[100]

Neoliberals accused earlier theories of neglecting relative price and of being interventionists. Their origin was a core of development writers such as Boyer, Balassa, and Lal, who brought to the fore the neoliberal revolution that had started in the United States and some other European countries in the late 1970s. They felt the need to ensure that capitalism did not yield to socialism in the Third World and to contain and reverse the state intervention that positivist orthodoxy had helped to establish. Neoliberals asserted the primacy of economic growth, believing that poverty is most effectively

reduced through economic growth. They believed that any benefits of intervention have huge costs attached. Rent seeking, a dominant feature of aristocracy, for example, is a cost on efficiency. The direct impact intervention has on prices, they say, shows the differences between market and "shadow" prices, resulting in the market not being able to facilitate efficient factor allocation

Neoliberals' central theme is that long-run economic growth will occur provided everything possible is done to achieve short-run allocative efficiency. They grudgingly acknowledge that because of initial imperfections, freely working markets may not necessarily achieve this goal, but they insist that the market provides the best way of approximating allocative efficiency, since conventional intervention strategies will always be less satisfactory. Imperfect markets, they say, are better than imperfect states in settling matters of resource allocation.

As neoliberal economists remind everyone, there is a well-established methodology provided by welfare economics for dealing with deviations from the optimum as a result of market imperfections. This involves comparing the welfare gain from correcting the initial distortion with the inevitable welfare loss that is caused by intervention. "Get prices right" was the basic message of this group.

Basic neoliberal theory, deriving from neoclassical economics, is founded on the pivotal role of the marketplace. This forms the basis of their claims to scientific and intellectual centrality within the sphere of social science. The core elements of this model of a satisfaction-maximizing automatic asocial mechanism are fundamental natural scarcity, private ownership of means of production, and competition to supply sovereign consumers through the ordering mechanism of the market. External finance, for example, is unimportant for development, since foreign exchange or savings bottlenecks can be eliminated by changes to domestic policy. In particular, interest subsidies, which have depressed savings and have little impact on real investments, should be removed. Aid diverts resources from more profitable uses to less profitable ones. Thus its short-run impact, in a global sense, is usually negative. Its maximal benefit to its recipients is the avoided cost of borrowing.[101]

In order to support the workings of the market, neoliberals advocate free trade and outward orientation of national economies. They insist that whatever the degree of competition in the home market, an open, export-oriented economy ensures international competition, providing stimulus for productivity gains. It also ensures that local prices at least can be close to the opportunity costs and determined by world prices and domestic scarcities; by implication, this goes hand in hand with price liberation in foreign trade.

The neoliberals say that governments do too much and that public expenditure should be reduced if economic growth is to be accelerated. For example, they would even advocate user fees for such services as education and health care.

By the early 1980s, neoliberals' views had gained favor, to the point that the thrust of the World Bank Development Report of 1981 was that governments had failed to improve economic performance by allocating resources through means other than market mechanisms. The World Bank's 1983 report remarked that "economic output will be maximized only when resources are allocated by a mechanism that takes account of their relative scarcity and costs . . . government intervention can result in large losses of efficiency . . . today's widespread reexamination of the role of the state is evidence of a new realism."[102] Much of the influence that neoliberalism has gathered to date is not due to the scientific and analytical strength of its prescriptions. Weaknesses in neoliberal theory are many.

There is no significant difference between the proportion of GDP accounted for by public spending in the sub-Saharan region (about which the above World Bank generalization was made) and that in other parts of the world. Among the sub-Saharan countries there is no apparent relationship between the GDP growth rate achieved and the proportional importance of public spending.[103] A comprehensive study carried out by Ram concluded that across the world, government size is positively associated with economic performance in the overwhelming majority of countries, especially developing countries.[104] It therefore appears that there is no conclusive evidence that government size and spending on their own account for low economic growth.

The claimed importance of competition is also doubtful. That competition spurs growth in productivity and incomes is based on empirical evidence from only a few cases rather than comprehensive cross-country data. Aghion and Howitt concluded that product competition is unambiguously bad for growth.[105] There is no theoretical argument that establishes unequivocally the connection between competition and high growth in productivity.[106] It is a question whether the possible duplication of resources and overcapacity that might arise from competition outweigh the benefits due to an economy where resource utilization maximizes overall national economic growth and productivity. Examining openness (another word for competition), it is difficult to identify a priori the effect of trade policy on long-run per capita income and growth. Aghion and Howitt concluded that while much empirical work supports the idea that openness is growth-promoting, the conclusion is controversial and subject to a lot of criticisms. One main problem they point out is that the definition of an open economy is not clear. Although it is convenient to classify countries as either open or closed, in practice this conceals a wide variety and extent of interventions.[107]

The neoliberal economists went from claims about the relationship of trade policy to growth to the assertion of a causal linkage between export growth and total output. They also jumped from results of empirical work on trading regimes to the generalized conclusion that free trade was desirable for growth.[108]

In his report Kruger acknowledged that available trade and growth models provided little indication of the quantitative importance of trade as a contributor to growth and still less insight into the losses in attainable growth that may be incurred with a departure from free trade.[109] The wide influence of neoliberalism in world and national economies, despite its thin theoretical base, is due to a number of factors. Neoliberalism gained prominence with the increased number of conservative governments in metropolitan countries in the 1980s. The failure of France, with its socialist regime, and other socialist groups to resist pressure to join other OECD countries in their acquiescence to this neoliberalism movement in 1983 was pivotal.[110] We will come back later to the U.S. role in this.

Assisting this political momentum was the fact that the changes of the 1980s offered significant opportunities for transnational capital, represented by financial institutions, bond holders, foreign exchange traders, and private investors. These dominant forces thus added their considerable weight in favor of neoliberalism.

James Tobin, a Nobel laureate in economics, observed that South Korea and other Asian countries —like Mexico in 1994–95—were victims of a flawed international exchange system that under U.S. leadership "gives the mobility of capital priority over all other considerations."[111] Jagdish Bhagwati, a professor of economics at Columbia University and a champion of free trade, commented that "Wall Street has become a very powerful influence in terms of seeking markets everywhere. Morgan Stanley and all these gigantic firms want to be able to go into other markets and essentially see capital account convertibility as what will enable them to operate everywhere. Just like in the old days there was this 'military-industrial complex,' nowadays there is a 'Wall Street–Treasury complex' because Secretaries of State . . . come from Wall Street. . . . So today, Wall Street's views are very dominant in terms of the kind of world you want to see. . . . They want to take capital in and out freely. . . . It also ties in to the IMF's own desires, which is to act as lender of last resort. They see themselves as the apex body which will manage this whole system. So IMF finally gets a role for itself, which is under-pinned by maintaining complete freedom on capital account."

Bhagwati added, "In my judgment, it is a lot of ideological humbug to say that without free portfolio capital mobility, somehow the world cannot function and growth will collapse."[112] Yet neoliberal pressures helped push the amendment of IMF's articles of agreement to require member states to remove capital controls and adopt full account convertibility. These pressures worked to promote the World Trade Organization's agreement on liberalizing financial services. These changes were incorporated into new measures adopted as part of the IMF's efforts to rescue the East Asian countries. By December 12, 1997, more than seventy countries had signed the agreement that commits them to open their banking and insurance sectors and their securities markets to foreign firms. These events—the revision of the IMF's articles of agreement, the WTO's financial services agreement, and the OECD's Multilateral Agreement on Investment—are expressions of a big push from international organizations, backed by government and corporations in the rich countries, to institute a regime of capital mobility that allows easy entry and exit everywhere.[113]

Another reason for neoliberalism's attractiveness is that it is a social theory dressed up as an economic theory. It adopted a simplistic recipe—less intervention, in favor of the market—in order to avoid the intellectually more difficult task of elucidating the details of the social process it has in mind. The market is largely undefined, but we are given to think that the market is rational and controlled by the "invisible hand." In this context it has stolen the dress of the rationalists and is able to appeal to and take advantage of the wide (but unmerited) support rational theory enjoyed in the United States. Indeed, much of neoliberalism is rooted in institutional theory. Institutional theory, as we pointed out earlier, carries a great deal of cultural baggage. So does neoliberalism. The stolen economic dress is neoliberalism's use of the concept of competition as a centerpiece of its theory. Rational behavior (as part of rational theory) requires seeking the best for oneself. Competition is a magic word in economics. As Krugman said, "Most people who use the term 'competitiveness' do so without a second thought . . . competitive images are exciting, and thrills sell tickets."[114] He said that "one of the remarkable, startling features of the vast literature on competitiveness is the repeated tendency of highly intelligent authors to engage in what may perhaps most tactfully be described as 'careless arithmetic.' . . . Assertions [about competition] are made," he said, "that sound like quantifiable pronouncements about measurable magnitudes."[115] The false impression that competition is the key to growth and is measurable is reflected in Michael Porter's statement that "vigorous rivalry is the only path to economic vitality. . . . Ultimately a country's productivity is the sum of its corporate productivity."[116] These are mere assertions that have no scientific validity, as will be apparent later in this book.

While nature itself has established a regime of competition—sometimes called "the survival of the fittest," in which, for example, animals eat plants or other animals—this is a necessary progression that adds value (is not wasteful). Competition in the marketplace is sometimes falsely presented as if it were like this natural phenomenon. Indeed, competition in the markets involves considerable "destructive destruction": duplication of resources, overcapacity, and waste. Kuttner pointed out that "the market [competition] does not care if beef was produced by a system that over-consumes water, causes deserts to encroach irrevocably on forest or throws subsistence farmers off the land." He adds, "If an economy has 20% unemployment, the price system may be operating normally but it is producing an outcome that is collectively inefficient because it leaves 20% of human resources needlessly idle."[117]

Despite the fact that neoliberal economics has no strong theoretical foundation or merit, its position since the 1980s has greatly strengthened thanks to the United States. Although there is no simple correlation between a laissez-faire economy and political democracy, in a false intellectual leap the United States has championed democracy as a precondition for sustained economic democracy. It is true that a command economy certainly tends to require a command state. Capitalism, by contrast, has coexisted nicely with the stable parliamentary democracies of the North—but it has also dwelt all too easily with the Nazis, fascists, traditional despots, and military dictators. Indeed, early capitalism existed with slavery, and today multinational corporations often enjoy the enforced social peace and low labor cost associated with dictatorship.[118] If democracy meant rapid economic development, India—the second largest democracy for nearly a half century—would be one of the world's richest nations. It is therefore a mistake to assume that free markets equal political freedom, just as it is to assume that laissez-faire policies maximize growth. The need to push democracy on its own merits, not as part of an economic plan, cannot be overemphasized.

Despite this, America has pressed ahead with a neoliberal world economic agenda. The collapse of communism has been seen by economists, business leaders, and commentators as a vindication of laissez-faire policies. Now, with the end of the cold war, there is the risk that a triumphant United States will want to impose a single economic model with doubtful economic validity on a diverse world. The serious obstacle such an attitude presents to the adoption of a scientific theory of economic development, if and when one is available, is illustrated by the words of Jeffrey Sachs:

> America has wanted global leadership on the cheap. It was desperate for the developing world and post-communist economies to buy into its vision, in which globalization, private capital flow and Washington advice would overcome the obstacles to shared prosperity so that pressures on the rich countries to do more for the poorer countries could be contained by the dream of universal economic growth. In this way, the United States would not have to shell out real money to help the peaceful reconstruction of Russia or to ameliorate the desperate impoverishment and illness in Africa. In essence, America has tried to sell its social ethos: the rich need not help the poor, since the poor can enjoy rising living standards and someday become rich themselves.
>
> Washington became skittish at anything or anybody that challenged this vision. When developing country leaders pointed out that development was harder than it looked; their economies were falling further behind in technology; that they were being destabilized by financial flows they could neither track or understand; that falling commodity prices were taking them further from shared prosperity that they had been promised; that unattended disease was ravaging their societies; that the wreckage of Soviet communism would take real aid not just short-term loan to overcome; or that they were still drowning in debt ten years after America acknowledged the need for debt relief—all these honest reflections were taken as hostile challenges to the vision of shared prosperity, because they put at risk the notion of cost-free American leadership.[119]

Kuttner was right when he said that the United States was superb at exporting "economic dogmas."[120]

The popularity of neoliberalism in the poor countries no doubt stems from heightened expectations of what capital inflow can do their economy, as they have been told that the one thing their economies need and lack is capital. If this hope is combined with the expected opportunity to sell to the rich countries the products of their new industries, poor countries hope everything will be wonderful in a global economy, and despite setbacks in the short term, they are urged to believe it will work in the long run.

A certain feeling of inevitability about globalization has been inculcated among ordinary people (whether in the advanced economies or the underdeveloped economies). With increasing rapidity the world is said to be contracting into a "global" village. In this view, the economies of different countries must, of necessity, be dealt with as a single unit. This argument has no economic basis.

For a theory of economic development to be scientific, it will have to define growth more precisely than neoliberals care to. For example, what precise formula and composition of factor inputs and what associated precise economic criteria constitute growth? Neoliberal economics lacks this expertise. It instead says that the hidden hand of the market will do the job. Krugman has said that no reasonable economist can claim to have an accurate accounting of the value of the sources of growth. He also conceded, "We can't really say . . . how much better our [U.S.] productivity growth would be if we did everything right."[121] It is only when we have developed precise prescriptions and formulations about growth as part of a scientific theory of economic development that the exact role of government in promoting growth in particular countries will be more easily determined. Until then, neoliberal economics waxes strong, precisely because of this lack of a scientific definition of growth.

Neoliberalism incorrectly equates growth with competition. But the market has many limitations and can overreach itself. According to Kuttner, "Mistakes that result are not instantly corrected by other market forces."[122] He asserted, "In the past twenty years, far from optimizing world growth, turning to laissez-faire has instead produced high unemployment, high interest rates, rising inequality both between and within nations, and a defamatory economy that often seems operated in the interest of bondholders. We have lost a decade of development for the South."[123]

It will be shown in the following chapters that a scientifically defined growth formulation contains full provision for equity and environment. On the other hand, according to Kuttner, neoliberal economics maintains that a fully competitive market makes the economy use its resources efficiently. "It is being implied by neoliberal economics that unemployment and inequality may be the legitimate price (trade-off) required to pay for this 'efficient' use of resources."[124] This applies in both rich and poor nations. In a way, it can be said that the World Bank's emphasis on poverty reduction since the 1980s is an acknowledgment that its economic development policy necessitates this trade-off. Recent neoclassical theorizing has, however, suggested that selective price distortions can improve purely market-based solutions to economic problems under conditions of uncertainty and differences in access to information among economic actors. To date, market-friendly policy advocates have treated such ideas as academic "curiosa."[125]

Standard neoliberal theory asserts that marketization will lead to convergence: Investors in capital-rich countries will seize the opportunities for growth in poor countries and will send them their capital, realizing high profits while the poor countries reap high growth. This theory, as we have already affirmed, is faulty—it relies on the concept (recycled from positivist orthodoxy) that capital is the source of economic growth. Indeed, we are reminded of Angus Maddison's OECD study, which confirmed that evidence from recent decades suggests that marketization results in divergence, not convergence.[126]

The contrast between the founders of the Bretton Woods institutions (the World Bank and the IMF) and those who operate these institutions today is striking. Kuttner observed that in 1944 the architects of Bretton Woods understood the risk of competitive devaluation. They understood that private global financial flaws, left on their own, would cumulatively lead to collective deflation. The original purpose of the IMF was to allow countries to stabilize their currencies without contracting their economies. The idea was to inject an expansionary bias into the system rather than a contractionary one so that each nation could pursue full employment at home. With stable currencies and full employment, the founders thought, nations would be in a position to accept free trade. But free trade and free movement of capital were not the summum bonum of the system. Indeed, the regime of fixed exchange rates tolerated and sometimes even required limits on the free movement of capital.[127]

It has been suggested that the World Bank, the IMF, and the rest of the development community had to fall into line with new right-wing governments' neoliberal philosophy because he who pays the piper dictates the tune.[128] Yet the collapse of Bretton Woods combined with the debt crisis of the least developed countries and abrupt increases in interest rates also created a new geoeconomic situation, one that produced new political leverage for the World Bank and IMF.[129] The result was policies now known as the Washington Consensus. The Washington Consensus recipe has been applied to nations as diverse as the former communist countries, Latin American nations, and countries in sub-Saharan Africa. The approved recipe ("getting prices right") normally calls for reductions in public sector outlay—frequently through devaluation, deregulation, and privatization—along with opening national capital markets and making domestic economies friendly to foreign private investment. The Bretton Woods institutions, instead of providing a needed counterweight to the tendencies of global financial austerity and contraction, have become agents of austerity and contraction. As a result, the Washington Consensus treats development problems as amenable to the type of applied macroeconomics deployed to analyze growth issues in the mature industrialized countries. A growing branch of the profession has also tended to apply sophisticated microeconomic tools to development problems very much as it would in any other setting.[130] These produce what we have already described as quick-fix solutions, relying on the notion that capital accumulation will lead to growth.[131] But, to reiterate, what is lacking is a scientific prescription for growth to replace the Washington Consensus prescription.

New Growth Theory (Endogenous Growth Theory)

The 1980s saw a resurgence of research by economists on economic growth theory and the birth of what has come to be called new growth theory or endogenous growth theory. This provided economists with a much-needed escape after about fifteen years without any major breakthrough in adapting the neoclassical growth model to fit present-day economics. According to the neoclassical growth model, long-term growth is effectively pegged by the rate of exogenous technology. But does endogenous growth theory provide a viable account of economic growth?

Aghion and Howitt assert that "by focusing on innovation as a distinct economic activity with distinct economic causes and effects, [endogenous growth theory] opens the door to a deeper understanding of how organizations, institutions, market structure, market imperfections, trade, government policy, and legal framework in many domains affect (and are affected) by long-run growth through their effects on economic agents' incentives to engage in innovative (or more generally knowledge-producing) activities."[132] This statement has a lot in common with North's concept of institutional economics, used to explain the radically different performance of different economies over long periods of time. North, it will be recalled, argued that the difference in performance hinges on the differences between institutions and organizations and on the interaction between them, which shapes the direction of institutional change. According to North, institutions determine the opportunities in a society. Organizations, he stated, are created to take advantage of those opportunities, and as the organizations evolve, they alter the institutions. He asserted that "the resultant path of institutional change is shaped by (1) the lock-in that comes from the symbiotic relationship between institutions and organizations that have evolved as a result consequence of the incentive structure provided by the institutions (2) the feedback process by which human beings perceive and react to the changes in the opportunity set."[133]

Aghion and Howitt stated that the purpose of endogenous growth theory is to fill the gap in neoclassical theory, "to open up technological progress and innovation to systematic analysis and to study their effect on growth."[134] "The excitement of the endogenous growth theory," they claimed, "is that it provides the tools to handle endogenous technological change and innovations within a dynamic general equilibrium setting."

In contrast to neoclassical theorists, who assume that technology is exogenous, endogenous growth theory according to Aghion and Howitt holds that innovation is created by people in several different ways: while trying to solve production problems, while learning from previous experience, to find more efficient ways of doing things, to gain profits from new activities, and at times out of curiosity. They described innovation as a social process subject to laws, institutions, customs, and regulations that affect incentive as well as the ability to appropriate rent from newly created knowledge, learn from others' experience, organize and finance research and development, pursue scientific careers, enter new markets currently dominated by others, accept working with new technologies, and so on.[135]

Let us examine endogenous growth theory more closely in the context of the theme of this book, summarizing the application of the theory in three areas of socioeconomic activities—education, inequality, and the market.

New growth theory, peculiarly, sees education as closely intertwined with the process of technological change, considering it to be a type of human capital. There are two basic approaches to analyzing human capital. One, the Lucas approach, followed the pioneering studies of R. E. Frank.[136] He concluded that accumulation of human capital constitutes an alternative to technology as a source of sustainable growth, and that there were two main sources of human capital accumulation (skills acquisition): education and learning by doing.

The relationship between education and growth has been modeled under two basic frameworks within endogenous growth theory. Lucas' model is based on the idea that growth is mainly driven by accumulation of human capital. It follows that differences in growth rates between counties are driven by differences in the *rates* at which they accumulate human capital over time. The second basic approach, arising from the work of Nelson and Phelps, treats economic growth as being driven by the *stock* of human capital, which affects a country's ability to innovate. Differences in growth rates are due mainly to differences in human-capital stocks and in those countries' ability to produce technological progress.[137]

Many empirical studies have been carried out to study the relationship between education and growth. These have displayed various correlations between education policy and growth.[138] One testable prediction of the Nelson-Phelps approach is that marginal productivity of education attainment is an increasing function of the rate of technological progress. Another testable prediction is that education should allow countries with less advanced technologies to learn more from the advanced countries and achieve higher levels of productivity by innovation.

Aghion and Howitt made a study of inequality as a social factor that can affect economic growth.[139] On inequality, endogenous growth theory postulates that individuals differ in their initial endowments of human capital, and this difference apparently causes inequality. It is postulated that these differences determine how an economy grows. As a policy, the ex ante redistribution of human capital endowments consists of taxing highly endowed individuals directly on their endowments and using the proceeds from this tax to subsidize human capital improvement in the less endowed. It is postulated that when credit markets are perfect, individual investment and (future) output do not depend on the distribution of human capital endowments across individuals. Because of this, they concluded, inequality and/or any redistribution designed to ameliorate it has no impact on growth. Thus it is claimed that wealth distribution policies cannot positively affect aggregate output and growth. On the other hand, when credit markets are not perfect (for example, credit is scarce and costly), equilibrium investments are supposed to differ from individual to individual because such investments consist of an increasing function of each individual's initial endowments in human capital, which in turn depends on the extent of redistribution. With such a heterogeneous human capital endowment scenario, the theory maintains, suitably designed redistribution policies will enhance aggregate productive efficiency and growth. In other words, redistribution programs are supposed to create investment opportunities and enhance equity in the absence of a well-functioning capital market. The underlying assumption is that marginal productivity for the rich is low while for the poor it is high. It is argued that the incentive effect on the poor caused by redistribution may sometimes enhance growth prospects. Thus reduced incentives to the rich as a result of redistribution should be weighed against increased incentives to the poor. There is a heavy dose of positivist orthodoxy here.

Tracing the effect of technology on inequality, it is postulated by the theory that technology change may itself cause an increase in wage differentials because technology is said to be generally biased toward specialist skills and so enhances new differences in abilities. This conclusion is based on a technology that is labor-saving.

On the whole, endogenous growth theory asserts that it has the necessary tools to analyze these and other similar sociopolitical issues as a way of understanding the growth process.

In regard to markets, the theory also claims the ability to deal with the consequences of the postwar liberalization of trade. Endogenous growth theory states that growth in investment is led by market growth and market size. It is then stated as a general principle that in any country, accumulation of capital leads to a fall in its marginal product, as capital becomes more intensively used. In a small open economy, Aghion and Howitt argue, the marginal product of capital is determined by the world's capital because goods can be exported from that country at prices given by the world conditions. They argue that as a country accumulates capital, it can shift into more capital-intensive export sectors, as occurred in some of the East Asian countries. By this strategy, a small open economy can evade diminishing returns even when ordinarily its technology would not support sustained growth. Ventura had argued that when economies trade and some form of factor price equalization occurs, the resultant interdependence can lead to growth in the countries involved.[140] Endogenous growth theory maintains that continuous market widening (in terms of geographical size, purchasing power, and diver-

sity) and quality improvement all help to offset any inherent tendency for individual product market saturation. This is supposed to encourage vigorous competition in terms of both product differentiation and cost reduction, causing a speeding up of technological and organizational innovation in terms of potential productivity gains and adaptation to more diversified demand. This speeding-up process, it is claimed, will require increasing amounts of resources devoted to research and development in the scientific and high-technology sectors. It is claimed that the increased complexity and diversity of science and technological capacities have resulted in growth of networks, alliances, and technological and scientific exchanges—that is, in growth in the external effects of technology. While dissenting voices argued that increased product market competition is detrimental to growth, endogenous growth theory insisted that the intensive production of the latest technological novelties tends to accelerate the acquisition of new equipment, thereby increasing physical investment. This increase is said to be enhanced by macroeconomic liberalization, that is, by the liberalization of capital markets and internationalization of financial markets and investment, all leading to increased internationalization of technology and globalization of enterprises.[141] There are still many aspects of the relationship between international trade and growth that remain to be investigated by endogenous growth theory, but by and large the theory assumes that globalization is good for countries.

As we shall see, like the other theories discussed in this chapter, endogenous growth theory has a number of shortcomings. All endogenous growth theory economists freely use the word *technology* as a centerpiece of the theory. But nowhere did these economists define what they meant by the word. The terms *technology, technological progress, technological change,* and *innovation* all have been used, sometimes leaving the impression that they are interchangeable. This is unscientific. A theory cannot stand on the basis of trying to be all things to all persons. Despite Aghion and Howitt's stated intention to "open up technological process . . . to systematic analysis," they and other economists writing on this theory leave the impression that the common accusation that economists treat technology as a black box in which something goes in and something comes out is still true. To imply that technology is what enables one to obtain greater output from a given input or to obtain a given output with less input is not a definition of technology. In other words, some economists seem to believe that *technology* and *productivity* mean the same thing. One does not scientifically define a phenomenon simply by describing what it does.

Aghion and Howitt wrote, "In our view, capital accumulation and innovation should be regarded not as distinct causal factors but as two aspects of the same process." They provided no (scientific) proof for this assertion. One gets the impression that they treat new physical capital as innovation. We are not told what is being innovated. They went on to say that "new technologies are almost always embodied in new forms of human and physical capital that must be accumulated if technology is to be used."[142] Here their sudden introduction of the word *technology* seems to mean that they regard technology and innovation as the same thing. Elsewhere these authors say that technological change (technology?) is experienced through its effect on productivity, improving the quality of machinery and equipment. This time *technology* seems to refer simply to improved quality. Elsewhere it was claimed, quite surprisingly, that technological progress is labor-saving —a claim that indicates a limited understanding of the issues involved.

In another section of their book, Aghion and Howitt discuss the possibility that technology is a kind of capital good and can be used in combination with other factors of production to produce final output. They did not say what those factors are. They claim that technology can be stored over time because it does not get completely used up whenever it is put into a production process, and that it can be accumulated through R&D and other knowledge-creation activities.[143] Here they refer to technology as knowledge. Elsewhere technology is linked to human capital,[144] referencing the claim by Lucas that differences in growth rate across countries are primarily due to differences in human capital stocks and thereby these countries' abilities to generate technical progress (technology).[145]

Freeman and Soete pointed out that endogenous growth theory views technological change as a good, "which has to be produced in the same sense as other goods, but also contains some typical features of public good."[146] This time technology seems to be a final good, not capital. The earlier strand of endogenous growth theory (the so-called AK approach) says that "technological knowledge is intellectual capital, which can be lumped together with computers, crankshafts and other forms of capital."[147]

To add to the confusion, Ghosh defined technology as "the whole range of technical inputs other than raw materials and labor which go into each economic activity, in particular the processes, building plant, machinery equipment and tools for each segment of production."[148] Clearly Ghosh did not know what to make of technology. This sad state in which people write about technology without clear definition of what they mean is also visible in Freeman and Soete's statement that "there has been an extremely important change in the way we order our knowledge of techniques used in producing, distributing and transporting goods." "Some people," they said, "call this change simply 'technology,' others prefer to talk of 'advanced technology' or high technology to distinguish those branches of industry which depend on more formal scientific techniques than the older arts." On second thought, they conceded, "in a sense human societies have always had technology; some people see little new in modern technology."[149]

Elsewhere in the same book, Freeman and Soete commented, "Strictly speaking, as the word itself implies, technology is simply a body of knowledge about techniques. But it is frequently used to encompass both the knowledge itself and the tangible embodiment of that knowledge in an operating system using physical production equipment. In this book the expression 'technical innovation' or simply 'innovation' is used to describe the introduction and spread of new and improved products and processes in the economy and 'technological innovation' to describe advances in knowledge."[150]

Here "technical innovation" contrasts with "technological innovation." To completely seal up the black box of technology, which Aghion and Howitt claim that endogenous growth theory will open to systematic analysis, the OECD in 1990 instead defined technology as "a social process which by meeting real or imagined needs changes those needs just as it is changed by them," adding the clarification that "society is shaped by technical change and technical change is shaped by the society. Technical innovation—sometimes impelled by scientific discovery, at other times by demand—stems from within the economic and social system and is not merely an adjustment to transformations brought about by causes outside that system."[151] No viable theory can subsist on such an unscientific foundation.

Earlier the similarity between the statement about the structural framework of endogenous growth theory and that of North's institutional theory was pointed out. North's institutional theory treats "organizations"—that is, the collection of individuals, entrepreneurs, rulers, and so on—as the most important set of economic agents. He also introduced the concept of institutions (rules) as constraints on agents' choices. Rules are supposed to be capable of influencing efficiency positively by reducing transaction costs and promoting predictability and stability. It is in the nature of rules to penalize deviant behavior. The existence of formal rules can be inferred from legal and other documents. The rules (institutions) create incentives, and opportunities secure property rights, which was a fundamental requirement in establishing incentives. In a study of the causes of increasing productivity in ocean shipping between 1600 and 1850, North suggested that it was not technological progress but decreased transaction costs (due to a decline in piracy) that reduced expenses for manpower, armament, and insurance.[152] Endogenous growth theory utilizes the same structures of institutional theory—organizations, institutions, government policy, and legal framework—but whereas institutional theory says economic performance is determined by the rules in the system, endogenous growth theory says it is technology (innovation?).[153]

North commented on this matter when he said, "We are wondering: if all that is required for economic growth is investment and innovation, why have some societies missed this desirable outcome? The answer, we contend, brings us to the original thesis. . . . Growth will simply not occur unless the existence of economic organization is efficient. Individuals must be lured by incentives to undertake socially desirable activities. Some mechanism must be devised to bring social and private rates of return into closer parity."[154]

It is institutional theory that gave endogenous growth theory the analytical tools it needed in order to break out of the same dead end neoclassical theory found itself in with regard to technology. Barro and Sala-i-Martin indirectly admitted this in their comment that "probably because of its lack of empirical relevance growth theory effectively died as an active research field by early 1970 on the event of rational expectations revolution and the oil shocks. . . . Major contributions [i.e., in the period following 1970] included the incorporation of rational expectations into the business cycle model, improved approach to policy evaluation and the application of general equilibrium methods to real business cycle theory. . . . Since the mid-1980's research on economic growth [i.e., endogenous growth theory] has experienced a new boom."[155] The theory's explicit emphasis on structural aspects of innovation is what is supposed to allow it to bridge the gap between theory and various strands of empirical and historical literature.[156]

Endogenous growth theory inevitably suffers from the same weakness as institutional theory, namely, its large sociocultural content. It therefore cannot acquire the generality it seeks to achieve.[157] Freeman and Soete commented that "growth theory attempts to generalize about all countries or at least large groups of countries. The sheer variety of culture, of political institutions, of economic and social structures, of scientific and technical institutions, of policies and of their interdependence makes this an inherently difficult project."[158] As Leys noted in describing the apparent attraction and weaknesses of institutional theory (which applies equally to endogenous growth theory): "Perhaps it is the occupational hazard of the hypothetico-deductive mind, which may be especially reluctant to accept the limited degree to which the social world is ultimately ordered at all."[159] Nelson pointed out that "despite the insights such a view of the interaction between technology, investment and growth contains, particularly with respect to some of the increasing returns of features of technology change, it will be obvious . . . that new growth models remain practically by definition rather schematic presentations of the complexity of interaction between technology and growth."[160]

Perhaps the most troubling question about endogenous growth theory is its claim that technology (which is undefined) is the major source of growth. The growth models put forth by Romer and by Grossman and Helpman insist that technology drives long-run growth independently of capital accumulation.[161] A contrary view among some of the theorists is that capital accumulation and innovation (technology?) are complementary processes. Capital accumulation stimulates innovation by raising the equilibrium flow of profits, just as more innovation stimulates capital accumulation by raising the rate of productivity growth. Neither process could, it is claimed, take place without the other, since without innovation, diminishing returns are said to choke off net investment, and without net investment, the rising cost of capital would choke off innovation. Either way, the powerful effect of technology on long-term growth is affirmed.[162]

The claim that as income rises Solow's residual accounts for an increasing share of growth may have helped willing theorists to give the central place to technology. This residual has sometimes been called productivity. Technology has often been equated with productivity, as in claims that technology affects productivity by improving quality of machines and equipment, or that technology is labor-saving. All this seems to have accounted for the elevation of technology (as described in endogenous growth theory) to the principal source of growth. The claim that Solow's residual accounts for most of the long-run growth in per capita income is not compelling evidence of the primary importance of technology (undefined) to growth. Solow's residual is just, as Abramovitz put it, "a measure of our ignorance," and evidence that it "explains" a lot is just evidence that the ignorance is very large.[163] Growth-accounting exercises by Young and Jorgensen portray technology as an unimportant source of economic growth compared with capital accumulation.[164] Jones has claimed that even though R&D inputs have increased a lot over the past century, there has been no visible tendency for growth in output per person or productivity.[165] While the initial growth achieved by East Asian countries has been taken by some people to imply that technological progress was unimportant for growth, others claim that the collapse of that growth process was due to the absence of technology. The central importance of technology (as described in endogenous growth theory) has not been established. This doubt goes to the root of the theory itself because technology is the centerpiece of the theory.

Indeed, Abramovitz was correct in calling the residual a measure of our ignorance, because, as will be shown in later chapters, the concept of total factor productivity (TFP) is severely flawed. TFP is not productivity, as is claimed by growth economists; rather, it is simply another black box in which something goes in and something else comes out at the other end.

Another troubling aspect of endogenous growth theory is the reliance by all its models on the assumption (recycled from positivist orthodoxy) that capital drives growth. Most models of growth theory are an attempt to reconstruct various principal variables in order to classify them as one form of capital or the other and so claim that the variables are growth-promoting. For example, as we have noted, technology is said to be embodied in new forms of human and physical capital and experienced through the improved quality of machinery and equipment, or it is said to be a kind of capital good that can be used in combination with other factors of production, stored, and accumulated. Other models treat education and knowledge as human capital. Haig-Simons wanted the creation of knowledge to be treated like the creation of capital goods, because in either case there is an expenditure of resources that could have been devoted to produce current consumption but instead have been devoted to the enhancement of future consumption opportunity.[166] This, it seems to us, is stretching the argument. Aghion and Howitt argued that "new knowledge should also be counted as output when it is created, just as physical investment is counted when it is created even though it eventually has a further effect on GNP by increasing the potential to produce

other goods." This is again stretching the argument in order to establish some kind of capital out of knowledge. Elsewhere these authors say, "There are many ways in which a piece of knowledge thus defined is like a capital good."[167] The arguments adduced for treating the variables as capital are not always convincing. Quite apart from questions already raised about endogenous growth theory's definition of technology, it does not seem correct to regard education, innovation, and knowledge, for example, as simply geared to economic ends only. If they are also related to purposes other than economic ones, we do not know where the proponents of the theory wish to draw the line.

Fukuyama, a former U.S. top advisor, has argued that the ethical habits and rèciprocal moral obligations internalized by each community member are a form of capital, which he called social capital.[168] We can go on with this kind of reasoning until practically every social activity becomes some form of capital and manipulated through a play with statistics to correlate with growth.

This leads to the problem of measurement. Endogenous growth theory proponents are trying to measure things that are not measurable. For example, attempts by various models to quantify efforts devoted to the creation of technical knowledge by standard measures of R&D activity cannot succeed because the theory's description of technology is inadequate to quantify R&D expenditure. Nor can the assumed output of technology be measured by such data as patents, introduction of new goods, new firms, and new jobs. It is clear that we do not have any adequate measures of the theory's main concepts: stock of technical knowledge, human capital, resource cost of knowledge acquisition, rate of innovation, obsolescence of old knowledge. The theory's proponents themselves have admitted that the situation is one of theory before measurement.[169] Scott went further. After reviewing the difficulties of measuring the various components of TFP—

capital input, labor input, and so on—on which the theory is built, he concluded, "Faulty materials have been used to construct faulty models of economic growth."[170]

On the whole, it seems to us that endogenous growth theory has gone about the search for growth theory the wrong way. Perhaps a useful analogy is to liken the situation to a case in which a water source is being contaminated with a chemical. It is obvious that if one wants to find out what the chemical is, one should go to the source and carry out the necessary tests there. It would be foolish to take samples of the water at various points downstream in order to determine what the chemical is, for there will be varying proportions of the chemical at different points and also other substances introduced at other points. Similarly, if economists want to discover the sources of growth, their effort should be directed toward a scientific search for those sources, as we intend to explore in this book. Proponents of endogenous growth theory should realize that searching for sources of growth in socioeconomic institutions, organizations, trade market structure, legal framework, market structure, and so on cannot provide them with a macro theory of growth. For example, while the theory seems to paint a rosy picture of the growth and technological achievements that a global market is supposed to bring to all countries participating in it, this does not accord with the experience of poor countries.

A conclusion reached by microanalysis, as occurs with many of the endogenous growth models, will not necessarily remain valid on a macro basis because there may be interactions between components of the microanalysis that may render them invalid on a macro basis. The nature of these interactions will be examined later in this book.

It needs to be stressed that to many economists it often comes as a surprise that there are many innovations that, as pointed out by Freeman and Soete, have widespread social effects but whose economic effects may be small or indirect in macroeconomic terms. The measurement problem well illustrates the common misperception in economic analyses that technological change and its social impact can be correctly assessed only economic terms.[171] The serious danger is that economists may attempt to weigh in on sociocultural and political issues (such as education, research, or inequality) in which they are not qualified and in which economic measurements alone may be misleading.

The point can be made in another way. Growth is an economic formulation. Social and political factors create an environment that will assist with or hinder the rapid establishment of this formulation. To attempt to quantify these social and political factors (which are not measurable) and seek to make them an economic quantity is basically misleading and fruitless. We will be dealing with the economic formulation of growth in coming chapters.

2

Science and Economic Development

The basic reason why the theories of economic development and growth we reviewed in Chapter 1 are not viable is because they are not scientific. Each theory set out to show that the one before it was defective. Each lacked permanency. Agreement can only be attained when economic development experts establish one common reference point, putting their inquiry on a scientific basis.

There are economists who believe that economics is not and should not be a science. Godelier, for example, believes that economics finds its foundation on ethical and philosophical ideology. "In the end," he comments, "the problem of economic rationality at its most complex level appears to escape the domain of economic science in general and to be related to a free adhesion to 'ethical values' which are put forward as true values, those that correspond to 'true human nature.'"[1] Leys, himself a professor of political studies, believes that economic development theory is a sociopolitical subject. Weber says that the economic sector is a cultural being that acts from "the capacity and the will to take a definite attitude towards the world and lend it significance."[2] Buchanan believes that with regard to what he called "economic order" and "social order," it is the role of the economist to contribute something to the questions of "is" and "ought"— his view is that these answers cannot be only scientific, because science cannot say much on the question of value and desirability, nor merely philosophical, because "we must understand the

mechanics of economic interaction and production."[3] Like many, Buchanan thinks of science only in mechanical terms.

Despite the views represented by people such as Godelier, Leys, Weber, and Buchanan, the bulk of present-day economists like to think of economics as a science. That, after all, makes the profession more prestigious in an era in which science dominates everything. But the problem is that economists mean different things when they claim that economics is a science. Buchanan himself claimed that "scientific economics is a by-product of social philosophy."[4] The well-known British economist Robbins defined economics as "a science which studies human behavior as a relationship between ends and scarce means which have alternative uses."[5] Landes described economics as "a discipline that would be a science." He claimed that the paradox in economics as a discipline is that it "would be up to date, yet it is always rediscovering yesterday's discoveries—often without realizing it."[6] Samuelson and Nordhaus described economics as "an inexact science."[7] Hausman claimed that economics is the most "advanced" of the social sciences and is "a particularly interesting science for a philosopher to study."[8]

With such wide variation in how economists think of economics, it is necessary to delineate the territory. We have identified four essential characteristics of science. The first is that the human mind cannot alter its laws and theories but can only study them, discover them, and ally itself with them in order to achieve desired results. Gower put the position simply when he said that "science is something apart from us."[9] A second relevant characteristic of science as summarized by Davies is that "scientific activities entail entities sometimes called laws. Laws are constructs associated with scientific enterprise and the identification of regularity in the natural world."[10] Hanson similarly stated that "science enterprise is interested in the unique and individual instances (e.g. models, empirical research, etc.) only in so far as the latter illuminate and throw light on the general and assist in understanding the unifying principles."[11] Third, Van Doren observed that a main characteristic of science is that "it deals with things, not ideas or feelings."[12] Ideas and feelings belong to the domain of humans. Fourth, O'Hear pointed out that a scientific theory "has . . . no essential purpose."[13] A purpose may arise, but only after the facts are established. The Nobel prize winner Friedman summarized the third and fourth characteristics in his methodology of positive economics when he said that positive (that is, scientific) economics deals with what is, not what ought to be. "Its task," he explained, "is to provide a system of generalizations that can be used to make a prediction about the consequences of any change in circumstances."[14] A common theme running through these four criteria is that science deals with the study and understanding of nature and things that derive from nature.

Nature is not based on rationality. Hausman has observed that "throughout its history, economics has been concerned mainly with understanding how a capitalist system works. A capitalistic economic system," he explained, "is a market economy in which the means of production are privately owned and workers are free to accept or decline offers of employment." He observed that ever since Adam Smith, a particular vision of the economy has dominated economic theorizing—that of an economy made up of a number of separate agents, including individuals, households, and firms—whose only interactions with one another are voluntary exchanges of goods and services. Hausman added, "Everybody knows people have all sorts of other interactions with one another but the economist assumes, as a first approximation, that these other connections among agents can be ignored. Economic agents are conceived of as well-informed, rational and self-interested maximizers."[15] With this basic rationalistic view of economic agents, most economic theorists have sought to expand knowledge through rational analysis buttressed by intellectualism. The economist Kenneth Arrow, a Nobel laureate, once declared, "An economist by training thinks of himself as the guardian of rationality, the ascribes of rationality to others and the ascribes of rationality to the social world. It is this role that I will play." But scientific laws are not necessarily subject to rational deduction. Paul Krugman's book, *Accidental Theorist,* is the latest authoritative account on the present state of economic theorizing. According to him, "A real economist starts not with a policy view but with a story about how the world works. That story always takes the form of a model—a simplified representation of the world which helps you cut through the complexities. Once you have a model, you ask how well it fits; if it fits them reasonably well, you ask what sorts of magnitude, what sorts of trade-offs it implied. Your policy opinion then flows from the model, not the other way round."[16] But this approach will be faulted on the second characteristic of economic science, namely, that a model is useful in a scientific context only if it throws light on the general and assists in understanding the underlying principles. For example, the model of the U.S. economy, as pointed out by Krugman in the book, showed that it could not achieve 4 percent growth. This has been disproved by recent experience, and so the model did not provide a system of (scientific) generalization. Intellectualistic theorizing is best illustrated elsewhere in the same book by Krugman, who stated,

"The central ideas of economic theory are very simple: They boil down to little more than the proposition that people will usually take advantage of opportunities, plus the observation that my opportunities often depend on your actions and vice versa." Applying these ideas to particular cases "requires some close, hard thinking in which a bit of maths and some specialized jargon can help you stay on track."[17] And he pointed out that "economic theory is not a collection of dictums laid down by pompous authority figures. Mainly, it is a menagerie of thought experiments—parables, if you like—that are intended to capture the logic of economic processes in a simplified way."[18] It is clear that economic theories arising from such rational (or intellectual) analysis cannot meet the criteria of science.

Robert Solow summarized economic theorizing by saying, "All theory depends on assumptions which are not quite true. The art of successful theorizing is to make the inevitable simplifying assumptions in such a way that the final results are not very sensitive."[19] But scientific theorizing will want first to verify that all the assumptions made are correct. Many of Adam Smith's ideas still serve as reference points in economic thinking. Numerous advocates of laissez-faire (toned down today and renamed the free market) are wearing what Samuelson and Nordhaus call "Adam Smith's necktie."[20] Buchanan observed that when Adam Smith was putting forward his explanation of how markets work, he was primarily interested to press home his argument for dismantling the mercantilist regulatory apparatus of his time. Buchanan argued that some of Smith's followers' concepts of the classical political economy overextended Smith's teaching and proceeded to treat the subject as an inflexible natural science. He argued that whereas the mercantilists had failed to understand how the free market generates order, the extremists among the classical economists failed to understand that the institution of markets were not themselves immu-

table. On the first and the fourth characteristics of science alone, then, Adam Smith's ideas and those of his followers cannot pass as a scientific theory, for they had a "purpose." Like Smith, Karl Marx was a philosopher-economist with a political agenda, and the same can be said of today's political economic theorists, left-wing or right-wing. In contrast to conventional economic theorizing, as described by Krugman, the scientific researcher is seeking to find out what natural laws govern the subject of his study.

Many economists have successfully argued that substantial aspects of economics derive from natural laws. They have then proceeded to argue that economics is a science. The theory of value, for example, rests on the fact that individuals can arrange their preferences in an order and that in fact they do so. As another example, the main postulate of the theory of dynamics is that individuals are not certain regarding future scarcities. These are not postulates that admit of extensive dispute. Robbins observed, for example, that the law of diminishing returns is simply one way of stating the obvious fact that different factors of production are imperfect substitutes for one another: "We do not need controlled experiments to establish the validity of these theories—they are so much the stuff of our everyday experience that they have only to be stated to be recognized as obvious. . . . Indeed, the danger is that they may be thought to be so obvious that nothing can be derived from their further examination." Yet, he went on to argue, "in fact it is postulates of this sort that the complicated theories of advanced [economic] analysis ultimately depends." He concluded that "it is from the existence of the conditions they assume that the general applicability of the broader proportions of economic science is derived."[21] The theories Robbins mentioned are (as acknowledged by Robbins himself when he admitted that some may think nothing can be derived from these theories) not exclusively economic. They are matters of everyday experience throughout ages and in all cultures, in both economic and noneconomic situations. It therefore does not follow that the complex theorems derived from them will necessarily constitute economic science. They may or may not. Even Robbins' basic contention that economics is the science that studies human behavior as a relationship between ends and scarce means that have alternative uses is rationalistic in its content. Robbins stated that "economics does depend, if not for its existence, at least for its significance, on an ultimate valuation—the affirmation that rationality and ability [of the individual or groups] to choose with knowledge is desirable."[22] It is possible that while various concepts in economics can be said to be derived from natural science, the full body of economics itself may not be a science.

It is clear that whatever one is studying in economics—the law of scarcity, the law of diminishing returns, the market mechanism, GNP, macroeconomics, microeconomics, unemployment, inflation, and so on—is subsidiary to the underlying basic subject of economic development and growth. It is economic development and growth that constitutes the arteries of any economy. It supplies the blood that sustains the economic body. Whilst there are natural laws in some of the subsidiary issues, such as the law of scarcity and the law of diminishing returns, the whole of economics cannot be scientific until theories of economic development and growth have attained a scientific position.

Some economists have argued that economics is or should be a social science, not a natural science. Their position is based on their view that economics deals with human beings and their social interactions, which seem "different from the study of planets or proteins."[23] Friedman argued that economics encounters "special difficulties" because it deals with the interactions of human beings and because the investigator is himself part of the subject matter being investigated in a more intimate

sense than in the physical sciences.[24] This distinction between economics as a social science and physical science is unfortunate. In the first place, it is wrong to claim that economics has mainly to do with human beings. Human beings are only one component out of the three production factors that form the basis of economic development. It is true that economic development and growth is for the benefit of human beings. But the results of the so-called physical sciences are also for the benefit of human beings. It is therefore not correct to claim that in economies the investigator is more specifically part of the investigation than in physical science. Indeed, the attempt of economists to distance themselves from physical science has diverted attention from the urgent need to integrate the system of physical science (technology) into the theory of economic development and growth.

One can venture to suggest that the notion of economics as a social science has flourished because the adoption of nonscientific theories of economic development and growth theories, discussed in Chapter 1, has created many social problems. The economist gained respect because he has gone on to profess expertise in social problems such as poverty, unemployment, inequality, wages, and welfare—issues that in many countries have become more intricate because of nonscientific economic theorizing.

Substantial numbers of economists are today using the tools of economics in fields on or beyond the traditional borders of their discipline. They now study subjects traditionally studied by sociologists, political scientists, educators, epidemiologists, and even criminologists. Researchers have studied issues as diverse as AIDS transmission, financing for the illegal drug trade, the demand for religion, models of elephant survival, tax reform, urbanization, and the work ethic. But, by and large, these kind of subjects have local rather than national or universal application, which means that they do not have generalized value—they do not meet the criteria of science. Behind all this, the researchers (knowingly or unknowingly) justify their probing into these nontraditional subjects on the ground that because each topic involves limited means and ends—a typical Robbins situation—they constitute the study of the human behavior that Robbins considered economic science. As Hausman pointed out, the decision to have children or to be unfaithful to one's spouse is, on Robbins' definition, part of economics.[25]

In their treatment of economics as a science, economic researchers have over time developed and accumulated highly sophisticated analytical tools that have been greatly enhanced by ever-expanding computing capabilities, and recently they have used these analytical tools to enter new and nontraditional subjects. Economists now use ingenious models to analyze new subjects and find creative techniques to test the models' validity. So-called behavioral economists are attempting to loosen the assumptions about self-interested, rational individuals and groups that up till now have underlain mainstream economic models. Their apparent success brings up the possibility that nature has allotted discretion to human beings in a way that cannot be fully accounted for through natural science. An article on this trend in *The Economist* of December 19, 1998, concluded that if these trends continue, a decade hence it may be hard "to disentangle economics from other strands of social science."[26] In the process, economics would have lost any hope of being a natural science.

Nature

Science, therefore, has to do with discovering those laws and principles that the human mind did not create. As O'Hear put it, "A scientific theory will characteristically attempt to explain some natural phenomenon by producing a general formula or theory covering the phenomenon of that particular type."[27] Ellis said, "Science aims to provide the best possible explanation of natural phenomena."[28]

The notion that economic development and growth can derive from natural laws will strike many economists as strange, used as they are to the idea that economic theories are man-made. It is therefore significant that some well-known economists have lately emphasized that nature is the ultimate mainspring of economic growth.[29] They unfortunately did not take the analysis of this further.

Production is the source of all economic development. It is a technical process by which man transforms materials from nature to meet a desired end. In order to achieve this transformation, man must have some knowledge about the materials. This is science. It is through science that man is able to predict that if he does this or that, he can transform the materials in a particular way so as to achieve a specific end. It follows that science is a necessary ingredient of all production, without which man could not achieve production. Many economists agree that there is science of materials—that infinite range and depth of technical mysteries locked up by nature in and about materials and which man has been "discovering" since he appeared on earth. But not many economists will readily agree to the fact that nature could also have established laws governing the use of these materials in order to achieve man's maximal satisfaction of his needs. However, if it is possible to find these laws, then it might be possible to formulate immutable theories of economic development and growth.

Primal State

The main problem facing the project of discovering immutable theories of economic development is to get a clue as to what nature intended. Man has already made a lot of discoveries about natural resources. He has also developed the money economy. The problem is how to strip basic reality of the appearances covering it like a veil. In other words, so much has been man-made in the area of economic civilization that it is difficult to identify in the midst of so much clutter what nature has intended. However difficult it is, this quest is the only viable approach if we are to put economic development and growth theory on a scientific footing.

To do this, it becomes necessary to go back and study man's primal state, when formal science as it is now defined[30] was not in existence and when the money economy as it is presently constituted also did not exist.[31] Some of the world's poorest communities, where economists would say that economic development has not occurred, provide us with the best locations to initiate our study of primal societies. If basic characteristics and patterns of human economic behavior identified in primal societies can also be identified in present-day modern economies, we will be well on our way. It may then be possible, by studying and comparing these two patterns more closely, to attempt to fashion a theory of economic development and growth deriving from natural laws.

What will now follow is a study of primal societies. Black Africa is the poorest region of the world, with virtually no economic development in many areas. Much of the study of the economics of primal societies should therefore rightly concentrate on Africa, with occasional reference to the experience elsewhere. As a scientific inquiry, the study of primal societies is concerned with what is, not with what should or should not be.

Study of primal societies is essential because many deductive errors about them dominate current economic literature.[32] Primal societies have one thing in common: Their members carry out economic activities necessary to meet the basic human needs—food, shelter, recreation, and security—and generate material surpluses. In some of them, the surpluses are marginally enough to maintain the society's infrastructure—community meeting centers, paths, shrines, streams, rivers, and so on. In some, especially nomadic societies, the surplus is hardly there. Other societies have larger surpluses, which make possible their maintenance of institutions such as a standing army, the erection and maintenance of architectural structures such as palaces, stadia, paved streets, and other major works of statecraft that have in the twentieth century engaged archeologists in their increasing finds of old civilizations in various parts of the world.

To begin, imagine what human beings needed to do to survive. They needed to protect and shield themselves against the weather—cold or heat, rain, wind—and they needed to eat. Intuitively and instinctively, they used the vegetation around them to create shelters that could withstand the elements.[33] Some of the plant items and their fruit could be eaten; some, in fact, tasted nice. Water to quench their thirst could be found in springs, streams, or rivers. They came across wild animals, some indifferent, others threatening. Humans' survival instinct required that they find ways to defend themselves against these threats. Because of their superior intellect vis-à-vis these animals, they were able to outsmart some of them and kill them with stones; consequently they found that these animals were good food. They noticed that objects such as stones could be used to kill some of the more dangerous animals. Starting with a stone blank and removing bits and pieces, they ended up with a scraper, a hammer, an ax, a blade, or some other tool. By rubbing pieces of certain kinds of stones together, they discovered that they made a spark that lit fire when dry grass was introduced. Over time, they found that the heat generated could be used not only to burn things but also to assist in transforming many things: Food could be cooked, and natural substances such as minerals could be used to make tools.

Early humans also faced a threat from members of their own species, as other humans near and far engaged them in quarrels and bloody encounters in disputes arising from land, grazing, and water rights.

It became necessary to develop sharp objects of wood or metal to harm or kill both classes of enemies—animal and human.

Every primal society has its endowed natural wealth or capital—its stock of naturally given assets such as land, forest, wildfire, water, and manpower. The first thing to note is that whatever the composition or size of its natural wealth or capital, a primal society adjusts itself to utilize it in a balanced, ongoing manner. Second, and closely related to the first, is the primal society's intuitive and instinctive study of its natural capital. Under the concept of natural capital, we identify a subcategory we call raw materials, which constitute direct input into production processes. Raw materials are relatively scarce and constitute what we call a factor of production.

Manpower and Labor in Primal Communities

Labor and manpower in primal communities are basically the same. In general, the one who does the work is part and parcel of the knowledge system relevant to the work being done. There is therefore a psychological harmony between the object of the work and the individual carrying it out, because the one doing the work was usually involved in selecting and identifying the inputs.

In a primal society, there is considerable specialization along a whole range of related activities. A traditional wood carver in a primal society produced a wide range of domestic wooden furniture as well as works of art. He was a man of many skills. He was not only a botanist and a lumberjack but also a designer. As a botanist, he understood the various types of trees in the forest. He was able to identify various woods and determine their suitability for his carving.[34] He understood which wood needed to be carved soon after the tree was felled and which needed seasoning for a number of years before being ready for use.

The smith in the primal society, responsible for ironwork, was a man surrounded by mystery and magic. He was responsible for a wide range of specialist activities, both utilitarian and ritual, other than simply forging metal. The mythology that separated him from the rest of the society provided the very elements that, in the eyes of his clients, invested special powers in the knives, swords, and other metal objects he forged. Provided with a supply of iron for smelting and with charcoal (only a few species of trees were suitable for this purposes), the itinerant smith could set up his forge and begin work within a few hours. He would use an anvil of stone, hammers made of stone and iron, tongs that might be no more than a split stick or piece of bent iron, and bellows that might consist simply of a pair of animal-skin bags or, in more complex forms, two or four solid chambers covered with a loose diaphragm of skin, each pierced at the center with a long stick, which the smith's assistant would pump to produce the necessary blast. With the aid of these relatively simple tools, the primal society's blacksmith mastered all the techniques of his trade.[35]

In the more affluent primal societies, military engineering, needed for defense of the society, was a highly skilled profession. Geography played a significant role in military engineering and warfare. Even though the materials for military fortifications are provided by the environment, military engineers in precolonial Nigeria ensured that the constructed fortifications had properties and features that made them strong and resistant to fire, weather, and mold. In the open savanna area of precolonial northern Nigeria, cavalry with long-range missiles or shock weapons was possible. Labor was important in the task of fortification and defense. This was because the whole building project was nonmechanized. In Hausaland, building specialists were classed hierarchically in categories with titles such as *sarkin magida, madakin gini, galadima gini, makaman gini, turakin gini,* and *shamakin gini.* By the nineteenth century, the specialist called *gwani* (genius) had emerged in military engineering. These were appointed by the *saki* (king) and occupied a special place among palace officials. The *sarkin magida* was empowered to appoint subordinate titled officials in all towns under the control of the *saki*.[36]

In some instances, particular clans in a primal society are known for specializing in a certain trade. For example, among precolonial Nigerian Yorubas, the Oluogboro was one of the most important local deities in Ile-Ife. According to local myth, painting started as a system of writing invented by him. While he was alive, he is said to have used paints of several colors for writing scripts on the walls of his house. After he died, his wives attempted to imitate his script. They began an annual festival in his memory during which they attempted to imitate his scripts, but they always ended up with pictures, not writing. Myth had it that these pictorial compositions eventually metamorphosed into actual mural paintings over the years. The descendants of Oluogboro now are a paint clan, painting and making paints produced from reddish soil *(itepa),* kaolin *(efun),* and charcoal *(dudu)* mixed with the *igbole* plant.[37]

A deeper insight into the scope of technology in African primal societies is provided by the main theme of a lecture of the renowned historian Ajayi in a lecture titled "The Cultural Factor in Technical Development," given at the University of Lagos in April 1994:

> To say that there is a cultural factor in technological development is in fact to emphasize that the state of technology in any society is the result of the historical experience of the people. . . . There was a flourishing silkworm industry (the original Sanyan) in parts of Cendo and Oyo which (later) the colonial powers tried to cultivate during the Second World War when there was a high demand for strong fiber for parachutes. They kept the operation secret and no one has studied why the industry went out and we now accept imported yarns

for Sanyan. . . . Dyeing involved considerable skills in the technology and chemistry of colors. Colors ranged from black, blue, purple, to red, orange and yellow. Dyes were applied either to the yarn or the woven cloth. Technology was involved in the preparation of the dye and bonding it to material such that it does not damage the fiber and retains permanent coloration throughout the useful life of the fiber; that is, it has to be resistant to both water and light. Indigo was perhaps the most widespread source of dye in Africa and there are varieties of indigo-fera which occurred wild but were also often cultivated. Preparation of the dye involved breaking up the plant structure to facilitate the fermentation process and preparing the alkaline medium which in addition to encouraging the release of the indigo-blue, also acts as a mordant to fix the dye color. Yoruba dyers built furnaces of up to four feet high and five feet wide to prepare the potash for the alkaline medium. The dye pits of Kano were famous since the 17th century. The red Karan dafi from the dafi plant was very popular and, by the Laso pit technology, not only were they able to increase production of indigo dyed cloth, they were also able to produce a variety of colors not only for textiles but also for leather goods as well. By the mid-19th century, there were about 2,000 pits (in Kano) each holding between 400 and 1,000 gallons of water.

Iron smelting was a major industry in Africa. There is a study (carried out) of a site in Ajilete, in Egbado area of Ogun State in Nigeria, where pits of up to 8 feet in diameter and depths of 50 to 60 feet exist and [the area] was known to have produced good iron ore. The smelters generated heat by burning charcoal, hardwood, and shells of palm nuts. The domed furnace could get up temperatures in excess of 1500 degrees Celsius, capable of turning smelted iron into liquid iron. The quality of the resulting iron depends on the construction of the furnace and the technology of the particular process adopted, relative to the nature of the ore and the intended use. The idea is to reduce impurities and other substances such as carbon or phosphorous. One authority says that Saki smelters developed a technique of using slag from a previous smelting as flux which helped to decarbonize the iron and absorb other impurities, thus increasing the quantity and quality of the yield. When this cinder flux was used at a low temperature, for example, it helped to reduce the phosphorous content of the iron. If the same had been put through an ordinary English blast furnace of the period, it would have produced pig iron of .06% phosphorous. While with the African process, phosphorous was kept at .01% and finished product after puddling was a good steel of .22% carbon. . . .

There were other techniques and innovations in African metallurgy. In one method, tuyeres (pipes) were fitted deep inside the furnace, which allowed the preheating of the air in the tuyere to very high temperatures before it entered the chamber. "This constituted a significant technological innovation unique to African industries." . . . This encouraged Childs and Schmidt to argue the hypothesis that the operation of preheated furnaces in Africa likely produced iron in a process altogether distinctive from Europe, and more efficiently. . . . the African technology represents a separate evolutionary branch in iron technology. . . .

Indeed, the general verdict seems to be that in the 19th century, "African smelting was technologically in advance of European, Middle Eastern or South Asian smelting techniques." . . . Besides iron, tin was mined in open shafts and smelted. Some of the furnaces studied indicate that some could take up to 140 lbs. of tin-ore and eleven furnaces could be put in full blast at once, employing a staff of up to 100 people. . . .

As for salt, the Jukun salt mine and those of Oguta are well known. Using different technologies, varieties of salt were produced in various parts of Africa, especially in Western and Central Sudan—sodium chloride, sodium phosphate, sodium carbonate, potassium sulfate and calcium sulfate in various concentrations. Salt was used not only for flavoring, but also various medicinal salts—bruises, infections, venereal diseases, ailments associated with pregnancies, etc. Some were used to enhance virility and others to treat dandruff. The "industrial" uses of salts included the use as mordant in fixing dyes, tanning hides and dyeing leather. It is typical that an American author who has done much to draw attention to African technical achievements says that "many and varied, indeed often ingenious uses of salt, is

a direct consequence of retarded technology." That seems to be another synonym for "traditional technology" but at least he does not deny that there was technology in traditional crafts and artisanship. . . .

If you insist that cooking is an art, you will not deny the technology involved in the construction of post harvest maize and yam barns and the preservation of food especially in the absence of freezers and refrigerators. Various salts and herbs were used, combined with drying in the sun, heating, smoking, etc. Food preservation was particularly important for armies undertaking military exercises and for distance travelers. . . . My aim is to demystify technology and insist that we should not confuse technology with the mechanized and capital intensive factory.

The skills in a primal society were not static. For example, it was the introduction of iron and other kinds of metal—copper, bronze, and gold—that significantly changed skills originally based on wood. The stronger and sharper instruments that resulted from the use of metals facilitated the growth of traditional wood carving. It became possible to erect large wooden structures, as it was now easy to cut trees that could withstand heavy weights. The use of mud and mud-burning techniques led to permanent buildings that weathered better. The availability of metal led to the growth of the lost-wax technique for casting. In some primal societies, new technical breakthroughs were held in high regard and were sometimes attributed to named persons. The Yoruba oral tradition (oriki) has been exploited as a means of eulogizing certain indigenous inventors. According to Moyo Okediji, some of these inventions in traditional Africa were "accidental," while in others the inventors "proceeded from cautious attempts to test certain hypotheses."[38] It was largely a trial-and-error process.

Mat weaving among the Yorubas is a well-developed skill practiced mainly by women in Ipetu-Ijesa and Ipoti-Ekiti. Eearan is a special plant with long and supple stems used as a raw material in weaving; it is cultivated in large plantations in farmlands and villages around Ipetu-Ijesa, and its leaves are used not only for wrapping food but also for making roofs. The origin of the technique for mat weaving is traced to the myths of Ipetu-Ijesa. A legendary ruler is said to have given the seeds of the *eearan* plant to his son, who told his son that planting the seeds would bring prosperity to the people of Ipetu-Ijesa. His son, in turn, gave the seeds to his right-hand man, who introduced it to members of the community. Soon the farmland around Ipetu-Ijesa was full of *eearan,* but nobody knew what to do with it. At this point, the son's right-hand man decided to consult the leader of the women of Ipetu-Ijesa. According to the myth, she started conducting experiments with the plant. One day when she went to pick a few leaves of the plant, she noticed that the inside of the stems was fragile, soft, and fleshy. She calculated that the weight of the plant could not be resting on the soft, fragile core and that the main support must come from the outer part of the stem. She therefore decided to experiment further. She cut off a stem and split it, observing that it easily separated into two halves. She scraped out the soft flesh of the core and discovered that what remained was a flat, slim, but very strong and flexible fiber. This encouraged her to continue her research, and she was able to produce the first mat. Mat weavers are said to have continued with her methods, which are now well established.[39] Research was therefore a strong feature of primal life, and innovators were held in high esteem in many primal societies.

However, in the exercise of their skills and application of techniques, the primal state craftsmen and innovators base their priorities on meeting and supporting the basic needs of the society—food, shelter, recreation, and security. In the "brutal" state of nature, it is reasonable to expect security to be high on the agenda. The political, cultural, and religious structures of primal societies are an essential support system for internal and external security.

Religion and culture are geared to defining conduct, establishing dos and don'ts. The skills and techniques of warfare are integrated with the political hierarchy to establish internal order and maintain external defense and military capability.

It is clear that technological change in primal societies is an indigenous process. Its development does not depend on financial considerations.[40] Thus the craftsman's production is geared not to commercial consumption but to the maintenance of the political, cultural, religious, and defense fabric. The arts and crafts (which dominate the work of the smiths, casters, and carvers) are geared toward the mystification of religion, culture, and political authority, with this end (social maintenance) in view. Whereas, for example, in the modern setting the wood carver and smith will concentrate on making utility goods, in the primal society their works were instead dominated by artworks depicting royalty, deities, and cultural events, all acting as instruments of order, security, and leisure. In some African countries, while sculptors have the materials and tools to perfectly represent a human being in its normal proportions, the head is made a third or quarter the size of the whole body. For mythic purposes the sculptor ignores the actual proportions. The head is treated differently from the rest of the body, reflecting the contradictions that help maintain order in a primal society, namely, reminding everyone that people are not equal.[41] The chanting of a wood carver before he ventures to fell a tree is not different from early Japanese society, where many of the myths that surrounded technology survive ritually in present-day Japan.

The mystic political, cultural, and religious context does affect technology. The taboos associated with the upkeep of the political, cultural, and religious system can limit experimentation and innovation. Most persons in primal societies will therefore more likely be content to apply existing technique in their works and not break new ground.

They will make use of new inventions only after these are pioneered and well tested by others and seem to be in line with the ethos of the system.

Primal societies nevertheless were often amenable to outside ideas and techniques (what in this day and age may be called technology transfer). But except where outside conquest was involved, primal societies selected from the outside techniques and ideas they wanted and adapted them to their sociocultural technical system, in which they were championed by local technicians and often adapted to local materials. For example, it is thought that the Tuaregs' knowledge of silver gilding was probably brought across the desert from Moknine in Algeria, while their neck "cross" was influenced by people of Niger. Among the people of Senegal, the heart and club motifs found in their jewelry are believed to be copied from images in playing cards from Asia.[42] According to Davidson, the "metal age cannot be said to have begun in continental Africa, as a distinct cultural period involving new forms of society and social organization, until the working of iron became common . . . knowledge of iron-working may probably have reached west and central Africa from Kush in the last years of the pre-Christian era."[43] On the other hand, smelting furnaces excavated in Rwanda by archeologists were said by Spring to have been dated to 800 B.C., well before such technology was established in Britain and only marginally later than in ancient Greece or Italy. By the third or fourth centuries B.C., Spring said, ironworking technology was being employed in northwest Tanzania and Meroe in Sudan: "It seems likely that iron technology developed independently at these sites rather than being diffused from the North Africa coast and Egypt."[44] The lost wax method of casting bronze was said to have been learned in the old Benin empire when their king, the *oba,* invited a Yoruba smith from Ife. The method was known to have originated in the Middle East and been brought to West Africa through the trans-Sahara trade. Benin

was later on to become very famous for its bronze casting and became the center of this technique in the sixteenth century. Indeed, the palace of the *oba* was decorated with bronze heads.

The importation of finished goods from advanced economies into primal societies tended to break down their system of technology.[45] In the lecture referred to earlier, Ajayi observed that "colonialism had a devastating effect on African technological development because colonial rulers were no longer satisfied with the only commercial weapon of competition in the open market. They used their control of power to enact and enforce legislation intended to discourage if not to destroy technological innovation. They forbade war and outlawed military technology; they gave tin fields as concessions to European firms of prospectors and outlawed African participation in tin mining; they copied our texture patterns and colors and imported cheap machine-made textiles using these patterns and colors to compete. They discouraged internal trade, crafts and manufacturing while they tried to focus attention on producers and traders only for export/import trade. Colonial control weakened our capacity to innovate and to cope with such ecological factors as dwindling sources of charcoal in the face of the importation of cheaper though inferior iron. In East, Central and Southern Africa, some indigenous food crops and methods of processing food were discouraged so as to promote dependence on [foreign] factory-produced mealy maize."

The smiths of the pastoralist Maasai people converted imported Western agricultural tools into bladed weapons. They began to use imported files to finish their work, though traditionally the final polish would be painstakingly applied with local abrasives such as sand. Often the colonial powers banned locally made weapons, and so the Maasai smith forged bladed weaponry that was now only used for ritual, ceremonial, or religious purposes.

Nigeria provides another good example of

changes in iron technology. Following the beginning of the colonial period, different types of oils, chemicals, and paints in iron containers were imported by the colonial power to the colonized areas. As soon as the contents of the containers were used, the iron from them (as well as from motor parts such as flat springs and sheet metal) became available as raw material for the primal society's smiths. Imported iron bars and rods were also available to the smiths for purchase; initially they were more expensive than locally smelted iron, but gradually imported iron became ubiquitous and cheap. Smiths naturally used the cheaper sources of raw materials, which meant that demand for locally smelted iron gradually diminished, leading to the shutdown of the local iron smelting industry.[46] Also, the imported iron was easier to work, as it did not need refining before use, and was often found in flat pieces, which could be used straightaway to produce flat tools such as hoes more easily. Tools made with imported iron were said to be inferior to those made with locally smelted iron, but that made it even more profitable for the smiths to use imported metal, because the inferior tools tended to break more easily and needed to be repaired or replaced. And as the demand for the smiths' services increased, those services became more expensive.

Ohiare reported how dyers in the Yoruba areas abandoned traditional indigo dyeing when imported synthetic indigo became available. The British ruler of Okene popularized the use of British imported yarns and in 1922 established a local store where imported cottons, wools, and silks were made available to the women. These imports resulted in the abandonment of native production of hand-spun yarns, forcing local cotton growers out of business and threatening local dyeing.[47]

In many instances it seems that primal indigenous industry and technology exhibited initial resilience and adjustment in the face of Western products but finally collapsed.[48] Isolated pockets of indigenous

technologies seem to have survived to date because they meet special cultural and religious needs. But there is no doubting that new religions from outside, for example, Christianity, weakened the beliefs of traditional religion and culture, which in turn were the support mechanisms for traditional technology —thus sowing the seed for weakening the base of that technology.

Capital in Primal Societies

In trying to transform natural raw materials into other uses, man in the primal society is often forced to realize that his labor alone is not enough. As a human being, he has a number of limitations. His height is sometimes too small for certain operations. There are weights that are too heavy for him to carry. His physical strength is inadequate to undertake certain tasks. His dexterity is limited. The raw material he wants to work on sometimes needs to be held in positions that are awkward for him. He cannot stand high heat. Fire will burn him. In order for man to undertake the transformation of natural resources (production) and because of his limitations, nature seems to have provided a solution: Man can select needed items from the natural raw materials at his disposal to construct production aids, called capital. The *Oxford Dictionary of Economics* has defined capital as the man-made means of production. As production aids, capital shows up in various forms in a primal society: parts of the human body, animals, and natural materials.

The human body can be used as a production aid in several ways. One common way is to hold or support a material being transformed. In Figure 2.1, the woman is using her left hand to support the clay that she is working on. Her left hand acts as her production aid, keeping the material in the position required for her right hand to work on it. In Figure 2.2, the left hand is simply keeping the material in position to enable the rolling being performed by

Figure 2.1 **Left hand is used as a production aid (capital).**

Figure 2.2 **Here again the left hand, as production aid, supports work being done by the right hand.**

the right hand to take place correctly. The left hand is an aid to production. In Figure 2.3a, the man's toes are used by him to support the loom. The toes act as part of his capital—an aid to production.

Animals act as capital in some primal societies. Elephants, cows, horses, camels, and dogs can act as a source of motive power and can bear loads. Selected animals do not suffer man's limitations—they weigh more, can reach higher heights, can carry heavy weights, have more raw power, can work longer, and can run faster.

Natural materials also can be converted into aids to production. The conversion may involve minimal

work, such as cutting tree trunks and branches and trimming them with a knife or machete so as to use them as a weaving loom (Figure 2.3b) or a mortar and pestle (Figure 2.4). On the other hand, a grinding stone (Figure 2.5) can simply be picked up from the environment, with no conversion work needing to be done on it. At the other end of the scale, the conversion may involve a number of work processes, such as with the production of iron tools and implements.

In a primal society, capital produced from materials is intended as a means of cooperating with labor only to the extent that it helps man to overcome the basic human limitations earlier listed. In primal

Figure 2.3a **The toes and legs are the production aid.**

Figure 2.3b **The legs and toes, together with the loom (made of tree branches), constitute the production aid.**

societies where population is sparse, there is a greater tendency to make more use of material production aids in place of human labor. Where there is great abundance of population—high-density population tends to go hand in hand with low density of natural materials—there is a tendency to make greater use of human and animal capital. Capital in a primal society need not have a long life. A stick used as a spindle can be discarded immediately after use and another one made up when it is required again. The stems used for a loom could be discarded at any time. If the owner chooses to keep them, it is most probably because of the convenience of not having to look for another set of items next time. The mud and earthenware material construction used for iron smelting furnaces is likely to be destroyed after each smelting and another one constructed next time. The mud construction used in lost-wax casting was usually discarded after each wax pouring. More durable production aids such as stone and iron tools were generally used until they were worn out.

Production aids, whatever form they take, are usually affordable. If there is a need to increase production, more production aids can be made or fabricated, or existing production aids can be used more intensively. In many instances, it is the craftsman who produces his own production aid, so the know-how for capital production was not always a specialist function. In sum, then, in primal societies the capital needed for production is readily avail-

Figure 2.4 **Wooden mortar as capital equipment.**

Figure 2.5 **Grinding stones as capital.**

able and affordable, though the expertise for producing capital is different from that for producing goods.

It is clear, therefore, that Samuelson and Nordhaus were incorrect when they claimed that "in the poorest regions, urgent current consumption competes with investment for scarce resources." "The result," they claim, "is that too often there is too little investment in productive capital as necessary for rapid economic progress."[49] Todaro claimed that the essential feature of capital accumulation— which he regards as the base of economic development in conditions of underdevelopment—is that it involves a trade-off between present and future consumption.[50] Samuelson, Nordhaus, and Todaro were here introducing positivist orthodoxy through the back door. Samuelson and Nordhaus saw a nonexistent vicious circle when they claimed that in poor

societies, the standard of living is so near to subsistence that they could not reduce consumption without great hardship.[51] In actual fact, primal societies did not lack natural resources. The surplus the two economists have in mind is not natural resources but the financial resources with which to manufacture and procure capital equipment from an advanced economy. So in their attempt to push their positivist orthodoxy argument, they claimed that poor countries have one advantage: "They can hope to benefit by relying on the technological skills of more advanced nations. . . . In a machinery catalog they can find tractors, computers and power looms undreamed of by the great inventors of the past."[52]

Primal societies are not money economies. So it is clear that the statements of these authors and their recommendations do not apply to primal societies, which in general are self-reliant.

If we were to follow Samuelson and Nordhaus' positivist orthodoxy prescription and introduce a power loom into the indigenous weaving industry of a previously primal society—a society entering industrialization, in the modern terminology—a number of consequences will follow. There will be a need to provide electricity to power the loom. The society will need to seek outside loans or aid for this. The power loom will render redundant all natural and manpower resources used in producing the preexisting indigenous looms. It may turn out that the power loom that has been procured is not adaptable to the local yarn. This may mean the importation of outside yarn. The power loom will most probably produce far in excess of what the society can consume. The society will therefore need to look for outside markets on which it will now depend economically. In the end the introduction of the power loom will turn a previously self-reliant society into a dependent economy. This is the typical dependency scenario discussed in the first chapter.

Materials in Primal Societies

The heart of all economic activity in the primal society is its natural material endowments, not capital, for capital is primarily developed from raw materials. It is therefore an analytical mistake to give pride of place to capital vis-à-vis materials, as do many current economic texts.

Conventional economists could learn from noneconomists who have studied primal societies. Spring, a sociologist, described her findings in remote areas of Africa. She said, "Traveling in this remote area was like stepping onto a different planet." Writing mainly with respect to jewelry production in primal African societies, she said:

Never before had I imagined such a variety of peoples, all distinguished by their striking and often strange body decoration. Some were covered by beads, others patterned with ritual scars, their ears and lips distended and plugged with ornaments. Ochre highlighted the graceful bodies of young girls, while some elders wore remarkable hairstyles packed in blue clay. Led on by my newfound curiosity, I began to discover that all these exotic fashions—in jewelry, body art, and even clothing—were not merely adopted for beauty. . . . I found that throughout the vastness of the continent the jewelry continued to change according to materials available, the lifestyle and cultural contacts of the people. It even changed with the terrain in which they lived, differing from desert to forest, savanna to mountainside, between settled and nomadic groups of one tribe. In some areas . . . plant and animal materials were predominant until recently: belts might be made from ostrich eggshells or fine antelope bones, bracelets from leather, necklaces from fiber of palm trees. Elsewhere people had access to elements more precious by Western standards: ivory, bronze, silver and gold. Materials, designs and techniques might be of local origin, or brought along trade routes centuries old; certain pieces might be inspired by the achievements of an illustrious chief, others by legend or simply by creativity of a local craftsman. As I delved back through the oral and written history of Africa, I became increasingly aware of refinements in form and technique achieved in parts of the continent—of ten centuries ago and sometimes well in advance of similar developments in Europe.[53]

Economists need to know that what matters is not whether a poor society is endowed with natural resources or not—much of their pronouncements on this are often based on limited information. What Spring was emphasizing is the ability of primal societies to adapt to their local factor endowments to enable them to meet their needs.

Economists fall into two groups—one group that says that poor societies have abundant resources but don't know how to use them, and another that says that poor societies are poor because they lack the natural resources. Say Samuelson and Nordhaus, "Some poor countries of Africa and Asia have been poorly endowed by nature, and such land and minerals as they possess must be divided among dense populations. The romantic notion that there remain in these countries areas of overlooked valuable resources has largely been exploded by geographers."[54] But each of these two groups misses the essence of economic development: balance and adaptability.

There is abundance of raw materials in nature. For example, there are stalks of raffia, evea, and ronier palms, tropical palm leaves, long ropes of phrynium, rattan vines, millet, and millet grass— all for different types of weaving in different climates. In the savanna areas, millet is used as a food, for making beer, for thatching, and for baskets. In the tropical areas, palm trees provide palm oil, palm kernels for eating and for producing oil, palm wine, palm leaves for roofs, oil for soap, palm branches for fencing and structures, and shells as a source of heat. Palm leaves can be twisted into a spiral and made into a broom, or bark can be made into cord and fiber.

To find use for available natural resources is a specialty of primal societies. For example, appearance and personal decoration, as Spring noted, were important in primal societies. She failed to state that before imported beads from Europe were readily available in any quantity in East Africa, jewelry was made sometimes of iron and clay but mainly of animal and vegetable substances: bone, horn, hair, wood, roots, and seeds. Ostrich eggshells were chipped and rounded into beads, a process used in Kenya since at least 7000 B.C. Some women of Kenya wear their hair in a cockscomb-like arrangement made with mud, animal fat, and ochre.

Clay generally is traditionally used by the Turkana tribe to fashion their elaborate hairstyles. The hair is twisted into small plaits that are covered with clay and shaped into a bun on top of the head.

The hairstyle may take up to three days to perfect and is meticulously remade every three months.[55] Dinka men bleached their hair yellow by applying a paste of cow's urine and ash. Although primarily done for beauty, it is noteworthy that this also acts as a disinfectant.[56]

When a society is not well endowed with any particular material, it finds ways to economize or do without it. For example, with water scarce in the desert, Tuareg indigo-dyed fabric is a deep color with a metallic sheen, the result of the dye being beaten into the fabric.

Alcoholic drinks were produced in primal societies, using grains or other suitable vegetable products. Okagbue described two alcoholic drinks produced in the middle and middle western parts of Nigeria, each produced from available natural products—malted sorghum and a combination of sorghum and maize.[57] In malting, appropriate grains are steeped in water for one to two days and then allowed to germinate for up to five days. Germination is arrested by sun-drying for one to two days, after which the malted grain is dried and then ground into powder. In Ibadan, *gari* (a fermented cassava product) is mixed with malted grain and water in the ratio of 1:2:6, stirred vigorously, and left to ferment for two days. The mixture is then boiled for about four hours and allowed to mature for another two days. In Lanai, Okagbue described the system by which ground malted grain is mixed with water, stirred, and fermented for twenty-four hours. One-tenth is withdrawn, and then the rest is boiled overnight to concentrate it and cooled. The unboiled fraction is returned to the main mash as a starter. Another forty-eight hours' fermentation is required to produce the beer. In *pito* production, malted grains are ground, mixed with water, and boiled. After cooling, the mash is filtered through a fine mesh basket. The filtrate is left to ferment until it becomes sour in taste. Then it is concentrated by boiling and cooled. A starter from a previous brew is added and further fermentation is allowed to proceed overnight. The final product is a dark brown beer.

Among the Tuaregs in the desert zone, where the camel is the key animal, their artisans made arms such as lances and *lanti* shields. The latter is made of the skin of the camel called *lanti,* which is tanned with milk and the shells of ostrich eggs for a whole year. Spring reports that iron makes no impression on such leather. If it is struck by swords, the swords glance off. If the *lanti* should suffer a scratch or cut, it could be dampened with water and rubbed with a hand, and the marks disappear.[58] As usual in many primal societies, the Tuareg shields were, despite their technical base, inextricably linked with myth and religion, as the shields were also intended to protect their owners from physical harm and from enemy curses.

These examples illustrate the vast application of knowledge of natural resources in primal societies. In the case of the different beers described, the science is the microbial conversion of sugar present in a potable liquor into alcohol. In each of the cases, the science was the result of knowledge gained by trial and error. In the case of northern Nigeria's *bukuru* beer, made from sorghum, the fermentation is carried out by yeasts that also produce lactic acid, which increases considerably the acidity of the fermentation mixture, whose pH falls from about 6.4 to 3.7 in forty-eight hours. The yeasts are responsible for converting sugar to alcohol, and after fermentation is complete, boiling kills the yeasts and evaporates the lactic acid. These principles are the same for the industrial Western production of beers using barley and wheat. Yet in many former colonial territories, large modern beer plants have been built, flooding the markets with beer made of imported grain. Sophisticated advertising of the introduced beer has seen the demise of primal society beer-making techniques based on the same science.

Education in primal societies is largely informal, with knowledge, values, and beliefs passed on through oral culture. In oral cultures, knowledge, values, and beliefs exist primarily in the form of practices, and their preservation is a by-product of repeated usage. In primal societies, change occurs gradually, sometimes so gradually as to go unnoticed. One learns by watching the older ones and participating. The fact that what is learned is not stored and passed out as knowledge does not make the process any less an education than what obtains in industrialized societies. In primal societies, techniques and craft knowledge are inextricably woven with sociocultural and religious structures. It is therefore wrong to generalize as Aghion and Howitt did when they claimed that technology change and capital accumulation are economic decisions. This does not apply in primal societies. They assert (incorrectly) that as a general rule, "new ideas generally need new vintage of capital goods for their implementation."[59] In primal societies, new ideas are essentially new takes on the nature and properties of materials, and these ideas do not necessarily create new capital. The claim of a direct link between new ideas and capital in modern economies is also misleading because new ideas in modern economies start with the discovery of new materials or new properties of materials and may or may not lead to new capital to exploit them.

Agricultural Economy?

It is clear from all we have said so far that it is not correct to regard all primal societies as agricultural, as many economists do. While many primal societies rely on organized agriculture, others are in tropical forests, where people survive through collecting food from the wild. In arid areas, which may not be conducive to cultivation, people survive through nomadic living. If by describing a society as agricultural one means that its technology depended on the use of raw material arising directly from agriculture, this is still wrong because much of the raw material in a primal society is (as we have seen) processed industrially into various end products using traditional techniques. Other economists describe primal societies as agricultural because they incorrectly associate science and technology with modern industry, discounting the science and technology that are produced and used in huts, in residential compounds, and under the shade of trees. Perhaps the notion of agricultural economies comes from the 1950s, when Lewis was writing about the abundant labor to be transferred from rural agriculture to urban industries; by this time primal industries had already significantly diminished, leaving primal societies with only survival agriculture and high unemployment.[60] However it developed, the notion that primal societies were agricultural has contributed to economists' neglect of the vibrant science and craftsmanship that kept these societies functioning.

Amato wrote, "Trial and error and accidental discovery: these are the procedures by which for the last 2.5 million years, humanity and its hominid progenitors slowly acquired the skills needed to transform raw materials into stuff for constructing things—for the first makers of stone tools; for early metallurgists who learned to combine copper and tin ores to make more workable and harder bronze alloys; for the Samurai sword makers who learned and then ritualized the transformation of iron into the superior steel edged sword." He added, "The original noisy act of material engineering—striking a stone where before there had been a dull surface— is no different from what people in Silicon Valley do when they implant boron and phosphorous atoms (stepping stones for electrical charges) into pristine wafers of crystalline silicon to create the semiconductor of the microelectronic revolution. The goal of both procedures is the same: to alter materials so that they can perform in new technological ways. Despite the apparent crudeness of chipping stones to make tools, the kinship between the

original stone flakers and the most modern materials engineers goes atomically deep." In the area of chemistry, he remarked, "For centuries alchemists, chemists and sundry tinkerers [including the brewers in primal societies] pulverized, mixed, boiled, distilled, roasted, extracted, electrolyzed, and otherwise fiddled with whatever substance they could find in the mineral, animal and vegetable domains."[61] It is clear that science was very much a part of primal societies and that present-day science derives from and is rooted in their science—each generation building on the last, block upon block. Studying science and technology as if they are recent innovations—as many economic texts seem to imply —is bound to give misleading conclusions.

Heat

In primal societies, the importance of heat was recognized as soon as primal man was able to produce a spark. As Amato observed, "the use of fire to change the stuff of the world" was one of the major turning points in human history. "Fire's heat has the capacity to reach down to the molecular identity of a material and then jumble, reorient and rearrange it to yield almost magical transformations. Wood becomes smoke, heat, invisible gases and ash. Dull, crumbly ore becomes lustrous metal. Wet, malleable clays become hard pottery. Sand becomes glass. It may all have been accidental in the hands of the first users but the consequences were and are world-changing."[62] It is to be expected that the quest for sources of heat has long been on man's agenda.

Recall Goucher's account that Africans installed tuyeres (pipes) fitted deep into the smelting furnace; this was because they wanted to achieve higher temperatures than could be obtained with the small hand-bellows kind of furnace. They must have known that a given temperature rise yields a more than proportionate increase in heat.[63] Goucher pointed out that the preheating of the air blast by inserting numerous clay tuyeres deep into the base of the surface also created "temperatures sufficient to produce a form of mild steel which for many centuries was preferred to brittle imports from overseas."[64] Heat energy was abundantly used in crude fractionation columns. It was used to achieve desired chemical reactions such as in the production of traditional beer. We will later take up the central role of energy in economic development and growth.

Factor Substitution

The fact that in primal societies capital (aids to production) was produced by utilizing natural materials or provided by human or animal power means that capital, labor, and material were substituted for one another in these societies.

Capital was often used to substitute for material when the amount of material used in production of a given item needed to be reduced or controlled. If a large object such as a bronze mask was to be made, it became necessary to reduce the quantity of bronze to be used by producing it as a hollow object. This was made by a complicated form of lost-wax production known as hollow casting. As distinct from the ordinary lost-wax method for producing solid objects, hollow casting required extra capital in the form of an extra inner core made of clay or sand of about the same size as the object desired but without the details of the final object. This substitution of capital for material is also seen in the production of hollow bricks, a product of early Roman times. As another example, recall that in Figure 2.1, the left hand of the pottery maker acts as a production aid. It enables the right hand to reduce the amount of clay used, so as to produce a thin, light pot used for carrying water on the head over long distances from a stream or river. Too, the clay tuyeres used in the iron smelting furnaces made it possible to achieve higher-temperature operations, which reduced input of ore per unit of output of iron.

Labor was also used to substitute for materials in primal societies. In societies where the supply of limestone and other paint-making materials was scarce, people acquired expertise in using labor more intensively so as to economize on paint used for shrines and other traditional structures. Traditional papermaking in a number of primal societies used a lot of labor in order to ensure that the appropriate thickness of paper was made and avoid excessive use of materials. In traditional Japanese papermaking techniques, the *tororo* and the basic fiber concentrated in the vat were provided and put in place in minimal quantities and forceful labor action was applied in order to provide a clean and even writing sheet. This is because the *tororo* and the fiber have amounts of hemicellulose that quickly build up into thick layers resistant to the passing of more stock. The labor-intensive activity helps save on raw material usage. The Maya people used a wooden mallet on a stone to vigorously and consistently work a bark paper strip with a thin white plaster coating in order to conserve coating material.

In a primal society, the primary objective of substituting capital for labor is not to displace labor but to undertake tasks where human labor is inadequate. Figure 2.6 shows a machine used in Kenya to extract the juice from sugar cane. The liquid sugar produced was used as a component for the local production of local liquor through fractionation. The machine, which is made of wood and locally smelted iron, extracts more juice from the cane than is possible with human manual labor alone. As another example, notice that in Figure 2.5, the two pieces of stone are arranged in a way that turning one resulted in a finer grind of millet through an ingenious gear ratio action. And Figure 2.7 shows a simple mechanical device in a shanty workshop that drives a metal pin into wood.

It looks as if in general, nature has established that man within limits can substitute labor, capital, and material to meet varying requirements depend-

Figure 2.6 **Wood metal-drilling machine.**

Figure 2.7 **Extracting juice from sugar cane using capital made of wooden trunks.**

ing on the production function and the relative factor endowments of the location. In a primal society the substitution is sometimes an instinctive act and sometimes based on trial and error.

If the inputs in a primal society are labor, capital, and material, what about land? Todaro defined factors of production as "the resources or inputs required to produce a good or service." He listed what he called "the basic categories of factors of production" as land, labor, and capital.[65] On the surface of it, land seems to be a necessary input in production in primal societies. After all, traditional societies were generally thought to be dependent on land for their survival. But production is a technical process by which man seeks to alter the physi-

cal or chemical character of natural materials to meet his needs. Land is not a component of this transformation. Land, like water, is important from the production point of view only insofar as it holds many natural materials. In some primal societies, peasants paid rent for land. With the beginning of the Industrial Revolution, entrepreneurs paid rent for industrial land. So rent was part of the production cost. This is, however, not a reason to list land as a production input. In calculating production costs, many an entrepreneur includes as overhead items that are only incidental to the essential technical process of production. That does not mean that these items are production inputs.

The inclusion of land as a production input has a historical origin. The classical economists, of whom Adam Smith, David Ricardo, and John Stuart Mill are the most prominent, laid emphasis on production and on the factors that influence the supply of consumption goods. In their view, there were three components of this system, each bringing along its basic inputs into the system: capitalists with their capital or stock of accumulated goods, landlords with their land, and workers with their ability to work. The neoclassical economists never took technology seriously, and so it is understandable that their analysis of production was not a technical one.

It is noteworthy that in his well-publicized account of the U.S. economy from 1929 to 1986 and in a similar study he conducted for the U.S. Department of Labor analyzing sources of growth of the U.S. economy over the period 1948–1986, Denison concluded that land made zero input into the U.S. growth despite that country's abundance of land.[66]

Basic Personality

In Chapter 1, we pointed out that the relationship between a developing economy and an advanced economy was like the development of a human being. Although the outward features may appear different from stage to stage, at each stage we are dealing with the same individual with the same basic personality. Within the realm of the science of economic development, it is the primal society economy that "grows" into an advanced economy. We are interested to find out what constitutes the "basic personality" of economic development and growth.

The Japanese and Chinese economies are today regarded as the only non-Western economies capable of self-sustaining economic growth. McRae called the two countries "two giants."[67] He reckoned that in economic terms China's economy would be the largest in the world of 2020, while the richest would be Japan. Since political power follows economic power, McRae reasoned that by 2020 China and Japan will be joining the United States as the dominant political force in the world.[68] The route to this position for China and Japan has been long. Let us trace the link between primal societies of Japan and China and their present economic achievement in order to identify their basic personality, if any, and how these set the character of their present.

Japan

Japan's early socioeconomic history is well documented.[69] Humans are thought to have arrived in Japan more than thirty thousand years ago. Evidence from the Jomon culture, beginning around ten thousand years ago, shows that this early population supported itself by hunting and fishing, living in pole-and-thatch dwellings in small and scattered communities, mostly near the coast. They caught fish and shellfish by netting, diving, digging, and fishing from small, maneuverable boats about the inlets and bays, with occasional forays farther from shore. They supplemented this fare with forest fruit and game, including deer and wild boar. Over the next seventy centuries improvements were introduced into domestic architecture and daily life. The simple room was enlarged and its framing was reorganized so that a center pole was no longer needed to support the roof. House heating was introduced. Drier stone floors replaced bare earth. Pottery firing provided more serviceable utensils. An increasing variety of tools and pottery facilitated daily activities such as cooking, washing, mending, hunting, and fishing.

Around the third century B.C. emerged the Yayoi culture—basically agricultural, growing paddy rice as well as dry-field grain and storing the harvest in their villages in elevated granary buildings. As time passed, people acquired the potter's wheel and improved kiln techniques, and developed spinning and weaving technology. They refined and improved tools of cultivation, replacing stone implements with metal ones. Initially importing their metalware, they eventually acquired a bronze and iron technology of their own, which in turn made possible superior craftsmanship. As elsewhere in other primal societies, craftsmanship was for functional purposes but more particularly for ritual and religious purposes.

By the sixth century A.D., during the Yamato era, a new technology of warfare had made its appearance. According to Totman, "Those who employed it were able to impose on Japan a radically new phenomenon: political consolidation. . . . It is not clear whether these fighting men were large numbers of invaders from the continent or mostly, as seems more probable, natives of the islands who acquired continental weaponry and for their own use."[70] This period provides evidence of a pattern of aristocratic leadership. The splendor of those early rulers is immortalized in huge burial mounds, some of them surrounded by wide moats.[71] The great size of the tombs demonstrates the immense workforce that the rulers of those days were able to employ year after year. Buried with the dead ruler were implements of his life: helmet, armor, sword, bows, arrows, knives, beads, pottery, decorative designs, wall illustrations of his glories. Around the tomb were placed clay figurines of warriors, horses of many sorts, furnishings, and so on. These remains demonstrated the military character of the elite with their associated technology and craftsmanship.

Continental influences also played a broader historic role by helping make the centuries of Yamato rule ones in which the economy of Japan expanded. Simple production aids, such as the use of draft animals (notably horse and oxen) and the better use of hoes, spades, and sickles, increased per capita productivity. Enriched by Chinese techniques, Yamato-era Japanese used better carpentry tools, including saws, clamps, and nails. They mastered the casting of precious metals and the technique of gilding. More varieties of silk and hemp weaving and dyeing became established.

Until the end of the sixteenth century civil warfare was almost continuous in Japan, yet, according to Roberts, "these troubles did not check the consolidation achieved so far of a Japanese culture which remains across the centuries a brilliant and moving spectacle and still shapes Japanese life and attitudes even in an era of industrialism. It is an achievement notable for its power to borrow and adopt from other cultures without sacrificing its own integrity or nature."[72] Primal Japanese society was dominated by the *daimyo* system, in which the country was divided up into quasi-independent domains. Each barony strove to increase its wealth by developing its own resources and becoming as far as possible self-supporting. It did this by erecting barriers both physical and political against intrusion from other domains. According to Sanson, while this system hampered the growth of a large national market, "it did on balance contribute to an all around increase in production and in the administration of their fiefs, the daimyos paid special attention to economics."[73] The small market of each barony, coupled with the country's relatively low amount of natural resources, called for a different technology from that of the West, which has served the country well in modern times. Japanese imports of technology were combined with domestic innovation, not substitutes for it, and largely eschewed the Western labor-saving innovations of the eighteenth century, which meant standardization, economies of scale, and the introduction of more productive machinery but made little sense in a country where restrictions on overseas trade and a stable population limited the growth of markets and where a complex status system fragmented the domestic market into a mosaic of small niches. Rather than attempt large-scale production of standardized goods, it was more profitable to pursue what would now be called product differentiation: creating distinctive local specialties often using a particular local raw material and aimed at a specific segment of the social order. During the Tokugawa era, inventiveness was channeled toward small-scale, labor-intensive innovation rather than labor-saving modernization.

These characteristics were partly a reflection of Japan's natural endowment—its shortage of most raw materials and its abundance of labor.[74]

It is clear from this summary that in many ways Japanese and European development patterns had substantial differences, many of them rooted in the regions' early history. Japan, from its primal days, has had to adjust to a relatively inhospitable mountainous setting with very few natural raw materials; it is a relatively small land, not as large as France and not even the size of California, with less than one-fifth of the country level enough for cultivation. Thus it is much smaller in usable land than it appears on the map.

By the early twentieth century, the Japanese advantage, according to Landes, was that it could build on "those branches of industry already familiar and changing even before Meiji—silk and cotton manufacture in particular but also processing of food staples immune from foreign imitation. . . . In short, the Japanese pursued comparative advantage rather than will-o'-the-wisp of heavy industry. Much of this was small scale."[75] That is, Japan developed in accordance with its factor endowment.

It is therefore simplistic to ascribe Japanese economic success in the twentieth century to the copying of Western technology, as many scholars even today still do by arguing that it was the Meiji government that started early Japanese industrialization by selecting and importing foreign technology. Others who still insist on this theory of copying claim that cultural tradition in Japan paved the way for this success, as individual initiative is suppressed and the Japanese family hierarchy makes for a lifelong commitment that enables them to adapt to the technological demands of the modern world. These authors do not give consideration to the possibility that copying is the Japanese way of asserting their supremacy, because they end up making something better and more suited to their requirements than the original thing. After all, early Japan looked to China for a long time for ideas and practices, but eventually Japan was able to militarily overwhelm China.

The Japanese have been so successful with this copying because throughout history they have been aware that many of their fundamental objectives and problems are different from those of the foreigners. Landes writes that when the Japanese first encountered the Europeans, the Japanese "went about learning their ways. They copied their arms; they imitated their time keepers; they converted in large numbers to Christianity. And still felt superior."[76] Landes was convinced that many of the Japanese who converted to Christianity did so because it "provided a channel for European trade and technological assistance in a tough political arena."[77] However, Landes' claim that copying the West never made the Japanese feel smaller misses the point. It was not a matter of feeling smaller or bigger; rather, the Japanese realized that theirs was a delicate balance in which technology was woven within a sociocultural, political, religious, and security matrix, one that foreign influences could upset.

Why, after Japan began to persecute and expel Christians and ban foreign trade (a move that caused the Japanese march of technological progress to falter), did the Europeans not fight the Japanese into submission? One reason given is that Japan's isolation as an island nation provided a sort of natural protection—what Roberts called "the passive advantages conferred by seas around Japan which kept out invaders." Another possibility is that "there was no real danger of foreigners exploiting internal discontent" in Japan.[78] Can it be said that the Japanese were lucky?

China

China has many features that make its economic history different from that of the West. Chinese primal society goes as far back as 10,000 B.C. China is bigger in size than the United States, with four or five times the U.S. population, but on a per capita basis, China is very poorly endowed with resources compared to the United States. The huge expanse that is China contains many climates and many regions. There is a great divide between its north, scorching and arid in summer and cold and bare in winter, and its south, humid and flood-prone in the summer and green in winter. The country's major internal divisions are set by mountains and rivers. Three great river valleys (the Huang Ho or Yellow River, the Yangtze, and the Hsi) drain the interior and run across the country roughly from west to east. Much of China is mountainous, and except in the extreme south and northeast, its frontiers still sprawl across and along great ranges and plateaus.

As far back as Neolithic times, there was evidence of jade and wood carving, production of wooden vessels (some utilitarian but mostly ceremonial), use of chopsticks, and silkworm cultivation— all activities that to date form the continuing characteristics of Chinese industry. Millet was becoming a widespread crop, and was to serve as the staple of the Chinese diet for a long time. Bronze casting and pottery making also developed early on.

The first documentary and archeological evidence of Chinese civilization comes from the Shang dynasty, which began somewhere around 1700 or 1600 B.C. Several small objects from the Shang dynasty "reveal a civilization . . . [that] is capable of exquisite work, above all in its ceramics," according to Roberts. Chinese ceramics matured much earlier than those of Europe, and "pride of place must be given . . . to the great series of bronzes which began in early Shang times and continue thereafter uninterruptedly. The skill of casting sacrificial containers, pots, wine bars, weapons, tripods was already at its peak as early as 1600 B.C." Bronze casting appeared so suddenly and at such a high level, according to Roberts, that historians have long sought to explain it by transmission of the technique from outside. But there is no evidence for this, and the most likely origin of Chinese metallurgy is in locally evolved techniques in several centers in the late Neolithic.[79]

The Shang showed evidence of being able to mobilize large amounts of labor for the building of fortifications and cities. These grand projects were continued under the next dynasty, the Chou, when a big effort was made to build canals for transport. This grand-scale project management competence also led to the building of the Great Wall to provide a continuous barrier against the barbarians, much of which was accomplished in the decade beginning 214 B.C. under the Chin dynasty. It was with this same human-labor-dominated technique that the Communist regime, much later, was to construct dams in which every piece of stone was carried on the head or shoulder by a human being, but it is clear that several great determinants of the future of China had already been settled in outline by the end of the Chin period.[80]

The introduction of iron in about 500 B.C. had a noticeable effect on agriculture in China, as it did in many other societies. Iron weapons soon followed. Chinese technique in handling the new metal was advanced even in those early days, probably based on experience with bronze casting and experiments in which it was found that high temperatures could be produced.

The invention of brush calligraphy in the third century B.C. was enthusiastically adopted. At first it was practiced on woven cloth, but around A.D. 105 the Chinese eunuch Ts'ai Lun proclaimed his marvelous invention of true paper—a thin felted material formed on flat, porous molds from macerated vegetable fiber. Despite its early emergence in China, papermaking did not reach Europe until the thirteenth century.

China's problems in dealing with the balance between natural endowments and population was always a source of social and political instability, as circa A.D. 281–302, when serious famine, plague, locust attack, and flooding in the agricultural north caused a significant population shift toward the south and political upheavals. In the south, rice was the prevailing crop, rather than the millet, wheat, and bean crops typical of the north. While the soil of the south was well watered and fertile, it required raw human muscle to clear the land, channel and control the floodwaters, and subdue the aboriginal inhabitants. Apart from rice, other new crops became available, and together these made possible the overall growth of China's population.

Industry continued to make advances. Sericulture, an ancient industry, assumed greater economic importance as dyeing techniques improved and the quality of colored silk became better. Tea had become a popular drink, and new skills were introduced for processing the leaves and preparing the beverage. Chinese porcelain manufacture continued to improve, with Lo Yang in the north making chinaware for the royal house and Chekiang province in the south specializing in dishes that, according to contemporary description, "look like ivory, but are as delicate as thin layers of ice." Artisanship progressed in the working of bamboo, leather, metal, ivory, and precious stones.[81]

Wright has observed that but for the success of the Sui dynasty in China in reuniting north and south China, the Chinese world might well have been divided into independent successor states, perhaps four of them, each with its own vernacular and culture.[82] The Sui has been likened to the Chin dynasty, which eight hundred years before united the north and south for a short time. As in all primal societies—the Chinese were not an exception—the Chinese emperor was not simply the head of the apparatus of state. He was at once cosmic pivot and moral lawgiver, the guardian and interpreter of ancient cultural traditions from which the norms of proper behavior, public and private, were ultimately derived.[83] All technology and science in a primal society, as already pointed out, were designed to

derive and support the basic needs, of which the mystic, religious, political, and security matrix was the central core.

The early technical competence and achievement in China was best demonstrated by the naval expeditions made between 1405 and 1433 under Yung-lo of the Ming dynasty and his immediate successors. The first of the Chinese fleets consisted of 317 vessels carrying twenty-eight thousand men. Some of the vessels were among the most seaworthy the world had yet seen, with the largest having a length of about 517 feet and a width about 212 feet. With favorable winds, they could make speeds of six knots an hour. The compass, which was independently discovered around this time in both China and Europe, became an indispensable instrument for navigation.[84]

These flotillas surpassed in grandeur the small Portuguese fleets that came later. They were probably the largest vessels the world had seen: "multideck junks" acted as floating camps each carrying hundreds of sailors and soldiers testimony to the advanced techniques of Chinese shipbuilding, navigation and naval organization. [These] were the so-called treasure ships, built for luxury and fitted with grand cabins and windowed halls. . . . Other ships met other needs: eight-masted "horse ships" . . . [that also carried] building and repair materials; seven-masted supply ships, carrying food; six-masted troop transport; five-masted warship for naval combat and smaller fast boats to deal with the pirates. The fleet even included water tankers to ensure fresh water for a month or more. . . . The whole seaboard was drawn into the effort, while inland forests were stripped for timber. Hundreds of households of carpenters, smiths, sail makers, rope makers, caulkers, craters and haulers, even timekeepers, were moved by fiat, grouped into teams, domiciled in yards next to their work. Since the shipwrights and their apprentices were generally illiterate, learning proceeded by example, using hand-crafted models whose parts fitted perfectly without nails. No detail was too small to escape the planning of the shipwrights: overlapping planks, multitude layers, joints between planks caulked with jute and covered with sifted lime and tung oil, iron nails sealed against rust, special woods for every purpose, even large "dragon eyes" painted on the prow so that the ship should "see" where it is going. . . . The work itself was done in huge dry-docks (China anticipated European technology by hundreds of years) opening on to the Yangtze. In this way, over a period of three years, the Chinese built or refitted 1681 ships. Medieval Europe could not have conceived such an armada.[85]

When Europeans arrived in China in the early sixteenth century, they found a society that was inward-looking and closed in on itself. They met what Landes called "an unaccustomed shock of alien condescension."[86] The Chinese had an overwhelming confidence that they knew best what they were doing and what they needed. The first Portuguese visitors in combination with Catholic missionaries that came to China wanted access. The Portuguese merchants wanted trade and the missionaries wanted to establish their religion, and hoped to use Western technology to win the attention of the Chinese. But the Chinese response was a repudiation or depreciation of Western technology, and eventually the Europeans finally blasted their way into China (using gunpowder, a Chinese invention that China did not develop for use in weapons, relying instead on incendiaries because these seemed better suited to their superior numbers).[87]

China had to make territorial concessions, and in 1861 a treaty brought to nineteen the number of treaty ports open to Western merchants. The defeat made it impossible to contain the slow but continuous erosion of Chinese sovereignty. Never a formal colony, China was beginning nonetheless to undergo a measure of colonization. European statesmen began to envisage the partitioning of China.[88] Mosher observed that "by the turn of the century, China was prostrate, unable to defend itself against predatory attacks by Great Powers. All wanted to carve out spheres of influence, and Russia and Japan appeared intent on dismembering the ancient empire."[89] China

was fortunate that at this critical juncture, America intervened, taking upon it what Mosher called "the role of protector of China's territorial integrity," culminating in the U.S. secretary of state's two notes addressed to the Great Powers in 1899–1900 stating the U.S. intent to guarantee China's freedom and independence. America also assumed a kind of moral guardianship for China. For example, the heavy indemnity that the Manchu regime was to pay the Great Powers as a result of the Chinese movement against foreigners that erupted in north China in the summer of 1900 was later set aside by the United States.

What has this review of China's history and technology revealed to us about the country's basic economic personality? Many Westerners have produced extensive historical assessments of Chinese economic structure, with the verdict of most being that China lost valuable centuries and fell behind Europe. A Jesuit missionary, Louis Le Conte (1655–1728), was quoted by Landes as saying that Chinese "are more fond of the most defective piece of antiquity than the most perfect of the modern, differing much in that from us [Europeans] who are in love with nothing but is new."[90] Landes observed that "China lacked institutions for finding and learning. . . . The sense of give-and-take, of standing on the shoulders of giants of progress—all these were weak or absent—they let the findings of each new generation slip into oblivion. . . . The history of Chinese advances, then is one of the points of light, separated in space and time, unlinked by replication and testing, obfuscated by metaphor and pseudo-profundity . . . limited in diffusion . . . in effect, a scattering of ephemera."[91] He stated that Chinese "cultural triumphalism combined with petty downward tyranny made China a reluctant improver and bad learner."[92] The secretary to Lord Macartney, Britain's first emissary to China, was disheartened by what he regarded as Chinese indifference to suggestions for improving their canals, lamenting that in China "they think that everything is excellent and that proposals for improvement would be superfluous if not blameworthy."[93] The thing to notice in all these comments is the assumption that the Westerner knew better what should be done and was a civilizing influence.

A closer look into what these commentators had to say about Chinese technology over these centuries is revealing. Landes commented that "the rejection of foreign technology was more serious because China itself had long slipped into technological and scientific torpor" and claimed that Chinese anger "blocked economic modernization. . . . Mechanization, discouraged by an abundance of cheap labor and reluctance of women to work, was tarred with the same brush." He was of the view that, "as a result, factory industry barely had a foothold at the end of the nineteenth century."

It is clear that Landes, whose views are fairly representative of Western economic commentaries on Chinese science and technology, was looking for mechanization and labor-saving technology. Factory-based industry and science and technology have always been closely linked with capital investment. Aghion and Howitt, as noted earlier, believed that investment and technological progress are tightly linked; that capital accumulation and innovation should be regarded not as distinct causal factors but two aspects of the same process, with policies that favor capital accumulation generally also stimulating innovation and therefore long-run growth; that research and development requires a lot of capital; and that new ideas generally need a new infusion of capital goods for implementation.[94] Productivity—that is, producing more per unit of labor by placing more capital equipment at the hands of each worker—has been stressed as the basis for economic development. Schumpeter's notion of "constructive destruction" has caught the imagination of writers on economics, so that any society that looks "conservative" cannot, by their reckoning, be technologically progressive. Landes wondered why China was not curious about nature nor wanted to understand it, and, more significantly, why China did not want to do more work with less labor through mechanization.

Roberts, like many other writers, lamented that masterpieces had been cast in bronze in the second millennium B.C. in China and that Chinese knew how to cast iron fifteen hundred years before Europeans, "yet much of the engineering potential of this metallurgical tradition was unexplored." He regretted that coal was being burned in China when Marco Polo was there, yet there developed no Chinese steam engine, and he observed that the list of lost technological breakthrough opportunities by China was much longer than just these.[95] Many Western "experts" have set out to probe the Chinese mind, and of course Confucianism, in an attempt to explain this Chinese lack of scientific orientation. "All in all," declared Riencourt, "the Chinese display the complete lack of logic which makes them shun deductive argumentation."[96] Each of these claimed failures by the Chinese is ascribed to the fact that the Chinese did not seek "advanced" technology from their Western visitors. To reject offered Western technology was thought to be foolish and could only be put down to what Landes called Chinese "intellectual xenophobia."[97]

It is important to note that Chinese factor endowments and factor proportions are vastly different from those in the West. Landes pointed out that China at the time was seesawing between labor-hungry soil and food-hungry labor. He quoted a Chinese memorialist who around A.D. 300 suggested that all grazing lands for pigs, sheep, and horses should be done away with so that provision could be made for people with no or little land. Landes pointed out that in economic terms, the Chinese substituted labor for land, using sixty to eighty persons per hectare (where an American wheat farmer would use one) and obtaining excellent yields, as much as 2,700 liters per hectare. He observed that at the maximum, a thousand people could live on food produced per square kilometer. By the thirteenth century, he stated, China had what was probably the most sophisticated agriculture in the world.

The point is that China had to deal both with the population pressure on the land and with its relatively low endowment of natural resources.[98] Material production aids (capital) derived from natural raw materials were available only in insignificant quantities. There was therefore a greater need to use manpower and animal-based capital.[99] These things seem old-fashioned to mechanization advocates, but the Chinese were doing quite well with science and technology that were in line with their factor endowment and proportions. Landes provided a detailed description of Chinese craftsmanship, science, and technology based on the resources available to Chinese industry at the time, but he and other scholars like him, together with those early Western visitors to China, failed to see that Chinese industry was growing, albeit on the back of technology that was not in vogue in the West. It is no wonder that Elvin writes, "It would seem that none of the conventional explanations tells us in convincing fashion why technical progress was absent in Chinese economy during a period that was, on the whole, one of prosperity and expansion."[100] They could not understand how economic prosperity and expansion could result from an environment that was thought deficient in "technical progress." Yet the Chinese themselves recognized this; the emperor told the Western visitors that "even though some of the Western methods are different from our own and may even be an improvement, there is little that is new," meaning that the Western methods were mechanical advances deriving from scientific principles of which the Chinese were already aware.[101]

The Westerners who came to China wanted trade. By this they meant the sale of Western manufactured products in exchange for Chinese raw materi-als. But the Chinese did not want Western manufactured goods. As Roberts said, "Nearly three centuries of trade with China had failed to reveal any manufactured goods from Europe which the Chinese wanted except the toys and clocks which they found amusing. . . . European trade with China rested on export of her silver and other Asian products."[102] It seems that the early Chinese industrial base, established from its primal society, survived through self-reliance to present times in line with their factor proportions.

Africa

Africa was not as lucky as Japan or China. When the Europeans reached Africa in the early nineteenth century, the continent was far advanced in iron smelting. Some date the origins of iron technology to 800 B.C. based on excavations in Rwanda.[103] Others such as Davidson believe that ironworking reached West and Central Africa in the last years of the pre-Christian era.[104] We are told that iron technology was introduced into China about 500 B.C. Taking into account the difficulties of reconciling dates and the state of iron knowledge involved, it can at least be said that iron smelting was known in Africa about the same time as in China.

The Europeans who arrived Africa were, like those who went to China and Japan, looking for conquest and profit. They allied with missionaries to win indigenous people away from their traditional religions. In 1883, the *Times* of London devoted three columns to the journeys of Lieutenant Cameron, a British explorer who reached the west coast of Africa after a three-year journey across the continent. Said he, "The interior is mostly a magnificent and healthy country of unspeakable richness. I have a small specimen of good coal; other minerals such as gold, copper, iron and silver are abundant, and I am confident that with a wise and liberal (not lavish) expenditure of capital, one of the greatest systems of inland navigation might be utilized, and from 30 months to 36 months begin to repay any enterprising capitalist that might take the matter in hand."[105]

In the late Middle Ages, two-thirds of the European gold supply came from West Africa. By 1480, for example, the Portuguese were loading their ships with gold in the Senegal River. In 1497 Vasco da Gama had rounded the Cape of Good Hope and opened up the seaway to India. Despite these relationships with Africa, Pakenham noted that in the mid-1870s Africa was still a mystery in Europe.[106] It was known only that Africa straddled the Equator. Europeans spoke of Africa as a "dark continent."

The slave trade involving Europe and Africa began as early as 1444, when a consignment of slaves was taken north of the Senegal River and put ashore in Lisbon. By the early sixteenth century, there were ports in Portugal where there were more African slaves than native Portuguese. But demand for slaves in the Caribbean and Brazil was infinitely greater, and soon millions were taken away or perished in the wars that overseas slaving provoked. Davidson remarked that the full effects of the slave trade "were ruinously destructive of society and civilizing growth—at many times fatal to both. . . . The slave trade strained and ruined much of the fabric of African society while permitting nothing to replace it." He pointed out that "from the beginning vast numbers of the Negroes refused to accept slave status."[107] They did not accept inferior status when they reached America. Some African chiefs and peoples of the coasts were corrupted into wholesale slave trading, but in the main, as Pakenham pointed out, "Europe had imposed its will on Africa on the point of a gun." In China, too, Europe tried to impose its will by force of firearms, but there it did not damage the fabric of Chinese primal society; in Africa it did. Africa was not the relatively homogeneous unit China was, and it was geographically more accessible to Europe than the Far East. In Africa it

was easier to liquidate isolated kingdoms and partition the continent. Strong rulers were humiliated and dispersed into exile or diminished to a shadow of their former greatness.

In partnership with trade (on Europe's terms) and imperial power, Christianity dealt a blow to many African societies' sociocultural fabric, around which their technology was based. Europeans regarded African society as uncivilized, and Spring was of the view that it was the ease and savagery with which the Europeans exploited Africans that helped make them perceive Africans as savages.[108] The notion that Europeans had a duty to "civilize" Africa played a role in European activity on the African continent. Said King Leopold of Belgium in 1876: "To open to civilization the only part of the globe where it has yet to operate, to pierce the darkness that envelopes whole populations, it is, I dare say, a crusade worthy of this century of progress."

The devastation of African primal societies was in many ways irreversible. A report to Britain's Foreign Office in 1903 remarked on the chaos the rubber trade had caused in the Congo: "Of all the shameful and infamous expedients whereby man preyed upon man. . . this vile thing [the rubber trade] dares to call itself commerce." The writer of the report had seen a boy of sixteen with his hand severed at the wrist, and he wrote, "In the Lake districts, things were pretty bad . . . whole villages and districts I knew well and visited as flourishing communities in 1887 are without a human being; others are reduced to a handful of sick and 'harassed creatures' who say of the [British colonial] government: Are the white men never going home, is this to last forever." An African was quoted as saying, "We said to the white man: we are killed by the work you make us do, by the stoppage of our plantations and the breaking up of our homes." Another said: "We used to hunt elephants long ago and there were plenty in our forest and we got much meat. Bula Matari [Europeans] killed the elephant hunters because they could not get rubber and so we starved. We are sent to get rubber and when we come back with little rubber we are shot."[109]

Pakenham reported that in 1899 Morel, the leading British authority in West Africa, commented acidly that when the king of England talked of the "blessings" of civilization in the Congo, he was thinking of his own profits. As for ill treatment of natives, he was supposed to have asked, "What European nation which had undertaken the heavy responsibility of introducing the blessings and vices of civilization into the Dark Continent can claim immunity for its representatives in this respect?"[110]

The destruction of the continent's primal economic fabric is at the root of Africa's present inability to achieve economic development. The African economic child died an early death. At best, it can be said that economically Africa is like a man who suffered severe mental and psychological damage when he was young.

3

Theory of Factor Proportions

Chapter 2 analyzed socioeconomic structure in the context of the successful economic development of China and Japan. We observed that development in these countries took a different path from that of the West and that the differences originated in the factor proportions of their primal society structures.

This chapter examines the structures of modern economic systems in order to see what similarities there are between them and those of primal societies. It is the contention that any common characteristics between the two can rightly be ascribed not to modern economic ideas but to natural (scientific) economic factors.

Factors of Production

Economists writing on today's modern economies seem not to be clear about what constitutes the factors of production. Most seem to work on the basis that capital and labor are the recognized factors of production, and many economic models are based on this two-factor position.

We indicated above why in early times land was regarded as a factor of production. Agriculture was predominant, and the early factories required land and associated facilities such as water. Today a lot has changed, and reference to land as a factor of production increasingly sounds hollow. Indeed the neoclassical growth model was meant to close the chapter on land as a major and necessary input for growth. According to Samuelson and Nordhaus,

"history records how entrepreneurs and capital—not landowners and land—have called the tune since the nineteenth century. Land did not become increasingly scarce."[1]

Production, as described in Chapter 2, is a technical process, not a financial transaction. Its financial aspects derive from the technical process. Land is not an input into this technical process.

It is therefore clear that the specific factor model is for this reason misleading and scientifically unrealistic. The model assumes that there are two factors of production, land and capital, which are tied permanently to particular sectors of the economy. It asserts that manufacturers produce goods using capital and labor (not land) but that food is produced using land and labor (not capital). Labor is therefore said to be a mobile factor, while capital and land are said to be specific factors in that each can only be used in production of one type of product. The falsity of this is that not only is capital used in production of food—a hoe, for example, in a primal society, or a tractor in an advanced economy—but also land is never (technically) input into the production of agricultural products. What is input are materials—nutrients and other chemicals (artificial and natural)—hosted by land. It is therefore clear that any economic theory developed from this intellectual analysis cannot pass a scientific test.

Whereas Todaro in his economic text defined what he called the basic categories of factors of production as land, labor, and capital, Samuelson and Nordhaus in their own text defined as productive inputs the machinery, equipment, tools, labor services, land, and raw materials needed to produce foods and services.[2] They might have grouped machinery, equipment, and tools together with knowledge as capital. Land is, for reasons we have stated, not a factor of production. Raw materials are correctly described as a factor of production. So if land is eliminated as a production input, the analysis of the two authors could be accepted as describing the three factor inputs of labor, material, and capital.

Yet in another part of their text, curiously, they listed production inputs as only labor, capital, and land and left out raw materials.[3] However, in another section of their book, they classified factors of production into three broad classes: natural resources, labor, and capital. Conventional economics regrettably puts great weight on capital as a factor of production, to the neglect of raw materials. Mikesell drew attention to this when he commented that while theories of sustainable development tend to regard natural resources as the primary limiting factor of production, conventional development emphasizes the availability of capital as the primary limiting factor.[4]

There is a tendency among conventional economists to consider raw materials as inventory and therefore as a kind of capital. In the second confusion that exists, the term *circulating capital* has been coined by some to mean inventories of produced goods that are wholly used up in producing the next period's output, but it is misleading, because while inventory is consumed in production, capital is not. The two have different and distinct factor characteristics. Also, as a production factor, capital cannot be equated to money. Money is coins, paper, instruments, and so on. Capital is a prior claim by a society to the raw materials and labor needed to produce production aids, without which no production can take place—irrespective of the stage of economic development of that society. Conventional texts have equated capital with dollar values. This has unfortunately moved theoretical analysis on factor utilization off course.

From our analysis so far, it is clear that capital (production aids) was installed by nature as a necessary ingredient of any production process. While it is correct in both primal and modern society to treat capital as a factor withdrawn from potential consumption, it is wrong to treat capital as savings or as a sacrifice of present consumption so as to gain higher consumption later. Doing so gives the impression that the act of capital formation is optional and could be avoided if the society so wishes. To argue that poor countries lack capital because they cannot save is misleading. For every stage of economic development, there is a corresponding level of capital that is adequate to meet consumption needs. Below this level, the economy cannot attain the level of production to meet its current demand. Above this level, there is too much capital—idle factors. We will call this adequate level of capital the economy's optimal or threshold capital stock.

It is necessary to illustrate the deep roots of the incorrect idea that capital is a feature that appears in an economy only after there has been a savings or denial of present consumption. Figure 3.1 is reproduced from Samuelson and Nordhaus' *Economics* and is supposed to represent two islands with exactly the same amount of available labor and land area. Island A uses these items, what the authors call primary factors, directly to produce consumption goods such as food and clothing, without using what the authors call "produced capital goods." Island B, on the other hand, during a preliminary period sacrificed current consumption and used some of its land and labor to produce capital goods such as plows, shovels, and looms. As a result, B ended up with a variety of capital goods. The authors state that by using "capital-intensive methods of production," Island B will enjoy more future consumption than Island A.

Figure 3.1 **A Tale of Two Islands: Two islands begin with equal endowments of land and labor. Spendthrift Island A invests nothing and shows a modest growth in per capita consumption. Thrifty Island B devotes an initial period to investment, forgoing consumption, and then enjoys the harvest of much higher consumption in the future.**

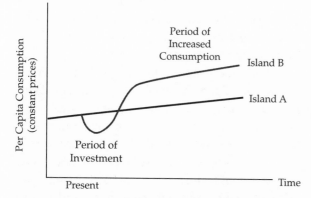

Source: P. Samuelson and W. Nordhaus, *Economics*, 14th ed. (New York: McGraw-Hill, 1992), Figure 16-4, p. 273.

The authors were wrong to think that Island A did not use "produced capital goods" (whatever they mean by "produced"). Nature has it that man cannot produce anything without capital. Island A could not produce clothing without some kind of elementary loom. The impression the authors gave that capital-intensive production was the ideal next step is misleading. What to do depends instead on factor endowments, not on preconceived ideas. Is there the demand for the increased output from the capital-intensive production? We are not told whether there was enough capital-intensive equipment to keep everyone on Island B producing or whether there are people who now have no work.

Lipsey and Chrystal identified four types of factors of production: all those gifts of nature, such as land, forest, minerals, and so on, commonly called natural resources but which they call land; all hu-

man resources, mental and physical, both inherited and acquired, which they call labor; all man-made aids to further production, called capital; and entrepreneurs or innovators, those individuals who take risks by introducing new products and new ways to making old products, organizing the other factors of production and directing them along new lines. But clearly in this classification they were thinking not of what actually are inputs in a technical process of production but rather anything that is a financial cost to the producer.

From this analysis, it can be concluded that in both primal and modern economies, production inputs are a three-dimensional relationship of materials, labor, and capital. Three-dimensional production input structure is therefore a natural phenomenon.

Substitution

We have shown that substitution among the three factors of production occurs in the primal economy. Substitution allowed man to undertake difficult and awkward tasks and to economize on relatively scarce factors as necessary.

In modern economies, the substitution between capital and labor is quite common; we need not elaborate on it. It is stated that as the quantity of capital per worker increases, output per worker rises. As the capital component increases, an activity is said to be capital-intensive.

With regard to the substitution between capital and material, this is common in the area of heat-generated material transformation. As noted earlier, heat radiation, which is the preponderant means of heat transmission, is proportional to T^4 where T is the temperature of the heat source. That means that if a large furnace is operating at a temperature twice that of a smaller furnace, the total heat actually transmitted from a large furnace is not twice but sixteen times that of the smaller furnace. Therefore, one-sixteenth of the amount of fuel used in the smaller

Figure 3.2 **Savings in fuel consumption due to increased aircraft size.**

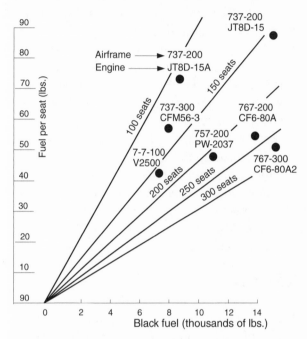

Source: Boeing (Aircraft Industry Survey, *Economist*, June 1, 1985), p. 7.

furnace will do the same amount of work in the larger furnace. More investment of material and labor is required to build a furnace that is bigger and able to contain the increased heat being generated. The gains from T^4 are subject to decreasing returns due to increased heat losses that set in as temperature increases. As another example, Figure 3.2 is a display of fuel consumption versus aircraft size, showing reducing fuel consumption with the increased capital investment associated with increased aircraft size. In a third example, for some products, undertaking industrial processes at higher pressures means reduced material consumption in substitution for the higher capital investments needed to create and control the higher-pressure conditions. There are also various material substitution schemes aimed at reducing waste by trapping and recycling potential waste, which requires intensive capital investment.

In regard to the substitution between labor and material, this takes place most commonly in the area of dispersion technology. For example, if a limited quantity of a chemical needs to be dispersed into a liquid over a large area, either because the solution strength needs to be controlled or because the quantity of chemical is limited, a vigorous side-to-side or rotary movement of the hand over time is required to ensure full dispersal of the chemical. The vigorous movement may in some instances generate some heat, which further helps dispersion and absorption of the chemical into a solution. These manual actions were used in primal societies in mixing dyes and other ingredients. In modern societies, this necessary movement is often mechanized.

In primal societies, where labor was used to coat a surface thinly with a substance such as paint, long and meticulous hand application was needed. This intensive action, substituting for material, has increasingly been mechanized in modern settings through the use of special sprayers that atomize fluids or solutions for use in coating technology.

In many manual operations, the hand is used to squeeze liquid from items such as fruits. In a typical palm oil industry, manual presses are used to squeeze palm oil out of boiled palm nuts. A diminishing quantity of palm oil is obtained as labor input is increased. Thus by increasing labor input, material input per unit of output is decreased. Again, in the last couple of decades, this labor has been substituted by mechanized presses.

In general manufacture in the early 1960s in Europe and the United States, a lot of manpower was deployed in order to reduce material input by time devoted to manually setting jigs to required tolerances and related tasks. Sizable amounts of manpower also were deployed on inspection and quality control in order to reduce net material input. Through increasing use of automated control technology, many of these labor activities, meant to substitute for material, have themselves been substituted with capital investment.

It is clear, therefore, that the scope for substituting between material and labor in today's economies is vast, especially in those economies where labor is plentiful. It can therefore be said that in both primal and today's economies, factor input substitution among the three factors of production is the basis of production. Factor substitution should therefore form part of any scientific theory of economic development/growth.

Conventional economists have sought to establish a theory on how factor substitution works. The general equilibrium theories are, according to Hausman, applications of (and thus not identical to) equilibrium theory.[5] An economic equilibrium is supposed to be the state of affairs in which there is no excess demand—a state of affairs in which at the going prices nobody wants to go on exchanging. Conventional economics assumes perfect competition in which the agents of production are rational. Their actions are geared to maximizing utility and their profit. They will adopt factor combinations that minimize cost. Accordingly, the price of factors is supposed to reflect their relative scarcity. Prices are supposed to help producers select the combination of factor inputs most appropriate to the society's factor endowments.

We are back to the recurring issue of rationality of economic agents and Robbins' wrong contention about what economic science is. The claim that the choice of factor utilizations is based on human rationality immediately qualifies the result of that choice as not necessarily scientific, because nature is not rational. The theory of maximizing earnings and profit, which no doubt accords with reality, is not necessarily therefore scientific.

In regard to the assumption that there is perfect competition—in which the ratio of marginal utilities of inputs for all consumers is equal to the relative prices of the goods, the ratio of the marginal costs of goods produced by agents is equal to the relative prices of those goods, and the marginal products of all factor inputs are equal for all agents and all goods are equal to those inputs' relative prices.

Hausman stated that "the stipulations [economists] make concerning information, markets and the like are ill-suited" for explanatory or predictive purposes. He went on to say that "theories of intertemporal general equilibrium assert or assume that agents have complete and accurate knowledge concerning the availability and prices of commodities and concerning production possibilities both in the present and future. They also stipulate a complete set of commodity features market on which present commodities (or titles to future commodities) can freely be exchanged for titles to future commodities of every kind and date." He observed that such claims render the theories "obviously either false or inapplicable to real economics . . . the fact that we cannot satisfy, even approximately, such assumptions of the theories leaves abstract general equilibrium theories with little if any predictive worth. Given the falsity of such stipulations such as perfect competition, one wants to know what the point is of abstract general equilibrium theories."[6]

Samuelson and Nordhaus have correctly observed that, "taken literally, there is no doubt that a perfect and absolutely efficient and competitive mechanism [for factor input selection] differs markedly from the real world." But they added that "in a broader sense the insights of the competitive theory retain a great deal of validity." "While oversimplified," they argued, the "competitive model points to many important hypotheses about economic behaviors."[7]

Replied Hausman, "Many economists, particularly when they are concerned about how to justify their theories, are tempted to say that they only provide us with some sort of logic of economic phenomena or that they are merely bags of tools into which we dip when convenient."[8]

Like Hausman, we ask: What is the point of a theory if its basic premises are incorrect? Even if we assume that perfect competition assumed is possible, there are some basic problems in the rationalist explanation of factor substitution. A basic requirement of competition is that the agents must know that the items are, in fact, in competition. In the present state of knowledge, producers are not aware that materials are in "competition" with capital and labor. Nor do the factors that determine the price of material in the market reflect a competitive position between these three factors.

Indeed, capital, on one hand, and labor and material, on the other hand, are not in competition in the marketplace. Capital is a different face of labor and material. Daly has in fact suggested that there is more complementarity than substitutability between capital and material.[9] At any given moment, if the demand for capital increases in a financial economy, the supply of labor and material in input factor terms will be reduced, so that while the price of capital rises because demand has increased, the price of labor and material will also increase because supply is less given that, at least in the short term, the overall availability of labor and material in the economy is fixed.

All these and similar arguments serve to destroy the whole basis on which the general equilibrium theory on factor inputs is erected.

The factors of production—capital, labor, and natural resources—available in any economy comprise the essential tools with which economic development and growth can be accomplished. The factor proportions of one economy distinguish it from another economy. The success of economic development and growth depends entirely on how a society adapts to its factor proportions.

The law of diminishing returns is a basic natural law, and Robbins was correct when he said that such

a law is so much a part of our everyday experience that it can be thought of as obvious. In further considering the relationship between the three factors, we now need to apply this law. Each of the three factors is always present in any production process. Each is scarce in that its supply is limited at least in the short term. The relative scarcities differ from one place to another. They mutually substitute for each other. The law of diminishing returns applies to their relationship with each other.

A number of economists have in the past attempted a three-factor trade analysis but have not developed this in other areas. Lal and Myint, however, concluded that "in searching for the deeper causes for growth and poverty redressal . . . we show how a three-factor classification of countries by their initial factor endowments, in terms of a three-factor trade—theoretic framework . . . is a useful starting point."[10] Elsewhere they said, "Nevertheless, we have found the three factor framework of the development of an open economy to be the most useful in making comparisons from our country studies." They pointed out that, "unlike the two factor (labor and capital) case, the three factor framework yields a much richer means of alternative efficient development paths depending upon a country's initial endowments."[11]

Leamer pioneered a triangular resource endowment model involving three factors—land, labor, and capital. The main point of Leamer's analysis of resource endowment is that there is a triangle of three factors in which every factor endowment point on the straight line emanating from one corner of the triangle has the same ratio of the other factors. For this reason, the scales of the three factor ratios can be placed on the edges of the triangle.[12] These three-factor inquiries were, unfortunately, never followed up.

In his book *Economics of Development,* Hagen attempted to show that under certain conditions capital-intensive development might lead a capital-

Figure 3.3 **Two-sector capital-labor relationships, under varying capital-labor proportions.**

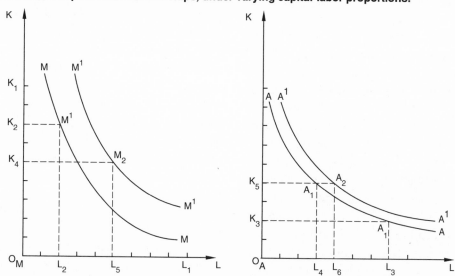

Source: E. Hagen, *The Economics of Development*, 3rd ed. (Homewood, IL: Richard D. Irwin, 1980), fig. 20–2 (A&B), p. 366.

labor allocation that is less than optimal (he called it "economic loss").[13] Here we explore his analysis further. Hagen concentrated on two sectors, manufacturing and agriculture. Suppose the total amount of capital and labor inputs in the economy is $O_M K_1$ and $O_M L_1$. In Figure 3.3, let the bulk of this capital, $O_M K_2$, and only $O_M L_2$ of the labor be used in manufacturing, in which case output in manufacturing is at the point M_1 on isoquant MM. The remaining capital $K_1 K_2 = (O_A K_3)$ and labor $L_2 L_1 = (O_A L_3)$ are available in agriculture. As the relatively steep negative slope of the isoquant MM at the point M_1 shows, production methods using a moderately smaller amount of capital (say, $K_2 K_4$ less) would not require much more labor to produce the same volume of output. On the other hand, if the capital saved were transferred to agriculture, isoquant AA can be reached at A_1 with a much smaller amount of labor.

If the net amount of labor thus saved from those transfers (the difference between labor freed in agriculture and that added in manufacturing to maintain the same output in each) were divided between agriculture and industry, output in both could be

increased above the original output to points M_2 and A_2 respectively. In geometric representation, it means that no further shift will permit increased output in both sectors when production rises at points at which the slopes of the two isoquants (drawn to the same scale) are equal. This is true at M_2 and A_2, respectively.

For maximal output, therefore, the factor proportion will be equal for manufacturing and for agriculture. After his analysis, Hagen wondered, "Economic theory assumes the possibility of an indefinitely large number of alternative methods of production, each using a little more or less capital, a little less or more labor than another. But the history of economic growth in the West has been a history of more and more capital-intensive methods. Today only capital-intensive methods are known in most Western manufacturing." As a result, he thought (perhaps wrongly) that "production isoquants [like in Figure 3.3] may not exist." But Hagen was on the right track.

Hagen's excellent and realistic analysis was limited because he also fell into the same trap as many others, assuming that manufacturing is capital-intensive and agriculture labor-intensive and that there are only two factors, capital and labor. Had he realized that manufacturing is not necessarily capital-intensive and that agriculture need not be labor-intensive, then he would make his study an analysis of any number of production activities: 1, 2, 3, 4 . . . Z activities. Hagen somewhat timidly acknowledged that "empirical investigation [over the past twenty years] has produced increased amounts of evidence that alternative methods of production of varying degrees of capital- and labor-intensity are available in manufacturing." If he also realized that instead of a two-dimensional factor structure there is a three-dimensional factor structure including material, he would have widened the scope of his analysis. He would therefore have arrived at similar conclusions whether he was considering the relationship between capital and labor, the relationship between labor and material, or the relationship between capital and material, namely, that for maximal output (if capital, labor, and material are labeled C, L, M):

$$\frac{C_1}{L_1} = \frac{C_2}{L_2} = \frac{C_3}{L_3} = \frac{C_4}{L_4} \cdots \frac{C_Z}{L_Z}$$

$$\frac{C_1}{M_1} = \frac{C_2}{M_2} = \frac{C_3}{M_3} = \frac{C_4}{M_4} \cdots \frac{C_Z}{M_Z}$$

$$\frac{L_1}{M_1} = \frac{L_2}{M_2} = \frac{L_3}{M_3} = \frac{L_4}{M_4} \cdots \frac{L_Z}{M_Z}$$

The situation, it is clear, is one of the same kind of exchanges as in welfare economics, in which relative allocations of factors are altered and adjusted until maximal utility is achieved. In other words, we could have reached this conclusion on the relationship between factor proportions vis-à-vis maximal output by looking at the position simply as one of the law of diminishing returns. The relationship

between factor proportions is a law of nature with two objectives in mind. The first objective is to ensure the optimal use of all factors of production so as to secure maximal productive output. It can be said that the natural law of production is based on creating a "big push" on all fronts of factor availability. Early theorists such as Paul Rosenstein-Rodan, Richard Nelson Singer, and Ragnar Nurske, who advocated a big-push policy as a means of initiative and maintaining economic development, were basically right, but wrong in that they wanted to create a big push on the capital front. What natural law (science) required is a push on all factors in their relative proportions.

The second objective was to ensure balanced development. This does not mean balanced capital investment programs. Nor is it the neoclassical definition of balanced growth. A balanced economy means that all economic activities make the same proportional demand on the factors of production and their operating factor proportions are equal.

So far we have concentrated on the microeconomic side. We now turn to the macroeconomic side. If the nature of the equality of the different factor proportions for all activities is considered, it will be clear that in the aggregate, the same equality should apply for the macroeconomic structure, since it can be considered as one very large economic activity. Every economy stands on the props of the three factors—labor, natural resources, and capital. The proportions between a macroeconomy's factors are called natural factor proportions, since these factors derive from an economy's natural endowments. We therefore labeled these as:

$$\frac{C_n}{L_n}, \quad \frac{C_n}{M_n}, \quad \frac{L_n}{M_n},$$

with L_n and M_n as the natural labor and material endowments and C_n as the natural capital. It is important to note that Hagen's analysis was seeking the basis on which to achieve full utilization of all the capital and labor in the economy—$O_M K_1$ and $O_M L_1$ of Figure 3.3. In our extended three-factor analysis, it means that the relationship we have established is based on full utilization of all available factor inputs in the economy.

Labor constitutes the adults in an economy able to provide the manpower required to carry out its production activities. Nature recycles the labor force in an economy, but its size remains largely stable in the very short term. It increases, or in some cases decreases, in the medium or long term. The supply of labor is designated L.

As with labor, nature—with the cooperation of man—will recycle the supply of raw materials. In the very short term, the quantity of raw materials is largely stable. It increases, or in some cases decreases, in the medium or long term. The available supply of raw material is designated M.

The supply of capital is subject to different conditions. Nature specified production aids as a necessary prerequisite to any production. The position was fully described in the discussions on primal societies in Chapter 2. The stock of capital of an economy started being built when its primal economy began; at that point it consisted of raw materials that either were already production aids (e.g., stone) or were worked on by man (using man or animals as a production aid) to produce capital. Thereafter an economy's capital stock is increased by further diversion of raw material and labor into the capital stock. The diversion also helps replenish losses arising from depreciation and to meet the need for upgrading the capital stock. Capital stock can therefore generally be represented in a dynamic context by the formula $C = pL + sM$, where p is the proportion of labor utilized in creating capital and s the proportion of raw materials utilized in creating capital.

Accordingly, the relevant factor proportions of the macroeconomy for sustainable growth in a dynamic context are:

$$\text{capital/labor} \quad = \frac{pL + sM}{(1-p)L} = \frac{p}{1-p} + \frac{s}{1-p} \cdot \frac{M}{L}$$

$$\text{capital/material} = \frac{pL + sM}{(1-s)M} = \frac{s}{1-s} + \frac{p}{1-s} \cdot \frac{L}{M}$$

$$\text{labor/material} \quad = \frac{(1-p)L}{(1-s)M}$$

At this point of equilibrium, p and s are of such values that $C_n = C_t$ (the threshold capital).

The essence of sustainable maximal economic development and growth requires that all along:

$$\text{(a)} \quad \frac{C_1}{L_1} = \frac{C_2}{L_2} = \frac{C_3}{L_3} \cdots = \frac{1}{1-p_t}\left(p_t + s_t \frac{M}{L}\right)$$

$$\text{(b)} \quad \frac{C_1}{M_1} = \frac{C_2}{M_2} = \frac{C_3}{M_3} \cdots = \frac{1}{1-s_t}\left(s_t + p_t \frac{L}{M}\right)$$

$$\text{(c)} \quad \frac{L_1}{M_1} = \frac{L_2}{M_2} = \frac{L_3}{M_3} \cdots = \frac{(1-p_t)L}{(1-s_t)M}$$

where p_t and s_t are threshold proportions.

We have to emphasize here what should now be obvious: that capital (production aid) has no independent existence and in the science of economic development and growth can be quantified and evaluated only in terms of labor and material input.

The above formulae provide a snapshot of factor relationships at any given time. We therefore arrive at the scientific theory that for sustainable economic development and growth in any economy, proportions between the three factors of production must be equal for all economic activities and equal to the economy's factor endowment proportions using threshold capital. Comparing these factor proportions with the actual factor proportions of an economy can tell us how far the economy is from sustainable growth.

All factor proportions, it is seen from these formulae, can be evaluated on the basis of the ratio between M and L. The path of economic growth in the last analysis depends on the ratio of its material and labor endowments, not capital.

The factor proportion relationship we have established on both the micro and macro levels leads to a fact of very great significance: For maximal output, all input factors must be fully utilized. The position does not therefore admit of idle resources. It does mean that the trade-off between growth and employment (and therefore inflation) is evidence of wrong economic growth strategy. These conclusions are the basis of the Nobel laureate Timbergen's conclusion "that total national product is maximized if employment is maximized, which happens if relatively labor-intensive industries and technologies are selected. Out of maximal national product more can be used for investment and hence for growth; so the future national product can be maximized."[14] If Timbergen had not, like many other economists, neglected material as a third factor, he would have most probably urged not only labor-intensive but also material-intensive activities simultaneously. Timbergen was in effect ruling out the strategy of capital accumulation as a prior requirement for achieving growth. Timbergen was seeking to reach the same conclusions as we have but did not have the analytical tools.

Natural factor proportions differ from one country to another. It is this difference that distinguishes, and should distinguish, one economy from another. It is the factor proportions of an economy that should determine its basic "personality." Lal and Myint concluded, "Our hypothesis is that initial factor endowments, rather than size of a country, are more relevant determinants of both economic policy and the political economy of countries. The initial endowments are analogous to the genetic endowments of individuals, which partly (but not wholly) determine their behavior. Countries with similar endowments are expected, at a first cut, to behave in similar ways irrespective of their size."[15] These deep insights by Lal

and Myint are fully in line with our theme of the basic personality of economies in Chapter 2.

Factor Supply

Yet no economy is in equilibrium. General equilibrium theories, as their name implies, base their claimed validity on an economy in which all goods markets are simultaneously in equilibrium.

One major weakness of general equilibrium theories is that it seems, as Hausman said, to have "the form of explanatory arguments where the explanation is the existence of this economic equilibrium. . . . Yet construing it as explanations of economic equilibrium with various properties is implausible since no economy is ever in a state of economic equilibrium. . . . There is no fact of equilibrium to be explained."[16]

The nineteenth-century French economist who is credited with discovery of the general equilibrium theory, Léon Walras, sought in vain to provide a proof that there is an equilibrium of the competitive system. In the middle third of the twentieth century, what was said to be a complete proof of this equilibrium was provided by J. Von Neumann, A. Wald, and the Nobel laureates Kenneth Arrow and Gerard Debreu. They claimed to have discovered that there will always be at least one set of prices that will balance exactly supplies and demands for all inputs and outputs—however many inputs and outputs, locations, and times there are, even if the goods are produced and sold at separate times.

The incorrectness of this proof was shown by the fact that it assumed conditions that, like the concept of perfect competition, were unreal—perfectly flexible wages and prices, no externalities, no increasing returns anywhere, and so on. In actual fact, no economy is in a state of (static) equilibrium. Each economy's supply of labor (L) and material (M) is constantly undergoing incremental change, with differing quantities of L and M being converted into C.

The labor supply of most economies—primal or not—increases in small increments over time as a natural phenomenon. In some advanced economies of the West, there has been steady or declining population, which may be due to the natural interaction with achieved prosperity. In the less developed areas, natural disasters and disease have the effect of reducing the labor supply. Modern medicine and health care may have interrupted the natural cycle, so that population growth has been assisted. In this respect the introduction of modern medicine and health care in the less-developed areas, especially those already coping with high population density, is a mixed blessing, as it will tend to change the natural population trend. The large increases in population being witnessed in some poor countries may not be unconnected with large-scale poverty arising from failures in present-day economic development strategies (or nonstrategies) deriving from the application of nonscientific theories of development (growth). Ironically, therefore, it seems that the large population explosion, which conventional economists regard as a curse on and a detraction from economic development and growth, can best be tackled by incorporating the population (labor) into the development formula—as we have just done.

It has also been claimed by some conventional economists that the quality of labor is the most important barrier to economic development. Said Samuelson and Nordhaus, "Virtually every other ingredient in production—capital goods, raw materials, and technology—can be brought or borrowed from advanced countries. But the application of high-productivity techniques of production to local conditions almost always requires management, production workers and engineering know-how found only in a literate and highly skilled workforce. Modern technologies are often embodied in capital goods . . . but these capital goods require complementary trained labor for effective use and maintenance."[17]

There is a lot wrong with this view. We are reminded of those European visitors in Chapter 2 who told the early Chinese in the nineteenth century that they were using outdated techniques; the Chinese ignored them. Samuelson and Nordhaus were saying that what the poor countries need is modern technologies, which for them meant capital goods from advanced countries. They wanted poor countries to adopt factor proportions out of step with their factor endowments. It is not, therefore, the quality of labor that is the problem in poor countries but the adoption of development strategies that are out of tune with their factor proportions and seeking to exclude that labor from economic participation.

In this matter of underdevelopment we said in our last book:

> A major ingredient of development is that the development process cannot truly get under way until it is indigenized and participated in by the mass of the people themselves. The fact that take-off cannot occur without a big push based on the least scarce resource (quite often manpower) means that to achieve the development effort needed the entire population of the area must participate actively and meaningfully to the utmost of their powers. Thus development must be indigenized if there is to be a take-off. . . . This is a social question as well because people tend to be psychologically more used to the factor proportions which derive from their immediate environment. Activities with such factor proportions are more within the financial and administrative [management] reach of such people. Within these factor limits, people react to economic incentives and only then do market forces become an instrument of development. Outside these limits, reaction is inhibited by psychological barriers. . . . Mass involvement . . . in the development process will evaporate as soon as factor proportions . . . move away from what is immediately within the psychological and mental reach of the masses. Development from that point becomes the preserve of the "intellectuals" and "elites" with consequent mass apathy.[18]

Each economy, primal or advanced, operates with a certain amount of division of labor and specialization. There is specialization, we pointed out, in primal societies. Often the craftsman both made and operated the production aid he needed. As the scale and volume of production activities increase and as one approaches the scale of an advanced economy, specialization becomes very pronounced and necessary; the worker who makes the production aid is not the one who uses it. As this separation takes place the relative fraction of the total production knowledge that the worker needs to acquire decreases. The need for the worker to understand and learn how to operate the capital equipment becomes more important than in early times, when the initiative of the early craftsman was more relevant than training.

In regard to material, the indigenous material supply of any economy also changes in small increments. The changes arise from the conversion of existing raw materials into new uses, the creation of new materials from existing materials, and the discovery of new raw materials. Each of these has a tendency to increase the demand and consequent possible increase in the supply of materials. In aggregate it is this increasing demand and supply that brings to the fore the issue of sustainability in environment terms. Resource depletion has become a topic discussed with considerable heat by people seeing the matter from different points of view.

The formula now set by way of factor proportion relationships has the advantage that for the first time a link has been established between economic development and material endowment. Economic production activities are now supposed to take account of the material factor endowment, whereas conventional economic theories either ignored the issue of material factor limits or even seemed to assume that material was inexhaustible.

M needs to be evaluated and quantified in order to give value to the factor proportions in any given economy.[19] Most economies do not currently know the value of their M. This quantification and evaluation can be carried out in the context of natural resource accounting, which environmental economists have been seeking to establish as a norm. Mikesell in his book *Economic Development and the Environment* called for a comprehensive treaty on sustainable development, which should integrate the macroeconomics of conventional development with the special concerns of natural resource sustainability and environmental protection.[20] Pearce, Markandya, and Barbier in *Blueprint for a Green Economy* put it differently: "The simple logic underlies the importance of valuing the environment and integrating those values into economic policy."[21] The scientific formulation presented in this chapter goes a long way toward meeting these needs. Given the harmful effects of present conventional economic development on the environment, it is clear that nature meant that the limits it imposed on resources must be used as a guide to the use of these resources. Primal societies constituted an example of how nature and man worked in harmony to preserve and rejuvenate the environment. Any science of economic development must encompass the issue of natural endowments.

The formula we have established also sets up the relationship between the microeconomy and the macroeconomy so as to achieve maximal growth potential. This connection has eluded theorists. Economists are much better at predicting and explaining what goes on in individual markets than what happens in the economy as a whole. In an attempt to bridge this gap, or to pretend that the gap does not exist, there has been an attempt since the late 1960s to make a micro/macro distinction. Monetarists and neoclassicists, in particular, have attempted to explain all economic phenomena in terms of theories based on the experience of how individual markets function, that is, microeconomic theory. To monetarists and neoclassicists, macroeconomics is simply "bad" microeconomics. It is clear from the formula established that their approach is wrong and simplistic. Other economists have behaved as if the macroeconomy is the net total of the pluses and minuses of the micro-economies.

The relationship we have established means that, for example, what microeconomic study regards as growth-inducing for firms may not be growth-inducing for the larger economy. The general equilibrium theory is trying to explain how a market economy as a whole would operate. But general equilibrium is a microeconomic topic in that it studies the allocation of resources by firms as determined by relative prices. In the process it ignores the problem associated with the disequilibrium between aggregate supply and demand. The result is that general equilibrium theory has no contribution to make to the science of economic development and growth.

Taking up where we left off, it should be clear that since L and M (and ipso facto capital) are not static in any economy, the equilibrium needed between factor proportions as the formula for maximal sustainable economic growth is dynamic, constantly being adjusted as the basic inputs change.

What, then, are the factors that in practice will make economies not achieve the factor proportions required for maximal sustainable growth? It should be immediately apparent that a situation in which factor inputs have market price tags will distort achieved factor proportions away from optimal values if these prices do not reflect the economy's natural endowment factor proportions.

Conventional economics has aggregated capital in terms of dollar values. In doing this, it treats capital as "a produced factor of production," in line with the incorrect claim that capital is sacrificed consumption. They could not provide a theoretical framework for evaluating capital in terms of factor inputs. It therefore approximates this product as the total dollar value of capital goods. This is an empirical solution and not natural (scientific). This financial evaluation means that the total dollar value ascribed to capital comprises other costs that do not form part of a technical factor input into the capital good production, such as rents, transport, and other financial overheads. On the other hand, we have correctly treated capital as the accumulation in an economy over time of labor and material diverted from the overall supply for capital formation. The determination of the price of labor in the United States, for example, is characterized by market imperfections. Labor markets in the United States are a blend of competition and monopoly elements. The level of wages is determined by factors that do not depend directly on the size of the labor supply. Different levels of labor earn different wages.

The price of raw materials depends on many factors—including the cost of extracting the resource and the demand. In high-cost oil fields, the cost of crude oil is high because of high exploration and extraction costs. If the demand for crude oil is high, this immediately sends crude oil prices climbing. When the demand is low due to a spell of warm weather in Western countries, the price of crude drops. In some instances prices rise even when there is an oil glut. Material supply is usually dominated by a lot of monopolistic practices. Many times politics plays more part in the availability and price of particular resources than supply and demand.

All in all, prices are not a good indicator of the relative factor endowments of an economy. It follows that theories of factor utilization based on prices will divert economics from the requirements of economic science. Prices are the shadow. The factors and their efficient use are the substance. A shadow is often not a true reflection of the substance and may in fact distort it.

Another cause of distortion in factor proportions away from an equilibrium position is the view, widely held among conventional economists, that the technology for a wide range of activities is given at a particular time. Ask any chip maker; he will prescribe the technology and the range of capital cost it takes to produce chips. Economists in the car industry will readily quote the range of capital cost it will require to set up an efficient car plant. In this view, car manufacturing is regarded as always capital-intensive and textile manufacturing as always labor-intensive. When there are large numbers of different activities in an economy with widely differing factor proportions, based on such fixation of technology, the result is a macroeconomic structure with low growth.

In most countries, in the belief that the mobilization of capital is the key to economic development, financial institutions have been created that in effect collect deposits from individuals and households with a view to lending these to businesses. In all instances the system is biased in favor of those with a good capital base, who ironically receive the bulk of this capital. As a result, factor proportions are distorted in favor of capital-intensive activities, leading to an unbalanced economic structure.

Going back to the issue of factors of production, recent literature seem to have adopted capital, labor, and technology as the factors of production. The major new ingredients in the neoclassical model are capital and technology. These shifts in position do not represent a better understanding of the issues. For example, there is, as pointed out in Chapter 1, no clear definition of what technology is. One does not scientifically define what something is by telling what it does. To argue that technology results in obtaining more output from a given quantity of input is not a definition of technology. The newly baptized inputs of capital, labor, and technology gave birth to what is now called "growth accounting," meant to analyze the ingredients that lead to observed economic growth. Total factor productivity (TFP) is supposed to show the efficiency with which all inputs are utilized in a production func-

tion. Whereas a partial productivity index measures the value of output per unit of input (capital or labor), TFP index sums the partial productivities of all inputs in the production process. Both input growth and TFP growth contribute to output growth simultaneously. The purpose of TFP is said to be to separate from these two forces. This percentage change in TFP equals the percentage change in output minus the percentage change in inputs times the elasticity of output with respect to inputs. Elasticity of output with respect to each input—that is, the percentage increase in output that is achieved from a 1 percent increase in input—is said to be econometrically obtained from the production function. It is reasoned that the change in output between any two periods can be obtained from the standard economic statistics of a country. Any other change in output that occurs in addition to this is said to be due to TFP; that is, it is a residual.

The concept of TFP has been represented by the production function as in Figure 3.4. It assumed constant returns to scale in capital and labor. The function f_1 is said to be the best-practice production function and relates output per worker to capital input per worker. Here the notion of capital is supposed to cover both physical and human capital. Economies that are technically inefficient are said to operate on the production function f_0. Catch-up is achieved by moving from a point such as A to D, combining accumulation with a movement toward best practice.

This reinterpretation of TFP change is said to be useful in understanding the sources of the rapid catch-up exhibited by some technologically backward countries, as witnessed in East Asia. Industrial economies that employ international best practice are limited to rates of TFP change determined by the rate of technological progress. On the other hand, it is said that economies that do not employ best practice can have growth rates exceeding the rate of technological progress only if tech-

Figure 3.4 **Concept of best practice function.**

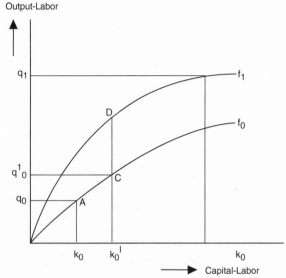

Output-Labor

nical efficiency change is positive. It is also argued that TFP change can be negative if technical efficiency change is negative and greater in absolute value than technological progress. A rapid shift from average practice to best practice—positive technical efficiency change—is claimed to provide a powerful engine of growth, which can show up in recorded rates of TFP change.

The concept of best practice is absurd. It is clear from Figure 3.4 that those propagating the concept have in mind a capital-labor relationship in which capital plays the primary role. In the context of the idea that factor proportions should determine a country's economic policy, it is incorrect to talk of the best-practice production function. It is wrong to talk of catching up to the best-practice position. Conventional economic growth assumptions that do not give center place to the basic personality of each economy and the differences that should arise as a result are bound to be misleading and thus nonscientific.

Despite these problems, many attempts are made to evaluate and classify countries in a kind of TFP growth league. In a well-known study of the rela-

tionship between TFP growth and total factor input growth in seven developing countries, TFP growth was said to be between 0.5 and 2.0 percent, and much of the growth in output between 4 and 6 percent was accounted for by total factor inputs. Hong Kong alone was found to have both higher factor inputs and higher factor productivity. In contrast, developed countries (except Japan) had a much higher share of TFP growth rather than total factor growth in their rate of growth in output, which was said to be typically lower than those for developing countries.[22] The "developing" countries with lower TFP than developed countries significantly in Chenery's study included, according to him, Hong Kong, Taiwan, Korea, and Japan.

On the other hand, World Bank estimates over a similar period claim that a number of developing countries show higher rates of TFP growth than the industrial countries, consistent with claimed large catching-up gains. The East Asian countries were said to stand out with high absolute levels of TFP. Six of them—Hong Kong, Japan, Korea, Thailand, Taiwan, and China—were said to be in the top decile. Three others—Indonesia, Malaysia, and Singapore—are said to be closer to the rate of TFP growth of the high-income economies (1.5 percent).

The study claimed that "in the high income economies most of the estimated TFP growth is due to advances in best practice, which explains their relatively compact distribution of TFP growths around 1.5% a year." It asserted that there is a tendency for TFP growth to decline with rising income. In low- and middle-income economies, it stated that change in TFP "must reflect more than technical progress otherwise we would never find negative TFP growth rates. We have already argued that TFP growth for low and middle income economies contain an element of catching up to (or falling behind) best practice technology."[23]

Against this background are economists such as Krugman, who determined that the growth in most of the East Asian countries can be fully accounted for by factor inputs. The World Bank has criticized such economists on a number of grounds.[24] First it argued that there were some centrally planned economies that save aggressively, like the East Asian countries, but did not grow like them because they invested their savings inefficiently. Second, it argued that it takes time for investments devoted to closing the knowledge gap (by investing in worker training and new equipment or by purchasing technology licenses) to show up in TFP growth. Third, it argued that when the effect of TFP growth on capital accumulation is taken into account, the contribution of TFP to growth is significantly greater than that of factor inputs of capital and labor. Finally, and very significantly, it argued that TFP calculations are highly sensitive to how one measures physical and human capital and how weight is assigned to them. It argued that the conditions in East Asia will tend to underestimate the role of TFP growth. Much of this line of reasoning is defective. It is based on the usual assumption that capital accumulation is the prime mover of growth. To claim that centrally planned economies invested inefficiently while East Asian countries invested efficiently is somewhat surprising in the face of the recent collapse of those East Asian economies. The World Bank could not take cover in the claim that it takes time for TFP to optimize because they were discussing figures covering the period 1966–1990. Their last reason, that a lot depends on the weight attached to various factors, is precisely why most quoted TFP growth figures are not to be relied on.

The lack of confidence in the exercise is reflected in Ray's summary of the way to determine the TFP of an economy. He described TFP as the measure of technical progress of an economy. In order to determine it, "using a production function and supposing that all factors are paid their marginal products, we can estimate the increase that *'should be'* due to accumulation of product factors alone. If we

see output growing faster than the production, then that *must* be due to TFP." He remarked that in considering labor, one must make assumptions about "participation rate."[25] He used the words "production function" guardedly because much depends on what production function the analyst chooses to use. Considering the different factor proportions of countries, an assumed single production function for all countries is bound to invalidate the exercise.

In the case of the Asian countries, the confused message coming from a TFP analysis is typified by Lingle's conclusions. He noted that several studies which appeared by the late 1970s brought the high growth of East Asia to the attention of the world. But most of their analysis did not confirm the World Bank's claim that the growth achieved was due to high TFP.[26] These studies, he said, found that about half of the reported increase in growth was due to TFP, not the high percentage the World Bank would like to adduce. According to him, another survey by Chowdhury and Islam found "quite mixed results across countries and over time." "Although improvements in TFP appear to be an important source of growth, there is also an indication that distortions in capital and labor market led to a decline in efficiency," he wrote, and claimed that this latter point was confirmed by several economists who analyzed "a more current data base." These economists were of the opinion that East Asian growth could not be sustained because it was only due to a "dramatic rise in quantity of inputs," which soon runs up against the law of diminishing returns. All these conflicting TFP-related explanations of the East Asian growth and decline are defective because TFP as a concept is defective. The true causes of this growth and decline will be taken up in Chapter 6.

The reality that TFP calculations are not to be relied on prompted Solow to say, "I don't find this a confidence-inspiring project. It seems altogether too vulnerable to bias from omitted variables, to reverse causation and above all to recurrent suspicion that the experiences of very different national economies are not to be explained as if they represented 'points' on some well-defined surface."[27]

There are more serious problems with the concept of total factor productivity, and we will take these up one by one. Significantly, conventional economists need to take more serious notice of Solow's concern that the TFP concept is being turned into what it is not—a science.

The World Bank stated that from the 1960s to the 1980s, the Soviet Union accumulated more capital as a share of GDP than Hong Kong, Korea, Singapore, or Taiwan, and increased its education in no trivial measure, but generated far smaller increases in living standards during this period than these four East Asian countries. It concluded that this was so not because the East Asian countries worked harder but that they worked smarter. Without saying what it meant by "smarter," the World Bank then took an analytical leap by asking whether knowledge could have been behind East Asia's surge. It answered the question by asserting that if their surge is due to knowledge, the implications are enormous, for it would mean that knowledge is the key to development. However, we are not told what this knowledge is about. Yet the World Bank went on to pose a number of other questions: "How, after all, does one put a price tag on and add up various types of knowledge? What common denominator enables us to sum the knowledge that firms use in their production processes; the knowledge that policy-making institutions use to formulate, monitor and evaluate polices; the knowledge that people use in their economic transactions and social transactions? What is the contribution of books and journals, of R&D, of spending, of the stock of information and communication equipment, of the learning and know-how of scientists, engineers and students? Compounding the difficulty is that many types of knowledge are accumulated and exchanged exclusively within networks, traditional groups and professional associations. This makes it impossible to put a value on such knowledge."

The World Bank then concluded that in view of the difficulties in quantifying knowledge, efforts to evaluate the aggregate impact of knowledge on growth have proceeded indirectly by postulating that knowledge explains the part of growth that cannot be explained by accumulation of tangible and identifiable factors, such as labor and capital. But this is merely an assumption. In complicating what is already a maze of assumptions, the World Bank added that even the residual that is ascribed to knowledge may not be due to knowledge alone after all, "for there may be other factors lurking in Solow's residual."[28] Basu was of the view that Solow's link between technology and growth was an assertion rather than an explanation.[29]

The World Bank's macro-oriented description of knowledge supposed to encompass technology—the TFP—contrasts with the micro-oriented concept, used by the OECD, that regards knowledge as assets needed by the firm in line with modern management theories to improve competitiveness: technological capacities, human capabilities, and organizational capabilities. Following this micro definition, the OECD immediately added that "at a macro level, we could similarly assume that TFP growth is the result of an accumulation process of intangible (technological, human and organizational) capital." It added, "This intangible capital is mostly complementary to tangible capital and is probably a substitute for labor (a country such as the United States with relatively low TFP growth also exhibits a relatively low growth in labor productivity; Europe with relatively high TFP growth rates faces serious unemployment problems)." It concluded that, "in general, there is no expansion without tangible investment and no innovation without intangible investment."[30]

There are clearly wide differences in the interpretation of TFP between the World Bank and the OECD, between those who take a technical interpretation of the residual and those who adopt a socioeconomic or political view of it. Such large latitude is indicative of a concept that attempts to be all things to all men.

If the residual is a measure of our ignorance, to use Solow's phrase, then the knowledge the World Bank is talking about is knowledge about that ignorance. The World Bank quickly added that many other things do contribute to growth—institutions, for example—but "they are not reflected in the contribution of the more measurable factor." It therefore concluded that institutions' effect "is inextricably woven into TFP growth."[31]

Recall that in the TFP concept, capital formation is not the primary source of growth in a country such as the United States. In his Nobel prize acceptance lecture, Solow said, "In the beginning, I was quite surprised at the relatively minor part the model ascribed to capital formation. Even when this was confirmed by Denison and others, the result seemed contrary to their common sense." He went on, "The fact that the steady-state growth is independent of the investment quota was easy to understand. . . . It was harder to feel comfortable with the conclusion that even in the shorter run increased investment would do very little for transitory growth. The transition to a higher equilibrium growth path seemed to offer very little leverage for policy aimed at promoting investment."[32] In his determined attempt to elevate capital to the high position in which, according to him, common sense would place it, Solow wanted evidence that technological progress—at least most of it—could find its way into actual production with the use of new and different capital equipment. Therefore the effectiveness of innovation in increasing output would be paced by the rate of gross investment—what he called "embodiment." After checking, he came to the conclusion that there was "no explanatory value in the embodiment idea" and that "it could be the case that some countries are better able to exploit the common pool of technological progress than others for reasons which have nothing to do with the rate of capital formation."[33]

Yet many conventional economists still stick with the concept of embodiment, as if to think otherwise will shatter their tightly held basic principle that capital formation is the key to growth.[34] The point being made here is that—arising from what we have already said about the role of capital—it should not have surprised Solow that capital has only a limited role, for according to the theory of factor proportions there is an optimal (threshold) capital stock level for each economy.

There are still other more fundamental problems with the TFP concept. One of them is that the "growth accounting," on which the TFP concept has flourished, is faulty. Conventional economists think of production as a financial transaction in which one simply adds up the cost of the input factors. As pointed out already, production is a technical process in which inputs behave like substances involved in a chemical reaction. Production is all about transforming materials into a useful product. In the product, as with the result of a chemical process, it is therefore not possible to isolate each of the constituent substances within the new chemical—which is different from each of the original constituent substances. Production, which growth accounting wants to analyze, is a different "chemical substance" from labor, capital, and raw material added up arithmetically. It is therefore not possible to break output into its constituent elements. As Samuelson and Nordhaus remarked, "It is generally impossible to say how much output has been created by any one of the different inputs taken by itself. The different inputs interact with each other."[35] The fact that the quantity of capital, labor, education, and so forth, increased over a given period in the same direction as a given increase in GDP is not a sound basis on which to conclude that the increase in input caused the increase in GDP. Yet this is the approach growth accounting depended on.

The problems of TFP multiply when it is recalled that it only recognizes capital and labor as physical inputs. It ignored the three-dimensional factor structure. The three-dimensional input structure has been recognized in this book as the only arrangement in tune with economic science. If material is therefore included as the third factor within the TFP theory and substitution is all the time taking place in the economy (not just between capital and labor but among the three factors), it will be evident that TFP has failed to identify a factor as important as, if not more important than, labor and capital—material. Since material is a factor input, it seems clear that the residual is nonexistent.

Recall that the OECD position is that there can be no expansion (i.e., growth) without tangible investment and no innovation without intangible investment. If intangible investment, according to the OECD, is TFP, then it means that there is no direct link between growth and TFP. This is in agreement with our view that growth derives from production and no production can take place except by the interaction of three physical factor inputs—labor, capital, and material. Human "capital" cannot cause growth on its own.

We note that Denison in his pioneering study of the U.S. economy classified the components of the residual into a number of components—increased educational qualification of the average worker, improved allocation of resources, economies of scale, growth of knowledge (or technological progress in the narrow sense, as Solow called it). Let us examine two of Denison's sources of the residual: improved allocation of resources and economy of scale.[36] Denison held that misallocation of resources could be measured by the amount by which the actual allocation of resources departs

from the income-maximizing allocation. In other words, an economy's growth will increase when inputs are selected on income-maximizing criteria. We had already claimed that income-maximizing criteria for selecting of factor inputs can distort factor proportions and will detract from maximizing the growth of the whole economy. So Denison is not on a firm footing here.

Denison's other component of the residual is economy of scale, which is said to boost growth because one obtains a greater than proportional increase in output from a given increase in input. Economy of scale derives from activities whose factor proportions are heavily biased toward capital intensity. The bias increases structural imbalance. While at the micro level the firms concerned gain in output, that is overbalanced at the macro level by a net loss in macroeconomic growth. Denison's evaluation of economy of scale as a source of growth was at best an assumption.

The case for TFP, from whatever angle one examines it, is very weak and confirms that it is essentially a concept confirming our ignorance. The acknowledgment of our ignorance is the greatest credit that can be ascribed to TFP as a concept—it was confirming to us the scientific fact that nature alone confers bounties, but TFP could not put its finger right on what those bounties are. It is to Solow's credit that he acknowledged that there was some unknown out there.

It is now necessary to examine the possibility that the technology factor (which Solow regarded as the third factor after capital and labor) might in fact be material, therefore taking the matter back to the conclusion already reached that there are three natural factors of production—capital, labor, and material. To do this, we must first examine the role of knowledge, which various writers give different names—research and development, human capital, science, technology, and so on. Many conventional economists act as if they believe that all these knowledge activities are new and have arisen as a result of modern economic development. In other words, they say that economic growth has gained increased momentum since investments in science, technology, and human capital became the focus of economic policy, particularly in the latter half of the twentieth century. What can be easily agreed is that the professionalized R&D system, as Freeman and Soete called it, is recent. Growth in this system "was perhaps the most important social and economic change in the twentieth century industry."[37] But this cannot mean that research and development is a twentieth-century invention.

Research and development are said to be pioneered by large firms. As Galbraith put it, "A benign Providence . . . has made the modern industry of a few large firms an almost perfect instrument for inducing technical change. . . . Technical development has long since become the preserve of the scientist and engineer. Most of the cheap and simple inventions have, to put it bluntly, been made."[38] This statement is interesting for the words Galbraith chose, suggesting his view of the origin of science and technology—it is modern, it is the preserve of scientists and engineers (also modern), and what was available earlier was cheap and simple and dismissible. It is capital-intensive, which is why only a few large firms can take it on. It is ideas such as these that have most probably led economists to seek to quantify knowledge, human capital, science, and technology and accept technology as another factor of production, where previously they had maintained there were only two (or three) factors—capital and labor (and land). These nonscientific thoughts about science and technology have regretfully been passed on to public leaders even in the poor countries. The minister of science and technology of a West African country once said that technology was expensive and capital-intensive.

Recently Oswald and Blanchflower have sought to quantify the happiness marriage provides. Using a randomly selected sample of 100,000 people in Britain and the United States, they compared the amount of happiness generated by a lasting marriage compared with the amount of happiness produced by a change in financial circumstances. Their statistical calculations claim to have shown that a lasting marriage brings as much happiness as an additional $9,000 a year in income. They also claim that the graph of happiness over a lifetime is U-shaped, falling on the average to its lowest level at about the age of forty and increasing after that point. Said Oswald, "It is measuring the really important things in life. Some people think economists are dull people but I want to give economists a broader, more humane face who care about more things than just money." Economists have a right to exercise their intellectual analyses provided they do not seek to make "science" out of it. One can go on in this way, trying to measure everything in the mistaken belief that in nature all goods are scarce, everything has a financial value, and economics consists of choosing among these scarce resources.

The knowledge the World Bank highlights encompasses so many subjects—a firm's production process, policy making, even social interactions. It is so diffused that it is neither possible nor desirable to compartmentalize the different types of knowledge. There are no doubt branches of knowledge, but they are what they are—branches. The essence of knowledge is that it is the intellect given to man—the ability to observe, think, and store information. It is a natural endowment without which the whole package of man's existence would greatly approximate to that of animals. But that does not make knowledge a factor input into production. Knowledge provides an enabling environment for man's economic, social, cultural, and religious activities. Just as we argued in Chapter 1 that institutions could help create the enabling environment for economic growth but are not in themselves economic development, knowledge creates enabling conditions for economic development but is not itself a factor input.

On the other hand, the World Bank claimed that it found three indicators related to knowledge that, it claims, significantly correlated with growth rates: education, openness to trade, and availability of the communications infrastructure (as measured by telephones per capita). It claimed that these three "partial proxies" for knowledge are by no means all there is to gauging knowledge or the ability to use it, but they do provide a rough approximation. It claimed that a country can add substantially to its growth rate by increasing the education of its people, increasing its openness to international trade, and improving its telecommunications infrastructure. The impact on growth, it claimed, can be as much as four percentage points. The authors of this document forget that some Third World countries have devoted large portions of their income to education. Some of these countries have had long traditions of free education and support many universities, but still have become poorer. The claim for openness to trade is based on the notion that openness relates to the opportunity to tap foreign knowledge embodied in trade goods and services, and it does not tally with experience in Third World countries, where openness has rather encouraged dependency. The World Bank claimed that telephone density relates to the ability of people to access useful information when needed. It did not say what that information was, nor how the information was quantified. Such is the sense and nonsense that surround TFP discussions that to an observer it seems that all one has to do is initiate a conjecture and add it to the heap of the unknowns ascribed to TFP.[39]

It is incorrect to think that science and technology are recent developments. It is this thinking that has led some economists to write about economic development and growth in terms of new things that societies are supposed to do in order to "modernize." People are told to regard activities that do not incorporate modern capitalist methods as inconsistent with economic development. Our detailed examination of primal societies revealed that they also depend on science and technology. They do not have research laboratories with million-dollar budgets nor professional scientists and engineers. Their science and technology developed through trial and error, but it is nevertheless painstaking. Amato commented, "To this day in the scientific age . . . trial and error remains a cornerstone in the quest to discover and invent. . . . As the twentieth century reached middle age, the era of trial and error in material-related research was reaching a point where the law of diminishing returns became operative. The days were over when an individual working solo stood much of a chance of coming up with dramatically better steel alloys or magnetic materials for motors or a semiconductor for switches. To people in power in countries this was an alarming reality. One big lesson from World War II was that staying on the strategic cutting edge of warfare technology would mean having a reliable supply of research teams that could create materials with an unprecedented combination of properties."[40] Amato's point was that the basic techniques of research had not changed; rather, new methods have evolved. The original noisy act of striking a stone against another in primal societies to produce a sharp cutting edge where before there had been a dull surface is no different from what modern Silicon Valley engineers do when they implant boron and phosphorous atoms into wafers to create semiconductors.

As revolutionary as the present information age is presented as being, Hobart and Schiffman in their book *Information Ages*—a historical survey of information through the ages—remarked, "Ours is trumpeted as the 'information age' and on the face of it, the claim requires no justification. . . . Yet . . . our electronic, computer culture has so mesmerized us that we fail to recognize other information ages associated with earlier technological changes and to appreciate the historical nature of our own era."[41] They contend that our present information explosion is part of a series of information explosions: "By the end of the eighteenth century, the [present] modern information age was in place."[42]

It is necessary to examine in more detail the role of material as a more important factor than capital in economic growth. This is best done here by quoting what Amato had to say about material:[43]

> Stop reading this book. Instead hold it in your hand. Feel its weight. Run your fingers over a page and feel its smooth texture, its dryness. Sense the page's compliance to the pressure of your finger. See how its whiteness is punctuated with black symbols printed in ink in a few dozen rows. If you sniff the page, you may even smell some aromatic chemicals still fleeing from the ink. Rub the page between your thumb and forefinger and hear that familiar papery noise. Twist a corner and see how the page crinkles. Now examine the book's fabric to which the pages are attached with an adhesive. The stack of pages in turn, attaches to the back and front covers of the hardcover edition by way of sheets of heavier-gauge paper that flank the book's first and last pages. At the bindery a machine pasted these flanking sheets to the rectangular paperboard. . . . Soft or hard, this book is made through and through of stuff.
>
> And so is everything else. Human beings extract about 15 billion tons of raw materials—that's 30 trillion pounds—from the earth each year, and from that they make every kind of stuff that you find in every kind of thing. Mined ore becomes metal becomes wire becomes part of a motor becomes a cooling fan in a computer. Harvested wood becomes lumber becomes home. Drilled petroleum becomes chemical feedstock becomes synthetic rubber becomes automobile tires. Natural gas becomes polyethylene becomes milk jugs and oversize, multicolored yard toys. Mined silica sand becomes silicon crystals becomes the base of microelectric chips. Each stuff is a link to enormous industrial trains whose workers process the world's raw materials into usable forms that constitute the items of our constructed landscape.
>
> Each kind of stuff also is a palimpsest of innovation in the use of materials, some going back to primal times. The wood-pulp paper from which books are made today comes from a pedigree of cotton and linen rags, animal skin parchment, Nile-reed papyrus and Sumerian clays tablets. The ink, a black pigment made from ground ash of some carbon-bearing fuel and suspended in a rapidly evaporating solvent, has its roots in crushed ore and charcoal mixed with spit or animal grease for use on cave walls and faces.
>
> It is the same for every other material that you encounter. Train your attention on the stuff of things rather than on their function. What you see is a rich medley of materials: the liquid crystal display of your laptop computer; the gritty concrete sidewalk on which you are strolling; the nylon of your raincoat zipper; the carbon-fiber-reinforced epoxy polymer of your tennis racket; the Kevlar polymer in your police force's bulletproof vests; the oak of your dresser; the diamond in your engagement ring; the nickel-based superalloy in the turbine blades in the engine of an airliner you are flying; the warm supple skin of your newborn; the cool, transparent glass of your office window; the combination of slick, high-density polyethylene and stainless steel that make up the artificial hip which a surgeon may have implanted into you; the cotton of the shirt you are wearing; the aluminum of the can you just drank from.
>
> In a single day the thousands of materials that you encounter, engage, manipulate and use display a diversity every bit as wondrous as that found in another set of material—this time found in living organisms (including man) which are composed of the most of all the world's most miraculous of all the world's materials—skin, bone, tendon, muscle, hair, and scads of other biological tissues— all of them honed by evolutionary engineering into a beautiful marriage of form and function.
>
> That books and buildings and the things in the world are supposed to be made of materials suited for their functions is so obvious that it almost goes without saying. But things that go without saying long enough are readily forgotten. That is why the materials that make up the world are most often not on people's minds. . . .
>
> But materials are too far central to our lives and

too fascinating to remain out of our mind until they become sensational headlines. Paying attention to materials in your life spawns an endless stream of questions (and even more fascinating answers). Why is a skyscraper's frame made of steel, not copper or polyethylene? What is so special about silicon crystal that it became the foundation of a society-changing electronics revolution? What kind of materials does it take to build a plane that can take off like a jet, accelerate 20,000 miles per hour, zoom into outer space and then land two hours later in an airport on the other side of the planet?

Simply noticing the diversity of stuff in materials of the world can evoke an open-mouthed sense of wonder akin to visiting a zoo filled with animals that you had never really seen up close. That sense of wonder might even grow in awe when you consider this: the constructed world brims with metals, ceramics, plastics, fabrics, glass, and thousands of specific materials that are found nowhere in the wilderness. . . .

Silicon atoms, when combined with oxygen atoms to form specific minerals, are the basis of one of the most coveted materials of the first stone tool makers—flint. Because of the arrangements of internal mineral grains in flint, the stone can cleave conveniently in a shell-like pattern that leaves sharp edges. Moreover, its edges are hard and tough enough to remain sharp even after cutting and scraping into tendon and bone. Silicon has been a celebrity element even from the beginning.

The vast stretches of time during which primal societies saw a number of major turning points, each leading to entirely new powers of material transformations that have changed the course of individual lives and of the global history. The use of fire to change the stuff of the world had already been mentioned. . . . Another major turning point was the development of a more deliberate type of chemistry and its far more extensive ways of reaching into and transforming the anatomy of material. For centuries alchemists, chemists, and sundry tinkerers pulverized, mixed, boiled, distilled, roasted, extracted, electrolyzed, and otherwise fiddled with whatever substance they could find in the mineral, animal, and vegetable domains. Out of this obsessive quest came a myriad of previ-ously unseen substances—solid, liquid, and gaseous—some of which harbored uses by themselves or as participants in new chemical reactions.

Along the way, chemists also learned about the limitations of their business. Despite the two-thousand-year alchemical quest to transform base metals into gold, no one ever succeeded in transmuting one element into another. At least on earth, under normal conditions . . . scientists realized that they would never become alchemists—they would never change lead into gold or oxygen into carbon or any one element into another element. The hard-won insight that the vast menagerie of materials in the world is the result of a small pantry of elements, that the personality of each material is the result of an inner hierarchy of physical and chemical structures, has become the principle of a new alchemy practiced by people known as materials scientists. Rather than gold from lead, their trophies are numerous, ranging from new lightweight alloys to build a next-generation fleet of superefficient jetliners to harder-than-diamond materials for industrial machine tools to polymeric drug-soaked medical implants that can release their cargo into diseased brain tissue.

In the past half century a field known as materials science and engineering has emerged as a powerful hybrid of many other technical fields. The practitioners of the field are coming to a point where they are gaining the ultimate level of control over the material world. No longer contented to manipulate "stuff," they have tools for seeing, moving and understanding individual atoms and the ever larger atomic collections that become the materials we use. The emerging ability to micro-manage materials even at the atomic level is giving researchers unprecedented access to the mostly untapped wonders of the periodic table of the elements. Even compared to today's most sophisticated materials, like semiconductors in a computer or the gallium arsenide in a CD player laser, materials scientists say we still haven't seen anything compared to the materials that will come.

The development of today's breathtaking speed of information technology depended on man's ability to move from the macrocosmic material world into the microcosm. With macrocosmic electromechanical machines, the speed of calculations stayed subject to factors governing the friction and inertia of mechanical parts. In the microcosmic universe of the vacuum tube, later taken over by the transistor and later by the silicon chip, the only elements in motion are electrons, whose mass is so tiny that virtually no friction or inertia impedes their flow. For practical purposes, their movement is nearly instantaneous. In the macrocosmic world, switching took five microseconds. Today the times are measured in nanoseconds—billionths of a second.

New developments in the medical field in the last ten years or so have occurred in gene therapy arising from the new vista of knowledge about genes. Drugs consist of molecules that now can be targeted to specific genes identified as responsible for certain diseases and deficiencies. The breakthrough is due to better knowledge of materials.

In general, therefore, material development has been geared to increasing the scope of man's economic activities by meeting new needs and tackling limitations that prevented the realization of many desired economic activities. For example, when iron was introduced, it was possible, using it to replace wood in many areas of activities, to increase output (e.g., train loads increased because of stronger iron carriages). It was possible to build iron bridges capable of supporting higher loads than wooden bridges. Steel alloys increased other desirable material qualities, such as ductility, which iron did not have. Aluminum combined light weight (compared with iron and steel) with ductility and enabled a significant reduction in the weight of structures, leading to higher outputs. New heat-resistant materials permitted higher-temperature processes that resulted in higher outputs. The discovery of heat-absorbing membranes helped to increase output where heat emission was a limiting factor.

When researchers perceive a new need, the first question is whether the right material is available or could be made. This material, when available, is invariably incorporated in a new production aid and/or in new material input. Labor—which is the other natural factor input—has not materially changed in its physical output, as barring malnutrition and poor health, man's physical strength is the same in all races and over time. We are not materially more intelligent than our predecessors. Each generation adds to what it receives and adjusts itself to meet the needs before it. A minister of religion put it this way: "We are a part of a long chain of humanity, which stretches from generation to generation. We stand on the shoulders of those who came before us, and we create a world for those who will be coming."[44] These are humbling thoughts for economists who would have it that present human knowledge is at its peak.

Those who argue that changes in technology are incorporated in capital equipment—if by this change they mean increases in output per unit—are therefore not 100 percent wrong, since new material is often incorporated into new capital equipment. It is, however, also incorporated in new material factor input.

It is therefore clear that materials are at the center of all economic activities and that advances in knowledge of materials hold the key to increased economic development and growth. The means by which a certain process or a certain configuration of material yields certain desirable properties that enhance output potential is not always clear to man. They do not follow rational lines. The human mind did not formulate them and cannot alter them. The human mind can only discover them (these days mainly through research) and ally itself with them. Therefore the recognition and integration of the role of material into the formulation for maximal sustainable growth is a necessary ingredient of the science of economic development and growth. Solow's residual is material, not the ambiguous phenomenon

Figure 3.5 **Advances in knowledge of materials shift the production function upward.**

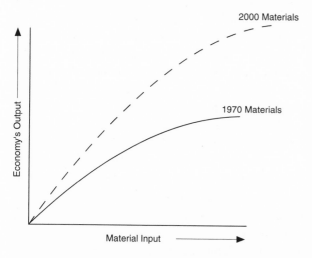

called technology. The changing material content of an economy therefore has an immediate and direct positive contribution to its growth, an effect far more profound than increases due to labor utilization. The general relationship between total output and materials is shown in Figure 3.5. This is a rearrangement of a similar relationship curve in which Samuelson and Nordhaus sought to locate technology (residual) as the determinant of growth.[45]

Some economists have neglected the central role of materials. For example, Samuelson and Nordhaus said of the history of economic growth: "History records how entrepreneur and capital . . . have called the tune [in terms of economic growth] since the early nineteenth century . . . inventions and new machines led to the introduction of power-driven machineries, factories that gathered teams of workers into giant firms, railroads and steamships that joined together far points of the world, and iron and steel that built stronger and faster locomotives. As capitalists' economies entered the twentieth century, important new industries grew around the telephone, the automobile and electric power. Capital accumulation and new technologies became the dominant

force affecting economic development."[46] This view is wrong because it seeks to derive its authority from the reconstruction of history instead of from science. It confuses the shadow with the substance. For example, it was not the steam engine that was the innovation. Rather, the steam engine was the consequence of innovation in a material—the discovery that when water was heated to a high temperature, it produced a surge of power that could not be equaled by horses or a flow of water. What is more, the character of the new material meant that it could be used anywhere without being tied to a location. The mobility of steam power untied a lot of economic activity from specific geographic features such as canals and rivers.

To use another example, the telephone was the shadow, and the substance was the discovery that a wire had the property to transmit signals over distances. Innovation need not be capital-based. It could be labor-intensive or material-intensive. It may not need a factory, as it may be a simple craft activity.

It is therefore not capital accumulation and new technologies that are the dominant force in economic development, as claimed by Samuelson and Nordhaus, but the discovery of new materials in the context of appropriate factor proportions. In any case the development of appropriate capital (production aids) both utilizes and depends on new materials. In other words, capital is nothing on its own. It is essentially a device dependent on the selection and development of the right material in order to provide the appropriate production aid.

It is material that is at the front end of economic development/growth. Growth of any economy is initiated by increases in quantity or quality of M, even if there is no increase in L. It is therefore a useless exercise to attempt to quantify knowledge, science, or technology and seek to ascribe growth values to them—as new growth theory (also called endogenous growth theory) seeks to do—because growth takes place only when this knowledge or science or technology results in an increase in M. Solow himself admitted that "very little is known about the exact connection between research and actual technological progress as it enters models of production."[47] Knowledge of this connection is difficult to obtain because whether a particular research project succeeds or not is unpredictable.

From our analysis so far of factor proportions and how they relate to economic development/growth there are a number of inferences we can make. First, the material of an economy is practically fixed in the very short term. In the medium and long term it increases or decreases for reasons already discussed. The rate of increase depends increasingly on research and development (these terms are used in their widest meaning). The more rapid the increase in M, the greater the output benefit to that economy. The absolute value of M is important. Every economy starts off endowed with materials. There are changes in the composition and quantity of this resource mix over time as some materials are depleted and new ones are discovered or developed. In Europe today, wheat is a material that is so common that the average European hardly gives it a thought. Yet the discovery of wheat as a material, back in primal days, must have been an important event. New uses for wheat through the years have no doubt increased both the demand for and the supply of wheat. New materials are "created" from existing materials. The production of steel is another example of the discovery of a new material.

It will be noted that the three basic factor proportions—capital/labor, material/capital, and labor/material—were each expressed in a formula that has the variable M/L (ratio of material/labor) or its inverse. This, as we stated earlier, is in confirmation of the fact that capital as a factor has no independent existence of its own. Capital cannot exist without M and L. And if you consider that to the

extent that man produces the input L (labor), L itself is produced by the "material" of man's body. So it is clear that no matter the economy, increases in output—that is, potential output—predominantly arise from changes in material (M). It is not a residual. And because M is a cumulative process, economies evolve from their primal state by building upon the stock of materials.

The labor stock of an economy is also a cumulative process. The social, cultural, and demographic characteristics of the population from which a society's labor is drawn can be best ascertained by tracing these back to its primal people. The knowledge that some people refer to as human capital is accumulated in a society over time and has a cultural and historical content that Western-trained economists ignore. Landes has observed that for many Western economists, culture simply gets in the way.[48]

Bean had this to say from his study of industrial relations across many countries: "The main characteristics of national industrial relations, their dominant and distinctive feature, seem to be established at a fairly early age in the industrial development of a country. . . . Subsequently in the absence of major dislocations such as wars or revolutions, the provisions appear to show a good deal of tenacity, retaining many of their early characteristics and institutions despite subsequent evolution. . . . Employment relations have been," he argued, "influenced not only by environmental or contextual variables . . . together with a country's history but also in some societies by distinct value systems and cultural features."[49]

The Confucian outlook of the Chinese, which still plays a significant role in that society's approach to economic development, was founded in Chinese olden times. The Japanese emphasis on the group derives from Japanese history and arguably has served Japan well. American liberalism was founded in the history of the nation's establishment and is today the basis of its economic principles. It is these historical, cultural, institutional, and social characteristics that help indigenize economic development in each society and provide the reference against which it copes with changes. The common feature of the cultures that achieve economic growth is that they mobilize all their factor resources through correct factor proportions.

Like the other factors, capital too is a cumulative process. It has been stated many times already that capital is an essential part of all production and was established when the primal societies were created. The stock of capital increases as the society progressively takes material and labor out of the system to create new production aids—to meet changing production needs, as M increases, and to replenish the existing stock of its capital. Financial value is not an essential characteristic of capital within the science of economic development. In early societies that had no money system, capital was not assigned a financial value, but it was capital nevertheless. Capital accumulation does not lead economic development but follows economic development and growth. Too much capital accumulation is a waste of factor resources and leads to imbalance in an economy.

To sum up, economic growth is a cumulative process over time. Its links to history are part of its present and form its base. It is a building process that involves erecting more bricks on top of the ones earlier generations put in place. There is no doubt that sometimes what we have is a tearing down of some of the bricks that were originally installed. But the process, nevertheless, is that of building on what was in place before. This is the way nature has it: Within the context of the three factors of each economy, there is a growth process with a basic personality.

The dynamic process in the factor proportions of an economy thus has a lot to do with the economy's rate of growth. This point can be made in another way by saying, as Michael Porter did, that "the stock of factors at any particular time is less important than the rate at which they are created [and] upgraded." Porter is right if he meant to stress that growth requires creation and upgrading of factors. However, Porter got it wrong when he differentiated between what he termed "basic factors" and "advanced factors." Advanced factors, in his view, include "modern digital data communication infrastructure, highly educated personnel such as graduate engineers and computer scientists and university research institutes in sophisticated discipline." He said that it is the advanced factors that make for economic growth. He argued that the importance of basic factors has been undermined by either their diminished necessity, their widening availability, or ready access to them through foreign activities or sourcing an international market." He argued that advanced factors are "scarcer because their development demands large and often sustained investment in both human and physical capital."[50]

It is not correct to say that the importance of basic factors has been reduced, because the advanced factors are produced from the basic factors. What is created (produced) must fit the stage of the maturity of that economy. For example, while Porter's advanced factors (digital technology, computer scientists, and university research institutes) may constitute what is needed in a capital-intensive advanced economy, they will be almost irrelevant in a labor-intensive economy.

Potential Capacity

The question of an economy's potential capacity has long been of interest to economists. This has also turned into another related question, how to increase the long-term rate of growth.

Those seeking to identify the potential capacity generally are looking to provide a policy guideline because it seems to set a target against which the results of policy measures will be assessed. In studies of the U.S. economy, potential output was originally considered to be the largest output that could be obtained without inflation. But such a definition was acceptable if it meant low unemployment, because potential output implies that the economy was using all its supply capabilities fully. Indeed, "output at high employment" was used as a synonym. Potential output was also regarded as the desirable level of output that provided suitable targets for fiscal and monetary policy. Underneath all this was the assumption that maximal output and inflation were pulling in different directions. In other words, the economy achieves high employment at the risk of inflation. The belief that there is a natural level of unemployment along with its output twin, potential GNP, has permeated much of conventional economic thinking. Samuelson and Nordhaus said that the concept forms "the central core of modern macroeconomics." They defined the natural rate of unemployment as the lowest level of unemployment that can be sustained (in the case of the United States, 6 percent); because this represented the highest sustainable level of employment, it corresponded to the nation's potential output.[51]

Krugman defined U.S. potential output as what the country could have produced each year if it had been at more or less full employment, which he thought corresponded to a 5 percent unemployment rate. Curiously, he went on to say that the measurement of potential output is "one of the more solid and uncontroversial pieces of modern economic analysis."[52] But this claim is not correct. The 5 percent rate was a bad guess, as in recent years the increasing output of the U.S. economy with lower levels of unemployment showed that the trade-off between growth and inflation, which had been the cornerstone of conventional economic theory, is not a valid conclusion.

In the United States during the 1950s and 1960s it was assumed that it would be possible to achieve price stability with low unemployment. Potential output was regarded as a desirable level of production that would be consistent with low unemployment and price stability. A higher output, it was claimed, would cause inflation, while lower output would result in excessive unemployment. Said Denison, "The conditions that determine the appropriate level of unemployment were not precisely formulated. Some regarded unemployment present under potential conditions as consisting of types of unemployment that would not be reduced much by stronger demand—at least not quickly and without exerting upward pressure on wages and prices. Others regarded the unemployment rate as corresponding to potential conditions as simply a rate low enough to be generally acceptable."[53] The U.S. president's Council of Economic Advisors (CEA) at the time considered potential output to be the output that would be obtained if 4 percent of the civilian labor force were unemployed.

Price stability is also not easily defined. Often price increases of 1 and 2 percent were considered to qualify as price stability. But in the late 1960s, price increases broke this range. In the 1970s significant price increases and unemployment above 4 percent occurred together. The 1970s and 1980s, therefore, led to confusion in the use of the term "potential output" because one series of numbers could no longer have all the old meanings. In its January 1979 annual report, the CEA used 5.1 percent as the potential unemployment rate (the rate of unemployment that would not change the present rate of inflation) in each of the years from 1975 to 1978 in the belief that a weighted unemployment rate provided a better measurement of the tightness of labor markets than the simple unemployment rate.[54] But using a weighted unemployment rate to define potential output does not make it possible to regard potential output as consistent with price stability or even as being much closer to consistency with price stability than if the unweighted unemployment measure was retained.

Faced with what they regarded as the incompatibility of high employment and price stability, some economists chose to retain price behavior as a criterion for potential output and to discard unemployment. However, none of them attempted to measure potential output as the largest output obtainable with price stability. Such a figure may not even exist within their conventional theory, and even if it did, it may be too small and imply such a high unemployment rate as to make it infeasible. Instead, this group introduced a new criterion, potential unemployment, and defined potential output as the output consistent with the potential unemployment rate. But unwittingly they had introduced another change in the whole concept—they had the underlying rate of inflation in mind rather than the actual rate.

This definition, based on stable inflation, had little resemblance to the idea of potential output as the highest output consistent with price stability. But the adherents of this new definition had other things in mind as well, namely, how it would be possible over time to reduce inflation associated with a particular unemployment rate and achieve an acceptable rate of inflation with low unemployment.

In the midst of these controversies, the CEA and many economists have resorted to defining potential output in terms of the economy's ability to produce. The 1977 CEA report, the last by President Ford's council, states: "Potential GNP is a measure of the aggregate supply capability of the economy or the amount of output that could be expected at full employment. More precisely, potential GNP is the output the economy could produce with the existing technology under assumed conditions of high but sustainable utilization of factors of production—labor, capital and natural resources." It added that potential GNP "does not represent the absolute maximal level of production that could be generated by wartime or other abnormal levels of aggregate demand but rather that which could be expected from high utilization rates obtainable under normal conditions."[55] This description, it will be noted, did not mention prices. Two years later, President Carter's CEA stated, "Potential GNP is defined as the level of real output that the economy could produce at high rates of resource utilization."[56] The unanswered question is how high.

But on the whole, it is clear that the question of the potential output of the U.S. economy has eluded conventional economists. There are still many unsettled issues—employment, prices, price stability, and so on—and these occur at a time when the relationship between unemployment and inflation is changing. Until a few years ago, typical estimates in the United States suggested that unemployment below 6 percent would lead to what Krugman called "a gradual but inexorable acceleration of inflation." But at the end of 1998, with an unemployment of 4.3%, an average for that year of 4.5% (lowest for almost three decades), prices were still stable.

Conventional economists leave us with no answer to what constitutes a situation of "high but sustainable utilization of factors of production" (the CEA's stipulation of 1977) or "high rates of resource utilization" (the CEA's definition of 1979). Attempts at defining these only on the unemployment front are definitely off the mark, because there are three factors, of which labor is only one.

Economists in the United States have sought relief from this problem by seeking approximations through empirical effects. Krugman asserted that "the unemployment rate turns out to be a pretty good indicator not only of the utilization of labor force but of the utilization of the economic capacity in general."[57] He sought justification for this claim by what he called "a remarkably good, though not exact, rule of thumb known as Okun's law," which suggested that each extra percentage point of economic growth is associated with about a 0.5 percent fall in unemployment (and conversely, a 1 percent fall in unemployment is associated with about two percentage points of economic growth). This law, when applied over the period 1973 to 1997, produced what he and many others thought was ("by standards of the inexact science of economics and normal fuzziness of economic statistics") a close fit to actual U.S. statistics.

But in our quest for a science of economic development and growth, this empirical approach is of limited use. Okun's law clearly does not apply to all economies. Indeed, in economic science there is no such trade-off. Therefore it does not help in ascertaining what the potential output of any economy is.

In an attempt at defining potential output without reference to the U.S. economy, Lipsey and Chrystal said that potential output occurred when all resources—land, labor, productive resources—were employed at their normal level of utilization. They did not define what the normal level is.

Krugman defined the U.S. economy's productive capacity as the number of employable workers multiplied by output per worker (productivity). But this does not tell us anything—it does not specify what the potential output per worker can be, and without this it cannot say what the potential capacity of the economy is.

Productivity as it is often defined is GNP divided by the total workforce. Economists regard productivity as a measure of the productive capacity of the working force. There are said to be three prescriptions for raising productivity. One is to increase the quantity and quality of business capital. Another is to improve the public capital that supports the private economy. The third is to improve the quality of its workforce, what is sometimes called human capital.[58] But this is easier said than done. Krugman himself agreed when he said, "No reasonable economist can claim that we have any accurate accounting of the value of each of these three sources of growth." We too will not expect accuracy. It is not possible. But Krugman went further to say that

"most estimates of the effects of both business and human capital on growth are based on their market return; yet it is a well-understood point that the return to the society from an investment may be either much less or much more than their payoff to the private investor. When it comes to public investment the position is even worse, since there isn't any market return to use as a benchmark."[59] He added, rather ominously, "So we can't really say what rate of productivity growth the United States is 'earning' by its investments or how much better our productivity growth would be if we did everything right."

Krugman's very candid statements confirm the view we have previously expressed, that treating capital as investments in dollar terms is not scientific and that the introduction of dollars into the analysis is bound to yield results that do not accord with the science of economic development and growth. Good returns to the private sector, as Krugman implied, can cause distortions in factor proportions.

There is another serious problem with the idea that in order to improve productivity, an economy needs to increase the quantity and quality of its capital. We have previously expressed the view that capital accumulation is not the prime mover for economic growth. The idea that all one has to do is to deprive the society of present consumption so that it will rise tomorrow in economic triumph persists (see Figure 3.1) in conventional economic literature. Solow called it the "draconian" path to economic growth: reduce consumption drastically, invest rapidly, and reach the (growth) target rapidly.[60] And the reference to the "quality" of capital is presumably another way of bringing in "technology." Therefore, to increase economic productive capacity is supposed to require three inputs—labor, capital, and technology (Solow's residual). We have argued that the residual is, in fact, material.

If that is the case, improving productivity from a labor point of view has two components: a unit of labor working with increasing quantity and quality of capital, and a unit of labor working with an increasing quantity of material. Why, then, can we not also examine the effect on growth of one unit of material working with an increasing quantity and quality of capital or one unit of labor working with an increasing quantity and quality of material? Surely all these are different faces of growth. It is to be reiterated that when one increases capital, it is not an issue of financial investment. It is the transfer of materials and labor away from factors available for producing consumption goods. That is why the production activities can become less labor-intensive and less material-intensive simultaneously. Obviously if this substitution reduces costs for the private producer, he will go for it, even if from the point of the factor endowment of the economy this creates factor proportion distortion. Since it is possible that in this whole triangular relationship between factors, there might also simultaneously be a substitution between labor and material, it seems somewhat odd that so much emphasis is laid in conventional economics on output per unit labor—productivity—as indicative of the productive performance of an economy. Current labor productivity figures on their own tend, therefore, to give a distorted view of the working of the economy.

Returning to the 1977 and 1979 CEA definitions of potential GNP, the 1977 definition specified that potential output is the capacity that could be expected with full employment, and then amplified this by saying that it is output under assumed conditions of high but sustainable utilization of factors of production. In 1978, the Full Employment and Balanced Growth Act (known more generally as the Humphrey-Hawkins Act) established new quantitative goals for U.S. economic objectives—a 4 percent unemployment rate and an interim target of 3 percent inflation. It is clear that U.S. politicians and economists were agonizing over what full employment meant. In the 1980s, the United States followed a deliberate policy of reducing output relative to past trend in order to trim inflation. The cumulative "output gap" resulting from this policy amounted to more than 20 percent of a year's GNP.[61] It was reasoned that to reduce U.S. inflation by 1 percent, the economy had to run something like 4 percentage points below its capacity—an estimate that soon was titled the "sacrifice ratio."

The 1979 CEA definition of potential output talked of output at "high rates of resource utilization." Unemployment was not mentioned, but it is clear that the performance of the U.S. economy did not meet their criteria for attaining its potential capacity.

The potential growth of an economy, therefore, is achieved when all its production factors are fully utilized. In the context of the theory of factor proportions, a position in which all factor production factors are fully utilized means that at the macroeconomic level, the operative factor proportions are:

$$\frac{C_n}{L_n}, \quad \frac{C_n}{M_n}, \quad \frac{L_n}{M_n},$$

Conventional economics argues that an economy can produce more than its potential output and that when this happens there is an inflationary gap that is the difference between the new increased output and the potential output. But it is not stated where the factors of production required to create this gap will come from, nor precisely what state of production techniques (that is, the relative availability and utilization of the factor inputs in the economy) is being considered. It is clear that inflation cannot be explained by reference to an inflationary gap. There is, therefore, no trade-off between employment and inflation. Conventional economics also considers that a recessionary gap exists when an economy's resources have not been fully used, but it is not stated what could cause this. It is clear, however, that the recessionary gap must arise because the technology left resources unused as a result of wrong factor proportions. In the end, it is clear that inflation and recession are essentially structural problems traceable to factor proportions.

Potential output cannot be achieved only by macroeconomic manipulations. The science of the situation is that maximum output of an economy can be achieved only when there is equilibrium between factor proportions at the macro- and microeconomic levels. When economies are not run on a scientific basis, the resulting disequilibrium creates inflation. In turn, people then blame inflation as the reason the economy does not attain the maximum output possible. The attainment of maximum output has nothing to do with fiscal management.

In the final analysis, therefore, an economy on a path toward potential capacity is like one huge chemical reaction in which the inputs are constantly changing, both in quantity and in composition. Though the factor proportions are changing all the time, such an economy maintains a highly dynamic equilibrium, though the particular features of this equilibrium will vary from one economy to another. Many conventional concepts in economics fail to grasp this dynamism.

In practice an economy on a sustainable growth path will have differences in factor proportions between activities. What matters as a practical guideline is that factor proportions cluster around the natural factor proportions.

We have gone into such detail to demonstrate weaknesses in current economic theorizing. Not only were economists quoting different figures for the limits to employment in the economy (which some regarded as full employment), but they made different stipulations as to what they considered were the factors of production. Even when some economists acknowledge that potential output requires full utilization of factors, they could not say how that full utilization was to be achieved.

In summary, there are two ways (which can operate simultaneously) for an economy to attain sustainable growth. One is to attain its potential growth, that is, growth that involves equalizing its factor proportions in both the microeconomy and the macroeconomy. The second is to keep increasing its potential growth level to new levels by continuing efforts to create new materials and upgrade existing ones. These efforts are enhanced through science and technology (used in the widest sense).

Productivity and Technology

The issue of productivity and technology has been viewed from a slightly different angle as a result of the birth of new growth theory. It is now generally thought that if technological progress ceased, economic growth would also stop. Krugman pointed out that "technology in the broad sense—not just hardware, but also 'soft' innovations like just-in-time inventory management—is crucial to productivity growth." He added that "analysts of long-run growth have been aware that long-run growth would grind to a halt without continuous technological progress and that much progress is the main source of productivity increase." Elsewhere Krugman said that "productivity is the single most important factor affecting our economic well-being."

Here what Krugman had to say about technology, society, and productivity is relevant:

> Economic historians have observed that it [technology] often takes a very long time to make a major impact on productivity and living standards. For example, the crucial technological breakthrough that launched the Industrial Revolution was arguably Hargreave's invention of the spinning jenny in 1764; yet the wholesale industrialization of Britain did not begin until around 1810 and real wages did not begin to rise significantly until the 1840s. Electric power was introduced in the 1880s, yet the historian Paul David has argued that it had little positive impact on productivity until the 1920s.
>
> The reason for these long lags is that a technology often does not have its full impact when used in isolation; it is only when it becomes broadly

applied and interacts with other technologies that its true potential can be exploited. An automobile is a plaything of the rich when it is a rare item; it becomes much more when there is a network of paved roads, gas stations and repair shops are universally available, and the biggest department stores are in suburban malls rather than traditional downtowns. And there is a circularity: the network of support and reinforcement that makes technology fully productive is both a cause and a result of that technology's widespread use. So a new technology, no matter how marvelous, may have only superficial effects for decades, then flower as it finally reaches critical mass. . . . Think of the twinned growth of the oil and transportation industries: superhighways, supertankers, and giant, super-efficient refineries did not involve any radical intellectual breakthroughs; even jet aircraft had been possible in principle since the 1930s. It was the implementation of known concepts, and mutual reinforcement of growing linkages among these industries, that made rapid productivity growth possible. The same may be said of the nexus amongst private automobiles, refrigerators and supermarkets that sharply increased productivity in the retail sector. Much of the productivity growth in manufacturing came from the replacement of the old-style multi-story, cramped factory —designed to allow a massive steam engine to power many machines and to allow a single railway to spur to deliver raw materials and take away shipments—with single-story, open-plan plants designed around electric power and road transport. The ideas were not revolutionary; their impact on productivity was.[62]

All that Krugman had to say can be summarized in one sentence: Human beings need time to get used to new things. If you move to a new city, it will take you time to get used to it. You may initially harbor a feeling of anxiety in your new environment, but over time, as you explore the town, you will gradually make the new town your own. New parents feel a lot of trepidation when they are expecting their first baby. But given time, they soon get used to parenthood and even come to enjoy it.

Krugman was therefore telling us what we all already know. What he is talking about is not a characteristic exclusive to technology. The main issue of concern—a point raised in a general way in Chapter 1—is that it is not clear what exactly he meant by technology. He talked about the hardware and software of technology; can it be that the superhighways, supertankers, and automobiles are the hardware, while just-in-time is an example of software? Romer and Nelson contended that "technology needs to be understood as a collection of goods," so they would probably accept that superhighways, supertankers, and automobiles are technology. They added that "other parts of technology are produced primarily through learning by doing and learning by using, both of which interact powerfully with research and development." So technology is a product, but it interacts with research and development. They further classed this product (technology) into three categories—hardware, software, and wetware. Hardware apparently includes "all non-human objects used in production—both capital goods such as equipment and structures and natural resources such as land and raw materials." This time technology is not a product but something used in production. Land and raw materials are apparently hardware technology. Software technology represents knowledge or information stored in a form that exists outside of the brain and which can be copied, stored, communicated, or reused. Wetware is anything stored in the human brain, "so human capital is now only a part of wet technology."[63]

On the other hand, Sloman said, "The technology employed in a country depends on the type of development strategy it is pursuing. Some strategies lead to the adoption of labor intensive technologies, others to relatively capital intensive ones."[64] In this view, technology will emerge from the development strategy selected. Still, he did not say what he thought technology is. Other authors avoided defining technology at the same time as they were telling us what technological change is. Samuelson and Nordhaus define technological change as changes in processes of production and introduction of new products such that more or improved output can be obtained from the same bundle of inputs. It is not clear whether they mean that it is technology change that causes improved output or technology itself, but other people, as we have seen, lay everything at the doorstep of technology, not change in technology. Landes wrote a 566-page book entitled *The Unbound Prometheus: Technological Change and Industrial Development in Western Europe from 1750 to the Present* without saying anywhere in it what technology is, though he freely used the term "modern technology." The economists Rees and Smith went further afield in their definition of technology: "Technology is hard to define but it is linked to the idea of applied science, that is, the use of human scientific knowledge to produce goods and services. It is more than applied science, however, because technology in its broadest sense has economic, social and even cultural and artistic purposes."[65]

The essential character of science is clear definition of concepts. Without a clear definition of what technology is, conventional economists' analysis of technology and its role in productivity cannot have a scientific base. There is no proof so far of any direct link between technology and productivity. Even though new growth theory claims to have endogenized technology, conventional economics has been unable to bring this technology into the mainstream of economic analysis.

It has been emphasized that (labor) productivity as a stand-alone index gives a distorted view of the workings of the economy. Just-in-time (which Krugman quoted as an example of technology) derives its importance from the fact that compared to previous production paradigms, it not only improved labor productivity in many areas but also reduced capital and materials (inventory) inputs. Just-in-time introduced significant changes in factor proportions compared with original mass production techniques. Picking labor productivity as the only innovation of just-in-time misses the point.

Krugman remarked in his book *The Age of Diminished Expectations* that "production isn't everything, but in the long run, it is almost everything. A country's ability to improve its standard of living over time depends almost entirely on its ability to raise its output per worker." He thought that the overwhelming importance of productivity should be obvious.[66]

The great importance attached to labor productivity in advanced countries is understandable but not totally justified. Economists and public authorities in Western economies have emphasized economy-of-scale techniques. What matters is how many products were turned out per hour to support the mass market. Not only is labor provided per hour, but the flow of material per hour is also important. Certainly in less advanced economies, as we will show, capital-intensive production will cause serious distortions in their economic structure. The economists' overwhelming interest in labor productivity cannot be accepted as part of a general theory of economic development and growth supposed to apply to all countries.

Krugman and Obstfeld did seem to accept that bias toward capital-intensive activities exists when they stated that high value added per worker is largely a function of capital intensity and that it is a dubious criterion on which to judge the desirability of industries. They added, "High industries with high value added per worker are typically capital intensive, that is, that they have low value added per unit of capital."[67] The question that is not answered is what value is added per unit of material. If material has a central role in economic growth, then material productivity (output per unit of material) is as important, if not more important, than labor productivity for development economics.

Krugman's comments on the time it takes for a new technology to mature before it shows up in increased productivity and living standards are interesting for another reason. He argued that during this maturation time, the technology needs to interact with other technologies in what he called linkages. But the historically observable sequences he mentioned do not provide us with a scientific basis to include them in economic theory. New discoveries can never stay in isolation because discoveries historically occur haphazardly—some might be related, some not. The problem for conventional economics is that, as Krugman implied, economists have no way of knowing whether a new technology can produce productivity gains until it has been out there in the society for some time. This is not economic science. A science of economic development and growth studies the factor proportions of a new technology and provides an immediate answer as to whether a new technology is growth-inducing or not in a particular economy. Not all technologies are growth-inducing because their factor proportions may be out of line with the natural factor proportions. Yet some economists tend to give the impression that all technology in whatever form or shape leads to growth.

Because of a lack of clarity about what technology is, many economic conclusions are reached through rational analysis (not science) and sometimes guesswork. Economists have, for example, attempted to explain the "productivity growth slowdown" in the 1970s in this way. There were three main categories of explanation, listed by Krugman as technical, social, and political. The technical explanation holds that the "productivity growth slowdown" arose because "the vital engine [technology] ran out of steam." It is claimed that this was not because there was anything wrong with the basic structure of the economy but simply because, "the technologies that were the basis of the post-war boom had pretty much by the 1970s reached their

limits . . . and so productivity growth fell off." "In effect," Krugman concluded, "productivity slowdown can be attributed to an exhaustion of ideas."[68] Krugman used the Boeing 747 as an example. When the Boeing 747 appeared in 1969, it was a triumph of engineering but according to Krugman, today's version of the 747 is improved "but not radically different." The technologies of the late 1960s, according to him, had approached their limit.

The engine analogy is attractive but lacks a scientific base. The theory of factor proportions states that when factor proportions are equal, the economy will attain maximal growth because all the factor inputs are fully used. The theory says that the greatest source for economic growth is through technical advances in the material factor apart from increases in quantities of the three factors.

Because economists concentrate their analysis on capital investments and not on the factor proportions behind the production of these capital items, they fail to grasp the great changes in production techniques that are taking place. Yes, today's 747s may look like the earlier version, but the production techniques have witnessed some revolutionary changes.

In a comprehensive survey of the aircraft industry in 1985, *The Economist* stated that it was the jet engine (more precisely, the gas turbine) that revolutionized the aircraft industry.[69] Improvements in jet engines came in stages. The turbojet (now used mainly for combat aircraft) was the first and simplest. Then came the turboprop, which proved very efficient at low speeds and low altitudes. Then came the turbofan, which dominated the industry for more than two decades because it was quieter and more efficient. The pressure now is to obtain even more performance out of turbofans; after fifteen years of development, one company produced dramatic improvements based on improved materials (a titanium sandwich filled with a honeycomb core), and GE produced an unducted fan engine, both of which have resulted in major savings in fuel. The survey concluded that the future challenges facing aircraft makers is "better aerodynamics, advanced composites, thermoplastic techniques." All these are issues, it will be noted, deal with materials and their behavior and characteristics in differing circumstances.

Figure 3.6 shows trends in fuel effectiveness of aircraft airframe/engine combinations over time, from which the changes caused by production techniques (represented by the different plane designs) is evident. All these developments involved changes in factor proportions in production. Said Keith Man, the director of the Royal Aeronautical Society, "Aerospace encompasses a lot of different leading-edge technology which have to be integrated to provide a successful produce. Often there are completely different and new disciplines. Software and systems engineering, for example, not thought of twenty or thirty years ago is having quite a dramatic effect on how we construct an aircraft, how light they are and how they are controlled."[70] It is thus evident that a claim that a jet aircraft of 1969 is not radically different from present jet aircrafts is true for a layman but widely off the mark in economic science.

The inability of conventional economics to deal with the cause of the productivity growth slowdown of the 1970s becomes more glaring if it is noted that the period coincided with a period when the U.S. economy placed about as high a share of its resources into investment and a higher share into education than it did in the 1950s and 1960s, which were years of rising productivity. If investments were supposed to be the engine of growth and the embodiment of new technology, why, then, did productivity growth fall when investments stayed steady or even rose?

Denison, who studied the causes of the slowdown in productivity growth in the United States over the same period, considered whether the drop was due to a slackening of technical knowledge input into the economy. He quoted Mansfield and colleagues

as saying that "many of the available bits and scraps of data point to a slackening in the face of innovation in the United States [during the period]. But the data are so crude and incomplete that it would be foolish to put too much weight on them."[71]

On all scores, it is evident that there is no proof that the slowdown in productivity growth in the 1970s had anything to do with any slowdown in technological change. The special status given to technology—not a definition in the scientific sense—results in the assertion that technological improvements result in more output from a given set of inputs. Productivity growth is considered to be an increase in output per worker. The attempt to explain the slowdown in productivity growth as the result of a slackening in the pace of technological change is therefore like arguing in a circle, because productivity growth and technological change are more or less the same thing.

The pessimism that surrounds the achievement of labor productivity as an instrument of policy for promoting economic growth is understandable. Krugman forthrightly stated that "productivity is not simply a matter of public ignorance." "Even among the experts," he remarked, "be they think-tank intellectuals or academic economists, stagnant American productivity is not a fashionable topic. Of course it's important, agrees anyone who thinks about it, but there is nothing much to do about it, so why make a fuss. . . . This apathy among experts becomes a little more comprehensible if we ask how economists answer two central questions about America's productivity slump: Why did it happen? And what can we do about it? . . . The answer to both is the same: We don't know."[72] A good reason for this apathy and ignorance arises from the need to understand and probe the science of production. It should be clear that low productivity has nothing to do with the prices of inputs. Prices may cause substitutions between factors but do not lie at the base of output.[73]

The other Krugman prescription for increasing

Figure 3.6 **Fuel effectiveness trend of airplane airframe/engine combinations.**

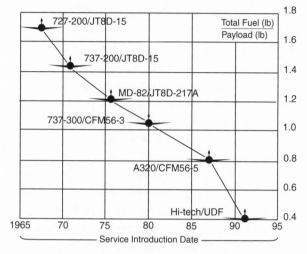

Service Introduction Date

Source: General Electric, "The Aircraft Industry Survey," *The Economist,* June 2, 1985, p. 19.

productivity is to increase the quality of the workforce. This prescription is not as simple as it sounds. The L (labor) in our factor equations expects that each unit of labor is capable of providing the physical input expected of a normal adult human being. The physical abilities of human beings have not changed in any appreciable way through the ages, and over time the owners of businesses have concentrated on how to utilize these limited physical abilities. In times that followed the Industrial Revolution, much mechanization was geared to limit the abuses that occurred when the workforce was being pushed beyond these limits. According to Klemm, the intention was to "relieve the workman from adjustments which exhaust his mind and fatigue his eyes or from painful repetitions which distort or wear out his frame."[74] In other instances, mechanization was pushed when businesses considered the wage being demanded for this input as excessive.

The attention being paid to the issue of how to maximize a worker's input has a long history. The specialization and division of labor was practiced as early as in pre-Hellenistic Greece. When Adam Smith was writing, automatic machinery was hardly known, and so he was properly led to regard the division of labor as a grand principle of manufacturing improvement; and he showed in the example of pin making how each craftsman, being thereby enabled to perfect himself by practice in one point, was able to work more quickly and at lower cost. Later still, toward the end of the nineteenth century, Frederick Taylor led a new attack on the problem of the efficiency of the worker. A distinguished engineer who was also a co-inventor of a new high-speed tool steel, he studied the worker as a important element in production. By a factual study of the worker's movements, Taylor was able to increase labor output per man without adding to the worker's physical burden. The time-and-motion studies he and his followers introduced are not now in vogue, but much of what was learned from them was incorporated into present-day factory planning. His greatest contribution lay in that for the first time, someone directed attention to the industrial process as a whole, of which the worker was treated as an integral element. The weakness, according to Mumford, was that it accepted as fixed "the aims of capitalist production" and relied upon "a narrow pecuniary incentive—with piecework production and bonuses."[75] Since the 1950s the same problem of worker output has been tackled through various training schemes said to increase the quality of labor through more humane means (and now called human capital development).

These various efforts described are intended, as already stated, to keep the worker's input value at a consistent, optimal level. Such improvements in performance that may result are therefore meant to prevent the value of L from falling and adversely affecting maximal potential output capacity of the macroeconomy. These measures therefore cannot be represented as a means of increasing the maximal output capacity of the economy. They are rather required so as to prevent the economy from falling below its maximal growth position as indicated by its factor proportions.

When attention is paid to the quality of the workforce, training is geared to enable the worker to understand and tend to the needs of the plant he is monitoring or operating, in which much of the production is mechanized or even automated. Invariably this involves labor being substituted by capital and/or material. In such a case the factor proportions in the microlevel case are altered. That in itself may distort factor proportion equalization and lead to loss in macroeconomic growth even though the producer might have achieved considerable financial savings in his production cost as a result of the factor proportion change.

Human Capital

The importance of training and education has been recognized since the earliest primal societies, which paid a great deal of attention to it even if their training and education were not formal. Adam Smith put considerable stress on education and training as a way to facilitate division of labor and enhance efficiency of factors, and it is perhaps to economists such as Schultz and the Nobel prize winner Baker that recognition must be accorded for establishing the basis for studying training and education as investment. Kuznets estimated in 1966 that the typical share of conventional capital formation in developed countries in the postwar period was about 30 percent of GDP, with private and public consumption taking 70 percent, but that if one allowed for "investment in man" through formal schooling and on-the-job training, the capital formation proportion rose to 47 percent, leaving only 53 percent for consumption.[76] Becker's theory of human capital helped to bring human capital to center stage.[77] In his 1964 book *Human Capital: A Theoretical and Empirical Analysis, with Special Reference to Education*, Becker rather disappointedly wrote, "Probably the most impressive evidence [that the growth of physical capital explains a relatively small part of the growth of income in most countries] is that most highly educated and skilled persons almost always tend to earn more than others."[78] Conventionally, capital formation refers to "any deliberate employment of income to increase productivity of resources, including uses which are not tangible but rather embodied in knowledge, skills, energy, strength, location or other qualities of people."[79] This very wide definition of what comes under the umbrella of human capital makes the list of what can pass as contributing to human capital limitless. Lipsey and Chrystal, for example, regard human capital as encompassing improvements in health and longevity.[80] But Samuelson and Nordhaus define human capital as the "stock of useful and valuable knowledge built up in the process of education and training."[81] The term *valuable* is not defined.

The appearance of endogenous growth theory has given new importance to the concept of human capital, as the theory attempts to show that all things it regards as technology are endogenous and can be manipulated to determine economic growth. The various models of economic growth, with their wide and sometimes inconsistent definitions of what passes as human capital, take on different assumptions. In many models, human capital is the major input in R&D. It is responsible for innovation. It is assumed that human capital is also employed in the production of consumption goods, but that there are big differences in the quality of labor employed in R&D and that employed elsewhere. It is thought that having a larger number of researchers causes an increase in the growth rate. It is also thought that, for institutional reasons, it is possible that a larger investment in R&D may not lead to greater employment in the research sector and that the research will not achieve a scale effect. There are also claims about diminishing returns. (Though there is great diversity in how various models deal with R&D, there is also wide variation among models as to how they deal with education and learning, too.)

The problem with human capital is that it is not measurable. In order to get around this, those seeking to quantify it resort to financial evaluation, as Kuznets and Becker had to. But financial valuation cannot measure what essentially are thought processes. As soon as financial evaluation takes center stage in a study of human capital, that study loses its scientific status.[82] Inputs of production are physical, so human capital is not an input of production, and growth arises only from production. So, despite the persuasive nature of the argument, human capital does not *cause* economic development and growth, contrary to claims such as those of Nelson and Phelps.[83]

There is a sometimes rather embarrassing effort to draw on conventional ideas about physical capital and prepackage them as new insights into the characteristics of the principal components of human capital. Aghion and Howitt asserted, in common with many others, that in a steady state, the economy's growth rate is equal to the growth rate of general knowledge.[84] They then asserted that economic growth can expressed as a concave function of the level of research H^r. They concluded that the level of research can conceivably be pushed so far at the expense of production that the steady state of growth goes down. They asserted that having too many fundamental innovations at the expense of secondary innovation (supposed to derive from production) can make research sterile by depriving it of feedback from experience. The concave relationship is claimed to apply also to things such as investment by government in education. This line of reasoning has a very close parallel with the concave function of economies of scale in production, when one starts with a decreasing unit cost that first bottoms out and then increases beyond a given output. There is no scientific basis for the originating

assumption of this analysis, that in a steady state an economy's growth rate will equal the growth rate of general knowledge. Even if this assumption is correct (which it is not), that does not make knowledge the cause of growth.

The term "human capital" is recent, meant to assist in conceptualizing the quantity of knowledge a society has. We know that the knowledge a society has cannot be physically touched. Yet we think of it as something that can be stored, that is available to be used, that depreciates and gets replenished and is accumulated. Though every society has its store of this capital, it is natural to imagine that an advanced economy will have a larger quantity of knowledge than a primal economy.

Economists, however, get it wrong when they seek to compartmentalize knowledge and when they assert that human capital is economic in character. Education in a society is not geared only to economic growth. Human capital is a socioeconomic and cultural phenomenon. Lucas's claim that human capital accumulation constitutes an alternative to technology (undefined) is clearly misplaced but shows the extent to which economic romance has gone. Human capital arises because man has been endowed with a mental faculty. Human capital is the lubricant that facilitates man's existence. While aspects of it deal with men and matter, other aspects deal with many nonmaterial but equally important facets of life. Each aspect mixes and flows into the other. It seems, therefore, somewhat futile to seek to turn it into what it is not—a physical input into production.

What Is Technology?

We have shown that technology is still a black box to economists. The first issue is whether science and technology are two separate systems that develop autonomously and independently. In Derek Price's famous analogy, science and technology are two partners in a dance, and while they are dancing to the same music, each has his or her own interpretation and moves in a different way.[85] At the other end, some historians and economists, such as Musson and Robinson, Hessen, and Jewkes and colleagues, will say that there is great interaction between the two.[86] At one time, the expressions "science-related technology" and "science-based technology" sought to demonstrate this difference of approach. It is clear from all this that a definition of technology must for completeness connect it in some way with science. Ghosh's definition of technology (cited in Chapter 1) as referring to a whole range of technical inputs other than raw materials and labor that go into each economic activity was confused. But it recognized that technology has got to do with inputs into each economic activity. Freeman and Soete's statement that technology is simply a body of knowledge about techniques is confusing, but at least it recognized that technology is a body of knowledge. Freeman and Soete and many others often talk of technological change as encompassing changes in processes and methods. The problem is that they could not specify what constitutes a process. Indeed, some people will call a process a technology.

We have seen that a production process is the interaction between the three factors of production in which a physical or chemical change occurs in the material to produce a new commodity or commodities called intermediate or final goods.[87] In order to produce the desired good or goods, these factors have to interact in a given factor proportion, determined by the producer taking many issues into consideration. To do this, he needs to have knowledge about each of the factors as well as knowledge of what will happen if they combine in varying proportion. To do this, he will rely a lot on experience and/or available scientific data and knowledge governing the material factors that are input, in the process itself, in the production aids, and in the role

of labor. Technology, therefore, is a science with a narrow aim in mind—to achieve production of the desired good or goods—not a science with no immediate end use. It is not possible to separate technology from science. The science we are talking about is what we can describe as disciplined knowledge. It is not science confined only to laboratories and institutions. A definition of technology must package all these bits, and so we define technology as the science (knowledge) of factor inputs and factor combinations.[88]

With such a definition, it is now possible to strip the mystery from technology—to identify its elements and put it at the center of a scientific theory of economic development and growth. If properly exploited (that is, if correct factors and factor combinations are identified), technology is the source of economic development and growth. It should now be obvious that not all changes or innovations in factor proportions brought about by technology are growth-inducing, as most conventional economic literature seems to imply. It is reasonable to think that the greater the number of innovations, the greater the chance that some will induce growth (at least those that accord with the natural factor proportions of the economy).

Technology is not an input itself. It is not production or capital. Technology, like every other human activity, derives from human capital but it is not human capital. It feeds back into and widens human capital. In the field of economic development and growth, technology can be said to be a kind of tool that can be employed however the user wants.

It is therefore clear that it is incorrect to talk of technological change. Whereas there are changes in techniques, technology is the science covering changing techniques.[89] Lipsey and Chrystal, as we noted earlier, have talked of "embodied technology change," which they defined as "increases in productive capacity that are created by installing new and better capital goods," and "disembodied technology change," which is "changes in the organization of production that are not embodied in particular capital goods," such as "improved techniques of management, design, marketing, organization of business activity and feedback from user experience to product improvement." Followed to its logical conclusion, it means that anything a company does to reduce its costs—for example, improved marketing and publicity—is technological change. This is incorrect. If technology was embodied in new and better capital goods, as they say, they should be saying that new materials and new material techniques are embodied in new production aids. If capital is embodied technology, why is it that it contributes so little growth according to Solow's residual theory? We conclude by saying that technology is the science that enables us to select and identify production techniques. It provides the launching pad for the choice of factor proportions as a means of promoting scientific economic development and growth.

Inequality and Competition

Perhaps the greatest sociopolitical problem caused by conventional economic strategies for development is the social inequality it creates. Conventional theory assumes that there is a trade-off between growth and employment—the so-called natural unemployment level. It also assumes growth (and productivity) is maximized when more capital is associated with each unit of labor—a position that distorts factor proportions, creating imbalance and therefore producing inequality. Unemployment and income inequalities remain the plague of both the advanced countries of Europe and the less advanced economies. In the United States, the so-called New Economy has produced favorable trends away from unemployment. Conventional economists, therefore, as we have seen in Chapter 1, regard inequal-

ity as a necessary outcome of the conventional pattern of development and have instead urged political action to reduce poverty and inequality.

The equality required of factor proportions between all microeconomic activities as the basis of scientific economic development and growth is a recipe for balanced growth. This balance provides the means through which inequality, which afflicts almost all present economic strategies, can be curtailed. In conventional terms, equality of factor proportions means that financial returns to factors should be equal. While there are still many economists out there who argue that inequality is the price for rapid economic growth, our analysis shows that such a conclusion is wrong. Some recent empirical studies now suggest that a better income and wealth distribution helps growth.[90] And the very concept of equality of factor proportions denotes lower inequality because, among other things we will discuss in later chapters, it eliminates unemployment, which is a key determinant of inequality. It should level the returns to factors in different economic activities.

It thus appears that a scientific theory of economic development and growth not only maximizes growth in a dynamic context but also ensures full utilization of all input factors (including labor) with inequality squeezed out. It should be possible to identify the factors that cause inequality. To the extent that all economic activities need to have equal factor proportions, this is not a competitive economy in Michael Porter's sense. On the other hand, it should be remembered that we are only talking of factor proportions, so the absolute size of specific activities can differ substantially. But the competition for resources will be such that it always tends toward a dynamic equilibrium of factor proportions. It avoids the destructive effects, duplication, and waste of factor inputs that the competitive style advocated by Porter entails.

Is this economy one in which government plays

a major role, or is it the economy that neoliberals advocate? It seems that in identifying, quantifying, and monitoring L and M as well as in their preservation in a diverse and dynamic situation in any modern economy—advanced or not—government has a central role. It may even be that in this role a government has to set and monitor guidelines for investment, so as to see that conditions for equality of factor proportions in a dynamic setting can be created, but that thereafter the economy may be left to the "hidden hand." State intervention in the style of the Asian countries in their "tiger" days will seem to be against the requirements of a scientific theory of economic development/growth. But these views are not conclusive.

Neoclassical Growth and New Growth

How does the theory of factor proportions fit into the history of theories of economic growth over the last two centuries?

Smith was the one who formalized the concept of economic growth. To him is attributed the theory that economic growth arises from an increase in the quality and quantity of three main factors of production: labor, capital, and land. In this view, economic development is driven forward by the accumulation of capital through high levels of savings and investments and by increased efficiency through division of labor, increased foreign trade, better education, improved soil and climate, laws and institutions, or any other means that increase the productivity of labor, capital, or land. Smith's point about the benefits that flow from the division of labor has a wide embrace. For example, his idea that foreign trade facilitates further division of labor because of an enlarged market implies that foreign trade increases economic growth. It is argued that an increase in the labor force does not really count as a source of economic growth because what matters is a country's standard of living.[91]

The criticisms made of Smith's stipulations are not well placed. Increased input of labor, cooperating with appropriate factors, should increase output. The issue of output per capita raised by Gylfason is not relevant. It arises only when people assume incorrectly that a possible change to a more labor-intensive production due to increased population will automatically reduce the standard of living. Smith accepted that population increase is a vital input to economic development and not a thing to be wished away. In regard to land, Gylfason's criticism that Smith should have realized that land was fixed is incorrect. Smith regarded land as something to be worked on and improved. Smith devoted the whole of Book II of his *Wealth of Nations,* aptly titled "Of Nature, Accumulation and Employment of Stock," to his thoughts on the natural sequences of wealth creation. In the world in which Smith lived, which was to a large extent not very industrialized, his views reflect much of the position in primal societies. It is not definite that Smith regarded land as a factor of production. Of land, for example, Smith observed that "the rent of land, it may be thought, is frequently no more than a reasonable profit or interest for the stock laid out by the landlord upon its improvement." He observed, however, that this is not often the case: "The landlord demands a rent even for unimproved land, and supposed interest or profit upon the expense of improvement is generally an addition to this original rent. . . . He sometimes demands rent for what is altogether incapable of human improvement." Smith complained that "the rent of land, therefore, considered as the price paid for the use of land is naturally a monopoly price." It seems that for Smith legitimate rent is the price paid for improvements made to the land, that is, capital improvements.

Smith was fully aware that land was limited and hence complained of the "small quantity of land . . . which is brought to the market and the high price of what is brought thither." He also said, "Land, mines and fisheries all require both a fixed and circulating capital to cultivate them; and their produce replaces with a profit, not only those capitals; but all others in the society." Here Smith seems to be talking of land as if it is a production facility like a fishery or a mine, not a factor input. He further stated that "the produce of land, mines and fisheries, when their natural fertility is equal, is in proportion to the extent and proper application of capitals employed about them."[92] The emphasis here is on "natural fertility," which encompasses the raw materials of the land.

Smith did not specifically equate capital with high savings and investment in Book II, though he recognized the role of what he called "stock." He traces its origin by noting, "As the division of labor advances, therefore, in order to give constant employment to an equal number of workmen, an equal stock of provisions and a greater stock of materials and tools . . . must be accumulated. . . . As the accumulation of stock is previously necessary for carrying on this great improvement in the productive powers of labor, so that accumulation naturally leads to this improvement." He divided the stock a man has into two broad categories—the stock he consumes (his immediate consumption) and the stock that affords him revenue, which Smith called capital. He explained that there are two ways in which capital can yield revenue or profit. The first is the case in which capital continually goes from a man in one shape and returns to him in another. Smith called this circulating capital. The second is to use the capital for the improvement of land or in the purchase of useful machines and instruments of trade. This Smith called fixed capital. "Provisions, materials and finished work are . . . regularly withdrawn . . . and placed either in the fixed capital or in the stock reserved for immediate consumption. . . . Every fixed capital is both originally derived from, and requires to be continually supported by a circulating capital. . . . No fixed capital can yield any

revenue but by means of circulating capital." Smith emphasized, "To maintain and augment the stock which may be reserved for immediate consumption is the sole end and purpose both of fixed and circulating capital."[93]

Smith's prescriptions are very much in line with the scenario we have described as the essential ingredients of a science of economic development and growth, namely, that material is a vital factor input. Land is not an input. Capital is essentially material and labor whose sole purpose is not to sacrifice present consumption for sake of future larger consumption but rather to meet the needs of immediate consumption.

Smith's prescription had only one major limitation that stopped it from being a full scientific theory of development and growth: It did not prescribe how labor, material, and capital were to be combined in order to achieve economic growth.

Smith later made what appears to be an attempt to relate his prescriptions to financial management. It is this aspect that has unfortunately commanded all the attention of conventional economists. The neoclassical theory of growth lays emphasis on saving and investment, which leads to capital accumulation. Dickey has observed that when Smith wanted to move from observations of natural processes into matters of money, capital accumulation, and saving, another force for growth came into the play—frugality, which had a moral tone to it. An individual saving for a rainy day and creating maximal financial wealth for himself is not necessarily Smith's prescription for an economy. Smith was simply making assumptions that savings in the wider economy will also lead to growth and wealth. Smith, therefore, sought to make a connection between capital accumulation and frugality. Dickey pointed out that the emergence of the concept of frugality raises a pivotal question as to how to interpret *Wealth of Nations*. He observed, "If we approach [the relevant parts of *Wealth of Nations,* or WN] with the idea—inculcated in generations of readers of the WN by economists—that Smith is developing the 'normative' core of modern economies in these books," the three main theoretical props of frugality (saving), capital accumulation, and division of labor will have tremendous coherence as a prescription for fostering and sustaining economic growth. Dickey said that the inclination to read *Wealth of Nations* in this way is compelling but to do so misses a lot of what Smith was doing.[94] In effect, Dickey is decrying many economists' attempt to present the neoclassical theory of growth and its descendants as if they were a core of systematized (scientific) knowledge.

Robbins, who showed much interest in economics as a science, said of Smith's stipulations on these matters of money (in particular Smith's objective of dismantling the mercantile system of his time), "Adam Smith's *Wealth of Nations* is not wholly or nearly scientific. . . . It was a mixture of polemic and scientific work."[95] It is also noteworthy that all conventional abstractions of Smith's works that have emerged as neoclassical growth theories have substituted a two-factor concept for Smith's original three-factor concept.

Neoclassical ideas about savings and investment behavior and the nature of the production function have a number of characteristics and assumptions supporting them. Because savings are equal to investment, an increase in the savings rate leads to an increase in capital stock, which rises more than needed to keep up with population, productivity gains, and depreciation. The resulting increases in capital/output ratio then decelerate until the capital/output ratio stops moving, as a result of which output per head and capital per worker are said to be increased. In the short run, it is said, an increase in savings will reduce consumption, reduce demand, and initially reduce output, which later will rise to new levels.

There are immediate weaknesses in this position.

It is positivist orthodoxy, pure and simple, in which the assumption is made that it is capital accumulation that is responsible for growth. Savings is, therefore, supposed to be its torchbearer. Less important is the assumption that what is saved is automatically invested. This assumption has been stoutly defended by neoclassical economists in ways that do not accord with reality. For example, it is argued that any increase in savings tends to reduce the rate of interest, which makes it more profitable to employ the savings in investment. But the science of economic development is concerned only with capital involved in actual production process. Therefore, as Chaudhuri put it, neoclassical theory had to make yet another assumption—that when total savings are equal to total investment, all the investment will be in such forms of capacity as produces marketable output.[96] There is another corollary assumption, namely, that savings may accrue initially as unspent income in various financial forms and that investment must transform these into some physical production capacity before output can be produced from the savings. Neoclassical theory assumes that such transactions are costless in terms of both money and time. Neoclassical efficiency—also a concept of positive orthodoxy—is supposed to follow from the increase in output produced by given inputs. This again derives from the increase in savings and investment that yields per capita increases in output and capital. Per capita growth is, however, restrained by the exogenously given rate of technological progress. Population growth is supposed to reduce output per head, because current savings and investments will not be enough to maintain the same amount of capital per worker.

The economy is, however, supposed to adjust to any increase in the rate of population growth. If the rate of population growth rises from the previous exogenously determined rate, the immediate effect is that the volume of savings is inadequate to meet the capital-widening needs of the growing labor force at the existing capital/labor ratio. This ratio will fall, as will the per capita output, with population growth. However, once the adjustment has taken place, the economy will grow at a higher rate, set by the population growth, so that output and capital stock grow in equilibrium. Population growth has a depressing effect on the standard of living of the current generation but does no cumulative damage in the long run. In the language of the factor proportions approach, the effect of population growth is to alter factor proportions, and it does not have any damaging effects.

On the whole, neoclassical theory holds that continuously augmenting the capital stock relative to output, even at nonexpanding levels of savings and investment, will drive output higher and so produce economic growth. A high level of efficiency achieved through a high level of foreign trade or education will stimulate growth by enhancing the effects of a given level of savings and investment. An increase in efficiency will increase economic growth. However, growth in output does not require a continuous improvement in efficiency. All that is needed is a steady accumulation of capital. A given level of efficiency will lead to economic growth through capital accumulation. It will be noted that throughout, efficiency in relation to what has not been clarified. The result is that much of the concept of efficiency, when taken together with the lack of clarity as to what technology meant to the theorist, lacks scientific authority.

The Harrod-Domar model expressed the dynamic relationships of neoclassical thinking in a simple formula by which economic growth depended on three factors: (1) the savings rate, determined by the division of income between consumption and savings, (2) the capital/output ratio, and (3) depreciation, which is partly the result of the quality of investment decisions in the past. In particular, an increase in the savings rate will increase the rate of economic growth. An increase in use of capital rela-

tive to output will reduce growth because of the need to use more capital to produce a unit of output. Increased depreciation will also reduce growth because it reduces net capital and signifies reduced capital utilization. But this differs in some significant ways from Smith's natural (scientific) prescription that there be just enough capital to satisfy immediate consumption needs.

The positivist orthodoxy of the Harrod-Domar model apart, this model did not even leave much role to a second factor input—labor. But more important, it treated capital/output ratio as an exogenous behavioral parameter—the ratio of two financial quantities. This is not scientific. Within the science of economic development it is not possible to keep capital (even as a composite of M and L) in a fixed ratio with output. New materials and enhanced materials provide the promise of higher output at given factor proportions. The capital/output ratio must necessarily be endogenously determined.

Scientific Economic Development/ Growth Is Exogenous

Solow's neoclassical growth model treats technology as exogenous. Solow was right that economic growth is exogenous, because in our view the factor proportions formula that determines growth is independently determined. It is this exogenous nature of factor proportions that makes economics a science. Solow was also right that savings behavior is not relevant for growth, nor is the so-called efficiency of factors except insofar as efficiency can help ensure the attainment of correct factor proportions. As factor proportions are not subject to policy discretion, economic growth is exogenous and therefore independent of economic policy—good or bad and independent of political or sociocultural factors. These Solow prescriptions are in general scientific if the residual is now assigned to material (natural resources). The exogenous nature of economic growth deriving from predetermined factor proportions has made it possible for economic growth to thrive under very different economic, social, and political environments and policies, a point the World Bank indirectly accepted in *Entering the 21st Century:*

> In recent decades both experience and intellectual insight have pushed development thinking away from debates over the roles of states and markets, and the search for a single, overarching policy prescription. Investment in physical and human capital, for example, should encourage economic growth, and as a general rule, empirical evidence supports this proposition. But in a number of cases, high rates of investment and education have not been enough to deliver rapid growth. A similar lesson holds true for industrial policies. Many countries decided, after experimenting with export subsidies, that the subsidies enriched business owners but did little to speed economic growth. They saw well-intended and industrial subsidies turn into a costly form of corporate welfare, an expensive way of providing tax-payer support for private jobs in a narrow range of industries. Yet East Asian economies, making active use of export subsidies and credit allocation, experienced the most powerful sustained economic development the world had seen in decades. And China, which alone includes 40% of all the inhabitants of low-income countries in the world, has had remarkable economic success with a development strategy that involves only a limited dose of market liberalization and privatization. The failure of centrally planned economies to keep pace with their market oriented counterparts has demonstrated clearly enough that planning entire economies at central government level is not a productive path to long-term development. But the experiences of Japan, East Asia and China make clear that it is possible for a country to have an interventionist government and still enjoy extremely rapid economic growth over a period of decades. Brazil also grew rapidly in the 1960s, in part by making widespread use of import-substitution policies. These policies certainly appeared helpful to Brazil at the time—at a minimum, they did not prevent a surge of rapid growth—but

this success does not mean that similar policies would make sense in other countries even in Brazil three decades later. Similarly, certain policies that helped Japan develop in the 1950s and 1960s and generated growth in East Asia in the 1970s and 1980s and 1990s were specific to time and place. They may not have worked well in other countries nor are they likely to be appropriate in the opening decades of the 21st century.[97]

Endogenous growth theory, unfortunately, arose from what was perceived to be the inability of neoclassical growth theories to answer several burning questions. We will review some of these questions as summarized by Gylfason.[98] The pace of technological change, it is argued, is bound to have an economic explanation, at least in part. If output per capita grows at a rate that depends solely on—in fact, is equal to—the rate of technological progress, then why do the growth performances of different countries differ so radically over long periods? Is the rate of technological progress really that different in different countries? Why is growth not more similar across countries? Does economics really have so little to say about these issues? And what does the neoclassical model tell us about relative growth performance, anyway? In particular, do poor countries grow more rapidly than rich ones? What is the empirical evidence?

These questions lose their legitimacy when one realizes they are being asked with no clear definition of technology in mind. It is evident, however, that those asking think there ought to be some identifiable relationship between technological change and growth. They also question the widely differing economic growth rates between countries and why these differences exist.

We have defined technology as a science. On this basis of this definition, these questions lose relevance. The science of factors and of factor proportions (technology) cannot of its own cause differences in growth performance between countries. If, on the other hand, we focus on the different factor proportions of each country, the answers to these questions become obvious. Different economies have different factor proportions and different countries are in different relative positions to their operating within their natural factor proportions. Thus, if a country such as India wishes to pursue research and development to reinforce a capital-intensive production paradigm, as that country is doing, its growth will suffer. Countries differ as to how focused and successful their technology is in generating growth-oriented work, namely, work that encapsulates factor proportions set exogenously.

We also emphasized earlier in this chapter that each economy has its individual economic "personality." Any attempt to standardize and compare personalities is usually full of pitfalls.

Looked at in this way, it is clear that new growth theory did not have a valid base for challenging Solow's basic neoclassical model. New growth theory quite simply says that technology is not exogenous because it assumes that technology depends on economic and social factors that then determine the amount of capital available to workers, that is, the capital/labor ratio. It reasoned that learning by doing improves capital utilization efficiency. It has been argued that new growth theory can in somewhat arbitrary ways show that the capital/output ratio (in line with the assumptions of the Harrod-Domar model) is fixed.[99]

Barro and Sala-i-Martin defended the need for new growth theory because they said that economists needed to "escape the straight jacket of the neo-classical growth model in which long-term per capita growth is pegged by the rate of exogenous technological progress."[100] This is wrong; the fact that technology is exogenous does not mean that growth is pegged. Within suitable factor proportions, we have shown that an economy is dynamic and can achieve sustainable growth. Barro and Sala-i-Martin claim that under new growth models, growth can go on indefinitely, "because return investment in a broad range of capital goods which included human capital does not necessarily diminish as economic development proceeds." Their reason is that technology yields greater output for a given set of inputs. This brings us back to square one.

New growth theory's view is that desirable structural changes are more likely to occur under conditions of disequilibrium, in which a shift of factors occurs from more productive sectors to less productive sectors, and that such disequilibrium will accelerate economic growth, but this is incorrect. The view is essentially a microeconomic stipulation that does not take account of the scientific stipulation that structural macroeconomic balance is a sine qua non for sustainable growth. In the twenty years of its existence, new growth theory has not provided powerful answers to the questions that created it. All the theory has done is throw all the windows on development theory wide open.[101]

Is the Technology There?

The conclusion has now been reached that the science of economic development and growth is based on the premise that every country, like every individual, has a basic personality. A country's basic economic personality is determined by its factor endowments. Growth and development can be maximized by the judicious application of a country's factor proportions as the base of its economic activities. The question here, then, is whether there is the technology (that is, the science of factor proportions) to meet this need. If the present state of conventional economics does not meet this need, what can be done to effect the desired changes?

In the interest of clarity, we will call a given factor combination a technique, so that within the field of technology there is a menu of techniques corresponding to different factor combinations.

The fixed or near-fixed coefficients of factors of many present-day industrial activities are grouped loosely as capital-intensive. Capital-intensive technology constitutes a web of ideas that claim to explain how industrial society works, where it came from, and why it has to be as it is. They seek to offer a theory of economic growth that links changes in the marketplace with changes in the use of capital and labor. They seek to explain the startling success of the leading industrial nations and want to emphasize the limited plasticity of technology. Conventional economic writers often adopt models using fixed assumptions about technology. In their detailed examination of the place of mass production in its economic and historical setting,

Piore and Sabel concluded, "From the perspective of late 20th century scholarship . . . the success of mass production seems less the outcome of mechanization than that of interplay of social and political forces. The historians' assault on the popular understanding [of mass production] has many objectives: a professional passion for detail; a suspicion that technological development has been manipulated to serve powerful interests; perplexity of the diverse national styles of machine operation in the face of competitive pressures for uniformity." They asserted that regardless of its motives, "research has uncovered preconditions for success of mass production . . . in the politically defined interest of producers and consumers—rather than in the logic of industrial efficiency," and concluded, "The obstacle to the progress of mechanization on craft lines lay not in some self-blockage of this model of technological development. Rather they lay in the unfavorable environment—political, institutional, economic—with which craft production had to contend. . . . [H]istory suggests—under different circumstances—the craft sector could have played a stronger role in economic development."[1]

With regard to the underdeveloped countries, the argument for capital-intensive development goes like this. There is a lot of imperfect competition in these countries. The situation results from economies of scale that characterize modern (capital-intensive) industries coupled with the relatively small market for manufactured (capital-intensive, nonlocally produced) goods, which limits the number of firms that can compete under perfect competition.[2] Despite having a higher capital/labor ratio, the capital-intensive activities have a low capital/output ratio. That is, even though the equipment is expensive for a poor country, it would yield high output and therefore cost less per unit of output. If foreign multinationals had to bring in the much-needed capital, the choice was not between labor-intensive development and capital-intensive development, as Sloman argued, but between having extra capital or no development.[3] This view is as old as it is entrenched. Kaldor lent his authority to the call for capital-intensive activities in conditions of underdevelopment when he declared, "You should not go deliberately out of your way to reduce productivity [in underdeveloped countries] in order to reduce capital per worker. This seems to me nonsense because by increasing capital/output tenfold, one may increase output per worker by twenty-fold."[4]

The course of the history of the dominance of mass production over craft production, as will be shown, is not based on economic scientific justification. Craft production in its environment is essentially based on a choice of factor proportions that is in line with factor endowment proportions. The craft producer brought in his skills and those of his assistants and sought to use materials either as capital or as production material, usually in relative quantities that intuitively reflected the abundance or scarcity of materials in his environment. His immediate concern was not his selling price, nor was he calculating prices so as to determine whether more or less of his labor skills needed to be exchanged with capital. Craft production culture was essentially flexible, involving quick and inexpensive shifts from one product to another within a family of goods and permitting constant expansion in the range of materials worked and operations performed in order to facilitate the transition from one whole family of products to another. In primal societies, economic growth was stunted not because of incorrect techniques (factor proportions) but because there was no constant expansion in the development of materials worked. The technology needed to sustain correct factor proportions must necessarily be flexible and, according to Piore and Sabel, needs institutions "to create an environment in which skills and capital [and materials] could be constantly recombined in order to produce a rapidly shifting assortment of goods." They were of the view that as a precondition for this, firms need to be "discouraged from competition in the form of wage and price reduction, as opposed to competition through innovation of products and processes."[5]

Mass production does not meet these criteria. The group of techniques that qualify as mass production do not have much flexibility. Indeed, in the short and medium term they are fixed. If this is the case, it becomes important to examine in some detail why mass production and capital-intensive techniques have come to predominate despite this defect.

The early-nineteenth-century American economy came close to being one in which resources were general-purpose. Firms using the most specialized resources were generally small, and many were founded and went out of business each year. Adjustment to shifting demand could take place through normal turnover. As equipment wore out and skilled workers retired, they could be replaced by machines and labor suited to the new, more marketable tasks.[6] As the century wore on, these forms of adjustment were increasingly foreclosed by the growing size of productive units in relation to their markets and by the increasing specialization of resources associated with this change in the scale of manufacturing. From the late nineteenth century on, this organizational form spread. Almost all the fifty largest U.S. corporations in 1917 appear in today's financial pages. By 1930, about half of the manufacturing output was produced by them. Despite these trends, one is struck by the persistence of craft economy and small production runs in the United States. Piore and Sabel have observed that "throughout modern industrial history, observers have been repeatedly struck by the persistence of small firms despite increasing prediction of their disappearance . . . instead of dismissing it as a historical vintage, observers started to look for systematic reasons for its continued vitality."[7] It is, however, necessary to caution here that small firms do not necessarily adopt techniques based on natural factor proportions. A small firm may indeed be capital-intensive. Capital intensity is evaluated from factor proportions and not by the absolute amount of capital invested. Small companies are usually classified by the number of persons they employ, usually a maximum of 100. This classification has no practical scientific use and is misleading because some of these small companies are indeed capital-intensive.

Early attempts to explain the persistence of small firms, which some equate with craft activities, despite the overwhelming predominance of mass production, relied on the theory of dualism. The theory asserted that mass production and craft production need each other, with the latter playing a subservient role. A similar idea pervades much of present-day conventional economic thinking, with the notion that small and large businesses can coexist and serve each other. The theory has no scientific basis; it is simply an empirical attempt to explain the existing structure of industry. The thinking is that mass production is the creation of general goods using specialized resources. The more general the goods, the more extensive is their market, the more specialized the machines used to produce them, and the more finely divided the labor that goes into that production.

Observation seems to suggest that an economy cannot depend entirely on mass production, as the specialized machinery used in mass production can-not itself be mass-produced. Mass production machinery must, in fact, be built according to the logic that is the mirror image of mass production: the production of specialized goods through general resources. Because the product is a specialty with a limited market, production must be continually reorganized and workers must have a range of skills and a general understanding of the processes that are currently attributed to preindustrial artisans. Thus according to the theory of dualism, as industrialization along the lines of mass production proceeds, craft production will be revitalized.[8] It is also argued that craft production is a necessary fringe component of every industry to take care of fluctuations in demand.

Within the concept of industrial dualism, small firms are said to be sustained by arrangements such as subcontracting and supply contracts from large firms. Many economic writers extol the virtues of what they see as the coexistence and cooperation between the small and large companies in economies such as Japan's.[9] The case of the survival of Chrysler has often been cited as example of the mutual advantage between the small and the large firm. Chrysler was for a long time the weakest of the then three top U.S. auto firms. It then deliberately attempted to emulate the Japanese strategy of working with its suppliers. In a study of this relationship, Dyer described this as the creation by Chrysler of an "American *keiretsu*" and showed that Chrysler's profit per vehicle went up from an average of $250 in the 1980s to a record for all automobile firms of $2,110 per vehicle.[10] Many of the suppliers made numerous suggestions for improvement. Freeman and Soete, who emphasized the virtues of such a relationship, nevertheless admitted that the main benefits of this arrangement went to Chrysler.[11] Mass production is therefore seen as the technologically dynamic form and specialty production its subordinate.

These views are mistaken. Their propagators seek

to justify the existing industrial structure for no reason other than that it seems to work. Yet this dualistic industrial structure is the consequence of the initial action, concentration of capital, leading to the distortion of factor proportions. When extra capital is transferred into capital-intensive activities, the factors of production associated with other activities are bled away, either further reinforcing the capital-intensive activity, creating idle resources, or both. The extent to which this takes place depends on the ratio of the third factor—materials—to the other factors of labor and capital. A dualistic industrial structure is, therefore, not the best macrostructure for achieving maximum economic growth. It creates instability arising from microeconomic imbalance. The point to reemphasize is that what is good for the firm at the micro level may not be good for the economy at the macro level. What conventional economic analysis may pass off or even applaud as competition between firms may in fact be harmful to the growth potential of the whole economy.

Piore and Sabel have argued that the eventual triumph of mass production occurred not because it was necessarily the one best way but because of the conditions of the moment. "An advance in a particular direction can choke off promising experiments with alternatives, since threatened competitors choose to emulate a proven approach rather than risk failing to find one more suited to their needs. There is, therefore, no guarantee that competition drives society to the frontier of its productive capacities; ironically, even the victors in this kind of competition cannot be sure they have hit on the approach that best serves their interests." This bandwagon effect, which may have helped reinforce the dominance of mass production, is what Piore and Sabel called a world in which technology could have developed differently from the way it did—a world with a history of abandoned but viable alternatives to what exists.[12]

At the point where the direction of technology could have swung either way, it is to be expected that relatively short periods of diversification in techniques will punctuate longer periods of uniformity. The technical knowledge that is accumulated during those interludes of diversity creates the possibility of divergent breakthroughs. At these technological divides, the different political circumstances in different regional or national economies move technology down correspondingly different paths. Competition will eliminate some of the technological experiments and bend others toward a common goal. Growing investments in the dominant technology reinforce the constraints of competition by giving even those who may once have opposed its introduction a stake in its perpetuation. The tendency to uniformity is reversed only when some combination of development in the market and in the capacity to control nature makes it economically feasible to disregard the sunk costs and technically feasible to strike out in new directions.[13]

Microcosms of innovation in the automobile, aircraft, and computer industries show that industries in the formative stages had a great abundance of competing solutions to technical problems. Each variant was potentially better on some dimension; its advantages reflected particular circumstances and favored the interest of some group over others. The proponents of each solution were reluctant to abandon it, but at the same time they were leery of proceeding because of fear of failure or because initial mistakes in implementation might teach others how to construct a superior model. Typically, an exercise of financial power ended the impasse—some firm or group that was able to establish the minimum market it needed and that had enough capital to cover mistakes pressed ahead and imposed a plan.

For the automobile industry, the United States did not lead Europe in the early days. In fact, virtually all the early inventions and innovations were made in Germany and France. By 1905, however, hundreds of small companies were producing automobiles in the United States as well as in the main European countries. They all used craft techniques and general-purpose machine tools scattered in small machine shops, employing highly skilled workers whose work was coordinated by the entrepreneur.

At the turn of the twentieth century, it was not clear whether the internal combustion engine would be preferred to the steam or electric engine; indeed, in 1900 steam and electric vehicles accounted for about three-quarters of the four thousand automobiles produced. However, by 1917 about three and a half million automobiles had been registered in the United States, and fewer than fifty thousand were electric and steam vehicles. The last major steam manufacturer, Stanley Motor Carriage, produced 730 steam vehicles in 1917—fewer than Ford produced in one day before lunch.

In the early days, both steam and electric cars had many technical advantages over internal combustion automobiles, which had problematic features including the sliding gear transmission and the starting handle. The starting handle soon disappeared after the first electric starter was invented in 1912. Even though steam cars and electric cars ran more smoothly, they suffered the disadvantage of short operating range due to the weight of their boiler or batteries and consequent refueling problems. The dashboard of the "Stanley Steamer" was festooned with various gauges for boiler water level, steam pressure, and so on, and just to start the engine required the manipulation of thirteen valves, levers, handles, and pumps. The electric car was simpler to start and drive, having no clutch or transmission. It was quiet, reliable, and odorless. Longer operating range was undoubtedly one of the decisive advantages of the internal combustion engine, but this was not purely a technical matter. The chain of refueling stations and repair and maintenance facilities could conceivably have been organized on a different basis given different strategies and policies of the utilities, manufacturers, and regulators.[14]

The lock-in to the internal combustion engine and its mass production was achieved by the financial success of Ford's assembly line, which reduced the cost and price of the Model T. Notably, Ford had the ability to finance such a major, risky venture. The Model T fell from $850 in 1908 to $600 in 1913 and $360 in 1916. By comparison, the price of electric cars was $2,800 in 1913, in part because of the introduction of new batteries. Not surprisingly, sales of Model T increased fifty times, and market share increased from 10 percent to 60 percent in 1921. Clearly the triumph of mass production of internal combustion engines came about through price reduction, not innovation of products or processes. Freeman and Soete noted that Ford's success was in one sense purely an organizational innovation but which in turn later stimulated a great deal of technical innovation among automobile firms.[15]

Thus, as Piore and Sabel point out, whereas a winning technology had to meet some minimum performance standard, "the sweep of its success was not a proof of unrivaled technical superiority nor of the existence of a narrow track of progress: other variants could have served as well. Power in the market, not efficiency [in the sense of appropriate application of technology] decided the contest."[16]

Technology paradigms played a major role in creating the dominance of mass production techniques. A paradigm creates the preconditions for a new orthodoxy. Piore and Sabel have observed that in regard to technological paradigms, the new orthodoxy is exemplified in model machines and factories whose producers and owners never tire of advertising and promoting it. Its structuring principles are propagated in textbooks and in economic literature. They note that technologists, at best half aware that their imagination has been circumscribed by convention, push down the new path; "so long as they feel that they are meeting the (frequently lax) test of international competition," they ignore the hints of alternative possibilities that are constantly unearthed by their experience with markets and machines. According to Piore and Sabel, machine makers, consultants, and theorists were fantasists—blind to reality of the times: "If machine makers tried to build automatic equipment and exaggerated their success, it was because they were correctly convinced that many manufacturers wanted such an equipment. If theorists accepted the advertising as truth, it was because what they had already seen then convinced them that the claims were plausible."[17]

The move to mass production occurred in part with the encouragement of governments. In the 1960s, the French state sponsored a campaign of mergers and restructuring that recast production techniques. Local firms came under the control of French-based multinationals. Craft industries were broken up, and the components of production that they had provided were integrated into the divisional structure of new corporate parents pursuing mass production techniques in the world market. Today the encouragement of capital-intensive techniques by governments has become general. Tax and other financial incentives, for example, are frequently based on the amount of capital invested in plant and machinery.

This review of the trend toward mass production techniques and the many nontechnical reasons for it reinforces Piore and Sabel's conclusion that these political and social forces helped the triumph of mass production technology. But Piore and Sabel did not attempt to explain these nontechnical forces —for example, why the French state pushed for mergers or why advertising promoting mass production was effective. We maintain that these nontechnical forces were not a cause of the triumph of mass production but the consequence of structural imbalances, described earlier, which results from

increasing capital concentration and which favors the capital-intensive activities to the detriment of low-capital activities. The political and social factors Piore and Sabel identified are reactions to a situation in which craft activities were losing ground and it appeared that the move to mass production was inevitable.

Mass production offered industries in which it was developed and applied enormous gains that increased in step with the growth of these industries. Progress on this technological trajectory brought higher profits, higher wages, lower consumer prices, and a whole range of new products. However, mass production is capital-intensive and requires very specialized equipment and narrowly trained workers. It is profitable only if the market is large enough to absorb the enormous output of a single standardized commodity and stable enough to keep the resources involved in the production of that commodity continuously employed.

Piore and Sabel represented the relationship between mass production and craft production as indicated in Figure 4.1. The curve shows how average unit cost varies with output. The fixed sum *ab* represents the variable-cost technique, which they state is for craft production. The mass production technique is represented by *cde,* where the initial fixed cost is at the point *c*. As mass production develops, *cde* will progressively move to the right. The shaded area represents the cost savings associated with the firm's move from craft to mass production technology (provided the level of output sustains the change). They state that the savings represented by the shaded area provides the incentive for firms to organize the market so as to avoid fluctuations and permit investment in mass production.

They claimed that the savings depicted "do not accrue only to the firm; they represent real gains to the society as well." They explained that the shaded area "permits a reduction in the resources required for the production of the commodity in question,

Figure 4.1 Cost characteristics of mass production/craft production.

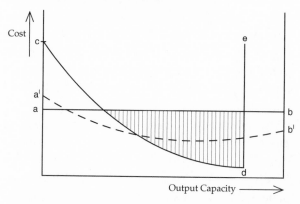

Source: M. J. Piore and C. F. Sabel, *The Second Industrial Divide: Possibilities for Prosperity* (New York: Basic Books, 1984), figs. 3.1 and 3.2.

making these resources available for other purposes." However, "the cost of freeing up these resources . . . is proportional to the risk of unemployment of the specialized resources that mass production entails." Piore and Sabel went on to say, "The social problem, then, is how to organize the market to reduce that risk and lower the cost."[18] But they are not on firm ground to claim that the savings represent resources freed up to be used elsewhere. In line with our earlier analysis, these savings actually come from the dislocation caused to the craft economy by the transfer to mass production. By asserting that the resources are being freed up for use elsewhere, Piore and Sabel sought to give the impression that on a macro level total growth is enhanced—the typical belief that what is good in the micro sense must be good for the macroeconomy.

Nor is it clear what the authors meant by saying that the cost of freeing up the resources is proportional to the risk of unemployment of the specialized resources employed in mass production. They seem to give the impression that they regard the freeing up of resources as a good, counterweighted by the negative possibilities of unemployment of the specialized resources. If we return to our theme that a balanced macroeconomic structure is a condition for maximum growth, it will be seen that the issue of proportionality does not arise and that the authors' suggestion that there is a social problem as to how to organize the market to reduce the risks and lower the cost is empty—just one more example of how economists focused on development and growth consign their lack of understanding of the science of the economic issues before them into topics to be fixed by economists specializing in welfare economics.

The choice of technique should not be determined by market size. It should derive, as we have argued all along, from endowed factor proportions. Mass production is not macroeconomically growth-inducing because it is especially sensitive to the level of demand for the product. Individual productive units often become so large relative to the total market that the propensity to invest in manufacturing plants is determined by the prospective level of capacity utilization, not by considerations of the best factor combinations.

Nevertheless, the authors' assumption that craft production does not require capital is wrong. We have continued to stress that in the science of economic development and growth, nature has stipulated that whenever there is production, capital must be used. One cannot produce without capital. The true position for craft production is therefore more likely to be a relationship like $a^l b^l$ in Figure 4.1, from which it can be seen that many theoretical studies exaggerate the price advantages of mass production, the more so if the endowed factor proportions have a significant capital component.

The modern American corporation is the baby of mass production. The early corporations developed in order to organize the market so as to cope with the pressures mass production techniques were putting on producers. When small producers who initially did not concern themselves with the market because their production constituted such a small part of it began to find that the minimum size of a plant was becoming larger and larger, their need to create bigger units of production became imperative.

At the same time, new ways to manipulate the market in a monopolistic manner appeared. Two basic approaches were discernible: segmentation of the market and production for inventory.[19] Segmentation was aimed at dividing the market so that the mass producer retained the base market while the fluctuations over this base were left to the small producers. The mass producer was able to achieve this objective because of lower price, which in turn assured him the full capacity he needed. The creation of an inventory sufficient to deal with fluctuations in demand—a mirror image of segmentation—was another way of ensuring full capacity utilization of a plant. It followed that once mass production strategies were established as a way of life, they came in handy in creating markets for new products.

The industrial countries, especially the United States, did enjoy a long period of prosperity in the first twenty years following World War II. This was the period of what has come to be called Fordism, in which mass production was coupled with mass consumption in a virtuous circle of growth.[20] The model of development expressed by the system was centered upon a regime of accumulation, which is the stable allocation of factors between investment and consumption. Under Fordism, this regime involved continuous innovation in the capital goods sector, leading to a kind of growth in labor productivity and output that was balanced by rapid growth in consumer demand. The relationship between production and consumption was stabilized and regulated by a wide variety of social norms and institutions. Gibson-Graham described the position as that of large firms, markup pricing, wage-price indexing, and collective bargaining working together to keep demand growing, productivity increasing, wages rising, and inflation creeping. New

Deal–type social insurance measures, such as social security and unemployment compensation, ensured that workers could continue consuming even when they were not working. At home the unquestioned hegemony of the nuclear family (manifest in the notion of a "family wage") generated a mass market with a voracious appetite for standardized consumer durables.[21]

All this functioned more or less smoothly until the 1970s, when a number of national and international developments disrupted the system. The Fordist technique's lack of a scientific base immediately became apparent, because it could not cope with an economy that was changing fundamentally from the one regulated to suit it. The market growth on which increasing mass production depended slowed; by the late 1960s, the growth in domestic consumption of consumer goods, which pushed the postwar expansion in the industrial countries, had begun to peter out, as the market was reaching saturation. Because domestic consumption was no longer sufficient, these countries overnight found themselves facing each other in competition for one another's markets and for those of the underdeveloped countries that were drawn into this. There was no instrument in place to ensure that the world economy would grow to justify new investments.

By the 1970s, certain groups of developing countries had joined the advanced countries in the competition for markets—the East and Southeast Asian countries and the larger countries of Latin America. This event coincided with the time when consumers began to turn away from standardized mass-produced goods; diversity and even customization increasingly became the order of the day as income increased and social and cultural values asserted themselves. Workers had become averse to the stultifying efficiency of the Taylorized labor process, which was itself resistant to further Taylorization. Niche markets for specialties and luxury goods were growing faster than the mass market for standardized products. Stagnating demand and import competition drove industrialists to seek concessions from their workers. After years of collective bargaining and cost-of-living adjustments, they reverted to union busting and takebacks. Fordism had broken down.

The second oil shock arising from the Iranian revolution sent the world economy into a state of panic, and a worldwide recession ensued.[22] The resulting inflation forced Western economies to restrain domestic demand.

One immediate result of this was an unprecedented level of mergers and acquisitions among mass producers, in which the dominant motive was either to secure new markets or to hedge risks in their primary market by diversifying into others. The incompetence of these efforts is obvious. The conglomerates continued to think that the problem was markets, but it actually arose from the structural problems of the economy, the effects of which were distributed across markets. The problems the companies involved in mass production were facing had, in fact, to do with technology—with the increasing adoption of the mass production paradigm, with factor proportions out of line with the economy's natural factor proportions. In fact, long-term benefits to the firms and increased macroeconomic growth can go together if the centrality of correct factor proportion choice is recognized in the context of what has been called the technology focus.[23]

Multinationalization was another way in which mass production producers sought to deal with the market problems they faced in the domestic economy. In short, by seeking foreign markets they attempted to achieve the economy of scale they could not be sure of domestically. The strategy required the producers to extend their operations into at least some parts of the underdeveloped world. The underdeveloped countries would provide the expanding margin of demand they required in order to achieve further economies of scale.

In order for this strategy to succeed, it required the integration of the developed countries with developing economies. Between 1970 and 1981, for example, investment by U.S. enterprises overseas rose from $75.5 billion to $227.3 billion. At the same time, direct foreign investment in the United States rose from $13.3 billion to $89.8 billion. It was thought that an arrangement in which the advanced countries would exchange sophisticated products for raw materials and simpler manufactured goods from the underdeveloped countries was the solution. Such a plan needed institutions and systems that facilitated international trade. It is clear that this arrangement was promoted at the behest of the mass production paradigm, but some economists have sought a theoretical justification for this pattern of international trade.

What emerges from the discussion so far is that the craft production has been largely neglected since the development of mass production. It is regarded as inferior, not modern, not scientific, by economists and policy makers alike. This neglect has meant that craft production has not been the subject of theoretical analysis. In particular, as already pointed out, craft production had been looked down upon by development economists because they wrongly believed it was outside their two-dimensional factor analysis—because it is supposed not to use capital—and so is not analyzable.

However, craft production, put in its right context, involves R&D, as we saw in the study of the primal society. The R&D is undertaken by the craftsman, who also provides all or part of the labor input. He uses capital, but his capital is general-purpose, not specialized, providing him the flexibility to produce different products or variations within an area of expertise. In poor societies, the market is highly customized, and the quantities demanded do not permit mass production. Craft production is therefore a type of flexible specialization.

The failure of Fordism has brought with it serious debate as to what the future holds. There are those who feel that craft production has won through low profile and patience. There are those who feel that the jury is still out. There are those who feel that a modified form of mass production is the answer—there is a noticeable tendency toward what Piore and Sabel called greater "technological sophistication rather than regression to simple techniques," which is the conventional economist's way of saying that the trend to capital-intensive techniques has to continue.

While it may seem that the survival and renewal of craft production to date is something remarkable, whole regions in the industrialized countries were untouched by mass production and escaped the mass production stagnation. Industrial districts in Emilia-Romagna (the so-called third Italy) and regions in Austria and western Germany pushed ahead with new products and processes based on craft production. The view at the time was that the successful were lucky.[24] When economists have no answer, they seek to dismiss the matter.

Piore and Sabel concluded that in the eclipse of mass production as the dominant paradigm, "the spread of flexible specialization suggests that the way out of the crisis requires a shift of technology paradigm and a new system of regulation. If recovery proceeds by this path, then 1970s and 80s will be seen in retrospect as a turning point in the history of mechanization: a time when industrial society returned to craft methods of production regarded since the 19th century as marginal—and proved them to be essential to prosperity."[25] However, they added that under some conditions, an extension of the mass production system could be as stable and coherent as the local systems that went before. Looking at the current relations among machines, workers, and economic institutions, they did not see any reason why the triumph of one or the other is more probable.

The death of mass production as a dominant para-

digm will be caused by the very thing to which it owed its early preeminence—the market. In the contemporary world, markets for many products are changing with great speed and product cycles are shortening, making it less appropriate for firms to invest in product-specific machines and workers that are capable of doing only one thing. Furthermore, mass production depends for its competitive advantage on its ability to spread its fixed costs across countries. As markets expand, the importance of scale economies decreases and so does the global producer's ability to spread his fixed costs across the border. Increasing scale activity aids the global product because it raises the average significance of fixed costs, whereas increasing market size hurts globalization by reducing their significance.[26] This is not good news for the mass producer seeking a global market. New developments in technologies are moving rapidly to reduce minimum scale in many industries, making the mass production paradigm increasingly outdated.

The paradigm of flexibility specialization, which is coming into prominence as the mass production paradigm recedes, covers a broad range of production, from pure craft production at one extreme to modifications of mass production at the other. These modifications have come in different names and descriptions. For example, flexible mass production is claimed as an attempt to preserve gains from economies of scale while exploiting and expanding economies of scope. Diversified quality production is supposed to achieve optimum quality in the context of flexible production.

The common feature of regimes that are based on modifications of mass production is that they consist of a systematic pursuit of scale effects of mass production while taking on an exceptionally high level of product differentiation. "Using the car industry as example, Coriat observed that car makers, subcontractors and assemblers are 'pressured into becoming bigger, more concentrated and more multinational.' The requirement for standardized elementary parts has demanded greater cooperation among firms as they jointly design and produce certain parts" in search of economies of scale.[27] Coriat was of the view that another distinct feature of regimes that seek to modify Fordism was the central role they give to just-in-time procedures and protocols, but this is not correct. While this class of regimes uses just-in-time, his claim can give the impression that just-in-time cannot play central roles in other regimes, when in fact it is a principle that can and should be given central place in almost all production management.

Considering the variety of flexible specialization, there has been a lot of sense and nonsense written about it. Among industrial practitioners, the emergence of flexible manufacturing systems (FMS), flexible mass production, numerical control (NC), and other regimes has caused confusion. The market among economists and industrial practitioners has been oversold on these manufacturing innovations and undersold on flexibility. Bignell and colleagues have correctly emphasized that "flexibility in manufacturing is a goal about which it is worth putting forward views. To dispute whether a system is FMS or not FMS is not worthwhile."[28] They were of the opinion that systems are things marketing and academic people sell, and that to concentrate the discussion on systems, institutions, and so on, rather than on flexibility, is to move away from what matters. The essence of post-Fordism is therefore flexibility. Flexibility is used in different ways, all of which boil down to producing in a manner that is determined by the circumstances in which one finds oneself. Post-Fordism is a move away from the near-fixed factor proportions of many mass production industries and toward the application of flexible factor proportions. It is a departure from the view that certain countries are best at producing high-technology goods while others are assigned low-technology goods. It is a departure from claims that one production function is preferred to another. It denies the claim that so-called lack of capital is an impediment to growth. The essence of the science of economic growth is the adoption of a technology (science of factor proportions) in which the choice of factor proportions is flexible in order to match the varying natural factor proportions of different economics. Flexibility therefore provides the production paradigm that meets the requirements of scientific economic development and growth.

Flexibility is attained in several principal ways:

a. *Flexibility in the use of equipment.* An attempt must be made to use general-purpose equipment in the specific application. The plant should be designed to have a low break-even point.[29] This can be achieved by keeping the cost of plant and equipment low and being aware that there is substitutability between the cost of plant and labor and material consumption. The purpose of production is reliability and low waste. An effective plant does not have to be the state of the art in technology.

b. *Process flexibility.* Process flexibility, or the ability to produce items with different materials, increases as machine setup costs decrease. Each item can be fabricated individually and not necessarily in batches.[30]

c. *Product flexibility.* This is the ability to change over to produce a new product economically and quickly. A variant of this is called "action flexibility." Included in this is another variant called "design-change flexibility." This heightens the producer's responsiveness to competition or in cases where demand for different products is low.

d. *Volume flexibility.* This encompasses both flexibility in the use of equipment and product flexibility, but it also includes the ability to cope with changes in demand. This flexibility can be measured by how small the volumes can be for all types of the product with the production still operating efficiently. Volume flexibility can be enhanced by having a layout that is not dedicated to any particular process.[31]

e. *People flexibility.* This applies more particularly to craft production. Inflexible workers have a stultifying effect. The Japanese gave labor all-around training and implemented work rotation. People willing and able to do whatever is within their capabilities make the balancing of sequences of operation easier.

These five broad flexibility criteria provide the vehicle for each economic unit to select the production technique best fitted to maximize economic growth. It is noteworthy that many of the kinds of flexibility being discussed have always been available in traditional manually operated job shops.

With the growing scope of flexible specialization production, statements such as that by Allsopp that in certain industries only large-scale output can be cost-effective will increasingly be consigned to history.[32] The same is true of comments such as Samuelson and Nordhaus': "Competition by numerous producers would not be efficient in many fields and will not last."[33]

Flexible specialization can be regarded as a rewriting of history in order to show economists that there are a variety of options in economic production. But unfortunately, despite the availability of options, many in the field are confused about the merits of flexible specialization over mass production. For example, Hirst and Zeitlin began with the premise that "neither mass production nor flexible specialization . . . is inherently superior to the other." "Each model," they claim, "is theoretically capable of generating a virtuous circle of productivity improvement and economic growth." They further complicated matters by holding that "the practical realization of either possibility depends on a contingent and variable framework of institutional regulation at the micro level of the firm or region and the macro level of the nation and international

economy." They asserted that "the technological dynamism of each model and its potential for sustained development cannot be evaluated outside of definite institutional and environmental contexts." To them, "flexible specialization emphasizes that each social 'world' contains a number of possibilities [i.e., of different strands of specialization]." Here institutionalism is making a comeback into what is basically an issue of choice of technique.

Hirst and Zeitlin felt that flexibility specialization has so many variants that a variety of possible outcomes can be constructed from the basic idealtypical concepts of it and that each can produce a different set of relationships between social objects and outcomes. They thought that it was important that people should be alert to the competing strategies—mass production and flexibility specialization—and assess outcomes "in terms that do not predetermine which of them will prevail." Part of the evidence they thought was needed was that "other alternatives were possible, that they coexisted with the dominant paradigm and that they offer distinct routes to innovation and change should the specific complex conditions favoring the dominant paradigm cease to apply." In their view, part of the role of theory is to identify instances or cases of progressive flexible specialization to show that they are socially possible and to investigate whether they can be generalized given appropriate policy commitments and satisfactory condition.

They view the issues concerning the two paradigms from another angle. "Flexibility specialization theory," they said, "includes a battery of concepts drawing attention to a number of distinct ideal-types of production systems, progressive and stagnant variants of the same, possible forms of hybridization, and also ways in which various systems can be combined in large and small companies, as well as national and regional economies." The result, they said, "is a very large range of possible situations and complex cases, a wide range of types of hypotheses." Thus they argue that it will not do to select one of these types of hypotheses and seek to refute it without reference to others.

Third, they felt that even if flexible specialization was not all-inclusive, it could still be valuable. This is because, in their view, it could help unearth other reasons why mass production gained a foothold other than its "technological necessities" and economy of scale.[34]

It is clear from all this that Hirst and Zeitlin, along with others who view the issues from the point of view of conventional economics or institutionalism, do not get the essence of flexible specialization. For a start, they are wrong to assert that flexible specialization as a general theoretical approach is compatible with a broad spectrum of possible forms of productive organization—"including the continued dominance of mass production." Flexible specialization and mass production are entirely different production strategies. They themselves earlier admitted the distinction (and competition) between the two. They envisage the possibility that flexible specialization can lead to the continued dominance of mass production as a paradigm because they have the wrong meaning of flexibility. In the ordinary meaning of the term, an idea can be so flexible that it could validate its opposite. Flexible specialization in its technical sense does not include the specialized structures of mass production, which assume for their validity a given minimum market size. The "battery of concepts" involved in flexible specialization is not as complex as they imagine. Flexible specialization boils down simply to recognizing that markets are not and cannot be packaged to suit any given production technique. In a way it is taking us back to man's primal origins, in that man's requirements are varied and that societies and individuals have customized desires. In primal societies, the market was varied, selective, and often customized. If after a spell of mass production modern signals are pointing to increasing local preference, special-

ties, and customization, it means that man is returning to his original roots and that the production paradigm now emerging is likely to be in line with the science (nature) of development/growth.

Without knowledge of the theory of science of economic growth as it is stated in this book, Piore and Sabel summarized what they envisaged as the benefits of flexible specialization to the macroeconomy. In parentheses accompanying each benefit will be the aspect of the theory of factor proportion to which their summary refers.

1. If economies of scale become less important, units of production will become smaller and the number of young, middle-aged, and old plants will be approximately equal (factor proportions will tend to equalize).

2. Minor imbalances between supply and demand will be corrected by attrition and replacement as well as by the migration of resources between alternative uses (factor proportions equalization leads to balanced development).

3. The economy would be more responsive to a truly internal stabilizing mechanism (equilibrium in factor proportions).

4. Demand for investment funds will decline, pulling down interest rates and whetting the appetite of entrepreneurs who were previously hesitant to go forward (increased economic participation and full use of resources).

5. Because relative wages and other returns to cooperating factors are taken out of competition, the economic system will not be as stable as pictured in models of a competitive economy (factor proportions in use will reflect natural endowments and equilibrium will be dynamic instead of static).

6. It will be possible to maintain full employment without artificial means (full utilization of all factor of production).

7. It imposes fewer constraints on the scope and character of the international economic order. It could operate effectively in a large, open world economy, but it does not need the markets that such an economy would provide. The more technology renders economies of scale irrelevant and raw materials substitutable, the more likely it is that each nation can produce a wide range of products on its own (present theories of international trade are deficient—a topic to be taken up in future chapters—and growth should be based on factor proportions of the endowments of each country, not on international transfers of capital or a brand of technology).[35]

Hirst and Zeitlin felt that large amounts of data were needed to test the flexibility specialization hypothesis. Such data were to come from both micro and macro levels of analysis. While data from the micro level are useful—and there is a lot of it already available—they serve little purpose in developing a theory of development and growth, because if flexible specialization did not have any validity at the micro level, it would not have improved firms' competitive position and they would not have engaged in it. On a macro level, Hirst and Zeitlin stated, "Reliable data . . . are likely to be difficult if not impossible to obtain," but from an economic development point of view, what the theory should be seeking to establish is whether flexible specialization promotes economic growth. The answer already provided is that to the extent that flexible specialization enables firms to choose factor proportions suited to the growth needs of the micro and macro economy, it provides the basis for achieving sustainable economic growth in varying conditions. But a hybrid system based on mass production techniques is not likely to be using factor proportions that are in consonance with macroeco-

nomic growth because factor proportions for the mass production component are likely to be set by market considerations.

How Hirst and Zeitlin got it wrong was by mixing institutions and social analysis with the economic and technical issues involved. Institutions are not economic growth. Correct choices of factor proportions is economic growth. No doubt institutions can provide, promote, or discourage propagation of a particular technology paradigm. The whole point of Piore and Sabel's book is that postwar Western societies and institutions chose wrongly by adopting mass production technology. Hirst and Zetlin's claim that "technological dynamism of each model and its potential for sustained development cannot be evaluated outside of definite institutional and environmental contests" is therefore not necessarily true. Since it is now possible to evaluate a technology paradigm and say whether it can promote sustained development, it is possible also to do so on a sound theoretical basis outside the institutions and environmental contexts.

It is from this point of view that the dangers in prescribing what institutions are necessary for flexible specialization become apparent. The industrial districts of small and medium-sized cities along with large, decentralized companies or groups have been identified by Piore and Sabel, and by others, as the institutional framework for flexible specialization. Said Hirst and Zeitlin, "In the industrial districts, geographically localized networks of firms subcontract to one another and share a range of common services, such as training, research, market forecasting, credit and quality control. Successful districts are also typically characterized by collective systems of conflict resolution that encourage firms to compete through innovation in products and processes rather than sweated wages and conditions." In large, decentralized companies, autonomous productive units are said to resemble the small, specialized firms or craft workshops, relying on other divisions for research, marketing, and finance. The danger of analyses such as these is that they create the impression that it is the institutions that originated flexible specialization, which is not true. It is the flexible specialization technology that gave rise to the institutions being described. In other societies, flexible specialization may create different kinds of institutions.[36] This is not to deny that the institutions in this case were instrumental in choosing the right paradigm.

The sociological or institutionalist viewpoint will want to put technology and social science on the same level in the search for economic development. The argument typically runs as follows: The performance of contemporary economies depends on production. But production involves more than technology; it involves social structure. The same equipment is operated quite differently in the same sectors in different countries. Variations in production and process technologies are influenced partly by variations in social environment. A social system of production is of major importance in understanding the behavior and performance of an economy.

This argument is defective. Our theory of the science of economic development and growth says that equipment suitable for one location may not be appropriate for another location because of factor proportions. This is contrary to the sociologists' belief that equipment, being a fixed device, should perform equally in all locations. Therefore they seek to argue that any difference in performance must be due to social and institutional factors.

There is no doubt that the social system is of importance in understanding the behaviors and performance of an economy. It gives an economy its distinctiveness and color. However, a scientific economic formulation that promotes rapid balanced growth is more likely to engender social systems and institutions that accord with it than not.

This social/institutional approach has in its economic analysis sought to divide production systems

into what has been called social systems of production. While Fordism seems to be labeled on its own, there are said to be around six or so types of flexible systems of production, "each tending to produce a wide array of products in response to different consumer demand supported by a skilled workforce with the capability of shifting from one job to another with the firm." It is said that these systems of production "are not meant to be descriptive statements about specific firms, industrial sectors or individual firms at specific periods of time." Rather, according to Hollingsworth and Boyer, "they are heuristic devices to sensitize us to possible interrelationships that might exist among a broad set of variables or social categories," and "neither type existed alone in space or time."[37] In another instance, the various identified models of production are said to have emerged from an analysis of local structural conditions and are concerned mainly with the coordination or relationship among actors, less so with technology or innovation. The different social systems of production (flexible and nonflexible) have been broadly identified as Fordist mass production, diversified quality mass production (DQMP), craft production, flexible mass production, and flexible specialization. To support their claim that none of these has existed alone in space or time, the social analysts cite the fact that mass production and flexible specialized production have existed together, the former predating the latter. But they do not take account of the fact that the coexistence was not necessarily good for economic growth, as it distorted prospects for factor proportion equalization. Since sociologists admit that these interrelationships are more concerned with social interactions than technology or innovation, it follows that these social systems of production have little to contribute to a scientific theory of economic development and growth.

The case of Japan has been a point of debate in the search for the availability and appropriateness of competing production paradigms. Japan's phenomenal growth in the 1970s and 1980s was due to its innovative production methods. Indeed, it is these new Japanese production strategies that expedited the collapse of Fordism as a preeminent model. The question is, how far can the success of Japanese firms be properly interpreted as evidence of the diffusion of flexible specialization or that of increased flexibility within mass production? Attempts to label large-volume production as a form of mass production are mistaken. Mass production is geared to achieving maximum capacity output because that is when it can fully exploit the economy of scale. That is what the Japanese call overproduction. In his book *The New Manufacturing Challenge: Techniques for Continuous Improvement,* Kiyoshi Suzaki said, "One of the most important concepts of JIT [just-in-time] is flow production. Here 'flow' refers to the movement of material through the plant. It is assumed that material will not be stagnant at any point in time from receiving the material to the shipping of finished product." He stated, "In JIT philosophy, overproduction is one of the chief obstacles to achieving efficient production activities. Because overproduction hides other problems, it is difficult to target areas for improvement." He affirmed, "We [the Japanese] . . . aim to produce only the amount required by the customer. When we produce goods required by the customer (by 'customer' we mean the immediate user of the product; in this case the next production process), the machine utilization rate should become a secondary concern. When sales volume is high, the utilization should go up; when sales volume is low, the utilization rate should go down. It is a big mistake to produce goods solely to increase machine utilization. . . . What is important, however, is to be able to use the machine wherever you need to produce products. We define this event as the on-demand utilization factor. We want to achieve a 100 percent on-demand utilization factor, rather than a 100 percent machine utilization rate."[38]

O'Grady, talking of Japanese production techniques and just-in-time, said, "JIT . . . means investing in low-cost machines that are flexible in their response to change in product volume and product type. There is little point in investing in specialized machinery if demand falls for those products the machinery is designed to produce. JIT implementations are characterized by flexible machines that can quickly be altered from one product to another."[39]

There is considerable confusion on the subject of what constitutes mass production. There is a tendency for some writers to assume that when production is in large volumes, it must be mass production. However, in technical usage it refers to the nature of the plant: a specialized plant set at a very high break-even point solely to gain the largest feasible scale advantage. The plant is designed not with a view toward dealing with fluctuations in demand but to operate at a constant high break-even capacity.

The fact that with Japanese automobiles and consumer electronics, for example, there is a "limited range of variation on certain models and long production runs and the relatively narrow skills required for many jobs leads to the dominance of large firms over their subcontractors"[40] (which some writers describe as a form of mass production)[41] does not on its own make such production mass production. It is therefore wrong to assert that the Japanese system is one of increased flexibility within mass production, because these two features cannot be achieved in the same machine.

The early success of Japan stems basically from a progressive pursuit of flexible specialization in which factor proportions changed as the economy developed from the factor proportions of labor intensiveness, material scarcity, and low capital giving way to factor proportions with moderate capital, moderate labor input, and material scarcity.

The central issue of adopting the appropriate factor proportions in each case was summarized by

Freeman and Soete in the context of flexibility when they said that "just as specific national circumstances strongly influenced the evolution of industrial technology in eighteenth- and nineteenth-century Britain or capital-intensive, material-intensive and energy-intensive production systems in the United States, so undoubtedly the lean production was powerfully influenced by the various Japanese national institutions."[42] They pointed out that at the time the Japanese decided to go into automobile and commercial truck manufacturing, they faced shortages of both materials and capital.

The Japanese pioneered FMS, an integrated, computer-controlled complex of automated material handling devices and numerically controlled (NC) machine tools that can simultaneously process moderate volumes of different items. It is designed to attain the efficiency of well-balanced, machine-paced transfer lines while utilizing the flexibility that job shops have to simultaneously make multiple part types. In recent times, many manufacturing facilities have been labeled FMS. This has caused confusion as to what constitutes FMS. Flexibility and automation are the key conceptual requirements. It is the extent of automation and the diversity of the parts that are important. Regrettably, some systems are called FMS just because they contain automated materials handling. For example, dedicated transfer lines or systems containing only automated storage and retrieval cannot, as is often the case, be classed as FMS. Other manufacturing that contains several (unintegrated) NC or CNC machines, or that uses computers to control the machines but often requires long setups or has no automated parts transfer, has all too often been labeled as FMS. Some systems have been called flexible just because they produce a variety of parts (of very similar type) using fixed automation.

Broadly speaking, the flexibility claim of any FMS can be judged by the level of flexibility achieved in line with the criteria already stated. It

is evident that because of different choices of flexibility level, there are different designs of FMS.

Despite the attractions of FMS, it is essential to point out that it is not all things to all men. The pursuit of the right factor proportion combinations must be unrelenting. Said Bignell and colleagues in their assessment of FMS by various technical specialists, "The shiny plastic bag of FMS around the parcel of flexibility may not be as valuable as the authors think."[43] The only thing that separates FMS from flexible specialization is automation. The level of automation can help determine the amount of flexibility.

On the other hand, it is essential to point out that smart automation is not high-speed equipment but rather equipment that will do what is needed at the time. For example, a great deal of automation only involves moving something; an ingenious layout can go far to prevent unnecessary movement, which otherwise might need to be automated.

Sometimes flexible machines work well, sometimes not—it comes down to whether, following the selection of the right package, the producer can overcome the technical and human issues involved. Fundamentals of people preparation, quality, layout, maintenance, and so forth make the difference. Both computerization and the price tag make FMS high-profile, garnering much management attention, but the success factors are often buried in low-profile activity. Indeed, in countries with high L, flexibility should derive from good utilization of the human skills available. The principles of flexibility are the same everywhere. It is clear, considering our detailed examination of flexible production, that the technology is there to make factor-proportions management a reality.

Economy of Scale

Apart from consideration of mass production, economy of scale is an important topic in conventional economics. The standard textbooks to date usually have listed what they consider to be different sources of economy of scale in an attempt to show that in conventional economics it pays to be big. The various sources can be summarized as (1) three-dimensional geometric factors, (2) one-time costs, (3) technology of large-scale production (alternatively called indivisibilities), and (4) economics of large-scale business.

Three-Dimensional Geometric Factors

Here economic texts refer to what they say is the engineers' use of the rule of thumb on geometrical relations of shapes. According to Beardshaw, this "law of two-thirds" states that as the volume of a container doubles, its surface increases by only two-thirds. Doubling the volume of a ship, for example, doubles its ability to carry cargo but only increases its construction cost by about two-thirds because the amount of material required to build it (and hence the cost) is related to the area of its surface. Hence, he argued, large ships are more efficient than small ones, and he concluded that this explains the development of massive oil tankers, bulk cargo carriers, and jumbo jets.[44] Begg stated that the cost of a factory building rises by only two-thirds as much as the output of the factory.[45] Using a smelter as an example, Lipsey and Chrystal stated that heat loss in a smelter is proportional to its surface area, while the amount smelted depends on its volume. They detected an economy of scale because the heat needed per ton of ore smelted decreased as the size of the smelter increased.[46]

The geometric world is an age-old phenomenon. Man has always needed containers for storage, preservation and safekeeping, and transport. Man in the primal society used hollow trunks, gourds, animal skins, and holes in the ground to store items, and developed techniques in pottery to make different shapes of clay vessels to meet different storage and transport needs. For example, a clay pot used in many traditional societies to carry water over distances is almost a sphere, whose volume is $4\pi r^3/3$ and surface area $4\pi r^2$ where r is the radius. Thus if those carrying the pot of water can bear the weight, they can carry eight times more water simply by doubling the diameter of the pot. If the container is a cone of diameter two feet and height three feet, increasing the diameter by 50 percent, to three feet, will increase the volume of water 2.25 times. For a doubling of volume, that works out to a 1.4-fold increase in material used. Therefore, the gains made in volume in relation to material content vary with the shape of the container, assuming other characteristics are constant. It is clear from these examples that, contrary to Lipsey and Chrystal, what is involved here is not a production process; containers are not productive capital, and the storage capacity of a container is not an output in any economic sense.

Another factor to consider is the nature of what is being stored—gas, liquid, or solid. If the weight of the solid is in excess of the bearing capacity of the material intended to carry it, it will be impossible to store or transport it in that container. If the material to be stored or transported is gas, its volume alone is almost meaningless; one cannot talk of the volume of a gas without specifying its pressure.[47] In that case, one needs to ask whether the material of the container can deal with the pressures and temperatures involved. Liquids come somewhere in between gases and solids.

The point to make here is that the claim that the cost of producing a container is determined by or even proportional to the surface area of the material used may be misleading. For the same volume of container space, material type (yield strength, elasticity, density, stiffness, thickness, etc.) is a prime consideration that will significantly alter the cost. For example, the strength-to-performance cost ratio (in U.S. units) of aluminum 2024–T861 is 1.51,

Figure 4.2 **Cost of shop-fabricated tank in mid-1980 with 1/4" walls.**

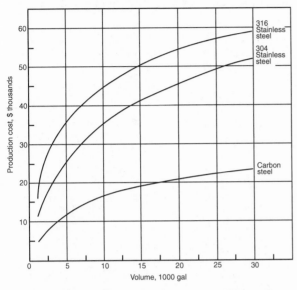

Figure 4.3 **Cost of small field-erected tanks in mid-1980.**

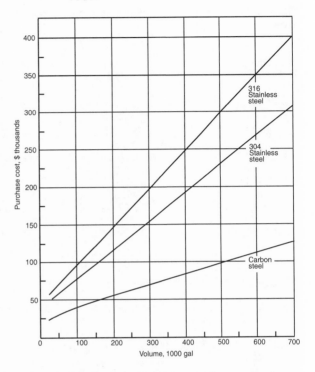

Source: R.H. Perry and D.W. Green, eds., *Perry's Chemical Engineers' Handbook*, 7th ed. (New York: McGraw-Hill, 1997), fig. 10-184.

cast iron (gray) 2.25, and steel 1015 1.54. Different aluminums have different strength-to-performance cost ratios: aluminum 3003-H18 is 3.11, aluminum 7075-T66 is 1.66, and stainless steel 304 is 6.75. The stiffness-to-performance cost ratio for aluminum 2024-T861 is 9.52 compared with 2.57 for steel 1015 and 3.00 for cast iron (gray).

The cost of producing a container is not just the cost of the base material. The same quantity of base material used in producing different configurations will entail different methods of fabrication. The relationship among cost, shapes, and material has been the subject of study by engineers; the best advice is to obtain prices over a number of years and see what empirical relationship there might be. The results of two such studies are shown in Figures 4.2 and 4.3. It is clear that the cost of the container was in some direct proportion to its volume. It shall be evident from Figure 4.2 that doubling the volume of a tank results in a price increase that is less than

Source: R.H. Perry and D.W. Green, eds., *Perry's Chemical Engineers' Handbook*, 7th ed. (New York: McGraw-Hill, 1997), fig. 10-185.

the increase in the surface area by as much as 30 percent below the rule-of-thumb prediction. Figure 4.3 concerns field-erected tanks, where costs include the cost of stairs, platforms, nozzles, and so on; this is more representative of actual usage. Here doubling of the volume of a tank tends to lead to an increase in price that is more than the increase in surface area by up to 12 percent of the rule-of-thumb prediction. The point is that the cost relationships depend very much on the storage needs and the configuration and material of the storage vessel.

The position is different when the container also serves as a means of transporting material. In the specific cases of oil tankers and jet aircraft, referred to in some texts as examples of economies of scale, there are design issues that may in practice not pro-

Table 4.1

Summary of Average Dimensions and Speed Against the Dead Weight Size Groups of Tankers of Various Design

Size Group tons d.w 1	Average Dimensions 2	Volume cu. ft. 3	Surface area sq. ft. (a) 4	Surface area sq. ft. (b) 5	Weight/ Vol (tons/ 1000 c.f.) 6
5000–9999	370x55x22.6 15.5	459,810	59,910	59,910	16.3
10,000–19,999	495x70x28.4 15.5	984,060	101,392	102,087	15.2
20,000–29,999	571x82x33.5 15.3	1,568,537	137,395	163,460	15.9
30,000–49,999	607x94x36.9 15.3	2,105,440	165,850	219,411	19
50,000–69,999	736x107x41.4 15.3	3,260,332	227,304	339,765	18
70,000–99,999	798x129x44.5 15.4	4,580,919	288,387	477,385	27
100,000–199,999	891x143x53.6 15.4	5,517,691	365,671	575,008	19
200,000–239,999	1058x170x64 15.7	11,511,040	516,904	119,958	—
240,000 and above	1130x183x69 15.5	14,268,510	594,774	—	—

Source: [Column 1, 2, 3]—*Clarkson Oil Tanker Databook*, p. 208; Table II, p. 149, (London: Clarkson Research Studies Ltd., 1993).

duce the economies expected. We will take the case of oil tankers first.

Table 4.1 is a schedule summarizing average dimensions and speed (in knots) against the dead weight (tons) size groups of tankers of various designs. The dimensions in feet are average length, average external breadth, and average summer draft. For simplicity, a rectangular shape has been assumed. Column 4 is the surface area of the tankers. Column 5 is the calculated surface area of the boat if the engineer's rule of thumb (a twofold gain in volume for every two-thirds increase in surface area) holds. Column 6 is the approximate values of the dry weight/volume ratio in tons per thousand cubic feet of the tankers. It is noteworthy that the achieved actual surface area of tankers (column 4) was in

general less than the surface area predicted by the two-thirds rule.

It is clear from these values that the designers of the tankers were attempting to adopt tanker shapes and configurations that would maximize volume and economize on surface area while achieving increased weight/volume ratios that would assist the dynamic balance of the tankers at the speeds specified as the quantity of oil carried increases.

The dimensions of a ship are determined by what it is supposed to carry. In the case of cargo ships, it is the cargo carrying capacity. In the case of passenger vessels, dimensions are influenced by the height and length of the superstructure containing the accommodations. One does not just, for example, increase the length so as to gain increased volume, as some economic texts imply. Where the length is not specified as a maximum, the length adopted should be consistent with required speed and hull form. Increased length produces higher longitudinal bending stress, requiring additional strengthening (and hence additional costs) and greater displacement for the same cargo weight. The breadth must be such as to provide adequate transverse stability. The minimum depth selected will be controlled by the expected draft plus a statutory freeboard, but increased depth will result in a reduction of longitudinal bending stress, providing an increase in strength or allowing a reduction in scantlings. Draft is defined by the needs of the area of operation, but it can be increased, as greater depth is a design stability advantage.

In regard to jet aircraft, total mass at takeoff is limited to a specified maximum by the structural design and by the requirements of takeoff, in particular the need for clearance of the screen height and attainment of an adequate angle of climb after the failure of one engine. The structural limitation is dependent on the assumptions made in relation to the average weight of passengers and the average density of baggage and freight in the hold. The assumptions about these weights determine the mass distribution throughout the fuselage and have a direct influence on the structural design. A basic aim is to define the maximum allowable payload and also to show how the combination of payload and fuel must be optimized. The issues are not those of area and volume of the aircraft.

Stretching is the term given to techniques for increasing the fuselage volume. This immediately increases the payload and the fuel load capacity, both of which increase the all-up weight. Increased fuel loads involve overload tanks, hung beneath the wings and the fuselage, or designing wings with larger dimensions. Increased weight with unchanged wing area increases the wing loading, which may be regarded as a pressure applied to the supporting

air by wing surfaces. There is a relationship between wing loading and dynamic pressure that must be maintained if the plane is to fly at the most efficient angle of attack to the air. If the wing loading is increased, then it must be met with increased dynamic pressure, and this can be done only by reducing the height of the plane. To increase speed at the same height without a balance between load and dynamic pressure involves the engines being off-design. Hence it will be operating inefficiently.[48] Enlarging the fuselage and the wing increases not only their total mass but also their moment of inertia; these in turn increase the size of the tail control and stabilizing surfaces. The larger the aircraft, the more powerful the flywheel effect about the axes through its center of gravity. Increased inertia makes the aircraft more sluggish and difficult to control. Stretching the aircraft increases risk of a tail strike on takeoff and landing. The undercarriage has to be strengthened if they and the supporting structures have insufficient reserve strength. This may require an increase in the number of wheels.

It must not be forgotten that the first generation of powered aircraft was built of wood and canvas. Though the use of wood persisted until the Second World War, aluminum took over in the 1930s and dominated until the 1980s, when titanium and various composite materials increasingly came into use. In practice, nothing still prevents the use of wood in aircraft of appropriate design. It is the use of different materials that greatly impacts production costs, because production methods depend on the nature of the material and how the design issues sketched here are tackled. For example, all metal-frame aircrafts constructed from thin materials require a large number of jigs and tools if they are produced via craft production. As the quantities increase, fittings machined from solid metal can be replaced by forged or cast fittings, which have an increased capital cost but may eliminate labor-intensive activities and the need for items such as stiffeners and fasteners. As aircraft size increases, the number of parts will not increase in proportion, and there are few parts of minimum gauge, so a relatively smaller unit weight can be expected. Larger parts required for larger aircrafts may be easier to fabricate and allow better access to riveting during assembly but are heavier to handle. Relative costs of production for small and large aircraft will depend upon the choice of factor proportions arising from choices made about the relative proportion of assembly to machining in frame production.

Having reviewed the storage and transportation issues arising from various economic texts' pronouncements on geometric relations, the question that is relevant here is whether their claim of economy of scale is justified. Economy of scale as a concept should not be treated so lightly. Even in conventional economics the notion of substitution is basic. One gives up something so as to get some other thing or more of something. It is theoretically wrong to regard economy of scale as a win-win concept. Economy of scale recognizes that as one seeks more capital input, operating costs increase, except that the unit total costs reduce progressively up to a point. To invoke geometric relations on their own as an example of economy of scale is likely to loosen economic debate, for after all, geometric relations apply to everything in life that has a three-dimensional existence—cars, houses, garbage bins, human beings, books, and so on. Where does one stop?

From the point of view of economic development and growth theory, geometric relations have little relevance. For example, if a cylinder is considered as a container, it is evident that its price is a function of its volume: $P = f(V)^c$, where P is price, V is volume, and C is a coefficient depending on the material. But for a cylindrical item used in production as, say, a heat exchanger, $P = f(q,T,p,M_cC_1)$, where q is the capacity of the heat exchanger (say in tons per year), T is its temperature of operation,

p is the operating pressure, M_c depends on the material of construction, and C_1 the relevant cost index of the material.[49] Other methods of estimating the cost of a heat exchanger make it a function of the heat exchange area but not the surface area or weight of the vessel. It is clear, therefore, that economies of scale delineated as arising from geometrical relations do not apply here.

The error of analysis in economic texts extolling claimed economies of scale arising from geometric relations is clear in its direct reference to production activities. Lipsey and Chrystal claimed that in smelting there are economies of scale. They pointed out that heat loss is proportional to surface area. Therefore, the larger the volume of the smelter, the lower the heat loss per unit weight of smelted material. There are three wrong analyses in this assertion. The first is the assumption that the volume of the smelter is the same as the volume of the smelter output. The second is that in a smelter, the more predominant loss of heat is by radiation. This is a function of the difference of the fourth power of the absolute temperatures of the smelter and the surroundings, not the surface area. As air is a poor conductor of heat, heat loss by convection, which is proportional to surface area, is small. The third is the assumption that heat loss in a smelter is inevitable. A well-designed smelter should eliminate the heat losses referred to or at least reduce them significantly. A smelter that has the heat differential claimed cannot be regarded as well designed.

Begg's claim that the cost of a factory building rises only by two-thirds as much as the output of the factory is another attempt to introduce geometric relations into production. It is true that as a rule of thumb what is sometimes called the 0.6 factor estimate can give a rough indication of the capital cost of a plant. In the equation $C_n = C_k (V_n/V_k)^F$, where C is the capital cost of a new plant, C_k is the capital cost of an existing plant, and V_n, V_k are the capacities of the new plant and the existing plant, respectively.

F is a factor that varies between 0.4 and 0.9 depending on the type of plant. The wide range in the value of *F* is evidence that this is not a strict result of geometric relations. But more important is the distinction already drawn in Chapter 3 between production in conventional economic terms and production in terms of the theory of factor proportions. Whereas the former is concerned solely with a financial or accounting analysis of costs so as to determine the cost per unit of output, the latter is concerned about the utilization of factor inputs (factor proportions) that go directly into the process of production. The former is a financial inquiry. The latter is a technology inquiry. The former took the technology as given. The latter inquired whether the technology was adequate. Thus it can again be said that geometric relations have nothing to do with science of economic production and its related choice of technique.

To repeat, none of the activities cited as an example of economy of scale arising from geometric relations is a production activity. Rather, economy of scale involves some fixity of factor proportions. Second, in extrapolating geometric relations into activities such as tanker and air transportation and assigning money values to them, economists ignored the fact that other practical design (scientific) factors come into play that may not always yield the economies of scale being claimed. Third, economies of scale assigned to geometric factors are likely to face the same fate that befell the Fordist style of economy of scale when the nature of the market on which they rely changes. To take one example, the collapse of the supertanker market started with the first oil crisis in 1973 and accelerated with the second several years later.[50] Early forecasts of the quantity and location of oil reserves have proved wrong, and with oil more available outside the Middle East, supertankers to carry it from the Middle East to Europe and America have become largely unnecessary. Also, consumption in the Western world is not growing as much as previously thought. In another

example, the fragmentation of the market for passenger air travel has changed, and different sizes of planes are better suited to various segments of this market; Boeing, for instance, now has a strategy based on different airplanes serving routes of different lengths.

We can summarize our discussions on economy of scale, insofar as production in concerned, in a few sentences. First is that economy of scale is a vital national phenomenon without which many everyday activities would be impossible. It is not an essential part of the production process. Conventional economists and designers of product processes wrongly treat economy of scale as manna from heaven—something for which one need not pay anything. When applied in production, economy of scale implies giving up something to get something. The thing given up is the right to choose the factor proportions best suited for the economy.

Economy of Scale and Factor Proportions Theory

The obstacle presented by the concept of economy of scale for the development of a science of economic growth can be gauged by the following statements by Todaro: "The gradual integration of less developed economies is a long-term dynamic one: Integration provides the opportunity for industries that have not yet been established as well as those that have to take advantage of large-scale production made possible by expanded markets. Integration therefore needs to be viewed as a mechanism to encourage a rational division of labor among a group of countries, each of which is too small to benefit from such a division by itself. In the absence of integration, each separate country may not provide a sufficiently large domestic market to enable local industries to lower their production costs through economies of scale. In such cases, import-substituting industrialization will typically result . . . in the establishment of high-cost, inefficient local industries. Moreover, in the absence of integration, the same industry (e.g., textiles or shoes) may be set up in two or more adjoining small nations. Each will be operating at less than optimal capacity." Many underdeveloped countries have in their zeal to grow taken steps to form economic groupings that implement a division of labor. The arguments for the adoption of export strategies by underdeveloped countries are regrettably often based on their need to secure economy of scale by grafting foreign markets onto their local small markets. Many Third World countries have in effect been told that their hopes for rapid economic growth cannot be realized because their markets cannot sustain viable industries.[51]

Economics of Large-Scale Business

The other sources of economy of scale frequently identified are essentially empirical observations. It is claimed that large companies enjoy managerial economy of scale, financial economy of scale, marketing economy of scale, and risk-bearing economy of scale, and that as businesses specialize in particular tasks, people become more efficient and cost falls.[52] Samuelson and Nordhaus' admiration of large, highly capitalized business is clearly evident from the following statement: "The question of returns to scale is of great importance for economic growth of nations. Most countries have experienced steady increases in their population, capital stock, available land and other resources. In the course of their growth, firms have expanded, with production levels of typical firms many times larger than those of large firms half a century or centuries ago. What would be the effect of a general increase in the scale of economic activity of most firms? If increasing returns prevailed, then the larger scale of inputs and production would lead to greater productivity. This . . . suggests that increases in nation's per capita output and living standards may result in part from

exploiting economies of scale in production as the nation grows."[53]

New changes being witnessed in the U.S. economy cast doubt on these claims. The organizational changes already caused by the Internet economy should clearly show that most of the economy-of-scale theories are incorrect. A *Wall Street Journal* writer observed that with the new information-technology economy, "the more evolved financial markets are better at nurturing new companies with good ideas. . . . Chubby bankers, who are more likely to support large established companies than struggling start-ups, have less control over capital. Venture capitalists, eager to find the next Netscape, have more."[54] Internet marketing will increasingly result in a shift away from the traditional pattern of marketing, which Lipsey and Chrystal had in mind when they claimed that there is a marketing economy of scale. For all the conventional economists' admiration of large-scale business, Petzinger was right when he observed, "Though official statistics understate the story, there is no doubt that the [U.S.] economy is splintering into ever-smaller and more specialized pieces." He quoted a corporate official as saying, "At one time [in the U.S.] if you had 50 or 100 giant companies doing the same thing in lockstep at the same time, you could destroy an economy. . . . But you don't have that anymore." Petzinger correctly observed, "Because of downsizing and outsourcing, the 1990s in the United States have witnessed a massive breakup of decision-making authority from a small number of monolithic corporations to an untold number of small firms and individuals."[55] These are just a few of the changes indicating that the net production factor proportions in the U.S. economy have been altered.

Across a wide range of industries where economy of scale was a growing trend, the 1970s heralded a change. Freeman and Soete summarized it this way: "There were signs in the 1970s that diseconomies of scale were beginning to affect the construction and operation of some of the larger plants. . . . But the slow down in economic growth in the 1970s together with the bunching of major investment decisions affecting very large plants, led to the emergency of serious over-capacity in several branches of organic production. . . . Prolonged below capacity working has an extremely adverse effect on the economics of large plant operation because of the high fixed capital costs. Such below capacity working may be induced either by the failure of the market to grow sufficiently, rapidly or by technical problems in construction, commissioning or operation of the new types of plant. In either case, losses can be on a very large scale. Similar problems of diseconomy of very large plants set in during the 1970s in electric power generation and in steel after a period of rapid scale-up in size. In the steel industry and several others, as well as some types of chemical plant, new processes and new designs restored some advantages to smaller plants."[56] It is clear that until recently, R&D has neglected to pay attention to the design and operation of smaller-capacity plants. Conventional economics has been content not to lead in making a case for this new R&D stance—maybe because it has not got the expertise—or is content to extol the large-size activities. It also lacked the theoretical framework to judge what engineers were up to.

Economy of Scale as a Production Input

Economy of scale is regarded as a very important development strategy in conventional economics, and indeed Samuelson and Nordhaus' comments and those of economists involved in growth accounting suggest that they regard it as a very important source of productivity and technology. But, to summarize from the preceding chapters, economy of scale is a growth-retarding phenomenon. First, it has been demonstrated that capital-intensive activi-

ties do not just coexist with non-capital-intensive activities at the micro level; rather, there is a struggle for factors in which the capital-intensive activities attack the non-capital-intensive activities, denying them factor inputs and seeking to reduce the scope of the non-capital-intensive sector. What results is economic structural imbalance, which, while it creates rich rewards and profits for the capital-intensive industries, retards the potential for higher macroeconomic growth. Second, economy of scale assumes that production technique (loosely referred to as technology) is given and fixed. It then joggles the relative quantities of inputs, using their prices as indicators, to achieve minimal cost for each level of output. But the prices almost always do not reflect the relative availability of factor inputs. Therefore, a combination arrived in this way will not ensure that factor proportions on the micro level are equal to the natural factor proportions. Proponents of economy of scale have, it should be noted, indirectly accepted the principle that all factors inputs can be varied in order to arrive at least cost. A third problem is in the analysis of the structure of economy of scale. It is argued that the long-run average cost curve is a boundary between attainable and unattainable levels of cost and that at its lowest point output attains the lowest possible per-unit cost of production. Thereafter, diseconomies are said to be encountered. But so far the theory seems to have only identified management problems as the cause of the diseconomies. Is the theory saying that there are no other factors that give rise to diseconomies? The concept itself is weak and largely an empirical construct.

Optimization

In considering whether the technology is there to meet the stipulations of a science of economic development and growth, the comments of Hawken, Lovins, and Lovins provide the key as to how techniques can be the servant, not the master, of economic development and growth: "Every naturalist knows that nature does not compromise—nature optimizes."[57] The change to flexible manufacturing techniques arising out of the ashes of Fordism has in its wake inspired a new attitude among designers of production systems and processes. Instead of a rigid attachment to methods, there has been a rediscovery of the notion that the designer should pick and choose from a set of parameters what best suits the varying objectives he may want to achieve. In other words, he needs to optimize.

Within a given area of knowledge (technology), there is considerable flexibility, and it is possible to vary factor input proportions to suit desired ends. The chemical process industry will be used as the example. Chemical process is traditionally regarded among economists as modern, highly specialized, and capital-intensive—so it comes as a surprise to hear that "chemical process equipment is basically the same now as it was in the 1930s or at least the 1950s. The trays, KO drums, compressors, heater, steam system have not—and probably will not—change. The fundamental nature of the process equipment has been established for a very long time."[58] This underlines the basic principle behind all choice of technique—namely, the need for the designer to identify and be guided by the scientific principle behind the process being designed. Within this constraint the designer has a wide choice of factor proportions.

Contrast this approach with its opposite: "If we are to design a new plant to meet an expanding market condition, as a first guess of the production rate, we consider the largest plant that has ever been built. With this approach we obtain the greatest economy of scale. . . . The maximum size of a plant is usually fixed by the maximum size of one or more pieces of equipment. Often this maximum size is fixed by restrictions on shipping the equipment to site. That is, only a certain size of compressor or whatever will fit on the railroad car or truck. We also consider the possibility of exceeding the maximum size of an existing plant. This approach always requires the development of new technology and this has higher risk. However, by gaining a larger economy of scale it might be possible to gain a greater share of the market and thereby justify the additional risk. However, if a project gets too large, new types of management problems might lead to significant increases in cost."[59] This scaling-up approach has dominated much of the territory for quite some time.

An industrial chemical reactor is a complex device in which heat transfer, mass transfer, diffusion, and friction may occur along with chemical reaction. In large vessels questions of mixing of the reactants, flow distribution, residue time distribution, and efficient utilization of the surface of a porous catalyst also arise. A successful chemical plant is an "economic" balance of all these factors. Optimal design requires the designer to select process alternatives that satisfy the desired factor proportions. Despite his championing the scaling-up approach just referred to, Douglas agreed that "a wide variety of problems in the design, construction and operation and analysis of chemical plants (as well as in other industrial processes) can be resolved by optimization."[60] The determination of the optimal operating conditions or design is complicated, however, because the various stages themselves are integer quantities and conditions to be set for each stage are interrelated. What is an optimal design for one set of conditions may not be optimal for another. In a chemical process plant, it is essential that according to the chemical reaction anticipated (the science of the process), the conversion process (initiation and completion of the chemical reaction needed) and the separation process (obtaining the desired product in an acceptable purity and disposing of unwanted components) are achieved in an "economic" fashion.

In the reactor stage of a process, the intention is to allow the input constituents to achieve the desired reaction with each other. As the reactor conversion desired by the designer increases, the reactor volume will necessarily have to increase; hence the reactor capital cost increases. At the same time, the amount of unconverted feed needing to be separated decreases; hence the cost of recycling unconverted feed decreases. Here substitution between material (feed) and capital is at the discretion of the designer.

Another major component of the process plant is the furnace. The higher the flame temperature, the more fuel consumption can be reduced by reducing excess air and combustion preheating. This in turn reduces heat loss through the stack. But the higher the temperature, the greater the need for special construction of the furnace walls. Too, a high furnace temperature is environmentally harmful, as this increases the formation of oxides of nitrogen. In any case there is a limit to which flue gas can be cooled without running into the problem of corrosion caused by condensation. The provision of heat recovery systems, which increases capital output, will have to be weighed against the availability of fuel materials in the economy. If fuel is abundantly available, use of large amounts of capital to recover heat lost can be avoided. Also, the design of the furnace operation (automatic, semiautomatic, or manual) will be based on availability of labor in the economy.

Separation is an important phase of all chemical engineering processes. Separators are needed because chemical species from a single stream must be sent to multiple destinations with specified concentrations. To achieve a desired allocation, one has to determine the most suitable types and sequence of separators to be used. Material endowment of the economy will have a role in this.

In the design of the distillation system, as distillation pressure is raised, separation of constituent chemicals becomes more difficult. Relative vola-tility decreases, which requires the provision of more plates (more capital) or more reflux. As the reflux ratio is increased from its minimum, the capital cost decreases initially, as the number of separation plates reduces from infinity, but then energy costs increase as more reboiling and condensation are required. Here again substitution between material and capital becomes central to the design process. As distillation pressure rises, the latent heat of vaporization decreases, so reboiler and condenser duties become lower, lowering capital cost. As distillation pressure rises, vapor density increases, giving a smaller column diameter—contrary to what would be expected on the basis of economy of scale. A smaller column diameter reduces capital cost. On the other hand, reboiling temperature can increase, but up to a limit often set by thermal decomposition of the material, which can cause its vaporization, leading to fouling. High pressure will cause the condenser temperature to rise. If, on the other hand, pressure is lowered, the reverse of all the things indicated will occur. It may, for example, be essential for reasons of factor availability to increase reflux, or because of the lack of energy resources to lower distillation pressure. The lower limit to pressure is set by the need to avoid vacuum operation or the use of refrigeration in the condenser—both incur capital and operating cost penalties and increase the complexity of a chemical process plant. The issue of substitution between factors throughout design is evident in this quote from Douglas: "We decrease losses of either materials or energy by installing additional equipment."[61]

Most process plants in the United States have a computerized control room with instruments to measure, record, and control. In the separation process, for example, it is necessary to control fluid flow so as not to permit unexpected failure to turn into fire or explosion. It is necessary to control the heat transfer process by checking the condition of the heat exchanger against designed specifications. Distillation can now be modeled and optimized with a computer so as to separate distillants and use depressants to control the volatility of any one of the components. Absorption is used to separate high boilers from gases. However, at the other extreme, many of these functions can quite easily be undertaken by labor with suitable training and established procedures, in a substitution between capital and labor; indeed, originally many of these functions were carried out by process plant personnel. It is clear that the processes described involve continuing substitution choice between labor, capital, and material.

In general, chemical process plants are divided broadly into continuous process and batch process plants, the latter regarded as best for smaller quantities and variable production rates. As in many other industries, the chemical process industry passed through a phase in which it shifted from a craft type of production (which was basically batch production) into what was called flow process (the industry's own type of mass production), with the usual claims of economy of scale. Freeman and Soete, for example, pointed out that flow process had the advantage of "preventing heat losses and in facilitating the monitoring and control of chemical reactions."[62] But the fact that nothing was done in those days to tackle the issue of heat loss and the bias that good monitoring could not be achieved with batch production was to a large extent due to the fact that people chose to turn their back on craft-style batch production as outdated. But today much has been achieved in greatly increasing the utilization of batch process plant along the lines of flexible production. In his book *Chemical Process Design*, Robin Smith identified six methods of doing this: overlapping batches strategy, parallel operation strategy, multiple operations strategy, step-by-step batch plant expansion, step-by-step decrease of batch plant size (the last two aimed at reducing dead time in the processes), and intermediate storage strategy.[63]

Each of these provides ample room for use of labor because automation aimed at integrating these activities is difficult and expensive. Where, for example, the equipment needs regular cleaning due to fouling or the need for sterilization, labor-intensive methods can have a role in suitable locations. There are now a wide range of choices in optimization design in the chemical process industry. In their book *Optimization of Chemical Processes,* Edgar and Himmelblau identified at least nineteen different optimization choices and techniques covering objectives as different as maximizing separation, minimizing capital cost, maximizing product recovery, minimum ideal work for separation, minimizing sums of squares of composition deviation from product specification, total number of theoretical stages, and maximizing separation.[64] The opportunity to select factor proportions to meet varying requirements is evident from optimization techniques. It should be clear that in this case it is not the volume of the equipment that is important (that is, the quantity of raw chemicals fed into the system) but how far the design has been optimized along all variables in achieving the objectives set out.

So far we have looked at the chemical process technology from the top down. To look at it from the bottom up, in Chapter 2 we referred to chemical technology in traditional societies, with which different kinds of dyes and alcohol-based drinks were produced. Distillation was the manufacture of intoxicating spirits under four processes: mashing the vegetable materials, cooling the works, exciting fermentation, and separating alcohol from water. The issue of mashing and mixing the chemical elements is very important. The degree to which physical (labor) input was expended to achieve more thorough mashing and mixture of the vegetable materials determined the material input per unit of final product in a labor-material substitution. The well-known *Perry's Chemical Engineers' Handbook* noted that "batches are suited to small production rates and to long reaction times or where they may have superior selectivity. . . . They are conducted in tanks with stirring of content by internal impellers, gas bubbles or pumparounds." These mechanical actions were originally manual ones. An engineer trained in the traditional chemical technology could mix and match these operations and be more flexible and resourceful in his approach to problem solving than one with only top-down experience. Most important, he is equipped to take methods from one area of industry and transfer them to other areas unrelated in terms of final product. This is a sort of diffusion of technical knowledge that is characteristic of primal societies.

The issue of optimization may also be examined from another perspective. The cement industry, for example, is generally regarded by economists as a "heavy industry"—capital-intensive and one in which economy of scale plays a pronounced role. In the past, Third World countries such as India regarded the development of heavy industries as a basic requirement of economic takeoff. Minimal optimal scale for the industry is said to have climbed from 300,000 tons per hour in the early 1950s to 50,000 tons per hour in the 1960s.

But take a look at the processes that constitute the production of cement. Calcium carbonate (from chalk or limestone) is mixed with silica (from clay or shale) into clinker. The clinker is ground, gypsum is added, and the mixture is then heated to combine into what is known as cement. The aim is to produce a consistent mixture.

The basic items of machinery now standard in the industry are crushers, grinders, and rotary kilns. But it is immediately clear that crushing, grinding, and burning are labor-intensive activities and need not be mechanized or automated. A mechanized cement plant is a high energy consumer. About 40 to 50 percent of the total cost of mechanized cement production is energy cost. Grinding equipment is an appreciable consumer of this high energy cost.

Also, the mechanical and electrical equipment needed in order to substitute for labor account for the greater part of the capital cost. The continuous rotary kiln was an attempt to break with batch production and was necessitated by the secondary effort to control loss of heat and save the labor involved in using an intermittent kiln. Kilns, grinders, crushers, magnet systems for eliminating iron, and filter systems in turn need peripheral equipment to support and drive them. At a smaller scale, the cost of this peripheral equipment can be a significant portion of the total cost of the equipment, and might be expected to increase in direct proportion with scale; but as scale increases, equipment designers can take advantage of various refinements of the basic technology (for example, changing of the shape of the rotary kiln) in order to increase the output. Beyond a certain scale, however, the cost of peripheral equipment may increase more than in proportion to the increase in kiln capacity, offsetting the savings.

The cement industry need not be capital-intensive; there is room to introduce differing factor proportions. The fact that economists have accepted a technology as given—say, in their analysis of economy of scale—has boxed them in and reduced their ability to seek generalized theories of growth.

Processing of Materials

The processing of materials is at the heart of economic production—and therefore at the heart of economic development and growth. It is the effect of the input of labor and capital in processing material that constitutes the base of development and growth. It is therefore useful to examine the nature of materials processing in the context of the theory of factor proportions so as to see whether the technology is to implement our theme of factor proportions.

The broad categories of materials processing are

casting, forming/shaping, machining, joining, finishing, and chemical. Casting involves altering a material under temperature so as to conform to a certain shape. This is achieved through an expendable or permanent mold. Forming/shaping covers the whole field of material rolling, drawing, sheet forming, and powder metallurgy. This process may or may not involve the application of heat. Machining consists of mechanical changes to a material by way of boring, drilling, planing, shaping, or grinding. Chemical and electrical or electrochemical machining and high-energy beam machining are relatively new developments in machining. Joining consisting of physically putting together two items of material by melding, soldering, diffusion, adhesive bonding, or fasteners. Finishing consists of honing, polishing, burnishing, deburring, surface treatment, coating, and plating.

It is noteworthy that every one of these seven basic materials processing techniques originated in the primal/traditional societies. What has happened over time is that knowledge and practices in each area have been refined, expanded, and deepened in order to meet new needs, reduce labor cost, increase quality, reduce material consumption, and deal with new environments. Each human generation has obviously gained from the experience of the preceding generation; overall progress in materials processing over time is usually exponential.

The lost-wax method of casting and sand casting are almost as old as man. Today lost-wax methods have developed into what is called investment casting. Well-established lost-wax processes are now used for high-quality, intricate castings in high-strength steel-, nickel-, and cobalt-base alloys and aluminum- and copper-base alloys. Complex shapes —for example, internally cooled gas turbine blades —are produced by investment casting without the need for external final machining or finishing. An accurate mold is produced by injecting wax blends into a die cavity that has been made by machining

metal or casting a low-melting-point alloy of bismuth or tin around a master pattern. Dies can also be produced using resin.

Sand casting can be used very cheaply for all kinds of metals, various sizes, and differing quantities. Sand has the ability to withstand high temperatures and to retain its shape under the action of flowing metal; it is permeable (allowing the escape of gases and vapors developed during pouring) as well as collapsible (permitting the mold to be broken up and separated from the casting). Sand casting can range from simple and cheap to complicated and costly.

In traditional societies, two iron pieces are joined by melting a portion of the iron pieces and mixing the molten iron with a filler material that forms a solid joint between them after cooling. With the advent of electricity, electric welding became common. Later developments such as metal inert gas welding and submerged arc welding are suitable for certain circumstances and materials but carry an increased capital cost. Electron beam welding is used for welding in a vacuum reactive metals such as titanium, which readily reacts with oxygen, and zirconium, which reacts with oxygen, nitrogen, and hydrogen—again resulting in increased capital cost. Spot welding has become a highly automated process for the mass assembly of automobile body components. Seam welding offers the advantage of producing a gas- and liquid-tight environment at relatively high welding speeds. Ultrasonic welding has been developed to deal with a wide range of dissimilar metals suitable for small parts, such as electrical connections including attaching of leads to transformer coils and joining miniaturized components of semiconductor materials or printed circuits. It is very useful for hermetically sealing a range of metal packaging for contents that cannot be exposed to the heat associated with other joining processes or in ambient conditions. These packaging applications are used for food preservation, protection of living tissue cultures, explosives, and propellants.

Four points need to be made from this brief review of materials processing. The first is that each of the seven materials processing techniques started as craft production. The second is that many of the developments in materials processing were driven by the need to change what was originally labor-intensive work into mechanized, automated work, the need to save material, or the need to reduce the finishing needed. It follows that there is a wide range of choice of factor proportions in material processing. The third is that to label any of these processes as inherently capital-intensive is to ignore the history and the developmental purpose behind them. The fourth is that none of the seven functions could have, even at the primal stage, been performed by man alone. They were tasks for which he needed production aids (capital) to accomplish even the most simple of the processes, in the same way as his modern counterpart needs capital for them. Each involves a three-dimensional factor input arrangement.

The emergence of an economy from primal structures necessitated the search for sources of power to supplement labor and production aids. Water mills were the most sophisticated source of mechanical power and one of the most advanced "technologies" of the eighteenth-century world.[65] Initially, then, most new economic activities developed around a source of water: streams, rivers, and canals. With the development of steam as a portable source of power, economic activities could move into a wider area and opportunities arose to do things previously impossible. It also made it easier to obtain coal, the source of heat used to provide that steam power—deep seam mining became possible with steam-powered water pumps, and steam-powered transport made it easier to transport the fuel. Steam-powered railways helped to open new internal markets. Steam-powered machinery made it possible to engage in large-scale manufacturing.

The discovery of electricity and the ability to generate large quantities of it through the use of steam marked another stage in providing transportable power. The *New York Times* in 1929 described the era of high-voltage electric transmission lines as the second industrial revolution, which had as much far-reaching consequences as the first: "Power is no longer confined. Already we are immersed in a vast unseen ocean of it that can be tapped by the farmhouse or steel mill. . . . Unlike the first industrial revolution the age of superpower, of energy shot with the speed of light into thousands of small towns and villages was foreseen. President Hoover foresaw it and welcomed it. . . . As central stations grew in size and it became possible to flash energy at more than 200,000 volts up and down the Pacific Coast, engineers began to plan the second electrical revolution—the revolution which was to free energy from time and space."[66]

The advantage of electricity over all other means of energy is its ability to travel at great speed. It is on this advantage that digital technology has been built. But even with electric transmission and distribution, electricity is still limited in that in order for it to be used, an outlet has to be available where the power is needed.

Production requires that certain designated actions be taken in prescribed sequences. Information is needed to tell the next sequence that the earlier sequence was completed and that it is now its turn. In a labor-intensive production, humans carried out these information transfers, often according to rules or maps.[67] At other times the information transfer is carried out through machines that operate in preset sequences.

In the field of production, we are constantly dealing with quantities—measuring, monitoring, recording, observing, manipulating. These quantities constitute information, which provides the producer with better insight into the production process. Production has always required a lot of communication to describe what goes on and how to make the product. Communication also constitutes the tools with which production can be controlled. Information is therefore a vital tool with which factor proportions can be controlled. From early times production has been information-intensive, and information management has been at the center of production.

Digital technology has radically affected information management, and certainly one can say that the birth of digital technology was accelerated by the information bottleneck facing production following the collapse of the Fordist production paradigm. Specifically, Turing and von Neumann stand out as the principal early architects of the new information age. Information's power, the two men stressed, derives from yoking logical operations to electronic circuitry.[68] Digital technology is not new as is generally thought, but it remained unutilized for nearly a hundred years until the arrival of electronics.

As information management in production moved away from being labor-intensive, it shifted into an analog regime. But there are a number of limitations. For example, analog machinery cannot easily simulate production functions, and so devising the required controls and process manipulation was often difficult. Analog machines also suffer from a certain amount of noise—influences that disturb the machine's attempt to provide a shadow image of the quantities being monitored. Too, analog equipment cannot store information. Another issue is that the machines used in analog control of production information may be mechanical, hydraulic, pneumatic, or electromagnetic, and so their efficacy is affected by numerous factors affecting all material, such as friction, inertia, and so on. The devices are also relatively slow—electromechanical equipment, for example, works by creating a magnetic field that mechanically operates a control device, but the buildup of the required magnetic field is not instantaneous. Analog machines consume a lot of energy and are relatively heavy and bulky. Finally, analog management of production information is not sophisticated and versatile enough to enable the process designer to fully understand the inner workings of processes, meaning that designers must often solve process design problems by employing additional capital equipment.

These problems did not matter a lot if production was in fixed regimes such as the Fordist mode. But as flexible production came into vogue, the need for faster and more reliable information management became urgent. This need was met with the development of digital information management. The electrons used to transmit information are so tiny that there is virtually no friction or inertia to impede them. For all practical purposes, their movement is nearly instantaneous.[69] The digital regime also increased the accuracy and precision achievable in production information management. And rapid progress in miniaturization and chip design has led to remarkable increases in computing power.

The effects of these developments on production were equally remarkable. Digital technology has replaced hydraulic, pneumatic, mechanical, and electromechanical features in a wide range of established production systems, drastically reducing not only capital but also material inputs. For example, Boeing's 777 aircraft eliminated many heavy cables linking mechanical systems. And, as Greenspan acknowledged, new chips require much less material than earlier control systems with their extensive reliance on copper wires.[70] As the size of chips gets smaller and output increases, designers may push for increasing automation of the operations. But the nature of the chip involves assembly. Assembly provides opportunity for increased labor input rather than mechanical or automated assembly. The production of chips is therefore capable of allowing a combination of less capital, less material, and more labor input.

The reduction of the relative input contribution of material in the U.S. economy is coming not from digital technology alone but also from other fields. Metallurgy has given mankind new materials that combine different desirable characteristics in unique combinations. Composite materials have reduced the weight of jet aircraft and other items. Lasers and fiber optics have caused a reduction in physical weight in many areas.

Despite these changes, economists have been unable to accord material a place alongside capital and labor in economic analysis. Samuelson and Nordhaus ascribed the changes to capital and labor: "Miniaturization and laser-etching allows, for the same input of capital and labor, 100 times more information to be stored in computer memories compared to two decades ago."[71] And although Greenspan acknowledged that new chips displaced a huge tonnage of copper, he too did not intend to acknowledge the role of material: "Since the dawn of the industrial revolution, there has been an inexorable drive to leverage physical brawn and material resources into ever-greater value added or output. . . . Almost all the rise in value added relative to physical input has reflected the substitution of ideas—new insights—for brute human effort and material bulk. . . . By far the largest contributor to growth of our price-adjusted GDP or value added has been ideas—insights that levered physical reality."[72] It is not clear how substitution of ideas (new insights) could have caused changes in material input, unless *ideas* and *insights* refer to science and technology. But in the science of factor proportions, reduction in material input as an end in itself is not correct, because to reduce material input you have to substitute it with something else. We know that physical brawn was replaced in the United States by substituting capital for labor. But the impression given, that physical brawn is outdated and undesirable in production, is not an example of thinking in the economic-science mode.

The substitution of capital for labor and material reached its peak in the 1980s, and since then it can be said that the role of capital has decreased in the U.S. economy.[73] Indeed, Greenspan observed that "the newer technologies are spreading to firms not conventionally thought of as high-tech."[74] The reason should be self-evident from our analysis of the way information management in production is changing because of digitization. Instead of the fuzzy way in which Greenspan tried to explain the change in material input, the analytical vista would have been opened up much more widely if a three-dimensional factor analysis had been substituted for the traditional two-factor (capital, labor) analysis, ridding economics of the idea of technology as a black box.

The new directions in production techniques, especially in the United States, reflect a leveling process in which capital intensiveness is shrinking at the upper end and increasing at the lower end. This process has been well served by development in microelectronics technology. Further, its effect on the U.S. economy has been positive, as it pushes the economy into a more balanced state, as we will be examining in more detail in Chapter 9. It is clear from these discussions, however, that the technology of material provides a rich area for choice and substitution of factors of production.

In principle, modular and flexible manufacturing has reduced entry costs into mass-market business. Mass customization has reasserted itself, thanks to the use of microelectronics. With computer-controlled production, for example, Nippon Denso, Japan's leading car-component manufacturer, can make radiators to fit any car in the world. Contract manufacturing is less a question of cutting costs than of the ability to get products to the market as the market demands them, which depends on the ability to effect design changes quickly.

As another example, consider the compact disc (CD). With its miniaturized laser and special microchips, a CD player has very few moving parts. Overnight all the skills painstakingly acquired by the big names in the record-player industry counted for nothing. Any backstreet firm, with little audio experience and still less engineering savvy, could buy the parts and plug them together to build a CD player that makes the traditional hi-fi sound like a scratchy echo.

Much contract manufacturing and final assembly have been automated because of their need to maintain high output volume. *The Economist* commented that contract manufacturing has grown thanks to "improvements on the shop floor" whereby "high-tech gear is no longer put together in a low-tech way by hordes of young women wielding soldering irons." The workers "could not pack electronic components densely enough for today's small mobile phones or video cameras," and most of the firms "now use surface-mount technology—robots that place the components directly on the circuit board without wiring and soldering." The noticeable prejudice against labor-intensive activities here is clear, and it is shared today by many technical designers and conventional economists with a Western orientation. This bias contaminates their technical and economic theorizing. This prejudice has unfortunately been passed on to technical designers and economists in the underdeveloped countries. But it is not shared in Japan—in 1999, the Japanese Labor Ministry designated 397 workers in the auto and electronics industries as "supertechnicians," recognizing some of the uncanny human skills that developed on its factory floor as Japan rose to become a great industrial nation. Bill Spindle of the *Wall Street Journal* described it as follows: "Rocking slowly back and forth, he [the "supertechnician"] shaves off long curlicues of hot metal that settle off, hissing and smoking around his black boots. When he finishes the hours-long process, the shaft will fit so snugly within its casing that pulling the two apart produces a satisfactory 'pop' of pressurized air. . . . Need a perfect photocopier lens, scratch-free down to a hundred-thousandth of a millimeter? How about a semiconductor chip so smooth that a speck of dust on it would loom like a mountain? Or a drill bit capable of boring 3000 holes through a fingernail-size flake of plastic?" Bill Spindle also wrote about the special skills of several workers, including Chizuru Hisatomi of the Mitsubishi Electric Corporation, Tatsunobu Tanaga of Matsushita Electric Industrial, and Teruo Noda and Yoshio Tamagawa at Ricoh. Hisatomi "smears diamond dust on a semiconductor die, then polishes its surface with a whittled chopstick—an innovation he and his coworkers cooked up—until flaws invisible to the naked eye are buffed away. A few years back, Mitsubishi Electric tried replacing him with a machine. No luck." Tanaga "fashions drill bits capable of punching 3,000 holes through a piece of plastic half the size of a postage stamp. He does the drilling himself, and then dabs each hole with a speck of solder the size of the head of a pin, so that electronic parts such as integrated circuits can be attached." And "robots are no match" for Noda and Tamagawa, who produce dies for photocopier lenses that are so smooth, "the lenses are nearly scratch-free; any flaws can be seen only with an electron microscope."[75]

This account illustrates the analytical mistakes that conventional economists make. In current production practice in the United States, the activities of the Japanese technicians would be automated. It is therefore to be expected that an economist in the United States would conclude, wrongly, that the capital investment for this automation was a necessary condition for achieving the technical innovation in the processes described. Such an economist has failed to separate the science of a process (its technology) from the choice of factors required to achieve that process. We also see that labor-intensive activities do not mean less technical content.

Virtual Reality

As a product of digital technology, virtual reality has caused dramatic changes in manufacturing. A computer-generated simulation of a three-dimensional environment provides the designer powerful tools with which to understand a process better. Two examples will suffice. Up till recently, chemical process designers had a limited ability to play out the different scenarios needed in order to obtain a deeper insight into the processes involved. But with digital technology, it is possible to "view" the results of simulated changes in different parameters; this has meant that instead of solving one problem at a time, which sometimes creates another problem elsewhere, holistic solutions can be adopted. This can only help in reducing capital costs. More important, it provides the best tool for optimization studies meant to allow designers to select factor proportions best suited to their needs.

The mundane action of grinding is another example of the use of virtual reality in manufacturing. Nobody really understands fully all the intricate physical actions that take place when an operator performs the simple task of grinding a component. The operator is trying to control motion along three axes as material is being ground away. The process in turn produces internal stresses and heat in the part, wheel, and table. The temperatures and stresses can be computed and selectively displayed as the simulation unfolds. We are therefore in a better position to understand labor-material substitution better—what in conventional economics is called "saving material." The opportunities for applying virtual reality in a wide range of production activities are immense, as they lead to a better understanding of the natural forces one is dealing with, widening the practice and knowledge of factor substitution.

It is true that microelectronics have reduced capital requirements. They have also, as we have already discussed, reduced material requirements. A

lot of things have been said in the resultant euphoria. In the apt words of Mitchell in his recent book *E-topia*, "Information has become dematerialized and disembodied." He, however, ended up with some far-reaching generalizations about digital technology: "The dumb machines of the industrial era gave us economies of standardization, repetition and mass production but the smart machines of the computer era can now provide us with different economies of intelligent adaptation and automated personalization. We can play silica and software on a vast scale to enable automatic custom delivery of just what is required in particular context and no more. . . . Today . . . information era projects . . . have begun to demonstrate a radical new resolution of the problem; they exploit the capabilities of a computer-controlled production machine to create compositions of non-standardized, non-repeating elements that respond precisely to their particular functions and contexts."[76]

Here Mitchell has made some unrealistic claims. First, it is not the "dumb" machines that gave us the economies of standardization, repetition and mass production. It is men (businessmen and academics, supported by public policy) of the era who created the "dumb" machines.[77] The smart machines of the computer era are created by men of the present era. In effect, it is for man at each turn to select the techniques he thinks fits his problems. If man is wrong—and Mitchell seems to be implying (perhaps correctly) that those who chose economics of standardization, repetition, and mass production were wrong—he has only himself to blame. The essence of a science of economic development and growth is to help elucidate the choices. Mitchell is also wrong to give the impression that the industrial era belongs to the past, now apparently replaced by a computer era. The computer is a child of industry and part and parcel of industrial production. The parents are the mistakes and triumphs of the past. Production throughout the ages has always been information-intensive. What is changing is the way this information is manipulated and managed. Attempts to make it that information has taken over from production are now common and tend to be aimed at sensationalizing the issues. Information without actual production is futility.

In the recent book *Building Wealth,* Thurow claimed, "The heart of the problem is that growth lies not in how much new plant and equipment an economy adds or even workers but in the knowledge embodied in it. . . . In the past, when capitalists talk about their wealth, they were talking about their ownership of plant and equipment and natural resources. In the future they will be talking of their control of knowledge. . . . More information is now more important than new materials, new biological entities or new robots in building this new knowledge-based economy."[78] These comments show a failure to realize that from early times production had always been information-intensive. Thurow in his efforts to show how things have changed because of "the information age" stated that unlike in the past, when plant and machinery and labor were all-important, everything in economic life except knowledge is subject to the laws of diminishing returns. But this has always been the case. In a book about the supposed overtaking of manufacturing by the information economy, Fingleton said that the United States was heading toward a competitive crisis caused by its "faddish" choice of unsustainable postindustrial activities—finance, computer software, and information.[79] There is in all this a nonrecognition of one fact: that the information age is the result of and depends on production. The physical components of the Internet and devices to access it are manufactured by the relevant combination of labor, material, and capital. So plant, machinery, material, and labor are as important as ever. Thurow's comments amount to saying that what matters is the skill of a pilot, but the skill will come to naught if no airplanes are manufactured.

Perhaps the most worrying aspects of Mitchell's observation is the impression he created that computer-controlled systems are the answer for everybody anywhere. They are not. Digital technology has brought vast changes in factor proportions. It is clear that in some economies the effect of such changes may be growth-inducing. It is also possible that in other economies digital technology can be growth-retarding if it leads to structural imbalances.

India, as an illustration of the point just made, has made tremendous strides in software technology and has been selling its wares in the global marketplace and creating wealth at an astonishing rate. But a *New York Times* article reported, "At a time when India's software industry is creating glamorous digerati and driving a dizzy escalation in stock values on the Bombay exchange, the boom has stirred a debate about the counting social and economic priorities." Some people worry that "the boom may be distracting the country from its chronic problems and fear that the last decade's more rapid economic growth—spawned by India's loosening of restrictions on trade and investment—is leaving the poor and poorer states further behind." Said Indian president Narayanan, "We have one of the world's largest reservoirs of technical personnel but also the largest number of illiterates, the world's largest middle class but also the largest people below the poverty line. . . . Our giant factories rise out of squalor. Our satellites shoot up from the midst of hovels of the poor." The article concluded that most economists in India believe that the country needed to attend to the "fundamentals."[80] To a democratic country that since its independence has sought to be at the front of modern technology, with its steel plants, cement factories, satellites, software technology, and one of the largest collections of scientists in the world, rapid economic growth is still not within its grasp. Despite its large population, India is well endowed with natural resources on a per capita basis. Its problem is not to economize on materials. It needs to mobilize all its resources with appropriate factor proportions.

A lot of nonsense has been written in regard to the relevance of digital systems in poor countries. Bill Gates thought that information technology will enable such countries to achieve lower costs. "Less developed countries," he noted, "may assume that a digital approach to government is out of reach, but countries without systems can start fresh with new technology, which is less expensive than manual approaches."[81] Freeman and Soete claimed that "microelectronics in so far as it is characterized by a radically different resource saving potential might be more 'approximate' in its application as well as production to the situation of a large number of semi- or newly industrializing countries . . . the locational advantages of these countries could be higher than with regard to many previous technologies. In particular, the capital-saving potential of information technology seems to be of relevance to countries where growth has been hampered by general capital shortage." They saw microelectronics as providing the potential for poor countries to catch up with richer countries, arguing that the "de-skilling" effects of microelectronics might be particularly relevant in regard to a wide variety of highly specialized technical skills that "form at this moment probably the most specific human capital bottleneck in most semi- or newly industrialized countries." They concluded that "the 'wrong' skills and 'irrelevant' experience could well amount to a more significant bottleneck and diffusion reduction factor in the advanced countries than in many industrializing countries."[82]

There are a number of misleading elements in the views of Gates and of Freeman and Soete—which, incidentally, are widely representative. First, the science of economic development is not about finding cheaper alternatives to a country's own resources. It is about using all of one's own resources.

This leads us to a fact of current economic development wisdom that simplistically regards the problem of poor countries—following the reflection of positivist orthodoxy—as that of reducing capital requirements, as Freeman and Soete think. It is therefore said that what these countries need are low-capital activities. Going by the way we have defined capital in the scientific sense in this book as the combination of available material and labor, it cannot be said that a poor country necessarily needs low-capital activities. It is the endowed factor proportions—in particular, the L/M ratio—that will determine capital needs.

To summarize this chapter with a number of concluding points: As we have seen in this chapter, particularly with Piore and Sabel, the postwar history of technology (the science of factor proportions—production) is marked by the unjustified adoption by the United States of the mass production paradigm. It led to economic growth, but it was not sustainable growth. The slowdown of the 1970s and what economists claim to be the sharp loss in productivity of that era are traceable to an untenable (nation-supported) production regime. That regime was based on fixed or near-fixed factor proportions. Nearly fifty years on, the United States has retracted its steps somewhat. U.S. industry leaders are today falling over each other to show who is best in lean strategies.

This chapter has shown that technology (science of factor proportions) is immediately available to meet any factor proportions. It means that the theory of factor proportions is a new but practical way to immediately move self-sustaining economic development and growth forward everywhere.

5

International Trade Versus Economic Development and Growth

This chapter examines the contribution, if any, international trade can make to economic development and growth.

Trade: Comparative Advantage

Most economists support trade and regard it as an important vehicle for economic development and growth. In general, trade is supposed to allow each country to specialize in those things it does best and let others provide it with those things in which it is not best.

In order for trade to pass the test as a vehicle of economic development and growth, it is necessary that the definition of "best" and the criteria for selecting those things a country does best have valid scientific credentials and that when countries trade on this basis they do in fact witness growth.

The essential concept that has dominated economic history in this analysis is that of comparative advantage. Krugman and Obstfeld quoted Samuelson as having described comparative advantage as the best example known of an economic principle that is "undeniably true."[1] A country is said to have a comparative advantage in producing a good if the opportunity cost of producing that good in terms of other goods is lower in that country than it is in other countries. David Ricardo's idea of comparative advantage was based on international differences in productivity of labor. So a country was best at producing a good if the labor needed to produce it there was less than anywhere

else. Because any economy has limited resources, it is argued that there are limits on what it can produce. The total labor in the economy is said to set the limits of production. In the Ricardian model, it is claimed that a country will, in a trade-off, produce those things in which the prices are equal to their opportunity cost and the relative prices of goods are equal to their relative labor requirements.

There are already problems here. Ricardo did not concern himself with how the goods he was talking about are made. Each of them requires a certain combination of capital, material, and labor to produce. It is obvious that for the unit of goods he has in mind, the one in which the labor proportion is least, will be said to have been produced with less labor and so come out on top in terms of Ricardo's comparative advantage. It seems that the Ricardian model is biased toward techniques requiring low labor input techniques. As we have already shown, however, a country's growth potential is maximized when the factor proportions of all activities are equal to the economy's factor endowments, and what is required is equal factor proportions for all activities. Whereas in the Ricardian model, which assumes an economy is unbalanced, labor supply is said to place a limit on the economy's production, in the new economy we have in mind, labor does not set a limit because the factor proportions, from which production techniques are determined, are based on the economy's supply of labor.

Each economy should have a basic personality

of its own, with its growth taking root in this personality. This brings up another issue on which the Ricardian model (like other trade models we will talk about later) is wrong. It is a static model, and no economy is static. If an economy is growing in the new context, its factor proportions are changing all the time. It is therefore wrong to slot a country's production pattern into boxes.

Samuelson and Nordhaus illustrated the law of comparative advantage by reference to the lawyer who is contemplating whether to hire a typist for the law office or do the typing himself. The question whether or not to hire a typist rested on the law of comparative advantage, and according to Samuelson and Nordhaus, it is apparent that the income the lawyer will forgo by spending the time to do his own typing rather than his legal work is greater than the cost of paying for the typing services. The lawyer makes more money by specializing in the production of legal services, "exporting" these services to others and "importing" typing services. This "free trade" arrangement pays the lawyer and pays the typist. If we assume that the lawyer is absolutely more efficient at typing than the typist (that is, he has an absolute advantage), this still does not mean the lawyer should in fact do the typing. It should be left to the less efficient partner, and this ensures a market for the typist's services. The typist willingly provides this service; specializing in typing, because alternative uses of the lawyer's time have less economic value both to the society and to the typist.

This simple example brings the basic issues home. It is true that both the typist and the lawyer have income and that their new combined income following the hiring of the typist is higher than before (analogous to the growth that results from trade). But the arrangement is that the lawyer will remain a lawyer and the typist will remain a typist. This is a static arrangement. In a dynamic setting—assuming there was only one lawyer and one typist to the arrangement—if the lawyer knew that the

typist might one day become a lawyer too, or change careers and take another job as an accountant, it may have suited the lawyer to keep his typing skills from getting rusty by doing some of the work, or to learn word processing on his computer.

The issue was dealt with by Krauss in his forthright book *How Nations Grow Rich: The Case for Free Trade* when he declared that there is a fundamental misunderstanding about the nature of the gains from trade. He pointed out that "free trade does not create jobs—it creates income by reallocating or transferring jobs from lower-productivity to higher-productivity sectors of the economy. The argument for free trade—at least in the standard theory—is an efficient allocation of resources argument. Such an allocation increases income by increasing the average productivity of the nation's stock of productivity resources." He adds a caveat: "Claims that free trade can make both trading partners better off are not the same as claims that free trade can equalize the standard of living in both partner countries."[2]

It is clear that if the poorer trading partner wishes to move in the direction of equalizing its standard of living (growth potential) with that of the more affluent partner, it cannot achieve this from free trade. Another way to put it is that free trade changes the microstructure of economies but not necessarily in the direction of macroeconomic growth.

Samuelson and Nordhaus summarized what they considered as the economic gains for trade as follows: "When trade has opened up, and when each country concentrates on its area of comparative advantage, everyone is better off." They define "better off" as a situation where "workers in each region obtain a larger quantity of consumer goods for the same amount of work when people specialize in the areas of comparative advantage and trade their own production for goods in which they have relative disadvantage. When borders are opened to international trade, the national income of each and every trading country rises."[3] Seen in the context of the issues raised, it can be seen that the root to economic growth of poor countries does not lie in international trade.

Economists have analyzed international trade in terms of a two-factor economy, rather than Ricardo's one-factor economy, because Ricardo's model fails to capture the changes trade can make in income distribution. Bowen, Hollander, and Viaene have indicated that "overall, the Ricardian model seems to raise more questions about the sources of comparative advantage than it answers" and that it "provides no guide as to how labor productivity and comparative advantage can be expected to evolve since it gives no explanation of differences in labor productivities across countries."[4] More serious is a point we had made in earlier chapters that labor productivity is not a suitable economic index when countries differ widely in their factor proportions.

In what is called the specific factors model, the assumption is that an economy produces two goods and that we can allocate labor supply between the two sectors. Unlike the Ricardian model, this model provides for the existence of factors besides labor, but whereas labor is said to be a mobile factor, the other factors are said to be specific.[5] The model analyzes an economy that can produce two goods—manufactures and food. Manufactures are said to be produced using labor and capital, and food is said to be produced using land and labor. A specific factor is defined as only being capable of producing particular goods.

There are immediate analytical problems with this model. Manufactures cannot be produced only with labor and capital, as the model assumed; material is an essential input. It is also not possible to produce food without capital (tools, implements, and—in more capital-intensive food production—agricultural machinery), and land is not a factor input.

Krugman and Obstfeld argued that "when economists apply the specific factors model to economies

like that of the United States or France, they think of factor specificity not as a permanent condition but as a matter of time. . . . In practice, the distinction between specific and mobile factors is not a sharp line. It is a question of the speed of adjustment."[6] But matters are not as simple as that. When one talks of capital as specific and able to produce only particular goods, one is talking about equipment. But equipment is not capital in a macroeconomic context. Capital in a macroeconomic context is not specific. Capital, as we have seen in Chapter 3, is the total accumulated labor and material input factors drawn out in the economy to create production aids. It is therefore clear that the specific factors model, in which it is assumed that a country has only two sectors, one sector producing manufactured goods with specific capital and the other with a specific factor (land) with labor being mobile, has no relevance in the quest for a viable theory of development and growth.

Despite the irrelevance of the specific factors model, international trade theory moved on to apply the results of its analysis in a one-country context to trade between different countries. It started with what was essentially a microeconomic analysis and then transferred the result to the macroeconomic perspective. As if that was not bad enough, it sought to claim that the results apply not just to two countries but to all countries. Here is a case of making analytical assumptions so as to suit the conclusion one wants to reach. The model therefore is not scientific, and is untenable and misleading.

The economists Lipsey and Chrystal gave the name "fixed production" to a situation in which the production function of a country is said to be fixed. They argue that with a fixed production function, there are gains to trade because the country can still decide to export some of its limited production in exchange for imports from the other country. The concept of fixed production is vague and self-serving. In the authors' words, the gains from trade under this condition arise because "consumers are no longer limited by their country's production possibilities. . . . They have achieved a gain from trade by being allowed to exchange some of their production of good Y for some quantity of good X and consume more of good X than is produced at home."[7] It is all about increased choice and consumption. We are in the area labeled "welfare economics." The theory assumed quite wrongly that increased consumption means increased income as well as sustainable increased economic development and growth.

The analytical problem facing Krugman and Obstfeld on their specific factors model showed up when they sought to transfer their data from a single economy to trade between two countries. In the case of the specific factors model, they said that "for trade to take place, the two countries must differ in the relative price of manufactures that would prevail in the absence of trade."[8] They ignored their earlier criterion that trade arises from differences in factors and appear to have abandoned their contention that output of manufactures will increase as labor is transferred from the food production sector, now saying that the only way to increase manufactures is if the relative price of manufactures increases. Hence, for trade in manufactures to take place between their two chosen countries, they maintain that the relative price of their manufactures must be different. Krugman and Obstfeld therefore needed to focus on the differences in the relative supply due to the difference in relative price of their manufactures. It is the change in relative prices, they maintain, that will make investment in one sector more attractive than the other and (in case of increase in price of manufactures) result in an increase in the capital supply to manufactures and draw in more labor to increase the supply of manufactures. They concluded that from their specific factors analysis, "Trade benefits the factor that is specific to the export sector of each country but hurts the factor spe-

cific to the import-competing section with ambiguous effects on mobile factors."[9] They were aware that if their specific factors model for one country was transferred to two countries, one with specific capital in manufacture and the other with specific land in food, the one with specific capital cannot increase its production of manufactures by drawing labor from food production in order to supply the country with specific land food with manufactures.

The difficulties facing economists undertaking a theoretical analysis of international trade should by now be apparent. Analysis of an economy using a one- or two-factor model fails substantially to reflect reality. After their effort with a one- and two-factor analysis in Chapters 2 and 3 of their book *International Economics: Theory and Policy*, Krugman and Obstfeld stated in Chapter 4 that "in the real world, however, while trade is partly explained by differences in labor productivity, it also reflects differences in countries' resources. . . . A realistic view of trade must allow for the importance not just of labor, but of other factors of production—land, capital and mineral resources."[10] They therefore devoted Chapter 4 to an explanation of what they called "the role of resource differences in trade." They indicated that they needed to consider a model "in which resource differences are the only source of trade" to show that comparative advantage is influenced by "the interaction between nations' resources (the relative abundance of factors of production) and the technology of production (which influences the relative intensity with which different factors of production are used in the production of different goods)."[11] On a similar note, Lipsey and Chrystal saw the "differences among regions of the world in climate and resource endowment as leading to advantages in producing certain goods and disadvantages in producing others."[12]

Despite Krugman and Obstfeld's reference to "many" factor inputs, in Chapter 4 of their book they proceeded to adopt only a two-factor analysis, the sole change being that the resources were not now specific. They decided to move away from considering financial costs as the key criterion. The new criterion is the factor inputs required to produce a given quantity of goods. They emphasized that in this revised two-factor model, "there may be some room for choice in the use of inputs." In each sector, they said, "producers will face not fixed input requirements but tradeoffs . . . which show alternative input conditions."[13] Curiously, the two factors they selected for their model were land and labor. They claimed that acres of land and hours of labor are inputs used to produce cloth as well as food. The use of land as a factor input in producing cloth seems strange. We find it difficult to see how land and labor are substitutes in a technological sense. Producing cloth is not farming. The farmer produces cotton, not cloth. Though Krugman and Obstfeld said, "A farmer . . . may be able to grow more food per acre if he or she is willing to use more labor input to prepare the soil, weed and so on." The farmer, they maintain, may be able to choose to use less land and more labor per unit of output. The authors sought by this example to illustrate what they called "trade-offs" that the farmer can utilize between labor and land.

Despite these preliminary weaknesses in the model, arising from the strange use of land as a factor, we need to carry out a more detailed analysis of it. The two-factor analysis using land and labor assumed that a_{TC} = acres of land used to produce one yard of cloth; a_{LC} = hours of labor used to produce one yard of cloth; a_{TF} = acres of land used to produce one calorie of food; a_{LF} = hours of labor used to produce one calorie of food; L = economy's supply of labor; T = economy's supply of land.

It was emphasized that the definitions speak of the quantity of land and labor used to provide a given amount of food or cloth, not the costs of producing that amount. This is important, as we had already

pointed out, because the model avoids the conventional criterion that the producer chooses and substitutes factors in order to minimize the cost of production and maximize profit.

Next the authors assumed that input decisions depend on the relative cost of land and labor. They had earlier explained that in the model producers will not face fixed input requirements but will exercise trade-offs in the face of alternative input conditions. But then they were faced with the problem of how to determine the relative contribution of the two inputs into production.

To solve this problem, they claimed that the relative price of the factors has a one-to-one relationship with the relative price of the goods produced, which they say is equal to the relative cost of producing them. So while the model started off identifying the amount required to produce as their criterion, the price of the product (surprisingly) came back into the center of the analysis. The price of the products, it is clear, is dependent on many factors, some of which have nothing to do with production.

As another major assumption, the model sought to classify cloth production as labor-intensive and food production as land-intensive. The authors had forgotten the initial stipulation that inputs were not to be decided on basis of price of factors and that producers are not to be faced with fixed input requirements but have ample trade-off opportunities. The authors had thus discounted the real possibility that in their financial analysis wage rates can be so high that cloth production can equally be land-intensive and that land rents can be so high that food production can be labor-intensive. They argued that the actual land/labor ratio used in the economy is directly proportional to the wage/rent ratio but that the actual land/labor ratio at each wage/rental ratio is different for cloth and food simply because the authors had preordained that cloth production is labor-intensive and food production land-intensive.

In other words, the actual land/labor ratio for cloth-ing is smaller than the land/labor ratio for farming. They then sought to argue that an increase in the supply of land in the economy will expand produc-tion possibilities disproportionately in the direction of food production while an increase in the supply of labor expands them disproportionately in the di-rection of cloth production. But the issue is not one of what happens if the supply of land and labor in the economy is increased; rather, what is of imme-diate concern is how the existing factors of land and labor are used.

The scenario played out is shown in Figure 5.1 The axes measure the economy's total supplies of labor and land. Inputs into cloth production are measured from the lower left corner and those for food production from the upper right corner. The slope of the line O_cC, which is supposed to repre-sent the cloth industry's use of resources, was pre-ordained because the authors said that cloth production is labor-intensive. The slope of O_FF is also preordained because the authors said that food production is land-intensive. The allocation of land and labor in the economy is said to be determined.

In trying to move the analysis into its interna-tional trade context, the authors were forced into more assumptions, including that the two countries, Home and Foreign, are "similar along many dimen-sions." The countries have "the same tastes and therefore the same relative demand for food and cloth when faced with the same relative price of two goods." These are very serious assumptions in a work attempting a general theory of trade involv-ing countries with very different social, political, and cultural conditions. Their third assumption is even more significant: that Home and Foreign have the same technology—that is, a given amount of land and labor yields the same output of either cloth or food in the two countries. The only difference between them, they say, is in their resources. They argue that since Home has a higher ratio of land to

Figure 5.1 **Krugman and Obstfeld's two-sector allocation.**

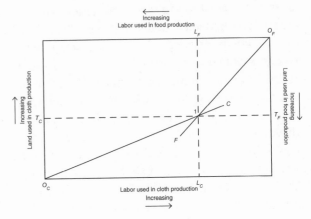

Source: P. Krugman and M. Obstfeld, *International Eco-nomics: Theory and Policy*, 4th ed. (Reading, MA: Addison-Wesley, 1997), fig. 4.5.

labor than Foreign, Home's production frontier rela-tive to Foreign should be shifted "more in the di-rection of cloth than in the direction of food." Home is supposed to produce a higher ratio of cloth to food. They conclude that "countries tend to export goods whose production is intensive in factors with which they are abundantly endowed."[14] They say this because they believe that a country's compara-tive trade advantage is in factors they have in rela-tive abundance. But this ignores the serious structural economic imbalance created when fac-tors are drawn further away from some sectors to those already well endowed.

Krugman and Obstfeld were well aware of some of the serious limitations of their trade analysis.[15] First, they agreed that factor price equalization be-tween trading countries—which is a central base for their claims of mutual benefits arising from trade—will often not work out. They acknowledged that factor price equalization occurs only if the countries involved are sufficiently similar in their factor endowments, but that factor endowments are indeed very different. They said, for example, that "a country with a superior technology might have a higher wage and a higher rental rate than a country with inferior technology,"[16] and pointed out that "recent work suggests that it is essential to allow for differences in technology to reconcile the factor proportions model." They were in fact hinting at the basic theme of science of economic development and growth. They finally admitted, "In the real world, prices of goods are not fully equalized by international trade."[17] So it seems that one of the main gains claimed from international trade cannot be substantiated.

The Heckscher-Ohlin theory is the closest attempt at invoking a three-factor model. The theory, by Swedish economists Eli Heckscher and Bertil Ohlin (later refuted by Paul Samuelson), is based on the concept of comparative cost and states that competitive trade position depends on supply conditions (proportions of factors) in different countries. Unfortunately, Heckscher and Ohlin were not clear what the factor delineations were. They referred to the factor supplies as mainly land, labor, and capital. The theory attempted to describe analytically the impact of economic growth on trade patterns and the impact of trade on the structure of national economies and on the differential returns and payments to various factors of production.

The theory is a bold one. It is a major departure from the current thinking that it is the price of factors that determines their combination. However, it suffers from defects in its main assumptions, which it shares with the two-factor analysis just reviewed. First, it ignores material as a major factor input and wrongly calls land a factor input. Second, it assumes that products are either labor-intensive or capital-intensive. Third, it assumes that countries have the same technologies. Given different countries' factor supplies, relative factor prices will differ (e.g., labor will be relatively cheap in labor-abundant countries), and so will domestic commodity price ratios

and factor combinations. Countries with cheap labor will have a relative cost and price advantage over those with relatively expensive labor in commodities that make abundant use of labor. This reveals the fourth weakness, which is that what matters in the theory is the price of the factor (whereas we hold that factor proportions are determined by the relative macro factor endowments, and so the price of the factor is not relevant—a country may well be relatively well endowed with labor and yet the price of its labor may be high). Fifth, it restricted its ideas on factor proportions to international trade.

Many tests of the Heckscher-Ohlin model have been carried out over time. In what has been called the Leontief paradox, U.S. exports were found to be less capital-intensive than U.S. imports. Table 5.1 is a summary of the factor content of U.S. exports and imports for 1962. Here again, despite evidence that U.S. exports were more labor-intensive than the imports, utilized more skilled labor, and had more engineering content, the lower capital/labor ratio of the exports continued to baffle many. According to Krugman and Obstfeld, the Leontief paradox "is the single biggest piece of evidence against the factor proportions theory."[18] They were wrong in determining the relative contribution of factors only in a two-factor context of capital and labor. In assessing the true contribution of each factor, assessment only in financial terms throws in serious distortions. For example, the relative material input will be greatly diminished if material prices are low. Valuation of capital in financial terms distorts the true contents of the capital assets, and labor can be assessed in financial terms in any number of ways. The proportion of inputs of capital and labor per unit output is dependent on the proportion of material in the unit of input.

It is not often realized that much of the United States' economic history in the late nineteenth century and a good part of the twentieth century was what Abramovitz and David described as "natural

Table 5.1

Factor Content of U.S. Exports and Imports for 1962

	Imports	Exports
Capital per million dollars	$2,132,200	$1,876,000
Labor (person-years) per million dollars	119	131
Capital-labor ratio (dollars per worker)	17,916	14,321
Average years of education per worker	9.9	10.1
Proportion of engineers and scientists in workforce	0.0189	0.0255

Source: Robert Baldwin, "Determinants of the Commodity Structure of US Trade," *American Economic Review* 61 (March 1971): 126–45.

resource-intensive, tangible-capital using and scale dependent in its elaboration of mass production and high throughput technology."[19] Brindle stated that the thrust of early American technology "was far more often directed towards substituting abundant resources for both scarce capital and scarce labor."[20] This picture of material abundance only started changing in the middle half of the twentieth century. Abramovitz and David called it "a resource-intensive technology." In a comprehensive study of U.S. postwar competitive advantage, Porter remarked that "the economic strength of the United States after the war was unique in modern times. . . . The United States enjoyed a unique combination of circumstances that spawned and sustained internationally competitive industry. . . . The explanations for America's success begin with factor conditions. The United States has been well endowed with natural factors, among them an exceptionally large supply of arable land, abundant forests and indigenous deposits of many resources such as phosphate, copper, iron, ore, coal, oil and natural gas." He stated that "America stands alone among nations, with the possible exception of Sweden, in possessing abundant national resources."[21]

Porter listed the top fifty American industries according to their achieved percentage of total world trade in 1971. These fifty industries were where the United States had "the most commanding interna-

tional position and accordingly an unusually strong international competitive edge." Of these fifty, the following achieved more than 50 percent of total world trade in their industry: soybeans (97.4 percent), natural phosphate (93.3), coloring compounds (81.9), aircraft (77.5), radioactive elements (76.6), rough-sawn veneer conifer logs (75.5), office machine parts (55.9), coal (53.4), and stable isotopes and compounds (50.4). They were followed by aircraft parts (49.3), animal oils and fat (47.4), organic chemicals (44.1), rice (42.4), vegetable oil residues (41.6), and nonchemical coal and petroleum wastes (41.2). It is clear that with the exception of a few items such as aircraft, these products depend on material abundance. Taking this factor into consideration, one sees why the capital/labor ratio of exported products will be smaller than that of goods imported from countries with smaller material endowments. It should be evident that if one was comparing only the capital/labor ratio of the U.S. economy and those of the countries it was trading with, the U.S. ratio would most probably be higher.

There have been other attempts to overturn Leontief's paradox and prove the Heckscher-Ohlin model right by suggesting that U.S. exports contained a lot of human capital, which accounts for their relatively low physical capital content. This is incorrect because, as explained in earlier chapters, human capital is not a production factor input.

It is clear that Leontief's paradox was misplaced, as it failed to accept material as a third factor input in production. What difference does the recognition of material as a major factor input make on the theory of trade in the context of a three-factor system? Recall Lipsey and Chrystal's comment that "differences among regions of the world in climate and resource endowment lead to advantages in producing certain goods and disadvantages in producing others." Differences in climate will mean that certain natural material inputs are available in only some regions and that producing them in other regions will be difficult. Tea, for example, can be more easily harvested in India than in the United States, and the same holds for cocoa in Ghana and Nigeria. But considering the economic development and growth needs of India and Ghana and Nigeria, it does not immediately follow that they will gain macroeconomic advantages by producing these goods. Despite the relative abundance of tea and cocoa in these countries (which take inputs to grow), these countries may not qualify as material-abundant economies, even though in a microeconomic sense the factor proportions suggest such abundance. The reason is that producing these materials will disrupt the existing equality of factor proportions of all sectors, which is required to achieve macroeconomic growth. In this case, export revenue from that sector simply increases national income, with which the country will augment its import consumption propensities. This objection goes to the heart of economists' urgings that Third World countries export their raw materials to earn foreign exchange.

We have gone into some detail in our consideration of the analysis of the theory of comparative advantages of trade as presented in Krugman and Obstfeld's book, which is one of the best theoretical texts available on international trade. We are faced with a situation in which the theory has not passed the litmus test of whether it is a tool for economic development and growth of countries.

The first problem is that the theory of comparative advantage is a financial, not economic, analysis of trade and production. Bowen, Hollander, and Viaene explicitly stated that theories of trade on the principle of comparative advantage are effectively theories of related price determination.[22] Prices of factors and products in the real world are a wild card and create many analytical problems for those seeking to promote comparative advantage. The multifactor models they set up assume that the factors are costlessly mobile within a country. According to Bowen, Hollander, and Viaene, recent empirical evidence on the dispersion of wages and capital returns—they did not mention material prices because they do not regard material as a factor input—questions this assumption. "Even after correcting for differences in worker ability, persistent wage differences across industries . . . over time have been found," they say, and conclude, "The findings suggest that both capital and labor may be relatively immobile between industries, even in the long run."[23] The specific factor models were an attempt to circumvent the analytical weaknesses of the assumption of mobility. Price differences between countries can only partly be accounted for by economic factors.

Economists have sought to bolster the theory by claiming that trade is another way of trading in factors. Although there might appear to be economic similarity between trade and so-called factor movements, such similarity is superficial and has no economic basis. Goods imported into a country for consumption have no effect whatsoever on the factor proportions of that country, whereas capital, labor, or material imported has serious consequences for the factor utilization in that country.[24] These are issues we will take up later in this chapter. Bowen, Leamer, and Sveikauskas set out to test the Heckscher-Ohlin theory on the assumption that calculating the factors of production "embodied" in a country's exports and imports will show that a country is a net exporter of factors if it has them in relative abundance and an importer of factors if it has them in relative scarcity.[25] This assumption is defective, and so it is not surprising that they initially concluded from their survey of twenty-seven countries and twelve factors that Leontief's paradox was confirmed. Recently, however, they have stated that Leontief's ratio is wrong and ought to be replaced by countries' net trade in factor services.[26] But this is still not the issue.

The comparative advantage theory has been bolstered by wrong assumptions about production characteristics. Much of the theory is based, as we have seen, on the mistaken assumption that production techniques are fixed in the sense that particular production activities have been arbitrarily labeled as capital-intensive, labor-intensive, land-intensive, and so on. Comparative advantage based on discussing the relationship between such production activities is misleading.

The theory cites benefits to trading partners that are not relevant to economic development and growth. Trade, it is claimed, increases the choice of goods available to consumers in each trading country. Comparative advantage, it is said, enables each trading economy to consume more of both goods of both trading countries than would be possible in the absence of trade. It is argued that this makes individual consumers in both countries better off. This has nothing to do with economic development and growth. It is claimed that when two countries trade, the international free-trade price ratio will settle somewhere between their domestic price ratios. As a result, a labor-abundant country will get more manufactured goods (the production of which is supposed to be capital-intensive) from the capital-abundant trade partner in exchange for a unit of agriculture (the production of which is supposed to be labor-intensive) than would be the case in the absence of trade. The capital-abundant country will obtain more agricultural production in exchange for

manufactured goods than it would at domestic prices. It is claimed that since countries will want to specialize in products that use their abundant resources intensively, they will compensate for their scarce resources by importing products that use these scarce resources more intensively, but rising domestic costs (and therefore prices in excess of world prices) will prevent complete specialization from occurring. This theoretical claim is faulty because it assumes—as the whole theory of comparative advantage does—that production techniques are fixed. We have stressed that production techniques are flexible and derive from each economy's factor proportions. If a country has abundant labor, it does not need to compensate for its scarce capital by importing capital-intensive products said to be manufactures. The science of economic development stipulates that such a country ought to produce those manufactured goods with labor-intensive techniques. It does not need to export those things that comparative-advantage theorists label as labor-intensive, such as agricultural goods.

Comparative advantage has been analyzed in the context of its effect on income distribution in the wrong belief that trade confers overall development and growth benefits. Krugman and Obstfeld pointed out that "the benefits of trade are often distributed unevenly."[27] It is clear that income inequality can be increased by international trade. Income inequality is one face of structural economic imbalance, which, as we have shown, blocks economic growth and development. Income inequality arises because in poor countries factors tend to be attracted to the export sector, which receives increasing income compared to the nonexport sectors. Regrettably, some economists prefer to ignore the income distribution effects of international trade. Krugman and Obstfeld gave three reasons why economists can be justified in ignoring the income issues: international trade is not the only course of income distribution differences, political action can be taken to compensate those who are hurt, and those who lose from international trade are typically better organized than those who stand to gain. These reasons are unsustainable. Are Krugman and Obstfeld saying that one additional cause of income inequalities does not make any difference? Technological progress, shifting consumer preferences, exhaustion of old resources and discovery of new ones—examples Krugman and Obstfeld gave as other causes of income distribution effects—can be loosely regarded as leading to constructive destruction, whereas international trade leads to destructive destruction. The second and third reasons they cite are essentially political arguments, not economic ones. Economists such as Ricardo present their arguments for trade in a way that assumes away the economic structural imbalance that international trade increases.

The theory of comparative advantage has usually been couched in terms of different economic groups: wage earners, owners of capital, and landowners. This has made the theory increasingly irrelevant in modern settings, where economic groupings have moved away from the old historical arrangements. Owners of capital and land are depicted as owning financially valued assets. But in the context of factor proportions, capital is not dollars but material and labor withdrawn from consumption as production aids. Land is not a factor input. Bowen, Hollander, and Viaene have correctly accepted this conclusion by pointing out that the specific factors model used by international trade economists has helped to show that "coalitions for or against trade policy issues would form on the industry affiliations rather than on factor ownership."[28]

The futility of economists' advice that political action can resolve the inequalities between social groups caused by trade is evident. The theory of comparative advantage, as already pointed out, is a static economic concept. It neglects the reality that factors and factor proportions of economies are in perpetual change. Poor countries desirous of economic development and growth (and desirous of closing the economic gap between them and the richer nations) need a theory asserting that as a country's factor proportions change, the economy's technologies should be changing as well.[29]

Porter acknowledged the static nature of conventional trade theory and advised poor countries to create for themselves what he called "advanced factors."[30] We have in Chapter 3 declared that Porter's differentiation between natural factors and advanced factors has no economic basis. The so-called advanced factors are themselves produced from natural factors, though many of them seem to call for capital investment, which is really what Porter was advocating without saying so.

On the whole, the theory of comparative advantage has survived because it has derived strength from positivist orthodoxy. As we saw in Chapter 1, positivist orthodoxy continues to dominate conventional economics because it has been repackaged successfully in different ways over the years. It was Adam Smith's view that savings, investment, and trade go together. Gylfason aptly described Smith's influence on trade and capital when he said that, "like Hume, Smith regarded savings and investment as by-products and precursors of domestic and foreign trade and, moreover, as a means of enlarging the market and increasing the division of labor and thereby efficiency."[31]

Adam Smith declared, "When we compare, therefore, the state of a nation at two different periods and find that the annual produce of its land and labor is evidently greater at the latter than at the former, that its lands are better cultivated, its manufactures more numerous and more flourishing, and its trade more extensive, we may be assured that its capital must have increased during the interval between these two periods."[32]

The Harrod-Domar model emphasizes domestic savings as the major constraint on an economy's rate of growth. In regard to developing countries, economists who see international trade as a major determinant have added that, apart from savings constraints, the growth of developing countries is also hampered by scarcity of foreign exchange from international trade. Therefore, as the Harrod-Domar model contends, these countries suffer two gaps that need to be filled—a foreign exchange gap and a savings gap. Harrod and Domar have constructed what they call the two-gap model in an attempt to study the situation. In an open economy—which the theory of international trade advocates—and assuming that the country is specialized in the production of a single commodity that it both consumes and exports (which is often the case), domestic investment is obviously export-dependent. They assume that "technology" is fixed, as is often the case, being relatively capital-intensive. Domestic capital investment comprises capital imports as well as domestic output, which must be combined in fixed proportion between consumption and savings in order to produced the desired savings. Lower import input of needed capital implies a decrease in domestic investment, because of a lack of foreign exchange reserves. Bowen, Hollander, and Viaene concluded that such an economy cannot achieve the targeted rate of growth unless the propensity to save is increased by shifting a proportion of domestic output from consumption to exports.[33] A limited output results from the savings gap or the foreign exchange gap. Another solution in the attempt to achieve target growth would be for the country to seek foreign aid. This vicious circle is the fate of many poor countries that have adopted a positivist-orthodoxy-oriented open-economy strategy. Their "growth" depends on investment arising from capital import, savings, and foreign exchange reserves from trade. The debt burden on many of the poor countries to date can be traced to this vicious circle of unsustainable growth.

Comparative advantage has also flourished because of the idea's simplicity. Division of labor—

specialization—has been around for a very long time. The doctor, the lawyer, the farmer, the African rainmaker, the artisan, the native smelter, the Bangladeshi charmer—each is a specialist but needs another for his well-being. It is so easy for anyone to understand. Krugman and Obstfeld declared: "Everyone knows that some international trade is beneficial—nobody will suggest that Norway grow its own oranges." This simple idea has enabled economists to tell noneconomists that nations should specialize in a similar fashion and get on with what they are best at. It is in this simplicity that the danger of carrying the theory of comparative advantage into broad economics lies. It has been easy for economists and leaders to talk up trade as if it is another word for economic development and growth.[34]

Kreinin carried this layman's simplistic explanation of comparative advantage further when he said, "Trade compensates for national deficiencies whether in capital, labor skill management or technical sophistication."[35] The words *compensate* and *deficiencies* are wrong because they suggest that some countries are innately unable to achieve economic development and growth. On the contrary, the science of economic development and growth states that every economy has a personality of its own, reflecting its unique factor proportions, and that each economy is at a different stage of maturity at any given time. Their continued ability to mature depends on building upon this basic personality, growing through the full utilization of their factors in the proper portions and not through compensation by trade.

Economy of Scale and Trade

Krugman in 1987 wrote, "Growing discomfort with the incongruity between traditional analysis of international trade, which assumes small producers and pure competition, and the reality of huge volumes of exchange involving related products and powerful multinational firms have sparked off the development of new theories based on economy of scale and departures from atomistic competition."[36] Table 5.2 shows a hypothetical example of the gains from economy of scale arising from market integration in automobiles. If two countries—one with sales of 900,000 vehicles manufactured by six firms, and the other with sales of 1,600,000 vehicles made by eight firms—integrated their markets, the merged market would have ten firms. On the basis of this hypothetical example, Krugman and Obstfeld concluded that "clearly everyone is better off as a result of integration. . . . In the larger market, consumers have a wider range of choice, yet each firm produces more and is therefore able to offer its products at a lower price."[37]

Krugman and Obstfeld stipulated in their model that in order to achieve economies of scale, each firm must concentrate its production in one country, either Home or Foreign, yet it must sell its output to customers in both markets. So each product will be produced in only one country and exported to the other. Figure 5.2 reproduces Krugman and Obstfeld's graph of the effects of this larger market. The model asserts that under conditions of imperfect competition—and competition under economy of scale falls into this category—the greater the number of firms (n) in the market, the greater the competition, so that price P is reduced and vice versa; hence the curve PP, which represents price according to the number of firms. At the same time, if there are many firms, the market will be more fragmented, and so average costs will rise; hence the lines CC_1 and CC_2, which represent cost according to the number of firms (the model stipulates that when the market increases, each firm is able to produce more and thus achieve lower cost, represented by a downward shift from CC_1 to CC_2, but the result is a simultaneous increase in the number for firms from n_1 to n_2 because a larger market

Figure 5.2 **Claimed effect of size of larger market on gains from international trade.**

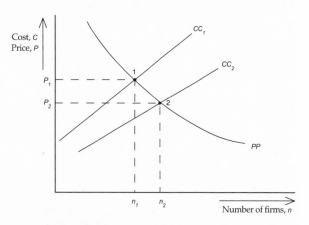

Source: P. Krugman and M. Obstfeld, *International Economics: Theory and Policy*, 4th ed. (Reading, MA: Addison-Wesley, 1997), fig. 6.4.

usually attracts new entrants; the result is a simultaneous fall in price from P_1 to P_2). At the point at which CC intersects PP, price is supposed to be equal to cost, at which point the number of firms in the market is determined.

Table 5.2 started off by assigning to Home a market of 900,000 sales of automobiles and to Foreign 1,600,000 sales. The model used a number of important assumptions. The demand facing each firm is stipulated as $Q = S[1/n - b(P - \mathbf{P})]$, where Q is the firm's sales, S is total sales of the industry, n is the number of the firms in the industry, b is a constant representing the responsiveness of a firm's sales to its price, P is the price charged by the firm itself, and $\mathbf{P}$ is the average price charged by its competitors. In dealing with their hypothetical example, Krugman and Obstfeld assumed that the firms in each country were charging the same price, $Q = S/n$—that is, the market is divided equally by the firms. This is because the model assumes that all the firms are symmetrical and that the demand function and cost function of all the firms in the industry are identical. Accordingly, the curve PP applies to all the

Table 5.2

Gains Said to Arise from Market Integration

	Home Market Before Trade	Foreign Market Before Trade	Integrated Market After Trade
Total Sales of Autos	900,000	1,600,000	2,500,000
Number of Firms	6	8	10
Sales per Firm	150,000	200,000	250,000
Average Cost	10.00	8.75	8.00
Price	10.00	8.75	8.00

Source: P. Krugman and M. Obstfeld, *International Economies: Theory and Policy* (Addison-Wesley Longman, Inc., 1997), Table 6-2, p. 136.

firms. For the cost function, the actual figure at each point is dependent on the number of automobiles (fixed cost F for all the firms is $750 million and marginal cost c is $5,000 per automobile).

However, this model does not provide us with a proof that economy of scale is an independent source of mutual benefit from trade. In the model, the number of firms was reduced from fourteen to ten after the two markets, Home and Foreign, were integrated. This contradicts the stated basic premise of the model, namely, that increased market size supports more firms. Going by the model's general assertion, one would have expected that the number of firms in the new, enlarged market would actually exceed fourteen.

We are concerned about some of the assumptions that had to be made in the model. Krugman and Obstfeld accepted the unreality of these assumptions when they admitted that the appeal of their model is not so much "its realism as its simplicity."[38] For example, the model assigned the same cost structure to all firms in both markets as well as the same price behavior. This contradicts the very basis of the model, which presumes imperfect competition on the basis of differentiated products; if price and cost characteristics of firms are the same, what else is there to compete on? That the cost of production in Home and Foreign is the same is also unrealistic, as is the assumption that all firms share

the market equally. The basis on which the model determined the number of firms in a market—namely, that price is equal to average cost, with zero profit—also contradicts the basic character of a differentiated product market. Porter has correctly stated that "it is difficult, though not impossible, to be both lower-cost and differentiated relative to competitors. Achieving both is difficult because providing unique performance, quality or service is inherently more costly, in most instances, to seeking only to be comparable to competitors on such attributes."[39] In a differentiated market, the notion of an average industry cost that applies to all firms loses its meaning, because the automobiles that the different firms are offering provide different performance, quality, and service.

The authors claimed that as a result of integration, everybody in both Home and Foreign countries is better off because of increased choice and lower price, and that these gains were still worth pursuing for each country irrespective of where the ten firms in the integrated market were located. These views run counter to our view of the science of economic development and growth, which requires the mobilization of the input factors in each economy. In short, being better off in Krugman and Obstfeld's sense is not development- and growth-inducing.

To what extent is the achievement of lower price by firms through economies of scale the driving force in their international activities? Porter has said that "economies of scale in production or R&D . . . are in and of themselves country neutral . . . because a large-scale plant or research center can, in principle, be located anywhere."[40] If firms were simply seeking economies of scale, they would locate anywhere they could derive this benefit. And Krugman and Obstfeld had said that it did not matter where all the ten firms that emerged from integrating the Home market and the Foreign market located. But we know that where the firm locates is a major consideration of today's mass producers, even if there were no trade barriers.

Let us explore the question posed at the beginning of the preceding paragraph using the automobile industry as an example. The Big Three automobile companies were founded in the United States in the early twentieth century. As *The Economist* put it, "The companies were national champions and they had an unwritten contract with the government. America's big companies organized the production of goods in huge volumes; the economies of scale brought down costs of production; the American purchaser could go on shopping more cheaply. . . . By the time of the New Deal in early 1930s, these giant corporations were national institutions."[41] In his 1991 book, *Work of Nations,* Richard Reich wrote, "The system [in the United States] contained its own internal logic. Big Business, Big Labor and the public at large would subsidize high-volume production in order to gain greater efficiencies of scale which in turn would employ a growing middle class of Americans capable of buying the expanded output."[42]

While all this was happening, these same companies had gradually put down roots abroad. In addition to its U.S. plants, General Motors had by the early 1930s already set up twenty-nine subsidiaries in Europe, including Vauxhall Motors in England and Adam Opel AG in Germany. In Ford's case, even though there was worldwide demand for the Model T, the company's 1928 Plan was intended to "Europeanize" Ford operations in Europe. Ford USA was to design the cars, while a plant in Dagenham, England, was to be the center of its European automobile manufacturing. It was to manufacture both knocked-down components and complete models, and Continental companies were to assemble the parts and distribute the products. The assumption was that British manufacture would be cheaper than American and that the concentration of European work in Dagenham would permit the adoption of mass-production methods "while labor would cost less and no transatlantic freights need be paid."[43] But by the time the Dagenham plant was to begin operation, in the United States Ford had staked everything on the Model A car, which was too large for the narrower English roads and too costly. The existing British firms Morris and Austin were meeting the local demand for small, economical cars. Eventually Dagenham retooled to produce a "baby Ford"—a car with a smaller wheelbase and lighter weight—which fared well compared to its competitors. In 1937, Dagenham's modern, well-planned factory (which had its own 1,440-pound-pressure power station, new coke ovens, and a blast furnace) introduced the 10 hp De-Luxe Ford, and the following year it created a sensation by pricing its 8 hp automobile at £100 (less than $500). None of its English competitors could sell a fully equipped car at such a low price. This was to be the beginning of Ford's chain of successful small cars in England.

Despite Ford's 1928 Plan to use Dagenham as its European hub, many of the Ford subsidiaries did not find it convenient and profitable to buy from Dagenham rather than from the United States. First, the small English car did not always suit Continental buyers as well as the American type of vehicles. Their greater distances, different tax structure, and established tastes still made the heavier automobile preferable in many of their markets. Since output for this kind of vehicle in Dagenham remained low by American standards, its unit costs were high, which offset the cost of importing vehicles from America. Ford had to yield by allowing them to buy from the United States—a major modification of its 1928 Plan.

Ford, like many other firms, found that what was most important to host country governments and publics was not so much the variety of automobiles and their low price but rather how much local content was in the manufactured automobile. As Nevins and Hill put it, the Ford subsidiaries "had to manufacture for themselves or perish."[44] By 1935, for example, the cars produced by Ford France had motors, transmissions, and rear axles made in Strasbourg, and much of the body work was done by French suppliers. It was on this basis that Ford France competed with Renault and Peugeot. By 1939 Europe was dotted with Ford factories and assembly plants.

The end of World War II, which left much of Europe in economic ruin, gave Ford another opportunity to integrate the European market with its U.S. plants, which had not been as affected by the war. In 1949, Henry Ford II and his adviser Graeme Howard left for Europe to assess wartime damages, inventory the remaining assets, and assess prospects for new growth in an environment where there were still acute shortages of materials, manpower, and credit.[45] Henry Ford II intended to base fundamental policy changes on their tour. He was increasingly determined to tighten both ownership and administration of Ford activities in Europe. But with an intensified sense of national identity and clamor for local content in European countries, Ford and Howard had to deal directly with each country. The plan to strategically locate plants to serve a single European market had to be discontinued. The Dagenham factory needed to establish itself further in Britain; in France, they hoped to gain a stronger position vis-à-vis French rivals such as Renault by

merging Ford France with a local small car maker, E. Mathis; in Germany, they explored the possibility of acquiring a 51 percent stake in Volkswagen. Holland, Belgium, Denmark, Sweden, and Finland were to continue being served by assembly plants which drew their parts in the main from Britain rather than the United States.

Notice that, instead of pushing economy of scale in Europe by using its U.S. plants, Ford opted to establish manufacturing plants in Europe, where the market was considerably smaller than in the United States. It is too simplistic to say that they were obliged to do this because of freight and other costs of shipping products from the United States, as later in the century foreign small cars invaded the United States despite freight rates and other costs. The U.S. automobile companies set up plants in Europe because they wanted to tailor products to meet national markets in Europe. The adventure with the Model A, for example, brought Ford England to the verge of receivership. But the "baby Ford" that later became successful in England did not provide everything some other European countries wanted.

According to Porter, the strategy of tailoring to suit reduces scale advantages that can be achieved by operating a single large plant.[46] U.S. companies wanted to enhance local marketing in the different European nations and to "Europeanize" their operations in Europe. England, France, and Germany each had home-based automobile plants, and so a strong motivation of the U.S. automobile companies was to fight these competitors in their home territory in order to reduce the competitors' resources and their ability to compete with the U.S. companies in Europe. The American companies' foreign plants had much higher costs than their U.S. plants, but what mattered to the U.S. companies was their share of the market.

However, American carmakers forgot the lessons they learned in Europe. In the ensuing years, Western companies missed a chance to have pushed hard to buy the weaker Japanese companies—Isuzu and Suzuki and Mazda. They ceded that regional market and instead were pushing for trade liberalization so that they could sell finished cars and parts in Japan when they had nothing to sell to Japan that was competitive either in price or in quality.[47] For large companies that want to capture a substantial part of any regional market, the lessons are clear: There is no substitute for producing in the market you think is important.

The lesson, however, was clear: If a car company thinks a foreign market is strategic, it will go along with requirements to increase the local content of its operations. For example, in 1962 Mexico prohibited the import of finished vehicles and imposed high local-content requirements. The five foreign multinationals with operations there—Ford, GM, Chrysler, Nissan, and Volkswagen—complied. By 1980, Mexico had a 500,000-unit industry shared by these five with over 50 percent local content. With the five producers making three or four models each, average annual production of each product was around 25,000 units, judged to be too low for mass production by these companies.

It has also been suggested that by establishing multinational operations, automotive producers are protecting themselves against regional cyclicities in the motor vehicle market.[48] Sales of motor vehicles, which are durable goods, tend to be more volatile than the general economy. And because the world markets don't go up and down at exactly the same time, a company with a presence in all major markets has more protection against cyclicity.

The problems and strategic issues we have sketched for the car industry are similar in many ways to those of other international mass producers. We can see that these issues work against the idealistic notion of the gains to be made from economy of scale in international trade.

Ford was aware that it could not use its plants in the United States as a springboard for international trade economy of scale. That is why it went to Europe. In principle, the theory of economy of scale in international trade claims that it does not matter where the plants are located in the enlarged market. So according to this theory, Ford could have served all Europe from the United States. But this is not true in the real-life situation. Even within Europe, which is a smaller market than the United States, Ford at the time could not gain any advantage by strategically locating plants in Europe to take on the entire continent as one market. As it found out, it was unable to compete with local European manufacturers.

Today car manufacturers have moved on from the production paradigm that the economy of scale theory was based on. With flexible manufacturing now the predominant paradigm in that industry, it is clear that the economy of scale model for international trade belongs to a past era.

Despite this, economists still shout from the rooftops about economy of scale as a major factor in international trade, albeit with a slightly different twist to their argument. Lipsey and Chrystal praised economy of scale as a means of achieving economic development and growth of nations small and big: "The larger the scale of operations, the more efficiently large-scale machinery can be used and the more efficient the division of labor that is possible. ... Smaller countries such as Switzerland, Belgium and Israel whose domestic markets are not large enough to exploit economies of scale would find it prohibitively expensive to become self-sufficient by producing a little of everything at very great cost." They concluded, "Trade allows smaller countries to specialize and produce a few products at high enough levels of output to reap the economies of scale."[49] They stated that one of the important lessons learned from the pattern of world trade since the Second World War resulted from imperfect competition and product differentiation. According to them, virtually all of today's manufactured consumer goods are produced in multidifferentiated product lines. In some industries, many firms produce this range; in others, only a few firms produce the entire product range. In both cases, firms are not price-takers and they do not exhaust all available economies of scale. Lipsey and Chrystal thought that by expanding the market through trade, firms would be able to exploit some "previously unexploited scale economies." Third World countries have been urged that they need to get out of the vicious circle of low market and high cost and instead gear up to produce for the world so as to exploit economies of scale not ordinarily available to them and to open their markets to enjoy a greater variety of products at cheaper prices than they can otherwise dream of achieving.

The international trade model based on economy of scale urges countries to specialize in a limited range of goods by setting up large plants to take advantage of economies of scale. Lipsey and Chrystal, addressing countries they call "smaller countries" and poor countries with small internal markets, advise them not to attempt to produce a little of everything they needed to satisfy their small internal market. They should import much of these at cheaper price from large-scale manufactures of other countries and concentrate on few advantageous lines on which they can build large-scale plants for export. So they were in effect advising poor countries to engage in selected capital-intensive activities. Other economists like Todaro, on the other hand, disagree and contend that those countries that were first industrialized are normally able to take advantage of economies of scale and differentiated products backed by their superior resources of capital, entrepreneurship ability, skilled labor and ability to use these resources more intensively to perpetuate their dominant position in the world. Todaro will say that poor countries have to function in the imperfect and unequal real world of international commerce and will find themselves locked in a stagnant situation in specializing in prod-

ucts that use unskilled labor.[50] Each of these economists wrongly looks to capital-intensive production as the preferred production paradigm.

At this point, we are more concerned to examine in further detail the adequacy or otherwise of the concept of economy of scale production as the basis for championing international trade as an instrument of development and growth. To do this, we will resume our analysis of the automotive industry as perhaps the best industry with which to study the issues in a little more detail than we attempted in Chapter 4.

There is a fundamental misunderstanding by many writers who claim that Ford's Model T is a child of mass production (economy of scale). Upon its establishment in 1903, Ford Motor Company was capitalized at $150,000, of which only $28,000 was actually paid. Other automobile craft producers were building big cars under the logic that the bigger the car produced, the higher the selling price and the larger the profit margin. That did not fit Henry Ford's ideas. He wanted to build low-cost, smaller cars that the average man could buy. He was of the view that building more and selling less would balance out profits in the long run. The company's board of directors disagreed. Realizing that he was at the mercy of the board, Ford began buying up the stock. By October 1906 he owned 58½ percent of the stock and took over as president; now he could do what he wanted. In October 1908 he introduced the Model T at the price of $850, telling buyers that they could have the car in any color they wanted as long as it was black. The Model T sold well from the start, moving 10,000 units in the first year, even though the rest of the auto industry sneered at the Tin Lizzie as a pile of sheet metal held together with baling wire.[51] In 1909, he entered his Model T in a New York–to–Seattle endurance race open to all car makers, giving his critics a field day, but the Tin Lizzie proved equal to the task. Twenty-two days after the competition got under way on June 1, 1909, the car had conquered rutted, mud-filled roads, arriving in Seattle in front of the few others that were able to stand the rigors of the still-primitive American roads. Over 18,000 cars were sold in the second year, making Ford the leading manufacturer of automobiles in the country, in fact in the world. Model T sales continued to rise geometrically.[52]

The Model T owed its success not to the fact that it was a good car in the engineering sense but to the splendid value it gave—low price, high power-to-weight ratio, foolproof controls, and nationwide (indeed, almost worldwide) availability of cheap spare parts that could be fitted by the unskilled laborer or farmer. There was no point cosseting a Model T or laboriously repairing worn or broken parts when it was possible for the owner to walk into any hardware store and ask for a part, secure in the knowledge that there was only one type of Ford and a dollar or so would buy the necessary piece.

Ford's first efforts to assemble his car, beginning in 1903, involved setting up assembly stands on which a whole car was built, often by one fitter. The assembler received the necessary parts, filed them down so as to fit (Ford had not yet achieved the perfect interchangeability of parts of mass production), then bolted them into place. Rae has pointed out that mass production too often has been incorrectly equated with quantity production and cheap production. He stated that true mass production requires the integration of five components: precision, standardization, interchangeability, synchronization, and continuity. He pointed out that "all these existed in the industrial world before the automobile came on the scene. . . . These components of mass production were known and used in the American industrial system well before 1900."[53] The significance of this is that economic historians who give the impression that Henry Ford originated these production practices in his operation are wrong. Another important point is that these five

components existed as part of the craft production paradigm that dominated America in the 1800s. So when Henry Ford came to the conclusion that a much larger market could be obtained if he could make the Model T cheaply enough to sell it at a price below $600, Rae concluded, "all the pieces necessary to the solution of Henry Ford's problem were in existence and well-known. . . . What was needed was for someone to put these pieces together into an integrated technique of production."[54] The phenomenal success of the Model T enabled Ford to build up the capital needed to implement his new mass production techniques. After much experimentation, the moving assembly line came to fruition in 1913 (with an obvious debt to the time-and-motion studies of Frederick W. Taylor).[55]

In the first ten years of the twentieth century, the American automobile industry consisted of an astounding assortment of hundreds of firms. It was a classic case of a free market. Entry into the industry was easy and cheap, competition unrestricted. Womack, Jones, and Roos put it succinctly: "Between 1914 and 1924, Henry Ford's and Alfred Sloan's industrial innovations destroyed a vigorous American industry, the craft-based motor vehicle business. . . . During this period," they stated, "the number of US automobile companies fell from 100 to about a dozen, of which three—Ford, General Motors and Chrysler—accounted for 90 percent of all sales." Womack, Jones, and Roos suggested that the reason why there was no panic, no protest, and no call for government intervention because of the changes taking place was that even as Ford and Sloan were demolishing one industry, they were creating a second—the mass production motor industry—and they were doing it in the same city "where craft-based industry had flourished vigorously." The growth of this second industry was so dramatic that practically all the skilled workers of the craft-based industry could find jobs building tools and doing other skilled tasks to support the new system. For example, the upholstery department used special molds to eliminate the skilled job of hand-stuffing. Seat cover sewing was standardized and simplified. In the body shop, stamping presses eliminated skilled panel beaters. A paint spraying system substituted for the skill of the brush painter. The authors commented, "No one has repeated Ford's and Sloan's ease in supplanting one type of production method with another."[56]

The small firms lost out financially not so much because of the capital intensity of the Big Three but because of what conventional economics calls economies of scope. Yates noted that the early automobiles were essentially functional—simply motorized carriages. As wooden frames gave way to all-steel bodies, style was largely limited to distinctive radiator shells, Art Nouveau hood ornaments, and such things as headlights mounted on fenders. For the most part, the cars were tall, angular black boxes. It was Sloan who was convinced that technical advances should be de-emphasized in favor of styling and marketing. His strategy was to tap the hunger for status among the rising middle class, and he never hesitated to credit GM's success to their "Hollywood styling." It was clearly cheaper to stamp out a new sheet of metal skin each year than continually to tool up to produce new engines. In the late 1930s, for example, the Cadillac styling team was fascinated with the rakish, organic lines of the Lockheed P-38 fighter plane, and so a new generation of automobiles featured such fillips as pointed noses, long sweeping pontoon fenders, curved windshields, and so on.

With what were essentially sales and marketing strategies, then, the Big Three constantly filled showrooms with collections of redesigned cars that were in Yates' words "devastating weapons against the smaller, weaker car makers who could not compete with the new styles and collective marketing power of the Big Three. The once-proud competition —Hudson, Packard, Willys, and Nash as well as such postwar upstarts as Kaiser-Frazer—could not generate funds to annually revamp their lineups."[57]

One point to gather from this review of the U.S. automobile history is that Ford's mass production, copied by the rest of the Big Three and later by European automobile firms, is not the only production technique for making automobiles. Craft production before Ford's assembly line was already using the five production components of precision, standardization, interchangeability, synchronization, and continuity, contrary to the impression that craft production features low standards and inconsistent quality. The Model T was not a success because of Ford's assembly line; it was already a success under craft production. Ford merely used mass production to exploit his success to the fullest. It is clear that the Big Three adopted factor proportions that were too heavily capital-intensive at the time. In this example, mass production, because of its financial success, attracted additional capital from persons and groups seeking to set up operations; through combining their financial resources, initiating public offerings, or getting assistance from the banking sector, they diverted essential factors of capital and skilled manpower away from the smaller, less strongly capital-based craft production sector.

It is therefore worrying that conventional economists seem to want to institutionalize mass production (economy of scale) on an international scale and squeeze out craft production, as happened in the United States almost a century ago. Nearly all small-scale car producers in Europe had disappeared by the end of the last century. The very few that survive are struggling in niche markets. These economists and their new theories of international trade constitute the best weapon the mass producers have in their quest to install and strengthen imperfect competition in a world in which inequalities in economic prospects are already intolerably great.

Prospects for the International Economy-of-Scale Paradigm

As the century progressed the U.S. automotive industry had become even more capital-intensive. In 1947, for example, Ford created an Automation Department to help evolve an efficient method of handling material that would reduce lifting, turning, feeding, and stacking. The automation movement gained momentum industrywide; Nevins and Hill used Drucker's words to describe it as "a major economic and technological change, a change as great as Henry Ford ushered in with the first mass production plant fifty years ago."[58] They said, "In the post-war period of scarcity of labor, rise in real wages, high consumer demand encouraged experiments with manufacturing processes which employed conveyors, compressed air, hydraulic power and electrical devices to automate certain operations. This came to be known in the automobile industry as 'Detroit automation.' Ford engineers began work in 1949 on the first factories built for extensive use of automation."[59] All these were to push the capital-intensive nature of U.S. mass production even further.

Over time, however, it became increasingly evident that automobile mass production was in some trouble. We have already pointed out how it started with a degree of capital intensity that was out of line with what was proportionally available at the time. In the early 1990s America was a material-abundant economy, and it did not matter that automobile mass production was material-intensive, with institutionalized maintenance of high inventories of materials and large rejects, because what mattered was to keep production uninterrupted. Come the latter part of the 1990s, America began to retreat from this position of material abundance.

While the immediate push came from the threat from Japan, the shakeout in the automobile indus-

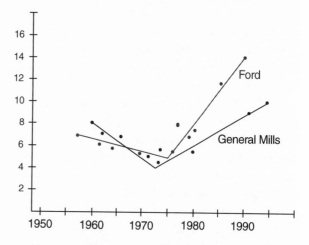

Figure 5.3 **Stock turn, Ford and General Mills.**

Source: R. Schonberger, *World-Class Manufacturing: The Next Decade* (New York: The Free Press, 1996).

try was long overdue. In a book titled *World-Class Manufacturing: The Next Decade,* Richard Schonberger illustrated what people were slow in realizing: that mass production was becoming an immovable mass. Writing in purely financial and commercial terms, he argued that the health of a manufacturer could be judged on one basic indicator: how many times in the year the company turns over its stock. The faster the turnover, the more financially healthy it is and, other things being equal, the more money it makes. Figure 5.3 shows turnover for two companies.

Mass manufacturers in the United States, according to Schonberger, had gone through decades up to about 1975 of lower and lower stock turnover rates. Spurred by competition from Japanese lean manufacturing, around then the companies started to imbibe the lean manufacturing techniques and use material more economically by cutting inventory and work in progress, which showed in their stock turnover. Not just auto companies took part in this trend; among the other companies that Schonberger cites are John Deere, TRW (electronics and engineering), Eaton (axles), PepsiCo, Caterpillar, Cummins Engines, Black and Decker, Motorola, Honeywell, and General Mills (food products). These companies learned the lesson that attempting to compete on the basis of achieving low price through mass production was not a guarantee of success.

While the changes reflected in the stock turnover rate partially address the issue of material utilization, in financial terms the other issue, excessive capitalization of Western automobile mass production, remained. After the American occupation following World War II, the Japanese sought to reduce capital and material input to suit their factor proportions, using several smaller general-purpose machines with specialized attachments in place of large special-purpose machines, perfecting quick die changes and machine setup, and assembling several different models on the same line. They also addressed the financial aspects of competitive strategy; for example, concerning the cost of factory buildings, they used much less space per unit of output than the equivalent American factory.

In U.S. automobile mass production, there is now a greater trend toward outsourcing and reducing investment in the internal production of components and parts. Ford's European management, for example, has a joint venture in the United States with a German transmission maker that will use a former Ford factory to produce a new generation of continuously variable transmissions. The joint venture will supply other companies as well as Ford. Ford Europe and Peugeot Citroën plan to produce diesel engines together. There is now a greater trend toward computer integrated manufacturing (CIM), a development of flexible manufacturing. CIM is capable of achieving breakeven at 30 to 35 percent of capacity, compared to 65 to 70 percent of capacity for a conventional mass production plant. GM in February 2000 announced plans to retool to meet the goal of allowing people to custom-order cars online and reduce lead time (order to manufacture) from ten days (minimum) in 1999 to three days in 2003 and elapsed time (order to delivery) from up to eight weeks in 1999 to between four and eleven days in 2003. All this is part of an effort to reduce capital-intensiveness. Modular manufacture is on the rise. GM's experimental modular assembly plant in Latin America is expected to convert the three thousand parts that now go into a vehicle into about thirty modules or major subassemblies. In reversal of the previous power-tussle relationship with its suppliers, GM wants its suppliers to be wired into its Web site, monitoring the order pattern so that they can stay on top of what is needed. Digital technology is also playing a major role in replacing various analog controls, as broadly described in Chapter 4. The net effect of all this is that economy of scale as a mass production paradigm in the industry is becoming less and less important.

In their effort to increase sales, the industry is going back to what it earlier abandoned, namely, renewed mass customization effort aimed at reducing investment in new production design. The "styling" era earlier in the century, when updating of style and detail was a way of increasing sales without major investment in new technological innovations, had gradually given way by the mid-1960s to an emphasis on aerodynamic efficiency, reduced weight, fuel efficiency, and nimbleness. In recent years, however, now desperate to connect with the twenty-somethings after courting the Baby Boom for so long, the Big Three along with Honda and Nissan are now racing to recapture styling initiative, folding it into souped-up versions of mainstream models. At the recent annual convention of the Specialty Equipment Market Association (which represents the automotive aftermarket industry), the major car companies were out in force, hoping to tap the association's knowledge of what is hot on the street and make arrangements to use the lower-cost facilities of the association's members to produce a new buzz around their models.

We have gone into this detail to show that the mass production paradigm in the U.S. automobile industry is under attack and that U.S. producers are still looking for solutions. The scope and scale of the challenge at GM is enormous. But this needs to be done, and economists need to link solutions to the competitive problems facing the U.S. automobile industry with Porter's prescription for international competitiveness: that in order to obtain and maintain international competitiveness, companies first need to establish domestically the required strategies and competitive styles with which to tackle international competition. As Porter said, "Global competition will not begin initially unless some firms gain advantage at home that allows them to penetrate the foreign market. Competitive advantage drawn solely from the home base is sufficient to lead to global competition."[60] Companies will slowly test the foreign market, always with only one foot at a time in the water, ready to adjust their home-grown competitive strategies to suit foreign markets. Womack, Jones, and Roos were probably wrong to call Japanese auto plants in the United States "transplants," as Japanese lean production has changed from its original parameters as it moved to the United States, featuring more automation.[61] Womack, Jones, and Roos must have been aware of this change in the characteristics of lean production when they declared that once lean production principles are fully instituted, companies would be able to move rapidly toward automation of most of the remaining repetitive tasks in auto assembly. "Thus, by the end of the century [they were writing in 1990] expect that lean-assembly plants will be populated almost entirely by highly skilled problem-solvers whose task will be to think continually of ways to make the system run more smoothly and productively."[62] This scenario is significantly different from the cord that Ohno at Toyota installed above every workstation to enable the Japanese worker to stop the whole assembly line if a problem emerged that he could not

fix. In short, the success of lean production in Japan was due to the fact that it derived from the factor endowments of the Japanese economy. They were then able to develop home-grown competitive strategies and knowledge that prepared them for international competition.

Economists who have extolled economy of scale as the foundation of international trade have urged countries to engage in free trade. They see the ideal world as one in which there are no barriers to trade. Krugman and Obstfeld referred to the North American Auto Pact of 1946 as an example of the benefits trade obtains from the economy-of-scale paradigm. Before the pact was put in place, the Canadian auto industry was a tenth the size of its U.S. counterpart. Initially Canadian auto manufacturing firms found that their small scale was a substantial disadvantage. While the U.S. plants were dedicated—that is, devoted to producing a single model or component—to exploit the economy of scale of the large U.S. market, the Canadian plants had to produce several things, "requiring plants to shut down periodically to change over from producing one item to producing another."[63] They also had to hold larger inventory and to use less specialized machinery. The productivity of the Canadian industry, we are told, was about 30 percent lower than that of the United States. Despite all this, because of tariffs between Canada and the United States, the Canadians found it cheaper to have their own, largely separate production system rather than pay the tariff to import vehicles from the United States. When the pact came into effect, removing the tariff, intraindustry trade increased. Canadian producers cut down on the number of models they assembled. The overall level of Canadian production and employment remained stable, and Canadian industry's productivity was said to have risen to become comparable to that of the United States.

Womack, Jones, and Roos maintained that the American and Canadian auto industries before and

after the implementation of the pact were inefficient mass producers. They found that in general
not only was productivity in lean production much
higher than in mass production, but they "could find
no correlation at all between the number of model
and body styles being run down a production line
and either productivity or product quality."[64] They
therefore argued that the stability of Canadian employment levels after the pact took effect was an
indication of low productivity both in Canada and
among the U.S. mass producers, and that the level
of activities reported both before and after the pact
was implemented could have been achieved under
lean production with less labor than was employed
in Canada. Had the Canadians converted to lean
production, they could have saved on their large
inventories and not needed to invest in specialized
machinery. Womack, Jones, and Roos unequivocally
stated, "Our conclusion is simple: Lean production
is a superior way for humans to make things. It provides better products in a wider variety at lower cost.
. . . It follows that the whole world should adopt
lean production, and as quickly as possible."[65] It
should be noted that their recommendation was
meant to apply to all production, not just that of
automobiles. It is clear that trade theories based on
economy of scale have been overtaken by changes
in production techniques.

International Trade Based on World Regions

On the basis of their conclusion, Womack, Jones,
and Roos proceeded to draw up a map of international trade patterns based on all automobile companies adopting lean production techniques. Unlike
conventional economists, who were urging the
worldwide free trade needed to accommodate mass
production, Womack, Jones, and Roos adopted a
more realistic stance that trade barriers and currency
fluctuations are a fact of life. They were of the view

Figure 5.4 **Cross-product regional flows of a company.**

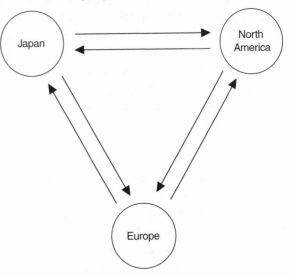

Source: J. Womack, D. Jones, and D. Roos, *The Machine That Changed the World* (New York: Rawson Associates, 1990), fig. 8.4, p. 206.

that all companies seeking global business need to
create a top-to-bottom manufacturing system in each
of the world's major markets in order to win competitive advantage over competitors manufacturing
and exporting to the world from a single region.
Figure 5.4 is their depiction of this global production system. The three regions in the figure, they
say, represent about 90 percent of the motor vehicle
market in the world at the time. The arrows show
mutual access across regions to systems for global
production, supply, product development, technology acquisition, finance, and distribution.

They adduced five reasons why such a strategy
confers competitive advantage. The first is that it
provides protection against trade barriers and currency shifts. A second advantage is that it provides
the company a rich product diversity. A lean production system, they said, "can gain most economies of scale at much lower volume per individual
product compared with mass production."[66] They
pointed out that the motor vehicle market in Eu-

rope, North America, and Japan was fragmenting. A lean production system can gain most economies of scale at much lower volume per individual product compared with mass production. Achieving this goal presumes that a variety of products can be assembled in sequence on one large production line using several different sizes of engine and transmission from a large engine and a large transmission plant. The authors argue that the three regions they depicted demand different types of products. Therefore an associated advantage is that it is possible to create a volume market in one region and export the product to a niche market in another region. Their example was Mercedes cars, which are used as taxis in Germany (volume demand) but sold in North America and Japan as luxury products. They also mentioned Honda, which built and sold its coupe at high volume in the United States but positioned it as a much more luxurious, limited-volume product for the Japanese market. A third advantage is that a multiple-region producer is capable of more sophisticated management than a single-region producer because of the interaction of management personnel across the different regions. A fourth advantage is that a multiregion producer is better protected against regional cyclicity in the market, as the world major markets don't go up and down at exactly the same time. The fifth is that developing a full-fledged production system in each region denies competitors defended markets from which to skim profits to fight battles elsewhere. In short, the strategy is for the major companies to have regional divisions able to conduct top-to-bottom design, engineering, and production of products that are sold primarily in their region of manufacture. Limited volumes are to be sold to other regions to serve niche markets there.

They ruled out the alternative (which they called extreme decentralization) of establishing regional subsidiaries that each develop their own products, manufacturing systems, and carrier ladders, saying, "This hermetic division by regions results in nar-

row focus, ignores the advantage of cross-regional integration," and "creates gilded cages for highly paid national executives unable to rise any farther in their organization."[67] They also ruled out strategic alliances with independent partners from each region, concluding that they leave the question of coordination and overall management between alliance partners unanswered and that, in fact, such arrangements are unmanageable except in perfectly stable market conditions.

The respect these proposals command is illustrated by the fact that many multinationals have adopted the multiple-region strategy as a basis for their worldwide operations. In 1997, there were 53,000 multinational corporations with 450,000 foreign subsidiaries. They accounted for one-third of the world's $2.2 trillion in exports.

However, examining the proposals closely, we have many unanswered questions. While the mass production (economy of scale) school needed the whole world as one market, presumably because of its larger volume requirements, it is not clear whether the regional arrangement was adopted because lean production needed less volume to achieve its own economy of scale. The authors, as we noted, say that each region demanded different types of products. Or is it because, as we indicated earlier, the authors wanted to work within the constraints of world trade barriers and currency fluctuations? If the latter, we face the next problem, which is that as of now, trade barriers and currency fluctuations are not regional phenomena alone. Surely Japan is not a region but simply a single, albeit large, market. The authors criticized Australia for viewing itself as part of the developed world and planning to develop its auto industry and ship to North America, Europe, and Japan. The difference between Australia and Japan seems to be that Australia has "a small and highly developed motor-vehicle industry with an insufficient domestic market."[68] It looks as if the regional strategy they recommend is based not really on geographic regions but on size of market, as is apparent from their references to the three regions (which don't include, for example, Asian and South American countries) constituting 90 percent of world demand. If the regional arrangement is primarily intended to ensure sufficient market for lean production, we have not made much progress, because we are back to the issue of economy of scale.

Lean production is, after all, a volume production, just like mass production, except that "lean producers employ teams of multi-skilled workers at all levels of the organization and use highly flexible, increasingly automated machines to produce volumes of products in enormous variety."[69] Trade barriers and currency shifts are still a country-to-country phenomenon—even within free trade areas, each country still decides the tariffs and quotas for products entering its territory and maintains its currency—and they were even more so when Womack, Jones, and Roos were writing in 1990. So it is not possible to see how the regions envisaged by these authors can work as described, except possibly in the case of the European Union, which, however, does not cover the whole of Europe. The only cases the authors quoted as examples of the risks arising from trade barriers and currency shifts—that of Jaguar in 1987 and Saab in 1989, each of which was nearly bankrupt—came about because of a weaker U.S. dollar vis-à-vis the British pound and the Swedish krona, respectively, not because of any interregional currency shift. The authors also seem to assume that the consumption patterns and consumer preferences of countries in one region are the same. But although Mercedes cars are used as taxis in Germany, they are luxury items in other European countries, just as they are in the United States.

Curiously, the authors condemned what they described as extreme decentralization by multinationals into regional subsidiaries, each capable of developing its own products. Their reason is flimsy. One suspects that the authors were trying to protect the financial interest of their sponsors, not wanting them to lose control. The authors would also no doubt shy away from contemplating a situation in which countries have many craft-car producers.

Meanwhile, changes in car manufacturing continue to move in the direction of the reduction of the scale effect. For example, it is estimated that a capital reduction item—microelectronics—component in car manufacturing from little or nothing a decade ago jumped to around 13 percent in 1991 and now is hovering at about 23 percent and set to increase.[70]

Market Fragmentation

The research by Womack, Jones, and Roos found that the motor vehicle market in Europe, North America, and Japan is progressively fragmenting, "with no end in sight."[71] In the auto industry as well as in many other industries, there is an increasing number of products and their varieties or substitutes on offer with the result that there is a continual decline in the number of sales per product. Womack, Jones, and Roos mused that in consequence, "the ultimate destination of lean production in terms of variety of product offerings is unknown." In the extreme case (although not for several decades), they say, "it is possible that we will return full circle to the world of craft production where each buyer was able to custom order a vehicle suited to his or her precise needs." This possibility is graphically portrayed in Figure 5.5, from which it can be seen that the team could not say in 1990 whether the following decade would continue on the path of lean production or lead back to craft production.

The doubts expressed by Womack and his team are of monumental importance because they were hinting of the possibility of a worldwide change in production paradigm. If that is a possibility, why did the team urge everyone to move over to lean production and abandon craft production?

The world does not want to make the same mis-

Figure 5.5 **The progression of product variety and production volume.**

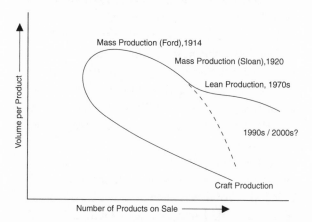

Source: J. Womack, D. Jones, and D. Roos, *The Machine That Changed the World* (New York: Rawson Associates, 1990), fig. 5.7, p. 126.

take as in the past, when a certain production technique prevailed because everything political and financial was geared to exterminate alternative techniques. Craft production seems always to be the victim. Listen to Womack, Jones, and Roos: "Our advice to any company practicing 'craftsmanship' . . . in any manufacturing activity, automotive or otherwise, is simple and emphatic: stamp it out. Institute lean production as quickly as possible and eliminate the need for all craftsmanship at the source. Otherwise lean competitors will overwhelm you in the 1990s. . . . We believe that lean production will supplant both mass production and the remaining outposts of craft production in all areas of industrial endeavors to become the standard global production of the twenty-first century. The world will be a very different and much better place."[72] Womack, Jones, and Roos might argue that this is so because lean production combines the best of both craft production and mass production. But this is not a good reason. How, we ask, did the uncertainty of 1990, displayed in Figure 5.5, now change to their certainty that lean production will be the standard global production of the twenty-first century?

Womack, Jones, and Roos were either against or ambivalent about craft production, as the following quotes from their book show:

> Crafts production methods were a well-known alternative [to lean production] but seemed to lead nowhere for a company intent on producing mass-market products.

> A number of craft production firms have survived up to the present. They continue to focus on tiny niches around the upper, luxury end of the market, populated with buyers wanting a unique image and opportunity to deal directly with the factory in ordering their vehicles.

Craft production had the following characteristics:

- A workforce that was highly skilled in design, machine operations and fitting. Most workers progressed through an apprenticeship to a full set of craft skills. Many could hope to run their own machine shops, becoming self-employed contractors to assembler firms.
- Organizations that were extremely decentralized, although concentrated within a single city. Most parts and much of the vehicle's design came from small machine shops. The system was coordinated by an owner/entrepreneur in direct contact with everyone involved—customers, employers and suppliers.
- The use of general purpose machines to perform drilling, grinding and other operations on metal and wood.
- A very low production volume—1,000 or fewer automobiles a year, only a few of which (fifty or fewer) were built to the same design. And even among those fifty, no two were exactly alike since craft techniques produced variations.

We all love the idea of craft production, but the problem with it is obvious: Goods produced by craft method . . . cost too much for most of us to afford.

We expect that lean assembly plants will be populated almost entirely by highly skilled problem-solvers whose task will be to think continually of ways to make the system run smoothly and productively. The great flaw of neo-craftsmanship is that it will never reach this goal, since it aspires to go in the other direction, back towards an era of hand-crafting as an end in itself.

Chinese industry is still focused inwards, pursuing a combination of extreme rigid mass production in its two volume production complexes . . . an inefficient low-quality craft production in about a hundred additional vehicle-manufacturing facilities spread out throughout China.

These "craftsmen" [in some assembly plants in Europe producing luxury cars] would be surprised to learn that they were actually doing the work of Henry Ford's fitters in 1905—adjusting off-standard parts, fine-tuning parts designed so as to need adjustment and rectifying incorrect previous assembly work so that everything would work properly in the end.

These comments show that the authors harbored prejudices about craft production. To condemn craft production because it does not serve the mass market is unwarranted. Nor is craft production necessarily confined to the luxury segment of the market, as the authors claim, or inherently inefficient and costly. The authors' study was intended mainly to deal with North America's and Europe's perceived competitive disadvantage in the automobile industry (and indeed in other industries) in the face of Japanese lean production techniques. It was intended to explain to interested parties in North America and Europe what lean production is and confirm its competitive advantages as real. It was to tell people and governments in North America and Europe that their only option to promote their own interest was to accept and embrace lean production to make a break away from mass production techniques.

Their recommended international multiple-region competitive strategy was intended to advise the sponsors of their research (which included car companies and component suppliers) how to compete on a global market. Unlike conventional economists advancing new theories of international trade, the authors were not interested in proposing strategies that lead to economic growth.

Let us, however, see whether the spread of lean production as the preferred production paradigm and international trade based on it will advance the course of economic development and growth of countries. To do so, we have to examine more closely the conditions under which lean production originated.

At the time lean production was being evolved in Japan after World War II, Japan was largely a developed country. During the 1950s, its real GNP almost doubled and annual growth exceeded 10 percent a year. By 1970, output was over six times what it had been in 1950. By contrast, U.S. GNP increased by only half in the 1950s and 1960s, with average annual growth of 3 to 4 percent. The size of the U.S. economy doubled in twenty years, whereas that of Japan doubled every six to eight years. At the time, Japan had subordinated other goals in favor of catching up with the U.S. economy. At the center of this thinking was an export promotion policy in which, by a combination of direct and indirect government intervention, incentives and strategies were put in place aimed at fostering an enlarged and protected home market. The companies were thus able to gain the necessary competitive strategy and strength at home in order to penetrate abroad.

By banding into *keiretsu*—huge business groups involving reciprocal ownership of stock and long-standing exclusive relationships—individual companies gained financial accumulation and connection that allowed them to undercut smaller domestic rivals and eventually foreign ones. Although the *keiretsu* themselves were stable, they created a business environment of extreme competition, especially in the sectors that targeted international markets. They went to great lengths to keep up with one another, copying new designs and practices.[73]

Lean production came directly from this environment. Lean production is mass-market dependent, though to a much lesser degree than mass production, and unlike craft production. Our estimate is that lean production in the automobile industry in Japan at the time was more capital-intensive and less labor-intensive than the general factor endowment in Japan dictated—even as the Japanese economy itself was already fairly advanced. The automotive industry in Japan, despite developments in lean production, is therefore one of monopolistic competition. This is a characteristic it shares with many of the Japanese export-oriented industries.

It is therefore evident that lean production cannot be the production technique every country should adopt because its factor proportions approximate in the main to those of capital-intensive, low-material, and lower-labor-factor economies.

The long-term prospect of the present monopolistic competitive structure of manufactures in international trade using lean production, in the face of increasing fragmentation of markets, is uncertain, as indicated in Figure 5.5. The long-term structure of international trade with fragmentation of markets will be one in which intraindustry trade may eliminate interindustry trade as we know it today. This is in line with our conclusion in Chapter 4 that flexible specialization (because it is flexible) provides the production paradigm that meets the varying factor proportions requirements of scientific economic development and growth. The flexibility will at one end accommodate a new craft production that has incorporated the new relevant technical developments that have taken place since 1913—new tools, new materials, new instruments, and so on, all of which will substantially improve quality, reduce waste and poor-quality work, and improve consistency and interchangeability. Production volume at this end will be in small quantities on a highly individualized basis. At the other end

will be automated flexible production producing in much larger quantities but with a wide variety of differentiated products with personalized features utilizing new features of information technology. We agree with Piore and Sabel that countries that pursue the strategy of flexible production could, as a result of the flexibility, substantially reduce their dependence on world trade altogether.[74] This is because such countries could find that the theory of comparative advantage and new theories of international trade, with the claimed trade benefits of economies of scale, do not apply to them. Such is the problem facing analysts in relating monopolistic competition (economy of scale) to international trade that Bowen, Hollander, and Viaene concluded, "These findings [of Hummel and Levinson, that positive correlation between trade-to-income ratio and size similarly holds for country groups of any kind] considerably weaken the earlier conclusion that the model of monopolistic competition and international trade is supported empirically." They further added that in an imperfectly competitive setting, potential gains from trade may flow from the elimination or reduction of distortions resulting from market power and from an increase in the size of firms that produce by means of increasing-returns-to-scale technologies. They say that gains may flow from the mere possibility of trade even if actual trade does not take place, but that "there is no guarantee that the gains will in fact be realized."[75] It is clear that the very base of the notion of gains from economy of scale as promoter of international trade is itself doubtful. In Chapter 6, we will show that investments of the nature Womack, Jones, and Roos have in mind retard economic development, especially in poor countries.

Infant Industry

There is hardly a book written on international trade that does not give prominent place to the infant industry controversy. The best statement of the position was that of Samuelson and Nordhaus, who reminded us that the origin of the infant industry concept was in Alexander Hamilton's "Report on Manufactures" (1791), which proposed encouraging the growth of manufacturing by protecting youthful industries from foreign competition. This doctrine received the cautious support of free trade economists such as John Stuart Mill and Alfred Marshall. Such supporters maintained that "infant industries would not be able to weather the initial period of start-up and experimentation if they are forced to face unprotected the gales of international competition." On the other hand, given some shelters, "they might develop economics of mass production, a pool of skilled labor, inventions adapted to local economy and the technological efficiency typical of many industries."[76] Samuelson and Nordhaus were talking of mass production industries, in which economy of scale was at the center. On the other hand, Kreinin saw in the infant industry idea the assertion that any industry that might benefit from large-scale operations because of the existence of external economies such as good transport facilities, well-trained labor, and learning by doing should be allowed to grow to optimal size under a protection tariff.[77]

Samuelson and Nordhaus were talking of internal economies, while Kreinin was talking of external economies—two totally different starting points. To further complicate the issue, it appears that when some authors talk of infant industries, they are including small-scale craft production activities in poor countries as infant industries, which they regard as inefficient and of low productivity. For example, Todaro included the production of bicycles as a local industry that falls into this category.[78] Therefore, in the general literature on infant industry there is a significant lack of agreement about what is being discussed.

Krugman and Obstfeld stated simply that according to the infant industry argument, "developing countries have a potential comparative advantage in manufacturing but new manufacturing industries in developing countries cannot initially compete with well-established manufacturing in developed countries."[79] Manufacturing, it should be noted, can be capital-intensive or labor-intensive.

From the point of view of a scientific theory of development and growth, the infant industry issue has two aspects—that of underdeveloped economies seeking to protect their new industries, and that of countries deciding to develop and grow in accordance with their own factor proportions and with little or no international market trade.

Samuelson and Nordhaus were right that the infant industry doctrine is about the development of mass production activities. This is because the building of a mass production industry requires a lot of time and money. It may require the cultivation of threshold market volume. The issue has become topical as the less developed economies are seeking ways to promote their own growth but are told that their home market is too small. Most of them—or at least the better-off ones among them—have been importing manufactured goods (through long-established colonial links) for quite some time. Their people have developed a taste for foreign goods and comforts. As world trade has grown and become more competitive, they have enjoyed high-quality goods and conveniences at very comfortable prices. But they are faced with the question of what to do to start local manufacture. Import substitution, which has over the past fifty years or so been a controversial issue, becomes a possible course of action under these circumstances. The issue is whether such countries should put up tariff walls to protect their infant capital-intensive activities. The issue of import substitution and the infant industry doctrine have therefore become inextricably linked. Import substitution has increasingly lost favor in recent years, but the issue is by no means finally settled. Let us look at the arguments against import substitution and infant industry protection and see how these stand up from an economic development and growth standpoint.

The arguments can very broadly be summarized under five headings.[80] The first argument is that it is not good for a poor country to move into industries in which it may have a comparative advantage in the future but does not now. As an example, if a country is currently labor-abundant and is in the process of accumulating capital, it should wait till it accumulates enough capital so that it will have comparative advantage in capital-intensive industries. The second is that protecting manufacturing does no good unless the production itself helps make the industry more competitive. For example, Pakistan and India have increased their exports of light manufactures and textiles but not of the heavy manufactures that their governments protected.

It is also argued that the problem in underdeveloped countries is market failure. If market failure did not exist, private investors would build the required industries, thus making protection unnecessary. It is therefore suggested that authorities should instead correct the market failure (for example, by creating financial institutions that can mobilize savings away from traditional sectors to the new industrial sectors). A fourth reason is that, as Krugman and Obstfeld remarked, "there are many stories of infant industries that have never grown up and remain dependent on protection" because they were protected from their inefficiencies.[81] The only ones who gain from such protection are the domestic producers (including foreign firms in the protected market), who charge high prices and penalize consumers. Indeed, countries that have started on import substitution have not shown signs of catching up with the advanced countries. India is a good example of this. After years of ambitious economic plans that emphasized heavy industry, India found itself still largely an underdeveloped country. It is argued that the failure of the Indian economy occurred because it lacked all the ingredients for running a modern industrial sector; it had nothing to do with trade. Import substitution is said to promote many negative features that impede efficient growth. Excessive and complicated methods to promote infant industries have distorted initiatives and have promoted what Krugman and Obstfeld called "production at an inefficient small scale."[82]

These arguments are deficient from the economic development and growth point of view. It is wrong to advise countries to wait to move into industries until they actually have a comparative advantage. Rather, they ought to start at once with local production through production techniques reflecting their factor proportions. On another issue, the concept of market failure derives from the conventional belief in the supremacy of the market, attached to which is a catalog of social, institutional, legal, and cultural stipulations that have been declared as necessary ingredients for economic development—a back-door introduction of institutionalism. Many of these stipulations derive from Western values. Their proponents regard a Westernized economy—capital-intensive in character—as best for rapid economic growth. Hence Krugman and Obstfeld incorrectly label small-scale production as inherently inefficient.

Many of the arguments against import substitution or protection of infant capital-intensive industries in developing countries are valid, but for different reasons than the ones presented by Krugman and Obstfeld. To the extent that they advise developing countries not to engage in capital-intensive industrial activities, they are sound. But when the arguments are intended to buttress support for the theory of comparative advantage and international trade, they are flawed. The reasons protection of capital-intensive activities in poor countries has neither succeeded nor helped such countries economically are fully discussed in Chapter 6. Economists who argue that there might be suitable conditions under which infant industry protection for capital-intensive manufactures is necessary in underdeveloped countries have also got it wrong.

But what of countries who wish to adopt a growth strategy based on their factor proportions? As a practical issue, the question is whether developing countries seeking such a change should be left alone so as to find their way. Virtually every country that has experienced sustained growth in the past, including the United States, Canada, and Japan, has done so using import substitution in the early stages of industrialization. These countries succeeded because they initiated sustainable growth utilizing their factor proportions. Failures occur when countries did not.

Lipsey and Chrystal have said that countries—United States, Canada, and Japan—that went on to sustained growth needed this protection to cope "with the enormous externalities involved in building up infrastructure of physical and human capital as well as required tacit knowledge and abilities."[83] It follows that countries that build on the basis of their factor proportions—a departure from their past—need protection. This gives a new meaning and purpose to infant industry protection—it is needed not to protect capital-intensive industries but to protect local factor-proportion-led industries. Some economists will call this "good import substitution practice," as opposed to what Krugman and Obstfeld called "bad import substitution policies."[84]

We conclude this chapter by stating that international trade is not an instrument of economic development and growth, especially between counties of widely differing economic status. Theories of international trade are empirical and lack scientific substance.

International Factor Mobility

The last chapter dealt with international trade. The theories of international trade claim, as we have seen, to be concerned with how to develop a global economy (world efficiency) in which economic activities take place where they have maximum potential (productivity). Each country is supposed to be relatively better off in the process (it is argued). The theories do not claim that international trade benefits countries equally.

A book on the science of economic development and growth, on the other hand, is concerned with how each country can sustainably maximize its growth. In Chapter 5, we showed that both the theory of comparative advantage and the theory of economy of scale and imperfect competition, on which current literature on international trade is based, are not suitable vehicles for promoting economic development and growth. In short, trade is not synonymous with economic development and growth.

Theorists advocating world growth will say that trade is a second-best substitute for factor mobility. The argument is that since trade has not succeeded in achieving factor-price equalization, free factor movements across countries in response to price incentives will increase world production possibility frontiers. In an ideal world, capital rent will be equalized and wages will be the same in all countries as a result of free movement of capital and labor. Trade is regarded as a substitute for international mobility of factors only if trade could achieve factor-price equalization. Being more or less sub-

stitutable, they are said to have similar effects. For example, capital could leave a capital-abundant country, where it has lower rent, and migrate to a capital-scarce country, where it will achieve higher rent. Labor would, as a result, have become more abundant in the capital-abundant country. Therefore wages will fall. But the income of the owners of capital will rise to become equal to that in the capital-scarce country. The opposite will happen in the capital-scarce country. Capital mobility, like trade, redistributes income from a country's relatively scarce factor to the relatively abundant one. It is argued that factor mobility in this way makes a country better off because the "ability to exchange factors, like the ability to trade goods, widens opportunities."[1] In effect, widened opportunities (whatever *opportunities* means in this case) are regarded as a requirement for economic growth.

Today, the factors that are regarded as transferable are capital, labor, and technology. Of these, technology has not always been regarded as a mobile factor. The importance of technology and its mobility seem to have increased with the emergence of new growth theory. Land is said to be an immobile factor. Recall that the conventional literature does not recognize material as a factor because of traditional economic ambivalence about the role of material. Instead, material is often classed in a characteristically unscientific language as a kind of working capital. Yet material is historically the oldest of the mobile factors.

Conventional economics takes the position that a country's factor endowments do not provide it with the best combination to maximize welfare. So, it is thought, each country needs to export and import products or factors. This is in direct contrast to the science of economic development and growth, which says that to achieve maximum growth each country should harness all its factors using factor proportions deriving from its factor endowments.

Trade economists assert that factor mobility between countries will increasingly reduce their comparative advantage differences such that they could end up with similar factor "endowments." The countries are then said to have minor comparative cost differences and will engage mainly in intraindustry trade. Any cost differences are said to be due to technological differences. In that case, it is asserted that trade and factor mobility become complementary.

Capital Inflow

The focus here is the effect of capital inflow on economic development and growth. By capital inflow, we mean any activity that increases the capital stock of a recipient country. A scientific analysis of capital does not involve finance because in science capital comprises only material and labor. Apart from external capital inflow, we can also treat capital inflow as capital in a country in a deliberate policy to increase its capital accumulation. Our interest is in capital as a production aid.

Foreign investment is often associated with import of capital equipment into a recipient economy. Foreign investment is usually undertaken by multinational corporations (MNCs) and can be directed toward either an advanced economy or an underdeveloped country. MNCs tend to obtain the capital equipment they need from advanced economies. It is, however, also possible to produce simpler types of capital equipment in developing countries. The NICs of East Asia initiated the recent trend of un-

derdeveloped countries engaging in foreign investment in advanced countries.

The issues to be raised may be best discussed at this point in the context of capital inflow from an advanced country into an underdeveloped country with a relatively low capital base. That presents a position of the widest gap in capital endowment between the sending and receiving countries. In other situations the capital gap will not be as great, so that the reader can treat those as a matter of degree.

Current economic literature, on the whole, regards foreign investment as an article of economic development and growth for the receiving countries. As a result, practically all countries, advanced and underdeveloped, are keen to attract foreign investment. The MNCs are not in the business of development and will go to countries and regions with the best financial returns and greatest perceived safety for their investment.

The arguments in favor of foreign investment with particular reference to poor countries identify broadly what are said to be four economic gaps that foreign investment is supposed to fill. The first is that foreign investment (in common with foreign aid) is a way of filling in gaps between domestically available supplies of savings and targeted or desired investment. In short, foreign investment adds to the host country's capital stock. A second gap, analogous to the first, is that foreign investment helps to fill the gap between targeted foreign-exchange requirements and those derived from net export earnings plus net public foreign aid—the so-called foreign exchange or trade gap. The third gap is that between targeted government tax revenues and locally raised taxes. By taxing MNC profits and participating financially in their local operations, poor countries are thought better able to mobilize public financial resources for development projects. Fourth, there is a gap that is said to exist in management, entrepreneurship, and technology skills, which can be filled by local subsidiaries of MNCs by means of training programs and the process of learning by doing and the demonstration effect, enabling local companies to copy the methods of foreign subsidiaries. MNCs are supposed to bring with them the most sophisticated and state-of-the-art technology and use best-practice production processes while transferring modern machinery and equipment to capital-poor Third World countries.[2]

Arguments against foreign private investment stretch from economic to philosophical and ideological. It is said that even though MNCs provide capital, they may lower domestic savings and investment rates by stifling competition through exclusive production agreements with the host government, by failing to reinvest their profits, and by inhibiting the expansion of indigenous firms. It is claimed that even though the initial impact of MNCs is to improve a country's foreign exchange position, their long-run effects may lead to reduction of foreign exchange earnings on both current and capital accounts. The deterioration may occur because of substantial importation of intermediate products, capital goods, and even raw materials, and through repatriation of profits, interest, royalties, management fees, and other funds. There are also many other financial leakages that the host government can suffer because of private foreign investment.[3] Liberal tax concessions, transfer pricing practices, excessive investment allowances disguised as public subsidies, and tariff protection are all means by which the revenue derivable from MNCs is whittled away. For example, in a report prepared as a background document to the ninth summit of heads of states and governments of non-aligned countries in Belgium in September 1996, it was said that there was a negative transfer of resources to developing countries from developed countries, and neither official and multilateral transfers nor commercial flows to these countries have made up for the gap.

Griffin and McKinley pointed out that the net flow of resources (foreign direct investment [FDI] minus profit remittances) typically is negative in developing countries. This, according to them, was clearly the case between 1965 and 1980. There were departures from that norm during the early and mid-1980s, when net resource flows were approximately zero, until 1987, when they then became positive. But they contended that these positive resource flows were about to become negative again because of "recent increase in profit repatriation." "Thus," they concluded, "in terms of net flows of external finance, FDI usually makes a negative contribution."[4]

The skills MNCs provide may have little impact on developing local sources of scarce skills and may in fact inhibit them, as will be discussed later.

According to Todaro, there are other, more fundamental criticisms of MNCs:

a. The effects of MNCs on developing countries are very uneven, and in many situations their activities reinforce dualistic economic structures and exacerbate income inequalities. They promote the interest of the small number of well-paid modern-sector workers against the interests of the rest by widening wage differentials. They divert resources from needed food production to manufacture of sophisticated products catering primarily to the demands of local elites. They worsen the imbalance between rural and urban economic opportunities by locating primarily in urban areas and thus contribute to the flow of rural-urban migration.

b. Multinationals typically produce inappropriate products (those demanded by a small, rich minority of the local population), stimulate inappropriate consumption patterns through advertising and their monopolistic model power, and do this all with inappropriate (capital-intensive) technologies of production.

c. As a result of the first two effects, local resources tend to be allocated to socially undesirable projects. This tends to aggravate the already sizable inequality between rich and poor and the serious imbalance between urban and rural economic opportunities. At the political level the fear is often expressed that powerful foreign corporations can gain control over local assets and jobs and exert influence on political decisions. They may even corrupt officials at the highest levels, directly (by payoff) or indirectly (by contributing to friendly political parties), thus subverting the political process of host countries.[5]

A fourth related criticism is that even the financial (capital) inflow which FDI is supposed to help boost growth is not always realized. The flow, it is claimed, remained concentrated among a few countries. FDI is of little significance to the majority of developing countries that have small markets, because MNCs are out looking for profits, not development of the recipient host country. Shunned by MNCs, such neglected countries will see no relevance in conventional economics, which urges underdeveloped countries to attract FDI in order to develop. The arguments in favor of and against foreign investment lack scientific content. Rather, the lines seem to be drawn on ideological tendencies. Those in favor seem to be coming from a neoclassical bias in favor of the free market, private enterprise, laissez-faire, and all that. They believe that private capital is badly needed in poor countries to make up deficiencies in savings. Governments should act in a hands-off manner. Theorists who are against foreign investment fret about possible loss of national governments' control over domestic economic activities. They see MNCs not as agents of economic change but more as vehicles of antidevelopment. MNCs, it is said, reinforce dualistic economic structures and exacerbate domestic inequalities with wrong products and inappropriate technologies.[6] While confiscation and nationalization of foreign-owned enterprises have waned in the past few years, there are calls for additional controls and more stringent regulation of such enterprises.

Opponents of foreign investment do not seem to be winning the argument—not because their case is weaker but because globalization seems to be saying to poor countries that a strong tidal wave is on its way and they cannot withstand it. The world's political and economic leadership—including that of the United States and development institutions such as the World Bank and the IMF—with their emphasis on openness, democracy, and free enterprise have successfully silenced the voices of those championing the power of host governments to control their economic life. As for the point that MNCs cause uneven development and promote duality, the accusation has increasingly become muted because there are economists, including international trade theorists, who believe that uneven development is an essential feature of economic growth and that inequalities spur growth. We are reminded of the old advocates of big-push development to be achieved through imbalances. We are also reminded of Leys' prescription, referred to in Chapter 1, that economic growth in poor countries will depend on identifying a new class of wealthy indigenous capitalists with access to local capital to spearhead home-grown economic growth initiatives. Such capitalists together with foreign investment will create oases of capital activities.

But it is clear that the argument has not been settled. Appleyard and Field expressed their relief that "research in this complex, important and controversial area continues."[7]

In order to further examine the case for and against foreign investment, we first look at the models often adopted in support. Appleyard and Field concluded that "restrictions on the flow of foreign direct investment have an economic cost of lost efficiency in the world economy and lost income in each of the countries."[8]

The marginal physical product of capital (MPP_k) schedules for two countries are plotted in Figure 6.1. The analysis assumes that there are only two coun-

Figure 6.1 Capital market equilibrium: The two-country case.

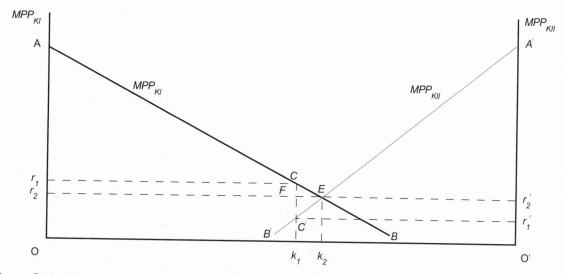

Source: D. Appleyard and A. Field, Jr., *International Economics* (New York: Irwin/McGraw-Hill, 1998, chap. 12, fig. 1).

tries in the world, I and II, and that there are only two factors, capital and labor. It further assumes that both countries produce a single homogeneous good that represents the aggregate of all the goods produced in the countries. In microeconomics theory, a marginal physical product of capital schedule plots the additions to output that result from adding one unit of capital to the production when all other inputs are held constant. With constant prices, this schedule represents the demand for capital inputs derived from the demand for the product. The demand for capital in country I is represented by MPP_{kI} and by MPP_{kII} for country II. The total amount of available capital in the two countries is represented by the length of the horizontal axis OO'.

The model assumes that at the initial pre-international-capital-flow situation, the capital stock in country I is Ok_1 and that in country II is $O'k_1$. With further assumption of perfect competition, capital in country I will be paid at the rate equal to its marginal product Or_1, which is associated with point C on AB. Similarly, capital in country II will be paid

at the rate equal to its marginal product $O'r_1'$, associated with point C' on the schedule $A'B.'$ The total product is equal to the area under the marginal product curve at the relevant size of capital stock. So the total output in country I is equal to the area $OACk_1$ and the total output in country II is equal to the area $O'A'C'k_1$. The world output is the sum of the two areas. The total output in country I is divided between the two factors such that rectangle Or_1Ck_1 is the total return (or profit) of capital (that is, the rate of return, Or_1, multiplied by the amount of capital, Ok_1), and labor receives the remaining output (or income), consisting of the triangle r_1AC. In country II, similarly, the capital receives total return (or profit) of area $O'r_1'C'k_1$, and labor receives the area of the triangle $r_1'A'C.'$

If the rate of return to capital in country I (Or_1) exceeds that in country II $(O'r_1')$ and there is capital mobility, then capital will move from country II to country I. Assuming the same degree of risks attached to investment in the two countries or that the rates of return have been adjusted for risk, the amount of capital in k_2k_1 country II will move to country I to take advantage of the higher rate of return. This bids down the rate of return in country I to Or_2. Since the capital is leaving country II, the rate of return there rises from $O'r_1'$ to $O'r_2'$. In equilibrium, the MPP_k in the two countries is equal, represented by point E, where the two marginal physical product of capital schedules intersect. At this equilibrium, the rate of return to capital is equalized at Or_2 to $O'r_2'$. There is then no further incentive for capital to move between the two countries.

The effect of capital flow k_2k_1 from country II to country I, it is claimed, is that total output has risen in country I. Before the capital inflow, output in country I was the area $OACk_1$, but now it has increased to the area $OAEk_2$. That is, output has gone up by the area k_1CEk_2. In country II, there has been a decline in output. The output before the capital movement was the area $O'A'C'k_1$, now reduced to $O'A'Ek_2$, a decrease of $k_1C'Ek_2$. The world output and efficiency of use of factor resources have been increased. World output has increased because the increase in output in country I (area k_1CEk_2) is greater than the decrease in output in country II (area $k_1C'Ek_2$). The extent of this gain in world output is indicated by the triangular area $C'CE$.

With regard to the total return to each of the factors of production in both countries, the total return to country I's owners of capital was Or_1Ck_1 before capital movement, but it has now fallen to Or_2Ek_2. The return to country II's owners of capital has increased from $O'r_1'C'k_1$ to $O'r_1'Ek_2$. The model is, however, unable to say whether the net gain of owners of capital in country II is less or more than the net loss of owners of capital in country I. Workers in country I have increased their total wages because they originally earned wages consisting of area r_1AC and later area of r_2AE, an increase in wages. In country II, the wage bill was originally area $r_1'A'C'$ and has now decreased to $r_2'A'E$.

This appears to be a solid case for foreign private investment as a means to achieve growth. But looking deeper into this model reveals its many serious weaknesses. The model is based on positivist orthodoxy's belief that capital accumulation is the source of growth. The claim that outputs were $OACk_1$ to $OAEk_2$ and $O'A'C'k_1$ to $O'A'Ek_2$ is therefore incorrect. Thus the claim about net increase in output is accordingly incorrect. Much of the analysis is based on the theory of maximum utility and price. The price content of the analysis makes it not a scientific study of the economic issues involved. The analysis is avowedly a microeconomic one.

There is a more important point, namely, that for the authors' claims to succeed, they have to show first that the growth in each of the countries was already at maximum before the mutual transfer of capital. They did not do this. Going by the principles established by the theory of factor proportions, it is clear that the injection of capital into an economy with its own distinct factor proportions is not what is needed to achieve increased growth. The receiving economy will face the type of structural imbalances that we discuss later in this chapter.

The analysis, therefore, sought to jump from a microeconomic level to a macroeconomic level. The marginal physical product capital schedule is essentially a microeconomic construction that cannot in any seriousness be said to be a useful tool for macroeconomic analysis. The analysis was supported by many assumptions that in practice are not realistic. The structural imbalances caused by the capital transfer were acknowledged by the authors' reference to gainers and losers in each of the countries. As is common with conventional economic analysis, this analysis was unable to conclude whether the losers were more than the gainers in each case, and characteristically the authors had to resort to the need for governments in each country to adopt an income redistribution policy to sort out the resulting economic mess.[9]

Krugman and Obstfeld put it in another way when

they (in what we consider an unsympathetic consideration for the losers in the world) said, "Because the world as a whole is producing more, it is possible in principle to raise everyone's standard of living."[10] But how can that be the case when some people's wages under the model we have just discussed have gone down? Appleyard and Field's statement that national income of the two countries increased as a result of capital mobility was based on assumed fixed prices. If prices vary, as one may find, the claim will not stand.

The model was therefore based on a fundamentally flawed assumption—namely, that because an underdeveloped economy has less capital, the rate of return, Or_1, is necessarily higher than that in the advanced country, $O'r_1$. Indeed, in many instances the financial rate of return to capital in the advanced country will be higher for many reasons. The instances where the rate of return in the underdeveloped country is higher—say, in regard to mineral extraction (the so-called enclave economies)—cannot apply in this model because such a high return arises not from the market in the underdeveloped country but from its material reaching the market in the advanced economy. It is thus a reflected rate of return.

Thus the model has not proved its basic theory: that capital movement from one country to another will benefit each of them and that world factors will be used at what is termed "higher efficiency."

Against this background, it is possible to revisit some of the claimed benefits of foreign investment to a recipient country. Appleyard and Field enumerated these benefits as increased wages, increased employment, increased exports, increased tax revenue, scale economies, provision of technical and managerial skills and new technology, and the weakening of the power of domestic monopolies. As we review this list, it is clear that foreign investment into a poor country has different effects from that into an advanced country due to differences in factor proportions. In pointing out increased wages as one of the benefits of foreign investment, Appleyard and Field were not on solid ground but were quick to add that they assume that some of the increase in wages will result from "distribution from profits of domestic capital."[11] They should know that this does not happen. In regard to increased employment, they pointed out that the gain is particularly important if the recipient country has an excess supply of labor due to population pressure. They should have taken account of the fact that capital-intensive activities have by their nature a low employment absorption. Increased exports are not an end in themselves. In this context, Appleyard and Field talked of the need to generate through increased exports the foreign exchange required to "import needed capital equipment or materials required to assist in achieving the country's development plans" or to pay "interest or repay some principal in the country's external debt." They were in effect interested in the conventionally prescribed but unviable development path for the poor countries, based on traditional theories of trade. Realization of scale economies, which they consider can arise when capital flows into a poor country, is not an advantage for a poor country, for reasons that were examined in the last chapter. A poor country should in the scientific context of development and growth keep away from scale economy activities.

Conventional economics is at loss to prove unambiguously that foreign direct investment increases growth in a poor recipient country. As is common, when conventional economists lack a scientific proof, they resort to the massage of empirical statistics backed up by correlation claims. Thus in regard to FDI the World Bank asserted in 1998 that "studies have consistently found a strong positive correlation between rapid GDP growth and FDI flows," although they quickly added that "the direction of causality is difficult to determine and may go in both directions."[12]

The report displayed a scatter table showing the

ratio of foreign investment to GDP of thirty developing countries against real GDP growth percentage based on its 1993–96 averages. The table showed, for example, that China achieved the highest GDP growth among the thirty countries, about 13 percent, but had only about a 6 percent ratio of FDI to GDP, whereas Hungary had a real GDP growth percentage of about 2 percent but an FDI/GDP ratio of about 11.5 percent. Vietnam, Peru, Malaysia, and Thailand were said to have had real GDP growth of around 9 percent, but ratios of FDI/GDP were about 10 percent, 9 percent, 8 percent, and 2 percent. Nigeria had a growth of less than 1 percent but high FDI/GDP of 6 percent. Mexico had negative growth, –1 percent, but an FDI/GDP of about 5.5 percent. With such inconsistent data, it is clearly incorrect to claim that FDI promotes economic growth. And if, after over half a century in development, this is all the proof the World Bank has about the relationship between growth in poor countries and FDI, this is depressing.

In another publication, *Entering the 21st Century,* the World Bank claimed that "foreign direct investment has a more profound impact on growth in countries that pursue policies promoting exports than it does in countries that follow import-substitution policies." "The reason," it says, "may be that foreign owned companies aiming at global competitiveness and international markets have a greater incentive to bring in technology and training—with accompanying spill-over effects." On the basis of this claim, the World Bank pointed out that in East Asian countries, foreign direct investment played an important role in bolstering advanced manufacturing exports and outputs. Foreign affiliates are supposed to have accounted for between 65 and 73 percent of output in the electrical and electronics sector. If the Bank had Third World host countries in mind, its claim is at best premature, especially considering that the jury is still out on what happened in Asia in 1997.

Having predetermined that foreign investment is essential for economic development and growth of countries that do not have much capital, the World Bank publication set out to list some of the policy actions that attract foreign investment. It claimed that an open trade policy is important. It pointed out that surveys of Japanese firms that decided to invest abroad found that a positive perception of policies governing such investment was a strong determinant of plans to invest and that low trade barriers made it more likely that companies would enter a country. According to the World Bank publication, "When first-rate information technology systems reinforce liberal market access, a country is further integrated into the world economy and becomes still more attractive as a destination for investment." It further pointed out that a survey of international firms in Hong Kong, Singapore, and Taiwan found that the presence of advanced infrastructure was the most important consideration in choosing where to locate regional headquarters and service and the second most important consideration in siting production. It claimed that foreign direct investment is increasingly connected more with trading opportunities than local market exploitation—hence Mexico, for example, has received a huge increase in foreign direct investment, as after NAFTA it is seen as a good base for supplying the United States. Export-oriented development means that investment decisions depend less on the scale of the home market, since firms are looking to sell in a global market. As a result, they are more flexible in choosing locations. It therefore concluded that "stable and attractive economic policies have become much more important [for attracting foreign investment]. . . . In fact, foreign direct investment seems to be responding faster to economic factors than it has in the past."[13]

The World Bank has played a significant role in promoting FDI in poor countries. It has been instrumental in setting up the Multilateral Investment

Guarantee Agency (MIGA) to provide investors with insurance against various possible losses. The Multilateral Agreement on Investment, an initiative of the OECD countries, is a comprehensive framework for protecting foreign investors, liberalizing investments, and settling disputes among all OECD members and other countries willing to meet its obligations.

The World Bank has direct guarantees intended to serve as a catalyst for private sector activities in the Third World. Bank group guarantees have increased steadily from $1.4 billion in 1991 to $4.5 billion in 1997, most of them by the World Bank's International Finance Corporation (IFC). The member groups themselves offer different kinds of guarantees. There is a widely held belief, not supported by scientific economic analysis, that private foreign investment is an important vehicle for economic development and growth in poor countries.

If the conventional model just examined and empirical studies do not provide us with the correct basis for examining the actual effect of capital injection into a poor country, we need to look for other ways of doing this. In underdeveloped countries, we find in regard to factors that, quite apart from the prevalent lack of mobilization of factors in these countries, economic activities are predominantly labor-intensive. It cannot be assumed that an underdeveloped economy is necessarily endowed richly with abundant natural resources (high M/L). The economic activities may be material-intensive or material-scarce, depending on the material endowment position. An underdeveloped country will probably, in the belief that its economic development and growth will be enhanced, seek to have a number of capital-intensive activities. It will be seeking increased capital infusion from other countries. It should be possible broadly to aggregate the labor-intensive activities through weighted averages and arrive at one factor proportion that represents the average for all the labor-intensive activities in

that economy. A similar exercise should broadly produce a factor proportion that aggregates the factor proportions for the capital-intensive activities in the economy. So we can end up with (1) a capital-intensive sector alongside (2) a labor-intensive sector, and (3) the possibility of capital inflow from outside to enable us to study the effect of increase in the capital stock on the relationship between economic sectors. This position is similar to that envisaged in the Rybczynski theorem somewhat combined with the Heckscher-Ohlin-Samuelson model, but the theorem/model combination focused on capital as a financial instrument with a price (rent). It is a two-factor analysis of labor and capital. It did not consider the material factor. A two-factor analysis is likely to miss out on the most important aspects of the consequences of capital inflow into an economy. The theorem assumed away price by positing that the relative prices of the products of capital-intensive and labor-intensive production remained unchanged. In practice, as we have seen in Chapter 4, conventional techniques are not determined simply by the relative prices of their products. The price of products is more usually a residual value after the production techniques have been chosen. Nor do the prices of products bear a direct relationship to factor prices.[14]

Capital is not a financial instrument but basically aggregated material and labor. The assumption of the theorem/model combination that techniques of production are subject to constant returns to scale is reasonable and could be retained in our examination of the issues involved.

The Rybczynski theorem, just like the Heckscher-Ohlin model, is usually analyzed in the context of international trade theory. The theorem states that a non-neutral growth in factors will shift the production possibilities frontier in an asymmetrical manner and alter the relative factor abundance in the country. The economic response to that change depends on the relative commodity prices, which are assumed to be constant on the argument that for a small country changes in its relative factor situation cannot affect world prices. The production impact of such factor growth is said to depend on whether the growing factor is abundant or scarce. If it is the abundant factor, there is said to be an ultra-pro-trade production effect, assuming that the country is exporting the commodity that is intensive in the abundant factor, in the manner of Heckscher-Ohlin. If it is the scarce factor, there is an ultra-anti-trade production effect. It is concluded that other things being equal, the expansionary impact on a country's trade is greater with the growth in the abundant factor than with the growth in the scarce factor. The various theorems and models proposed by conventional trade economists recognize that many things can happen to alter the factor allocation between economic activities and that these changes have important effects on growth behavior. Economists have usually introduced prices into these theorems and models, a situation that tended to force nonscientific matters (welfare, income distribution, consumer tastes and preferences) into the analysis. For example, conventional economics says that if wages rise, all sectors will be more capital-intensive as firms replace labor with capital. But it is not possible for all firms to move toward capital intensiveness if the amounts of physical capital and labor in the economy have not changed.

Figure 6.2 depicts two sectors—one capital-intensive and one labor-intensive—on a three-factor basis of capital, labor, and material. The economy's factor endowments before and after the increase in capital stock are shown by the boundaries of the modified multi-sector Edgeworth boxes OPQR, ORST, OTUP. The capital-intensive sector is depicted by OA, OB, OC, while the labor-intensive sector is depicted by OA^1, OB^1, OC^1. The lines OA and OA^1 in the Rybczynski theorem are said to be determined by the prices of products. But it is clear that OA, OB, OC and OA^1, OB^1, OC^1 are all deter-

mined by the factor proportions of the relevant production.

An increase in capital stock through foreign investment RR^1 (= QO^1 and SS^1) will be in line with the Rybczynski theorem result in a reduction of the labor content of OL_1 to OL_2 and material content from Om_1 to Om_2. Unfortunately, Rybczynski's theorem omitted the effect on material factor when factors of capital and labor are imported into an economy because the theorem was a two-factor analysis. The resulting reduction in capital in our analysis has two components: $C^1(L)C^2(L)$ and $C^1(m)C^2(m)$. The labor-intensive sector therefore loses labor, capital, and material to the capital-intensive sector. In line with the Rybczynski theorem, an increase in foreign investment will increase production in the capital-intensive sector by more than the increase in capital accumulated. On the other hand, as seen in Figure 6.2, it will lead to a contraction of the non-capital-intensive sector. It is clear from Figure 6.2 that the extent to which the output of the capital-intensive sector will grow and the labor-intensive sector will decline will depend very much on the endowed factor proportions of the economy as well as the size of incoming capital. If, for example, the country has a relatively low population, the line holding the point OA^1 will shift to the left and the reduction in the labor component will constitute a higher percentage of the original labor content of the labor-intensive sector and vice versa. So the effect of foreign investment will hit the local economy more severely if the country's population is relatively low. It is, however, a question of extent. If the incoming capital is highly capital-intensive, it will absorb less labor from the local economy. The overall effect, however, is to weaken the local labor-intensive sector. Similarly, a country with few natural resources will be hit severely because of the contraction resulting from materials being transferred to the capital-intensive sector. In many Third World countries, the extent

Figure 6.2 **Two-sector, three-factor construct receiving inward capital investment.**

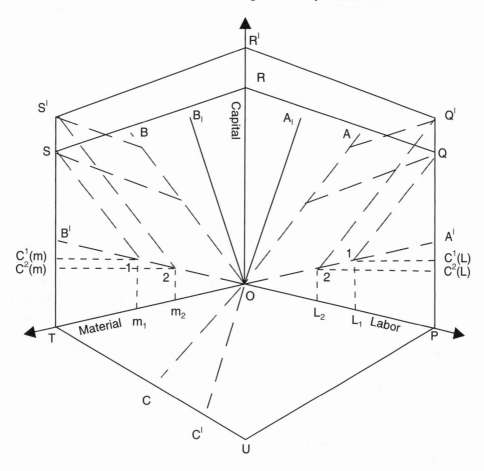

of foreign investment is limited because MNCs will go only where they expect high returns from their capital and many Third World countries do not qualify for this. The additions to the capital stock of many such countries by MNCs are therefore bound to come in small bits and will not make dramatic changes to the capital intensiveness of the capital-intensive sector. Nevertheless, when such foreign aid and loans are added, the total capital input will amount to a substantial portion of such a country's capital stock. This analysis will, therefore, be fairly typical of most underdeveloped countries.

There are, however, instances where foreign in-vestment is high for various reasons. Underdeveloped countries with mineral resources, including petroleum, are likely to attract substantial foreign investment because their market for such foreign investment is outside these countries. The forward and backward effects of these can also create an internal market to which further foreign investment will be attracted. Substantial foreign investment may be caused by the opportunity to pay low wages in order to sell more cheaply in the world market. The more economically viable "emerging" countries that have large markets, like India, are also likely to attract substantial foreign investment.

Figure 6.2a **Effect of increasing FDI in a poor economy, in a two-factor context.**

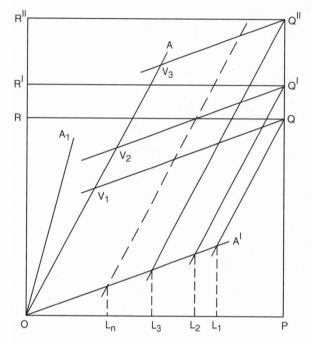

Let us consider the situation in which this considerable substantial foreign investment takes place. The result is likely to be an overall increase in the capital-intensive sector. This is represented in Figure 6.2 by two components of the increased capital intensiveness: that OA_1 (a more capital-intensive production technique) will replace OA, and OB_1 (a more capital-intensive technique) will replace OB in a capital-labor context. Now an entirely new situation arises.

In order not to clutter Figure 6.2 further, we will represent the ensuing relationship in Figure 6.2a and show only the Edgeworth box OPQ^1R^1 of Figure 6.2. Relationships similar to those indicated for box OPQ^1R^1 will be seen to apply to box OR^1S^1T.

OA_1 is the consequence of increasing the size of capital in the economy further beyond PQ^1 to PQ^{11} due to increased FDI. It is seen that this leads to an even greater contraction of the local economy which loses even more labor and material. Higher foreign investment grows at the increasing expense of the local economy, the labor reductions being at L_1, L_2, L_3 ... L_n with their material and capital component. All this exacerbates the economic structural imbalance of the macro economy.

Some underdeveloped countries such as India as well as the former Soviet Union sought to mobilize capital by building capital-producing industries. The capital items produced may not necessarily be very sophisticated, but they are capital items nevertheless. The building of capital is usually part of a deliberate economic strategy of building up what is generally called a modern industrial sector in the attempt to initiate capital accumulation. The result is that capital exceeds threshold level. Proponents argue that it is necessary to develop heavy industry because, through a push strategy, the forward and backward linkage effect is supposed lead to the creation of other new basic capital-based activities. This strategy emphasizes attaining economies of scale. This source of capital development is different from foreign investment capital because it requires that a portion of the economy's endowment of labor and material be assigned to it, leaving less labor and material factors available for production of consumption goods. This position is depicted in Figure 6.3.

In order to maintain and grow an increase in capital QQ^1, the factors of labor and material available for production of consumption goods are now reduced to OP_1, OT_1 because P_1P and T_1T are factors used in production capital QQ^1 ($= RR^1 = SS^1$). The factor endowment matrix of the economy now changes to $P_1Q_1R^1S_1T_1U_1$. The new factor proportion line between labor and material is now OU^1 instead of OU. The effect on a poor country such as India of pursuing a capital-producing strategy is that its disproportionate (that is what we call biased expansion in favor of capital) growth is intensified with the subsequent greater contraction of the

Figure 6.3 **Two-sector, three-factor construct facing diversion of resources into capital investment.**

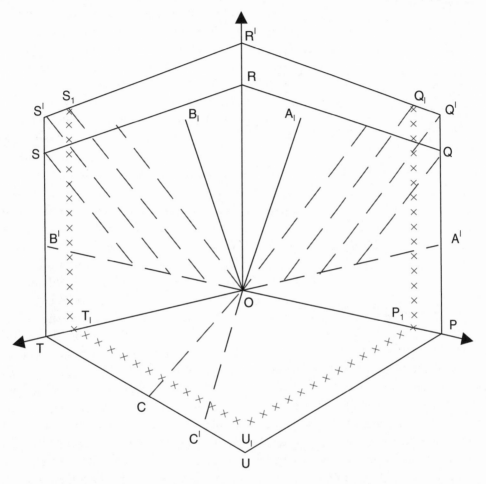

growth of its small-scale labor-intensive sector, as will be seen by comparing Figure 6.2 and Figure 6.3. It is clear that in a country such as South Korea, which has a low material/labor endowment ratio, the effect of pursing a capital accumulation strategy can be devastating for the non-capital-intensive sector of the economy, because it loses capital, labor, and material.

All in all, we see that contrary to conventional thinking, capital growth in underdeveloped economies (whether through foreign investment or a deliberate policy of internal capital growth) does not lead to balanced macroeconomic growth. It tends to exacerbate the factor proportion differences between sectors of the economy. Structural imbalances are worsened. The scale of the structural imbalance, as we have seen, very much depends on the size of the capital input. In any case these constitute impediments to the growth of the local economy due to the dislocation of its factor proportions.

Let us now examine the implications of the opposite policy to the deliberate capital creation and concentration, and seek instead to reduce the gap between the capital-intensive sector and the rest of the economy.

In Figure 6.4, unlike in Figure 6.2, development

Figure 6.4 **Effect of closing factor proportions gap between sectors.**

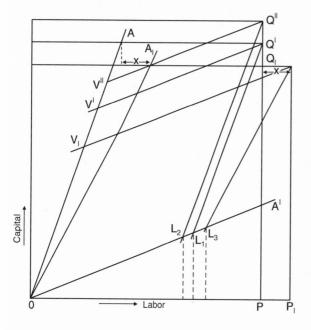

strategy is to bring the factor proportions between the two sectors nearer. This means that OA_1, which is more labor-intensive, replaces OA. The economy now has two sectors, OA_1 and OA^1. The gap between the labor-intensiveness of the factors has now narrowed. It means that instead of increasing the economy's capital beyond $Q^{1,}$ as in Figure 6.2a, we reduce the capital by Q^1Q_1 as shown in Figure 6.4— this is equivalent to the capital difference between OA and OA^1—and increase the labor boundary of the economy by, say, PP_1—this is equivalent to increased labor released by a change from OA to OA_1 (equal to x). It will be noticed that the new parallelogram based on OA_1 meets the labor-intensive sector OA^1 at a point L_3, thus reversing the encroachment on the local economy as compared with L_2 due to the original increase in capital to Q^{11}. The disproportionate growth of the economy's capital sector is reversed as we witness its reduction from a previous increase of V^1 to V^{11} to a reduction to

V_1. The macro economy now moves to greater balance and so has higher growth potential.

It is obvious from our discussions that in order to attain maximum potential growth in a dynamic situation, factors of production need to be flexible and mobile between sectors. For example, capital (which comprises the aggregation of labor and materials) can be constituted and used for practically any required production. In that sense, capital (production aid) is flexible and mobile within an economy. Appropriate materials can be selected by firms to meet their production needs with increasing outreach to alternative materials as well as substitutions with other factors as necessary. In general, factors within an economy, in the scientific economic context, are not, within a broad time horizon, specific, a theme that will be taken up in Chapter 10. Within an economy, factors are diffused and mobile. Increasingly conventional economists are recognizing that economic flexibility of factors is the key to long-term high economic performance.[15] It is flexibility in factor utilization that enables factor proportions to change and evolve as necessary. When this does not happen, an otherwise strong, balanced economy can in time become a weak, slowing, unbalanced economy. Conventional economics confuses mobility of factors as indicated with the effects of factor prices. They will argue, for example, that because of persistent wage differences across skills and across industries as well as persistent long-run differences in returns to capital, these factors are not mobile.[16] It is necessary in the context of economic science to see these price differentials as impediments to factor flexibility.

Foreign investment is specific, lumpy, and highly localized. Foreign investment, as should be clear from our discussions, cannot be a means of achieving maximal sustainable economic growth in poor countries. Its presence in a poor country will promote biased growth, skewed in character and incapable of promoting maximal potential growth. It increases economic structural imbalance in which an economy performs below its potential.

All in all, macroeconomic growth suffers in a poor country due to foreign investment. The foreign investor will gain high output because of the Rybczynski effect of his capital, though his returns may not always be as great as they would be in an advanced economy.

We need to look more deeply into the nature of structural imbalances that result when a poor country adopts either a pro-foreign-investment strategy or economic strategies based on promoting investments that are capital-intensive. Each of these strategies results in substantial capital stock formation.

What we have in Figures 6.2, 6.2a, and 6.3 is an economic dichotomy, which some economists loosely call a dual economy. They euphemistically label the capital-intensive sector "modern" and the other either "poor" or "traditional" or "informal." Such economists will say that the aim of economic development is to increase the size of the modern sector until in effect it squeezes out the traditional economy. We have seen that this aim is not achievable. This is because increasing capital input does not lead to the elimination of the traditional economy but only widens the gulf between the two, increasing structural imbalances, and in the end affects both sectors adversely.

The situation is exacerbated, as already hinted, by financial considerations. Because the worker in the capital-intensive sector has more production aids (capital) to work with, he is assumed to have an output value much higher than that of his counterpart in the other part of the economy. Consequently, he is paid at a much higher rate than his counterpart. One immediate result is that the capital-intensive sector acts to pull the best workers away from the rest of the economy. The centers of capital-intensive activity become centers of population as an uncontrollable informal society of hangers-on forms around the capital-intensive activities in towns.

In most poor countries, policy, following the dictates of conventional economics, is geared toward channeling funds to enable firms to procure and produce more capital equipment. Conventional economists emphasize the need for savings in these countries in order to promote growth, but they really mean that the savings of the bulk of the population should be mopped up and mobilized so as to underwrite "modern" economic structures. Financial institutions and instruments are the agents for mobilizing savings and foreign finance. These, along with other financial and fiscal incentives, are intended to facilitate either local production or the importation of capital equipment. We therefore see that apart from the structural imbalances that occur naturally through the interaction of factors as depicted in Figure 6.2 and Figure 6.3, financial factors tend to aggravate the position. Not only is skilled labor drawn away from the rest of the economy to the modern sector, but savings are also transferred to that sector.

Let us contrast the role of foreign investment in an advanced economy. The first major difference between an advanced economy and an underdeveloped economy is that the former is not a dual economy. Even the agricultural sector in an advanced economy is comparatively capital intensive. The difference between the capital-labor ratios of the most capital-intensive activity and the least capital-intensive activity is much smaller than in a poor country. Labor-intensive activities are not a common feature of advanced economies. The second difference is that in most advanced countries, capital equipment resulting from foreign investment constitutes a small percentage of the capital stock. Indeed, many foreign MNCs in advanced countries will source a substantial part of their capital plant from the host country. In practice, a greater proportion of the economy's endowment of material and labor is devoted to capital formation in an advanced economy compared to a poor one (that is, the capital/

Figure 6.5 **Two-sector changing factor relationships as foreign investment enters into an advanced economy.**

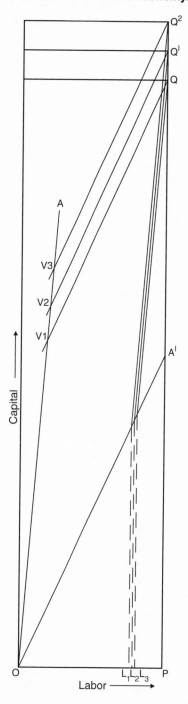

material ratio is generally higher). Third, broadly speaking, advanced countries have a higher material/labor ratio than poor countries.

Because of these reasons we see that when the capital stock of an advanced economy increases, the capital addition is likely to be spread over many more activities than in a poor economy. This means that an increase in capital stock is likely to raise the capital share of the factor proportions of the less capital-intensive activities as well. For example, as Freeman and Soete have pointed out, many service activities in the advanced countries are becoming more capital-intensive and clusters of new technologies cause constant technology diffusion across sectors of their economies.[17]

The position described is shown in a two-factor (capital-labor) analysis in Figure 6.5. Similar analysis on a capital-material basis can be carried out in relation to FDI into advanced economies. QP and OP are the capital and labor endowments of the advanced economy. The relatively "long" length of QP compared to the short length of OP indicates a high-capital/labor economy (advanced economy) unlike, say, Figure 6.2 which describes a low-capital/labor economy. The broad sectors representing high capital intensity and low capital intensity in an advanced economy are shown as OA and OA^1, respectively.

The distinctive feature of an advanced economy is that FDI, unlike that in a poor country, constitutes a relatively small portion of the economy's capital. This is represented by the relatively small FDI capital injections QQ^1 and Q^1Q^2 (compared to PQ).

It is clear from Figure 6.5 that additional capital injection through FDI takes relatively very little labor away from the less capital-intensive sector and moves it to the highly capital-intensive sector (L_1, L_2, L_3) compared with L_1, L_2, L_3 in Figure 6.2A. This is because of the low labor content of the highly capital-intensive sector. For equal quantities of capital injection QQ^1 and Q^1Q^2, it is evident that

$$\frac{V_1 V_2}{OV_1} \quad \frac{V_3 V_2}{OV_2}.$$

That means that incremental biased growth of the capital-intensive sector decreases with each additional capital injection. A comparison of countries makes it clear that the incremental biased growth of the capital-intensive sector in a poor economy is much greater than that in an advanced economy (see Figure 6.2a). In Figure 6.2a, a unit of FDI is a larger proportion of PQ than in Figure 6.5. OA^1 leans nearer to OP in Figure 6.2a than in Figure 6.5.

We therefore see that injecting FDI into an advanced economy causes very little change in the relationship between sectors and does not cause the large structural imbalance which it causes in a poor economy. To that extent, it cannot be said that FDI into an advanced economy can contribute to sustainable macroeconomic growth. It may be more accurate to say that FDI in advanced countries seeks to take advantage of the relatively more balanced economy in an advanced country so as to achieve a consistent profit profile. The increasing tempo and flow of FDI between advanced countries are therefore logical commerical strategy. We conclude in this section on international mobility of capital, by which recipients are enabled to increase their capital input, that capital movement across countries of different statures is not an instrument of economic development and growth.

Economic Hemorrhage–Business Cycles

Conventional economics operates on the basis that different productive activities of different sizes (approximating to different factor proportions) of the micro economy exist side by side and should cooperate. It assumes that the sum of the parts is equal to the whole. These assumptions are not correct. We will now turn briefly to look at the structure of the micro economy.

To do this, we need to examine the dynamics of factor change in the context of our discussion on the introduction of new capital into an economy above threshold value by way of international factor mobility (in this case capital injection through foreign investment or aid) and/or a policy of domestic capital formation, as shown in Figures 6.2 and 6.3.

We have seen that an increase in the economy's capital through new capital-intensive activities will poach labor, material, and capital from the less-capital-intensive sector. This contracts the less-capital-intensive sector and curtails its growth. We have seen that in turn the less-capital-intensive sector takes revenge on the capital-intensive sector because its ultimate demand for the latter's output falls. In turn the latter adds to the unemployment that results. Such is the push and pull between the sectors, which can get fiercer and fiercer depending on the gap in factor proportions. We therefore see that as more capital is introduced, the "chemical" composition of each sector is undergoing constant change, as the movement of factors in and out of sectors changes the preexisting factor proportions.

The economic gyrations so caused reflect adversely on the growth pattern of the economy. In an advanced economy, this shows up in what conventional economists call business cycles, whose gyrations do not always follow a pattern, as so much depends on the quantity and sequential timing of new capital formation. Economic decline will occur with high buildup of new capital. The decline peaks when the imbalance eases off, which occurs when capital formation shrinks because of falling demand.

At the other end are the low-level underdeveloped economies. They do not attract much foreign investment. They do receive some capital project aid and set out deliberately, because of conventional economic practice, to increase their capital base and engage in a number of "modern" projects. Their structural imbalance, however, is far greater than that of an advanced economy because the large difference in factor proportions between the "modern" sector and the rest of the traditional economy. The push-pull is there but causes smaller but serious gyrations because capital inflow and accumulation are small and spasmodic. There are therefore no noticeable business cycles because there is little economic activity to start with. What we have is an economy that is, in the medium term at least, in decline with no intrinsic growth prospects because of serious structural (factor proportions) imbalances.

It is the middle-income countries, the so-called emerging markets, that have each of the two evils that afflict the countries at both extremes of wealth. They receive continuous capital inflow, and they also share the wide differences in factor proportions with the poor countries. The gyrations are therefore far more severe than those of the advanced countries. In Chapter 2 we said that economic development and growth were like the arteries that carry vital blood for an economy. It seems that the best way to describe the situation in the emerging economies is that the gyrations, after simmering for a while, can sometimes erupt into what we will call "economic hemorrhage" when the economy suddenly loses large doses of blood (steep falls in growth rate), as the experiences of the East Asian and South American countries confirm.

Material Inflow

Mobility of material factor in international economics is older than capital mobility. Transfer of cotton, for example, into the United Kingdom set up the famous Lancashire cotton industry that was the strength of that country's industrial revolution. Today such materials as cocoa, coffee, and other agricultural items constitute important inputs into the production processes in the advanced countries. Crude oil and a wide range of minerals, whose exploration and extraction in the Third World countries is responsible for substantial proportions of

foreign capital investments there, are aspects of the transfer and mobility of the material factor. To the extent that the Third World countries exchange these materials for manufactured goods and services from the advanced economies, this is trade in the ordinary sense of the word. But in the context of traditional international trade theory it is not trade. Mining and oil extraction are among the most capital-intensive activities of modern times. Nor do cocoa, coffee, and so on fall into the same category as textiles and other traditional labor-intensive productions in which the Third World trades with the advanced economies.

It will be thought that for any country with few natural resources, conventional theory on the international factor mobility of materials will come to the rescue and make up for its economic "deficiency." All the country needed to do, according to this theory, is import the materials it needed as vital inputs to new economic activities. Japan, for example, being material-deficient during the early period of its industrialization, invested a lot in owning mines in foreign countries in order to assure itself of the supply of different types of industrial inputs.

Regrettably, Rybczynski's theorem comes back into play. The importation of large quantities of materials into a country causes the sector(s) into which these are deployed to grow at a rate faster than the growth rate of imported material supplies by taking away from the rest of the economy considerable quantities of capital and labor. The production aid (capital) that may be needed to utilize the increased material input either has got to be imported (as in the case of South Korea) or has to be manufactured by dipping into the economy's already limited material resources (as in Japan). In each case, structural economic imbalance results. It is no wonder that this aspect of Japanese international investment strategy has cooled over the past decades. The importation of significant quantities of crude oil by many countries (rich and poor) cannot therefore be justified on scientific economic grounds. However, it is a matter of necessity due to countries' adoption of capital-intensive technologies that require increasing inputs of oil and gas energy. But the international mobility of materials does not contribute anything to sustainable economic development and growth of countries.

Foreign Investment and Trade Between Advanced Economies

As we have shown, foreign investment into an advanced economy does not add to structural imbalance and can add to growth in the recipient economy. This means that by investing in each others' countries, advanced countries stand to gain mutual advantages. This because their factor proportions (though not exactly the same) are near to each other's.

These conclusions are not too dissimilar to recent modifications that conventional economists have made to their trade theory. It was becoming evident to them that conventional trade theory neglected many important things. They have reluctantly accepted that international trade tends to widen the gap between rich and poor. Appleyard and Field stated that recent new insights "do not lead to particularly optimistic conclusions about the future export performance of developing countries."[18] New theories suggest that the future of international trade lies in growing trade among rich countries and not in trade between the poor and rich. What this means is that trade among countries with similar factor proportions will increase provided they all have achieved sustainable economic growth. Similarly, foreign investment between advanced countries is increasing and is mutually beneficial. Freeman and Soete have gone even further to say that "it is primarily the internationalization of production over the past three decades which has led to catching up and rapid technological diffusion of 'best practice' production techniques and products

from the USA to a large number of OECD countries, and thus to the convergence of income levels, rather than just the actual international trade flows, as traditional trade theory would lead one to believe."[19] Today the flow of FDI to developing countries is indeed small in comparison to that among the rich countries.

The deep structural dichotomy between rich and poor countries has not interested conventional economists. As ironic as it seems, international factor mobility hurts poor economies and helps to widen the gap between them and the rich economies. This conclusion is coming at a time when poor countries are told that with globalization, their economic future lies in attracting foreign investment and seeking access to increased export of their primary products and home-produced goods, and when they are being required to maintain open economies.

In layman's language, it can be said that in economic development, when dissimilar things are juxtaposed, they react with each other not in a positive, cooperative way, but in a way in which the stronger tends to prey on the weaker, forcing it into a permanent subservient position. This occurs, as we have seen, between the so-called modern sector and the traditional sector in a poor economy. It is not hard to see this within countries in Europe. Despite over ten years of free movement of factors between eastern and western Germany since German reunification, with unprecedented inward capital inflow from West to East, the economic gap between the two has largely remained. Unemployment in the East is currently 17.8 percent—more than double the 7.8 percent in the West. Some DM40 billion ($18.5 billion) flowed into the East from the West in the eastern "reconstruction" and government support programs in 1999. In that same year, migration out of the East due to huge unemployment was the highest since German reunification. Northern and southern Italy have similarly remained permanently economically divided.

Foreign Direct Investment and Export of Manufactured Goods by Developing Countries

Economists have trumpeted the fact that the East Asian countries did not only succeed in developing exports in manufactured high-tech goods but followed this up by making some investments in Europe and America and elsewhere. In 1996, developing countries are said to have invested $51 billion abroad.[20] Like industrial countries, they invested predominantly in economies in the same region. The World Bank claims that these trends indicate "the growing integration of developing economies in the world markets."[21]

Three factors will show that foreign direct investment and export of manufactured high-tech goods by developing countries are not sustainable. The first is an aspect of Linder's hypothesis that successful potential exports are those goods for which a domestic market exists.[22] The knowledge of how to develop, produce, and market a product cannot be acquired without a local market to interact with; this helps an economy move up the learning curve.

Porter, as we pointed out in Chapter 5, also emphasized that multinationals succeed only because they have built up a home base market. The market in many developing countries for the capital-intensive production is small. These countries, therefore, lack experience at home in dealing with product differentiation, on which competition in the advanced economies depends. Indeed, because of differences in home and foreign markets, local home production is either a version of the foreign production or entirely different.

The second factor is one we have just examined, namely, that the establishment of capital-intensive home production faces the prospect of a local economic base that contracts (in the Rybczynski fashion) as the capital-intensive sector denies it the factors it requires in order to sustain itself. This might in the extreme case cause the whole economy itself to hemorrhage, with the capital-intensive activity in turn becoming a victim of inflationary pressures.

The third is the difficulty that faces such developing-country MNCs in keeping up with changes in the science of their industry, as they are not likely to have the same access to research infrastructure as those they are competing with in the international market.

To illustrate the factors just described, we will use South Korea just before the meltdown of 1997 as a representative example of a developing country that has been most successful in exporting high-tech goods and in making FDI. The chip business generated cash flow for South Korea in good times and kept whole companies afloat. Together Samsung Electronics, Hyundai Electronics, and LG Semicon represented 34 percent of the global DRAM market and accounted for 13 percent of Korea's 1997 exports. Yet current prospects are that Hyundai Electronics and LG, which together account for half of South Korea's production, may be unable to afford the transition to 12-inch wafer fabs that are critical to mass production of 156 MB chips. This is a big blow to the country. Park Joon Kyung of the Korea Development Institute (a government think tank) acknowledged that the chip-making sector was what he called Korea's core competence. Its collapse, he once said, "will have enormous consequences in the Korean economy. The semiconductor industry is key to telecommunications, multi-media and a wide spectrum of electronics."[23] South Korea is therefore likely to face a challenge that is difficult to meet as the speed of technological change and obsolescence accelerates.

Between 1983 and 1998 three *chaebols* in the semiconductor industry spent more than $4 billion on product equipment. This has been euphemistically called an "entry fee."[24] If catching up was already quite costly, keeping up and getting ahead brought an even higher fixed capital cost burden.

Korea's semiconductor industry is based on an extremely weak foundation in terms of necessary material and production equipment. In 1991, 90 percent of the production equipment had to be imported (50 percent of that coming from Japan). We have already studied the structural effect of the importation of capital equipment and material on a developing economy. Import dependency was embarrassingly high, particularly for high-value special material. In 1999, current annual consumption of material was about $600 million, with about 70 percent imported. While some progress has been made in domestic production of silicon wafers using foreign (capital-intensive) techniques obtained from licenses and joint ventures, most domestic production is restricted (as it should be) to relatively simple materials such as frame, bonding wire, and packing materials. There is therefore structural imbalance even in this sector.

Probably the major weakness relates to circuit design, which involves the country's limited capacity to broaden product portfolio and develop new products and markets. The narrow focus on memory products has negative repercussions for the overall structure of the electronics industry. Korea continues to export more than 90 percent of its total semiconductor output, while it imports more than 80 percent of its domestic demand. Such imbalance between supply and demand makes it difficult to broaden and deepen the forward and backward linkages within the electronics industry and give it the home base it needs to compete in the monopolistic international arena. In their book *Technological Capabilities and Export Success in Asia*, Ernst, Ganiatsos, and Mytelka concluded, "It is probably fair to say that Korea's semiconductor industry represents today a modern version of the classical mono-product export enclave characterized by a minimum of linkage with the domestic economy."[25]

South Korea's automotive industry faced similar problems, which resulted in its being largely sold off in 1999 to the automotive corporations of Europe and the United States.

In the end, it does not seem that developing countries have a lot of economic gain to derive by seeking to engage in foreign direct investment in capital-intensive production. It can be said that the international market in capital-intensive manufactured goods since the 1990s is not as welcoming to newcomers as was the case in the 1970s and early 1980s. Competition (monopolistic) has globalized and become more innovation-based, making it difficult for new firms to identify market niches and grow with them. Standards are more often than not set elsewhere, and firms find themselves under pressure to match the best. Catch-up strategies based solely on building production and investment can no longer enable the individual newcomer to keep up.[26]

In respect, then, to the World Bank claim that the developing countries were increasingly being integrated into the global economy, we can see that developing countries cannot participate in any meaningful way in a globalized economy for three reasons: (1) their economies cannot usefully accommodate foreign investments or engage in a capital-intensive industrial structure, because such investment cannot lead to increasing and sustainable growth; (2) they cannot engage in sustainable outward foreign investment because they lack the home base—the economies of rich countries are in any case dominated, almost to the exclusion of poor countries, by investments among the rich nations; and (3) regional economic blocs among developing countries only provide powerful MNCs the opportunity to establish capital-intensive activities because of increased opportunity to achieve economy of scale—the structural imbalances caused by such investments and local host economies is the same as if the regional grouping did not take place, because the natural factor proportions of a regional economic bloc will not materially differ from those of its members.

Technology Transfer

Apart from capital transfer (FDI), another factor that conventional economics recognizes as mobile (transferable) in promoting economic development and growth is technology. Here again, as always, no one cares to define in a scientific sense what is meant by *technology*. Before the industrial revolution, the income gap between the poorest and richest nations was relatively small, with a ratio between 1.5 and 2. Over the last century, following the industrial revolution, this ratio increased dramatically, and now the dominant pattern of economic growth is one of fast-increasing differentiation among countries and growth divergence.[27] Many authors, especially with the emergence of new growth theory, attribute these differences to the rich countries' success in using "science and technology." The endogenous role ascribed to technology by conventional economists has made it the determinant of whether a country forges ahead or falls behind or catches up according to them. Capital in the usual sense is absent in most new growth theories.

It is from this perspective that the concept of technology diffusion has gained favor. The idea of "foreign technology" as a vehicle for that diffusion has become a basic assumption of conventional economic development and growth theory. Foreign technology and its international diffusion, it is said, are historically a well-recognized factor in the industrialization of both Europe and the United States in the nineteenth century and, more strikingly, Japan in the twentieth century.[28] It is not often sufficiently emphasized, however, that while the United States had a diffusion of technology in its early years from Europe, it considerably adapted this to its relative factor endowments, which were different from those of Europe. Japan is said to have copied Western technology, but it too modified and changed it to suit its needs. The Asian tigers, unfortunately, attempted to imitate the foreign technology with-

out adapting it and failed after what seemed at first to be a huge success.

Freeman and Soete were of the view that international diversity in growth performance and "catching" up put the emphasis back on the "historical institutional framework within which the process of imitation/technological catching up takes place." Therefore, they said, "the international diversity in growth performance of countries demonstrated the importance of path-dependent development with many bifurcations and possibilities of 'locked in' development whereby some industrialized locations got 'selected' early." They argued that such locations may exert some "competitive exclusion" of other places by appropriating the available "agglomeration economies." They concluded that "it is the increasing returns associated with industrialization and development which make the conditions of development so paradoxical. Previous capital is needed to produce new capital, previous knowledge is needed to absorb new knowledge, skills must be available to acquire the new skills and a certain level of development is required to create the agglomeration economies that make development possible. In summary, it is to some extent within the logic of the dynamics of the system that the rich get richer and the gap remains and widens for those left behind."

Freeman and Soete indicated that development policies have in one way or another been concerned with how to break out of this vicious circle. Most of these policies have concentrated on tackling investment and infrastructure location problems, with less attention given to "knowledge and skills constraints." They argued that international diffusion of technology provides "a crucial ingredient in the debate on technological 'locking out' of underdevelopment." They were of the view that through the use of imported (foreign) technologies the poor countries would acquire some comparable industrialization advantage in low-tech, mature products and industries. On the other hand, they cautioned that insofar as "mature products are precisely those that have exhausted their technological dynamism," there was the risk of the poor countries getting trapped in low-wage, low-skill, low-growth development patterns. The authors finally concluded that "technological catching up will only be achieved through acquiring the capacity for creating and improving as opposed to simple 'use' of technology."[29]

Freeman and Soete's book on technology and innovation is currently regarded as comprehensive and authoritative. Their views can, however, be confusing to the student because some correct facts are mixed with incorrect facts and assumptions. As usual in conventional economics, the authors have assumed that Western-style technology is what every country should adopt in order to break out of the vicious circle in which the rich get richer and the poor get poorer. It is in that context that they refer to some technologies as "low-tech," which according to them entrap people in disadvantageous patterns of development, and argued that "Heavy reliance on imported technology is an inescapable necessity for most countries in the world."[30] They are right that the historical institutional framework is relevant, but only insofar as it can lay the grounds for a people to be self-reliant and evolve their own basic economic personality. So it is that the United States, China, and Japan have thrived in terms of economic growth. But there is no set of institutional parameters that is universally conclusive to economic growth, as institutions are socio-politico-cultural creations. To that extent, Freeman and Soete were right when they emphasized the need for a people to acquire the capacity to create and improve. But the result may not be "Western" technology.

It is true that some advanced countries seem to exert some competitive exclusion by appropriating the available agglomeration economies. It also looks as if existing capital is needed to produce new capital, existing knowledge is needed to absorb new knowledge, existing skills are needed to acquire new

skills, and a certain level of development is required to create the agglomeration economies that make development. In short, Freeman and Soete are suggesting that the rich countries have the start-up advantages that poor countries don't, and that lack of these advantages is a barrier to economic development and growth. But the apparent agglomeration economies enjoyed by the advanced countries do not result from the factors listed by Freeman and Soete. An advanced country is inherently growth-oriented and that of a poor country is inherently stagnating or growth-retarding. An advanced economy is more structurally balanced than a poor country seeking to grow by traditional conventional methods of new capital investments. Because the former is more structurally balanced, additional activities in an advanced economy induce greater growth potential.

It is incorrect therefore to claim, as the authors did, that the growth tendency of an advanced economy exists because its people possess more existing capital or knowledge or skills. Lack of capital by itself is not a handicap in economic growth. Claims that poor countries should acquire Western technology and skills have for a long time obstructed economic development theory.

We will examine a series of cases from Nigeria to throw some more light on aspects of the foregoing. Over the years, as the Nigerian economy's revenue from oil increased substantially in the 1970s, that country invested heavily in electricity infrastructure, which conventional economists and the World Bank regard as the key to economic growth. But then in the late 1980s oil revenues fell and the economy slumped. One result of this is that electricity demand fell as the few industries created by foreign investment lost their market. Often they were unable to find the foreign exchange they needed in order to import spare parts and raw materials. Despite this, the National Electricity Power Authority (NEPA) was unable to meet even the lower demand. Its system had collapsed because its capital-intensive structure was out of phase with an economy that was basically labor-intensive and material-intensive. A press release by NEPA's Technical Board in 2000 highlighted aspects of its organization:

- NEPA has ten power stations, with only six partially operational.
- The installed capacity is 6,000 mW, but current output is 1,500 mW.
- Fifty percent of existing substations are either overloaded or damaged.
- Most vehicles used for fault detection/clearing, including all its helicopters, are nonfunctional.
- The protection, communication, and automation systems for the transmission grid are obsolete and/or nonfunctional.
- The SCADA system, which is designed for data acquisition, control, and automation, is largely nonfunctional.
- The power line communication systems are down and unserviceable in most areas on the grid.
- The transmission grid is extremely fragile due to long years of neglect.
- The authority's rates are heavily subsidized.

As another example, in 1999 it became evident that Nigeria's five refineries, each of them built by reputable international companies with the latest technology, were largely inoperational. The country has, as a result of the oil boom of the 1970s, imported over the years many cars, buses, and trucks, and ambitious road building projects were undertaken in the belief that this would help lay the infrastructure for modernization of the economy. However, the country experienced the worst fuel shortage of its existence and had to resort to importation of gasoline, diesel, and kerosene. Ninety-five percent of the gasoline needed by the country was imported, as the refineries could produce only 5 per-

cent. At the same time, by 1998 most of the roads were in serious disrepair.

Despite its many years of refinery operation, by 1999 Nigeria had to put out tenders for proposals by international companies for what was euphemistically called "turnaround" of the refineries. As in the case of electricity, gasoline, diesel, and kerosene prices were being heavily subsidized by the government.

In the third example, in 1983, Benue State in Nigeria was able to borrow the sum of £67 million from international banks under the aegis of the United Kingdom Export Credit Guarantee (ECGD) to build a soybean processing factory. Farmers in the Taraku region of the state were soybean farmers, and the potential for expanding production was high. A state-of-the-art processing factory with a good deal of automation was designed and installed by a UK company. The capacity of the plant was designed with the expectation that the soybean oil produced would be exported. Local personnel were trained in the operation, maintenance, and management of this industrial edifice. After five years in which the fortunes of the investment went from bad to worse, the plant closed down. The plant now stands virtually abandoned. There are no resources to reactivate it.

As a final example, in the days of high oil revenues, Volkswagen established a state-of-the-art assembly plant in the country's administrative capital, Lagos. It provided employment for hundreds of Nigerians. With a similar assembly plant built by Peugeot of France, it looked for a time as though Nigeria had a vigorous car industry. But it imported practically all of its components, and for this it depended on obtaining access to foreign exchange. Efforts by the Nigerian government to get the industry to increase its local content were not very successful, as establishing the capacity for producing content locally would still force the country to rely on foreign technology and capital. Nigeria has since lost most of its foreign exchange income from oil. Volkswagen of Nigeria was therefore unable to import the components and parts it required to sustain its assembly operations. The factory has closed down, with the plant and equipment rusting away and all its former staff long retrenched.

The cases described were selected not because Nigeria's economy is structurally different from that of many other Third World countries—it is not—but because it happened to have oil, unlike many other Third World countries. It was, therefore, able to get hold of a lot of petrodollars with which it was able to engage in modern capital-intensive activities through inward investments and their associated technology transfer. But this pattern of development was obviously footless. It was based on factor proportions outrageously out of step with the economy's factor endowments. It was an easy kind of development, because others came in and did it for them, bringing in technology, material, and capital equipment. Engineers and leaders in Nigeria ironically revel in hobnobbing with the personnel of foreign technical companies. The pattern in Nigeria is based on the conventional economic principle that a modern economic infrastructure (power, roads, communications, etc.) will attract the foreign investment and technology needed to launch the country into the twenty-first century. The strategy did not involve the more difficult route of evolving production techniques that made maximal use of its factor endowments.

We have defined technology as the science of factors and factor proportions. Technology transfer should therefore be the transfer of knowledge (science) about factors and factor proportions. Drawings, specifications, processes, and methods do not qualify as technology transfer because they usually deal with specific production techniques; the recipient tends to go away with the idea that there is only one best way to do what has to be done. By using production techniques not suited to his own factor proportions, the receiver adds to the structural eco-nomic imbalance of his macro economy. He therefore misses the essence of the task before him because he has been unable to see the unifying principles on which what he received depends. The essence of technology transfer is to provide the receiver the knowledge (science) with which he can, in his own environment, decide how to accomplish certain tasks with the factors he has and not with the factor endowments of the giver. In our many years of observation, study, and research in economic development and growth, we have come to believe that what each society requires from the other—technology transfer—in order to achieve economic development and growth is the transfer and exchange of new knowledge (science) behind every production process to enable each participant to decide how best to apply it in his environment.

Freeman and Soete broadly accepted this point when they concluded that a suitable arrangement for a more equitable and mutually beneficial international division of labor in science and technology would be based, in principle, on all countries contributing to as well as drawing from the world stock of knowledge. They argued that "the greatest significance of fundamental research is that it provides a multi-purpose general knowledge on which to build a wide range of science and technical services. Every country without exception requires such a base even if only on a very small scale. Without it, there cannot be any independent long-term cultural, economic or political development."[31] They were in effect endorsing the principle of a basic personality of economic development for each country arising from its natural factor proportions. In poor countries, the small-scale base the authors advocated will necessarily supplement nonformal science initiatives.

Foreign Aid

Conventional economics envisages a world of international economic cooperation—a liberal, market-oriented global economic regime. The rules of the game should permit the unimpeded flow worldwide of goods, services, technology, capital, and labor (material is usually forgotten). No country should be allowed to ignore these rules with impunity. The rules are, after all, intended to make it possible for everyone to share in global opportunities. The intellectual (rationalistic) view is that in all but exceptional circumstances all parties to this transaction benefit. The benefits may not be equally distributed, but all parties gain. In the market for goods and services, both the vendor and the purchaser gain. In the capital market, both the lender and the borrower expect to be better off. It follows that if one party refuses to engage in a potentially beneficial transaction with another, he harms both himself and his potential trading partner.

Foreign aid is supposed to provide a global safety net for these who might lose out in this process. In a dynamic sense, therefore, it is a kind of tax on those who benefit most in order to transfer part of their gain (resources) to those who did not profit as much. Foreign aid is still based on a belief in the efficacy of transfer of resources from one place to another; in a static sense it is a transfer of resources from the rich to the poor.

These ideas do not derive from any scientific analysis. They appeal to our rational common sense, just as the idea that countries specializing in what they are best (comparative advantage) appeals to our common sense. A poor man who has a rich friend can help himself by obtaining a loan from his friend. He can use the loan to start a small business. He can prosper and pay back the loan with interest. Each will be better off: The poor man now runs a profitable business, and the rich friend has earned interest and feels satisfaction that he helped his poor friend to prosper. It does not make a difference if the poor friend had to buy his supplies from his rich friend, from which the rich one also makes additional profit. It is not inconceivable that the borrower can become so successful in his new business that he may end up as wealthy as or even wealthier than his benefactor. The borrower can, on the other hand, not fare well in his new business and end up in debt, accumulating unpaid interest. This everyday scenario is the rationale behind foreign aid. It is not steeped in any scientific analysis. But, as we shall see, conventional economists have sought to fit out foreign aid in scientific dress.

The idea that the whole of humanity is one and that a new world order is an important priority has gained strength with the leadership of the United Nations. As early as 1974 and 1975, the United Nations General Assembly in its sixth and seventh special sessions explored ways to develop an international order. The key arguments run as follows: Technological and ecological issues have shown the need to recognize the interdependencies of all parts of the globe. This has increased to a point where the welfare of humanity as a whole must be taken as the goal of the new order, and an integral part of this was the welfare of the poor masses in the developing countries. Foreign aid therefore derives in a significant sense from a humanitarian sense of obligation to help the unfortunate. Here again we are not dealing with a scientific endeavor.

Foreign aid seems also to derive from the claimed benefits of international mobility of factors. Where it appears that factors are in short supply, it is said that the deficiency can be made up by transferring factors from locations of plenty. This will kick-start economic growth in the receiver economy.

But the greatest factor that has given foreign aid the prominence it enjoys is the success of the Marshall Plan. This was the largest transfer of resources in modern times, and without this it would have taken Europe a long time to recover from World War II. In his book *Development Assistance Policies and the Performance of Aid Agencies,* Selim, then the adviser general of the Abu Dhabi Fund for Arabic Economic Development, argued that without aid the interests of the developing and the developed world would run in parallel rather than converge: "The problem is how to bring back some order into this great disorder in the aftermath of the Second World War. . . . We had the Marshall Plan for Europe but what we really need now is a Marshall Plan to abolish poverty or a Marshall Plan for Africa, Asia and Latin America."[32]

It seems therefore necessary to examine claims that the Marshall Plan saved Europe and, through the transfer of resources to the tune of over $13 billion, put Europe rapidly back on the track to economic growth after World War II.

William L. Clayton, the U.S. assistant secretary of state for economic affairs, in a famous memorandum in May 1947 that most scholars have seen as the start of the plan, gave his assessment of Europe: "Europe is steadily deteriorating. The political position reflects the economy. One political crisis after another merely denotes the existence of grave economic distress. Millions of people in the cities are starving. . . . The modern system of division of labor has almost broken down." Paul Hoffman, the first administrator of the Marshall Plan, stated that Communists in Western Europe were getting perilously strong: "They were busy exploiting the hunger and the hopelessness and the lack of jobs among tens of thousands of people. Broken factories were operating fitfully and often slowed to a halt for lack of raw materials and repair parts for equipment. Farmers raised little more than enough to feed themselves. The transport system was in too bad a state of disrepair to carry even the slight food surpluses to under-nourished city dwellers." It would appear from Hoffman's comments that the bulk of Europe's productive assets were present but damaged. They lacked parts and materials to get back to full production. Similarly, the infrastructure was in a state of disrepair. Lord Franks, who was the chairman of the Committee of European Economic Cooperation, set up in response to U.S. Marshall Plan initiatives,

later commented that "in the spring of 1947, the economic and social state of Western Europe was far graver than in the thirties," during the time of the Great Depression.[33]

On the other hand, Milward has contended that "as Marshall was taking his words from Clayton's memorandum, most European countries were still in a period of rising output and expanding foreign trade. It could not be shown that any population outside Europe was in danger of starving and even their diet was slightly improved over the previous year. There were no bank crashes and few bankruptcies. Profits and investments were high and so in most countries was the level of employment. . . . Only one phenomenon associated with previous economic crises occurred, a severe fall in gold and foreign exchange with acute balance of payment difficulties. . . . [This] had more in common with those postwar European crises still to come which were largely confined to areas of international financial transactions and were more associated with problems of adjustment to high output and employment."[34] Milward was of the view that the demands for reconstruction loans and trade credits from Europe needed to be backed by people like Clayton in the hope of painting a picture of a continent where economic and social discontent were mounting to levels so dangerous as to call into question the future of capitalism. For example, in countries such as France and Italy, Communist parties held powerful electoral positions. The military administration in Germany had also begun to feel itself in competition with the Soviets for the political allegiance of the German population.

These two extreme positions on the economic conditions in Europe in 1947 portray what are clearly different assessments. Even on the issue of the balance-of-payments problems, which did occur at the time, there are different schools of thought among economic historians about the causes. One is that the foreign exchange crisis was due to structural changes in the international economy brought about by the war itself. Whether these changes were permanent or temporary is still largely in dispute. Those who argue they were permanent put less emphasis on the specific events of 1947 and argue that it was the inevitable outcome of the failure of postwar settlements and the Bretton Woods agreements to tackle adequately the problem of reconstruction. Those who saw the changes as temporary blamed the European governments for pursuing larger spending and inflationary policies. It was asserted by one school of thought that there was a reduction in the outflow of U.S. aid to the rest of the world in 1947, which made it difficult for Western Europe to obtain from the United States the imports on which reconstruction depended, and that during the war the United States obtained a greater share of its primary imports from elsewhere, which made it difficult for European countries to earn dollars from exports. Others argued that during the war the United States' level of self-sufficiency made it impossible for any world trade and payment equilibrium to appear unless the United States committed itself to a long-term program of foreign investment combined with any other means of financing its export surpluses.

McWilliams and Piotrowski have argued that the Marshall Plan was intended to preserve the prosperity the war brought to U.S. society. They argued that at the end of the war the United States had taken the lead to establish free trade, and that needed a prosperous Europe. Therefore, the United States shored up the financial system of the Western capitalist world as a potential weapon in the containment of Soviet influence.[35]

Reducing these issues to their political aspects, we find a division of opinion among economic historians. If there was an economic crisis in 1947, was it because the dislocation caused by the war was greater than the United States had assumed in demanding allegiance to the multilateral trade and payment systems it sought as the basis of the postwar settlements? Or was it because European countries had refused to acknowledge the harsh economic realities facing them and embarked on ambitious national reconstruction policies, which made their economic situation worse?

On the other hand, some scholars believe that the Marshall Plan was in large part a humanitarian gesture for which the United States was able to draw a residue of goodwill for decades from Europe.[36] It was conceived in terms of an integrated Europe and eventually led to subsequent definite moves toward Western European economic integration later.

The Marshall Plan was not an organized, structured form of aid, as recipient governments were very much left on their own to determine what to do with the facilities made available. At home, the recipient government would sell the imported goods to firms and consumers. Under the provisions of the recovery program, the receipts from these sales accrued to the recipient government as counterpart funds. With the permission of the local Economic Cooperation Administration (ECA) mission, the recipient government would use these counterpart funds to finance essential needs. In some countries such as France, Germany, and the Netherlands, the funds made a significant contribution to long-term investments (for example, new electricity development in Germany).

France and Germany in effect used the aid to circumvent what they perceived as weaknesses of the private capital market and the difficulties posed by controls over government finance to help alleviate bottlenecks in the recovery process. In Austria, there was after a time a shift in allocation of the counterpart funds from the transport sector to basic industries. Britain used much of its counterpart funds to repay its national debt.

Milward argued that even if it was assumed that the whole of the Marshall Plan aid went into capital formation, it would represent in most countries a small percentage of the total: a third of GDP in Italy, a fifth in West Germany, a tenth in the United Kingdom and France. He concluded that there is considerable skepticism about the overall importance of Marshall Plan aid: "The main reason for the skepticism about the overall importance of the ERP [economic recovery program] has been that quantitative measures of its impact on the European economies suggest that its contribution to them was greatly exaggerated by Cold War historians and that it also brought few, if any, of the economic advantages to America which 'revisionist' historians suggested." "As a total sum Marshall aid does not look large in terms of Western Europe's total foreign trade or investment. American exports to Europe did not increase but fell during the Economic Recovery Program and American capital exports to Western Europe were at one of their lowest ebbs."[37] He was of the view that "the value of the Marshall aid to Western European countries primarily consisted in the fact that it allowed them to continue to maintain a high level of investments and imports and avoid the deflations or further increase in trade controls which were the only other possible responses to the crisis of 1947 and in particular permitted them to maintain a flow of dollar imports."[38] A similar conclusion was reached by Geiger: "By 1947, industrial production in many Western European countries had reached pre-war levels. In all likelihood, Europe's recovery would have continued even without Marshall aid—albeit at a slower pace."[39] Indeed, plans for economic reconstruction of Europe were in place before the Marshall Plan was conceived.

A number of conclusions can be reached from this review of the role of Marshall Plan aid in Europe. The first is that Western Europe was already in the midst of economic reconstruction when the Marshall Plan was conceived. Scholars differ as to the extent of this reconstruction, but it could not be said that Western Europe's economic condition was anything to compare with that of present poor countries. The reconstruction was largely a question of replacing what was damaged during the war and attempting to recover economic growth that had been lost. The second conclusion is that each recipient was left to decide what to do with the aid provided. There was therefore no doubt about the competence of each recipient government to manage its economic affairs. The third conclusion is that the Marshall Plan had a strong political motive, which contributed to early attempts to paint the economic and political scene in 1947 in such gloomy terms to win the support of the U.S. Congress. There was also a political need to claim all the credit for Europe's economic resurgence after the war. The fourth conclusion is that the aid was in effect a transfer of factors from an advanced economy to recipients who to all intents and purposes were also advanced economies.

From a macro point of view, the last conclusion is the most significant. Despite Milward's contention that Europe might have pulled through without Marshall Plan aid, he did confirm that "it permitted a level of import from the United States of investment goods appreciably higher than could otherwise have been the case."[40] The transfer of factors such as capital equipment and materials from the United States to Western European countries corresponds to the relationship depicted in Figure 6.5, where it was shown that capital inflow from an advanced economy to another advanced economy can produce growth in the recipient. Because the transfer of factors into a war-torn economy, helping to replace damaged assets and creating new activities, occurred at factor proportions not too dissimilar to those of the recipient economies, their growth was enhanced. The growth that this transfer of factors engendered in Europe helped to strengthen Europe and put it back on track, which leads to our fifth conclusion about Marshall Plan aid: that it was a short-term phenomenon. The aid was no longer needed after it made its contribution. During this period trade resumed between Europe and the United States following what we earlier called the structural changes in the international economy brought about by the war. These problems were the essence of the Bretton Woods agreements, which preceded the Marshall Plan.

Most people involved in foreign aid on both sides will readily agree that the essential purpose of aid is economic. Riddell observed that even though official development assistance funds have been continually subject to an array of non-development-related issues (political, strategic, commercial), "their stated purpose has been to enhance or accelerate the process of development (initially economic development) with the amelioration and eventual eradication of absolute poverty as a major objective. . . . For many donors, the notion that those with the means available should channel and allocate some of their human, physical and financial resources to those in dire need has provided a powerful (moral or humanitarian) justification for providing (and gradually increasing) aid."[41]

In *Assessing Aid*, the World Bank, on the other hand, said that foreign aid from its inception had twin objectives that are potentially in conflict. The first was, as above, to promote long-term growth and poverty reduction, the underlying motivation of donors being a combination of altruism and a more self-interested concern that in the long term their own economic and political security would benefit if poor countries were growing. The second objective was to promote the short-term political and strategic interest of the donors. As a result, aid went to regimes that were political allies of major Western powers. This, in the view of the World Bank, meant that the strategic and developmental objectives of aid "were potentially, but not necessarily, at odds."[42]

Any simple and direct link that there might have been between aid and economic development seems to have become increasingly more complex as the objectives of foreign aid were initially split into direct/near-term and indirect/longer-term objectives, with more and more direct/near-term objectives later added to those already present.[43]

Arising from this splitting process is the growing emphasis on poverty reduction as a direct/near-term objective of aid. The posture is that economic development is an indirect/longer-term objective beset by many problems, including those involving national host governments. The large aid projects are supposed to be essential mainly in the broader context of national economic development and growth in these countries and not immediately relevant at the grassroots. It has sometimes been claimed that the multiplicity of objectives has contributed to poor performance, as it is claimed that this necessarily means that some objectives are regarded as having greater importance than others. Riddell has observed that a majority of bilateral and multilateral donors would probably maintain that "one of the main, if not the main, contemporary objectives of aid is poverty reduction and elimination." Today, according to him, few donors would likely object to assessment of their development aid program in terms of its orientation towards poverty alleviation. Bilateral and multilateral donors therefore review, assess and judge their whole aid program through what he called the "poverty prism."[44]

But here is a problem. The splitting of the objectives of aid seems odd. Why is it that nearly fifty years after aid started, the aid community wants to distinguish between direct/near-term objectives and indirect/longer-term objectives? The poor man in an underdeveloped country wants to have the means through gainful engagement in economic activity to feed and clothe his family, educate his children, and have a roof over his head, but this can be achieved only in a growing economy that provides the necessary support services. Those who want to split objectives put the cart before the horse. The argument goes like this: In poor countries, the few rich individuals grab all the direct benefits of huge aid programs. Rapid economic growth does not automatically translate into rapid improvements in human development. The trickle effect does not work, and it is the poor people who suffer. While looking for ways to improve their economy, the immediate task is to help the poor. But those who make this argument and advocate splitting do not know how to improve the economic growth prospects for the poor sector of the economy. So they resort to direct funding of health care, education, water, and sanitation projects and other such items that are thought to be needed most by the poor. The advantage for the donor is that his aid efforts are immediate (near) and visible. Yet the World Bank admitted that "aid has done much less than might have been hoped to reduce poverty."[45] This style of poverty alleviation is easier to deal with than the almost insoluble issue of economic growth because it simply involves direct transfer of facilities and resources from the donor to the poor recipient. Increasingly, national governments are usefully bypassed in this transfer process, making the transfer easier and freer of bureaucracy. Unfortunately, only a growing economy can provide and sustain the growing social sector on a long-term basis.

In other words, social amenities are and should be the direct product of successful economic development and growth strategy. They are not a precondition for successful economic growth. But the nongovernmental organizations (NGOs), mostly from the North, adopted advocacy around poverty reduction in the 1970s and argued through the 1980s for a stronger focus on poverty, for more social lending, and increasingly for public (that is, NGO) participation in project planning and implementation. Poverty advocacy became international when the World Bank agreed to meet regularly with a standing consultative committee of NGOs. The NGO World Bank Committee became an official international venue for discussing poverty and partici-

pation issues.[46] An International Labor Organization document in 1975 listed a wide range of basic needs, from the minimum requirements of food, shelter, clothing, and access to essential services such as transport, sanitation, education, and health care to the expanded goals of an adequately remunerated job, a healthy environment, and popular participation in decision making. But most of these depended on a growing macro economy.

Robert McNamara, president of the World Bank from 1968 to 1981, pioneered the concept of "absolute poverty" and brought about a moral fervor to the task of eradicating "the extremes of privilege and deprivation [that] are simply no longer acceptable." The basic-needs approach was rejected by many developing countries in the 1970s when it was first formulated, since they saw it as a way of telling them that they could not aspire to true modernization and should remain satisfied if most basic needs were met.

It is clear that poverty alleviation as an aid strategy is based on moral and sociopolitical reasoning. It was not based primarily on economic theorizing about how to achieve macroeconomic growth. Perhaps the greatest deficiency of the basic-needs approach is that it wrongly assumed that macroeconomic growth in a developing economy is a long-horizon, capital-led phenomenon that depends on a delayed trickle effect to benefit the poor. The anger of Third World leaders with the strategy is understandable.

Today, a new agenda has been set out by the donor community in consultation with developing countries: (1) reduce by half the proportion of people living in extreme poverty by 2015; (2) achieve universal primary education in all countries by 2015; (3) achieve equality of the sexes and empower women; (4) reduce by two-thirds the mortality rate for children under 5 and by three-quarters the rate for infants by 2015; (5) provide access to the primary health care system for all women of childbearing age not later than 2015; (6) implement national strategies for sustainable development in all countries by 2005 to ensure that losses of environmental resources are reversed nationally and globally by 2015. It is not clear what any of these have to do directly with macroeconomic growth. They are an agenda for social reconstruction. Because macroeconomic growth strategy seems elusive, donors such as the World Bank like to say disparagingly that economic growth focuses mainly on growth of per capita income, attempting to give the impression that macroeconomic growth is only about money and not quality of life.[47] In another breath, however, the World Bank said that "if an economy grows rapidly, the return on investment in road rehabilitation, for example, is high. . . . Similarly, economic growth makes it easier for children to get into schools."[48]Elsewhere the World Bank clearly recognizes that without relevant macroeconomic growth, targeted poverty reduction is not possible.[49] Therefore, "organic" poverty reduction is possible only through a structurally balanced strategy of economic development and growth. What the present foreign aid poverty alleviation programs do is to throw external resources at the problem of poverty without the requisite macroeconomic development and growth. This is a recipe for continued dependence by the poor countries on outside aid. It is clear that foreign aid, if it is to claim a place as an instrument of economic development, must have to face this primary problem of how to promote long-term economic growth in poor countries.

In order to examine the ability of foreign aid to accelerate or promote long-term economic development and growth in poor economies, we need here to summarize our conclusions so far as they relate to the transfer of factors between an advanced economy and a poor economy, for that is what foreign aid is in economic terms.

The first conclusion is that conventional economic theories on development operate as if there is no preexisting economy in a Third World country, or if they do recognize one, they regard it as a nuisance. The second conclusion, related to the first, is that conventional economists have not studied the structural effects of the transfer of factors from one economy to another of different maturity. The greater the difference between the factors transferred and the existing factors, the greater the structural inequilibrium caused.

The third conclusion is a more fundamental one, namely, that economic growth formulation is exogenous. Institutions' policies are not a primary determinant of economic growth and are not specific. A wide array of institutions and policies, deriving from social and cultural characteristics, is possible in order to facilitate maximal economic growth arising from the adoption of proper factor proportions.

There is an urgent need to put away all the rhetoric that has surrounded foreign aid over the past fifty years. Aid has not been subjected to a theoretical analysis on a scientific basis. Riddell correctly pointed out that not only the birth but also the growth of the aid phenomenon was boosted more by an a priori assumption about its merits than by careful analysis of its overall impact.[50] He supported his claim by advancing three arguments. First, he observed correctly that it took almost a quarter century of aid giving before donors began seriously and systematically to appraise potential projects and assess the impact of the aid they provided. Second, while the growing number of impact assessments confirms that many discrete aid projects have managed to achieve the narrow objectives for which aid was provided, there is a paucity of evidence to confirm the view that aid in general is either sufficient or necessary to enhance or accelerate development or reduce poverty. Third, the evidence—or lack of evidence—of aid's development impact even at the project level has made no significant difference in the volume of aid provided by official donors.

There are two basic requirements in any assessment of the impact of aid. First, we must know its impact not only at the micro level but more importantly at the macro level. Second, the assessment must be done in a scientific theoretical framework. What is currently presented as evidence that aid works is essentially empirical. Empirical evidence without a sound (scientific) theory to support it is not useful. Up until recently, aid agencies have homed in on the success rates of individual projects, but lately there have been attempts to claim macro-level benefits that, regrettably, stand on weak and unreliable empirical assumptions. As if he saw the need for good theory, Booth has urged that the findings of empirical studies on aid be translated into theoretical formulations so as to achieve a sufficient level of generality—a sort of ground-up approach.[51] But Booth was talking in terms of social development research, which we have maintained has nothing to contribute to the formulation of a scientific theory of economic development, and in any case it is difficult to see how theory can be constructed from empirical findings, as no valid development theory has ever evolved from the abundance of empirical research that there is today on development.

Having a priori decided that aid was what poor countries needed in order to grow economically, donors have adapted aid strategy to changing economic development theorizing. At its inception, aid had essentially to do with money. It attempted to fill the gap between the capital a poor country was supposed to need to achieve economic growth and its very limited savings—not that such a country obtained much from its export trade. Poor countries were poor, it was reasoned, because they could not fill this gap. Institutions such as the World Bank now say they have discovered that they got it all wrong as to why positivist orthodoxy has not worked in poor countries —the real problem is that lagging economies are held back more by policy and institutional gaps than by a financial gap. The World Bank claims that foreign aid in the past concentrated too much on the transfer

of capital, and this "resulted from misunderstanding about development . . . and from external and internal pressures on aid institutions."[52]

Next, modernization theory took over aid strategy, attempting to identify and foster development and promote certain forms of government, institutions, and organizations—essentially to implement instant democracy. As the reasoning goes, "Development assistance is more about institutions and policies than providing capital."[53] Later more interest was shown in transforming "electoral democracy" into "real" Western liberal democracy, with an independent judiciary and restrictions on the powers of the executive branch.

It was believed that by restructuring the societies of poor countries along the lines of Western society, the basis for the success of aid programs would be ensured. It was no longer a matter of only "getting the prices" right but also the institutions.[54] The neoliberal theory of development in time made its impact and became central to aid strategy. These factors shaped the structural adjustment programs of the 1980s, which produced another change in strategy. The core theme of structural adjustment was "less government." Aid was to be provided only if recipients agreed to implement a package of donor-initiated conditions prior to the aid being given. Indeed, not only was aid the prize given for agreeing to carry out these policies, but in some cases significant amounts of aid were withheld from poor countries that measured by the original needs-based criteria would have been the first to qualify for aid. Thus the change meant that whereas one of the purposes of donors' project evaluations has been to use ex post data to improve the impact of future projects, the conditionality under structural adjustment tried to improve the impact ex ante. The 1980s saw the rise of the IMF and the World Bank to unprecedented preeminence in the development dialogue, attaining the status of global governance agencies by coordinating bilateral and private lending to indebted states on the condition of policy changes and by taking a leading intellectual role in defining the ends and means of development. But the World Bank's dream of structural adjustment turned into a nightmare as criticisms of the policy mounted from diverse circles.[55] Eventually the policy of structural adjustment was abandoned, and the 1980s was acknowledged to be the "lost decade" as it became clear that the neoliberal-oriented policies had not produced the results expected.[56]

Based on what Vandersluis and Yeros called a "decade of learning," the official theory of development assistance began to undergo yet another transformation.[57] For the first time, donors now pointed a direct accusing finger at the recipients: It was all the fault of the governments in the underdeveloped countries—they were corrupt, they had poor knowledge of governance, they wasted resources given to them. The World Bank complained that "many of the world's poor live in countries with weak governance and poor policies, so that aid agencies work primarily in difficult environments." Failures of donor-financed projects were blamed solely on "weak governments and public organizations."[58] The World Bank finally realized what had been long evident—that the state has a role in development— and decided that what was needed was not less government but better government, which concentrated its efforts less on direct interventions and more on enabling others to be more effective. The problems were, according to the World Bank, primarily associated with the inability to separate private and public, the failure to establish a predictable legal and political framework for development, excessive regulation, misallocation of resources, and lack of transparency in decision making.

The World Bank sees development thinking as having passed through three phases in its consideration of the market and governments. In the first, market failures in poor countries were seen as pervasive and complete. In the second, for a brief period, government failure was seen as pervasive and complete. The latest twist, "pragmatic but not ideologically satisfying," is that both markets and governments have pervasive failures. Governments should focus on areas where the problems are greatest—but they must have the capacity to improve the situation.[59]

The OECD normally takes a more political stance, its attitude being that governance criteria should be taken into account in foreign aid policies and that the World Bank criteria should be linked with participatory development, human rights, elements of democracy, and generally speaking legitimate government.

The new path in development thinking adopted by the World Bank assumes that what is important for long-term growth is a stable macroeconomic environment (whatever this means), an open trade regime, protection of property rights, and an efficient public bureaucracy that can deliver education, health care, and other public services. When developing countries have such "sound management," the World Bank thinks, financial aid will have a big effect on growth and poverty reduction, improving social indicators over and above what good management itself induces.[60]

We have gone into this detail to illustrate that aid is still regarded today as a major aspect of the economic development of poor countries. Riddell observed, "In the absence of persuasive evidence to the contrary, it could be argued that it was the ability of aid to change in relation to its objectives, the forms in which it is given and, to a lesser extent, the composition of recipients—in short, important attributes of flexibility—which played a decisive role in ensuring not only its perpetuation but its steady absolute expansion for over 40 years." He added, "It was not merely the attribute of flexibility which was decisive: it was flexibility combined with a strongly held donor view that aid was capable of making a positive difference to aid recipient countries" and pointed out that "it was the twin attributes that together provided the impetus to execute far-reaching adjustments to and changes in the aid relationship and which worked to try to ensure that the criticisms made of aid were deflated, deflected and largely neutralized, rather than built upon to expand the view of aid's (albeit divided) critics that aid did not and/or could not fulfill its (ever-expanding) development objectives." For example, when the NGOs promoted a campaign against the way aid was perceived and administered, a rising share of official aid was given to them to promote their own programs. Riddell summarized the flexibility: "Aid has continually responded to criticism by changing (or adding to) its objectives and the form in which it is given in an amoeba-like fashion, which in some measure absorbs and thus sanitizes the thrust and impact of at least part of the criticism made."[61] Vandersluis and Yeros, in a similar tone, have remarked, "The World Bank has often to shift from being the target of critics to claim a new status as an ally or even a leader in the [aid] effort."[62] It has often had to redefine itself and make its projects somewhat relevant to new realities lest it risk losing its leading intellectual role in the definition of development and in the coordination of world development programs.[63]

On the other hand, the World Bank, according to Vandersluis and Yeros, has "resisted critiques of adjustment lending that would diminish its influence and undercut its role in the implementation of neoliberal policy."[64] On the World Bank's new emphasis of governance, Peter Gibbon observed that governance "was part of the assertion of a claim by the World Bank to broader and broader areas of policy expertise, connected to and ideologically justifying expansion in the scope both of the [aid] regime and the World Bank's role in it."[65]

There is nothing wrong with flexibility. Indeed, leadership involves identifying basic answers but being flexible enough to apply these to suit different environments. The theme of the science of economic development and growth is that because factor proportions have been identified as the solution to economic development problems, each society should adopt whatever institutions it sees fit as long as these basic requirements for factor proportions are met. Looking at the flexibility exhibited in aid, however, it may seem that donors have no basic formulation about economic development and growth to offer and are out simply to preserve the sanctity of aid by shifting strategies to ensure "its perpetuation," to use Riddell's words. In the particular case of the World Bank it may be an attempt to retain "its leading intellectual role," to use the words of Vandersluis and Yeros. Looking at the different postures exhibited by the donors, the only discernible feature running through all their changes is the message that aid (finance) was what the poor countries need—whether by executing projects or by enabling them access to the elements of social infrastructure.

The World Bank acquired its intellectual leadership of development issues during the era of positivist orthodoxy, when everyone thought that aid was needed only to fill the capital gap facing poor countries. But since then, much has changed in economic thinking. Neither the institutional theory nor the neoliberal theory with which the World Bank is associated has any scientific base. And since then, conventional economic theory has moved on. Since the 1990s the proponents of new growth theory have taken over. In a way it is surprising that donor institutions have not incorporated new growth theory in their views about aid. Can it be because new growth theory is moving rapidly toward either eliminating capital as a promoter of growth or at best grudgingly giving it second place? That would make aid as we currently know it redundant.

Has it occurred to the donor institutions, in the search for what is wrong with aid, that *they* may be the problem and that the aid on which poor countries have become perpetually dependent is preventing those countries from fashioning their path to sustainable economic growth? Arnold put the position clearly: "[Under the Marshall Plan the] massive injection of American capital into economies [was to] enable them to get back on their feet again. It worked, although there were many factors to take into account. . . . It was never envisaged that aid [to the poor countries of today] would become a permanent feature of international dealings between states. Rather, aid represented a once-only effort whose provision might last somewhat longer than did Marshall Plan aid but nonetheless was only expected to continue for a limited period of time. . . . What has gone wrong? . . . Much disturbing is the fact that despite years of injections many developing countries appear no better off today than when the process began. In some cases there seems to have been an actual deterioration of the economy despite aid.[66] African countries are good examples of this situation.[67] Gibbon, Bangura, and Ofstad asked, "The habit of aid appears to have set for good. . . . Since the statement appears set . . . is there any point in continuing the dialogue [of aid]?"[68]

It is now our intention to show that the World Bank's newfound wisdom on aid will not work, just as the past wisdoms did not work. The institution has indicated broadly where its aid funds go and for what; "most aid is delivered as investment projects in particular sectors as roads, water supply or education."[69] The remaining funds go into the new role it has assumed since 1980 of "designer, financier and enforcer of a neo-liberal vision of integration among national economies."[70]

Aid, the World Bank has said, acts as a magnet for private investment, bringing in almost $2 in private funds for every $1 of aid. It adds that in countries "committed to reform, aid increases the confidence of the private sector and supports important public services." In the World Bank's view, therefore, foreign aid and foreign investment are two sides of the same coin.

By and large, the bulk of aid is geared toward specific projects. The projects, which are intended to facilitate foreign private investment, encompass basic infrastructures such as electricity, roads, and telecommunications. Other projects assist in the provision of public services in such areas as health care and water. All these require so much capital that they are beyond the reach of poor governments. Most of these projects are designed and their implementations undertaken by firms from member countries of the donor institutions.

In short, aid projects share with foreign investment the characteristics in Figure 6.2, from which it is clear that foreign aid produces the same structural imbalances in the economy of poor countries as foreign investment and has the effect of contracting the preexisting economy. Therefore, despite the good intentions of donors, foreign aid projects in general are not growth-inducing on a macroeconomic level. Worse, the more aid given, the more aid required, because sustainable economic growth is unachievable with foreign aid. Lack of economic growth in turn makes it impossible for countries to sustain the poverty alleviation programs that aid attempts to finance, thus enlarging the dependency syndrome. The problem with foreign aid is not whether the product is being packaged and marketed in the right way, or whether it is properly produced, or whether the customer is the right customer. Rather, the problem is that it is the wrong product. This is in sharp contrast to the experience with Marshall Plan aid in Western Europe.

From this, it can be seen that failure of foreign aid to date to achieve the economic growth of poor countries is not due to "bad governance," as the new wisdom of the World Bank seems to suggest. Corruption, waste, and lack of proper management of resources are not the cause but the consequences of large-scale projects and grandiose schemes that have no true growth in them.

When people in poor countries see projects running into the millions of dollars that seem to them to be out of proportion to the country's needs, it is not to be unexpected that some may feel that taking out a little for themselves will not seriously harm the original intention. We are reminded of Robert Klitgaard's account of Equatorial Guinea in his book *Tropical Gangsters*. When the World Bank decided to approve credit for cocoa farmers in Equatorial Guinea, government officials and ministers overnight turned into cocoa farmers and acquired large tracts of land. When harvest time came, they could not repay the loans for obvious reasons. In other situations, public officials will intercept some of the money on its way to the farmers. Our point is that even if corruption did not exist, the projects have little chance of succeeding.

In its latest attempt at a flexibility strategy, the World Bank in its publication *Assessing Aid* said that it has now found the secret to making aid work. Among its worrying claims are that a $10 billion increase in aid would lift twenty-five million people out of poverty if the sum was spent in countries with sound management, whereas if it was spent across the board it will lift only seven million people out of poverty. Another is that 1 percent of GDP in assistance will translate to a sustained increase in growth of 0.5 percent in GDP. It claimed that some countries with sound management that have received only small amounts of aid have grown at 2.2 percent per capita, while the high aid group with good management grew at 3.7 percent per capita. The World Bank also asserts that 1 percent of GDP assistance reduces poverty by 1 percent and that aid has a similar effect on infant mortality. On foreign investment, 1 percent of GDP in aid is supposed to bring in another 1.9 percent of GDP in private investment in "good management" countries; in "poor management" countries, 1 percent of GDP in aid is said to *reduce* private investment by 0.5 percent of GDP.

There are serious problems arising from a statis-tical treatment of the issues involved. It is understandable that with the spread of structural adjustment and other reforms that the World Bank and other donors at one time said were needed in order to promote economic development in poor countries, there was the pressing need for donor agencies to establish more precise links between policy changes and outcomes. Lacking the necessary micro-macro economic development and growth theory to back up these reforms, people were left with only two alternative statistical approaches—the country-specific and cross-country empirical models. The implication of country-specific models is that for economies suffering from external and internal imbalances, the range of policy reform options and thus the room to maneuver are very limited.[71] The World Bank therefore has had to resort to cross-country regression studies—which immediately run into problems. The multiple regression model the World Bank adopted has the problem of multi-collinearity in that many of the variables that are supposed to be independent variables are in fact correlated with each other. We are also dealing with many variables that are not quantifiable. For example, it makes no statistical sense for one to attempt "to measure democracy," to use the World Bank's phraseology. Yet this is what their analysts had to do by pulling together all sorts of judgmental indices that undermine the statistical quality of their regression model.

The World Bank needed to measure governance—a key concept in its new wisdom on how to make aid work. This is another unquantifiable variable. The World Bank argued that the performance of recipient governments could be measured by using the economic rate of return (ERR) of its projects—since the same project selection and implementation procedures are used across all countries, the differences in returns across those countries are an indication of how effective governments are in implementing public projects. But this is a wrong assumption, made in an attempt to avoid quantifying governance. The ERR includes policy variables (black market factors, fiscal surplus), economic variables (change in the terms of trade, GDP growth, capital/labor ratio), a dummy variable for "project complexity," and a set of dummy variables for the sector of the project. For the time-varying variables, it used the average value in the three years prior to the year in which the project was evaluated. It also added variables it said were for civil liberties. It is clear that the World Bank's governance variable is not an independent variable but a set of assumptions, and that its measurement of governance is largely subjective and unscientific.

Weiss pointed out that it is difficult to draw conclusions from cross-country studies on structural and political reform and macroeconomic performance. Such comparisons, he argued, can be little more than suggestive. The number and dates of loans a country has received are not necessarily an appropriate indication of the extent to which reforms have actually taken place, which is what the World Bank's country classification attempts to reflect. A serious limitation of cross-country studies is, in his words, "the relative arbitrariness of how individual countries are classified for country grouping." To him, comparisons of poverty across developing countries are highly problematic given basic data inadequacies.[72] Indeed, Mittelman and Tambe have argued that there is no consensus on how to measure poverty.[73]

From the point of view of economic science, the World Bank erred in lumping fifty-six countries into one sample labeled "developing countries" for its regression studies when each of these has different factor proportions. These countries in effect have different economic personalities; the only thing they have in common is that they are poor. The World Bank is therefore not justified to make its statistical claims, which it wanted to be accepted as general rules. While regression applies scientific methods,

it is not a science. Regression is a means of making an informed guess.

Hogben reminded us of the dangers of assuming that regression is a science and making what purports to be definitive (scientific) prescriptions for them:

(a) the theory prescribes a method of locating averages or specifying parameters of descriptive formulae referable to such averages, but the deviation of any individual score from such an average has no more title to be more or less near to a true value than any other. The descriptive formula which embraces them can rightly claim the title of law . . . only if we have some assurance that we shall meet a population described in terms of such averages in definable circumstances. In fact, we are rarely, if ever, able to do so in branches of inquiry relying on this procedure; (b) Laboratory or observatory experience may endorse with some plausibility the assumption that successive uncontrollable instrumental errors turn up random-wise; but the assumption that deviations of population scores from fictitious means are random variables derives its sanction from the arbitrary and Platonic concept of infinite hypothetical population; (c) Though the theory of regression makes use of the same formal algebra as the Gaussian theory of error, it derives no sanction from whatever claims to usefulness we concede to the latter.[74]

The World Bank's claim of a linear relationship between growth and aid, between poverty and aid, or between aid and foreign investments has no scientific basis and is indeed misleading. Paul Krugman once accused some economists of engaging in what he called "careless arithmetic," making assertions that are crafted to "sound like quantifiable pronouncements about measurable magnitudes, but . . . do not actually present any data on these magnitudes."[75] The World Bank in this instance can be accused of "careless statistics."

These regression claims portray an institution that has not given up positivist orthodoxy as a theory of economic development and growth. The World

Bank still sees lack of capital as the most important cause of underdevelopment and aid as a way to make up for this lack. It emphasizes that "money matters —but not in the way we thought."[76] In short, if you clear the garden of weeds, the seed will grow.

Positivist orthodoxy assumes that growth is directly related to capital accumulation. The World Bank gets to this position in a roundabout way. It states that the theoretical foundation for its empirical studies on the effect of aid on growth derives from the assumption that the accumulation of physical and human capital depends on the initial conditions, institutions, and policies that affect the return to savings and investment. Therefore it claims that growth is a function of those initial conditions, institutions, and policies plus external shocks.[77] This is positivist orthodoxy wrapped in institutional cloth with neoliberal colors.

Ingham was correct to point out that at the macro level, empirical studies have shown no significant positive relationship between aid and development. "If aid performs well at the micro, why is it there is no impact at the macro level?" she wondered. The answer, she felt, was that "despite a wealth of empirical work we do not really know how aid affects economies at the macro-level." Not only are there ambiguities in the theoretical models of aid and growth, but there is also the problem of correctly specifying the empirical test.[78]

To summarize, foreign aid, like foreign investment, injects structural imbalances into underdeveloped economies, which reduce their prospect of achieving sustained economic development and growth. Claims of a direct relationship between aid and growth are thus problematic and mislead policy orientation in both donor and recipient countries. In this instance any claimed micro-level success for aid programs is more than offset by deteriorating macro prospects. The position is troubling because lending operations of the World Bank are based on sectoral (micro-level) studies.[79]

Project Assessment and the Issue of Participation

The World Bank assessed the "success" of its individual lending projects through ex post evaluations conducted by its Operations Evaluation Department (OED) and also through its Annual Review of Portfolio Performance (ARPP). OED assessment covers the overall performance of completed projects. Indicators include an estimate of the economic rate of return when a project is completed, a binary measure (satisfactory or unsatisfactory) of the overall project outcome, plus an ordinary assessment (four levels, from highly satisfactory to highly unsatisfactory) of the project's sustainability and its contribution to institutional development of the recipient country.[80]

The determinants of the economic rate of return, as we have seen, include a whole set of policy, economic, and dummy variables. With so many unquantifiable inputs, the World Bank's estimate of a project's economic rate of return cannot be quantified, either. When an assessor has to choose among four levels, from highly satisfactory to highly unsatisfactory, the issue of bias and consistency across projects can destroy the regression results arising from such assessment. ARPP rates projects annually according to a number of criteria that relate to overall project performance (contribution to development objective and implementation progress) as well as what is called "intermediate" characteristics (compliance with legal covenants, project management performance, availability of funds, procurement progress, training progress, technical assistance progress, studies progress, environmental aspects, fiscal performance, and gender aspects). The minimal analytical rigor and poor informational content of these measures are obviously of limited use. The World Bank does not regularly rate these indices, resulting in large variations in the number of observations available for different indicators.[81]

In their book *Does Aid Work?* Robert Cassen and associates observed that although a large body of knowledge on project performance has accumulated over the years and much work has been done on refining the methods, there are several respects in which formal evaluations of the type described above are deficient. "Sometimes one cannot tell what an individual project has achieved," they said. "It is rarely possible to take a number of evaluations and assess the overall effect of what has been done in a given sector or country."[82]

The first and most important limitation of present project evaluations is that little is known about how projects are sustained after the initial phase in which the donor is active. "It is without question true," Cassen and associates said, "that a number of projects which look successful at the end of, say, five years when the donor withdraws do not maintain their promise, and if reviewed five years later give much less satisfaction."[83] The second is that there is no well-developed evaluation methodology that is universally applied to an individual sector, let alone several sectors. Even with the same aid agency—as we have observed with the World Bank—practice can vary considerably between similar projects, depending on the approach, the caliber of individual evaluation, and the specificity of the guideline provided. Third, the assumption of what would have happened without the project—an assumption that is theoretically crucial to a cost-benefit analysis—can rarely be ascertained. Fourth, projects may achieve useful results that nevertheless fall short of initially overambitious objectives, and even with the benefits of hindsight, it may be difficult to distinguish such overambition from justifiable aspirations.

Despite these serious limitations—which largely support our comments on the World Bank's evaluation methods—Cassen and associates, who are also employed in the aid field, concluded that "compilations of evaluation studies are valuable contribu-

tion arriving at sound, broadly applicable conclusions on project performance." They argued that "the compilations often point to generalized findings which are hard to ignore, and have the advantage of basing management and policy recommendation on actual and often persuasive experience." They concluded with an apologetic excuse for their lukewarm support: that "evaluation is an evolving art," and point out that only a few aid agencies evaluate all their projects.[84]

While, as we have seen, many aid projects are undertaken with no assessment whatever—sometimes because the operators think that existing evaluation methodologies are of no practical use, and other times because they would rather just carry on with the assumption that aid is good for economic development and growth—evaluations such as those of the World Bank are based on the endogenous view of economic growth. Economic growth is to the World Bank a dependent variable determined by a host of claimed independent variables that happen to be mostly unquantifiable. It is these unquantifiable factors that aid agencies' project assessments are supposed to quantify. The truth is that aid agencies have no valid basis to say whether their projects will add to macroeconomic growth—which, as we have insisted, is the only criterion on which aid should be judged. Within the theory of factor proportions, in which economic growth is treated as exogenous, the growth-inducing content of a project (that is, its success) is dependent on the extent to which its factor proportions correlate with the natural factor proportions of the economy. Based on these criteria, it is immediately evident that aid projects as presently constituted cannot be growth-inducing in poor economies because of their unsuitable factor proportions.

Sustainability and Participation

The words *sustainability* and *participation* have increasingly come into use in the vocabulary of foreign aid. Sustainability is an important factor in the World Bank's OED indicators of project success, and participation was mentioned frequently in the World Bank's publication *Assessing Aid*. An exploration of these concepts, however, reveals the contradictions that face aid, and the dead end in which the aid industry finds itself. We will use water and sanitation as an example.

At about the same time as the World Bank was publishing its *Assessing Aid: What Works, What Doesn't, and Why,* the UNDP–World Bank Group produced *Learning What Works: A 20-Year Retrospective View on International Water and Sanitation Cooperation*, which traced the development and historical and strategic changes that characterized water and sanitation aid programs during the years 1978 to 1998.[85] The 1977 World Water Conference adopted a declaration that was supposed to herald a new era of cooperation between poor and rich countries to work toward improved water and sanitation in the developing world. According to this declaration, the 1980s were to be the International Drinking Water Supply and Sanitation Decade, with the slogan "Water and Sanitation for All." The argument was made that the vast majority of those living in developing countries were "water-short" and that the countries had little to spend on public infrastructure.[86] In effect, the program was aimed at poverty alleviation. According to the report, "During the 1960s, the eradication of world poverty via development and aid had been seen as the post-colonial mission. The international institutions put in place after the second World War [World Bank, IMF] were—with some adaptations—applied to this task. The transfer of technology and resources to developing countries along classic Marshall Plan lines was to boost their immediate economic growth. But it swiftly became clear that in terms of the goal of poverty reduction the strategy was achieving little. Instead of wealth 'trickling down,' most of the poor were becoming progressively marginalized

from economies that were operating beyond their reach and often according to quite a separate set of norms."[87] As usual, the intention was the transfer of resources from the advanced economies to the poor economies. Other anti-poverty-oriented justifications for investment in water and sanitation in poor countries were based on the belief that there were certain basic services that individuals in any society were entitled to have provided by governments—health care, education, water, sanitation, and so on. Another case for aid investment in water was based on the belief that a good number of rural (and latterly urban) dwellers, especially women, spent many hours and much energy fetching water. The UNDP–World Bank report asserted that "lack of access to safe water is at the heart of the poverty trap" because "it is the poor, especially women and children, who suffer most in terms of illness and lost opportunities." It claimed that in rural Africa alone, forty billion hours are lost each year on collection of water from distant sources. (It failed to say, however, what these poor people will do with the forty billion hours saved.) Such are the sentiments that propelled the drive to "water for all."

The program of water for all kicked off with enthusiasm, with all those involved seeing technology from the advanced countries as the answer. But as time wore on, the international donor community was faced with the additional issue of the rapid pace of urbanization in the Third World—a pace that in many ways outstripped its historical counterpart in Europe and America. A very high proportion of the urban inhabitants were living in slums and shantytowns without water and sanitation.

In what the report described as the "appropriate technology phase" of the learning process, municipal authorities and aid agencies soon realized that the master plan prepared by donor country consultants, informed by concepts governing public health engineering in the industrialized world, would not provide lasting answers. Rather, they needed to seek what they described as "lower-technology, lower-cost" alternatives. Aid agencies soon realized that they were taking on something too big and costly, even with the less expensive approach.[88] In fact, the search for "appropriate technology" was faulty because it confused technology with cost. In other words, the fact that an installation is financially cheaper does not necessarily make it "appropriate technology."

Those dealing with the issues believed that wholesome water was synonymous with piped water, which of course requires pipes and pumps. Where it was believed that the water was contaminated, some sort of water treatment was added. The effect of this is that water collection and delivery, initially a labor-intensive activity, was now mechanized. The distances poor people walked to the source of water and transporting it back were now traversed by pipes carrying the water to the point of need. People who hauled water up from wells by manual devices were now provided with pumps (electric or manually operated). The factor proportions had dramatically changed and became more capital-intensive.

Those involved often rejected out of hand pre-existing traditional styles of water management, which were usually described as too informal. In some countries, such as Kenya, for example, post-independence laws helped to undermine the community's informal water management setup by eroding the concept of community ownership of resources.[89] Yet traditional water management, despite its apparent informality, was highly controlled, with rules about use of water, maintenance, hygiene, and right of access. In some communities committees were charged with supervision and management. All this suited the labor-intensive nature of the water supply operation. It is clear that when mechanized systems were introduced, traditional norms were immediately replaced, with resultant sociocultural discomfiture. Those who promoted these changes, including the aid agencies, were surprised that local inhabitants did not always identify with the new installations. Aid groups wanted to impose formal systems with legal structures that were alien.

This was happening at a time when the need for community involvement was proving most important, as the increasing number of isolated schemes could not be effectively run by a central authority. Even the central water and sewage systems financed by foreign aid in urban centers were, more often than not, not sustainable because funds were not always deployed and skilled personnel were not available to maintain the sophisticated equipment and to expand and reinforce the systems as necessary to handle the increasing influx of people to these centers.

Significantly, the World Bank–UNDP report pointed out that the availability of alternative technologies and their endorsement by heavyweight players in the international donor circuit did not lead to their enthusiastic acceptance by the authorities in developing countries. This was not surprising, because in many poor countries one of the greatest obstacles to the search for the necessary framework for the adoption of appropriate techniques are elites and bureaucrats who regard modern techniques as necessary vehicles for economic development and growth. Local NGOs also have the same basic attitude.

As the International Drinking Water Supply and Sanitation Decade drew to a close, it was obvious that its unrealistic goals were not going to be met. "The experts had been forced to recognize that past legacies had left a legacy of expensive and non-functioning systems all over the developing world which could not serve the poor."[90] Clearly these had a damaging effect on these weak economies, which suffered further structural imbalances. Also, the decade's failures brought home to the donor community the fact that the funds were not simply there. Around $10 billion was being spent on water and sanitation every year by the end of the decade. But this was a small fraction of what was needed to provide full coverage.[91] It also brought it home to them that the communities for whom these installations were undertaken were not always involved and often did not show a commitment to the upkeep and security of the facilities.

When the decade ended without achieving its objective, the next period (1988–1994) was what the report called "the era of 'hardware' to 'software,'" a change from emphasis on appropriate technology (hardware) to concern with institutional and service management issues (software) and attempts to show that the new ideas will actually work.[92] It could be said that a change of focus was forced by the lack of necessary funds and the low involvement of the beneficiaries.

The publication of the Brundtland Commission report on environment and development in 1987 reopened the issue of environmental resources, which led to the Earth Summit in Rio de Janeiro in 1992. The report focused on a new concept of sustainable development, defined in this context as development that meets present needs without compromising the needs of future generations. It urged that a scarcity value and a protection-of-quality value be attached even to resources that appear free—air, water. According to the World Bank–UNDP report, this means that service spread and management should be cost-effective, taking into account constraints on the resource itself and on the availability of financial resources. The report argued, in respect to water, that there was a need to be tough-minded, reinforced by the knowledge that the investment resources needed to provide full coverage from public funds, given the rate of population growth and economic setbacks many developing countries were facing, were never going to be available.[93] Given this interpretation, sustainability now meant that even poor people have to make a financial contribution to water programs. Cost recovery

became the watchword. Overnight the very basis of water and sanitation programs, as geared to primarily poverty reduction, was thrown in doubt. For decades, health criteria had been the unchallenged justification for foreign aid investment in water and sanitation services. But as the International Drinking Water Supply and Sanitation Decade was coming to an end, there was considerable debate among donors whether the provision of water to low-income communities actually made any marked impact on health. Some analysis concluded that using water in the home for washing and cleaning was more important for health than water quality—a position they could have come to much sooner if they studied traditional water management fully in the first place. It soon dawned on them that water use rose significantly when the source was very close to the point of use. Demand for a service, they now learned, depended more on water scarcity and distance from a source than the perception of its health-related benefits.

In the traditional setting, water was respected as a gift of nature. It was revered and in some societies defied. Water was not wasted, and traditional water saving and conservation methods were preserved (as we discussed in Chapter 2 in regard to the Tuaregs). In some societies, floodwaters were collected and used for tasks that did not require clean water. Rainwater was used for a set of designated purposes. When foreign aid made water abundantly available, delivered as an ordinary commodity at the doorstep, donors should not have been surprised that traditional communities did not rise in enthusiastic support of the programs. So the donor community now needed to make another turnaround in policy as the volume of demand rose at no cost to the communities. The Brundtland Commission came to the rescue with its call to revert to respect for the scarcity value of water as a gift of nature—which was all along the basis of traditional water management and utilization.

Thus arose the new concept of demand-responsive service. The need for any system of water provision, the new concept said, must now be justified in terms of effective demand or willingness to pay.[94] Willingness-to-pay surveys became a standard ingredient of feasibility studies. Cost-recovery mechanisms were featured at the center of policy and had to be realistically geared to family incomes in order to ensure sustainability of the services.[95] The upshot was that not every community, even if it was very poor, was eligible for services.

While this was described with the term *participation,* it was not participation as one would normally understand the word. Rather, it was another way of saying that communities would now share the cost of water schemes, and the extent to which they were willing to contribute would determine the service they got. They were to be considered stakeholders and take over some or all the cost and management of the installations. It was essentially participation built around financial imperatives. Participatory methodologies were designed to elicit information, build confidence and leadership, undertake tasks, select sites and sizes, and monitor results—but all based on technologies set by the donor. The demand-responsive approach holds that making people pay for a service allows them to decide how much they value the service compared to other outlets for their money. This was a complete turn away from the original justification for these schemes.[96] The idea was that those sponsoring the project would present the community with a menu of well-defined service options, and it would be up to the community in consultation with the donors to select what they can "afford."[97] The import of this—taking it to the extreme—is that very poor communities cannot have any service.

In the midst of a deteriorating water and sanitation situation in urban and semiurban areas, donors started wondering aloud whether they should not have sought solutions from indigenous practices.

The World Bank–UNDP report noted, "The challenge is to gain an understanding of how populations meet their needs for water and waste disposal, and then build on rather than replace what already exists."[98] The question is why not leave them to carry on uninterrupted by "new technologies" in the first place.

It is not often realized that the politics of foreign-aid-based water and sanitation promotion have had other effects on the economies and social structures of Third World countries. In parts of Africa, for example, there were thriving pottery-making industries based on local clay. These pots, produced in large quantities, were, among other things, used to fetch and store water. The pots were fragile but served the purpose of a water collector, scooping water with a clay cup into the pot or dipping it into a stream. But with the arrival of piped water, the pots were driven out of use because they could not withstand the high pressure of water coming out of piped and pumped systems. Water storage containers were no longer needed, as water was available on demand at the delivery points. So these clay pots have been replaced by metal and plastic containers manufactured with machinery imported from industrialized countries.

If water and sanitation are now "economic" services for which users have to contribute financially, they lose their original primary claim of being part of a poverty reduction program. Since such programs cannot induce macroeconomic growth, the question is, what then is the use for them? With this dead end in mind, we approached the World Bank and suggested a reexamination of their water and sanitation strategy in poor countries, focusing initially on eastern and southern Africa. If they wanted to continue loan financing of water projects, we thought that the emphasis should shift from a project approach—with designs by consultants selected from donor countries and construction contracts awarded to firms from donor countries—to one in which much smaller amounts were regarded instead as developmental catalysts. The provision of water would be no longer an end in itself but rather an "economic node" intended to assist communities to recapture the initiative in planning and managing economic activities. We pointed out that in all traditional societies, management of water affairs has been handed from one generation to another. We pointed out in Chapter 2 that Africa's poor economic performance arises from a basic economic personality that has suffered a mental and psychological disorientation. This disorientation saps confidence and initiative in doing and in innovating. Teaching and training by outsiders, however well intentioned, reinforces dependency and feelings of worthlessness. We opined that water programs provided an excellent opportunity to tap into communities' management and organizational traditions —in essence, the holistic management of water and sanitation. If communities can be enabled to enter into productive economic activities, the base for sustainable economic development and growth will have been laid. In turn, economic growth will allow communities to, among other things, service their water needs on a financially sustainable basis and do away with foreign assistance.

The World Bank enthusiastically praised the concept and said it accorded with the spirit behind its water and sanitation programs. But during our meetings with the key personnel in charge of various countries' World Bank water and sanitation programs and the Eastern and Southern African Regional Office of the UNDP-World Bank Water and Sanitation Group in Nairobi, we saw no evidence of holistic management or anything near it. In Nairobi, the regional manager boasted about their demand-responsive approach but did not have any response when the contradictions in the program were pointed out. A number of country representa-

tives of the World Bank expressed to us their anxiety about the increasing financial unsustainability of the aid-based water projects; only a few years after schemes were commissioned in urban and semiurban settings, many of the facilities had fallen into disrepair.

According to the World Bank–UNDP report, an extensive review of urban infrastructure programs, notably by the World Bank, revealed that many municipal authorities in developing countries were grossly inefficient and wasteful of scarce resources.[99] But much responsibility rested on those that introduced the inappropriate technologies. When we wrote a report to the World Bank informing them of the poor situations we had found and suggesting that we cooperate with them to provide the basis of a holistic water and sanitation management program, they wrote back to say that they were not set up to undertake such activities. We in turn talked to the World Bank's chief economists for Africa, forwarding these proposals as well as a chapter of this book, still in draft, pointing out the need for the World Bank to reevaluate its overall economic strategy and de-emphasize capital. Despite reminders sent to the economists concerned and the World Bank's vice presidents for Africa, no reply was received from them. We are reminded of Vandersluis and Yeros' comment that "the influence of the Bank over the shape of economic policy creates at least the perception of effective disenfranchisement of those who oppose it."[100]

In concluding this chapter, one must acknowledge the sincerity and devotion of many people, including the staffs of international institutions and agencies, in their quest to bring foreign investment and aid to poor countries. Unfortunately, they are like a devoted doctor who believes that when a patient is not responding to treatment, the answer is to increase the dosage.

7

The World Economy and Globalization

The theory of trade and the theory of factor mobility have won the day despite the serious and fundamental flaws in their claim to promoting economic growth. The next stage, that of globalization, has long been coming, because globalization epitomizes the virtues of free trade and free movement of factors. There are many claims that globalization is not a new phenomenon, that the world in the past has encompassed times of free trade and mobility of capital, natural resources, and people. This is true.

Never in history, however, has so much wealth been accumulated seeking further wealth. Well over $2 trillion a day now travels across the street and across the world at unimaginable speed as bits of electronic information. The need to amass large amounts of investment funds continues to encourage the consolidation of investment and banking corporations. Transnationals, a comparatively recent historical event, now straddle the globe and have forced major adjustments to the classical theory of trade.

The Asian Financial Crisis

On January 30, 1995, twenty-four hours before President Bill Clinton orchestrated a $50 billion bailout for the Mexican economy, the world financial system came perilously close to a meltdown. As news spread that Mexico was on the verge of defaulting on government bond payments, capital fled stock markets from Brazil and Argentina and even countries as far away as Poland and the Czech Republic. Asian markets were spared only because stock markets there were closed in observance of Chinese New Year.

When in 1997 the Thai currency crashed, it bankrupted most of that country's financial institutions and set up a wave across Asia. Capital went flying out of all Southeast Asian emerging markets. The recession that resulted had an immediate effect on commodity prices around the world. Asia had in its rapid economic growth become an important consumer of raw materials as well as semifinished goods and capital equipment. This had important consequences for countries in the advanced world that traded with the Asians. There was a race in these countries, the United States included, to erect walls to contain the so-called contagion within the troubled region. It was feared that the East Asian crisis would seriously dent the rising U.S. economy. People in Europe and the United States feared that cheaper imports from the shrinking economies of Asia would flood their markets and that the flood would turn into a tidal wave if Japan and China also sought new growth by cheapening their currency to increase exports. The fall in prices turned out to be the mechanism by which countries such as Russia felt the effect of the Asian financial troubles. Countries such as Brazil, just finding their feet, saw their stocks and bonds being sold by panicky investors. Investors cashed in Korean, Egyptian, and Israeli stocks and bonds for the safety of the West. In all cases the reactions were almost instantaneous, and it was clear that the world was far more interconnected than ever before.

It is important, therefore, to study the genesis of the Asian financial crisis to help us determine the effectiveness of this growing world economy system (globalization). Chris Patten, the former governor of Hong Kong, said that in all the countries of the Far East that were involved directly in the crisis, there were two basic and common causes. First was a failure to remember the importance of the economic fundamentals in a given region. He described the fundamentals of Asia as weak regulation of banks and the banks' cozy relationships with politicians and governments. Second, the development of Asia's economies and their increasing sophistication had raised expectations about openness and accountability that the system did not satisfy. He felt that the Asian economies had outgrown their political structures.[1] Friedman, in his well-publicized book *The Lexus and the Olive Tree,* put the global economic crisis down to "bad lenders" and "bad borrowers."[2] Simply put, Friedman said that too much credit went to the wrong people at the wrong price, in turn encouraging irresponsible business behaviors. Henderson asserted that despite a national savings rate of around 35 percent of GDP, Thailand still sought funds from abroad, since its domestic investment rate was over 40 percent. He claimed that the 40 percent was a result of the Thai government's grandiose economic plans, which relied on continued heavy flows of foreign capital and FDI. This funding shortage led back into Thailand's rising external debt in a vicious circle. He described investments undertaken in a number of Asian countries as "low-return, low-productivity projects."[3] The East Asian companies were therefore accused of operating on gearing ratios unacceptable in Western economies. It was said that the Asian countries lacked a deep domestic bond market because Asian companies needed access to a broad spectrum of

capital markets to supply their funding needs. Reliance on equity markets was said to be insufficient. The lack of a developed domestic market forced banks and companies to focus on foreign-currency-denominated bonds and loans.

Krugman claimed that "soaring investment, together with a surge of spending by newly affluent consumers, led to a surge in imports; the booming economy pulled up wages, making Thai exports less competitive."[4] He drew a triangular relationship between loss of confidence, financial problems for companies and banks, and a combination of plunging currency, rising interest rates, and slumping economy. He christened this triangle "the vicious circle of financial crisis." While economists knew of this relationship, they did not, according to him, realize how powerful this feedback process can be in practice. He concluded that market economies can be very unstable and the feedback relationship can create an explosive crisis, as occurred in the Asian countries.

Conventional economists' inconclusive attempts to explain the Asian crisis have led to a new set of additions to the economic vocabulary: *contagion, herd effect* (including *electronic herd*), *cronyism, transparency,* and so on. As usual, relying only on empirical data, economists cannot agree on what caused the crisis or even on how to avoid another one. Expressing his exasperation about this, Krugman would even say that some economists would argue that the economies were in very good shape and that the crisis was wholly gratuitous. "The real controversy—the one that is heated and often personal, because those who criticize the way the crisis was handled are also criticizing those who handled it—concerns policy," he said.[5]

Despite the quarrels, it seems most conventional economists are of the view that the solution to the economic crisis in Asia is to clean up a number of dirty patches but basically continue more of the same. Henderson said, "Asian countries and their governments will seek to restructure according to the prevailing necessities of the global economy. . . . The global economy increasingly requires uniform standards. Ideologically, emerging market countries may resent having to obey the standards of the West, but if they are to receive the West's capital, they have little choice." He likened emerging countries that tried to stop globalization to "King Canute trying to stop the sea coming in."[6] Indeed, the World Bank wants to promote the view that in many respects the crisis can be seen simply as the failure of the East Asian countries to manage globalization.[7]

Let us examine some of the claimed causes of the crisis. We shall assume that the cause of the crisis was bad lenders and bad borrowers as well as a lack of bank regulation. Before the crisis, the World Bank had this to say about financial institutions in these countries: "Central banks and departments of finance appear to have been greatly successful in supervising commercial banks which have reported a relatively low proportion of non-performing loans in their portfolio. . . . Generally, however, non-performing loans have been less of a problem in the HPAEs [high-performing Asian economies] than in many developing countries. . . . The more effective prudential regulation of East Asia banks is apparent in the ease with which most of them adopted international capacity adequacy requirements set by the Bank for International Settlements (BIS) to ensure that banks do not take on inappropriate levels of risks. . . . Most East Asian economies continue to rely on close contact between supervisors and banks to encourage prudence."[8] How can it be that less than a year later, the experts changed their tune to assert that banks in East Asia were not regulated and East Asian countries were a host of bad lenders and bad borrowers? The problem was not necessarily the banks, but a poor economy.

In June 1998, the Federal Reserve Board sent a circular to U.S. banks in which it warned that recent surveys had shown a drop in banking lending standards due to the healthy state of the economy and competition. It cautioned that this could cause problems if the economy turned sour. The circular observed that banks were loosening lending controls and taking greater risks in three areas: (1) lack of proper analysis of customers' future financial performance, with a tendency to base future performance on borrowers' recent performance, (2) insufficient attention to loan pricing, resulting in a failure to take account of greater risk in some lending, and (3) rapid growth since 1996 in unsecured loans to real estate investment trusts. It said that banks were too focused on rosy expectations and that banks' overall health owed much to the remarkable condition of the economy, not their prudent lending. The acting comptroller of the currency added in a separate statement that "the deterioration in credit-underwriting standards we are seeing in the banking system is serious." The executive director of the American Bankers Association urged U.S. banks to always look at lending standards "to make sure banks are in good shape for the coming downturn [in the economy] whenever it comes."[9] It is clear that the charge that banking regulations were absent in East Asian economies and that the banks were in the pockets of politicians and engaged in a habit in unprofitable ventures was not the cause of the crisis but the result of a rapidly deteriorating economy. The *Financial Times* of London pointed out following the Long-Term Capital Management collapse in the United States that the collapse "shows that it is not only in the developing markets that transparency, oversight and prudential controls have been wanting."[10]

Following sober reflection on the crisis, the World Bank noted that it was clear that segments of the financial system were performing poorly: "State-owned banks in Indonesia, finance companies in Thailand, and merchant banks in Korea showed increasing signs of weakened performance and increased risks. Fragmented financial systems (for example, commercial banks in Indonesia) and rules or other barriers prevented one class of financial services from competing against one another (for example, banks and finance companies in Thailand) further weakened competitiveness, and stability, and added risk. In Thailand, for example, finance companies could not raise deposits; as a result they needed to rely on higher cost funds which created incentives to lend for more risky projects. The large number of often weakly capitalized finance companies in Thailand and banks in Indonesia, for example, reduced the franchise value of financial institutions thus undermining the incentives for prudent behavior. The competitiveness and institutional development of the banking system was hampered by the local presence of foreign banks." But it concluded: "These weaknesses, whether considered individually or in total, were not sufficient to doom the financial system to immediate stress." It observed that all the countries had performed well over the previous decades in spite of these weaknesses; rapid economic development and high domestic savings had spared most of East Asia's banking system from the adverse consequences of such weaknesses.[11]

The charge that Asian companies adopted gearing ratios unacceptable in the West is also a superficial one. In a thriving economy, it hardly matters what the gearing ratio is. The Asian countries experienced their period of rapid growth with high gearing ratios. It was only when their economies started faltering that their high gearing ratio became a problem. It is wrong to treat the high gearing ratio as the cause of the financial crisis. One must look to the state of the economies in question.

Krugman asserted that soaring levels of investment and increased consumer spending drove up imports and that wages rose, decreasing the competitiveness of Thai exports. This analysis is stunted. Henderson has correctly stated that the situation in Thailand was far more complicated. Significantly,

he noted, "The problems were structural and potentially life threatening to the country as a whole."[12] Henderson's position contrasts with Krugman's caution that there is a temptation to regard economic downturn as evidence that the economy has structural problems that must be resolved before it can recover. Krugman was of the view that the economic downturn might just require a dose of demand stimulus. He felt that those who oppose stimulus would argue that it "would reduce the pressure for change." In one instance Krugman talks of stimulating demand, and in another he talks of high consumer spending arising from soaring foreign capital inflow. We do not agree; his assessment of the problem is an oversimplification of what was basically a structural issue.

Krugman wondered why countries in East Asia not equally far down the path of development all hit the wall at the same time, concluding that it was because opening their financial markets and running up a lot of outside debt made them all more vulnerable. He claimed that these factors intensified the feedback from loss of confidence into financial collapse.[13] In fact, as will become evident later, the East Asian economies—far being from at different levels of development, as Krugman suggested—had the same basic structural problems. But it is futile to blame the crisis on international investors, accused by conventional economists of causing what the World Bank called the "explosion of the crisis." The World Bank quite wrongly asserted that after receiving large capital flows for four years or more, the four countries affected, Indonesia, Korea, Malaysia, and Thailand, suffered heavy losses "following the sudden shift in investor sentiment."[14] The loss of confidence was the consequence of, not the cause of, the economic crisis. Some economists seek to explain the cause of the crisis with the most unscientific line of reasoning. For example, Bhagwati claims that capital markets are volatile: "You may be healthy but suddenly you catch pneumonia. And then you may have to do unspeakable things to your economy just to regain confidence because you are hooked into the system. Markets may do something when you have done nothing wrong and you may have to do something wrong in order to convince the markets that you are doing something right."[15] Was Bhagwati seriously saying that there was nothing wrong with the economies of these countries before the financial crisis and that it was all down to market sentiments? Krugman observed that especially when the subject is grave, economists are often afflicted with the temptation to use big words without saying anything; the alternative is to be entertaining, even to the point of levity, to illustrate the analysis and jolt the listener's mind into a different way of looking at the situation. True enough, but in many cases writers who take this tack are not illustrating any serious scientific principle, and this is the case for Bhagwati in his explanation of the Asian crisis.

Many pundits have argued that the crisis was one of liquidity—creditors "ran" on the currencies, leaving borrowers unable to finance their loans. The truth is that foreign investors fled because of poor economies that threatened their capital. In the case of Thailand, foreign investors watched for almost a year and a half as the economy declined, and started jumping ship only when it looked as though their investments were seriously at risk. So again the cause of the crisis is the economy.

We are left wondering where Krugman's famous TFP analysis of these economies has gone if he now feels that it was not the economy of these countries as such that was the real cause of the crisis. His opinion is that it was not that the borrowed money was badly spent; some of it was, some of it wasn't. Rather, while there were real problems in these economies, the main failing was, according to him, a "vulnerability to self-fulfilling panic."[16]

Some believe the crisis was the result of an overdependence on foreign finance. Henderson ar-gues that overreliance on external debt and the general weakness of the Asian banking system tied in closely with the general weakness of the banks.[17] But the truth is that except for Korea, Indonesia, Malaysia, and Thailand each had less than 5 percent of their total debt plus equities as external long-term debt in the period 1996–97. Korea had only 13 percent. With regard to their short-term foreign debt, in 1996–97 all these countries had 2 to 3 percent of their total debt plus equity as short-term foreign loans.[18] The accountabilities of external short-term debt were not the direct cause of the crisis.[19] It seems that the issue of external dependence has been overblown.

On the whole, the size of the short-term debt in these countries was not large by international comparisons. Indeed, the bulk of the foreign loans was made by the larger firms, export firms, and firms with foreign direct investment.[20] Foreign borrowing was therefore concentrated in a small number of firms.[21] Manufacturing does not seem to have been a major player relative to real estate and the financial services sector.

Some people have drawn similarities between Thailand's real estate collapse and the U.S. savings and loan crisis in 1980. Given that Morris described the $150 billion bailout of the savings and loan industry in a $7 trillion economy as not "such a big deal," Thailand could have weathered the real estate collapse in a strong economy.[22]

Some of those who attempted to explain the crisis in terms of the structure of the economy made heroic efforts to prove that the economies lacked an adequate technology base. Wade and Veneroso argued that the economies of Southeast Asia engaged in the world industrial economy largely as subcontractors to the Japanese, with relatively little technology spillover from these export-oriented subcontractors to the rest of the economy. The two economists argued that the industrialization of these countries was "technology-less" in the sense that even adaptive technology came from abroad. Throughout the region, they claimed, infrastructure was chronically congested, and the shortage of skilled persons had grown from a "critical emergency to a critical emergency."[23] These arguments have a lot in common with Krugman's TFP assessment of East Asian development, but they are countered by Henderson's assertion that these economies experienced major strides in technological advancement, innovation, and education that cannot be explained by input or funding.[24] Amsden claimed that Korea, for example, was a successful learner because it invested heavily in foreign technical assistance and education, which has acted as a determinant of economic development, driving the economy to the heights of per capita income achievable by a high level of formally educated human resources.[25]

The irony of the Asian crisis is that these countries had been, at the urging of the IMF, OECD, and Western governments, undertaking final deregulation, opening up their markets. In fact, in the early 1980s the Korean government was already promoting a policy of economic globalization on both domestic and foreign fronts, and by 1997 it had agreed to completely open up its economy by the year 2000 and eliminate all legal impediments to foreign private investment; at that time, FDI approvals were up to $3.2 billion from $1.9 billion in 1995. Seoul entered into the WTO, and by 1997 the OECD had bound it to specific schedules of market opening and deregulation. Kim Young-sam's adoption of *segyehwa* (globalization) as his watchword was supposed to indicate the country's enthusiasm for these steps.

Neoliberalism (Friedman would call it democratization of technology, finance, investing, information) depends on the belief that by allowing every potential participant in economic activity free access and free movement of factors, the sheer number of actors is likely to increase the possibility of hitting upon the right economic formulations (the invisible hand).[26] Democratic economic manage-

ment is in effect saying that the greater the number of participants and the greater their freedom of activity, the greater the chance of achieving economic growth in comparison to where action is regulated. The only problem with this neoliberal economics in a global setting is that the free transfer of factors from the richer areas to the poor areas creates structural problems that stultify the latter's economic growth. But what if in the absence of economic democracy, the few initiators (governments) were able to find the right economic formulation? Nature (science) has provided that economic growth is exogenous. This is to enable each society to achieve economic development with institutions that suit differing social and cultural norms. It seems, therefore, particularly unfortunate and off target that the experts are disdaining the so-called Asian values as being incapable of sustaining Asia's economic development.[27]

Many would prefer to think of the Asian crisis as a bad dream, something that will soon pass, like all the other financial crises of the past twenty or thirty years; in fact, in 2000 the World Bank declared that East Asia was once again the world's fastest-growing region, with the hardest-hit countries recovering nicely in terms of foreign exchange reserves (up), currencies (stable), and interest rates (down). But what else could have been expected after these economies reached their lowest levels? The World Bank further observed that financial markets were well above their crisis-induced nadirs and in some cases above precrisis highs. Equity markets rose by more than 40 percent in 1999. But the World Bank's optimism reflects a lack of scientific approach to economic growth issues. It is expressing satisfaction with what it regarded as recovery because of financial data that are in fact nothing but a shadow of the real economy. It is not surprising that the high levels of poverty and low industrial capacity that occurred in the East Asian countries in 1998, judging by their past economic profiles, must mean a reduction of imports. Low costs arising from lower value of the currencies will increase exports. The result has to be an increase in reserves. From a very low level of GDP, any increase will represent an exaggerated percentage growth. The World Bank may have forgotten that the precrisis numbers were already deplorable and were abysmally below their 1995 levels; for them, it is almost business as usual. The report quoted Alfred Ho of Invesco Hong Kong as having said in March 2000 that while the year before he had not been sure what to tell his clients, in the present year he and his colleagues were telling their clients that if they didn't want to lose their money at a time when many Asian markets were down by 80 percent from their peaks, the greater risk to investors lay in not investing.[28] Hoagland, in an article in the *International Herald Tribune* in September 1997, immediately following the crisis, correctly read the mood of global experts, predicting that globalizers no doubt would soon be claiming to have known all along that things would turn out this way. He thought a more likely outcome of the crisis would be minor tinkering with the assumptions already reached and blessed and a knee-jerk continuation of the policies, practices, and thinking that produced the crisis.[29]

Having stated that the Asian crisis was not a financial crisis but an economic one, it is now necessary to analyze what really happened. We will use Thailand and South Korea to illustrate the position. These two countries, in common with most of the Asian tigers, have had a checkered economic history since they decided to "modernize" their economies. Hoagland argued that the real wonder is that the Asian debacle did not occur sooner. His stance contrasts sharply with the impression created by those who dubbed the Asian economies as tigers in the first place. For example, the World Bank said, "East Asia has a remarkable record of high and sustained economic growth. From 1965 to 1990, the twenty-three countries of East Asia grew faster than

all other regions of the world. Most of this achievement is attributable to the seemingly miraculous growth in just eight economies. . . . The eight economies do share some economic characteristics that set them apart from other developing countries. . . . The eight high performing economies (HPAEs) have been unusually successful at sharing the fruits of growth."[30] But Korea's industrialization did not start with modernization. As Amsden noted, Korea's industrialization can be said to have begun in the 1870s, "when the 1,000-year old Yi dynasty began to shatter as a consequence of Japanese intrusion."[31] The country suffered economic damages because of World War II. Korea's economic rebuilding was initiated during 1953 to 1962.

Korea is a small country with limited natural resources. Arable land accounts for only 22 percent of the total area. The marked population growth since 1953 has left it with one of the highest population densities per acre of arable land in the world. In terms of factor proportions, Korea should have adopted a strategy of low capital input, low material input, and high labor input. It is necessary to bear this in mind in reviewing its economic structure up to the 1997 crisis.

According to Suh, the country in 1953 was "faced with a market too small to support the building of social infrastructure or attract investment, an inability to meet the basic needs of a rapidly growing and urbanizing population and generally low income levels and high unemployment, all aggravated by lack of natural resources."[32] The economic policy pursued in this period was essentially that of import substitution of nondurable consumer goods and intermediate goods. Because of the country's lack of resources, most of its reconstruction projects between 1954 and 1959 were funded by foreign aid, especially from the United States.

A new development strategy was adopted in the early 1960s. The new government of the third republic was intent on playing an active role in promoting growth and transforming Korea. It considered that with the country's limited natural resources and small domestic market, an outward-oriented development strategy that emphasized exports was the answer. The essence of this strategy was the promotion of labor-intensive manufacturing for export, in which Korea considered it had comparative advantage.[33] Suh explained that in keeping with its emphasis on stimulating exports, the government devalued the won by almost 100 percent and introduced a unified floating exchange rate system to eliminate bias against the export sector. It introduced a whole range of tax exemptions, lower rates for public utilities, tariff rebates for imports destined for reexport, and a wide range of other incentives for new export companies.

To mobilize savings and resources, it more than doubled interest rates on deposits, from 12.0 percent to 26.4 percent. Importing most of its raw materials and converting them first into light consumption goods and later durables, it enjoyed rapid growth. Total exports (mostly of labor-intensive products) rose at an annual average of 39 percent in the period 1963–71, spurred by incentives and devaluation at a time when world trade was growing at an annual rate of 11.6 percent. Average annual growth of GNP for 1963 to 1971 was more than double that of 1954 to 1962.

These options did, however, lay the country open to import dependence because of the need for large importation of raw materials. Nevertheless, the country witnessed impressive growth. The labor-intensive strategy had a significant influence on its social welfare, leading to a better overall income distribution.[34] The income share of the lowest 40 percent increased from 14.1 percent in 1965 to 18.9 percent in 1970, and that of the highest 20 percent declined from 47 percent to 43 percent. It is clear that the government partially got its economic growth formulation right in terms of factor proportion pattern of development.

The period 1972 to 1979 saw a change in strategy. The main objective of this change was a drive to establish heavy industry and a chemical industry for new strategic exports and the promotion of import substitution of intermediate materials and capital goods, which favored such industries as shipbuilding, automobiles, nonferrous metals, and petrochemicals by promoting large-scale investments in them. The country resorted to heavy foreign borrowing.[35] What Corbo and Suh called "hidden problems" soon emerged:

Below the surface, major problems were brewing. Excess capacity appeared in the heavy and chemical industries and the financial sectors were accumulating non-performing loans, primarily as a result of lending to those industries. Continuing incentives for these industries produced a substantial increase in private investment . . . and created an overheated labor market—unemployment fell from 3.2 percent in 1978, rising slightly only to 3.8 percent in 1979—that caused real wages in manufacturing and export activities to grow by 110.2 percent and 105.2 percent respectively between 1974–75 and 1979 . . . [and] led to a high average annual inflation rate of 21.3 percent . . . despite controls on many wage goods. A black market emerged and flourished. Moreover, the rate of increases in real wages was outstripping the rise in productivity. With domestic inflation higher than international levels, the real effective exchange rate appreciated 23.6 percent between 1973 and 1979. The rate of growth in output per unit of input slowed considerably by 4.9 percentage points during 1963–72 to only 1.6 percentage points during 1979–82. External debt was burgeoning at an annual rate of 28.8 percent. By the late 1970s, export performance was beginning to deteriorate; the rate of growth slowed to 8.4 percent per year and turned negative in 1979; meanwhile, export profitability declined continuously. The rise in wages and lack of access to bank credit hit the profitability of labor-intensive exports particularly hard and they lost competitiveness in the face of lower unit costs in other NICs.[36]

In effect, the government had mobilized the savings of the population but denied small businesses access to those savings.

> The high rate of inflation and unbalanced regional and sectoral growth of the 1970s ultimately led to a slight worsening in the distribution of income for three reasons: (a) with economic growth centered on large, capital-intensive projects, there were relatively fewer jobs for lower-income workers, a pattern that resulted in a wide wage differential amongst workers; (b) the government's industrial policy fostered the rapid growth of large conglomerates, so that the distribution of business ownership worsened; and (c) given the high rate of inflation of the 1970s, Korean companies and households found it more profitable to invest in speculative domestic ventures especially real estate.[37]

Korea's external debt grew rapidly, reaching $20.3 billion in 1979, a 372 percent increase over the 1973 figure of $4.3 billion. The subsidized loan policy had in effect resulted in overinvestment in some industries, and an imbalance developed.

The rapid growth in the heavy and chemical industries required large quantities of energy. Korea, lacking in natural energy sources, required vast amounts of imported crude oil. In 1979, along with other NICs, Korea was hit hard by the second oil shock. Export-led growth became export-led recession. Suh observed, "All these factors aggravated the mounting structural difficulties that resulted from policies such as the drive for heavy and chemical industrialization."[38] During the period 1980–88, Korea undertook its first structural adjustment, covering price stabilization and market liberalization (to give more autonomy to the private sector). Import liberalization was intended, in line with conventional development thinking, to introduce foreign competition in order to pressure domestic producers into raising productivity and quality, and it included partial deregulation of foreign investment. The claimed success of this structural adjust-

ment occurred against the background of increased world trade. The chronic current-account deficit improved. The massive investments in heavy and chemical industries had led by 1985 to an external debt of $46.8 billion. Riding on the favorable trends in the world economic environment since the September 1985 Plaza Agreement, Korea was able to reduce its foreign debt to about $31 billion in 1988, and between 1986 and 1988 it achieved a GNP growth rate of over 10 percent. Between 1986 and 1989, Korea achieved very favorable external surpluses. By 1990, however, Korea's trade balance had slipped into a deficit and exports had stopped growing in real terms. In 1992 real GNP growth fell to less than 5 percent.

The rapid economic growth from 1986 to 1988 resulted in worsening imbalances in income distribution, in regional and sectoral growth, and between large conglomerates and small companies.[39] By the late 1980s capital intensiveness had increased in the belief that efficiency and productivity would rise as well. Factory automation systems were introduced to reduce dependence on labor. It was estimated that more than two-thirds of South Korean manufacturing spent over half of the funds available for facility investment on automation.[40]

By 1989, nominal wages in manufacturing had increased by another 25 percent, while growth in labor productivity came to a virtual standstilll.[41] In that year Korea's exports posted a poor 2.8 percent rate of growth. Growth remained weak at 4 percent in 1990, with the trade account shifting back into deficit. When the trade deficit nearly halved from $9.7 billion in 1991 to $5.1 billion in 1992, it was due not to rapidly growing exports but to slackening imports, which fell from 16.7 percent in 1991 to a negligible 0.2 percent in 1992. Demand in the domestic market had decreased also. The decline in inflation and improvement of the trade balance in 1992 made policy makers confident about maintaining contradictory policy measures despite increasing numbers of bankruptcies and the rapid slowdown of GNP growth to 4.7 percent, the worst downturn since 1980, when the economy recorded a negative rate of growth.[42]

By 1993, the incoming Kim government was facing what Koreans regarded as an economic crisis. Low private consumption, meaning a weak local market, was a contributory factor. The government adopted business-propping measures just before Kim's inauguration. These did not have the desired effect; investors' confidence did not recover, as corporate plant and equipment investments declined by 5.7 percent. The government attempted to deal with the challenges it faced by encouraging labor-intensive producers that were no longer competitive to shift into other lines or transfer their operations overseas to lower-cost countries such as China.[43] It is surprising from a factor proportions point of view that the country, in the face of its industry's loss of competitiveness, opted for more foreign capital and increased flows of FDI and technology from the United States, Japan, and the European Community.

It is clear from this review of the Korean economy since World War II that the World Bank's statement that the East Asian countries (as exemplified here by South Korea) grew consistently between 1960 and 1990 was an exaggeration. South Korea did not achieve sustained growth during this period. It is also clear that the path Korea chose after 1972 embedded a sick profile into its economy that continued into the 1990s.

In order to analyze the structural economic problems inherent in Asian countries leading to the crisis of 1997–98, we will now follow closely the course of events in Thailand and South Korea in 1996 and 1997.

Thailand

In the first half of 1996, growth in domestic demand weakened, continuing a trend from the be-
ginning of the year. In short, the domestic market was weak. Despite faltering economic prospects, foreign direct investment remained bullish, as evidenced by the approvals given to such long-term projects as GM's regional plant and heavy industrial projects in steel, cement, and chemicals. In the first quarter of 1996, the current account deficit reached Bt 87.8 billion, 42.5 percent higher than in the same period in 1995, putting it on track to surpass 1995's deficit of Bt 333.7 billion, which was equivalent to 8.1 percent of GDP. The baht was weak against the dollar because of efforts to limit the damage to export competitiveness caused by the yen's even larger fall against the dollar.

After rising by 23 percent in baht terms in January 1995, export growth plunged to 12 percent in February 1996 and 3 percent in March 1996. The extent of the economic slowdown took business by surprise, according to the Economist Intelligence Unit (EIU). As the country was entering the third quarter of 1996, it was becoming increasingly evident that the main components of domestic demand were continuing to slow. The export slowdown prompted predictions that the period of export-led growth in Asia was coming to an end. It was noteworthy that a contributory factor to the export slowdown was the loss of an overseas market for labor-intensive and relatively smaller industries— the so-called sunset industries, such as textiles and footwear. The country's larger current-account deficit and a ballooning debt stock (expected at the time by the IMF to reach nearly $100 billion by the end of 1996) increasingly consisted of expensive commercial bank loans to the private sector. This raised Thailand's self-imposed external financing requirement over the next two years above $25 billion. A speculative outflow occurred in early August in response to rumors of a devaluation. The authorities, however, continued to insist that devaluation would not be appropriate since the benefits for exports would be nullified by the higher costs of imports. A substantial cause of the current-account deficit was the economy's heavy dependence on imported machinery and parts. As for manufacturing, declining domestic demand contributed to successive falls in output. The country's stock exchange slump continued unabated, and by August the index had fallen to 1,104.83, the largest drop since early in the year. A study of the earnings growth of listed companies showed a decline from an average 20.9 percent rate in 1990 to just 9.5 percent in 1995, and speculation was that it would fall farther. Most deterred by these unfavorable developments were foreign investors. Earnings growth per share fell, and by August the index was 5 percent below the level of November 1995. As the country ended 1996, the economic outlook remained gloomy. However, the year-on-year rate of industrial production index leveled off in the third quarter of 1986 after falling to a two-year low of 5.6 percent. The stock exchange continued to decline and by November 1986 it stood at 931.5, a slight improvement from mid-October.

By the beginning of 1997, more than half of the companies listed on Thailand's stock exchange reported failing earnings. The private investment index—a twelve-month moving average of such components as construction permits, capital goods import, domestic cement consumption, and commercial bank credits for manufacturing and construction—had continued to register progressively slower rates of increase. It was becoming evident that applications and approvals for foreign investment were beginning to go into decline. Since the end of 1996, the baht had come under repeated attack, but on each occasion the Bank of Thailand had successfully come to its rescue, albeit with serious damage to foreign reserves. The sharp slowdown in manufacturing that occurred in December 1996 dashed hopes that recovery was under way, even though the Ministry of Industry blamed the economy's problems on the export sector. The growth rate was also depressed by domestic fac-

tors, highlighted by weak demand for motor vehicles, cigarettes, and sugar. Clearly, capacity utilization in Thailand was steadily falling well before July 1997.

Output of the main exported industrial items such as electronics, textiles, and jewelry, however, remained stable. The government started an industrial restructuring program. It set up research institutes for four manufacturing sectors: textiles, food, electronics, and motor vehicles, emphasizing the introduction of technology, staff training, and provision of soft loans. Textiles, regarded as a sunset industry, was given special treatment. It was becoming clear that import slowdown was becoming more pronounced than export slowdown. In March 1997, a financial crisis was precipitated by the revelation that several of the country's financial companies were overexposed to the rocky real estate and installment buying sectors. The crisis, which the EIU described as the most serious in Thai history, was defused by a series of measures aimed at shoring up the financial and real estate sectors. On March 4, the day's withdrawals from financial companies amounted to Bt 9.4 billion.

The EIU reported that by mid-April 1997, the worst-case scenario, involving massive withdrawals of domestic and foreign capital from the bank's finances and the stock exchange and a forced devaluation of the baht, had apparently been averted. Between May 6 and 7, withdrawals were down to Bt 3.5 billion. Inflation fell in the early months of 1997 for reasons attributed to slower economic activity. The private investment index fell to about 7.3 percent, barely half of its level in 1996. Direct investment continued the decline that had begun in mid-1995. Most key sectors were reporting idle capacity and high inventories in response to poor export sales and weak domestic consumption. By the second quarter, the government announced the establishment of a Bt 25 billion fund offering low-interest loans for mechanization of some of the worst-affected sectors, especially textiles and garments. Most of the fund was to be used to import capital equipment. Evidently the government had decided that the cure to its problems was the introduction of further labor-saving techniques of production. But studies by the Federation of Thai Industries (FTI) claimed that outdated machinery was only one reason for the fall in textile exports; others included rising wages and high import duties for an industry that depended on imported inputs. The FTI warned that much of the Bt 187 billion ($7.2 billion) of planned investment in steel capacity was at risk because of import tariffs ranging as high as 20 percent. But the Thai government was caught between the demands of downstream producers, who wanted to tap into offshore materials, and upstream suppliers of intermediate products, who wanted to keep foreigners out. Despite this gloomy news, investment continued to flow into steelmaking. Also, it is noteworthy that according to the World Bank, personal consumption indicators in Thailand were already weak before the outbreak of the currency crisis.[44] Real GDP growth in 1997 was negative, at –1.7 percent, and fell even further in 1998, to –10.4 percent.

South Korea

Much of 1996 was a downward slide in South Korea. From the last quarter of 1995 economic growth slowed from 10.0 percent in the preceding quarter to about 6.8 percent but recovered in the first quarter of 1996 to 7.0 percent. The slight recovery in the next quarter to 7.9 percent led to optimism about the second half of 1996, and fears of a crash, which were prevalent, receded, according to the EIU. The government attributed the growing trade deficit to mounting trade disputes and massive inflows of high-priced luxury items. The EIU commented, "In reality, trade disputes are sporadic and insignificant while affluent consumers' growing appetite for foreign brands is not the whole story." In fact, consumer goods made up less than 12 percent of Korean imports. South Korea still had to import much of the plant and technology it needed to manufacture export goods. The deterioration in the current-account deficit to a record of more than $12 billion in 1996 was a shock to both the government and most economic forecasters.

Fixed capital formation, however, was still recording "positive" growth. It was this component that pundits thought contracted and caused a sharp slowdown in GDP growth in 1992, after the previous upturn of 1990–91. By mid-1996, according to the EIU, concern among stock market investors and policy makers appeared to have reached panic proportions. Despite falling long-term interest rates and the huge capacity additions of 1994–95, the steady trickle of the movement of labor-intensive industries to offshore locations continued. The current account deficit represented 2.3 percent of GDP. The won's weakness against the dollar was partly inspired by the government's need to limit the damage to export competitiveness caused by the yen's even larger fall against the United States and partly by the widening current-account deficit.

However, by 1996 the profits of the thirty largest chaebols (industrial groups) fell by 90 percent. The economists at Samsung were warning that South Korea "is at the brink of a crisis like that in Mexico." Multinationals in South Korea were also moving offshore in a bid to escape overdependence on a lackluster economy. With annual salaries in Korea averaging $24,000, South Korea's economic miracle was just about to come full circle.[45]

As 1996 was closing, it was becoming clear that domestic demand and private consumption were growing less quickly during the year than in the same period in 1995. The slowdown in investment was particularly marked, from a year-on-year figure of 12.4 percent in the first nine months of 1995 to 6 percent in the corresponding period of 1996.

The Bank of Korea, with an eye on the depreciating yen, allowed the won to slip against the dollar for most of 1996. The "success" of heavy industry at the expense of the light industrial sector continued. South Korea's vehicle industry was still investing heavily in new capacity both in Korea and abroad and was enjoying spectacular success in markets such as the United States and United Kingdom. Other capital-intensive activities, such as the expansion of capacity by oil refiners, were under way.

As the country started 1997, the EIU commented, "Historians may well look on 1997 (and the first quarter in particular) as the time when the chickens finally came home to roost in South Korea." For the first four months South Korea was preoccupied by the Hanbo scandal. On January 23, Hanbo, the country's second largest steelmaker, failed to honor promissory notes that had come due, precipitating bankruptcy of the group, with its twenty-four subsidiaries. As the full details became known, people wondered why major banks had lent vast sums apparently without proper inquiries into the steel mill's viability and the company's creditworthiness. Hanbo's debts were around twenty times its assets and roughly equal to the annual turnover of the entire group. To make matters worse for the banks, a second steelmaker went bankrupt weeks later. The steelmaker's trouble was partly due to losses on a speculative Canadian acquisition and unwise expansion based on debt. Fears of a domino effect were heightened in April when Jinro, the nineteenth largest chaebol, was revealed to be in trouble as a result of rapid expansion into unrelated fields. The large current-account deficit, scares over the financial health of banks and chaebols, and the financial scandals combined with yen-dollar depreciation to force the won down in early 1997. The deficit in the first quarter of 1997 stood at $7.43 billion, much larger than was recorded in the first quarter of 1996.

The EIU observed that with the reversal in fortunes, more and more cases of apparent reversion to economic nationalism were appearing. It noted that there was deep gloom about the country's economic performance in both 1996 and 1997. By the end of the first quarter of 1997, South Korea's corporate insolvency rate reached its highest level in fourteen years. The percentage of promissory notes outstanding that were in default stood at 0.24 percent, the worst since 1982. The figure had doubled since September 1996, when it was 0.12 percent.

By May 1997, over a hundred small and medium-sized companies had failed, compared with forty in 1996. Despite these economic woes, some large-scale investments were still coming in. For example, Ireland's Pan-Pacific bought a 31 percent stake in Samsung Motors for $29.1 million, a new French wholly owned bottler for Coca-Cola invested $210 million, and a U.S. firm paid $750 million for 80 percent of Bohyang. Such an upswing in FDI was attributed to the government's efforts. Aware of the need to limit the growth of debt and ever cautious about opening the country's capital market to volatile portfolio flows, it had made a greater effort to attract FDI, lifting some restrictions, simplifying procedures, and publicizing the attractions of South Korea.[46] For the first four months in 1997, direct investment inflows were worth $3.7 billion—a 585.6 percent increase over the same period of 1996.

As the last half of 1997 started, the country's economic position continued to deteriorate. Its twenty-five commercial banks posted a combined net loss of 77.8 billion won for the first half. Reserves for nonperforming loans were up by 150 percent, though some analysts criticized the accounting procedures and claimed that the banks' true level of exposure was several times the published figures. Despite the state of the economy, independent analysts were still forecasting that the economy would grow slightly in 1998 and more rapidly in 1999, in apparent disbelief of what was happening. They were forecasting that the current account deficit would fall as a share of GDP—to 2.5 percent in 1998 and 2.1 percent in 1999.

As 1997 was closing, exports grew and the trade deficit rose to a hefty $9.1 billion. Foreign investors in September sold about $33.16 million of shares at a net basis, the highest figure since March 1955. This was the second month in a row that foreigners sold more shares than they bought. In September, the Bank of Korea disclosed that the foreign exchange reserves at the end of August had fallen by $2.53 billion from July, to $31.14 billion. This was below the figure at the end of 1996, $33.2 billion. The decline was attributed to the foreign exchange support given to commercial banks that were experiencing difficulties borrowing from abroad as well as the central bank's market intervention to prop up the won. In December 1997, an average of 123 smaller companies failed each day, a 1,000 percent increase from one year earlier. It was being forecast that as many as thirty thousand small and medium-sized companies might wind up failing in 1997.

By the beginning of the second half of 1997, the won was fairly stable. The EIU was forecasting that the economy would shrink in 1998 before a recovery in 1999. It projected that in 1999, external demand would be helped by faster world trade growth of over 7 percent combined with a supply-side recovery of products such as automobiles and the 64MB DRAM chips. It forecast that exports in the national account would return to double-digit growth. In fact, real growth in 1998 was –6.7 percent, and the won declined further.

Pre-Crisis Economy of the Southeast Asian Countries

We concluded earlier that the Asian crisis was caused by the deteriorating economy. We now need to take a closer look at the economy of these countries.

The first thing to notice is that demand in these countries started to fall before the crisis and before investment rates dropped, as can be seen in our narrative of the economies of Thailand and South Korea from the end of 1995 to the third quarter of 1997. A World Bank report stated that a range of indicators in the region showed a weakening in domestic demand even before the outbreak of the crisis.[47]

The decline was a slow but steady process. In the case of Korea, capacity utilization for 1996 was already 85 percent. In the first half of 1997, it dropped another 1 percent, and by the second half of 1997, it was down to 81 percent. The machinery industry, for example, was hard hit since it depends on domestic demand rather than exports.[48] Even exporters cited a decline in domestic demand as one of the reasons for lowered plant utilization.[49]

In Indonesia, companies with no foreign direct investment were 20 percent below full capacity by 1996; those with foreign direct investment, often with substantial export production, were at 83 percent plant utilization. By June 1997, the non-FDI companies were down to 75 percent utilization, while FDI companies were at 75 percent. In each case, domestic demand was the most important cause of the low capacity utilization.[50] The Indonesian National Development Agency pointed out that the low capacity utilization in 1997 indicated "a possible slowdown in aggregate demand prior to the crisis."[51]

At the onset of the crisis in Korea, only 12 percent of the imports were consumer goods. In the case of Thailand, Henderson attributed the large monthly current-account deficit late in 1996 as due "not to [poor] export growth but to a collapse in imports as domestic demand slowed."[52] We can safely conclude that a main cause of the crisis was declining domestic demand in all the countries. Therefore, no economic explanation of the cause of the crisis is correct unless it explains why declining domestic demand started the decline process.

Another common feature of these economies was

the belief that they could beat the West economically by high capital-intensive growth. Despite their high savings rates, they sought foreign capital. Government intervention in these countries diverted domestic savings in the direction of the capital-intensive sectors. Small and medium-sized outfits were in effect denied access to the domestic savings that would enable them to adopt the requisite capital ratio commensurate to their economies' factor endowment.

The bulk of South Korea's modern industries are concentrated in a narrow corridor between Pusan and the capital, Seoul. It was a classical case of an enclave economy—high capital-intensive activities isolated from the rest of the economy. In Indonesia, the heavy capital-intensive mines and oil extraction sites and their downstream heavy activities have combined with large investments in a variety of preferred "strategic" sectors and ambitious power projects to produce a structurally unbalanced economy. Fallows described the Malaysian industrial structure as "very advanced within their special zones" but "largely represent[ing] the effects of innovation and investment somewhere else."[53]

In Chapter 6 we undertook a theoretical analysis of the relationship between economic sectors with wide differences in factor proportion. South Korea decided to import capital equipment and materials, procured with both foreign and domestic capital, in order to sustain its export-oriented strategy. It decided to make up for the relative lack of natural resources by importing material—a case of international mobility of factors. All this created, according to Rybczynski's theory, disproportionately rapid growth of the capital-intensive sector—industrial chemicals, transport equipment, car production and electronics and so on. It drew production factors away from labor-intensive sectors such as textiles, plastic products, shoe production, and so on, which at the beginning of the 1990s accounted for over 60 percent of Korea's manufacturing output. The same

thing happens when material imports raise the material stock of the economy.

In addition to draining capital and materials, this scenario affects wages as well. Capital-intensive activities traditionally justify themselves by high wages, and South Korea was no exception. The consequence is that the small and medium-sized businesses were faced with a climate of increasing wages, which contributed further to their instability and reduced domestic demand. Over 90 percent of Korea's businesses are sole proprietorships or unincorporated businesses. On top of that, the burgeoning services sector (the direct result of a capital-intensive sector) was competing with the capital-intensive sector for skilled personnel, so that by 1996 the capital-intensive sector was facing a shortage of skilled labor.

The injury to small and medium-sized businesses (which are mostly labor-intensive) and low material/capital factor proportions weakens the purchasing power there. That is the cause of reduced demand. It is not something to be cranked up. It is the loss in demand typically caused by structural imbalances that is usually the first noticeable factor that leads to the vicious cycle of depression economies.

An unbalanced economy, according to the theory of factor proportions, cannot attain sustainable economic growth. That is what was happening in East Asian countries ever since they opted for capital-based export-driven economy. The cyclical pattern of growth, with its upward and downward trends, is the result of repeated injections of capital and material into an economy with serious imbalances, each of which produces a short-term spurt of growth but is followed by an accelerating decline in demand.

It is therefore evident that the outward orientation of these economies was a major factor in their economic problems. Because of their dependence on imported capital equipment and materials, they were fluctuating between narrow trade surpluses and negative trade balances. The cost of the outside inputs put countries such as South Korea in a vulnerable position in which they could not compete in the long term with industrialized countries that produce their own capital equipment and enjoy large domestic markets. But more important is that with the resultant unbalanced economy, each of the countries is condemned to a path of unsustainable economic growth. East Asia's economic problems are therefore structural and long-term. When the collapse of 1997 occurred, it was a case of economic hemorrhaging. Conventional economists who say that the economic crisis of the East Asian countries was due to their weak financial sector or withdrawal of capital are only scratching the surface of the problem.

Many conventional economists claim that what the East Asian countries need in order to avoid future failures is to transfer from what they call low-value industrial activities (meaning labor-intensive activities) to high-value activities, where productivity is said to be higher. Henderson advised that Asian manufacturers have to go further up what he called the "added-value chain," producing "more technologically advanced" goods. He argued that Asian nations need to develop "a critical mass of production and funding potential" to achieve this. Low-added-value production "inevitably . . . results in low price, low margin businesses." High-added-value businesses had the opposite effect, "boosting long-term margins."[54] From our analysis, it is clear that things don't work out that way. It is not an issue of financial margins. It is also clear that economists who argue that the success or failure of the East Asian economies is due to their achieved TFP have it wrong because they too are in effect saying that high-tech is the way these countries should go. The more high technology the Asians adopt, ironically, the more intensive the vicious cycle becomes.

The scientific approach, rooted in the theory of factor proportions, should help clarify the analytical problems conventional economists face in dealing with economic cycles and depressions in East Asia, as many of them have difficulty understanding the structural issues discussed. For example, when Garnaut stated that the East Asian crisis started in Thailand because "that economy had symptoms of old-style crisis together with vulnerability to sudden large-scale reversal of capital inflow," he was not really in a position to tell us what was wrong with the Thailand economy.[55] On the other hand, some economists argued that there was nothing wrong with the macroeconomic structure of these countries. This view is exemplified by Garran, who argued that the fact that no one saw the Asian crisis coming reinforced the view that the crisis was largely "an irrational panic. . . . It was not a reflection of the underlying economic fundamentals of the East Asian countries affected." Garran was not aware of the scientifically analyzed structural defects of these economies. So he, like many others, thought that the crisis arose from a sudden, impulsive withdrawal of funds—that the problem was a purely financial crisis. He wondered how economists could have better designed their models so as to predict such a crisis. He, like other economists, was attacking the IMF and the World Bank for not sounding the alert signals. But those institutions, like Garran, were relying on financial data that were a shadow of the problem, not the substance of it. One cannot interpret the shadow without full knowledge of the substance. Garran pointed out that another contributory factor is that "the [financial] market operates with limited information and tends to come round to average views which can shift in a radical and unexpected manner."[56]

Garran argued that the European exchange crisis of 1992–93 was sparked off by poor macroeconomic conditions and the 1994–95 Mexican crisis by the government's high level of foreign debt, but that except for Thailand, Asian countries were not guilty of either of these. Hirst and Thompson argued that the sources of the crisis are essentially external: "The problems experienced are side effects of largely irrational and excessive capital flight and contagion that generalized the crisis." They claimed that "different countries have experienced different degrees of disruption, from what amounts to melt-down in Indonesia to what seems likely to be a major but salutary setback to a rapidly overheated economy in the case of Malaysia." They argued the sudden withdrawal of short-term funds severely disrupted the various Asian economies "without real domestic necessity." It was, they contended, "a crisis made in the volatile global markets."[57]

In a highly theoretical analysis of the crisis, Aghion, Bacchetta, and Banerjee argued that "slumps should be seen as part of the normal process in economies like these, which are both at an intermediate level of financial development and in the process of liberalizing their financial sectors." They warn against "seeing these emerging market economies as ones that have lost their way and are beyond repair and therefore must undertake in haste a radical overhauling of their economic system." They concluded, "Second, policies which allow firms to rebuild their credit-worthiness will at the same time contribute to a prompt recovery of the overall economy," for "credit-worthiness is the key element in the recovery from slump and suggests that a policy of never bailing out involved banks (or of closing down a large number of banks) runs the danger of making firms less able to borrow . . . thereby prolonging the slump." Aghion, Bacchetta, and Banerjee sought to provide a macroeconomic diagnosis of Asia's cyclical economic fortunes in order to justify their recommended policy, the rebuilding of creditworthiness. They stated that ex ante policies should recognize that unrestricted financial liberalization may actually destabilize the economy and bring about a slump that otherwise would not happen. Fully liberalizing foreign capital flows and opening the economy to foreign lending may not be a good idea, they argued, until the

domestic financial market is sufficiently developed. FDI, according to them, does not destabilize. There is therefore an a priori case for allowing FDI even at low levels of financial development. This is contrary to our scientific analysis. Aghion, Bacchetta, and Banerjee claimed that what brings about financial crises is precisely the rise in the price of nontradables, for example, real estate. They sought to explain these cyclical sorts of problems as follows: More investment leads to more output and so higher profits, which increases firms' creditworthiness. This in turn fuels more borrowing, which leads to more investment. Capital flows in to finance this boom. Then, according to them, demand for nontradable inputs rises at the same time and raises their price relative to tradables. This leads to lower profit in the tradables sector, reducing firms' creditworthiness, leading to less borrowing and so less investment. Of course, they argue, once investment falls, all these forces reverse, and eventually the price of nontradable inputs may fall enough to raise profits in the tradables sector and start another boom. In their model, they claim, "the interplay of these forces leads the economy to have stable cycles where the economy alternates between investment booms with high prices on non-tradable inputs and large capital inflows and slumps where non-tradable inputs are cheap and capital inflow is sharply reduced or even reversed."

Having completed what they regarded as a purely economic structural analysis of these economies, they then claimed that "when the monetary dimension is added, it leads to movements in normal exchange rate and central bank reserves." It was their view that FDI differs from foreign lending because it does not depend on the creditworthiness of the domestic firms. In a slump, cash flow is low in the domestic economy. They claimed that FDI actually prefers to come in then in order to profit from the low price of nontradable inputs. They were so sure of their theoretical analysis that they claimed these economies would have experienced the crises that hit them "even if corruption and panic selling were not there."[58]

Aghion, Bacchetta, and Banerjee's analysis is misleading. They adopted a too simplistic model in that they sought wrongly to transfer the conclusions they reached from a microeconomic analysis of firms into a macroeconomic frame. Their analysis ignored the essence of the theory of factor proportions, which is that there is a sort of "chemical reaction" between factors in different sectors that renders untenable the assumption that the macro economy is the arithmetical sum of the different microeconomic sectors. Theirs seems to be a determined attempt to provide a theoretical explanation for claims that the property bubble in Thailand started the downward chain reaction of the Asian economies. At best, the property bubble helped push the Thai economy (which was already in very bad shape) over the cliff. It was not the cause of that economy's long-standing cyclical characteristics. We would have thought also that FDI prefers to go into economies where the creditworthiness of firms is high, as that is an indication of a potentially profitable market. Aghion, Bacchetta, and Banerjee's distinction between FDI and foreign borrowing is scientifically not tenable. FDI, foreign borrowing, and some local savings all are deployed in procuring capital equipment. They all have the same economic effect in an underdeveloped economy, namely, promoting structural imbalances.

The basic conclusion that slumps are part of the normal process in the growing up of "intermediate" economies is flawed, because it has been arrived at with a flawed model. The East Asian crisis occurred because all the countries affected were pursuing aggressive, open, capital-intensive, and sometimes material-intensive development strategies that created serious structural imbalances in their economies.

In order to bring this section of the chapter to a close, we need to explore why Taiwan escaped the economic crisis. To do this, we will compare the economic structures of Taiwan and South Korea, one of the main victims of the crisis. Remember that the factor proportions theory says that an economy in which factor proportions of all activities are equal and equal to the endowed factor proportions will achieve maximum self-sustaining growth; one with wide differences in factor proportions will not.

Many of the countries in the region have chosen an export-oriented policy and have in the past twenty to thirty years pursued the development of new industries almost from identical shopping lists. But there were fundamental differences in approach. South Korea and Taiwan, for example, can be said to be pursuing their economic transformation from opposite ends. Korea is outward-looking, seeking new technology and outside capital. Taiwan is basically inward-looking; though it does export, it does not seek outside capital and is determined to implement techniques that are people-oriented. In both of these countries, government played a crucial role in economic strategy, but in Taiwan's case, government was operating in a decentralized system, whereas in Korea the system was centralized, with a directed shift in favor of the big companies.

Fallows has provided clear descriptions of some of the differences in strategy. Taiwan needs very little foreign investment to finance its development. It has mobilized its savings, but not in the direction of capital-intensive activities. It can be said that Taiwan is reluctantly an open economy. Interestingly, Taiwan has no term comparable to *keiretsu* or *chaebol* and because of this has no comparable economic structure like South Korea's. "Taiwan does have a few large firms with international scope. . . . But these are unrepresentative features on the country's economic landscape. . . . The archetypal Taiwanese firm is still a small manufacturing business run by an individual entrepreneur with his extended-family members, which concentrates on a few niche products and scrambles to survive." Yet it is this feature, small family-owned businesses, that some conventional economists will say is synonymous with inefficiency and low productivity because of their low capital investment. Fallows points out that the abundance of small and medium-sized businesses typifies Taiwan's manufacturing base and makes it exceptional among the four Asian NICs.[59]

The contrast between South Korea and Taiwan is a long-standing one. For example, in the period 1980–82, the top fifty firms in South Korea were responsible for 37.5 percent of that country's shipments and the top one hundred firms for nearly 47 percent. By contrast, the top fifty firms in Taiwan were responsible for somewhat over 16 percent of shipments, and the top one hundred for around 22 percent.[60]

Fallows pointed out that Taipei is home to a huge international trade center. One week it will host a convention of leather-goods makers; the next week it will show printing equipment, or food packaging machines, or computer parts. Week in and week out, the hall contains thousands of booths, each representing a company that makes a certain kind of copper pipe or computer keyboard and nothing else. Taiwan represents the closest thing Asia offers to Jacobs' dream in her book *Cities and the Wealth of Nations,* where she argues that city economies were healthiest when businesses were small, numerous, specialized, and agile. In such healthy economies, tiny firms are constantly appearing and disappearing, adjusting, thriving, and specializing "in the most arcane and bizarre ways." She admirably coalesced all this in a statement that puts in layman's words the message of this book when she said, "If one wanted to define economic development in one word, that would be 'improvisation.'"[61]

An article in *Forbes* in June 1998 describes the entrepreneurial situation in Taiwan this way: "Lit-

erally everyone in Taiwan wants to be his or her own boss. 'We have more of an entrepreneurial spirit,' says Paul Wang, chairman of Pacific Venture Partners and a former IBM executive. He contrasts this with Japan: 'You don't see many people quitting Fujitsu to start their own companies. There are new ventures set up here every day. It's even more dynamic than Silicon Valley.' A local joke making rounds in the industry is that if a roof falls down in Taiwan, it will kill at least four chairmen of electronics companies. . . . In Japan and much of Asia, capital flows to capital. In Taiwan, capital flows to talent. The capital market is very democratic in Taiwan. . . . Capital doesn't just flow to the big strong companies. . . . With plenty of equity capital available, Taiwan companies can avoid the debt burdens that now weigh so heavily on most other Asian companies. . . . Where does this abundant capital come from? At the startup stage, it traditionally came from the savings of family and friends. Now it is a self-reinforcing flood."[62] Taiwan, in effect, does not need foreign investment to finance its projects.[63] In contrast, in Korea—at least until the crisis—the average university graduate put his mind to getting a job in one of Korea's major groups.

Taiwan's policy to encourage the start-up and development of small enterprises is a deliberate one. Various measures have been undertaken since the 1950s; these were coordinated and brought into focus by the Small and Medium Enterprises Guidance Unit, introduced in the 1960s and formalized into an agency in 1981.

This is not to say that the other NICs have not at one time or another given consideration to smaller enterprises, but it was more usually done in reaction to political pressures. Meyanathan and Salleh noted that despite the proliferation of such programs in Malaysia, the development of small and medium-sized enterprises there was essentially peripheral to the buoyant, export-led, foreign-investment-dominated manufacturing sector. Only after the recession of the 1980s was a concerted effort made to refocus on the smaller enterprises by reducing the bias of fiscal incentives toward larger enterprises. In regard to Korea, Meyanathan and Salleh found that even though the importance of small and medium-sized businesses was recognized and a long-term plan for their promotion was drawn up in 1982, the main thrust of 1993's New Economy Plan was how to encourage competition in the international market through deregulation and removal of protections for those smaller enterprises.[64] In Indonesia, while several promotion programs for small and medium-sized businesses have been introduced, in practice the government's policies and regulations have resulted in unintentional discrimination against them. For example, the trade regimes produced by the Indonesian government in the 1970s and early 1980s tended to favor large-scale, capital-intensive manufacturing rather than small-scale, labor-intensive industries.[65]

Let us look at Taiwan's approach to production techniques by briefly focusing on two industries—one new, one old. Taiwan is very much involved in memory chip production. Whereas South Korea has invested billions of dollars in equipment-specific production, the Taiwanese have adopted a flexible manufacturing strategy. Most Taiwanese chip makers are still doing foundry work. Profits in that business are good, but nothing like the riches collected by firms that make their own memory chips when there is a shortage. But foundry work is a way of using spare capacity. So Taiwanese producers are investing in dual-purpose capacity that can be switched from logic-chip foundry work to memory chips. That means they can deal with small orders and diversify when the market for one product is bad. Said the *Economist,* "Taiwan spouts none of the dangerous talk of 'domination.' Its virtues of flexibility and profit over market share look a lot sounder by comparison."[66]

As a second example, Taiwan's machine tool builders are a very important link in the country's industrial growth. They find their niche in what can loosely be called "intermediate" techniques. These involve mechanical devices with a degree of electronic control. Such machines will obviously not operate in the same way as equipment that is fully microprocessor-based (and more capital-intensive). The Taiwan-made machines require a more skillful operator. The semiautomated machine that is in line with local factor proportions helps to improve quality and at the same time is suited to supplying a small market. In the shoe industry, for example, the design and production of a shoe-making machine is a combination of imitation and creativity. A shoe company may start with a shoe-making machine built in Britain. Then a local machine tool builder will reproduce the British machine, removing components that the shoe company does not need, ending up with a machine made with locally available equipment and components, adjusted to local conditions, and affordable to a small producer. This means that while a Korean shoe company would consider an overseas order for fifty pairs of shoes too small to produce economically, the Taiwanese shoe producer will be interested in filling it.

Fallows observed that in seeking advanced manufacturing processes, the Koreans were faulted by Japanese as well as Europeans and Americans for being "too sloppy and inattentive to detail"—an accusation Fallows says applies to the Japanese, Americans, and Europeans as well.[67] It takes attention to detail and creativity to take apart a piece of equipment based on different factor proportions, figure out the science (technology) behind it, and build a new piece of equipment that does more or less the same thing but is based on one's own factor proportions. But because Taiwan can do this, it has laid a basis for a more balanced economy than its fellow tigers. Such an economy was able to withstand the shocks of the 1997 crisis, even though it lost substantial export trade at the time. And with this balanced economy, Taiwan has consistently achieved a foreign trade surplus over the years, unlike its counterparts.

With a more balanced economy, the issue of fair income distribution becomes easier to deal with. Kuo, Ranis, and Fei said that their analysis of Taiwan's economy reveals that "it is possible for economic development to be compatible with improved distribution of income."[68]

World Economy

The concept of a world economy is now on the agenda of all international economic forums. Those who advocate it think all the world's resources can be mobilized to achieve maximum growth on a global basis, enabling everyone to share in a just and equitable way in the resultant wealth. But if we seek to apply the theory of factor proportions as the means to achieve maximum sustainable growth with a fair distribution of wealth, all countries will have to adopt ratios of capital to labor, capital to material, and labor to material that are different from those currently applicable to the United States or the other OECD countries. Production techniques will have to be much more labor-intensive than presently in vogue in the advanced countries, but not quite as labor-intensive as in the poor countries. Somewhat more material-intensive techniques than in the advanced countries will probably be needed. It will require retooling and retraining in all countries. Some supervising agency—an element of a world government—will be required to establish the game plan and rules for achieving the identified factor proportions.

It seems such a gigantic undertaking that no world agency as presently constituted will be able to undertake it. Nor does it immediately seem feasible that countries will cede all the required powers to any new world agency to undertake this task. It is unlikely that countries that are already wealthy will want to hand over their production regimes to such an agency in what will seem to them to be a gamble with the strong possibility that they may, at least initially, lose their superior wealth base. Reliance on market forces to establish a worldwide regime of appropriate factor proportions will not work.

What we have currently is an attempt at creating a world economy spearheaded by those who have achieved success in building their own economy. The reasoning is that useful experience goes with success and that such experience and the tools derived from it can be used to benefit everyone else. Globalization is therefore regarded primarily as a means of spreading the benefits of modern technology to all parts of the world. As Friedman succinctly put it, the "democratization of technology is the result of several innovations that came together in the 1980s involving computerization, telecommunications, miniaturization, compression technology and digitization." Because of this, "all sorts of countries have the opportunity to assemble technologies, raw materials and funding to be producers or sub-contractors of highly complex finished products and services and this becomes another subtle factor knitting the world more tightly together." He argued that this is how Thailand, which was fifteen years ago a primarily low-wage, rice-producing country, rose to become the world's second-largest producer of pickup trucks, rivaling Detroit, and the fourth-largest maker of motorcycles. According to Friedman, democratization of technology has meant that the potential for wealth creation has become geographically dispersed, "giving all kinds of previously disconnected people the chance to access and apply knowledge."[69] His opinion is that openness of all countries to technology will lead to convergence in productivity levels across all countries.

Apart from technology, said Friedman, capital has also been democratized. This began in the late 1960s with the emergence of the commercial-paper market, followed in the 1970s by the securitization of home mortgages. In the 1980s, democratization of finance exploded via the emergence of junk bonds and the issuance of corporate bonds, which now have become widely dispersed among individuals, pension funds, and mutual funds. All this coincided with greater freedom for international flow of capital and the opening up of financial markets worldwide. The argument goes that the free movement of capital is accompanied by the transfer of technology, and because differences in capital stock (physical and human) explain income differentials among countries, impediments to international capital mobility can slow or prevent convergence among countries.[70]

Friedman also attributed to globalization the democratization of information. The process started with the globalization of television, was enhanced by advances in compression technology, and has been topped off by the spread of the Internet. He says that the net effect of the democratization of information is that "the days when governments could isolate their people from understanding what life is beyond their borders or even beyond their village are over. Life outside can't be trashed or made to look worse than it is. And life inside can't be propagandized and made to look better than it is."[71]

Globalization could not have blossomed, according to him, during the Cold War era, when various barriers allowed countries to maintain widely differing and antagonistic economic systems—centrally planned Communist economies, welfare-state economies, socialist economies, free-market economies— each with a different political system, anything from democracy to dictatorship, from enlightened authoritarianism to monarchy to totalitarianism. He said that what blew away all these walls were fundamental changes in how we communicate, how we invest, and how we learn about the world— globalization.

Globalization has been highly politicized, and much of its present case is made in veiled political tones. Friedman's use of the word *democratization* is meant to link globalization with democracy. Democratization of technology, capital, and information should be an attractive slogan to the average American, who thinks that all countries should be democracies. The case seems to be that pro-democracy forces in non-Western countries need to embrace globalization because it is an instrument of democracy, and countries that embrace democracy are told that they can reap democracy's dividends, namely, Western technology, capital inflow, foreign investment, and access to the world market.

Friedman called those in the United States who do not embrace globalization isolationists and separatists. He accused them of still speaking the political language of the Cold War. He accused the separatists of believing that free trade and technological integration are neither good nor inevitable because globalization widens income gaps in the United States and leads to jobs being sent abroad, homogenizes culture into global mush, and leads to life being controlled by distant, faceless market forces. He accused them of being unconcerned about poverty in the world. This is political blackmail. It did not occur to Friedman that the people he calls separatists may have their reasons for believing that if countries are left on their own, they could develop their economic personality. Friedman is no more democratic than those who feel that each country should be allowed to develop its own resources.

The trouble with Friedman and writers like him is that they treat globalization as synonymous with digitalization and the Internet. They lose the essence of globalization in its economic sense, which is to treat the world as one economy. For example, his claimed democratization stands in sharp contrast with international monopolistic competition with its higher entry barriers, on which conventional trade theory depends.

In an article in the *Wall Street Journal* in April

2000, Easterbrook claimed that at the deepest level, much of what inspires the foes of globalization is a "fear of change"—world economic changes are occurring so fast that they can't keep up. He said that because of the rapid pace of globalization, nobody fully understands the process, including the World Bank and IMF. Frustrating as this may be, he argued, it might in fact be the proper way to proceed with globalization—with no one in charge. He reminded his readers that historically it was conservatives who most feared economic change. Conservative writers of the late nineteenth century, he said, were aghast at the factories of England and New England, fearing that the new industrial order, drawing workers from traditional agrarian communities to the central cities, would change women's roles, family structure, sexual norms, and many other aspects of society. But today, he claimed, it is the left that fears the spread of economic change. "It is no coincidence," he wrote, "that one of the complaints of the antiglobalization crowd is that modern economics is drawing developing-world citizens away from traditional agrarian communities toward the city center. . . . Antiglobalization sentiment stems in part from romanticized notions that the developing world would be better off if left untouched by the West." He asserts that for its own reasons, the left is unhappy that no one is in charge of globalization: "If there were multinational bureaucracies running the globalization show (instead of just granting licenses, as the WTO does), the left might feel very differently, since then it could lobby the agencies and attempt to dictate events. Instead the show is running itself."[72]

In sharp contrast to Easterbrook's happiness at the no-one-in-charge state of globalization, Garten remarked, "When all is said and done, the world economy is crisis-prone because it is evolving at a breakneck pace and has many seriously weak economic and political links. The crisis was the fruit of a general overestimation of the strength of the framework for global finance and—in Washington at least—a hubristic belief that emerging markets would adopt American-style capitalism and were close to doing so. Blind faith in the 'magic of the market' replaced any historical perspective."[73]

The democracy claims of Friedman and Easterbrook cannot stand side by side with threats that globalization is coming, whether or not countries like it, and that countries had better learn how to align with it. We are told that the Internet is already linking the world into a global village, capital is already flying all over the globe, and none of this can be stopped. Indeed, the IMF and World Bank have made globalization their key economic philosophy and the compulsory tonic for any country that comes to them for help. Tabb remarked, "Some agencies of corporate globalism are very much involved in pursing the emancipation of capital from popular control." The ill-fated Multilateral Agreement on Investment (MAI)—described by the director general of the WTO as the "constitution for a single global economy"—was negotiated in secret for many years. The agreement specified a five-year period before any country could withdraw from it, and no protection or privileges for foreign corporations could be undone for another fifteen years. Countries could lose control over their economies and could be sued for interfering with transnationals. Penalties would have to be paid if national policies caused such companies to forgo profit, and governments would be prohibited from making new laws that interfered with the right of capital to free investment where and when it likes. As Tabb remarked, even though MAI is off the immediate agenda—not least because the left was able to expose its aims and act as part of a broader opposition movement—many of its provisions are already enshrined in the WTO and are being imposed in the proposed IMF charter revision that would further the IMF's efforts to transform practices at the nation-state level.[74] The drive for globalization is a well-orchestrated action program; though it is sometimes fraught with selfish disagreements among the players, as Bhagwati has remarked, "Morgan Stanley and all these gigantic firms want to be able to get into other markets and essentially see capital account convertibility as what will enable them to operate everywhere." Wade and Veneroso have remarked that the revision of the IMF articles of agreement, the WTO's financial services agreement, and the OECD's MAI are the expression of a "big push" from international organizations, backed by governments and corporations in rich countries, to institute a worldwide regime of capital mobility that allows easy entry and exit everywhere. They remarked that if the agreements are ratified and enforced, "they will ratchet up the power and legitimacy of owners and managers of capital in the world at large."[75] Friedman himself advocated the use of American power to maintain globalization and the need to use that power against those who "threaten" the system.[76]

There is no doubt that some people who claim democracy as the guiding principle of globalization mean it. President Clinton, who did a lot to promote the ideals of globalization, meant it when in many of his speeches during his presidency he talked about humanity's common destiny, shared human values, and the fact that we are all living in the same global village. He talked of the need for countries to cooperate to solve common global problems, such as pollution and AIDS. The thinking goes that if the West has found solutions to poverty through science and technology, technology and capital (physical and human) should be transferred and shared. But such altruism does not match up with the prescription made by the science of economic development and growth. It looks as if nature intended for each group to be self-reliant while cooperating with others. Dependency is as undesirable as noncooperation.

It is this kind of altruism, coated with a bit of self-interest, that may have been behind Peter Marber's book *From Third World to World Class: The Future of Emerging Markets in the Global Economy.* Peter Marber is the president of a U.S. management firm devoted to investment in the Third World. He said, "As national income levels grow, developing countries will be integrated into the global economy and trading system. . . . Contrary to much populist rhetoric in the United States and other industrialized countries, global economic growth is not a zero-sum gain. Rising GDP will not come at the expense of the industrialized countries. . . . The First World will prosper from having access to new markets and cheaper production costs. The developing world will gain from having access to new markets for manufactured goods and raw materials and, perhaps most important, from access to capital for productive investment. . . . The process of global economic development over the next ten decades will be marked by synergy that in many ways resembles that which occurred in England and the United States early this century or more recently in Japan. The next wave of growth, based on today's Genius Technologies, will further propel the integration of the world economies, altering global geographic and financial landscape."[77] Marber was not writing economics. He was simply being philosophical. If we mix things up, he said, we will somehow benefit everyone by the interaction. But economic science does not work out that way.

In this context, an economic strategy of self-reliance is labeled isolationist. Friedman claimed that as more countries are plugged into the globalization system and what he called the "Fast World," a backlash group of "wounded gazelles" has formed. This group, he says, consists of people who tried globalization and got hammered by the system. He thought that such people should, instead of sulking and shutting themselves out, get up, dust themselves off, and do what it takes to get back into the Fast World. He affirmed—without any economic analysis—that "if you think you can retreat permanently into an artificially constructed third place and enjoy all the rising living standards of the Fast World without any pressures, you are really fooling yourself and your people."[78]

It is clear, therefore, that much of the rhetoric about globalization has little to do with economics and certainly leaves no room for scientific economic analysis.[79] Easterbrook's claims are typical of what some Western politicians and multinationals believe: "The changes wrought by globalization may be stressful and confusing, but so far, they are largely pro-people. Incomes and longevity are rising almost everywhere in the world, including most of the world's poor; food production continues to rise faster than population, staving off predicted Malthusian famines, and saving the life of billions . . . literacy rates and education levels are rising globally with the biggest gains amongst the worst off; communications technology is eroding dictatorships and empowering typical people throughout the world, including those people who oppose the WTO. . . . Suppose opponents of globalization managed to stop or severely restrict the chaotic, decentralized process of globalized economies and technology. The outcome would almost certainly be negative for everyone; it would be worse for the world's working class."[80]

The situation gets more muddied because of claims by multinationals about their contributions to economic growth in underdeveloped economies. Often they do so with the support of academics. In a recent study funded by Coca-Cola, carried out by a team of U.S. and Chinese researchers, it was reported that the benefits to China's economy from foreign companies are greater than the amount of money they invest. It found that Coca-Cola's spending in China yielded more than three times as much value in total economic output. Every worker Coca-Cola and its bottlers employ directly in China is said to support as many as twenty-nine more jobs

at other Chinese companies. The study found that the 8.2 billion yuan ($990 million) Coca-Cola's China operations spent in 1998 actually produced 30 billion yuan in overall economic output as the investment multiplied through a network of local suppliers and distributors down to the corner shops and restaurants that sell its beverages to consumers. Coca-Cola and its units paid 400 million yuan in national and local taxes in China in 1998, but the entire "Coca-Cola system" is said to have generated 1.6 billion yuan in taxes. The company and its operations employ about fourteen thousand Chinese workers, but the study found that Coca-Cola operations actually support an added four hundred thousand jobs in China.

The error in this type of typical pro-globalization analysis is that it is a microanalysis that does not accurately represent the situation at the macroeconomic level. It assumes that what Coca-Cola produced is immediately added to GDP. It ignores the structural imbalance Coca-Cola's capital-intensive activities create in an economy that is essentially labor-intensive.

The claim that FDI results in relatively higher wages in desperately poor countries and creates employment is not enough to justify FDI there. During the 1980s downturn, concern arose that the rapid rise of foreign investment in the United States would have adverse effects on the American market—it was feared the foreign firms would move "good" jobs to their countries and offer only "bad" jobs to Americans. However, most economists believe that FDI is a minor but positive factor in the United States economy. Foreign firms tended to offer higher wages than the U.S. average and were many times more productive than their U.S. counterparts. It was also noted that they increased their employment in U.S. manufacturing when the general trend was to shed jobs. The difference between the U.S. and developing-country cases is that when FDI comes into an advanced economy from another advanced economy (or at least an economy adopting factor proportions that are not critically different from those suited for the U.S. economy), it will not exacerbate any existing structural imbalances in the U.S. economy and may add to macroeconomic growth prospects.

Against this background of broad, unfounded, politically based, and sometimes misleading economic claims, Garten correctly remarked that the broad global economic picture still looks grim. Writing in 1999, he noted that developing-country growth in 1998 was only 2 percent, roughly half its 1997 level, and was not expected to improve much in the next year. Private capital flows, which global theorists say are on the move everywhere on the globe, have avoided many poor countries. Garten observed that some thirty-six countries, accounting for 40 percent of the developing world's GDP, probably suffered negative per capita growth in 1998. Poverty on a worldwide basis is increasing, not decreasing. "All across East Asia and Latin America, the social fabric continues to tear as poverty increases, with unforeseen economic and political consequences. Consider the situation in the five biggest emerging markets. Brazil is on the ropes. Indonesia is on the cusp of social revolution. Russia's economy is still in free fall. China's economic reforms are under great stress."[81]

Suddenly countries that were supposed to have graduated into the world's upper middle class were seeking foreign aid. For example, the 1997 crisis returned half of Indonesia's two hundred million people to destitution; 70 percent of the companies listed on the Jakarta exchange were technically insolvent. According to Indonesia's largest independent trade union, IPWU, more than 800,000 workers lost their job in the last months of 1997; this figure was expected to rise to about 1.5 million in 1998. Fewer than half of the 2.4 million young people entering the job market could find work.

A Korean generation that grew up taking rising living standards for granted is now throwing the old model out of the window. Out-of-work managers are rolling up their sleeves, leaving globalization behind, and starting their own business, reversing the path trodden by an earlier generation. After watching scores of big companies go under, university graduates are heading in new directions. A job in the chaebol is no longer seen as a ticket to the good life. Young Koreans are choosing small, healthier companies in which they can make a difference.[82]

We do not need to mention African countries whose economies have been pried open on IMF's bidding but are still waiting for FDI that never arrives. This is because the internationalization of production and trading activities remains extremely unequally distributed, dominated by Europe, Japan, and North America and a few favored less developed countries. The vast bulk of the world's population is heavily disadvantaged and almost ignored by these developments. Hirst and Thompson concluded that global inequality has increased, not decreased, since the 1970s: "All these," they stated, "go against the sentiment that benefits to the less well-off nations and regions will 'trickle down' as investment and trade are allowed to follow strictly market signals."[83] Globalization seeks to establish a global economy with factor proportions that are at variance with the overall natural factor endowments of the world—which is difficult to ascertain at the moment.

Garten observed that the Asian crisis has eroded the faith of many up-and-coming nations in modern capitalism itself: "Although most foreign officials and business executives are reluctant to publicly voice their deepest concerns, a backlash is quietly building up against unbridled economic liberalization and the chaos it has unleashed."[84] Krugman reflected the same unease when he said, "We had better start trying to find ways to get them [emerging countries] back to more or less full employment or the rationale for free-market policies is going to wear thin."[85] Is Krugman suggesting that he has doubts about international trade? In another article, published in 1999, Krugman remarked that "Asia has not emerged from this crisis with any clear idea about how to avoid the next one. . . . There is every reason to believe that Asia has emerged from the crisis with its long-term prospects less promising than they had seemed only two years ago."[86]

In its publication *Global Economic Prospects and the Developing Countries 2000,* the World Bank claimed that "globalization provides developing countries with significant benefits and spurs economic progress." Its claim was based on a 5 percent GDP growth rate in developing countries in the 1990s compared with 3 percent during the 1980s. The bulk of the claimed growth in the 1990s came from East Asia and some South American countries, but the report neglected to discuss the situation after the 1997 crisis. Poverty fell, according to the report, from 29 percent in 1990 to an estimated 24 percent in 1996, again omitting the post-1997 situation. The report quickly noted that "the financial crisis of the 1997–1999 period has shown how globalization, and in particular openness to external capital flows, can expose developing countries to increasing volatility. . . . The poor are especially vulnerable to this volatility."[87]

The report admitted that the crises of 1997–99 continued to persist in many aspects. In most developing countries, growth remained weak. Progress in poverty reduction stalled in the developing world at the end of the 1990s, and the number of poor was rising in most regions. The report downgraded its long-term projections for growth in developing countries from the previous year, suggesting that while the outlook for developing countries in the years 1999 to 2001 was of significant acceleration in growth due to "improvements in the external environment," that is, globalization, growth between 2002 and 2008 was likely to be lower than in the precrisis 1990s. The report gave several reasons for this. The first was that very same "external environment," though less favorable this time—in effect, factors that had nothing directly to do with these countries themselves. The second was what it called "prospects for a protracted workout of structural weaknesses—particularly in financial and fiscal positions—that have become apparent in the wake of the crisis." It is clear that the report is totally oblivious of the basic economic structural problems that caused the economic crisis.[88]

The theoretical foundation on which the economic benefits of globalization are premised is a mixture of the theory of international trade, the theory of the free mobility of factors, and the theory of convergence. Each of these theories says it provides the basis for a stable global financial architecture. Based on our analysis of these theories in earlier chapters, we say that none of these theories provides the basis on which the economies of emerging markets can be pulled up into the path of self-sustaining growth.

Table 7.1, displaying capital and labor endowments of the countries listed, is deficient from the point of view of a science of economic development and growth, in that the true values of the factor quantities are distorted by the prices assigned and by the differences among the countries listed. However, the proportions of capital to labor indicated can be considered approximations that give us some useful comparative data.

Those who regard the mobility of capital as the main source of economic growth in emerging economies will say that if a few chunks of capital investment from Switzerland, with a capital/labor ratio of 40,000, were to move to India, with a capital/labor ratio of 1,898, productivity in India will rise because the capital/labor ratio will increase. They will say that any movement of capital from countries in the lower half of the table to those in the top half will greatly increase economic growth in the latter group. In fact, before the East Asian crisis (when it was thought that the more capital

Table 7.1

Capital and Labor Endowment (1988)

Country	Capital Stock ($ billions)	Labor Force (millions)	Capital/ Worker
India	482	254	1,898
Brazil	507	53	9,566
South Korea	204	14	14,571
Mexico	353	23	15,348
USA	3,696	116	32,421
Canada	419	12	34,917
Germany	1,018	26	39,154
Japan	2,336	59	39,593
Switzerland	120	3	40,000

Source: J. Markusen et al., *International Trade: Theory and Evidence* (New York: McGraw-Hill, 1995).

an economy absorbs, the faster its growth), it would have been said that the greater the difference between the capital/labor ratios of the giving and receiving economies, the faster the growth of the latter.

The science of economic development and growth says it does not work that way. Any gains in growth in the receiving country will be more than offset by the losses caused by the wide structural differences between the sector with the much higher capital/labor ratio and the rest of the economy. What India needs in order to attain maximum sustainable growth is to create more activities that have a capital/labor ratio of 1,898 in a dynamic setting, not the transfer of production aids from Switzerland.

Those who see convergence as the benefit from globalization will say that capital movement from Switzerland brings to India the new technology that country needs. This diffusion of technology into the Indian economy will, the theory claims, increasingly pull India into a higher per capita income bracket at a pace that will close the gap between India and Switzerland. One guesses that a version of convergence theory will say that the smaller the difference between the capital/labor ratios of the giving and receiving countries, the slower will be the rate

of convergence. Despite the lack of empirical evidence to support this convergence hypothesis, a lot of globalists feel that capital mobility promotes convergence between countries of different income groups. This derives from claims that if production technologies are the same (the ultimate result of capital mobility) and innovations diffuse internationally, then the steady-state output per worker must also be equalized.[89] For example, it is claimed that OECD countries that were poor after World War II tended to grow faster than the initially richer OECD economies.

The science of economic development and growth replies that the convergence hypothesis is not a proven scientific fact. It is a conjecture. We have seen that a major stumbling block for the South Korean economy was its dependence on foreign know-how and imported capital equipment. This saddled it with import bills that constantly left it fluctuating between small trade surpluses and embarrassing trade deficits. The structural imbalances between the large chaebols and the small and medium-sized enterprises created the macroeconomic instability that started the downward slide.

As far as trade goes—and trade is a major prop of globalization advocates—a lot has changed since the heyday of the theory of comparative advantage. New theories of trade suggest, as we have seen, that production differentiation and scale economies—in which emerging economies are weak—play a larger role in the gains than factor endowment differences. The East Asian economies and the countries of South America are fighting a no-win battle to compete in the arena of product differentiation and scale economies because they are utilizing factor proportions that don't belong to them. To succeed, they need not only a large home market base (to allow them to practice and update the strategies) but also home-grown capital-intensive techniques and associated R&D investments. Without these, they will always be dependent and vulnerable because of their external trade balance and threats to their currency.

Of the twenty-four MNEs known to originate worldwide from developing countries in the period since the mid-1970s, there were two each from Brazil, India, and Taiwan, nine from South Korea, and one each from the Netherlands Antilles, Israel, Argentina, Chile, Colombia, Kuwait, Mexico, Philippines, and Venezuela. As of 1975, FDI from developing countries was a mere $3,304 million; that is between 1 and 2 percent of the world stock of outward investment. By 1989, direct investment from the developing countries had increased twentyfold, to about $61,662 million, representing an annual increase of 23 percent over 1975. Despite these increases, FDI from these countries constitutes a negligible fraction of the overall world outward investment. Many of these investments were in other developing countries. Any firm-specific or proprietary advantage of these developing countries in outside investment was often based on their ability to innovate along essentially different lines from those of advanced countries, that is, to innovate based on a lower level of research, size, technological experience, and skills, and in some cases on the basis of what Sengenberger and Wilkinson called "modernization of an older technique, including foreign outdated techniques."[90] Without having developed a strong reliance on R&D, a greater part of their innovating capacity and advantage results from production engineering, learning by doing and using, organizational capabilities, and having access to foreign but complementary techniques. The problem comes when underdeveloped-country FDI wants to "move up" to compete on the same league with advanced-country FDIs on the world market.

In the long run, the observation of Appleyard and Field that newer theories in trade do not portend well for the future export performance of developing countries needs to be taken seriously by those

pressing for increased globalization. Appleyard and Field suggest that these countries may be permanently condemned to exporting "older products rather than new high-tech ones."[91]

Imperfect competition has taken control of international trade. Starting in the 1980s economic activity in many advanced economies came to be driven by the spread of cost-reducing and quality-enhancing advancements in electronics-based industries (semiconductors, telecoms, computers, consumer and industrial electronics), which transformed the production processes of other industries. Information could now be carried around the globe in less than a second, enabling and accelerating globalization.

The technical changes in turn generated a new wave of automation, which put pressure on producers to cut fixed costs by boosting sales and broadening markets internationally. The more labor-intensive of the capital-intensive activities were farmed out by multinationals to a second tier of NICs such as Thailand and Malaysia, which offered lower labor costs. At the same time, the shortening of the production cycle in the rapidly changing science of factors (technology) and the concomitant accumulation of production innovation led MNEs to enter into strategic alliances, often with competitors from other regions, to share sharply rising R&D costs, pool resources, and gain better access to new techniques and markets. The linkages and interfirm networks created by such alliances and collaborative activities primarily spanned the United States, Europe, and Japan and involve only certain industries: electronics, aerospace, pharmaceuticals, automobiles. The growing links between multinationals have been accompanied by an increasing vertical disintegration by large firms, which began to retain in-house only those production stages essential to maintaining strategic control.

The rapid expansion of international investment dictated by these changes along with the assertive role played in it by the corporate strategies just described have led people to talk of the globality of the economy.[92] Globalization is seen as the third phase of cross-national economic integration, going beyond the international exchange of goods and services and direct foreign investment to include all phases of economic activity, including conception, development, manufacturing, distribution, and consumption. It is generally recognized that the interpenetration of markets, the generic nature of the new information technology, the attempt to harmonize consumer tastes and product standards, production on a worldwide scale, and mergers and acquisitions are leading to a worldwide economic reconstruction, leaving large corporations less dependent on any one nation's economy.[93] Chamberlain called the impending globalization "the theory of monopolistic competition in a world of giants."[94] The attempts of groups from the developing countries to join this club have not succeeded. The South Korean chaebols were only passing stars on the world scene.

We note, however, that despite all the press and academic interest in globalization, the internationalization of business activity has been exaggerated. It is not increasing at a particularly dramatic rate. It is reasonable to suggest that between 70 and 75 percent of all MNE value added continues to be produced in the companies' home territories. Hirst and Thompson assert that "MNCs still rely upon their 'home base' as the centre for their economic activities despite all speculation about globalization. And while FDI flows have increased since the mid-1980s, the bulk of it is still between the industrialized countries.[95] The inevitability of globalization is therefore by no means certain.

It is clear that globalization is driven in part by advanced-country MNEs wanting to exploit worldwide markets in response to new developments in technology and their need to exploit economies of scale. MNEs will be the first to say that the consumer is the winner from globalization, being of-

fered a wider variety of choices of differentiated products at very good prices. But that is not economic growth.

Claims that globalization is democracy seem to be unjustified. Its protagonists do not appear to accept that there are other viable alternatives to achieving maximum world economic growth. As we have seen, the protagonists, private and public, are doing whatever is possible to stop countries from straying from globalization. Rist asked, "What real chance is there for a policy of autonomy in a single country?" Since the present system (globalization) is based upon international division of labor and expanding trade, is it really possible to extricate oneself from the system and conduct a totally different policy in isolation? Rist concluded that the answers to his questions were probably negative. He argued that "the situation would be quite different if self-reliance could become as widespread as the market system. . . . The social autonomy strategy would not be limited to countries of the South, but would be a system in which each country tried to reduce social inequalities and use its resources to acquire means of existence. The aim would be to reduce the importance of international trade instead of promoting it further, to concentrate investment on the exploitation of local resources instead of playing on short-term productivity differentials in accordance with casino economics that govern the financial market."[96]

The point that the science of economic development and growth is making is that the system by which emerging economies are receiving foreign capital creates economic structures that are unstable. The quantity of this capital, its rate of accumulation, and its time sequence all determine the characteristics of the imbalance. Each receiving economy is suffering a hemorrhage, although to different degrees. Some, such as Russia, have a slight but continuous hemorrhage. Others have a slight but intermittent hemorrhage, like many South American countries. For others it is violent, such as what the East Asian countries experienced in 1997. But they all experience cyclical bursts of growth followed by a drop in the growth rate. This is the fate of all emerging economies presently hooked into the global system, whether they are South American countries or the East Asian former tigers or the former Eastern bloc countries of Europe. None is on the path of self-sustaining economic growth.

The massive amount of foreign capital that was poured into Russia since the Soviet Union disintegrated has further unbalanced that economy. Its financial market from time to time suffers what the *Wall Street Journal* once called "violent sneezes." Moscow—the failed enemy of old-world capitalism—is now exposing the weaknesses in the new (global) order that it has embraced. Russia's GDP is less than $500 billion, and it imports as much as Australia and exports about as much as Denmark. Its massive external loan of over $100 billion is supposed to get it on the path to sustainable growth.

In the second quarter of 2000, Brazil posted its fastest quarterly growth rate in three years The country was rebounding from the painful devaluation of its currency in January 1999. During the first half of 2000, following the IMF's pronouncement of Brazil's good health, many firms expanded their production capacity and invested in new (imported) equipment. The country was also making great strides in deregulation and opening up to foreign investors in key sectors. Brazil drew a record $30 billion in FDI in 1999. Despite all this, Brazil's output in 2000 was still a shadow of the $772 billion it had been in 1998. Like South Korea, Brazil's major capital-intensive industries are concentrated in one area; São Paulo state alone, for example, produces 50 percent of Brazil's industrialized output. And of course Brazil's poverty record to date is legendary.

There have been renewed attempts to trumpet Mexico as a shining example of the triumph of the new global arrangement. At the beginning of the

1990s the international press was talking of the "Mexico miracle"—not unlike the way it spoke of South Korea and the other tiger economies. Mexico, like South Korea, started the twentieth century with an inward-looking policy. As usual, in all conventional inward-looking strategy the mistake was to undertake import substitution through the installation and protection of local capital-intensive industries. As with South Korea, the Mexican government was happy to let its companies borrow heavily from U.S. banks. The 1970s saw a booming economy, thanks to new oil revenue and large loans from foreign banks. A new set of policies was introduced based on a free market, export-oriented growth economy (again paralleling South Korea). Mexico set out, in line with present-day conventional free market prescriptions, to sell off government enterprises and facilitate FDI.

The economy was structurally unbalanced and hemorrhaging. The "Brady bonds" (which constituted an American rescue by that country's Treasury secretary) saved the sick economy from a run by foreign lenders (unlike in the East Asian countries). Foreign investors (mistakenly) saw the Brady deal as the stability they needed, and so they were again prepared to pump in more funds. Thus by the early 1990s, Mexico was feted as the example of how a country can get its fundamentals right. NAFTA in 1993 was essentially a culmination of Mexico's new profile, and people talked of Mexico as having finally achieved the status of a first-class nation. But while all this was going on, the country's structural imbalance was showing in significant levels of poverty. Poverty in Mexico during the mid- to late 1980s was 27.5 percent and remained almost constant at 25.9 percent in the 1990s. The level of what the World Bank defined as "extreme poverty" actually rose from 7.7 percent in the mid- to late 1980s to 8.2 percent in the 1990s.[97]

In September 1994, the World Bank warned that Mexico was becoming extremely dependent on foreign capital inflow. Toward the end of 1994, Mexico's foreign reserves had fallen to just above $10 billion, and again investor confidence was slipping and short-term speculations were attacking the currency. By early 1995 Mexico again was in the throes of default. The U.S.-packaged $49.8 billion assistance plan gave Mexico a needed sedative. By 1997 Mexico was on a financial rebound, and once again foreign capital started flowing again. In 1999, Mexico was clocking a trade surplus of $15 billion with the United States; in the first half of 2000, the trade surplus was already $10 billion. Since 1993 and the passage of NAFTA, total trade between the United States and Mexico has more than doubled, from $77 billion to over $159 billion in 1999, putting Mexico ahead of Japan and trailing only Canada as the United States' leading trade partner. But this hides the true situation. NAFTA has turned the country into a dualistic economy. U.S. companies and other transnationals have rushed into Mexico to tap its relatively cheap labor, but that has added to the poverty problem, increasing income inequalities and social pressures. There is a growing gap between the capital-intensive border factories and foreign-owned assembly activities and the small and medium-sized local businesses sector. Mexico has a trade surplus with the United States because U.S. multinationals have shifted some parts of their production cycle to Mexico; in the second quarter of 2000 these companies sent nearly $24 billion worth of components to Mexico—the equivalent of Mexico's entire trade surplus with the United States over the previous eighteen months. Mexico is in effect assembling (mostly in U.S.-owned plants) components sent to it by the United States. Since the assembled product is always worth more than the sum of its many parts, the trade statistics will appear to favor Mexico. The apparent trade deficit with Mexico foretells a growing surplus worldwide for the United States as Mexico increasingly trades with Europe and South America. It can be said that some American multinationals are using Mexico as a trampoline to bounce hundreds of millions of dollars of U.S.-made components around the world. In Brazil and China, for example, the percentage of affiliate sales that remain in the country is high, often exceeding 90 percent. By contrast, the percentage of affiliate sales that remain in Mexico is dropping to less than 50 percent. So falling domestic demand will not show up in capacity utilization the way it did with the Asian tigers.

In a 1999 article, the *Wall Street Journal* had this to say:

> For most Mexicans these statistics offer little solace. In terms of what they can buy for themselves, most consumers are worse off today than they were a decade ago. Even those lucky enough to have one of the new assembly plant jobs can't buy as much as they could have five years ago before Mexico abandoned its fixed exchange rate. Since Mexico's big 1994 currency devaluation, consumers have suffered a staggering 39 percent drop in their purchasing power. Since June 1997, the number of people living in extreme poverty—defined as workers earning less than $2 a day—has grown by four million, or twice the growth of the population . . . Mexico's lesson for other troubled economies is something very different [from what pro-globalization economists prescribe] . . . [it is that] sometimes macroeconomic health is achieved at the cost of mass hardship—and even then timing may be as important as policy. After its devaluation, Mexico followed almost to the letter the advice of the International Monetary Fund and the U.S. Treasury—the same advice that has since been given to Asian countries. . . . Growth has been restored within 18 months of the devaluation and inflation fell dramatically.

The article mentioned that a recent study carried out by the United Nations Development Programme found that while just one of seven Mexicans lived in dire poverty before the crisis, two years later the proportion was one in five. "Adding those a rung up—workers living in 'moderate' poverty with daily incomes of $3—almost two-thirds of the citizenry is considered poor today. Fewer than half fit that description before the crisis."

The article pointed out that, assuming that the Mexican economy can keep growing at 5 percent a year, it will still take five more years for Mexico to reduce poverty to 1984 levels. In other words, despite three straight years of impressive post-devaluation growth, the peso crash virtually wiped out a generation of progress, leaving most Mexicans poorer than their parents. The danger, the article pointed out, is that many countries without the advantages Mexico had in its financial recovery are being exhorted to follow Mexico's example.[98]

It therefore appears that a free trade zone with the United States has provided Mexico some cushion against possible external financial shocks. Mexico is, however, another classical case of an enclave economy. Because of the cushion, it may not now experience the type of meltdown the East Asian countries went through late in 1997.[99] But that does not remove the fact that its basic economic structure is in many ways similar to those of the wounded East Asian countries. To economists who are concerned only with financial data, the macroeconomic fundamentals of Mexico are now satisfactory.[100]

The prevailing view of Mexico from Wall Street is that of a country that got over a bad patch a few years ago and whose experience should serve as a lesson to other emerging markets in the global economy. Krugman described Mexico as a basically well-run emerging market. From a structural analysis of the Mexican economy, however, it will be seen that the economy as presently constituted cannot achieve self-sustaining economic growth.

The fate of emerging economies in a global economy is not bright. The structural economic imbalance of the present global system is best described by Mittelman: "How is it that globalization which helps to alleviate poverty in some parts of the world is antithetical to poverty reduction on a world scale?" This is a rhetorical question, but he attempts to answer it. "It appears antithetical to poverty reduction because there is a shifting incidence of poverty, growing polarization among and within regions, and a reconstitution of wealth. In other words, global poverty comprises a downward spiral of economic conditions in some countries and elsewhere a sense of disjuncture between macroeconomic growth and persistent material deprivation for many. . . . Our core hypothesis is that although poverty is an age-old phenomenon, today it is better understood as the outcome of the interaction among globalization, marginalization and gender."[101]

In response to this not-so-good fate of the poor countries inside the global economy, proponents of globalization have proposed what is now called the "safety net."[102] Friedman defined those he called "social-safety-netters" as "people who believe that globalization will only be sustainable if it is democratized, both in an economic and political sense. Economically, this means designing trampolines and social safety nets that don't try to cushion the fall of the left-behinds, know-nots and turtles, but actually try to bring them into the system by helping them acquire the tools and resources to compete. And politically, it means encouraging democratization in the developing countries that are globalizing because there is no sustainable growth without the growth of personal freedoms as well." Friedman contrasts this group with its opposite group, the "Let-Them-Eat-Cakers," people who believe that globalization is essentially winner-take-all, loser-take-care-of-yourself: "They want to shrink government taxes and safety nets and let people reap the fruits of their own labor or pay the price of their ineptitude. There is nothing that focuses the mind more on getting a job and keeping it, say the Let-Them-Eat-Cakers, than knowing that there is no net under you."[103]

Friedman is essentially talking politics here, not economics. In any case, it is too simplistic for him to claim that his brand of safety net is not necessarily intended to cushion a fall but rather to bring the fallen back into the system by helping them acquire the tools and resources to compete. But this is in the first place what globalization is supposed to do. And if it does that, why should he be left with these people on his hands? The point is that the global economy is by its nature a structurally unbalanced economy that inherently leaves some groups behind. Providing these left-behind groups with what globalization offers—capital and modern techniques— results in a vicious circle that only increases the number of those left behind.

The World Bank safety net is different from Friedman's. The Bank seems to be focusing primarily on transfers through budgetary allocation. Where, therefore, there are declines in pubic spending, as in Russia, there is, in the Bank's view, no safety net for the poor. The Bank seems to be thinking that the provision of a safety net is a national responsibility, and so the nature of the safety net will vary in character: income transfers in Europe, public works programs in the typical Keynesian fashion in Korea, rice distribution schemes in Indonesia.[104]

The World Bank seems to take it as given that countries will, under globalization, have poverty as an essential part of their economic landscape. According to the Bank, "Any development strategy for stable and sustainable growth must include adequate safety nets and appropriate policies and institutions designed to prevent financial crises and respond to them when the crises occur." The Bank explains that safety nets, while not a substitute for sound pro-growth macroeconomic policies, can help mitigate the effects of economic crisis.[105] The idea of a safety net is anathema to the science of economic development and growth, which, through the correct factor proportions, ensures full utilization of all factors

and a balanced economy. It has been claimed by the Bank that foreign aid is a safety net, but we have established that despite the good intentions of donor countries, foreign aid to poor countries is not growth-inducing. It should not be a surprise that after almost half a century of foreign aid, the Third World countries still remain poor, with a growing gap between them and the advanced countries.

The idea of a safety net as an essential structure of a global economy is perhaps the single most important reason why globalization is an inadequate tool for economic development and growth. Globalization, because of its serious structural imbalances, cannot help countries attain sustainable growth. It cannot economically achieve takeoff because it has a lot of dead weight of unutilized resources—those that are the "left-behinds," "know-nots," and "turtles," to use Friedman's expressions.

Before we take up the financial aspects of the global system, we need to ask why China did not suffer the fate of the tiger economies with which it shares the same economic region, because in a way China is plugged into the global system. China is a major power whose international role will grow in the twenty-first century. What it does is of great interest. Why did China escape the crisis that engulfed most of its neighbors?

There have been suggestions that China might still be a victim, albeit not in exactly the same way as the tigers. As Krugman put it, who will be the next victim of depression economics?[106] He said there were three distinct groups of economies that have not yet had full-scale crises but still could: the good, the bad, and the wealthy. The good are emerging economies "who have tried from the beginning to live under the rules of the New World Order, that have sound money and sound budgets." He gave as examples Hong Kong, Argentina, Mexico, and Israel. The bad he did not specifically define, but clearly are the countries that don't live by the rules of the New World Order and don't have sound money and sound budgets. He thought China was a good example. The wealthy he named as the advanced economies of Japan, Europe, and the United States. Krugman left his readers with the impression that the good economies could fall into crisis because they might catch cold from the "chill wind" coming from elsewhere—and because a crisis did indeed happen to Japan.

If we stay with Krugman's analogy of a chill wind, we can say that an economy is like a four-legged structure. If the legs are equal and well balanced, the structure is less likely to be blown over from whatever direction the wind blows. If the legs are not of equal length, the structure is more likely to be knocked over by the wind. Therefore, an economy that can conventionally be said to be in good health (like Mexico's) but is actually structurally unbalanced can be blown over. The wealthy countries too could be affected by the wind, except that they have more balanced economies, as we illustrated in Chapter 4. Their crises, if they occur, are more likely to be milder and shorter.

Now back to China, which Krugman singled out as a "bad" economy. China has many of the characteristics that the conventional economic wisdom says were responsible for causing the East Asian crisis. Krugman accused China of cronyism; for example, licenses are required for practically everything, and in such a closed economy, the ability to obtain these licenses is based on political criteria. The country is also not democratic, and according to conventional neoliberal market philosophy, this lack should inhibit economic growth. Corruption and mismanagement may be seen to be responsible for a state industrial sector that is reportedly almost bankrupt. Many state enterprises cannot pay their debt and cannot meet banks' requirements for new borrowing, and so they are essentially insolvent (like the chaebols in South Korea during its crisis). For many decades, Beijing has acted as China's chief economic architect, deciding how many steel factories, auto

companies, or oil refineries are needed. While this top-down effort has made China the world's largest steel producer and a major player in other global industries such electronics, it has saddled the country with dozens of money-losing companies.[107] The top-down control in China parallels that in South Korea, where succeeding governments were accused of economic dictatorship. Many banks in China are technically bankrupt and are being pressured to modernize.[108] Again, this parallels the state of the financial sector in South Korea, which was said to have lent irresponsibly, on political considerations alone. China, like South Korea, also is export-oriented. Thus China at the time of the Asian crisis had most of the characteristics that were said to be responsible for the Asian crisis.[109]

But beneath these superficial similarities between China and the Asian tigers there are basic differences. Roberts observed that despite high-level statements to the contrary, Beijing seems to be pushing a "buy domestic" agenda for its industries. While foreigners are banging on the doors to be let in, China is instead reorganizing in order to give a big edge to Chinese companies. Whereas countries such as South Korea and Thailand tried to catch up with the West through capital-intensive industrialization, China stayed on course with techniques that emphasized maximum utilization of available local factors. Lin and Yao correctly identified the contrast between South Korea and Thailand, on one hand, and China, on the other, when they observed that by pursuing large-scale industrial development, South Korea and Thailand deviated from their comparative advantage.[110]

In 1998, the China State Power Corporation decided to end all purchases of foreign power generation for projects under 600 megawatts. In telecommunications, an internal directive ordered all local governments to purchase domestically produced switches and fiber-optic cables whenever possible; the Chinese minister in charge won't con-

Table 7.2

Capital/Labor Ratio (in yuan per workers) in China

	1978	1979	1980	1981	1982	1983	1984	1985	1986
SOE	7,090	—	7,582	—	—	—	9,255	10,435	11,489
Rural	643	777	887	1,024	1,100	1,153	856	—	—

	1987	1988	1989	1990	1991	1992	1993	1994	1995	1996
SOE	12,830	14,283	16,460	18,534	21,259	24,293	19,578	31,282	39,741	51,767
Rural	—	—	—	2,254	2,484	2,964	4,164	5,539	7,933	9,254

Source: SSB, *China Statistical Yearbook*, 1995, 1997; *The Yearbook of Chinese Township and Village Enterprises*, 1995, 1997.

sider giving free rein to foreigners until domestic companies are sufficiently competitive, which is considered likely to occur in 2020. Until then, foreign telecom operators must operate in a legal gray area. These examples show that China is continuing a historical policy of relying on itself and attempting to forge its own economic personality.

Let us resketch China's industrial structure as summarized by Neil Hughes, senior operations officer in the China and Mongolia Department of the World Bank. China is home to roughly eight million industrial enterprises, about six million of which are owned by a family or an individual and have fewer than eight employees. Nearly fifty thousand enterprises are classified as "other," including private businesses that employ more than eight people and joint ventures between Chinese and foreign businesses. The rest are publicly owned, as defined by the Chinese constitution, but there are important differences between them. Only 118,000 are owned by the government at the national, provincial, or municipal level; within this group of state-owned enterprises (SOEs), roughly 13,000 medium-sized and large state enterprises account for most of the output in this group. The rest of the 1.9 million public enterprises are owned by townships and villages and are classified as collectively owned. They are unregulated and rely on local savings and local en-

trepreneurship. These collectives account for about 40 percent of total industrial output, while the state-owned enterprises account for only 34 percent.

The state-owned enterprises dominate the major mining and manufacturing sectors: coal, ferrous and nonferrous metals, chemicals, textiles, pharmaceuticals, machine tools, food processing, printing, tobacco, capital goods, fertilizer, motor vehicles, electronics, and defense.[111] Hughes argued that because the state enterprises were tying up two-thirds of the industrial assets and contributing only one-third of output, they were "terribly inefficient." His conclusion was misleading because he was thinking that the SOEs were capital-intensive and therefore should in some way correlate positively with output and produce at much higher levels than the statistics say. What he should have concerned himself with was why the bulk of the output in China was coming from outside the SOEs.

Official statistical data in China and the use of the terms *light, heavy, rural,* and *urban* in relation to industry, used by Western economists in discussing China, do mislead. These economists give the impression of an economy with dualistic characteristics in which heavy industry dominates the scene. The Chinese attempt to venture into heavy industry, it must be emphasized, is historically a recent event, covering a period of about three decades just after they came under Soviet influence. But they did not import Soviet plant or machinery.

Table 7.2 displays published capital intensiveness (in yuan per worker) of the Chinese state-owned enterprises compared with that of the rural enterprises. This gives the impression of two sectors of different characteristics.

Lin and Yao concluded from these figures that net capital stock per worker in rural enterprises had never passed 20 percent of that of the state-owned enterprises. We need, however, to scrutinize these figures further before drawing conclusions. Averse as we are to evaluating production aid (capital) in financial terms, we need to convert the capital intensiveness of the state-owned enterprises to equivalent dollar values using the official Chinese exchange rate of 8.3 yuan to the dollar (an exchange rate that China has maintained since 1994). We see that the capital intensiveness of the state-owned enterprises grew from a little less than $3,800 per worker to a little over $6,000 per worker between 1994 and 1996. These figures are in the lowest quartile of the U.S. industrial sector's capital/labor ratios. Compared to their equivalents in the West, the Chinese heavy industries are essentially labor-intensive. Hughes complained that the state-owned Chinese plants were obsolete, inefficient, and highly polluting, and suggested that state enterprises should modernize by importing new technologies. In actual fact the state-owned enterprises are "heavy" only in terms of their physical size. In economic science this size is of little significance since what matters is the factor proportion.

A number of factors will tend to inflate official Chinese capital/labor figures for state-owned enterprise. Hughes noted that the state enterprises maintain hospitals, clinics, and schools and build houses for workers; they employ one-third of the nation's medical staff and six hundred thousand teachers and administrators. Workers in these enterprises regard health care, housing, and education

benefits as their entitlements. If allowance is made for such large overheads, it will be clear that a sizable part of the quoted financial investment has nothing to do with the actual production plant and machinery. Therefore, the physical size of the SOEs is large because of all these add-ons. On top of this is the problem of establishing asset values for the state industries in China. Hughes observed that many of the state-owned enterprises have revalued their capital holdings. According to him, the Chinese employ much longer depreciation periods than is generally acceptable.[112] This will inflate capital asset values. It is clear that the actual scientific capital/labor ratio of the SOEs will almost qualify as labor-intensive, contrary to what Chinese official statistics might represent it as. In any case, the number of medium-sized and large state-owned enterprises—about thirteen thousand out of six million industrial enterprises in China—is small. On a weighted average, their factor proportions are not likely to make much difference to the macro economy's factor proportions.

On the other hand, many factors will tend to lead to an underestimation of the capital/labor ratio of the so-called rural industries. According to Lin and Yao, the number of rural enterprises in China increased from 1.5 million in 1978 to 20.2 million in 1997. Six million are industrial enterprises. By 1996 only 30 percent of the rural labor force worked in rural industries. An average capital/labor ratio for all the 20.2 million enterprises (the bulk of which are nonindustrial) will obviously be much lower than the ratio for the industrial enterprises. In other words, lumping the industrial and nonindustrial enterprises together fails to take account of the fact that the industries normally have a higher capital/labor ratio. Also, much of the financing of the rural industries comes from savings, cooperatives, and contributions from friends and relatives. Rural industries' small plant and machinery are often fabricated locally by the entrepreneur and his friends.

Animal and human power are used as production aids. Given all these factors, evaluating the plant and machinery for these industries in financial terms is likely to underestimate the true size of the capital invested in rural industries.

The point we are making is that the factor proportions of state-owned industries and non-state-owned industries are not too different. This seems to be confirmed by Chinese government statistics showing that while state enterprises, which control 72 percent of the industrial assets, were responsible for 70 percent of total industrial employment, the rest of the economy, with 28 percent of the industrial assets, was responsible for the remaining 30 percent of total industrial employment. Clearly there is equilibrium of the capital/labor ratio in both sectors. This is economic structural balance.

China has more than ninety Chinese car and truck companies. The market is dominated by about ten major ones. But the bulk of these companies are craft-type production, geared to the needs of the Chinese economy. The relatively costly ($20,000) sedan market is small and saturated by foreign manufacturers who were seeking what they thought was a huge market. The real demand, in a balanced economy with relatively low income inequality, is for affordable basic vehicles costing about $3,000, which the Chinese car and truck companies produce and foreign companies don't.

In light of these considerations, it is clear that Lin and Yao's conclusion that the net capital stock per worker of rural enterprise never passed 20 percent of that of the state-owned enterprises was not academically useful and lacked thorough verification. It seems they recognized the superficiality of their assessment when they observed—despite the 80 percent gap in the capital/labor ratio that they claim existed—that "the gap between SOEs [state-owned enterprises] and rural enterprises [industries] in their capital intensities has narrowed through the years." They claimed that this could be explained by what they

ambiguously called the "rural enterprises' adjustment to changes in factor endowments (and thus the comparative advantages) in the economy." Lin and Yao conclude that urban-rural dualism in China's economic structure is disintegrating, and "industrial development in urban and rural areas are complementing and infiltrating each other."[113]

Yet China is not static in terms of production techniques. The economy is very dynamic, increasingly copying and adapting Western techniques and pushing ahead independently on all fronts. The Chinese are protecting their technology base, as indicated by their decision not to buy any generating equipment less than 600 megawatts because they have developed their production of this. They did not want to give foreign competitors free rein until 2020 so that Chinese companies can become competitive. In cases where they absolutely need goods or services that they cannot yet easily replicate and modify, they will use foreign suppliers until they can take control.

The Chinese economy is therefore relatively balanced, utilizing factors in its economy and downplaying foreign borrowing and foreign investment. As the *International Herald Tribune* said of China, "Post-Mao China has always managed to balance gradual reform with strong economic growth, one supporting the other."[114]

How much does China need the global economic system? Perkins was of the view that exports and foreign investment were of importance to China, and so the country needed "to abide by the rules of the international economic system, as embodied in organizations such as the WTO."[115] Are exports vital to the economic development and growth of China? When the East Asian economies collapsed, exports from China dropped sharply. But China did not devalue its currency in order to make its exports cheaper. Its economy was untouched by the loss of the export market that conventional economists claim was a contributing factor in the economic crisis in the East Asian countries. Exports are the things that the engine cranks out. The issue is not how much the engine cranks out but whether the engine is in good condition. Perkins was not correct in concluding that China needs exports for its economic development. His reason for this incorrect conclusion was that, as he put it, "For reasons that are poorly understood, but that probably have something to do with the productivity-enhancing influence of foreign competition, growth based mainly on domestic demand may not be able to sustain the high GDP growth enjoyed while exports were surging."[116] Perkins was concerned only with financial statistics and not with the structural economics of China.

What of foreign investment, which Perkins also states is China's need? A lot of current Western literature on the Chinese economy seems intended to give the impression that China is increasingly dependent on foreign direct investment and technology. By 1996, China had attracted about 280,000 foreign firms with a total investment valued at $176.6 billion. Today, total foreign investment is estimated at $450 billion. Some township enterprises and government departments were known to have shifted money secretly out of China and brought it back as foreign in order to enjoy tax breaks and other privileges. According to Li and Li, this and Chinese investment in China may account for the fact that 70 percent of officially registered FDI between 1979 and 1995 originated from Hong Kong, Macao, and Taiwan and nearly 60 percent of this from Hong Kong alone.[117] If we are to go by this, it means that something like only 30 percent of officially recorded FDI into China is actually foreign. It is therefore clear that most of the FDI is not so capital-intensive as to draw attention.

Li and Li's findings should help explain why a substantial portion of the so-called foreign investment into China ended up in firms in rural areas of the coastal areas, since it would appear that townships and government departments involved

in the shifting of money out of and into China were mainly located in the coastal areas.[118] Wang stated that FDI from such "investors" was more likely to enter into the labor-intensive sectors that dominated the rural enterprises.[119] These have over the years dominated Chinese export growth. According to official Chinese statistics, their share of exports rose from 9 percent in 1986 to about 46 percent in 1997. The relatively low impact of these FDI firms is further illustrated by the fact that in 1995, only about 28 percent of the output of firms at township and village level was created by them.[120] The bulk of foreign investment into China is from Taiwan and is not capital-intensive. It is therefore clear that Perkins' assertion that foreign investment in China played a central role both in marketing and in the restructuring of Chinese industry to produce quality products for international markets cannot be substantiated.[121] It is stretching the argument for anyone to imply that it is the overseas Chinese that sustained the export drive of China, as if native China lacked any ability to organize. Indeed, it is the labor-intensive nature of the Chinese rural enterprises that enhanced their position in China's export market.[122]

It is clear that China's economic development and growth do not need or depend on a global economy. It has surged ahead. To attribute this growth to what Lin and Yao called "the rapid growth of its rural industrial sector" is not strictly correct.[123] It is the adoption of factor proportions that approximate to the country's natural factor proportions that leads to a balanced development pattern, which in turn distributes development evenly in the economy, as it has done in China.

China—Whose Globalization?

The entry of China into the World Trade Organization (WTO) has given rise to two broad claims about globalization. One is that post–Deng China's economic growth is due to its limited forays into globalization prior to its entry into WTO. Economists quote China's increasing foreign trade in exports and its substantial FDI figures in support of this claim. The second, related to the first, is that entry into WTO will enable China to solidify and in fact increase these gains, particularly in exports.

China, as we have seen earlier, is a country whose history is inward-looking. "In the Maoist era of socialist self-sufficiency, China," as Studwell put it, "developed its technology for everything . . . the techniques were rudimentary by international standards."[124] This self-sufficient approach, which persists today, has been reinforced by what Chang called "two centuries of contact with foreigners [which] have left the Chinese humiliated and events long past [that] have been etched into their consciousness." Chang recalled that *Time* magazine once labeled China the "Worst Victim of Globalization" because Britain forcefully opened the Middle Kingdom with the opium trade in the 1940s. He added, "The Chinese, who have much history to boast about, seldom do. [They] express nationalism in terms of two hundred years of colonial encroachment, not the accomplishment of five thousand."[125] The Chinese inward-looking approach has a long history. It is risky for economists to make too much of China's WTO membership. It must be remembered that China has political aims and that along with acceptance as the site of the 2008 Olympics (Beijing), entry into the WTO underlines China's arrival on the world scene as emphatically as did its emergence as a nuclear power in 1946.[126]

Most emerging countries (if we group China as an emerging country) and advanced countries, especially of Europe, actively seek foreign investment and create conditions conducive to financial success. Most emerging countries seek FDIs because they are told that FDIs will be a source of technology transfer. We will take the cement in-

dustry as an example because it is classically regarded by economists as the best industry to illustrate the economy-of-scale paradigm. Studwell's account about the cement business in China is instructive. He writes that "in the cement business, four-fifths of Chinese output comes not from modern kilns but from vertical-shaft kilns similar to those that produced the first cement in the early nineteenth century. China makes one-third of all cement in the world using a process that is nearly 200 years old. The vertical kilns are generally small and housed inside low-rise buildings. Limestone, silica and alumina are shoveled on top of cheap—usually brown—coal which is ignited. Vast clouds of black smoke fill the air and the chemical process that creates the base for cement begins. When the process is finished, the kiln is cleared and refilled. The output of a vertical kiln is as little as 50 tons a day compared to 1,000 tons or more in a modern plant. The costs of building a vertical kiln are as little as $500,000 versus $100 million for a 2,000-ton-a-day rotary kiln. There are 7,000 vertical kilns in China—three in every county. The dream of every local government in China is to have its own industrial base—a car factory, a steel factory, cement factory and so on."[127]

A number of foreign-owned cement plants exist in China as well as those financed by the International Finance Corporation (IFC) with the most modern technology. According to Studwell, because of overcapacity arising from the proliferation of low-cost local cement production, the price of cement in China halved in the 1990s, reaching the lowest level in the world.[128] Many foreigners say that cement produced from vertical kilns is of poor quality. According to Studwell, the China chief of mission of the IFC and World Bank in a complaint written as a memo asked, "How can a large, world-scale plant, with the latest proprietary technology that is built to produce to the highest quality with lowest pollution and sponsored by an investor who has a return for its home-country shareholders and must pay its bank debt, how can such an investor get a decent return against competition that need not care about quality, the environment, providing an equity return, or repaying its bank loan?" In a later note, the chief of mission in 1999 was quoted as having said, "The half-reformed nature of China's economy has structural barriers to achieving fair returns [for foreign companies]. . . . Until these rules [business rules in China] are substantially changed, it will continue to be impossible to make a fair return, regardless of China's growth or exchange rate."[129]

When a French-owned cement company in China targeted some model Chinese projects in which cement quality might be an issue, it decided to expand its production by forgoing operating profit in the hope that such quality projects would change its financial difficulties. In 2000, the company estimated it had less than a 5 percent share of the Beijing cement market but a 50 percent share of the market's profit. Yet the return was still lower than could be obtained by making a deposit in a French high-street bank.

A *Financial Times* article quoted Michael Komesaroff, the managing director of Urandline, a consultancy specializing in capital-intensive industries in China, as saying that he is not sanguine about China's ability to attract foreign investors. "I think there are enough [foreign corporations] that have been burned. There will always be those who want to come in, but overall it won't be easy." The *Wall Street Journal* of March 2004 stated "as the world's consumer giants charge headlong into China, well entrenched [small] local brands are proving to be formidable competitors." The *Economist* stated that "few foreigners who have done well have ignored the domestic market and concentrated on China as a cheap base for manufacturing and exporting processing. . . . Many [foreign] companies are not covering their costs, much less getting

a proper return on investment." Some multinationals deliberately lower required rates of return and charge head offices to make projects more profitable than they are. The segmented market, such as China's large market, has reduced Rybczynski's effect, reducing the formation of a dualistic economy. Labor-intensive craft activities, in tune with Chinese factor proportions, have outperformed Western foreign investments that need large markets. With such a poor record, the $500 billion foreign investment in China cannot justifiably be claimed the prime mover of Chinese outstanding economic growth.[130]

The *Times* article argued that China had reneged on many power purchase agreements with foreign companies so that much of the burden of building a power infrastructure falls upon domestic companies. Starting in 2004, foreign makers of wireless equipment must revamp their software to meet Chinese standards because of "national security." China's "technology for market" policy attracts a range of advanced western manufacturing companies and forces them to reveal their technology in exchange for market access.

In the 1990s, counterfeiting of foreign branded products by firms in China was a major problem. Henkel, the German manufacturer of household products, found that it was "selling" 130 percent of what was leaving its factory. Enforcement against counterfeiting is not effective.[131]

In his book titled *Other People's Money,* Studwell suggests that foreign investments were being used in China to maintain its huge socialist bureaucracy, which employs over 200 million people, because FDI created numerous revenue streams that China needed for this purpose. So China was, according to Studwell, using other people's money for its own purposes.

In general, it is clear that foreign investments are discriminated against in China, and according to Panitchpadki and Clifford, many are hoping that "in its simplest outline the WTO will set out the rules for a market-based [China]. It will eliminate unfair treatment that favors state-owned firms and discriminates against foreign companies and local entrepreneurs."[132]

But China holds the trump card because the foreign investors are swarming to get a share of the action in what they regard as potentially the largest market in the world by the middle of this century. In mid-1990, Studwell says China was "a place of long and agitated queues as the surge of would-be investors competed for a limited supply of licenses and investment opportunities. As a result, market entry costs rose exponentially. Almost no one questioned the price being paid." He concluded that "the Chinese government would be due congratulations for continuing to woo tens of billions of dollars of foreign investment a year despite evidence that returns on much of that capital were either negative or below bank deposit rate."[133]

About the fact that WTO now has a role to play in facilitating foreign competition in China, Studwell says that the rekindled enthusiasm in China [due to its WTO membership] is "based on dubious analysis." He says that the inference that the Chinese government's decision to pursue WTO membership reflected a new willpower to enact change had nothing to substantiate it. In fact the evidence was to the contrary. According to him, ". . . the capacity of WTO to complete its task is vastly overestimated by both China's would-be reformers and foreign investors." "Although greatly strengthened by internationally agreed changes made in its rules in 1995, WTO," in his view, "is not equipped to tackle the domestic economic constraints that make China . . . so impermeable . . . to profitable international trade and investment. . . . China will pose unique problems to parties wishing to challenge its record of enforcement of WTO obligations."[134]

So what we see is globalization in Chinese style. China wants to use globalization to achieve its increasing export and political power. The rest of the advanced countries realized they could not leave the tiger to roam. They needed to bring it in and at least be able to watch it. The new Chinese leaders in Beijing will have to take care that their policies do not disturb the structural balance on which China's impressive growth has depended.

Interconnectedness

The world is increasingly an interconnected village, thanks to advances in communications—what Friedman called the democratization of information. The Internet has changed the way people see the world. Friedman quoted an Israeli philosopher who said that cyberspace is a place where all mankind can be unified and totally free. Friedman himself claims that as the Internet proliferates, it is going to become the turbocharged engine that drives globalization, because from the moment one logs on, one can communicate globally practically for free. The number of people connected to the Internet worldwide had grown from about 171 million to 304 million in just one year, and it is reckoned that the number will jump to a billion in five years. It took seven years for 30 percent of the population of the United States to connect to the Internet, compared with seventeen years for an equal proportion to get television and thirty years for the telephone. By 1999, more than half of the U.S. adult population was online.

When we talk of a village, we normally think of a close community that is knit by many bonds and in which interpersonal contact is close. Some villages in the past had squares where people meet to discuss and exchange views and reason together. Friedman says that the first rule of the Internet age is that "we are all connected but nobody is quite in charge." Unfortunately, Friedman's claim is not correct. This is because the interconnectedness globalization is producing is one in which the advanced countries are in charge. What is being proposed is to increase the access of the people of the Third World to the Internet so as to enable them to have access to modern technology, Western films, Western culture, and Western institutions. Small village computing centers in the Third World are being proposed and financed by aid agencies and NGOs from the advanced countries in order to bring remote areas in poor countries in touch with "civilization." The dialogue is essentially in one direction. The poor countries, because they are poor, are not in the position to provide the necessary infrastructure to make the Internet a two-way conversation and exchange. The domination of world media by the West has been a major complaint of the media in the Third World.

The problem is that most underdeveloped countries are poor because they have not mobilized their resources and have not set in motion strategies necessary to do so. The leadership in many poor countries is Western-educated and is focused on Western methods and technology; they have significantly failed to study their own factor needs and how to mobilize them. The danger of growing Internet penetration in these countries is a disoriented population that looks elsewhere for the institutions it needs for economic development—education, technology, culture, and orientation. For developing countries that are seeking self-reliant economic development and growth, free Internet access unidirectionally tuned toward the West is bound to produce some undesired consequences. When China wants to control use of the Internet in China, Western commentators unsympathetically see this as simply a denial of basic freedoms. It is the theme of this book that economic development and growth are exogenous and that each society should devise the institutions best suited to itself in order to promote this. It is our view that the science (nature) of economic development and growth was predicated on a world of variety in which each culture and people utilize their special socioeconomic institutions.

This is not saying that Internet penetration in non-Western societies is all bad news. Rather, the point being made is that in an ideal world, people everywhere should distill what is suitable for themselves from information made available to them in cyberspace. They will be better off if they have information about what other people are doing; however, the bulk of the people in poor countries are likely to regard what is done in the advanced countries as what should be copied, because Western economic success is the best testimonial for all its norms.

There is a gathering momentum from the international development industry to promote and finance the growth of the Internet in underdeveloped countries. Governments in the Third World are coming under increasing pressure by aid agencies, Western governments, and Western business to invest in the Internet. We are saying that on balance, it is not a priority.

The claimed inevitability of globalization is also based on the claimed inevitable growth of the Internet worldwide. Globalization promoters will argue that even in the poor countries, there is a great appetite for computers, satellite dishes, handheld devices, and so on. For those in these industries in advanced economies, this is a justifiable reason for wanting to expand their sales into poor countries and seeking ways to provide these services at affordable prices. But for the economic development and growth of these poor economies, the appetite is not a justifiable reason for investing in cyberspace.

In order to push the growth of the Internet worldwide, a number of claims are made about it. In this connection a new measurement has been designed by the industry to evaluate what they call the connectivity of each country.[135] Connectivity of a country measured in megabytes per capita is the installed megabytes divided by the number of potential users in the country. It has joined PCs per household as the key yardstick in the industry. Access to the Internet is concentrated within the rich countries. The OECD countries, with only 19 percent of the world's population, have 91 percent of the world's Internet users. It is immediately tempting because of this correlative relationship to say that the recent economic growth of the OECD countries is due to the Internet. The first claim made, therefore, is that jobs, knowledge, and economic growth will gravitate to societies with the most networks and largest amount of bandwidth, for these countries will find it easier to amass, deploy, and share knowledge in order to design, invest, manufacture, sell, provide services, communicate, educate, and entertain. The claim has no scientific basis. While it is true that the Internet and computers are inextricably mixed in with the longest period of sustained growth that the United States has witnessed in modern times, and therefore it is tempting to conclude that Internet use and connectivity in what some have called the "knowledge economy" will increasingly determine economic growth for all countries, there is no basis for such generalization.

The Internet has also been credited with assisting technology transfer. New technical information can be made available to subsidiaries, affiliates, subcontractors, and partners of multinationals in countries around the world. Production can be moved around from country to country in search of the best tax deals and the most efficient and lowest-cost labor force. It is possible to standardize technical specifications and designs worldwide and simply adapt them to local tastes. Globalized production has expanded vastly along with capital movements. From the moment one starts doing business on the Internet, one can think globally in terms of who one's competitors or customers are. We have already discussed the issues of technology transfer and capital transfer extensively and will only say here that the Internet's role in promoting global production adds to the structural imbalance of those countries whose factor proportions do not warrant the blanket adoption of the factor proportions of advanced economies.

This book has accused conventional economists of passing off what works in the advanced economy as general principles of economic development and growth. This is true also of the claims that are made about globalization. Theorists on globalization are attempting to erect a global economy patterned after the advanced economies. No one quarrels with people having dreams that one day the global economy will be one big advanced economy. But you do not achieve those dreams by pretending that it is simply all about the expansion of advanced-economy infrastructures in the hope of pushing underdevelopment out of the picture. Three examples will be given here of this pretense. First, as already discussed, is the claim that societies with high connectivity achieve higher employment and growth. This applies in an advanced economy for reasons to be discussed shortly but does not apply in poor economies. Second, as referred to in Chapter 4, is the oft-made assertion that digital technologies, which have contributed to growth in advanced economies, will automatically do the same in poor economies. A third and related claim, as stated by Friedman, is that the new technologies cause increased "productivity in a factory and living standards in a society because they displace labor." As he put it, "a robot does the job more efficiently than an assembly line worker. The voice mail chip in your phone does the job better than an operator. . . . In other words, the key to the information revolution is not that it increases labor output per unit, but rather that it reduces labor input per unit. The amount of physical labor required to do any task gets reduced."[136] From this he made the following mental leap: "If you have a culture and society that allows you to easily and freely displace workers with new technologies, then you will reap the benefits they offer in terms of productivity, improved profits, greater general prosperity, and ultimately more job creation. It adds to a more competitive country."[137] Friedman was correct when he talked of the effects of the reduction of labor input in an advanced economy, because there labor is relatively scarce. But he was wrong to generalize his conclusion to any "culture" or "society."

Friedman drew attention to cost reductions that have been achieved through digital technology, adding to his claim that "innovations in miniaturization can be taken to more and more far-flung places and afforded by people with less and less income."[138] He is no doubt referring to a new set of "development experts" who are now concentrating on the "grassroots" in poor societies through their "bottom-up" development strategies. But they are doing nothing different except to miniaturize advanced-economy strategies. For example, Barbara Crossette wrote in the *New York Times* that "there is no dearth of ideas about how to bring the benefit of globalization to the poor. . . . Computer technology, for example, can be brought to the poor regions at relatively low cost with the use of satellite telephones making available all kinds of information on health, education, agriculture and consumer advice."[139]

This sort of strategy is increasingly being combined with "miniaturized" lending in the rural areas of poor countries such as Bangladesh. With the failure of megaloans to stimulate economic development, a new set of development experts now seeks to set up online networks of microbanks in these countries, arguing that it makes it easier to keep track of hundreds of loans and reduces processing and transaction costs. Such microloans can now be bundled together and sold to major banks in the advanced countries. But such efforts fail to produce the needed mobilization of productive factors, as they are engaged in peripheral activities (trading, services, etc.) in which the emphasis is on a mini foreign aid through transfer of mini capital funds. And when one adds in the capital-intensive character of the Internet in these rural areas, the net result is not macroeconomic growth.

The bulk of pro-globalization literature unfortunately is infected with broad-brush generalizations that what is good for an advanced economy must be good for a poor economy. For a poor economy with an abundance of labor, it is obviously inept to adopt Friedman's labor displacement strategy. In regard to digitalization, the suggestion that Third World countries should embark on digitalization is naive; however much the capital component has been reduced because of digital technology, it is still capital-intensive in the context of many underdeveloped economies.

Two things have happened at the same time in the advanced economies as a result of the pervasive adoption of digital technology. At the lower end of their economies, that is, in the labor-intensive sector, there has been increasing capital intensity, as Friedman described, while at the upper end, in the capital-intensive sector, capital intensity has been greatly reduced. The result is that the macroeconomic structure in the advanced countries where digital technology is pervasive has become more balanced, leading to improved sustainable growth potential. But the broad differences between developed and underdeveloped economies must be borne in mind when one is evaluating claims about globalization. What is true about the effects of globalization on advanced economies is not, as a general rule, true for poor economies and therefore cannot pass as a general economic principle. Each type of economy has a different economic personality. To brush these differences away in the name of globalization is a recipe for further widening the gap between the rich and the poor of the world.

It should therefore be evident that information technology is not a viable option for many developing economies, as its relative capital intensiveness will worsen structural imbalances in the Third World. Therefore, when G-8 finance ministers at a meeting in Okinawa in July 2000 urged a faster integration of developing economies into the global economy, they were mistaken. They argued, "In view of the rapid progress of globalization and the IT revolution, it is important for developing countries, including the poorest, to harness the benefits of new advances in IT and prevent the digital divide. It is crucial that the international community emphasize capacity and institutional building including those related to IT" for developing countries. This recommendation by the finance ministers was later adopted on July 24, 2000, by the lenders in what is now called the Okinawa Charter, which set up an initiative to help poorer countries connect to the Internet more quickly.[140]

According to the *Wall Street Journal,* Europeans say a push for "information and communication technology" should focus not on Internet connectivity but instead on cellular telephone service. But, as is to be expected, the new initiatives found favor with many U.S. technology companies that attended the summit, as it obviously opened new business opportunities for consultancy, technology transfer, and profitable foreign investment. Indeed, some degree of a digital divide is necessary if poor countries' prospects for sustainable economic development are not to be further jeopardized, because it will enable these countries to concentrate on developing their own resources.

Financial Solutions in the Global Context

Throughout this book we have treated money as the shadow and not the substance of economic activity. In days gone by, people used to think of finance and financiers as being like the oil in an engine—necessary to make the engine work (a facilitator) but not part of the engine nor its fuel.[141] Economics lost its claim of being a science when it allowed finance and financiers to lay claim to being part of the engine, if not the engine itself. Finance can never be a science because it is an artificial illusion that,

although very useful, was created by humans for their own use.

The recent Asian crisis has shown how unscientific and shadowy the so-called global financial architecture is. Ranson and Russell presented two contrasting views of this architecture: the "house of cards" view and the "beehive" view.[142]

According to the "house of cards" view, countries stand to gain or lose when other countries gain or lose. The more Country A's prosperity depends on Country B, the more vulnerable A's economy is to the crisis and recession in B. Thus a bad bank loan in Indonesia throws people out of work in the United States. To this way of thinking, interdependence through global trading has turned the world economy into a house of cards. Disturb one card or two and the house teeters. Take out a few cards and the whole structure comes tumbling down.

The "beehive" view is that the destruction of a few bees has no noticeable impact on the hive. Even if a large fraction of the bees are knocked out, the hive will quickly regenerate its missing population. In the meantime, it will be business as usual for the hive. As far as the welfare of the hive as a whole is concerned, bees are interchangeable and easily replaced. The authors explained that in this view, "the world economic system does not need all its parts to be fully functioning in order to remain healthy. While one country is in crisis, it can be full steam ahead for another."

These are but two of the possible views of the global architecture; no doubt other people have different ideas. But the authors in this case were inclined to show that the global economy was like a beehive. Writing in 1998, shortly after the 1997 crisis, they claimed that the evidence was there in front of their eyes—that while there was no doubt that the global hive sustained some damage from the crisis, the Dow Jones Industrial Average "has recently rebounded to all-time highs."

The authors also were of the opinion that banks

are also like bees. A banking institution merely constitutes a package of assets and liabilities. The resources needed to run a banking industry—like any other—include its labor force, management talent, human knowledge, technology, physical premises, and equipment. In their view, as far as these resources are available and the incentive exists to put them together productively, a banking industry will continue to function. Wipe out some assets, reshuffle some liabilities—ultimately the ownership of these resources will simply be redistributed.

It seems that the authors used a debatable example to illustrate their case for a "beehive" global structure, for it is arguable that the Dow Jones highs were the result of globalization and did not occur in spite of it. The United States survived the global financial turmoil of 1998 and thrived afterward because its economic structure was strong. We have argued earlier that the East Asian economies suffered during the financial turmoil because their economies were already sick. In the face of international financial problems, the weak economies will collapse like a pack of cards and the strong ones will be like a beehive. It is clear that people who lean on the "pack of cards" view want to see vigorous action taken when the first signs of financial difficulty appear, while the "beehive" proponents would prefer to leave things to the market forces to sort out.

In a more serious look at the confusion as to what to make of the global financial architecture, Marber pointed out that the problem of the global financial architecture is that "different observers offer radically different recommendations because they define the problems differently because they have different views on how the international and financial systems work."[143] Eichengreen also complained that various proposals for the global financial system "are contradictory and mutually incompatible."[144] He noted that while some recommend that policy makers renew their efforts to liberalize international capital, others pleaded for the reimposition of capital controls. "Some suggest that international countries respond forcefully to crisis, others want them to stand back and let 'nature' take care in the form of market."

The IMF was created to help countries tackle balance-of-payments problems without resorting to draconian austerity measures, beggar-thy-neighbor exchange rate policies, or trade barriers. But now its role is supposed to be central to defending threats to the stability of the global financial system. Some people are saying that the IMF has exceeded its mandate, however. They say that it crossed the line in dealing with the former Soviet Union and Eastern Europe. These countries needed advice about their creation of basic market institutions. The IMF was able to get its advice accepted by offering financial rewards. In the next great intervention, the IMF was accused of continuing this extrajurisdictional behavior and imposing on the East Asian countries free market reforms as comprehensive as those it imposed on Russia "even though such reforms in the Asian context were not necessary to restart the flow of funds."[145] Some people, such as Sachs, accused the IMF of making the crisis in East Asia worse by shouting that the house was on fire, scaring away those who would have stuck around, and that its response was too slow, worsening the social consequences of the crisis. Others, such as a former U.S. secretary of state, even suggested that the IMF should be abolished. On the other side of the debate, the U.S. deputy Treasury secretary defended the IMF and lauded its prescriptions as crucial to Asia's recovery.

In this highly controversial atmosphere, global experts say they are studying ways to control future crises. But regrettably, they all have adopted a simplistic (and incorrect) view of the problem as being, in Friedman's words, one of bad lenders and bad borrowers. It has all got to do, they say, with just money—with projects and those who lend and borrow for those projects. If we can just create the necessary safeguards to ensure that those who lend make sure the projects are profitable and that the borrowers have in place contingent arrangements in case they find themselves in financial trouble, then all will be well and the world economy will be on the path for sustainable growth.

This simplistic view of prosperity is flawed because it is essentially a microeconomic analysis of what is a macroeconomic problem. It says that if each investment in the economy is productive and generates a profit, that will create maximum growth. Porter and Takeuchi put this mistaken view succinctly in the course of their argument that countries must allow free rein to competition: "Ultimately a country's productivity is the sum of its corporate productivity."[146] But a structural economic analysis says that this does not follow. A country's productivity derives not from the arithmetic total of its corporate productivity but from a "chemical reaction" of the factor proportions, as already discussed.

What conventional economists and the international financial world are doing in framing what they regard as the strategy for a stable global economy is to make us believe that if banks are lending to viable projects, the economy will achieve macroeconomic stability. It is no wonder that global economists lay a lot of emphasis on the financial institutional structure of countries.

If Japan had come to the rescue of the East Asian tigers in 1997 as the United States did for Mexico, probably the world, they argue, would not have woken up to the fragility of the global finance structure. Since 1997, there has been a scurry to find answers. Faced with the realities, neoliberal market ideology and positivist orthodoxy have had to retract some of their firmly held tenets. It used to be said that capital was what emerging markets needed badly, and if the poor economies were to bridge the economic gap, then the more of it the better. Since 1997 there has been a change. Emmerson said there have been what he euphemis-

tically called "inconsistencies between theory and practice—between free trade and available remedies."[147] Krugman called the change turning the clock back at least part of the way.[148] But in fact it is an about-face. People now say that some players in the market are irrational and that others have a herd mentality. Overnight people now talk of too much capital, but they are not able to figure out how too much capital affects the macroeconomic structure of a developing economy, so they blame banks for not being able to ensure that they lend only to profitable projects. Krugman talks of the need to limit capital flows to countries that are unsuitable for either currency unions or a freely floating currency, and of the need to regulate financial markets to seek low (but not too low) inflation rather than price stability.[149] Other economists want to explain away a position they don't understand by saying that too much of a good thing (capital) is not good.[150]

The free market ideology that wanted national governments not to meddle with the economy is now yielding to the need for national governments to intervene in a major way to establish capital controls. The World Bank was initially against capital controls, but like all cases in which people have no scientific theory guiding them, the Bank has changed its position and now says that safeguarding battered economies from the erratic movements of short-term capital is a key challenge for the global community. The safeguards it suggests range from the Chilean approach of controls on incoming capital to Malaysian-style curbs on outflow (even though Wall Street and Washington were initially appalled when that country's prime minister, Mahathir Mohamed, proposed global controls). But the Bank quickly made it clear that "none of these measures can substitute for . . . better macroeconomic fundamentals . . . they cannot protect countries against the consequences of large fiscal deficits or overvalued currencies." Some economists believe that the capital controls of Chile helped it escape the "tequila effect" of the Mexican crisis.[151] But it did not mean that the Chilean economy was healthy. Such is the controversy in the global camp that many people oppose capital controls on principle. They say that capital controls violate the basic principle of the free market and distort market signals.[152]

Stiglitz argued that the net benefit of short-term capital is small, if not negligible. He argued that when the net savings rate is already high and when marginal investment is misallocated, additional short-term flow increases the vulnerability of an economy.[153] Stiglitz should have said that when savings are high and marginal investment is misallocated, *any* kind of capital flow, not just short-term capital, will further harm the macroeconomic structure.

At the height of the East Asian crisis, President Clinton in September 1998 suggested that a distinguished private sector group assess the need for reform of the international financial architecture. An independent task force comprised of an impressive galaxy of twenty-nine of the most respected figures in academia, business, and diplomacy, sponsored by the Council on Foreign Relations, prepared a report on the future of the international financial architecture. The task force seems to define "financial architecture" as something that "strengthen[s] crisis prevention and management." But a piece of architecture is a defined whole with known scientific characteristics. It cannot be "architecture" without some basic scientific guiding principles.

The task force identified six principles that it said defined its analysis of the international financial architecture: (1) encouraging emerging economies to intensify their crisis prevention efforts, (2) permitting savings to flow into the countries and be used where they have the best return, (3) promoting burden sharing among private creditors, official debtors, and official creditors when a crisis does occur, (4) increasing the role of market-based incentives in crisis prevention and resolution, (5) making reforms of the architecture a two-way street, with the

major industrial countries of the IMF and the World Bank on areas they are equipped to address.[154]

One cannot prevent something if one does not know its cause. But in this case economists assumed incorrectly that economic crises are caused by financial factors. The financial signals of a poor structural economy are not always reliable and may show up late due to time lags; they are, after all, only a shadow of the real economy. In December 1997, at heavily depreciated exchange rates, we were seeing a big trade surplus of $3.7 billion in South Korea —equivalent to something like 15 percent of its GDP annualized at the postdevaluation exchange rate of 160 won to the dollar. Thailand ran a current-account surplus for several months in 1997. So did Malaysia. But these financial figures were deceptive. The economies of these countries were already collapsing. The only reason short-term capital did not fly out of South Korea fast enough is that financial statistics led to the belief that the economy was still healthy.

In the contentious atmosphere on globalization, not everyone agreed with the task force. Their report stated that they discussed "more radical alternatives which included comprehensive controls on capital flows, the adoption of a single currency, more far-reaching reforms of the IMF (ranging from its abolition to the creation of a much larger and more powerful fund) and the establishment of the new supranational regulatory institutions." It said that the more radical proposals seemed "either undesirable or impractical," and in the end it opted instead for what it characterized as "moderate plus" proposals —proposals that, taken together, would make a significant difference to crisis prevention and management but still have a reasonable chance of acceptance. The task force was in effect seeking a compromise between groups that hold divergent views colored by the political left and right.

But the task force did not achieve acceptance. Take, for example, the sharing of the burden among private creditors, official lenders, and debtors. The "moral hazard" continues to poison the private/public perception of the issues. Dispute persists on the question of who would construct rescue packages to manage crisis—the IMF and governments alone, or the IMF and governments together with private lenders and investors. Some people accuse the private sector of overlending and overinvesting and insist that they therefore have some responsibility for the ruin. Wall Street sees the position differently. It rejects the idea that the private sector does not sustain losses. It will not warmly accept the task force's claim that rescue packages allow private creditors to escape from bad landings at relatively little cost. The task force's report claimed that in recent years the balance between limiting systemic risk and encouraging market discipline has shifted too far toward market discipline. Wall Street will not accept the task force's recommendation based on this assumption.

Wall Street and people in Washington disagree on the public-private responsibility for providing financial data on emerging markets. Private lenders and investors think that the IMF should make public the financial information it obtains. Not only are many emerging markets not always accurate with their information, but the IMF also feels that disclosing information to Wall Street will mean that governments will no longer share politically sensitive or confidential information. But then where is the much talked-about transparency?

The fact is, they are all chasing the shadow. The substance (which is the real economy) can be easily assessed by anyone if and when attention is redirected to assessing micro- and macro-level factor proportions, enabling economists to rescue world economies from the hands of Wall Street and the IMF/World Bank.

There is nothing comprehensive nor scientific about the often talked-about international financial architecture. It is a set of speculative intellectual prescriptions, varying with who is making them, indicating their view about what might or might not help reduce and manage the effects of external financial shocks on emerging economies. All these various proposals share is that they are afterthoughts intended to patch up—albeit unsuccessfully—the basic weaknesses of a global financial structure. They all are also steeped in international politics and diplomacy. As Garten correctly pointed out, "The problems—and remedies—go beyond economics. The world of finance and foreign policy need to be bridged. . . . Better financial diplomacy could ease economic and political turmoil. Countries must 'buy into' the stabilization program at hand which may require extensive negotiations."[155] At a time when all other professional disciplines are seeking more scientific solutions, economics is getting more political because it has sidestepped into finance, with groups and governments fighting for global financial power.

The conventional globalization literature has increasingly become defensive, grudgingly accepting the inevitability of economic crises. The literature is now awash with advice on how to protect oneself from "unexpected" shocks. The task force spoke of countries joining a "Good Housekeeping Club." Good housekeeping involves, among other things, "holding enough international reserves and arranging contingent credit lines so that there is enough liquidity on hand to cushion against unexpected adverse shocks." Feldstein counseled the need for self-protection, which he said requires more than avoiding bad policies that make a currency crisis inevitable. "Liquidity," he said, "is the key to financial self-help." Liquidity provides a cushion in times of crisis, and, as he said, "like death and taxes, international economic crisis cannot be avoided."[156] But Feldstein's prescriptions make it obvious that most underdeveloped countries now forced to maintain an open economy have little chance of protecting their economies against the ravages of global financial problems. They routinely have poor reserves and no contingent credit lines.

It is clear in retrospect that the East Asian countries were shortchanged, though it may be argued that they deserved what they got. The IMF pressured these countries to open to capital even when they were awash in domestic savings. The IMF sought to impose free market reforms but did little to organize debt rescheduling negotiations, preferring to provide bail-out funds in return for structural and institutional reforms. Tobin wrote, "South Koreans and other Asian countries—like Mexico in 1994–95—are . . . but victims of a flawed . . . system . . . that under U.S. leadership . . . gives mobility of capital priority over all considerations." Tobin concluded, "Events like these in Southeast Asia call into question claims that liberalization and globalization of financial systems are the path to prosperity and progress."[157] Bhagwati observed that the IMF "want[s] the ability to take capital in and out freely. It also ties in to IMF's own desires which is to act as the lender of last resort. So IMF finally gets a role for itself, which is underpinned by maintaining the complete freedom of capital account."[158] We had already made similar observations about the World Bank with regard to foreign aid in Chapter 6.

It is clear that the IMF, the World Bank, Wall Street, and aid givers, all backed by governments and multinational corporations in the advanced economies, are pushing capital into emerging and poor countries for their own reasons. They are in effect creating economic structural imbalances that retard economic development and growth prospects in these countries.

Who are the winners? asked Wade and Veneroso. They pointed out that the IMF's prescriptions for reshaping Asian financial systems opted for a regime of higher interest rates, which tipped many companies with high debt/equity ratios into bankruptcy. Meeting Western standards of debt/equity ratio, as the IMF insisted, meant a swap of debt for equity that implied foreign ownership positions in Asian firms and banks. The devaluation has enabled foreign companies and individuals to pick up companies and stocks at what Wade and Veneroso called "fire-sale prices" or—in the current Korean phrase, reflecting a political backlash—"IMF cold wave prices." Wade and Veneroso say that "the combination of massive devaluations, IMF pushed financial liberalization, IMF-facilitated recovery may even precipitate the biggest peacetime transfer of assets from domestic to foreign owners in the last fifty years anywhere in the world, dwarfing the transfers from domestic to US owners that occurred in similar situations in Latin America in the 1980s or in Mexico after 1994." They recalled the axiom, attributed to Andrew Mellon, that "in a depression, assets return to their rightful owners'."[159]

The Way Forward

Globalization is basically a Western product for sale. Said Micklethwart and Woodbridge: "The process [of globalization] has not to do only with economic efficiency. It has also to do with international freedom. Globalization offers the chance to fulfill (or at least come considerably closer to fulfilling) the goals that classical liberal philosophers identified several centuries ago and which still underpin Western democracy."[160]

Involving the free movement of capital, globalization has different effects in different environments. Capital moving from one advanced economy to another adds to economic growth in the capital-receiving economy, and the owner of the capital earns a high return. Trade between advanced economies is set to increase and yield great benefits to participating trade partners. On the other hand, capital moving into underdeveloped economies with differing factor proportions from those of the advanced economies distorts and exacerbates their structural imbalances, leading to economic hemorrhages (masked by cyclical bursts of growth) that kill off any chances of their attaining higher sustainable growth. When a financial crisis occurs in emerging markets, a large proportion of their population is thrown into poverty, and people lose most of the gains made during the boom, with consequent social and political disruption.

The theory of factor proportions stays immutable. The structural imbalance that can be caused by too much capital is basically the same whether the capital (production aid) is owned by nationals or foreigners, private or public. It means that it does not make any difference, from a purely scientific economic standpoint, whether the ownership of companies or financial institutions in East Asia has changed hands from Asians to foreigners. Privatization is therefore not the cure for low economic performance. The basic economic structure of Asian economies has not changed, as all indications are that it is basically back to business as usual, with a few cosmetic but largely irrelevant financial and political changes. Because under globalization emerging economies remain inherently unbalanced, their future is not promising. Those who have used the fall of the Asian economy to acquire new ownership stakes face basically the same future the Asians did prior to 1997.

What is needed is time for the emerging and underdeveloped countries to put their economies on the path to sustainable growth through the development and mobilization of their factor resources. At the moment, emerging markets are relatively small boats in a turbulent sea.[161] If the poor countries can attain rapid growth and close the widening gap between them and the advanced countries, it will not be through trade and capital mobility. The irony is that in such a situation, those now seeking to invest in and trade with emerging economies would reap higher and more assured returns than they are presently getting under the present globalization paradigm. Real investors want stable economies in which to invest, not just short-term gain.

In the situation we are contemplating, there are still vast opportunities for countries to work together. The nature of international cooperation will need to change. So far, regrettably, economic relations between rich and poor countries have been shaped by the politics of finance. The promise of aid, or the threat of withdrawing it, has often been used by the rich countries to get the poor countries to do their bidding. But in the new relationship, cooperation and exchanges in science will need to be enhanced in order to enrich the science of factors and factor proportions (technology), enabling each country to better appreciate what its choices are. The solving of common problems such as disease, pollution, and war will continue to draw on cooperation between peoples.

Many policy makers in the West mean well when they press for faster globalization. The idea, however, that to leave poor countries to rely on themselves and solve their economic problems is wicked and selfish has to give way to the acceptance that nature (science) made it that way. It means, therefore, that the present drive for globalization is premature and is harmful to the prospects of achieving worldwide prosperity.

8

The U.S. Economy

A Historical Perspective

Unlike most of the advanced countries whose economic beginnings are shrouded in history, the U.S. economy has a discernible beginning because we know reasonably well that the first immigrants into what was essentially a virgin continent arrived in the early seventeenth century. Almost from the start, these immigrants were presented with a vast continent, irrigated by numberless rivers intersecting land and mountains that were rich in forest products and minerals. The flow of immigrants rose in good times and fell in bad times. It was also dependent on bad times and good times, both economic and political, in mother Europe.

Literature is replete with historians who argue that the immigrants that came to the United States were especially enterprising and were there simply seeking economic opportunities and economic freedom. Cochran and Miller claimed in their book *Age of Enterprise,* "We have been primarily a business people, and business has been most important in our lives. Abstracting colorful aspects of our culture, historians have interpreted them naively in terms of profit motive." In doing so, the historians "have ignored the most dramatic story in our history, the story of business enterprise itself, the story of the institutions, and their impact upon the American society."[1] John Chamberlain rephrased this sentiment when he claimed that America's success story owes much to its selective inheritance from the old world. "In crossing the Atlantic the 'new men' of America left behind them much that was to impede European development in the seventeenth and eighteenth century— vestiges of master-servant relationships, traditions of monarchical allegiance, a society of status and classes as opposed to a society of free men. . . . And in offering protection for the individual in all his rights, the Founders recognized that economic and political liberties stand or fall together . . . the stress almost from the start was on the individual— and the individual tended to make his own decisions if only because he could walk off into the forest if unsatisfied."[2]

The vast territory that was to become America was a challenge to its initial European inhabitants. The five million or so Americans in the late eighteenth century were scattered over an enormous country. Communications were poor. There were no railroads, no canals. American provincialism had its origin in this diverse but largely isolated living. Out of necessity, groups and units had to learn how to be self-sufficient. Naturally most of the colonial population was young. The cheapness of land encouraged people to marry early and strike out on their own. Therefore much economic activity was concentrated in home production and based on the use of production factors that were immediately available—largely wood. There was so much wood available that everything from door latches to ships were constructed from timber. Iron was imported and expensive in the early years; as time went on, finished metal products started appearing but were scarce, and mills and other industrial facilities remained small.

The diversity of industrial activity can be gleaned from the account of one of the earliest advocates of American manufacturing in 1794. "In the midland of Pennsylvania, many precious manufacturers have resulted from a flourishing agriculture and immediately on their birth have contributed to the property of the cultivators. The borough of Lancaster which is one of the largest inland towns in the United States is only sixty-six miles from a seaport, and ten from any practiced boat navigation. The number of families was in 1786 about 700 of whom 234 were manufacturers. The following is a list of them: 14 hatters, 36 shoemakers, 4 tanners, 17 saddlers, 25 tailors, 25 weavers of woolen, linen and cotton cloth, 3 stocking weavers, 25 white and blacksmiths, 6 wheel wrights, 11 coopers, 6 clock and watch makers, 6 tobacco and snuff manufacturers, 4 dyers, 7 gunsmiths, 5 rope makers, 4 thinners, 2 brass founders, 3 skin dressers, 1 brush maker, 7 turners, 7 nail makers, 5 silversmiths, 3 potters, 3 brewers, 3 copper smiths, 2 printers in English and German. There were in 1786 also within 39 miles of the town, 17 furnaces, forges, rolling mills, slitting mills, and within 10 miles of it, 18 grain mills, 16 saw mills, 1 fulling mill, 4 oil mills, 5 hemp mills, 2 boring and grinding mills for gun barrels, and 18 tanneries."[3] Lacking economic links with other centers of population, communities needed to be self-contained.

Improvements of roads and harbors lagged far behind European standards until the end of the colonial period.[4] The English political leaders, as we will discuss later, promoted legislation that hindered the export of tools and machinery from the home country. English or colonials who had savings to invest often preferred the safer investments in British firms.[5] As a result, "new technologies of the Industrial Revolution found fertile ground . . . the need for self-sufficiency in an age of slow and intermittent communication gave rise to local manufacturer.

. . . Every family had its workshop and anvil, its gadgets and cunning improvements."[6] A few machines came from England, but only a few, and the Americans were soon adapting them for their factor availability. It was estimated that by 1810 the gross value of American manufactures was just under $200 million.[7]

These developments were indeed the early beginnings of the U.S. economic personality, which later was to emerge as a force to be reckoned with. The fact that the early economy of the United States did not receive large doses of capital equipment nor foreign investment enabled it to proceed on factor proportions dependent on its factor endowments.

Even before the new U.S. government was set up in 1785, men such as Alexander Hamilton and Tench Cox had urged Americans to give up communal self-sufficiency for specialization and the national exchange of commodities. A little later, people such as Albert Gallatin, Matthew Carey, and Henry Clay took up the old arguments, urging their fellow Americans to diversify their economy, separating manufacturing from agriculture and removing the factory from the home. "The main obstacle was transport. However, between the founding of the federal republic and its near extinction in the Civil War, transport facilities were provided with startling rapidity. First were the toll roads, then the canals, then the rise of the river and lake steamers, then the first real roads which later were to consolidate and merge into huge transcontinental systems. With all these were increasing movement of people to the West. The land boom accelerated as new towns sprang into being in the West. Land speculation became rife. In accordance with the state of the land boom, banks flourished or failed and the currency alternately expanded or contracted. . . . Western 'currency' was seldom at a par with eastern bank notes."[8]

The expansion of transport in all its facets was such that by 1840 there were more than three hundred railway companies in the United States with about 3,300 miles of track. The great canal-building era (1815 to 1843) saw about $31 million in investments, nearly three-quarters of which were from government sources. In a second wave between 1843 and 1860 there was about $66 million in investment, nearly two-thirds from government. These gigantic leaps in transport were not a cause of America's economic growth by themselves.[9] But they did help to integrate the American market and above all to link America's diverse factor endowments into one economy.

The American colonies' economy and particularly their relations with other countries were regulated by the imperial authority. The Acts of Trade and Navigation of 1651, 1660, and 1663 were intended to establish the colonies' relationship with Britain. The colony was to export only certain commodities—sugar, tobacco, cotton, indigo, ginger, and various dye woods—and these were to be exported only to England or destinations within its empire. The list was from time to time lengthened and amended; for example, Scotland was added as a legal destination after 1707. Manufactured goods composed the bulk of England's exports to the colony. English manufacturers were granted special advantages over other European manufacturers in British American markets. The British manufacturers felt that the colonies should not undertake what they called "duplicate production" of manufactured goods. In 1699, a law was passed making it illegal for the colony to export wool, wool yarn, or finished wool products to any foreign country or even other colonies. Wool production in the colonies was limited to personal use or local trade. The Hat Act of 1732 prohibited colonial export of hats. Toward midcentury, pig and bar iron were admitted duty free into England, but colonial manufacture of finished iron products was forbidden. Walton and Rockoff have observed that these were the only prohibitive laws directed at colonial manufacturing, indicating Britain's lack

of fear of American competition. It was thought that England enjoyed a distinct comparative advantage in manufacturing and that the colonies' comparative advantage lay overwhelmingly in agriculture and other resource-intensive products from the seas and forests.[10] The laws prohibiting colonial manufactures were therefore loosely enforced. But less than a century later the United States had overtaken Britain industrially.

In passing, we note that present-day conventional economics still thrives on the principle of comparative advantage as a basis of the economic relationship between developed and underdeveloped countries. As Walton and Rockoff observed, in other colonial territories (for example, in Africa and India), Britain enforced these industrial restrictions more forcefully. If Britain had enforced these restrictions in America as in other colonial territories, the U.S. economy might not have achieved what it has today. Alternatively, if England had not enforced such restrictions on these other colonies, they could have been further advanced than they are today in developing their economic personalities.

The American Revolution began in April 1775 and lasted more than six years. Coastal trade was curtailed by a British blockade, a lack of vessels, and wartime freight rates. As exports and imports fell, import substitution abounded, and the colonial economy became considerably more self-sufficient.[11] However, this import substitution was based not on the factor proportions of Britain (the original supplier of the manufactured goods) but on those of the colony. There were substantial differences in the capital/labor ratio between Britain and the American colony, with Britain's about 40 to 50 percent higher than the colonies'. In Philadelphia, as an example, nearly four thousand women were employed to spin materials in their homes for newly established textile plants. A sharp increase occurred in the number of artisan workshops, and a similar rise in the production of a wide range of alcoholic beverages. Any capital plant needed was produced in the colonies themselves, as prior to the hostilities the English did not ship any there. This inward-looking self-sufficiency stance imposed by the war further reinforced the growing economic personality of America. It is noteworthy that after independence, U.S. trade was still based largely on export of agricultural products (tobacco, rice, wheat, flour, and maize, etc.), and the country still imported some manufactured goods.

The War of 1812 was largely a naval war, during which the British seized more than a thousand ships and blockaded almost the entire U.S. coast. As exports and imports declined to practically nothing, another boost was given to the United States' growing manufacturing capacity. The war-related spurts in manufacturing provided an important basis for further industrial expansion. Agriculture began to slip from its dominant position in the economy.[12] Thus by the early decades of the nineteenth century, the basic structure of the U.S. economy was substantially changing. Some business historians consider that an "American industrial revolution" occurred about 1820 and that it was well under way within twenty years.[13] Accompanying this was a shift to coal and steam as primary sources of energy, replacing water and wood.

Iron and Industrial Development in America

The transition to iron-based technology is a historical fact of most societies in the world, as we discussed in Chapter 2. How each society made this transition had a lot to do with its subsequent economic development and growth profile. The American colonies' iron industry was for a long time held down by Britain, but by 1775 there were more furnaces and forges in America than in England and Wales. It is estimated that America was then producing a seventh of the world's output of pig iron and iron bars.[14]

Utilizing new processes for puddling and rolling iron invented by Henry Cort in the 1780s, the British established a significant lead in the unfolding industrial revolution. So even into the early part of the nineteenth century, American ax makers, sewing machine makers, and railroad builders were dependent on British sources for good iron. The first ironworks in the United States, at Falling Creek in Virginia, was destroyed by Indians in 1622, but the iron age in America can be said to go back to the New England Puritans, who had a small blast furnace for the production of metals they needed for pots, skillets, and andirons. The Saugus works was producing some eight tons of iron a week by 1648. Over this period, the various activities in the industry have been described as "small-time stuff" providing "barely enough metal for use in blacksmiths' shops." However, Robert Erstead's development of the American Iron Company in 1771 came in time to provide iron for Washington's armies.[15] Much of the early American iron industry had to reckon with the British government's reprisals. J. Leander Bishop spoke eloquently of the "dexterity of Americans in the manufacture of scythes, axes, nails, etc.," but, "the flood of foreign iron . . . at the close of the war" kept American production from growing.[16] In effect, the American colonies' industrial development was stunted by a trade relationship in which manufactures from Britain were exchanged for natural-resource-based products. What the colony needed was more import substitution, and that is what it set out to do, utilizing factor proportions that suited its factor endowments.

We will continue with the iron industry to illustrate what happened. During the second half of the eighteenth century Britain led in major iron technical innovations: the use of mineral coal in place of charcoal as a blast furnace fuel, refinement of pig iron in the reverberatory furnace by puddling instead of in the open forge of ancient usage, and the use of grooved rolls in place of the hammer as forging equipment. One would have expected that when Americans had their freedom, they would have leapt to import plant from Britain in order to build up their iron industry, but they did not. Rather, they opted to develop along the lines best suited to their needs. For example, the iron manufacture for which Pittsburgh later came to be famous had its origins in the blacksmithing business attracted to that city by the needs of the westward-moving immigrants of those days.[17]

Explaining what happened in the iron industry, Hunter commented, "It is axiomatic that the results of European experience have rarely been incorporated unchanged in American life but have undergone greater or less modification in the process of assimilation." More pointedly, he observed that "the fact of transfer and introduction can by no means be taken as an indication of the existence of an urgent need for the thing transferred nor a guarantee of its general adoption or acceptance." Unfortunately, this theme underlies much of present-day conventional wisdom as to what constitutes technology transfer from developed to underdeveloped economies. Hunter argued that numerous monographic studies on U.S. industry have shown the danger of extending generalizations outside the field in which the monographs were originally formulated: "The study of each industry must be approached inductively in order that circumstances and conditions peculiar to it may be seen and their influence properly evaluated."[18]

Hunter pointed out that most American economic historians have, in their quest to generalize, ignored the technical problems posed by the refining of pig iron and rolling. They have instead focused on the financial issues of securing coke of the proper quality as part of evolving blast furnace techniques. The conventional literature, as will be seen, concentrated almost exclusively on production—for example, increasing the size of blast furnaces—and ignored other very important factors such as conditions con-

trolling the consumption and use of the product.[19] Hunter argued that conventional economic thinking would expect that the difficulties encountered in the introduction of these processes in the United States could be measured by the extent of the differences between the old and improved processes, and that the order of their diffusion would be the order of their original development.

This did not happen in the United States. Of the three British innovations, the use of mineral coal in place of charcoal as a blast furnace fuel would have been the easiest to adopt in the United States. After all, the country had lots of coal (40 percent of the world's known reserves, compared to 35 percent for the whole of Europe). There were no real obstacles, such as the introduction of unfamiliar processes or difficulty in adapting it to local conditions and materials. But as it turned out, it was the use of mineral coal in place of charcoal that was the last of the three innovations that was adopted in America. The first that was adopted in the growing iron industry center of Pittsburgh was rolling, in 1812. The first rolling mill was established to roll from the larger merchant bars or from bloom sheet iron to be used in the manufacture of nail rods, shovels, and other hardware. The use of grooved rolls for the production of bar iron took place as early as 1814 in a wire factory, but the first full-fledged rolling mill at Pittsburgh, rolling bar as well as sheet iron, was established in 1818–19. Except for a small fraction of the product that was made into nails, no finished products were produced here. The emphasis was on producing semifinished iron in bars and sheets of various sizes. The pace was being dictated by the increasing product variety demanded in the market. The roll in the rolling mill substituted for the vertically directed blows of the trip hammer, which required more labor input than the rolling process. In the preliminary stages of the introduction of the rolling mill, the hammer was still used to separate the iron from the slag. Gradually the use of the hammer was eliminated by the alligator and rotary types of squeezers, introduced in the 1840s. In short, the rolling mill was adopted at a time when the market for iron goods was expanding and getting more varied. Labor was beginning to be scarce. The rolling mill fitted the needs.

The puddling process came into vogue much more slowly than rolling. The refinement of pig iron by puddling in America was not essentially different from the mode of refinement previously in use, although the equipment and the fuel used were quite unlike those of the process it displaced. A lot of experimentation was done in the United States in order to modify the original British Cort puddling into a viable alternative to iron produced from the rural Juniata region of Pennsylvania.

The use of mineral coal (in particular bituminous coal) in place of charcoal was another matter. England did not have the wood and forest resources the United States had. On the other hand, the *Pittsburgh Gazette* claimed, "Both wood and coal are so abundant [in the United States] that they have scarcely any value beyond the cost of getting them to market and in neighborhoods where there are no iron works, from $10 to $15 an acre is paid to clear and burn off the land."[20] Another commentator at the time stated, "In the Western States, many charcoal furnaces are in operation and there is no limit to their extension, so far as raw material, wood and ore are concerned."[21] Wood was also easier to access than coal. Swank in an 1892 book titled *History of the Manufacture of Iron in All Ages* explained why, despite the availability of bituminous coal and despite the established British innovation replacing charcoal with mineral coal, blast furnaces in America stayed with charcoal: "There was a lack of transportation facilities for bringing iron ore and coke together; not all bituminous coal that had been discovered was suitable for making coke; the manufacture of coke was not well understood; the country had an abundance of timber for the supply of char-

coal, and finally a prejudice existed in favor of charcoal pig iron and of bar iron hammered in charcoal forges." In 1916 Clark explained that the application of bituminous coal and coke to the manufacture of pig iron, "common in Great Britain for many years[,] was deferred in America by the abundance of charcoal, the conservatism of iron-masters, and prejudice in favor of charcoal iron and lack of good coking coal, and by the fact that suitable soft coal did not, like anthracite[,] lie immediately tributary to developed iron mines and established furnace districts."[22] It is evident that America did not feel a strong need or desire to use British technical expertise in this instance (though if this situation occurred in the present day, the World Bank would be rushing to give America loans to purchase British plant and machinery to enable it to develop bituminous-coal-based blast furnaces).

Hunter thought Swank's additional claim that the manufacture of coke from bituminous coal was not well understood in America was merely an excuse.[23] In regard to transport, the Americans could have developed the transport facilities if that was the sole obstacle to bringing iron ore and coke together. Hunter maintained that the issue of lack of transport was not as critical as Swank made it out to be, as many ore-bearing areas were often not far from bituminous coal "measures."[24] The prejudice (as Swank called it) and conservatism (as Clark called it) are in effect a factor-proportions mode of thinking, in which a country should exploit what it has in abundance and shun techniques that depend on factors suitable to another country.

Clark pointed out that sources of bituminous coal, unlike sources of anthracite coal, were not particularly close to developed iron mines and established furnace districts. This means that anthracite coal was more immediately available to those producing pig iron. So the Americans' next step was not to bituminous coal but to anthracite coal.

As far back as 1768, one Obadiah Gore successfully used anthracite in blacksmithing. In 1805, James Woodhouse was said to have demonstrated that anthracite can be burned in an air furnace. In 1808, Jesse Fell designed a grate that was satisfactory for burning anthracite. In 1813, Joshua Malin used anthracite to melt several hundred tons of pig iron. By 1818, anthracite-burning stoves made by Texler Bethlehem were being sold in the Wyoming Valley. In 1828, James Neilson patented his hot-blast stove in Britain. In 1829, the Collin Company, a celebrated ax maker in Collinsville, Connecticut, replaced charcoal with anthracite in forge fires. By redesigning the firebox and adding a forced-draft blower to the English-designed puddling furnace (which was meant for bituminous coal), Americans added to the variety of equipment they had for anthracite-based furnaces. Americans achieved what was considered impractical in Britain and made possible large-scale production of iron in eastern Pennsylvania, where the bituminous coal needed for conventional puddling furnaces was not available.[25]

As is normal with economic activities that derive from appropriate factor proportions, the advent of stoves and gates suitable for burning anthracite in America created new opportunities. Proprietors of the new canal and railways systems benefited from the increased traffic between the coal fields and major eastern cities. Established industries based on water power adopted anthracite for auxiliary power to be used in case of drought or to expand the capacity of an existing plant beyond what could be sustained by its water source. As cheap coal became available in urban centers, proprietors of water-power-based industries were able to take advantage of urban settings for their works. By 1854, iron smelted with anthracite accounted for 41 percent of all pig iron made in the United States.[26]

Up to about 1859, the iron industry in America was controlled and conditioned by the needs and requirements of a pioneer agricultural population, which were met to a large extent by forges and rolling mills without the mediation of manufactories of finished iron products. The principal function of the manufacturer of wrought iron was to supply rural ironworkers, blacksmiths by profession or necessity, with bar iron to be shaped to meet the needs of the American farmer, wagoneer, and mill owner. This period in the iron industry in America has been called the agricultural era.[27] The equipment was simple and the process essentially labor- and material-intensive. For example, in Missouri, where charcoal was in use, 150 bushels of charcoal were used to produce a ton of product, whereas only 70 bushels of coal would have been required.[28] On the basis of cost at the time, the coal could have been cheaper. It can be said that up to about 1850 substantial increases in manufacturing output (from $20 million in 1810 to just under $2 billion in 1860) were achieved by craftsmen operating independently or in small groups and using little capital but significant amounts of raw material and labor-intensive techniques.[29]

The industrial era can be said to have been started with the rise of railways. First, the demand for rail iron was relatively large. Second, the need for specialization was becoming apparent. Whereas the blacksmith, a worker of iron in general, required raw material possessing a wide range of properties and therefore of the highest grade, the manufacturer of finished goods needed iron with specific properties. There arose, therefore, a demand for special grades of iron. Third, rails could be made from a wide variety of ores of different qualities. According to the *Pittsburgh Gazette* (July 13, 1853) the demand for railway iron was so great that it could absorb all the poor qualities of metal in the market.

By the late 1840s, the iron industry entered the stage of factories. New establishments dwarfed those of a quarter century earlier, and some of them passed beyond what could be called the mill stage.[30] The industry diversified as new demands were created in new areas such as locomotives, rolling stock, cars, sheet and boiler iron, and the petroleum industry. Blast furnaces, foundries, and rolling mills of increasingly large capacities emerged.

Similar developments were taking place in other branches of industry. Walton and Rockoff described the cross-fertilization arising from the growth of the iron industry in the following words: "How one industry could adopt new methods as a consequence of progress in another [in this case iron] is shown by the fact that as the sewing machine was produced on a quantity basis, the boot and the shoe industry developed factory characteristics. Carriages, wagons and even farm implements were eventually produced in large numbers."[31]

Further impetus in the iron industry derived from the introduction of the Bessemer process from England in the 1860s. Bessemer steel had greater tensile strength and hardness than wrought iron. The principles embodied in the Bessemer process had been discovered through trial and error by Bessemer and an American working independently. By 1880, more and more mass-produced steel was being incorporated into products other than rails: factory and office machinery, shops, construction and mining equipment, farm implements, cans, wire, bicycles, girders for skyscrapers, and after 1900 automobiles. Continuing improvements in steelmaking, such as the development of the open hearth process in Germany, increased the range of applications, including those in which high speeds and close tolerances were involved.[32] Steel production thereafter expanded phenomenally, from under 1.25 million tons in 1880 to over 10 million tons in 1900 and 26 million tons in 1910. By the turn of the twentieth century, the United States accounted for over one-third of the world's steel. In this key industry, America had a great advantage due to its abundance of iron ore and coal.

U.S. Economic Emergence

Despite rapid growth in all sectors of its economy, the United States remained a predominantly rural nation throughout the nineteenth century. This is in part because much manufacturing took place in what were essentially rural areas. The iron industry was mainly rural-based until the Civil War. Other industries were employing easily available factors of cheap and efficient water power and so remained rural even longer. Although steam engines gradually encroached on water power, it was the advent of central electricity-generating stations that caused the decline of rural-based industries. The westward movement continued after the Civil War, encouraged by the Homestead Act and the opening of the West by railways. By 1890, the United States had become the world's foremost industrial nation.[33] By 1910, the quantity of goods poured out by its factories was nearly twice that of Germany. In 1913, the United States accounted for more than one-third of the world's industrial production.

The central question is what caused the United States to achieve such fast growth. England provides the ideal benchmark, being the mother country of the United States. An abundance of literature asserts that the U.S. economy overtook that of England by the end of the nineteenth century because of its greater productivity. There are serious weaknesses in the productivity explanation, to which we shall return later. But for the moment, we need to examine the various reasons why people say that the U.S. economy achieved such a high productivity profile over these years.

Almost all economic historians who write on this topic seem to emphasize that the United States had abundant materials and scarcity of labor at the time. But that is where the agreement stops. We shall return to this later. A few economic historians, however, do not regard the abundance of raw materials and scarcity of labor as the essence of America's rapid economic growth. For example, Uselding argued that substitution between the factors of labor and capital played relatively little role in achieving high labor productivity in the U.S. economy between 1839 and 1899. In fact, it contributed less than 10 percent of the measured labor productivity of the United States in the last half of the nineteenth century. He argued that those looking at the divergence in technological development between the United States and Great Britain have tended to ignore the magnitude of two effects operating within the pre–Civil War American economy. The first is what he called the "social savings" accruing to the U.S. economy as a result of "having that portion of its productive population added by net immigration being raised to or near productive age by resources of an external economy, e.g., England, Ireland, Germany, etc." The second effect is that each immigrant entering the labor force, by virtue of such skills as he might possess, represented a transfer of human capital. He argued that when the social savings and human capital import were taken into consideration, less than 10 percent of the measured increase in labor productivity between 1850 and 1900 was attributable to factor substitution.[34] He later revised this conclusion: "For the period 1856–1900 factor substitution was consistent with something on the order of one-third to one-half of the increase in labor productivity [in the United States] when the advancing technology is viewed as bringing about variable and increasing rates of largely unbiased technological progress. . . . Substitution per se may not have been the most important element in productivity growth during the nineteenth century."[35] In effect, Uselding was adopting a TFP approach, saying it was not the physical factors of labor and capital that gave America its rapid economic growth, but human capital imported from outside as well the enabling environment so created.

Uselding got it wrong. As we showed in earlier chapters, what Uselding seems to be labeling as nonmaterial factors, apart from labor and capital, is in fact material in the context of a three-factor economic analysis. We shall return to this later. Uselding, like many other economists, abandoned

scientific inquiry by delving into nonscientific issues such as the financial considerations of prices, wages, and elasticities. Basic scientific economic analysis, being an inquiry into nature, does not introduce prices. Uselding admitted that "factor price ratios in money terms did not fairly represent the underlying marginal production ratios . . . changes in relative factor shares and relative factor prices may be imperfect indicators of the extent of substitution under certain conditions."[36] If, for example, the price of material increases, the nonscientific researcher will claim that the material factor input relative to other factors in a process has increased when in fact the amount of material input has not changed at all. Accordingly, the calculations on which Uselding based his studies are not scientific and not helpful.

Uselding's argument that social savings and human capital input due to immigration were a major source of productivity growth is questionable from the facts available. Skilled immigrants were less than 10 percent of total immigration in the first half of the nineteenth century. The bulk of the immigrants were officially classed as having no occupation—they were farmers, servants, and laborers. Against this background, it could not be claimed that America derived social savings or that it enjoyed higher human capital input in comparison with a position in which the total population at the time increased organically. It is true that American businesses profited financially from a seemingly inexhaustible supply of unskilled and semiskilled immigrants. New arrivals, whatever their national origins, largely filled the ranks of unskilled labor.[37] U.S. firms by the turn of the century, on the other hand, spent a lot of resources on the methodical recruitment and training of existing employees (the bulk of them immigrants) for more advanced and skilled positions.[38] While we can agree with Uselding that capital-labor substitution alone did not occupy the commanding heights ascribed to it in the United States, we disagree that the commanding heights belonged to the social savings and human capital input. Rather, the most important factor most probably was substitutions with the third factor, material.

We now return to the other explanations provided by economists for the rapid growth of the American economy. There are those who are so taken by the abundance of America's natural resources at the time that they present in sophisticated economic language what is basically the layman's conviction that if two people possess different quantities of wood, the one with the larger quantity will be able to put up a bigger house than the one with the smaller quantity. The one with the greater variety of wood will be able to put up a greater variety of structures.

Thus, Abramovitz and David stated that America's advantage stemmed first from "America's more abundant and cheap supplies of primary materials." They argued that such supplies had a more important bearing on the country's growth potential in the nineteenth and early twentieth centuries than they have had since that time, because food at the time constituted a larger share of consumer expenditure and GDP, and resources devoted to agriculture were a larger share of the total than they have been since then. They maintained that the profusion of forest resources facilitated the extravagant use of wood and iron in the manufacture of a wide range of finished goods and lowered their costs. Minerals—coal, iron, copper, and others—helped America to forge ahead. By combining what they called "technological borrowing" from abroad with the United States' extensive resources, the country, they said, embarked upon the exploration of a new "technological trajectory." In this trajectory, the cost of minerals "bulked larger in the total costs of finished goods than subsequently came to be true." Cheap supplies of these primary materials underlay America's growing comparative advantage as an exporter of natural-resource-intensive manufactures during the period 1880–1929.[39]

The authors' narrow outlook is further illustrated by their assertion that the "minerals-based, resource-intensive technology" proved to be what they called "the dominant path of technical progress in all the presently advanced countries." They attributed America's advantages to that country's embarking wholeheartedly on a path of infrastructural investments so as "to explore, develop and reduce the costs of access to her mineral resource deposits." They claimed that Europe as a whole possessed known reserves of a number of key minerals that were in 1910 as large as those identified in North America, and in 1913 the continent's rate of production of iron ore, coal, and bauxite exceeded that of the United States. When it came to other minerals, however, America was outproducing the whole of Europe, including Russia. They asserted that "there was no nation in Europe—to say nothing of Japan—that approached the United States in the variety of richness of mineral resources that actually had been developed, rather than remaining in 'reserve' status."

Brenner observed that it was the combination of these factors (that is, some social tracts in the United States that encouraged entrepreneurship) with the country's fortunate wealth of natural resources that helped the United States of America to develop from a thinly populated country into the economically most advanced country in the world within the relatively short period of less than 150 years. "In the sense that it is true that the economic progress of the United States was largely due to the abundance of natural resources, because had it not been for the large iron and coal resources, there would have been little chance of the machinery industry to develop the way it did."[40]

Brenner too got the issue wrong. What is of interest economically is not the abundance of natural resources per se, but the resources/population ratio. If the United States at the time was highly populated, it would not have abundant resources in relative terms. It is wrong to claim that because natural resources were in abundance, goods produced with those resources would necessarily be cheap, as one has to consider other cost elements. For example, the cost of obtaining such natural resources may be high, as in the case of deeply buried veins of coal. Furthermore, a scientific analysis of the economic issues involved has nothing to do with the cheapness or costliness of the natural resources. Abramovitz and David seem to have thought of natural resources mainly in terms of minerals, and so they focused mainly on mineral-heavy (supposedly capital-intensive) activities as the source of high productivity.

Indeed, we would argue the opposite, namely, that since labor was scarce at the time in the United States, wages were high. Overall production costs were high and forced industries to seek means of increasing their efficiency.[41] Abramovitz and David were wrong that America during the relevant periods in the eighteenth and nineteenth centuries depended on exports of manufactured goods for their economic growth. American exports never matched those of England during the period. Abundant land and rich natural resources may help explain why the United States (with a small population) had a higher per capita income than Europe but do not in themselves explain America's higher growth rate.[42]

Ratner, Soltow, and Sylla have correctly reminded us that large areas of the world have at one time or another in the last two centuries (and even now) been in very much the same position in respect to natural resources as was the United States in 1790 but have produced fewer advances in technological and economic development.[43] Many Third World countries are obvious examples.

The majority of economic historians (unlike Abramovitz and David, who look to the abundance of natural resources) see capital formation as the key to America's rapid economic growth, because capital growth is supposed to spur rapid growth of productivity. For example, Davis and colleagues estimated that in constant dollars, capital per per-

Table 8.1

Labor Productivity Changes in the U.S. Northeast, 1820–1860

Capital-intensive industries	% Change in labor productivity
Cotton textiles	2.2–3.3
Iron	1.5–1.7
Liquors	1.7–1.9
Flour/grist mills	0.6–0.7
Paper	4.3–5.5
Tanning	1.2–1.7
Wool textiles	2.7–2.8

Other industries	% Change in labor productivity
Boots/shoes	2.0–2.1
Coaches/harnesses	2.0–2.4
Furniture/woodwork	2.9–3.0
Glass	2.5
Hats	2.4–2.5
Tobacco	0.1–2.4

Source: K. L. Sokoloff, "Productivity Growth in Manufacturing During Early Industrialization: Evidence from the American Northeast, 1820–1860," in S. Engerman and R. Gallman. eds., *Long-Term Factors in American Economic Growth* (Chicago: University of Chicago Press, 1986), p. 698.

son in the United States increased about three times (from $2,100 to $6,400) over the last three-quarters of the nineteenth century. They concluded, "It is hardly surprising that the productivity of the American worker advanced spectacularly during the period."[44] Claims and explanations such as this still, unfortunately, dominate conventional economic literature.

Table 8.1 is the result of a study of productivity in the U.S. Northeast, 1820–1860, showing comparable changes in productivity between capital-intensive industries and other industries.

Walton and Rockoff comment that the "comparable rates of advance of labor productivity by both categories of industries would suggest that capital deepening was not a prerequisite to higher output per worker nor were high rates only for a few industries. A wide range of manufacturing industries exhibited high productivity rates, even shops, mills and small firms with limited mechanization and primitive power sources." They concluded, "This reinforces the perspective of economic growth as the cumulative impact of many incremental advances throughout the economy."[45]

We therefore can say that the enormous growth of the American economy over this period was due not to capital deepening, as Davis had thought, nor to America's abundant natural resources, as Abramovitz and David have claimed.

What Walton and Rockoff in typically nonscientific language called "primitive" power sources is what Habakkuk correctly interpreted as Americans' attempt to substitute material (natural resources such as water power and steam) for capital and labor.[46]

The pioneering study of factor substitution in the comparative position of America and England in the nineteenth century was undertaken by Habakkuk in his book, *American and British Technology in the Nineteenth Century*. Nineteenth-century America was short on labor but well endowed in land (natural resources), while England was short on natural resources but relatively abundant in labor. Habakkuk's basic labor scarcity hypothesis was intended to explain the rapid economic growth of nineteenth-century America.

In a broader context, the hypothesis is that factor scarcity is an important reason for the characteristic bias of technology change and that successful substitution for the relatively scarce factor should account for a substantial proportion of productivity gains in any economy. In short, according to this hypothesis, America grew rapidly because over time Americans sought to substitute for their scarce labor. Habakkuk's general line of argument is that "the high productivity of American industrial labor was due principally to the fact that it was combined with richer natural resources, rather than with capital, though sometimes more capital per head may have been technically necessary to combine labor with the resources." He was of the view that the Ameri-

can entrepreneur at the time consciously reflected on the resource-saving characteristics of different techniques: "Investment may have adopted itself to relative factor-scarcities by a process of natural as well as of conscious selection." He then made a statement of great significance: "If some manufacturers, for whatever reason, adopted improvements which were more appropriate to the factor endowment of the economy, these men fared better than those that made a contrary choice. They competed more successfully in product and factor markets and by expanding their operations came in time to constitute a larger share of their industry. Moreover, they brought influence to bear not only via the market but by force of example. Their success inspired imitators and shaped entrepreneurial attitudes toward the more likely lines of development."[47]

Habakkuk was saying that labor productivity was as much a matter of natural resources as capital, differing from conventional economists who put capital on top of the pile. He was also saying that the attitude of Americans at the time toward factor substitution was born not just out of rational market cost analysis but from natural and conscious selection. Habakkuk's views run very close to the basic principles of economic development and growth through the adoption of the natural factor proportions of the economy.

What happened in the United States was therefore a combination of indigenous technology and foreign-sourced technology, all geared to American-designed and built productive aids and methods based on its factor proportions. For example, inventions in the English textile industry were principally the results of attempts to save labor. Some of them saved labor but necessitated higher capital expense. However, some were able to reduce labor input without a great increase in capital input. Some of these new methods of production suited American circumstances and were rapidly adopted by Americans. For example, the principle of warp-stop motion was invented in England in the 1820s. The idea of automatically renewing the supply of weft was hit upon by William Rossentter about 1860. In another industry, the first practicable continuous mill for the rolling of iron was patented in England and later adopted widely in America. Many other examples abound in shoemaking, woodworking, signaling, and so on. Other inventions were made almost simultaneously in both countries but subsequently developed more rapidly in the United States.

We do not intend to give the impression that changes in techniques in the United States were orchestrated. The pressure to adopt techniques varied in different parts of the economy. It was greater where existing ranges of techniques afforded the least possibility of escape from scarce labor supplies. There were some instances where organizational changes by themselves afforded business considerable relief through better use of labor. In others, some time elapsed before the labor-saving possibilities of techniques imported from England were fully exploited. What mattered is that on the whole the overall tendency was to deal with the overall labor scarcity in the whole economy. Thus the timing of and extent to which the need to save labor bore fruit in the technical progress of America varied from activity to activity.[48] But as one of the commissioners sent to the United States by the English Board of Ordinance in 1854 commented, "The whole energy of the people [of the United States] is devoted to improving and inventing labor-saving machinery." The Britons who reported on the New York Industrial Exhibition stated in a similar tone: "The very difficulty in procuring human labor . . . may be attributed to the extraordinary ingenuity displayed in many of those labor-saving machines whose automatic action so completely supplies the place of the more abundant hand labor of older manufacturing countries."[49]

Habakkuk, himself English, claimed that the absolute amounts of mechanical experience and inge-

nuity, at least in the first half of the nineteenth century, were greater in England. According to him, it would be surprising if most seminal inventions had not been of English origin, but "the point is that the American inferiority on this score was offset, to an increasing extent, by the specific incentive [which the Americans had] to invent which their factor-endowment provided."[50]

In examining the position of choice of techniques at the time, Habakkuk observed that at the time "there were clearly several occasions on which one technique was manifestly superior for any range of factor prices and would therefore have been the most appropriate choice in England as well as America."[51] If we replace "factor prices" with "factor proportions" for reasons by now obvious, Habakkuk is saying that there are several occasions when one technique will be adequate over a range of factor proportions and that it will be up to each country, while using the same basic technique, to adopt factor proportions suited to its factor endowments.[52]

Habakkuk observed that the new techniques of spinning invented in England in the late eighteenth century were so much more productive for all factor combinations than the old spindle that they were the best choice whether in England or America, that is, with labor-poor or labor-abundant factors. He noted that on balance it seemed reasonable "to suppose that in the textile industry [in both countries] the range of possible methods of production was sufficiently wide and continuous in respect of the proportions in which they used capital and labor for the choice of techniques to be responsive to relative factor prices."[53] He noted that technical progress was still more empirical than scientific in that "it depended more on the response to particular and immediate problems of industrial practice than on the autonomous development of scientific knowledge. Technical development was, therefore, likely to take the form of slow modifications of detail, as opposed to spectacular leaps to a new technique decisively superior from the start to its predecessors; even most of the 'great inventions' of the period resolve themselves on close inspection into a perpetual accretion of little details probably having neither beginning, completion nor definable limits. For the same reason, the process of improvement was more likely to be sensitive to the factor needs of the economy in which they were made. . . . The existence of methods of varying the factor intensity of the basic techniques meant that there was usually a fairly continuous range of methods and the method which used a little more capital saved a little more labor. But the relative factor prices [factor proportions] would still be influential even if there were discontinuities."[54] He argued that the conditions of their labor supply gave the Americans a much stronger incentive than the English to leap such a gap in the spectrum of techniques. It is this that was at the heart of America's rapid economic development and growth. It is to be regretted that some present-day American economists cannot conceptualize a development strategy for poor countries to make the factor adjustments that suit their factor endowments, which may be different from those of the United States.

It is noteworthy that America achieved this economic leadership in a closed economy. As Cole put it, the "United States was [by 1850] already well launched on a policy of economic nationalism behind a high tariff wall and abundant natural resources which made it easy to pursue such a policy without lowering standards of life to any appreciable extent, if at all."[55] In short, the United States achieved growth by utilizing its factor endowments, adopting its natural factor proportions. Regretfully, the typical conventional economist now stipulates that countries with abundant natural resources should export them as well as products derived from them in exchange for imports that are ostensibly material-saving.

Substitution for National Resources (Materials)

Habakkuk recognized the effect of the relative abundance of natural resources in America on its technology at the time. He observed that in England and America, there were alternative techniques, the principal difference of which was in their possibilities of substituting between natural resources and either capital or labor. "Some techniques were more important principally because of the proportions in which they used capital and natural resources. Large blast furnaces may have allowed a substitution of capital for raw materials and the application of steam to water transport may have involved the reverse substitution—of capital. . . . There were also techniques in which there was substitution between natural resources and labor; in particular there were possibilities of using power from water and steam instead of manpower. The abundance of land and the nature of the American climate also enabled some substitution of natural resources for capital. The American railways were built in ways which, in effect, substituted land for capital as contrasted with English railways which were built with a disregard for natural obstacles, a disregard which increased their engineering cost. The Americans early developed high-pressure locomotives partly to overcome steep ascents but partly on account of abundance of fuel (wood). It may be that the mechanization of the Massachusetts cotton-textile industry was a substitution not so much of capital for labor as of water-power [natural resources] for labor."[56]

Habakkuk's contributions were significant. He recognized the importance of a three-factor technology-based model of economic development and growth. Unfortunately, in regard to natural resources, he made the common error of most economists dealing with factors. He argued that whatever force his argument—namely, that high labor productivity in the United States was a result not just of the combination of labor with more capital but of a combination with natural resources (materials) —may have, for the latter part of the nineteenth century the three-factor phenomenon was not predominant. He claimed that, with the possible exception of cotton and wood, "natural resources relevant to industrial manufacturing in the United States were at the time cheaper in relation with capital and labor in Britain than in America."[57]

As soon as Habakkuk introduced prices, he moved away from scientific economic theory. He cited examples suggesting that outside the fall line in America, power supplies may well have been dearer and less elastic in relation to labor and capital than in England, since supplies of coal were small. He argued that until the discovery of new sources of iron ore in the 1860s and 1870s, the same might have been true of iron ore. He asserted that "technical possibilities within an industry of substitution between natural resources on the one hand and capital and labor on the other were less in America than the possibilities of substitution between capital and labor."[58] He therefore concluded that he was justified to proceed in his book on the assumption that the dearness of American labor and its substitution by capital was the most realistic way to concentrate in examination on the economic influence on American technology. It seems that the conventional economic view that the replacement of labor by capital constitutes efficiency and is the core of modern technology had its beginnings in the early American economic success with labor-saving techniques.

Early English views on American techniques are useful because at the time there was a rivalry of sorts between England and America in technology. While Britons who admired U.S. techniques were effusive, those that were not expressed their dislike. Industrial exhibitions on both sides of the Atlantic became fashionable after the 1851 Crystal Palace Exhibition in London. The views of two small English commissions that undertook tours of

American industrial districts in 1853 and 1854 as well as another tour by the British Ordinance Department shortly after add to our knowledge of the position at the time. In all three instances, the visitors returned to England with similar views: "The eager resort [in the United States] to machinery wherever it can be applied and the extent to which U.S. industries were organized for mass production in large factories where in England outwork and handicraft persisted."[59] They were critical of the quality of machine tools in the United States but were nevertheless impressed with the production in large numbers of standardized articles in factories characterized by ample workshop room and admirable systems designed to assist the progress of materials through various stages of production.

The commissioners gave a wealth of illustration of the tendencies they noticed. They were impressed with woodworking machines and wrote about factories that produced doors, window frames, or staircases by self-acting machinery at a cost to builders less than that of producing the goods in their own shops. Such factories were not necessarily large— one with a daily output of a hundred doors employed only twenty men. They wrote about a factory where all plows of a given size were made to the same model and the parts were all alike. In the manufacture of locks, clocks, and small arms, machining methods were applied where accurate fitting of components was essential. In achieving these results, extraordinarily little handiwork was introduced.

On the negative side, the visitors were not as pleased with the American mode of making machines as with their resourcefulness in using them. The visitors thought that U.S. engine tools were similar to those in use in England some years earlier and were lighter in construction. Such claims about the apparent inferiority of the American tools were to be repeated many times. For example, James Montgomery, a witness before a parliamentary special committee in 1840, criticized American textile machinery as flimsy and less durable. The report of a parliamentary committee in 1850 thought that, in point of quality, American tools were inferior to English ones.

The Crystal Palace Exhibition of 1851 was the first time the British public had the opportunity to see what their cousins across the Atlantic could do. The *Times* of London sneeringly described the American exhibition as "mere machinery." At successive international exhibitions held in Paris and London in 1856, 1862, and 1867, the same theme continued: that American machinery was cheap, constructed too often with wood, and too light. This view was substantiated in a report of a parliamentary select committee in 1867, which stated that "English goods . . . are not altered to meet new requirements. . . . The United States' goods are rapidly changed. . . . The American sees the article will answer the purpose it is made for . . . he frequently omits a considerable portion of that which has been considered important to the construction of the article in England, and he contrives by some direct method to make it efficient for its purpose and generally more efficient than the Englishman makes it, it is often more simple in construction and always lighter in weight." But the more exacting standards of construction in England may well have been characterized by needless weight, unnecessary finish, and complicated movements.[60]

We have already noted Habakkuk's view that except for wood and iron, the cost of materials was higher in America than in England. Burn claimed that "English observers also stressed the relation between the characteristics of American industry and the peculiar difficulties which had to be overcome in order to establish it successfully." One of these difficulties, in his view, was the relative dearness of some of the United States' primary raw materials, including iron (though Habakkuk thought it was relatively cheaper), which he thought was responsible for the lightness of structure in Ameri-

can machines. He argued that the expense of raw materials in America was due to its high labor costs.[61] On the other hand, Brenner argued that "had it not been for its large iron and coal deposits, America would have had little chance of developing the machine industry the way it did."[62]

The point being made by these two men is not sustainable. Quite apart from the problem of deciding who is right on the relative price of iron between the two countries, none of them denied that America had relatively more abundant natural resources, including both wood and iron. If a machine designer finds that, in choosing between plentiful iron and plentiful wood, wood meets his requirements, then the issue of the price of iron is not important. If he finds that the purpose of the machine requires iron, he will have no alternative other than to use the iron. The trouble is that the English designers at the time were more inclined to regard strength, sturdiness, and the general engineering finish of their machine—a capital-intensive approach —as an index of sophisticated engineering.

The truth is that Americans were in fact adapting equipment in order to save on capital and labor. Nineteenth-century Americans, according to Walton and Rockoff, were short on labor and capital and long on raw materials and natural resources (water). American industrialists, as runners-up to British producers, had not only to copy English machines but to adapt them as well in ways that would allow them to economize on labor and capital, perhaps at the sacrifice of raw material usage.[63] Contemporary Europeans at the time viewed American production methods in agriculture and manufacturing as wasteful of land, wood, and mineral resources. But in the United States this was a rational response to their relative factor endowments. Ratner, Soltow, and Sylla observed, "Cheap natural resources were rationally substituted for more expensive capital and labor. American techniques often reflected capital scarcity as much as labor scarcity. . . . Within the United States there were regional variations of the same theme."[64]

Let us for a minute consider the claim that Americans were short of capital, a scarcity that was supposed to have made them seek to substitute raw materials for capital. That there was a shortage of financial capital is not borne out by the facts. Cochran and Miller made the following statements with regard to industries' access to funds: (1) Faced with a growing army of steady customers and with funds seeking investment, American industrialists in the 1820s and 1830s had the opportunity to mechanize their plant at a rapid rate. They took advantage of this, plowing profits and loans into new buildings and new machines. Between 1820 and 1840 investments in American factories rose from $50 million to $250 million. (2) Growing corporations benefited from the accumulation of large amounts of security capital in the great money markets of the country. (3) All these conditions brought businessmen swarming to the great cities of the East and Middle West, whose continual growth provided additional incentives by bringing more and more buyers and sellers together, enhancing the value of urban real estate, combining the funds of thousands into great capital available at reasonable rates for industrial and speculative enterprises. (4) Capital is a commodity dealt in by bankers, much as mine owners deal in coal or copper, or manufacturers in textile or shoes. And it was the eagerness of bankers to find markets for the funds deposited with them or with financial institutions available to them that gave great impetus to the consolidations that later occurred. (5) For a hundred years before the First World War, Americans had poured billions of dollars into transportation and manufacturing plants and into the exploitation of unparalleled natural resources. (6) The failure of American industry to utilize its usual proportion of American savings and the failure of foreign opportunities to take up the slack in our long-term investments left America in

Table 8.2

U.S. Consumer and Capital Goods as Percentage of Industrial Output, 1850–1914

	Consumer goods (% of total industrial output)	Capital goods (% of total industrial output)
1850	43.5	18.2
1870	38.6	23.3
1880	43.8	24.7
1890	35.6	23.6
1900	33.9	28.0
1914	31.1	34.3

Source: W. G. Hoffman, *The Growth of Industrial Economies,* trans. W. Henderson and W. Chaloner (Manchester: Manchester University Press, 1958), 96; S. Ratner, J. Soltow, and R. Sylla, *The Evolution of the American Economy: Growth, Welfare, and Decision Making* (New York: Basic Books, 1979), Table 12-2.

the twenties with increasing amounts of unused capital available for speculation.[65] In constant-dollar terms, capital per person in America increased by about three and half times in the last three-quarters of the nineteenth century.[66] There is, therefore, no basis to think that industries over the period were short of financial capital. Perhaps the position at this time in the United States helps refute conventional economists' view that the mere availability of financial capital and high savings in themselves determine the level of investment in capital equipment in industry.

Capital (production aids), as we have indicated in the early chapters, is not money but material and labor combined through productive process. One would ordinarily expect that with an abundance of natural resources, the Americans would combine the skilled labor they had developed in fashioning labor-saving techniques with massive, capital-intensive plant and machinery. This did not happen.

Table 8.2 shows the relative position of consumer goods industries versus capital goods industries in the United States as a percentage of total industrial output.

We had in the early chapters argued that an economy needs only such quantity of production aids (capital) as is necessary for it to meet its consumption needs. As we indicated, conventional economics, which advocates that societies deprive themselves of present consumption so as to increase their future productive ability, has no economic scientific justification. Capital formation beyond the natural threshold value creates structural imbalance vis-à-vis the natural factor proportions of the economy. It appears that even though the capital goods sector over the period 1850 to 1900 was growing faster than the consumer goods sector, during a good part of this period capital goods were comparatively modest vis-à-vis consumer goods. This is in line with our prescriptions on threshold capital.

What created the conditions in America for production for standardized demand during this period? Was it the cause or the effect of the beginnings of mass production at this time? Here again the English would at the time have asserted that standardization was attained in the United States not because of American ingenuity but because the society was well suited by circumstances to encourage and accept standardized production. Burn placed emphasis on the size of the population of the United States, "growing by emigration as well as by natural increase," which was, according to him, such that "whether the supply of goods is derived from home or foreign manufacture the demand cannot fail to be greater than the supply." He claimed that the opportunity thus created was increased by the higher average wealth of the people of United States compared to the population of England. He argued that the U.S. market was extremely receptive due to inadequate supply, and claimed that "the willingness on the part of the American public to buy what is offered them, has given the American manufacturer advantage over his European competitor who has to contend with habits and prejudice of centuries standing. . . . In the United States they overlook defects more than in

Europe, and are satisfied if a machine intended to supersede domestic labor will work even imperfectly while we insist on its being thoroughly well and efficient."[67] Ratner, Soltow, and Sylla suggested that the position might have worked because of "the substantially lower product prices generated by cost economies and market competition."[68]

All these explanations are speculative. Habakkuk answered the question more correctly when he stated that "a higher proportion of American demand for standardized goods was the result—direct and indirect—of the country's factor endowment." He argued that "the high price of labor, the abundance of land and the relative equality in its distribution went to the middle-income groups who demanded the types of goods which lent themselves to mechanization, and for the cheapness of goods ensured a high per capita demand for industrial goods."[69] Taking away the financial aspects of Habakkuk's reasoning, it will be clear that he was in effect making a point we had made earlier: that where production proceeds in line with natural factor proportions, inequalities are greatly reduced, a position which creates a demand pattern tending to greater leveling in demand patterns. We are also reemphasizing here that it is factor proportions (techniques) that should determine the nature of the demand and not the other way around.

We will now examine the relationship between factor proportions in the early economy of the United States and the course of its economic development and growth. All information available points to the fact that the U.S. economy took the world lead in the late nineteenth century. The quantity of goods produced in the forty-five years up to 1860 increased twelvefold. The total value of these goods, a measure retarded by sometimes drastic reductions in their average prices, rose eightfold. Allowing for some roughness in these estimates, the amount of goods available to an average American grew dramatically over this period, probably about tripling.

The demand for manufactured goods between 1815 and the 1840s expanded more rapidly in America than in Britain in relation to total factor supplies.[70] By any historical precedent, this was a very rapid increase for such a large sector over such a lengthy period.[71] America, as an economy, was a late starter, and the only way a late starter can overtake the early starters is by achieving and maintaining a faster average speed. The nature of the factor proportion changes in the United States over this period is therefore very important both as an important historical event and as empirical evidence that will contribute to our general theory of economic development and growth.

We will draw a lot from a paper by Cain and Paterson in the June 1981 *Journal of Economic History* titled "Factor Biases and Technical Change in Manufacturing: The American System, 1850–1919." They argued that the study of industrial growth and the direction of technological change (production techniques) have commanded persistent attention because of their role in the economic development of the United States, and that the economic forces that guided U.S. industrial development imparted a bias to the direction of technical change. Their paper was intended to examine the proposition that U.S. manufacturing experienced biased technical change during the period 1850–1919, although in our view the trends they noticed were a continuation of earlier trends in the economy. They set out to test for the presence of biased technical change in U.S. manufacturing at a disaggregated level. To do this, they adopted a gross-value model of the long-run production process as contrasted to the value-added model used in earlier two-factor studies. They created a new database consisting of nineteen sectors of the manufacturing industry with the appropriate SIC codes. An important set of data was factor shares and factor prices for each of the sectors they selected. Labor's share was equated to that of wage earners. The declared value of capital em-ployed was multiplied by an estimated rental rate for capital in order to generate an estimate of payments to capital, which was used to compute capital's share. The share of output given over to material consumption was taken as the value of reported material purchases as a proportion of the value of output. They decided that all payments otherwise uncatalogued should be grouped into a share that they called "residual." They faced the problem that "estimates calculated from census compilations are necessarily limited by available data—sometimes they are crude and sometimes they are only approximations." Census data are, of course, always subject to errors. From the quantification of the shares of each factor, the authors were, despite these limitations, able to track factor proportion changes that have occurred over the period they studied. But the authors faced a problem that was also the source of the weakness in their analysis, namely, that material consumption and capital were stated in monetary values. The inputs and outputs were also all in monetary values.

The basic thesis of the study was this:

> Although biased technical change may occur as part of general cost reductions introduced by entrepreneurs, it is more commonly argued in economic history that there is a historical relationship between the bias and relative factor prices. Based simply on an appreciation of past relative factor movements, entrepreneurs biased the combination of inputs to economize on the use of those inputs that historically had become expensive. Biases also may have been introduced when entrepreneurs were prepared to act on their own expectations of relative factor price changes. Expectations about future relative factor movements often are based on historical trends. Any entrepreneur who did not act to economize on the use of increasingly expensive factors bore a penalty in the form of higher per-unit costs. Such penalties . . . increased in severity as product and factor markets became less imperfect and as more and better information became available to potential innovators.[72]

This is a tall order. It assumed, as conventional economics does, that entrepreneurs are out to maximize their profit or, alternatively, compete successfully by achieving lower prices. It argued that industrialization in the United States was not a revolutionary development, as it was in England, and that industrialization in the United States was merely a cheaper method of providing goods.[73] In short, the consumer was supreme. Short-term adjustments in factor proportions to meet changes in factor prices do in the short term benefit the consumer, but since they do not affect all sectors equally, the differences in factor proportions that can be created in such a competitive atmosphere can adversely affect long-term growth prospects to the eventual disadvantage of the consumer. In any case, what the authors were basically interested in is the relative quantities of factors used and how these were affected by changes in factor prices. Unfortunately, the quantities were also in financial denominations (which were subject to changes that sometimes had nothing to do with quantities). Elasticity of demand varies with the nature of the factor. The authors noted, for example, that material demand was more inelastic than with other factors. Labor was the most elastic. Capital, being a financial quantity in their study, did not have any direct relationship with the demand for production aids (capital). It is therefore clear that the factor proportions resulting from the study will be somewhat different from factor proportions based on quantities. In a scientific study it is physical quantities that matter, not prices.

Associated with this weakness in their study is the difficulty of analyzing outputs in order to identify the shares of factors in them—a point we made in earlier chapters. Output is the result of chemical and/or physical reaction of inputs, and it is not possible to identify the share of each input factor in it. There are also always technical losses associated with each reaction, which are not always easy to quantify.

As with the factors themselves, Cain and Paterson had to evaluate output in financial terms, which make the exercises subject to the same analytical weaknesses we have already mentioned. Their conclusion that labor's share of gross value of output between 1850 and 1914 fell, whereas that of capital and material rose, must therefore be regarded with caution.

Despite these limitations, Cain and Paterson provided us with some important insights into the American economy at the time. Perhaps the most important is that "bias effects in a great number of cases were stronger than ordinary substitution effects, which contributed only modestly to the change in factor proportions in most sectors of manufacturing." This means that the economy grew principally through bias in sympathy with the factor endowments of the economy rather than the short-term financial manipulations of factor composition.

Cain and Paterson stated that the two-factor model of capital and labor accompanied by value-added assessments—which dominates conventional economic analysis—belies the true complexity of biased technical change. They stated that a historical tendency of manufacturers in some sectors to adopt technical change that ensured a material-using bias in the U.S. economy. They pointed out that claims under a two-factor model that the period between 1850 and 1919 was characterized by technical change based on labor-saving and capital-using techniques obscured the differences between various manufacturing activities and failed to take into account biases that exist with respect to factors of production other than labor and capital. Although labor-saving biases were evident in many sectors of manufacturing, they did not always coincide with a capital-using bias. In some sectors, they found that a labor-saving bias was accompanied by a material-using bias. In some others, capital-using biases occurred where labor neutrality was present. They emphasized, "The general dichotomizing of technical biases as labor-saving (as they often are) and capital-using (as they may not be) is misleading and belies the complexity of sectoral growth within manufacturing in the late nineteenth century and early twentieth centuries." Of the nineteen sectors they studied, the simple case of labor-saving and capital-using technical change alone was a feature of only three sectors.

The authors found that factors were both complementary and substitutes for each other. The degree of substitutability of one factor for another varied. Labor-capital substitution ranged from 3.8 in the tobacco industry to 0.5 in the instrument industry in 1860. In eleven of the nineteen sectors, the degree of substitutability between labor and capital was greater than that between any other factor. Substitutability between labor and material was often, they found, greater than between material and capital.[74] The main conclusion is that substitutability between any two factors varied from one activity to another.

The authors stated that the important role of material-biased technology change found in U.S. manufacturing as well as variations in elasticities of substitution across the different sectors call for a reexamination of existing international comparison of technical change, and observed that there is no particularly strong reason to believe that material prices varied less between countries than the price of labor. They should have said that material-saving or material-using biases applies to all countries depending on their relative material endowment. They emphasized that their study, applying a relatively new technique to newly compiled data, "afford[s] strong support to the traditional, three-factor textbook view of the process of industrial development and the direction of technical change than the earlier, two-factor empirical studies."[75]

Finally, the authors observed that no single sector of manufacturing was free from some biased technical change over the period of their study. In effect,

the dynamic nature of factor proportion changes was evident in all sectors, tending toward a dynamic equilibrium. The characteristics of biased technical change varied from sector to sector in such a manner that there was no general pattern, although sectors may have shared certain common features. "In summary," they say, "although labor-saving biases were present in most sectors of manufacturing during the period 1850–1919, the expected capital-using bias was not as pervasive. A material-using bias of technological change was characteristic of many manufacturing industries."[76] These features were in line with the relative factor endowments of the U.S. economy at the time. This accounts for the sustainable high growth rate the economy achieved.

If the U.S. economy surged ahead because of its correct factor proportions bias, it is important to find out why on factor proportions England's economy lagged behind the U.S. economy. To do this, we must first show what the overtaking of the British by American economy was *not* due to in order to illustrate the point Cain and Paterson were making about the inadequacy of all two-factor models in economic analysis.

Table 8.3 shows the capital/labor ratio indices in 1870–1979 for a number of European countries and Japan (United States = 100).

According to conventional economics, throughout most of the nineteenth century the United Kingdom achieved higher productivity than the United States. According to its own logic, productivity determines economic growth. So U.S. productivity must have been galloping ahead of English productivity in order to have overtaken Britain economically by the later part of the century. The only other conclusion that can be drawn from the table is that the English economy started facing a relative decline in economic growth later in the nineteenth century compared with that of the United States, even though its capital/labor ratios were higher than those of the United States over that period.

Table 8.3

Comparative Capital-Labor Ratios, 1870–1979
(US=100)

	Germany	Italy	UK	Average of three European countries	Japan
1870	73	—	117	—	—
1880	73	26	106	68	12
1913	60	24	59	48	10
1938	42	32	43	39	13
1950	46	31	46	41	13
1970	71	48	53	57	29
1979	105	66	64	78	52

Source: M. Abramovitz and P. David, "Convergence and Deferred Catch-up: Productivity Leadership and the Waning of American Expectionalism," in R. Landau, T. Taylor, and G. Wright, eds., *The Mosaic of Economic Growth* (Stanford, CA: Stanford University Press, 1996), Table 4. *Source of data:* E. Wolff, "Capital Formation and Productivity in the 1970's and 1980's," *The American Economic Review* 81, no. 3, Table 2, pp. 565–79. Reprinted by permission of the American Economic Association.

Explanations why the British economy stagnated that have been provided are mostly based on a two-factor view of the economy—labor and capital. As an example, Williamson claimed that labor market disequilibrium was produced in England because of unbalanced growth associated with an industrialization spurt after about 1820.[77] He argued that wage gaps existed in England as a manifestation of factor market disequilibrium and that industrial output and employment, though dramatic after the French wars (with their opening up of employment opportunities in England), were seriously constrained by factor market distortions. He argued that around 1831 nonagricultural employment would have been around 23 percent higher had factor market distortions been absent. The rate of industrialization, he said, was retarded on that score, and labor market failure contributed a good share to that. He also claimed that the rate of capital accumulation was slow in England during and after the French wars and explained it with the notion that that capital markets failed to accommodate investment demands in industry and that industrial accumulation

was constrained by profits. The results, he declared, suggest that labor market distortions contributed to low profits by making labor too expensive in cities and towns. Capital contributed to low profits by starving industry of capital. Nonagricultural profits, he said, might have been about 78 percent higher in 1831 had these so-called factor market distortions been absent. In addition, he noted what he called the "puzzling finding" that manufacturing capital was reluctant to move into the countryside in southern England so as to exploit surplus labor.

Table 8.3 clearly shows that, contrary to Williamson's position, England's problems at that time were certainly not due to lack of capital in industry, because England's capital/labor ratios were already the highest in Europe and higher than those of the United States. In introducing the issue of profits, Williamson was suggesting that low profits (incidentally, he had no basis to claim that profits were low) caused a slowdown in further capital accumulation. He was clearly confusing microeconomics with macroeconomics in this situation. Indeed, the truth—as we will see—is that in areas where regional labor shortages occurred, industries adopted labor-saving techniques. On the whole, his arguments were based on the wrong assumption that it is capital accumulation that creates economic development and growth.

England during this period was short of land (natural resources) but had an abundance of labor. As a country short of natural resources, it should be wary of diverting too much of its resources into production aids. It ought to have only moderate capital stock, which should not be classified as being capital-using. It will be shown that England's micro economy over this period was largely labor-saving and was structurally unbalanced, with factor proportions that were out of line with its relative factor endowments.

Cole has said that "the final indictment of the new industrialization in Britain in the nineteenth century is not that it actually reduced working-class standards of consumption. . . . The charge is rather that it created in town and country alike a vast mass of human unhappiness and disorientation. The villages, with their land enclosed, and the auxiliary earnings of domestic industry taken away, suffered from a loss of surplus of landless workers who lost their place in society."[78] Marshall was of the view that "there was a failure [in England] of economic progress and the increase of numbers [of people] to keep together. Perhaps for the country as a whole population outpaced economic progress."[79] Overall, therefore, unemployment and underemployment were common. Floud and McCloskey pointed out, "There seems little doubt that in areas like Lancashire the technological unemployment created by mechanization was felt more severely by the adult males."[80]

The country's problem was complicated by regional variations. Most of the rising industrial districts, where the demand for labor was greater, were in thinly populated parts of the country.[81] This accounted for the early introduction in many areas of industrial high-capital-using plants. Habakkuk remarked, "The long-term abundance of labor was compatible with complaints of shortage in particular industries and localities with a favorable bargaining position for particular groups of workers and even, on occasion, with a more general sense of shortage at the height of a boom. But, in general, the shortages were local and temporary."[82]

Labor in England always reacted negatively to the adoption of labor-saving devices. There were frequent attempts to destroy new machines in the capital-intensive textile industries, but this was probably a less powerful impediment to mechanization than persistent opposition on the factory floor. Owners of old machines incited workers' "combinations" to act against rivals who installed new machines, and a common object of strikes was to induce a manufacturer not to use a given sort of machine or generally to change his method of production.[83] Mechanical innovations such as the mule

and power mule were, therefore, slow to be introduced industrywide.

Machinery was often intended to save particular kinds of labor—usually replacing highly skilled adult males who were seen as not only relatively expensive but potentially threatening. The intention was to use machines to deskill labor by substituting cheap and docile women and children for fractious and/or expensive males.[84]

Despite all this, capital-intensive techniques were a distinct factor after the industrial revolution. Indeed, in the forty years prior to the First World War the number of persons employed had risen by 50 percent, while total capital invested grew by more than 80 percent.[85]

So in the country labor-intensive activities were competing with capital-intensive ones. Boot- and shoemaking were still done by workers on the domestic system. There were as yet no mechanical cutters nor sewing machines in the Leeds clothing trade. But the cotton industry was wholly mechanized, congregated into factories and focused in Lancashire and the west of Scotland. Side by side with Lancashire cotton mills and West Riding mills, thousands of weavers went on working at home at their hand looms. As textile factories continued to be biased against adult males, the retreat of unemployed males into hand-loom weaving was one of the most harrowing aspects of industrialization.[86]

Worsted was also a machine factory industry, except in combing, but this too was mechanized by 1857. The woolen industry, though largely mechanized, still had hand looms for another quarter of a century.[87] Habakkuk noted, "Over and above any increases in income, there was an increase in demand for products of the factory at the expense of English domestic industry."[88] He added that quite apart from increases in any sector, a considerable increase in income was achieved simply by shifts from less productive to more productive sectors, a claim typical of an unbalanced economy.

The large variations in capital intensiveness in Britain at the time were highlighted by Cole when he pointed out that during the nineteenth century, "although the number of mechanized industries increased, a very large proportion of total effort was concentrated in a few of these."[89]

In regard to material factors, shortages of fuel and water power were a feature of the English economic landscape. Many of the mechanical improvements to mills and mill wheels in the early industrial revolution resulted from attempts to make the most of a given stream. Much of the history of innovation in the primary iron industry in the eighteenth century can be explained by reference to fuel scarcity just as much as American development of this industry in the nineteenth century can be explained by reference to labor scarcity.[90] Also, native ores of nonferrous metals (copper, lead, tin) were gradually depleted.[91] Nevertheless, many new methods of production were wasteful of fuel, and because they were new and imperfect, some of the expense, according to Habakkuk, was unnecessary.[92]

Throughout the nineteenth century, fuel economy continued to be a most powerful motive behind innovations in techniques. There is no way of balancing the effect of British innovations that sprang from the limitations of natural resources against that of American inventions that sprang from labor scarcity. There is no reason for supposing that it was easier to relax a shortage of natural resources than a shortage of labor. There is, however, a reason for expecting that attempts to save natural resources should be less fruitful than attempts to save labor.[93] This is because labor is more homogeneous than natural resources—all firms use labor, but only some use a particular natural resource (with the exception of power)—and thus a shortage of it provides a more general incentive to invest techniques to offset it. But the contrast is not absolute.[94]

Nineteenth-century technical knowledge was also not particularly in a position to solve the problems of natural resource scarcity (to which solutions have since been obtained in new sciences of factors, as seen in Chapter 5). The upshot is that England was not particularly successful in achieving natural-resource-saving techniques in the nineteenth century and resorted to imports of raw materials. It was easier to relax natural resource stringency by tapping new sources of supply (for example, cotton from America and iron ore from Spain). In some cases, those foreign supplies were mined and imported by British firms. So material-intensive techniques took over, especially where imported raw materials were cheap.

The economic structure of Britain as we have just sketched it had a lot in common with what we saw in South Korea. Small labor-intensive industrial sectors existed alongside capital-intensive sectors, and entrepreneurs were pushing ahead with capital-intensive activities even when the natural factor proportions did not justify them (though in the Korean case the government was also involved). Material-intensive techniques, fueled by cheap imports of raw materials, were adopted in order to produce huge quantities of manufactured exports, on which the economy increasingly came to rely. The huge imports of raw materials naturally caused the economy to experience continuing Rybczynski imbalances, exacerbating the already unbalanced structural economic position, just as South Korea suffered relentless shocks, depending as it did on imported capital equipment and materials in order to keep up with exports of manufactures.

The structural imbalance of Britain worsened because the country soon came to depend upon and import American machinery and techniques in the belief (as many Third World countries presently do) that their economic salvation lay there. The attitude that labor-saving methods and high capital investment were the way forward was highlighted by Habakkuk when he argued that, "as a result of long pre-occupation with labor-saving methods,

Americans had developed types of engineering skill which were a prerequisite for development of new methods wherever they arose and whatever factor they saved."[95]

Burn said that beginning in the 1860s "machines developed in the United States had been frequently introduced into English industries. Sometimes the machines themselves were imported, more often they were manufactured here to American designs."[96] The United States led the way in sewing machine manufacture from the early 1850s. Large numbers of these were imported into England. Many were manufactured under patents purchased from Americans. The States continued to be home to novel types of machines. "We are accustomed," a British publication stated in 1863, "to look to America whenever a fresh desideratum in woodworking machinery makes itself felt in general practice."[97] The problem is that whereas in the early part of the nineteenth century, Americans depended on British techniques but modified them to suit their factor proportions, in this case the British regarded the factor proportions of U.S. techniques as the best, even though they were different from British factor proportions.

The resultant economic fortunes of Britain cannot be summarized better than Langer did: "In reviewing the amazing growth of British industry, one should not avoid the impression that the process of economic change was even or steady," as most texts on the industrial revolution and modernization of that economy seem to do. Langer went on, "The period was one punctured by booms and recessions which at the time were not understood and therefore provoked much discussion and inspired much uneasiness. . . . Modern studies reveal a strong upward trend in the period 1833–1836 followed by sudden depression and slow recovery to 1839 and then another period of hard times to 1842. There was a short period of prosperity which ended . . . in 1845 followed by . . . crisis years of 1845–1849. . . .

The final few years [up to 1853] marked a slow recovery from the turmoils of 1848. It is clear that the accelerated tempo of economic life and greatly enhanced rate of production presented the business world with problems of which previously it had only the barest inkling. . . . The industrial scene was as unpredictable as the harvests."[98] This description sounds in some ways similar to the experience of South Korea from 1880 to 1997. But America was to face its own depression early in the next century, as we will see.

Failing to see that the problem of Britain was the imbalance in its economic structure (wrong factor proportions), pundits claimed that the sociocultural structure of Britain was the cause of its economic decline, citing the country's lack of entrepreneurship or traditions that discouraged industry. Habakkuk stated that English social structure and public opinion were less favorable than those of America to entrepreneurship, in terms of both recruitment of ability and full ability once recruited. While the United States had no long-established class structure, Britain's strongly entrenched social system limited social mobility, and land ownership, bureaucracy, the army, and the professions were all powerful competitors of business for the services of able men. There was therefore a hemorrhage of capital and ability from industry and trade into land ownership and politics.[99]

But Habakkuk was wrong. The people who were pioneering industrialization in England were among the best entrepreneurs in Europe. In pushing for capital-using and labor-saving techniques, they were exercising initiative and talent, and they must have been surprised and disappointed at the results. In a way, it was unavoidable that in Britain, where the industrial revolution was born, the old and the new came to be juxtaposed. Perhaps structural imbalance was the price Britain had to pay for its initial leadership.

Many observers argue that the Americans succeeded because they were free and unfettered and had democracy and the freedom to explore and experiment. If America had failed, the same people would have argued that it was because of British colonialism, which limited freedom in the colonies. Fraser claimed that "the American was a believer to an unlimited extent in progress."[100] Another English expert held that sound practical education in America was fundamental to its industrial growth.[101] But the problem was not education, though many today think that what underdeveloped countries need is education.

Some have even argued that what the Americans excelled in was science and that the British lacked scientific know-how. Lewis argued that the British competitiveness weakness was not in the older industries but in the new ones, which were characterized by a higher scientific level than the old with one exception being the bicycle industry. He argued that "any intelligent and observant person with a stroke of genius could invent the steam engine or the flying shuttle or the hot blast." Innovation after 1880, he thought, required something more than genius. Scientific knowledge was needed to develop electrical machinery, organic chemistry, or a workable combustion engine. He believed that most of the important inventions of the industrial revolution originated in Great Britain but that they were quickly followed up elsewhere by others, and that the British lagged behind in exploiting them.[102] Lewis failed to explain what he meant by "following up" or "exploiting" British inventions, but what happened is that Americans and others modified what the British invented to suit factor proportions in the United States, while the original inventions did not all necessarily fit the factor proportions of the United Kingdom. It is incorrect, however, to assert that the reason is a lack of scientific knowledge on the part of the British. The Americans were driven by their needs and intuition to adapt inventions to suit what they were faced with. Need is the source of knowledge

(science). In this case, many of the original British inventions were geared to dealing with shortage of certain natural resources.[103] Lewis' views and others of earlier times have historically led economists to believe that technical progress is "simultaneously physical and human-capital augmenting."[104]

Anyone with an engineering background will appreciate that any attempt to adapt the enormous quantity of present-day capital-intensive techniques for use in labor-using environments will require a lot of engineering and science, as we saw in Chapter 5. This is because in the last two and a half centuries engineers have concentrated their science of factor proportions (technology) in the direction of labor-saving techniques.

The reasons given by various authors for why England lagged behind the United States—sociocultural norms, poor education, lack of scientific tradition, and so on—sound much like the current conventional economic literature's litany of causes of underdevelopment in the Third World, which adds a few of its own: bad governance, corruption, lack of democracy, and so on.

In a historical context, we think that in a situation in which economic development and growth theory is undeveloped, the empirical case of the American economic success in the eighteenth and nineteenth century on the back of labor-saving technology is the origin of conventional economists' view that it is technology that is the sine qua non for economic development and growth everywhere. Economists who relied on a two-factor model study of that economy were easily convinced that a capital-using and labor-saving technology approach was what economic development and growth was all about.

United States, 1890–1940

America entered another phase in the development of its economic personality as the nineteenth century came to a close. In the fifty years from about 1890 to 1940, Americans woke up to the rude shock that the economic success of the past century and a half was not to be taken for granted. *Iron Age*, a prominent journal of the iron and steel industry of the time, stated in a 1931 editorial that "the seemingly boundless markets that have stimulated the resourcefulness and energy of our people since they set foot on this broad continent, have been disclosed as having definite limit."[105] McCracken contrasted the post–World War I economy of the United States with the nineteenth-century U.S. economy, complaining that "the industrial system absorbed technological progress without serious difficulty before the war but not since. . . . Although the entire nineteenth century was continuously and incessantly dynamic, with machinery and labor-saving devices following fast upon the heels of each other in all branches of trade and commerce, yet jobs increased faster than population and a higher percentage of eligible workers was employed in 1900 and in 1800. . . . this trend continued up to 1914 or the beginning of the World War. But for some reason or other, the trend was reversed during the war with the results that progress did not repair itself nor the technologically displaced worker find re-employment during the prosperous decade of the twenties."[106]

The factor proportions of the United States were changing but seem to have reached a threshold at the beginning of the twentieth century. In describing the change that took place, Roosevelt many years later said, "In the first century of our republic, we were short of capital, short of workers and short of industrial production, but we were rich in free land, free timber, free mineral wealth. . . . But today the government no longer has vast tracts of rich land to give away and we have discovered that we must spend large sums to conserve our land and our forests from further depletion. The situation is different from old days because we now have plenty of capital, banks and insurance companies loaded with

idle money, plenty of industrial productive capacity and several millions of workers looking for jobs."[107] The population of the United States nearly doubled between 1890 and 1930, and a large proportion of this increase was due to immigration. It therefore seems that the material/labor ratio of the United States decreased. In line with our theory of factor proportions, what the United States needed was techniques that were more labor-intensive and less material-intensive in order to continue its sustainable growth path established in the nineteenth century (we will come to the capital ratio later). But this did not happen.

Cochran and Miller observed that in the three decades after the Civil War, "as confident entrepreneurs raced to take advantage of every ephemeral rise in prices, of every advance in tariff schedules, of every new market opened by the railroads and puffed up by immigration, they recklessly expanded and mechanized their plant, each seeking the greatest share of the new melon."[108] In effect, they were choosing their production technique based not on factor proportions but on the market. The pre–Civil War entrepreneurs chose their production technique in line with the economy's endowed factor proportions. Walton and Rockoff say in characteristically uneconomic language that these changes were "because the pace of technological change was so exceptional in those days."[109]

The United States entered the period of capital-intensive industrialization via mergers and acquisitions. These consolidation measures were viewed as either necessary or against the public interest, depending from what end they were being viewed at the time. The basic problem which the economy was facing (as was also true of South Korea in the second half of the 1990s) was declining demand, which was progressively getting worse as the 1920s drew to a close. *Iron Age* stated in March 1929, "Mass production after acquiring great momentum under the spur of ever increasing costs and constantly expanding sales has run into the stone wall of saturated demand. The savings accruing from rapid growth are now a thing of the past in many industries and future profits depend on replacement business and the slow increment that comes from increased population."[110]

Adams pointed out that the unemployment in the 1920s was due to the closing down of industry, itself a result of an "excess of goods in the markets which in turn is due to the shortage of purchasing power of American consumers."[111] Erickson pointed out that by midsummer of 1929 a number of signs indicated danger; the slowing down of consumer spending was one of them.[112]

On September 20, 1929, the president of the Standard Oil Company of Ohio told the National Petroleum Association at its twenty-seventh annual convention that the fluctuation of prices that had been occurring in the industry for a long time indicated "fundamentally unbalanced economic conditions." He said, "Ultimately our problems will have to be solved by economic evolution." He pointed out that the petroleum industry was entering the third stage of its development: "The first stage was characterized by rapid expansion and wide margins of profit which are needed to make possible such rapid expansion. . . . In the second stage there was an inrush of outside capital attracted by those wide profits, until the business became overcrowded and there was overproduction and demoralization of prices. Now comes the third stage: a period of sifting, survival, merger and getting down to brass-tacks efficiency basis—a hardpan proposition with the boom all gone. . . . Price cutting in our industry has a peculiar significance. Since it cannot stimulate the total demand, it tends towards industrial self-destruction."[113]

About the same time, the executive director of the American Institute of Steel Construction observed that the paramount problem in most industries in the United States was that of marketing. He

was of the view that producers must either maintain consumption on a basis equaling production capacity or ration their production in keeping with their ability to sell. He thought that through proper research, much could be done to increase markets. "We are at a stage of industrial development," he said, "where it is much easier to produce than to sell what we produce. . . . It is easier to employ scientific management in the factory and eliminate waste than it is to make profit on our goods. Efficiency in plant production has reduced costs to a minimum and therefore if relief is to be expected from the many perplexing problems it must come from similar attention to market and distribution." He further observed, "There are some industries where demand is declining or where it is impossible to increase it to any extent." He complained of the inability of business executives in industry to fully appreciate the problems of distribution, to have any known yardstick with which to measure market possibilities, to have any scientific approach to control of market costs.[114] In many industries the trouble was that as they mechanized and became more efficient, the greater the number of buildings and machines left idle when a new market approached the saturation point or the rate of expansion of the market declined.[115] In short, many of the large capital-intensive businesses were facing serious financial problems (much like the chaebols in South Korea decades later).

The expansions in capacity were possible because of the capital-intensive techniques. But in view of the complex nature of the situation and in particular the declining market demand, it is simplistic to accuse the businesses that were amalgamating or forming associations of a lack of patriotism. Nor does O'Brien's conclusion that "increases in concentration during the merger wave were motivated more by the desire to reduce price competition than the desire to exploit scale economies" show a deep understanding of the problems facing businesses at the time.[116] They invested in the belief of a growing and expanding market, but instead the market started to contract. This is not to say that there were not those who set out to corner and control the market and prices. But because of the complexity of the problem, succeeding governments in the United States as well as the Supreme Court had different attitudes toward business combinations.

The Hoover administration, for example, regarded trade associations as a vital instrument of stabilization. The stabilization of prices was seen as a means of preventing disorganization, hence a key to stable production and prosperity. McCracken said the choice was between "economic stabilization through price stabilization or stabilized production through price flexibility."[117]

According to Walton and Rockoff, it was clear as the United States entered the 1920s that "one of the great pre-1920 experiments in the social control of business achieved little. By the time a vigorous enforcement of the antitrust laws was undertaken in the 1930s it was too late to do anything about the problems of bigness in industry." What the courts did in the United States to help the establishment of big companies was in a way equivalent to what the government of South Korea did much later, actively encouraging the formation and growth of the chaebols.

Between 1890 and 1929 in the United States, fixed capital in manufacturing increased from about $5.5 billion to over $63 billion, the highest level for the next decade. Capital stock per capita jumped from about $1,090 to $2,500, while the capital/labor ratio went up in money terms from $4,010 to $9,090. Conventional economics would assert on the basis of such figures that productivity in the first decades of the twentieth century rose and that economic growth accelerated. Instead, growth was uniformly slower in these two decades.[118] Indeed, the Depression can be attributed to this change in capital intensiveness, as will be shown later.

So the American economy entered into what was variously called economic concentration or economic centralization. According to McElvaine, "The idealized American economy of small freely competing units upon which much of the nation's economic thought and social philosophy was based was largely a thing of the past by the 1920s."[119] McElvaine reminded us of the classic conclusion of two well-known economists in the 1930s, Adolf Berle and Gardiner Means, who carried out an exhaustive study of the growing corporate structure in 1932: "American industrial property, through corporate device, was being thrown into a collective hopper wherein the individual owner was steadily being lost in the creation of a series of huge industrial oligarchies."[120]

By the end of the 1920s roughly two-thirds of the industrial wealth of the United States had passed "from individual ownership to ownership by the large, publicly financed corporations." In 1929, two hundred corporations controlled nearly half of all American industry. The $81 billion in assets they held represented 49 percent of all corporate wealth and 22 percent of all national wealth. Three years earlier, the same corporations had held 45 percent of corporate and less than 20 percent of all U.S. national wealth.[121] The political impact of these developments was clear. In speeches in 1932 and 1933 Roosevelt was at pains to tell people how he thought industrial concentration was affecting society. Though concentration of financial power had not proceeded so far in 1912 as it had in 1932, he cited Woodrow Wilson, who had said, "No man can deny that the lines of endeavors have more and more narrowed and stiffened; no man who knows anything about the development of industry in this country can have failed to observe that the larger kinds of credit are more and more difficult to obtain unless you obtain them on terms of uniting your efforts with those who already control the industry of the country and nobody can fail to observe that every man who tries to set himself up in competition with any process of manufacture which has taken place under the control of large combination of capital will presently find himself either squeezed out or obliged to sell and allow himself to be absorbed." Roosevelt himself went on, "It is true that men can start small enterprises, trusting to native shrewdness and ability to keep abreast of competitors; but area after area has been preempted altogether by the great corporations, and even in the fields which still have no great concerns, the small man starts under a hardship."[122]

McElvaine pointed out that studies of the concentration of the economy in the 1920s concluded that the political economy of Adam Smith, which had dominated American thinking for a century and half, no longer applied. The competitive model drawn up by Smith as the "great regulator of industry" was based upon the assumption of numerous small units whose prices were determined by the market. They concluded that as this was no longer the case by the late 1920s, the market had lost its inherent tendency toward equilibrium.[123]

All evidence therefore points to the fact that (as Table 8.2 confirms) the capital goods sector overtook the consumer goods sector around 1914 and that this contributed greatly to the imbalance that people in 1920s America were complaining existed between production and consumption.

By the middle of 1929 the comparative indices of production of producer goods against that of consumer goods reached (1925 to 1929 = 100) was 113 to 104; by the end of 1929, following the crash, it had dropped to between 88 and 91. Capital investment therefore was at peak right up to the beginning of October 1929.

The investment position over the decade was succinctly summarized by Gordon:

> The outstanding fact about recent movement of total capital formation in this decade is the high level reached by 1923 and maintenance of this level

for seven years. We have here a prolonged period of high-level investment in producer and durable goods and construction. Inventory accumulation did not play the same important role it did in 1919–1920. For the period 1923 to 1929 as a whole total capital formation averaged about $19.5 billion (in 1923 prices) compared with $11.7 billion in prewar 1904–1913. It is significant that both producers and consumer durables formed a larger part of the GNP during the 1920s than any period before World War I. We have a period of prolonged investment boom which supported a steady expansion of incomes and consumer demand. . . . Mass production techniques were extended, greater use made of automatic and special purpose machines, radical improvement in material handling. Labor cost fell as wages failed to rise as rapidly which encouraged further investment. The former led to illusions in the midst of a spectacular boom for the late 1920s that "conditions were fundamentally sound."[124]

Gordon argued that the chief immediate cause of the downturn was the impact of what he called "partial over-investment."

Others have drawn attention to the decline in nonindustrial investments, such as the downward trend in residential construction. Walton and Rockoff observed, "The boom in building activity that began in 1918 had undoubtedly helped the economy out of the slump of 1920 and 1921; the downward phase of the same building cycle, coinciding as it did with other economic weaknesses, was a major depressing influence. What began as a gentle slide in construction from 1925 to 1927 became a marked decline in 1928."[125]

Atack and Passell on the other hand, stated, "Investment . . . had begun to decline well before the onset of the depression having peaked in 1926. Much of the change in investment spending in both the 1920s and 1930s can be traced to variations in construction. In each of the years between 1924 and 1927 the ratio of real residential construction to GNP was at a record level—in excess of 8% of GNP and it represented about half of gross domestic investment. That level, however, could not be sustained or justified and by 1929 residential construction was less than half its mid-decade peak." They added significantly, "In part, the decrease stemmed from declining demand for housing. Population growth was slowing down as fewer families were formed and fewer immigrants landed on these shores."[126]

By telling us why housing investment decreased, Atack and Passell have shown that decline in residential construction was not the cause but the result of depression. Fewer immigrants landed in the United States because the economy was in depression.

Against this background, it is clear that economists who argue that sacrificing current consumption for future consumption will result in an expansion in the capital goods industries, leading eventually to an increase in income and consumption, will find it difficult to explain why the sacrifice that started at the beginning of the twentieth century led America to a depression instead. People will say, in today's language, that America at the time had too much capital in its industrial sector, just as economists were charging that South Korea had too much capital in the early and middle 1990s. What was needed in each case (pre-1929 America and pre-1997 South Korea) was a threshold capital accumulation necessary for maintaining a structurally balanced economy, not more.

Pre-1929 America was also already suffering from another relatively new major economic crisis: unemployment. But how serious was this? Crowther put forth a familiar explanation of the cause of the Depression, namely, that corporations brought in so much machinery prior to 1929 that they rapidly cut down the number of their employees. He argued that a quick reduction in the number of wage earners while more goods than ever were being made was bound to result in a surplus of goods over buyers. Economists at the time were of two minds about what should be done. One group was for sum-

mary action, wishing to prohibit any important changes in the plant of the country for a period of years without approval from a government agency. The other would allow any or all improvement but would arrange for the benefit to be distributed in higher wages and shorter hours so that, according to Crowther, "the capitalists would not get all the benefit." He argued that sometimes changes to the plant do not result in any benefit to the capitalists because entrepreneurs have to incur large front-end costs in research, advertising, and marketing.[127]

In the first half of the 1920s, employment fell from the levels of the previous decade. It picked up slightly around 1925, but still not enough to keep up with the rising population. Indeed, by 1929 the ratio of total industrial employment to population was lower than what it was between 1910 and 1920. It is clear that beginning in 1925, unemployment became a very visible feature of the American scene.

On August 24, 1929, the Institute of Politics, saying that "certain indices show that the nation is headed for a depression," took steps to form a nationwide organization to develop plans for construction works. This organization, later known as the Planned Prosperity League or Prosperity Reserve League, was set up after a general conference on unemployment that cited unemployment as "the greatest communal crime of our civilization."[128] A participant in another conference around the same time asserted that employment was the right of all workers and that poverty must be abolished, declaring, "No policy is so unwise and extensive as our present practice of supporting a part of the unemployed with labor in return for such support, nor persons as vagrants and criminals, through public and private means and by individual and therefore necessarily indiscriminate almsgiving. Now is it that we cannot afford to employ the unemployed? . . . Will it not be a wise economy to obtain from the unemployed this same form of productive labor in return for their support. Employment is a great structural necessity of the modern industrial world. The consuming wage power of the worker must be built up to measurably equal the productive power of the modern machinery. Not to do this is to admit that we have created a modern Frankenstein which we are unable to control."[129] From the start of the 1920s unemployment increased steadily, and by the beginning of the last quarter of 1929 it had reached about 7 percent, a figure that increased steadily after the crash in October 1929. A contributing factor was company failures, which marked much of the decade. Lest monetarists attribute these failures to lack of credit, a major banker at the time said that many banks had increased their lending to peaks never before attained, and that he did not know of any banks that were refusing to make legitimate commercial loans.[130]

The general state of business was that of an economy in decline prior to October 1929. On September 23, 1929, the Federal Reserve Board reported in its monthly review, "Whilst production in basic industries increased somewhat in August as compared with July, the advance was less than is usual and the index of industrial production, which makes allowance for seasonal changes, showed a decline." In its review of trade and industry at the end of September 1929, the National City Bank declared that a slackening of trade and industry have been making records for the past two years. "The activity of manufacturing and trade continued to be at a high level [in September] but was not marked by the seasonal expansion which usually occurs in September." It remarked further that there was considerable speculation in banking circles that the upward movement of the total of loans may reflect in part "some unhealthy accumulation of inventory."[131]

The Department of Commerce's statement in September 1929 on production of motor vehicles announced that in terms of factor sales, the month of August reflected "accurately the dip in demand for new cars which developed after the turn of the

half of the year." It noted that in this connection, the small low-priced model cars were best in demand at the time. The summer season of 1929 showed a remarkable performance in steel output in view of the "present trend towards decline in the rate of steel output."[132]

In September 1929 the *New York Times* remarked, "While merchants are optimistic on trade prospects . . . some falling off in employment in important industries . . . may reduce purchasing power. . . . Contrast between the so-called key industries which furnished the main impetus to industrial operations and to general business for so many months, and the miscellaneous or lighter industries have grown more marked. Steel output has receded further and prices are weaker. Building as measured by contract awards is now running about 20 percent behind last year. Conditions in the automobile industry are less cheerful, the leading producer reporting a drop in retail sales of 11 percent last month as compared with the usual increase that is obtained from July to August. Sales were also 10 percent under August 1928."[133]

We have established that prior to the stock market crash of October 1929, the U.S. economy had already been in trouble for a number of years. Demand was in decline. Defaults, especially small ones, were increasing. Unemployment was increasing. Accordingly, any attempt to explain the Depression as the result solely of the crash is not useful. How the Federal Reserve handled the crash or whether the Fed helped to precipitate the crash is therefore not the main issue. As in the 1997 crisis in South Korea, factors that accelerated the economy's final collapse should not be confused with the initial factors that pushed the economy onto the path of depression.

We had argued in earlier chapters that some of the financial shocks that conventional economists claim caused the Asian crisis would not have affected the Asian economies if they were balanced economies. Temin has stated the same thing in regard to the stock market crash of 1929:

> Time has not been kind to the school of thought that blames the Depression on the stock market crash. The stock market has gone up and down many times since then. The most obvious parallel was in the fall of 1987. The isomorphism was uncanny. The stock market fell almost exactly the same amount on almost the same days of the year. If the crash of 1929 was an important shock to the economy then the crash of 1987 should have been equally disastrous. The stock market has grown in the intervening years in the intervening half century and news of the stock market was pervasive. . . . The stock markets around the world were more closely synchronized in 1987 than in the late 1920s. Despite a flurry of speculations, the world economy did not turn in the fall of 1987. The boom that was underway for five years continued apace.

Temin concluded, quite correctly, "The stock market is not a big enough event on its own to cause a depression," but added, "This is not to say that the crash of 1929 had no effect."[134] A stock market crash can worsen a depression that is already on but cannot on its own cause one.

Similar claims that the Federal Reserve's increase of the discount rate in 1929 helped start the Depression are equally unsubstantiated. For example, some economists claimed that throughout 1928 and 1929 both the Federal Reserve and the Federal Reserve Bank of New York acted aggressively to control stock speculation. They argue that those actions clearly failed to stop the market boom and did exert a steady deflationary pressure on the economy. Temin did not agree that the interest rate, 6 percent, could have caused the Depression.[135]

Keynes' perception was that the crisis was caused by a decline in confidence, which undermined investment spending. This is another example of an unacceptable explanation, because production of producer goods (which is what we are interested in) fell only after the crash. Right up to early Octo-

ber 1929, the index of production of producer goods was the highest it had been throughout the 1920s. Friedman and Schwartz's claim that the crisis was caused by the fall in money stock, using data on money and income from 1929 to 1933, cannot also pass as a useful explanation of the Depression, which, we have seen, started earlier.[136]

On the whole a substantial number of economists agree that aggregate demand fell in the years before the crash. Peter Temin, for example, believed that there was a collapse in consumer spending and attributed the Depression primarily to this "unanticipated" and "unexplained" decline in consumption. Temin was of the view that the decline in autonomous consumption expenditure was unusually large in 1929. Goods that could not be sold were not produced. The fall in aggregate demand spread throughout the economy.[137]

Perhaps the greatest weakness in current monetarist theories on depression is their inability to explain why aggregate demand suddenly fell. Joseph Schumpeter believed that the Depression was caused by underconsumption. Szostak observed, "Though the Depression is associated in the minds of most people with the stock market crash of October 1929, the downturn actually started some months earlier." More significantly, he concluded by asking, rather rhetorically, why consumption fell so much in the late 1920s.[138]

One cannot prescribe remedies if one is unable to identify the cause of this fall in aggregate demand. According to Krugman, the problem of getting people to spend enough to employ the economy's productive capacity is not, as one might think, always a problem with an easy solution.[139]

It is in this context that we have to see Keynes' prescription for depression: to make up for loss in aggregate demand through expenditures for welfare, public works, and so on. This prescription assumes that depression is caused by weakness in private investment and so the only way to stimulate investment is to increase consumer demand through government spending. This assumption is wrong. Though Keynes aimed to overturn classical economics, Adam Smith's model of a self-adjusting, free economy leading to full employment is not at fault in our view. The model served in its day because the economy had numerous small units. These small units were structurally similar in that their factor proportions were similar. We are of the view that the classical model still marches on as strong now as in the past provided that the model's underlying assumption—namely, similarity in the structure of production units—is retained. When the U.S. economy turned away from the balance that it had achieved during much of the nineteenth century and entered the period of centralization and concentration, it violated the basic principle of the classical economy.

So we arrive back at the theory of factor proportions: that if the factor proportions of all activities are equal to the economy's factor proportions, there will be structural equilibrium, which guarantees full employment. The contradiction in Keynes' prescription is evident from the fact that while it sets out to make up for investment whose decline he thinks caused the Depression, the public expenditure he champions tends to work at the wrong end of the production process. It is the capital goods market (especially the heavy manufacturing industries) that is hardest hit in the Depression.[140] For example, it was estimated that in September 1933, when public works programs were in place, there were about ten million unemployed. Of those, about half were producers of services. The other half were producers of goods. The producers of services were of course idle because their work had to do, essentially at the time, with the movement of goods. Of the five million unemployed producers, virtually all had been employed in making durables or capital goods. It was clear that it was this high-capital-using part of the economy that was not helped by

the government spending program. That was precisely what—in structural terms—the economy needed in factor proportions context to start the long process of moving back toward equilibrium, namely, a stop to further capital accumulation. But Keynes intended for his prescriptions to lead to the strengthening of capital growth. It will seem that what Krugman called "the success of Keynesian economics in damping down the business cycle" was achieved by default.

The fall in aggregate demand was the direct result of improper allocation of production factors in the economy. It is difficult to see how throwing money at the problem will solve it. But monetarist economists believe that the ups and downs of any economy can be solved by doing just that (or withdrawing money from it) in order to control demand and investment.

As Skousen says, "Today's economic writers, still dressed in Keynesian clothes, say they have learned the bitter lessons of depression. . . . What are the lessons? Primarily, they maintain that free-market capitalism cannot provide employment and a stable economic environment. Since capitalism is inherently unstable, government must therefore intervene and keep it from falling off the edge."[141]

Praising the role of Keynesian policies in damping the business cycle, Krugman said, "It was once again reasonable to assume that the economy would always tend quickly back to full employment—not because of any automatic mechanism but because intelligent policy makers would use monetary and fiscal policy to get it there."[142] But as Krugman recognized, the use of monetary and fiscal tools cannot always ensure that they can or will increase demand when it is needed. Dow saw the use of fiscal and monetary tools as necessary but noted that as means of control, they "may appear very crude."[143] For conventional economists who think that governments can prevent depression with monetary and fiscal tools, there is the problem that no macroeconomic forecasting model can accurately predict possible depression—such models only recognize depression when it has already started. Dow agreed that with available knowledge, "major recessions appear unlikely to be forecastable much in advance of their being manifest in a downturn of output."[144] It is only through structural economics that this forecasting model can be attempted. Phelps correctly pointed out that "the experience of the Depression needs to be re-studied with alternative interpretations, structural theory being a strong candidate."[145]

It is therefore clear that in our scientific analysis of the economic crisis that faced the United States in the 1920s and after, we should attach much less importance to the Wall Street crash of October 1929 than to the growing signals in the early 1920s. The Wall Street crash, like the Asian financial crisis nearly seventy years later, was a reaction based on people's reading of what was happening as the economic downtown grew and their self-interested anticipation of what might happen. It is therefore only to be expected that there is little unanimity among conventional economists about financial issues, explanations, or tests of the theories concerning the Great Depression. In short, there are many competing explanations, not all of which are mutually exclusive.[146]

It is noteworthy that in the 1920s and 1930s monetary and fiscal factors were not given the prominence they currently enjoy among conventional economists as being the cause of the economic problems at the time. There was instead greater attention on the structure of the economy. Unfortunately, it was only the financial structure they considered in their attempt to explain the loss of aggregate demand, the first sign of depression. The 1930s saw a lot of interest in what was called the "underconsumption/overproduction" theory of the Depression. President Roosevelt, in a 1933 Fireside Chat, attributed the collapse of 1929 to "overspeculation and overproduction of practically every article or instrument used by man . . . millions of people had

been put to work, but the products of their hands had exceeded the purchasing power of their pocketbooks." He observed, "Under the inexorable law of supply and demand, supplies so overran demand which would pay that the production had to stop. Unemployment and closed factories resulted. . . . If the government had a policy," he said in frustration, "it was rather to turn back to destroy the large combinations and return to the time when everyone owned his individual small business."[147] Adams pointed out very significantly that "in so far as we have a general overproduction situation in industry in the United States, it was brought about by diverting too large a percentage of the national money income in making new capital investments and too small a percentage of the national income into purchasing finished consumers' goods." Having correctly complained that there was too much capital, Adams unfortunately then embarked on a financial explanation. He argued that the supply-demand position he described could happen only "where profits have been too high and real wages slow, or where prices have not been adjusted to the lower cost of production during a period of economic progress." He complained that the monopolistic price controls in operation between 1922 and 1929 kept prices from being lowered as rapidly as the cost of production was dropping. What he called the "displacement of labor by automatic machinery" between 1922 and 1929 resulted in a surplus of labor, which kept wages from increasing as rapidly as did profits.[148]

This line of analysis was greatly expanded by McElvaine in his book *The Great Depression: America, 1929–1941.*[149] He claimed that no cause of the Great Depression was of larger importance than the growing maldistribution of income in 1920s America. McElvaine went into great detail to show this income inequality:

> According to the famous Brookings Institution study, "America's Capacity to Consume," the top

0.1 percent of Americans in 1929 had an aggregate income equal to that of the bottom 42 percent. Stated in absolute numbers, approximately 24,000 families had a combined income as large as that shared by more than 11.5 million lower-middle class families. Fully 71 percent of all American families . . . in what was generally regarded as the most prosperous year the country and the world had ever known had incomes of $2,500. At the other extreme, the 24,000 richest families enjoyed annual incomes in excess $100,000 and 513 American families that year reported incomes above $1 million. . . . The authors [of the Brookings Institution study] concluded, it appeared that income was being distributed with increasing inequality, particularly in the latter years of the period. . . . Late in the twenties, a larger percentage of the total income was received by the portion of the population having high incomes than had been the case a decade earlier. Between 1920 and 1929, per capita disposable income for all Americans rose by 9 percent but the top 1 percent of income recipients enjoyed a whopping 75 percent increase in disposable income. The share of disposable income going to the top 1 percent jumped from 12 percent in 1920 to 19 percent in 1929. Here in stark statistics was one of the principal causes of the Great Depression. Maldistribution of wealth in 1929 was even greater than that of income. Nearly 80 percent of the nation's families—some 21.5 million households—had no savings whatever. The 24,000 families at the top—0.1 percent—held 34 percent of all savings. The 2.3 percent of the families with income more than $10,000 controlled two-thirds of America's saving. Stock ownership . . . was even more concentrated. The top 0.5 percent of Americans in 1929 owned 32.4 percent of all the net wealth of individuals. This represents the highest concentration of wealth at any time in American history. . . . Clearly a major cause of the unstable foundation beneath the prosperity decade was the dichotomy between the reality of massive concentration in American business and the classical economic model upon which policy was still being based. Coolidge and Mellon were playing by rules of Adam Smith's pin factory at a time when Henry Ford's River Rouge plant was more indicative of the true nature of the economy. It would

have been remarkable if disaster had not resulted from this discrepancy.[150]

In order to advance his contention that inequality caused the Depression, McElvaine, like a number of economists in the 1920s and today, claimed that "a large part of the reason for the growing gap between the rich and poor was that productivity was increasing at a far faster rate than wages. In the decade ending in 1929, output per worker in manufacturing leaped upwards by a remarkable 43 percent. In only six years between 1923 and 1929 output per person-hour increased by almost 32 percent. During the period, wages also increased but only by 8 percent, a rate one-fourth as fast as the rise in productivity." He observed that "with production costs falling rapidly, prices remained yearly stable and wages rising only slowly, the bulk of the benefits from increased productivity went into profits. In that same six-year period ending in 1929, corporate profits soared by 62 percent and dividends rose by 65 percent. . . . The rich were getting richer at a much more rapid rate than the poor were becoming less poor."[151]

McElvaine next advanced his argument by stating that "any interpretation of the origins of the Depression that places significant emphasis on maldistribution must account for the peaceful coexistence of prosperity with maldistribution in the years preceding the Crash." He then reasoned that the poor (that is, wage earners in the lower three-fourths of the population, whose wages had not kept up with productivity) practically exhausted their wage income on both nondurable and durable consumer goods (food and clothing in the former, automobiles and houses in the latter). They could do no more for the demand side of the supply-and-demand equation unless they were paid more. On the other hand, the wealthy, although they also bought consumer goods in far larger quantities than their less affluent neighbors, could "be expected to eat only so much and buy only so many cars and houses." They put their income into savings and investments as well as luxury spending. The high rate of investment helped keep the economy in temporary balance during the boom years, but this was, he maintained, a problem in the long term, because it further increased productivity, and since the gains were not being passed adequately into higher wages, the income distribution worsened further. "The basic macroeconomic problem growing out of maldistribution was that those with the means to buy more of the products of mass production industry could satiate their desires by spending only a small fraction of their income while those whose needs and desires were not satisfied had no money," he concluded.[152]

Society attempted, he argued, to dispose of the excess supply through exports and credit sales, but when exports dried up and the supply of consumers who could be persuaded to make purchases on credit ran out, the problem reemerged. Under these conditions, the economy was peculiarly dependent on a continued high level of luxury spending and investment by those receiving a disproportionately large share of the national income. If something caused a sudden loss of confidence by these affluent Americans, the whole economic structure might collapse—a situation that McElvaine maintained occurred in the fall of 1929.

Sylos-Labini maintained a similar position: "It is precisely this phenomenal shift in the distributive share that is at the origin of the Wall Street crash." He denied that the crash was due to "the unexplained exhaustion of a wave of optimism followed by an equally unexplained wave of pessimism," however, arguing that even though economists believe that in the capitalist system an increase in profits (however criticizable from the social justice point of view) is favorable to economic development, the issue must be posed in different terms. He argued that what is needed is an optimum in the share of profits and in the rate of profit growth, especially in the industrial sector. A decrease will act as a brake on accumula-

tion, but an increasing rate indicates a fall in the share of income going to labor. This brings a weakening in the rate of increase in the demand of consumption goods and indirectly in the demand for investment goods, slowing down the whole process of development.[153]

There are many flaws in such attempts to explain the Depression. First is the wrong assumption that "productivity" growth—namely, an increase in production arising from a given input—should be credited to labor and therefore translate into higher wages. The assumption is based on a two-factor model of an economy.

Also, the monetary explanation of loss of aggregate demand as arising from low wages is not acceptable. National income in the United States in 1919 was $70,281 million and total payroll was $12,427 million. In 1929, the national income was $83,365 million while the total payroll was $14,284 million. The rough ratio between the national incomes in those two years is 1.186, while the ratio between the payrolls is 1.149, a mere 0.3 percent difference. It is clear that, broadly speaking, payroll over the period kept up with national income.

Second, wage earners connected with the capital-intensive sector, to which McElvaine's analysis was directed, averaged no more than about 30 percent of the total working population of the United States over the period.[154] McElvaine and Sylos-Labini argue as if workers in the capital-intensive industries represented the whole of the working population at the time.

Over the period 1922 to 1929 money wages across the board went up by 14 percent. In 1929, just before the crash, nearly four times as many employers reported increases in wages to the Bureau of Labor Statistics as reported wage reductions. In Ohio, a state with good statistics, the total amount paid to wage earners in 1929 was $1.49 billion. In 1932, it was nearly $607 million, a reduction of almost 60 percent. But during the eight years from 1923 to

1930, wage earners' incomes never fell below $1.19 billion, and averaged above $1.3 billion.[155]

It is noteworthy that when the crash occurred, there were calls for wages to be cut, as some felt that the weight of wages was a contributory factor to the Depression. This was opposed initially by government and leading employers in the hope that the maintenance of wage earners' income would prop up demand and help recovery. This does not seem to support any claim that wages before the crash were "poverty" wages.

Excess profits, if they occurred, may be due to the fact that in purely financial terms the price system was pricing materials cheaply in a comparative context—a situation that confirms that the U.S. factor proportions at the time were material-abundant. The position may also mean that prices were high, an accusation that was leveled at the trade associations and amalgamations. It was said that they did not pass on their lower costs (arising from capital-intensive production) in the form of lower prices. But it seems matters were not as simple as that. Recall the statement of the director of the American Institute of Steel Construction that while efficiency in plant production had reduced costs, similar attention needed to be paid to marketing and distribution, and his complaint that there was no scientific approach to the measurement of market possibilities and the control of marketing costs.[156]

A similar situation holds for the petroleum industry, where Halliday complained on September 12, 1929, that while there was overproduction of both crude oil and refining capacity, the industry was also facing overproduction of distribution facilities. This was caused by the need to put "new dealers into the retail business by the orgy of pump loaning and similar practices." "The result," he said, "was the reduction of gallonage of an average service station today compared with that of the horse-drawn tank wagon of twenty years ago." In effect, he is saying that new capital-intensive production was associated with higher distribution costs per gallon of product than before.

In the area of food production, it was reported in the same *New York Times* of Sunday, August 25, 1929, that owners of plants for processing foodstuffs and owners of sales outlets were merging, "but with different ideas of reducing costs by elimination of duplication and general economies that can be effected by efficiency of management."[157]

The director of the Steel Institute touched on a matter that only received full attention following the fall of Fordism some fifty years later: "Mass production is predicated upon constant production and it is expensive if the operation is halted or stopped. Under such a system, it not infrequently happens that 50 percent of the cost of an article is due to plan stoppage, for that cost continues no matter whether the plant is in operation or not. That is why a plant is often encouraged to sell its output at a loss. It is that much more reason why we should take steps to cut those losses before they start." He continued, "There are some companies still left which insist upon taking larger orders before it is realized that they are worth as much as zero with the rim ripped off. It is difficult for such a management to admit that a million times nothing is still nothing." He warned that a large corporation is at a disadvantage over the game of cutting prices because "whenever the selling structure is lowered so that it focuses attention upon nothing but price the small company has the advantage because it has the ability of maintaining personal contact with customers and such contact is often the balance of power in swinging a contract."[158]

It is clear that the twenties were a period of great change in which the growing capital-intensive sector was still finding its feet. Those who invested in it were pioneers and often incurred substantial preproduction and research costs, which they sometimes needed time to recover. Even though they had developed new and efficient production methods and achieved production cost savings, the same could not be said of marketing, where because of the sheer volume and variety of products, appropriate marketing and selling techniques were yet to be developed. As we can see, in some cases marketing costs were larger than before. It will appear from all this that with falling demand, the capital-intensive activities did not have all that much cost savings to pass on in reduced prices or increased wages. According to Blackford, "Scale economies proved more elusive in selling than in making products."[159]

Nor is it right to give the impression that all the inequality in income was only because of large business profits, which, according to the argument, led to new investments, which increased productivity further in a kind of vicious circle. Indeed, substantial wealth for the rich came from property speculation in the 1920s (as in Thailand much later) and from stocks. Almost 74 percent of all 1929 dividends went to fewer than 600,000 individual stockholders with taxable income in excess of $5,000. Just under 25 percent went to the 24,000 making over $100,000, and nearly 6 percent went to 513 individuals whose families reported an income of over $1 million a year.

So the charge that these amalgamations made huge profits cannot therefore easily stand up. Between 1924 and 1929 the rate of profit fell.[160] To put the matter in context, it must be remembered that as the United States entered the twentieth century, its wage rates were higher than those in Europe at the time. Real wages rose again in the United States between 1920 and 1923 but thereafter were practically stationary. In 1929, in fact, there was a noticeable rise in earnings and total wages, a rise that was bound up with the spurt in production that marked the final aggravation of the forces of cyclical breakdown.[161]

The charge that the few who received those profits amassed too much wealth for the good of the economy is not strong either. Smiley has told us that the upward increase in the share of income going to the rich at the time was biased upward because they were based on tax returns at a time when the rich found it advantageous to shift their assets into areas that yield taxable income and to report past incomes that had not previously been reported.[162]

Walton and Rockoff concluded, "A long-term trend towards increased inequality had been interrupted by World War I. So some increase in equality probably represented a return to conditions that were prevalent before the War. The distribution of income was far from equal in 1929, but little evidence exists that something drastic and unexpected had occurred that could explain that the depression that was to follow."[163] There was in any case improvement in the standard of living of a large section of the population over the period, resulting in the formation of a large middle class.

Common to all forms of overproduction/underconsumption theory is the idea that the industrialized system failed to provide the consumers with sufficient purchasing power. Therefore, according to this argument, consumers needed an ever larger income to buy goods; otherwise overproduction was unavoidable. There are three variants of this theory. The first stresses the apparent surfeit of goods, attaching secondary importance to income as such, and is generally known as overproduction theory. The second approaches the problem from the standpoint of the alleged shortage of consumer income—this is underconsumption theory proper. The third emphasizes the maladjustments in income distribution.[164]

What economists mean by overproduction is that more has been produced than can be sold at a price sufficient to provide adequate returns to the producers so as to continue producing at the same rate. But Corey pointed out, "There cannot be even a partial overproduction—or at least not for any appreciable length of time and not of sufficient dimensions to bring about a major industrial depression if prices are right. Much less of course can there be any such thing as 'general overproduction.'"[165] In 1931, an official of the Federal Reserve Bank of New York, charged with providing information on volume of production, stated, "The idea of an unusual rise in total production preceding the crisis [in October 1929], was so far as I can find, a fiction."[166] The overproduction-underconsumption theory, therefore, is unable to account for the loss of aggregate demand.

Temin put the matter in context when he drew attention to the fact that profits rose as a share of national income in the 1920s, the rise being about 5 percent of national income. According to him, if the propensity to consume was 10 percent lower among capitalists than among workers, the decline in consumption caused by the drop of income was about 0.5 percent of national income. He concluded that this was too small a decline to have been a potent factor in the Depression and that underconsumption and overproduction were not useful concepts in the investigation of its causes.[167]

Income inequality, as we earlier emphasized, is the direct result of a structurally unbalanced economy, because rewards for factors in different sectors become highly differentiated. While inequality is a consequence of an unbalanced economy, it is itself not the cause of that imbalance—in this case a depression.

Walton and Rockoff's theme that "something drastic and unexpected" needed to have happened to explain the setting in of depression agrees with Temin's view that something "unanticipated" and "unexplained" resulted in a decline in demand and caused the Depression. Hairault, Hénin, and Portier described this as a "shock" to demand.[168] Thus apart from valiant attempts by some authors to link income inequality with the cause of depression, much of the current literature on how to avoid depression (including Keynes' prescription, which still holds considerable sway) is suffering from a basic error.

In 1934 a psychologist named Morgan, analogizing to physical disease, pointed out there was profound ignorance of the cause of the Depression. "There was ignorance about the significance of the symptoms manifested and the treatments that should be applied and the prognosis for the disease. There is a great temptation to fall into the error of thinking that an accurate description of the symptoms constitutes an explanation; but it is just as much of an error as to think that we have explained a manic-depressive psychosis when we have made careful curves of changes in motor activity, rate of thinking of emotional reactions, and of bodily temperature in the different cycles through which our patient passes." He added, "A still greater error comes when one attempts to cure the disease by treating the symptoms." In many ways, he maintained, the differences between various theories about the causes and cures of the Depression are simply differences about how to treat the symptoms. He too pointed out that various warnings were issued before the crash of 1929: "The Federal Reserve Board tried to put on the brakes by raising the discount rate, by issuing warnings, and by selling securities. . . . Such restraints were about as futile as applying 'straitjackets' and 'restraining devices' on our manic patient. They may hold him down somewhat but they do not cure him."

When the crash came, the Board changed tactics: "They lowered the discount rates and bought securities, both of which processes were an artificial stimulant to businesses; but businesses declined faster. Their tactics were just as futile as the administration of artificial stimulants to the depressed patient in the psychopathic hospital." Then, according to Morgan, attempts were made to soothe the rattled nerves of businesses by optimistic pronouncements, but with about as much effect as "optimistic statements have upon a depressed person." "Then the group that had been imbued with the oversaving philosophy had their inning and people were urged to spend and buy their way back to prosperity. This makes one think of the optimist who tells the depressed patient to get up and dance so that his gloom will vanish." Then we are told that we have produced too much so we have "turned under our crops and killed pigs" on the theory that we must have rising prices to bring back prosperity. "Such destruction, however, did not enable the jobless to buy what was left after the destruction. . . . Then we are told," he said, "that the trouble was with the distribution of wealth and that by taxation, we must extract the savings from the thrifty and give jobs to those who had nothing but that those who were given jobs must not produce or we would have another glut on the market. Finally, the symptom of too little money had to be dealt with. This reminded one of the trick a father played on his son. The son was in deep personal distress because he wanted two pieces of candy instead of the one he possessed. The father broke the candy into two pieces and told the boy that he now had his wish—to dry his tears."[169]

The Great Depression was basically an economic hemorrhage. The capital-intensive sector of the economy at the time was juxtaposed with the low-capital-using sector at a time when the American population was growing significantly through substantial immigration (from 1920 to 1929, the population grew by over 14 percent). It is to be expected that at the low end of the economy, there would have been a substantial increase in labor-using activities, while at the high end, capital intensiveness increased substantially, which leads us to conclude that this sector was increasingly material-saving.

We need to go back to basic principles. In order to produce the enormous increase in capital that occurred during this period, the country needed to draw away from the economy substantial amounts of material and labor, over and above the economy's threshold capital accumulation levels. That violates the conditions required to set up factor proportions at the micro level that can equal the country's natural factor proportions.

It is not necessarily correct to claim, as many writers have claimed, that the increase in capital-intensive businesses over the period 1920–1929 caused unemployment. The era was one of rapid changes in new techniques, and many capital-intensive businesses were born or expanded through the floating of common stock, which was a popular technique at the time.[170] Each such new activity invariably recruited new workers, though not as many as a capital-saving alternative. But nevertheless, they increased employment at a time of high unemployment. How much of this increase in employment was retained depended very much on whether economic conditions favored or disfavored profitability. Total employment will also depend on the condition of the non-capital-intensive sector.[171] Thus employment figures at any given time will therefore reflect the state of the economy more than the direct consequence of enlarging the capital-using sector.

The increasing volume of capital-intensive activities drew not only labor but also material away from the labor-intensive, material-intensive sectors. These sectors comprised the bulk of business outlets and population in the economy. By drawing in labor and material from the rest of the economy, the capital-intensive sectors achieved large increases in output in line with Rybczynski's predictions. The production factor losses suffered by the non-capital-using, material-intensive sectors cut at the root of their economic growth and reduced demand.

In a nonmonetized economy, people pay for what they obtain with what they produce. The money economy does not vitiate this principle. Thus the loss of aggregate demand is not a matter of wages, as McElvaine and others would have it. It starts as a result of the collapse of productive capacity of non-capital-intensive, material-using sectors. It may in time result in increased unemployment in these sectors. However, in the U.S. economy from 1920 to 1929, such unemployment occurred alongside momentary increased employment in the capital-intensive sector. We know, however, that loss of output capacity in the non-capital-intensive sectors led to business closures.

The initial drop in aggregate demand shrank the market for the capital-intensive sectors, soon leaving them with excess capacity. As new waves of capital flowed into the economy, they further exacerbated the already weak production capacity of the rest of the economy. Each new wave of capital helped to widen the factor proportions difference between the high and low ends of the economy. This increased structural imbalance leads to a steady decline in macroeconomic growth.

The financial consequences are not as important as the consequences of the factor misallocation; they are at the edges, not the center, of the issues involved. For example, the capital-intensive sector is more likely to pay higher prices for labor and materials, as these are a smaller fraction of their cost than in other sectors. This tends to attract materials and labor away from the lower-end sectors to the high end, pulling in the same direction as the misallocation of factors and further aggravating the situation. The lower end of the economy is as a result faced with higher labor and material costs, which detracts from their profitability and ability to survive.

It should be clear, therefore, that over the period 1920 to 1929 capital-intensive businesses were engaged in a perpetual struggle against falling rates of profit. The rates fell 33.7 percent from 1923 to 1924, rose 14 percent from 1924 to 1925, fell 22.5 percent from 1926 to 1927, and rose 21 percent from 1927 to 1929.[172] The profit rates fell and rose according to the competition between the more-capital-intensive and less-capital-intensive sectors, while total output was increasing and decreasing in an environment of contracting aggregate demand.

It is therefore clear that what first showed up as an initial loss of productive capacity at the lower end of the U.S. economy not only increased the imbalance in the economy but also accelerated the loss in aggregate demand via a push-pull action between the different sectors. This is the economic hemorrhage that the U.S. economy suffered from at the time.

The stock market crash, which some conventional economists say caused the Great Depression, was itself caused by the state of the economy at the time. The push-pull between the sectors arising from economic imbalance and the ups and downs of the main Wall Street shares were at the heart of the uncertainty and speculation of the late 1920s. The *New York Times* of September 22, 1929, summarized the unsettling stock position of the time as follows: ". . . stocks moved in a very erratic fashion with some wide gains and equally sharp recessions but with the market as a whole revealing a singular lack of confidence in the immediate trend. The fact that leading stocks, such issues as United States Steel Company, General Motors, Chrysler and others of the sort, continue under definite pressure has been mainly responsible for the market's irregularity and lower trend. Some of Wall Street's favorite shares exhibit but feeble rallying power and the market as a whole appears, at the moment, to be without definite or organized leadership."[173]

The stock market crash not only had psychological effects but resulted in the loss of the necessary financial resources to support further common-stock financing. Each of these slowed further growth of the capital-intensive sector. As Keynes indicated, the crash discouraged entrepreneurs from seeking further financing to create more capital-producing aids or engage in new capital-intensive activities. Neither result of the crash had any effect at the low end of the economy, where financial capital plays a relatively small role. In a way, therefore, the stock market crash started the long process that eventually stopped the vicious circle of loss of aggregate demand followed by new capital-intensive activities that further intensified the loss of aggregate demand. To that extent, it can be said that the process is self-correcting. The bank collapses were the result of an economy that was in trouble, not the cause of the poor economy. As we have seen, it was not necessarily true that banks starved businesses of funds.

Economically, therefore, it can be said that recession or depression is a structural problem with a financial shadow. Financial solutions, therefore, may or may not work, depending on whether one picked the point on the shadow that happened to lead to the right spot on the substance.

It should be clear that the problems of an economy that had been structurally unbalanced for about forty years could not be corrected immediately. It is therefore surprising that economists over the years have wondered why it took so long for the U.S. economy to recover from the Depression. It is therefore doubtful that there was anything the federal government could have done in 1929 to stop the Depression. This puts into context the futility of the financial measures adopted after the crash, ostensibly to put the economy back on the track of sustainable growth. Many economists criticized the Hoover administration for not doing the things they thought would have fixed the problem. Walton and Rockoff have charged that "the major deficiencies of the Hoover administration were its persistent refusal to establish a desperately needed federal program of work relief even if it meant deficits, and its failure to press the Federal Reserve to expand money and credit."[174] "Orthodox Keynesians would add that the administration should have deliberately raised spending for whatever purpose and cut taxes to generate 'multiplier effects.' . . . What Hoover should have done was to cut taxes, increase spending to provide relief and demand that the Fed buy bonds in great volume to finance the deficits, bolster bank reserves and ease credit."[175] Autonomous private spending on investment and consumption between 1929 and 1938 totaled $7.1 billion. Because this was lower than the increase in federal spending, Brown concluded that

the attempts at recovery in the 1930s were unsuccessful because the Keynesian prescription was not given the preeminence it deserved.[176]

In effect, economists such as Brown were convinced that the solution was for capital investment to resume, leading to increased consumer spending by pushing money into the economy. But we have pointed out that what was needed was not capital investment. We have also pointed out that the drop in aggregate demand was not caused by lack of money in the pockets of consumers, especially when the cause of this lack has not been substantiated.

By 1937, net national product had risen to $75.1 billion from a low of $42.7 billion, though it was still below the 1929 level. Keynesian economists argued that this boom was the result of the expansion of government spending over the period for relief of the poor and other New Deal programs. All this, it is claimed, was stimulated by the expansion of the money stock from $32.2 billion in 1933 to $45.7 billion in 1937. The monetary expansion was the result of deliberate Federal Reserve policy to increase the money supply.[177] This increase was supposed to have caused the economic boom by enhancing confidence in the banking system and "encourag[ing] people to redeposit currency in the banking system. . . . The fractional reserve system that had worked to destroy the monetary system from 1930 to 1933 now ran in reverse. Even more important . . . was an increase in the monetary base, primarily because of purchases of gold by the U.S. Treasury."[178] This claim is unsubstantiated. If it is followed through, it would imply—based on the mistaken belief by its supporters that what was required to get out of the Depression was increased investment—that over the period 1933 to 1937, or better still from 1930 to 1937, there was an increase in capital investment in industry.

In fact the opposite happened. Yearly purchases of capital equipment, which were at a peak of $7.3 billion (in 1958 dollars) in 1929, declined steadily

Table 8.4

U.S. Savings Deposits during the Great Depression

	Total savings ($ millions)	Number of depositors (thousands)
1930	28,478.6	52,729.4
1931	28,219.6	51,399.4
1932	24,281.3	44,352.1
1933	21,125.5	39,262.4
1934	21,752.5	39,562.1
1935	21,730.1	39,793.6
1936	22,603.9	41,094.2
1937	23,425.3	42,645.0

Source: A Half Century of Progress 1894–1944: Facts and Figures about the Growth of Economic Life in the United States (Minneapolis Investors Syndicate, 1945), p. 4.

over the period to a low of about $2.6 million in 1935. The quantity of new yearly capital equipment introduced to the economy started to rise in 1936–37, a situation that naturally reversed the trend to structural balance that the drop in capital introduction over the previous six or seven years was creating.[179]

The claim that people increased their currency deposits after 1933 is incorrect. Table 8.4 indicates the level of savings deposits and depositors in U.S. banks over the period. Over the period, it is clear that deposits decreased and the number of depositors decreased.

Having explained the pickup in the economy up to 1937, these economists could not explain why the economy quickly reverted to its depressed condition after 1937. According to Walton and Rockoff, "Many attributed the renewed onslaught of depression to reform measures introduced and passed in 1935 and 1936. Social security and the new freedom granted to labor came in for some harsh words. But most of the criticism was directed toward the anti-business political climate created by the Roosevelt administration which . . . made vigorous business expansion impossible."[180] By business expansion, the authors were referring to capital investment. But their assertion is incorrect because

the introduction of new capital equipment into the U.S. economy increased from 1935 right up to 1941 ($2.6 billion in 1935, $3.7 billion in 1936, $4.7 billion in 1937, $2.9 billion in 1938, $3.5 billion in 1939, $4.7 billion in 1946, and $6.0 billion in 1941).[181] In conventional economic parlance, it can be said that the period from 1936–37 to 1941 was one of increasing investment in U.S. manufacturing.

World War II

World War II shaped the U.S. economy in distinctly new directions and left indelible marks on the body of conventional theories of economic development and growth. Keynesian economists, for example, have extended their reach into modern economic texts because they believe that the economic "success" of 1942–45 was the result of Keynesian policies. Vatter, who himself attempted a detailed study of the World War II U.S. economy, concluded that "only the onset of the war brought into operation Keynesian deficit financing of sufficient magnitude to end twelve years of mass unemployment."[182] One economist claimed that the war gave economists and statesmen everywhere an object lesson in the form of Keynesianism that was not forgotten.[183] And the fact that mass production techniques enabled the United States to meet wartime demands has simply reinforced economists' belief that capital-intensive techniques are what economic growth is all about.

The Keynesian explanation of the U.S. World War II economy has troubled some economists. Higgs worried that some analysts have blinded Keynesian and monetarists' explanations, treating them as complementary, to point to the rapid increase in the stock of money during the war as what finally got the U.S. economy out of the Depression. He argued that it was not Keynesianism that wiped out unemployment in the United States during the war. According to him, four-tenths of the total labor force at the time was not being used to produce consumer goods or capital capable of yielding consumer goods in the future, according to conventional economic wisdom, and in fact consumers were worse off during the war, though they felt wealthier because they were building up bank accounts and holding bonds.[184]

Keynes sketched out his ideas in a 1941 pamphlet, "How to Pay for the War." According to him, government-directed expenditures would produce the output necessary to create the material goods for war and civilian consumption and investment. Full use of the economy's productive capacity set an upper limit to what was possible. Since the money cost of war goods became spendable income in the economy at large and the war products did not enter that economy to absorb those expenditures, taxation, bond sales, and postwar credits (interest-earning deposits made by workers and frozen for the duration) must absorb the excess income or else inflation would result. Economists have wrongly asserted that "How to Pay for the War" is a direct application of Keynes' "General Theory of Employment, Interest and Money." But as Higgs was suggesting, Keynes' prescription is valid only if the increased consumer spending triggered new investments—which were supposed to get the economy out of depression and in the process bring back full employment. Higgs observed that between 1940 and 1944 unemployment fell by either 7.45 million (official measure) or 4.62 million (Darby measure) while the armed forces increased by 10.87 million. He concluded, "Even if one views eliminating civilian unemployment as tantamount to producing prosperity, one must recognize that placing either 146 or 235 persons (depending on the unemployment concept used) in the armed forces to gain a reduction of 100 persons in civilian unemployment was a grotesque way to achieve prosperity, even if a job were a job. . . . Whether the government ran deficits or not, whether money stock increased or not, massive military conscription was sure to de-

crease dramatically the rate of unemployment."[185] If the period 1942 to 1945 was one of economic growth, it certainly was not because it was consumer-led. It was not a Keynesian solution.

Higgs' analysis of the World War II economy typified the problems facing conventional economists trying to study economies. Higgs set himself the task of reassessing what he called the consensus view on the wartime economy. "For nearly half a century," he charged, "historians and economists, almost without exception, have misinterpreted the performance of the U.S. economy in the 1940s. The reigning view has two aspects: one pertaining to the conceptualization and measurement of the economy's performance; the other pertaining to the explanation of that performance in macroeconomic theory." Higgs presented six different published sets of financials of U.S. GNP from 1939 to 1949, some of which he described as "conceptually problematic." Higgs, in effect, showed that conventional economics lacked the conceptual framework with which to analyze a war economy. More important, Higgs reviewed the dilemma facing conventional analysts. The crucial question, he pointed out, was whether war spending purchased a final good and hence belongs in GNP or an intermediate good and so should be classed outside GNP.

Kuznet introduced—apparently from nowhere—the concept of peacetime and wartime GNP. He argued that while ordinarily goods that contribute to consumer satisfaction or add to the stock of capital from which future flows of goods are derived should be considered GNP, one must recognize that success in the life-and-death struggle of war and preservation of a country's social framework is, as a purpose, at least as important to the welfare of individuals as standard concepts of a good.[186] "When intended for defense," he claimed, "war production may be viewed as similar to other capital investments designed to avoid or mitigate the effects of calamities that threaten the production fabric of the country."[187] Dissenters to Kuznet were many; they wanted to eliminate from GNP anything that was not a direct source of utility, as well as anything that was a necessary input to activities that may yield utility. They wanted to count only activities that constituted a measure of what they called "economic welfare." This meant that they eliminated all defense spending, arguing that even though military spending was not wasteful, it nevertheless did not contribute directly to welfare. Others regard warfare as creating a difficulty in distinguishing between the final and intermediate output of government. Evaluation of the World War II economy has therefore been a subject of continued controversy among conventional economists.

These are all essentially sociopolitical issues and not scientific economics. Sociopolitical issues beg the question and provide an escape when macroeconomic analysis reaches a dead end. The result is a resort to economic intellectualism. There is therefore no conceptual basis in conventional economics to ascertain whether the World War II economy was one of growth or a slowdown, as proponents of each are equally strongly entrenched.

The macro economy of the United States during World War II is quite easy to examine in scientific terms. It consists simply of assessing how production factors were used and how far they complied with our factor proportions stipulations. Men and women in the armed forces constitute labor that "emigrated" out of the economy. War goods together with consumer goods constitute the level of demand in the economy, irrespective of their so-called welfare utility status. What was needed was capital at a threshold level vis-à-vis this demand in a dynamic context.

Different estimates have been made by economists about the growth of production output over this period in the United States. Cape estimated that between 1940 and 1943, output doubled in Germany and Russia. It quadrupled in Japan, but in the United

States, it increased twenty-five times.[188] Novick, Anshen, and Truppner indicated that the annual gross national product (output of goods and services) in the United States rose more than 50 percent after allowing for price changes. The volume of manufactures tripled, and output of raw materials increased by 60 percent. The volume of construction (mainly for new war plants) more than doubled from its 1939 level.[189] The War Production Board in a report in 1945 said that from 1940 to 1945 manufacturing capacity increased by close to half. Whatever the statistics, it is clear according to Vatter that the United States performed a miracle in outproducing the Axis powers so soon after entering the war.[190]

The impressive production record of the U.S. economy has been accounted for by conventional economists. Walton and Rockoff boasted that "under Roosevelt's leadership, the United States adopted a bold plan of economic mobilization and used its vast industrial might to mass-produce arms and overwhelmed the Axis with sheer firepower." Cape claimed that during the war "America mass-produced wonder drugs. Not only were supplies such as small arms and ammunitions mass-produced, but also planes and even ships to carry the arms to the theatre of war. . . . To some extent . . . mass production techniques were even used in producing destroyers."[191] Janeway stated, "The application of mass production methods to defense production problems . . . began to earn dividends in the form of manpower saved."[192] To a large number of economists, the production achievement of the war economy was due to mass production strategies in war industries.

Other economists have accounted for this by claiming vast increases in capital productivity, and/or labor productivity, and/or TPF gains. Vatter asserted that "output expansion for war, and to a small degree likewise for the civilian sector, was aided by productivity which rose over the years 1940–

44." He arrived at the figure of a 27 percent in labor productivity by dividing the sum of civilian production and military commodities purchased by the U.S. government (which he said rose by 52 percent) by private civilian labor hours. He claimed that total production expansion was also fostered by an accompanying 30 percent increase in output per unit of capital input in the total economy. He asserted that the capital productivity was abetted by two-shift and even round-the-clock operations in many cases. Using Kendrick's TPF indexes, where 1929 = 100, and defining increases in TPF as output rise relative to rise in all inputs, Vatter also asserted that there were proportionate increases in TPF to 131.3 (1941), 133.1 (1942), 137.3 (1943), 147.9 (1944), and 152.9 (1945), compared to 85.1 (1921 and 1922), 90.2 (1923), and 93.6 (1924 and 1925). He claims that overall productivity rose more during the period 1941–44 than in 1921–24 and was substantially better if the terminal date is extended to 1945. Proportionate increases in productivity, he said, were 10 percent in the 1920s and 12.6 and 16.5 percent in the periods 1942–44 and 1941–45, respectively.[193]

The United States' entry into the war resulted in a sharp drop in private investment as the government turned the resources of the economy over to the war effort. The expansion in private capital investment that occurred from the middle of 1940 to the end of 1941 was aborted by the attack on Pearl Harbor and the country's entry into the war. During the war, 2,265 industrial plants were authorized by the DPC at a total cost of over $8.3 billion, comprising military-related industries (aircraft, aluminum, aviation fuel, chemicals, machine tools, ordnance, communications, shipbuilding, iron and steel, other minerals, and synthetic rubber).[194] In general, private investment centered around the expansion of established concerns when they found a niche in the market. The overall macroeconomic factor proportion relationships are specifically of

interest. The drop in private investment meant that the source of capital concentration and intensiveness was largely removed.

Shapiro and Mendelson noted that "the private sector of the economy added virtually nothing to the fixed plant equipment during the war. The 70 percent hike in GNP from 1941 through 1945 was due mostly to a more extensive use of existing facilities rather than proportionate increase in physical facilities of the country. By the end of 1945, the net book value of the fixed assets of all non-financial corporations was below the figure for the end of 1941 and about the same as that of the end of 1939."[195] The real net value of manufacturing assets (1958 dollars) was $31.7 billion in 1945, compared to $32.7 billion in 1941.[196]

Vatter commented, "These great wartime production increases were attained primarily by employing more labor in combination with more energy and raw materials input, but with moderate addition to the pre-existing capital stock (which, of course, was underutilized in 1940). The civilian labor input increases were a combination of more employed non-agricultural workers and longer hours." According to him, "the large army of unemployed and attendant excess capacity in industry facilitated rapid conversion to a war economy in 1941 and 1942. . . . However, except in raw materials, what was more urgently needed for defense production was re-tooling, revamping and coordinating, rather than merely stepping up the rate of production and squeezing out excess capacity. In many lines of production, conversion was an agonizing task."[197] The gross flow of investment goods contracted to a low in 1943 that was only 37 percent of the 1940 level (and much below replacement requirements).[198]

Walton and Rockoff said, "The great bulk of the resources for the war effort were obtained by employing previously unemployed resources and by using already employed resources more intensively."[199] It is clear that since the amount of capital invested in industry over this war period had not grown to match the increases in output achieved, it seems somewhat simplistic to attribute the gains to labor or capital productivity simply by dividing the gains by capital invested or labor input. It is also simplistic to adopt a two-factor model, as Vatter sought to do.

Over the period 1942–45, vast changes occurred in U.S. macroeconomic factor proportions. The fact that only halfway through this period, the net capital increase was less than the wear and tear on existing capital (production aids) meant that the macroeconomic factor proportions were capital-saving. Taking the aircraft sector as an example, the value of the capital assets in that sector increased seventeen times between 1939 and 1945, whereas the labor employed in it increased over twenty-five times. Shipbuilding, with total capital invested of $2.1 billion over the period, had a total employment of 751,000, a capital/labor ratio of about $2,720, which is extremely low.[200] In short, both of these sectors, which economic historians have described as the core of World War II mass production, were essentially capital-saving.

The essence of most mass production during World War II was standardization. Janeway remarked that as the war was already raging in Europe and America was mobilizing to assist its allies in Europe, the Office of Production Management (OPM) realized it needed an executive engineering apparatus to stop what he called "two sources of immediate waste and future tragedy" in the country's mobilization—the first originating with manufacturers' specializing in government military work and the second in what he called a "group of businessmen who regarded defense contracts as a distraction." He said that as a class, manufacturers of war equipment had no conception of standardization (and therefore of volume). They developed a vested interest in their individualistic methods and

models, which they defended fiercely. The OPM counted no less than fifty-five different types of planes, and the number of parts and accessories was much greater. Janeway observed that many of the companies involving themselves in the war program approached their new assignments less as entrepreneurs, manufacturers, or creative engineers than as mere contractors. "Little wonder that skepticism greeted all assertions that mass production could revolutionize airplane and ordinance manufacturing. . . . Yet this was what they [the companies] soon began to do."[201]

In 1942, for example, the automobile industry pooled its production facilities, technical experience, and managerial talents for the manufacture of war materials by creating the Automotive Council for War Production. The council's formation "recognizes that with the country looking to the mass production industries for the utmost contribution to victory, it is imperative that, in addition to all that has been done, every cooperative facility should be utilized to attain maximum volume." The council set up committees on various subgroups such as bombers, airplane frames, guns, and other ordnance and military vehicles.[202] As a result, Boeing in January 1942 reported that it had stepped up plane output by 70 percent after remodeling its new Valtes plant at Downway, where it moved away from custom-building planes by developing the first powered conveyor that could turn out planes in mass production.

Mass production in shipbuilding also came into play. United States Steel and Bethlehem Steel were the dominant players in West Coast shipbuilding and steel marketing and regarded Henry Kaiser as an upstart contractor. They had fixed ideas about how much inventory was needed to support boat construction. Kaiser wanted to prove that he could produce ships faster. At a time when the experienced shipbuilding companies were refusing to commit themselves to the unfamiliar tasks warship building called for, Kaiser "reached out for every derrick, crane and bulldozer he could lay his hands on." He hired "every floater willing to take the highest pay, without regard to qualifications, on the assumption that everyone who could be had to be used."

He had a cost-plus contract with the government. It was an unbelievably extravagant plan in which the government was ready to gamble that higher pay would mean higher production output. Even Kaiser agreed that his ships "were not built for immortality." They fell far short of traditional shipbuilding standards. But on the other hand, traditional shipbuilding standards were much too high to meet the need to produce vast amounts of tonnage quickly. In such a desperate situation, Kaiser's drive and the scale on which he had the audacity to spend public money allowed him to improvise a new production technique. As much cutting, shaping, and fabricating as possible was done behind the ways, while the steel moved up the keel. This reduced to a minimum the time each ship delayed its successor in the ways. In 1941, it took 355 days to deliver a ship, but by 1942, Kaiser's yards could complete one in 14 days. By 1943, one ship was being produced every 12 hours. It is clear that this kind of mass production was achieved through work rearrangement in Taylor's style and did not need capital-intensive techniques. The age of the all-welded ship had arrived.[203]

War mobilization quickly changed the orthodox economic view, which came to regard people as production assets. All previously unutilized labor was brought into production. The resultant labor-using techniques that dominated the World War II U.S. economy can be illustrated by the following account of the role of women at the time:

> Women are now working as welders in shipyards, aircraft factories, machine shops, munitions works and on precision instruments. Despite the pre-war notion that to be adept at welding took years of experience, women have already effectively replaced men as welders in aircraft assembly plants and have mastered various types of welding—sport, arc and oxyacetylene welding—on engine mounts, manifolds and other airplane parts. They have out-produced men in such jobs as welding on wing panels and control surfaces. . . . At one shipyard, women welders were found to be working not only on the top decks of ships on the ways and the outfitting docks, but also on lower decks and deep in the holds, where they carry equipment up and down. For welding in cramped quarters one shipyard used women because they are generally smaller than men. . . . Welding involves much climbing and weightlifting. Frequently the women welders must carry their welding lines up and down stairs and ladders and along catwalks. In most yards, the smallest section of welding hose is fifty feet long and weighs thirty-five pounds. Sometimes the women must pull the welding lines out from under several other heavy lines stocked on top of their lines, often several times a day. In overhead welding, the lines must be on the shoulder to hold them in position and this also causes a strain. In some enclosed places, welders in addition to their welding regalia, often heavy and warm, must wear respirators.[204]

Novick, Anshen, and Truppner also pointed out that even the 7.5 million men and women added to the wartime workforce would not have been sufficient had not the length of the average manufacturing work week been increased by 20 percent, from 37.7 hours to 45.2 hours.[205]

Mass production required the development of appropriate engineering solutions and tooling to changes required in the plant and machinery. The conversion of auto industry plants to aircraft and aircraft component production required appropriate engineering solutions, as aircraft production required tolerances smaller than those in autos.[206] The challenge to find simple engineering solutions is further illustrated by the case of H. J. Heinz, a food product manufacturer, which converted its production lines to make wooden aircraft parts. Over a period of three months, all the building facilities were converted, engineering and research staffs were formed from regular employees, aeronautical experts were called in, supplies of plywood and glues were obtained, and even the old Heinz machine shop was called into service, shaping jigs to fit out various airplane parts.[207] The whole project was not capital intensive.

It is clear that tooling was a cornerstone of the United States' mass production achievements during the war, since this facilitated the production of standardized items and conversion of existing plant to war production requirements. Conversely, elimination of costly and elaborate tooling can sometimes facilitate a faster production rate. The machine tool industry was therefore a strategic sector of the war effort while the machinist was the essence of wartime production.

In war conditions, three factors tended to make for capital-saving production facilities. First, time was of the essence. What was needed was to erect a plant in the shortest time so as to obtain war goods as soon as possible. Second, such plants were generally viewed as short-term installations, to be dismantled or sold off after the war or converted to some other peacetime use. Third, with the critical material shortages during wartime, planners were loath to allocate needed material toward the building of plants. These factors were always balanced by the preference of military authorities to place procurement orders with large producers.

The wartime control of material was significant in that it sought to mobilize all material resources and expand the production of all needed materials. Rather than embark on vast plant expansion in order to produce needed materials, the role of wartime planning sought to divert materials such as steel and petroleum in a way that limited their low-priority consumption. The shortage of tin, for example, necessitated the shifting of food canning away from nonessential items to canned food for army rations. The container industry moved away from manufacture of folding boxes for civilian use to boxes for small ammunitions. A long list of civilian uses of tin were banned, while the allocation to others was drastically cut. The enormous increases in raw materials used for war-related purposes and the substantial rise in GNP, according to Vatter, were effected without any increases in the quantity of imports over the whole period.[208] Development of new materials and substitutes accelerated because of war needs. For example, production of synthetic rubber, a replacement for imported natural rubber, increased almost ten times during the war. And due to wartime shortages of relevant natural products, synthetic flavors were developed; their use has continued ever since.

The war brought increased production of some materials, such as vanadium, tungsten, nylon, and aluminum. The principal use of vanadium was in the manufacture of high-speed, low-alloy tool steels and high-speed cast iron and steel forgings, the demand for which increased because of war needs. All vanadium produced from December 1941 to February 1944 was sold to the U.S. government for war purposes. Tungsten was also used in steel tools. Increased production of nylon arose from a multitude of war needs, including parachutes, flak vests, airstrip reinforcement, and fibers for use in dollar bills. Similarly, aluminum usage and output increased because of the war. The production of aluminum, vital for airplanes, tripled in 1944, with nearly three hundred thousand planes built. Combining aluminum with such metals as beryllium, magnesium, copper, and zinc, as well as with silicon, it was possible to stave off metal fatigue and deterioration from high temperatures. Aluminum mat was produced for use in the construction of advanced airfields.[209] It is evident from these few examples that wartime material management achieved a more effective use of the country's endowed material resources. This significantly increased the economy's output.

The war accelerated the development of the electronics industry, which was to play a dominating role in the postwar U.S. economy. The customer for the industry in 1944 was the United States government and its allies. It was estimated that industry sales were $270 million in 1939, $300 million in 1941, and $4 billion in 1944. Such a dollar volume was almost equal to the third largest industry group in the United States, automobiles and automobile equipment. The products of the industry covered almost all aspects of the war, including aircraft, ground vehicles, ships, fixed communication equipment, radar, and artillery equipment. About 95 percent of the electronic product output was used in communications, but by 1943, industrial electronics had already started to shorten production schedules through elimination of mechanical systems. One application was radiothermics, used in "explosive" riveting during aircraft assembly because it simplified fastening problems and accelerated output almost a hundredfold. Radiothermics also found application in the manufacture of wooden aircraft parts, reducing the time it took to bring the wood up to the appropriate temperature. At the end of 1943, 1,618 companies in the United States had entered the electronics field, with 968 product trade names and 232 groups of products.[210]

Many texts on the World War II economy give the impression that the enormous production achieved between 1941 and 1945 was for large, purely military such as aircraft, ships, ammunition, and so on.[211] But mass production was also a feature of many other sectors of the economy. There were enormous demands during the war for very ordinary things such as leather goods, shoes, textiles, food products, and so on. In 1943, for example, a problem arose as to how to expand textile production as defense procurements increased. At the time, cotton mills were producing 11 billion square yards of cloth, a figure considered impossible a few years before (when the annual average was 8 bil-

lion square yards). Not only were textiles required for direct use by the military, but there were indirect defense needs, such as in cable insulation, motor vehicles, shoe linings, and so on.

Demand for paper shot up because of war needs, and so both "obsolete" production units and new units were brought into operation. Domestic mill production increased from 87.2 percent to 107 percent and paperboard output increased from 78 to 101 percent during the war years.

By 1943, the Machinery Dealers National Association in New York had set up a nonprofit clearinghouse to help ferret out idle machines that could be put to work in shops with war contracts. The association traced sales its members made to nonessential industries. Where the equipment was found idle, the owner was urged to sell or lend it to the government or a war contractor.

Plywood is another case. By 1942, fully 60 percent of production (already at record levels) was being used in defense, including in airplanes, torpedo boats, minesweepers, cargo vessels, chemical vats, and so on. The multiplicity of new uses to which plywood was put to during the war helped to release aluminum and steel for other purposes. "The industry is being asked to do jobs hitherto regarded as technically impossible," reported the *New York Times* of January 2, 1942.

Plant conversion during the war was not restricted to war vehicles, planes, and ammunition. Many small companies, for example, converted their facilities to make gas masks for use by civilians near the East and West Coasts.

There were complaints that small companies were overlooked by official procurement during the war. Of the $175 billion of prime contract awarded between June 1940 and September 1944, over one-half went to only thirty-three corporations; 70 percent went to a group of a hundred corporations. While a survey in 1943 found that 252 of the largest contracting corporations subcontracted about a third of the value of their prime contracts, three-fourths of that went to other large concerns (over five hundred employees).[212] The chairman of a U.S. Senate special committee noted, "The basis of free competitive enterprise has been practically suspended by the exigencies of war. . . . The trend towards the expansion of big concerns and the wiping out of smaller ones has been renewed with greater impetus than before."

But it was not correct that the war economy tended to destroy small businesses. A survey by the Office of War Information showed that half of the 3,446 small manufacturers contacted said they expected their business to be as good or better than in 1942, and two-thirds expressed satisfaction with their backlog of orders. About 58 percent were found to be engaged directly or indirectly with war production. Of the remaining, approximately 10 percent had been unable to get war contracts, and 32 percent said they had not tried either because they had enough civilian business or for some other reason. It was found that most of the businesses could not increase production much more with existing plant. Forty-three percent were unable to increase war production under any circumstances.

Vatter concluded that World War II weakened the market position of small manufacturing firms in the United States.[213] He observed that small firms accounted for about 26 percent of total manufacturing employment in December 1939 but that this share had declined to only 19 percent five years later. This reduction occurred in the context of a 55 percent jump in total manufacturing over the period. (His definition of small business included firms with less than a hundred employees, in contrast to other studies that classed as small businesses with fewer than five hundred employees.) It must be noted that small firms may well be capital-intensive, while a firm with more employees can be labor-intensive.

Vatter's conclusion is relevant only in the sociopolitical context. It does not help us determine whether the economy at the time was on a sustainable growth path or not. It does not inform us about the macroeconomic structure. Vatter failed to inquire into the production techniques that large firms used during this period in order to achieve the large increases in employment he mentioned. He unfortunately seemed to have assumed, without saying so, that big firms were synonymous with capital intensiveness. Only by analyzing the factor proportions of each activity vis-à-vis that of the total economy itself is it possible to give definite answers on the structural balance of the war economy and thus its growth potential. The irrelevance of Vatter's conclusion was all too evident when a few pages later he concluded that, "It would appear that some of the fear for the fate of small manufacturers during reconversion was exaggerated."[214]

Our review of the United States World War II economy shows that the economy moved toward a more balanced structure compared to the decade before it. The country resorted to production techniques that in broad terms sought maximal use of resources that the country had in abundance—labor and material. Indeed, the United States proceeded to expand the variety and amount of resources utilized and to economize on capital formation (which would have taken up much labor and materials during wartime). The result was an economy that, contrary to Higgs' contention, could rightly be described as "war prosperity." The shared prosperity of the United States over the World War II period was best summarized by Zinn: "The biggest gains in corporate profits occurred and rose from $6.4 billion in 1940 to $10.8 billion in 1944. But enough went to workers and farmers to make them feel the system was doing well for them."[215]

A number of observations can be made from this conclusion. First is that the war prosperity was not a Keynesian cure. The recovery of the economy during World War II was not engineered by increased demand arising from more money in workers' pockets. The economy thrived because it was more structurally balanced. Second is that a nonmarket economy can be as successful as a market economy. What Higgs and many others call a command economy, not subject to price mechanism, can achieve the result of steady sustainable economic growth. The type of command economy the United States ran during World War II may be what many poor countries need provided they get the principles of factor proportions and their appropriate production techniques right. The war was a time when the U.S. government marshaled all production factors in the economy and sidestepped all the inequilibria a price system would have caused in the economy. Those who insist that democracy and sustainable economic growth go hand in hand will have cause to pause and realize—as we have stressed all along in this book—that economic growth is exogenous and could be achieved in any socio-political environment. But the war demonstrated the Soviets' large war capability, and in the face of a Europe that was devastated by war, the threat of the Soviet giant framed America's postwar economic and military strategy, geared toward containing the socialist threat to the institution of private property and the capitalist order everywhere.[216] This was the start of the United States' internationalized campaign to link democracy with economic growth.

Postwar Economy

When the war finished, the men in the armed forces returned and the economy experienced an "external" input of labor, which in ordinary Rybczynski fashion would draw capital and material away from existing capital- and material-intensive activities in the economy—though there were not many of these at the time, by our analysis. But this input of labor would normally require across-the-board use of more labor-intensive techniques in order for the economy to continue in a more structurally balanced

state. Instead, the years after the war ended saw large increases in capital formation. Shapiro and Mendelson noted that U.S. corporate fixed investment was already rising when the postwar decade opened. The rate of increase slowed after a few years but continued to drift upward. By 1955 fixed investment was $24.5 billion per year, compared with $13.7 billion in 1946.[217]

Thus by 1950 the U.S. economy was becoming increasingly more imbalanced and was heading toward the boom-and-bust economic cycles that characterized its economy for most of the remaining part of the twentieth century. Periods of steady, sustainable growth usually provided businesses with an incentive to increase their capital formation in order to take further advantage of the boom. This worsened the structural imbalance, which in turn initiated trends toward recession. That reduced capital formation and over time moved the economy toward balance. The cycle then would start again. In the 1970s Mandel described it this way: "The upturn and the beginning of the boom are precisely the phases of the cycle in which massive renovation of fixed capital occurs in a manner rather concentrated in time, not staggered more or less proportionally over the years of its 'moral' duration. The cyclic movement is clearly stimulated and tends to be reproduced through its echo effects."[218]

When in time this trend was replicated in other Western advanced economies, the issues became internationalized. The postwar international financial arrangements between the United States and Europe were aimed essentially at solving the immediate problems that faced them at the time. For example, Britain desperately needed U.S. help and wanted trade with America expanded and facilitated. Lord Keynes, in urging the setting up of the IMF, argued that the Fund would give "everyone a breather": "If there were no Fund a crisis would ultimately arise because of the inability of the rest of the world to pay for exports from the United

States. . . . If the trouble were temporary, all will be well but if it got worse it would give all countries time to work out a solution together in a rational, friendly, orderly way."

Lord Keynes admitted that the proposals for setting up the IMF and the International Bank for Reconstruction and Development (IBRD) were subject to criticisms. In pressing for these proposals to be adopted, he said that even he could do a good job of criticizing these proposals but that "all the possible alternatives were so much worse that the world could not do anything else but accept if it wished to have a post-war era of expanded foreign trade, production and employment and avoid the monetary chaos, restricted trade, depression and unemployment that followed the last World War."[219]

The IMF and IBRD proposals were an attempt to establish a delicate balance. There were strong feelings in the United States that Europe was seeking ways to get the Americans to finance the war reconstruction of many countries. Some key Americans would have preferred that the United States lend Great Britain $5 billion and "let the rest of the world go hang," as Lord Keynes described the attitude. Keynes and his U.S. counterparts did a fine job of championing and pushing through these changes by a series of compromises and assumptions, many of which have not been borne out by history.

One postwar consequence of the economic recessions inherent in the boom-bust cycle is that capital-intensive companies in the West needed to find ways to reduce the cycle's adverse effects. They sought to do this both by diversification into unrelated fields and by internationalizing their businesses. The result was the beginning of concentration and movement of capital and internationalization of production.

These post–World War II changes form the base of the present day's international financial structure, now moving into globalization. It is clear from these historical considerations that these postwar changes in international economic relations and their wider effects are not the result of a scientifically reasoned economic theory.

9

New Economy

Third Industrial Divide

The U.S. economy, the most advanced in the world, grew rapidly for a decade starting in the early 1990s. The question is whether this spectacular growth heralds something different in the United States' economic structure. In a lecture in September 1998, in the midst of this spectacular growth, Alan Greenspan defined the issue as "whether there has been a profound and fundamental alteration in the way our economy works that creates discontinuity from the past and promises a significantly higher path of growth than has been experienced in recent decades."[1] According to him, it was not enough to say that the American economy is a new economy simply because it has experienced significant growth. To call it a new economy, it needed to be shown that the economy now works in a different way.

That something that had changed significantly was attested to in the 2001 *Economic Report of the President,* in which the president's Council of Economic Advisers said, "The remarkable economic trends of the 1990s took many by surprise. They represented a distinct change from the 1970s and 1980s, decades in which the economy was plagued by persistent inflation, periodically high unemployment, slow growth in productivity, rising inequality and large federal budget deficits."[2]

Greenspan's view is somewhat ambivalent. In 1999 he remarked, "We policymakers have engaged in a lot of on-the-job training in recent years. The remarkable American economy whose roots are still not conclusively known and the Asian crises that caught us by surprise, among other humbling experiences, have made policymakers particularly sensitive as to how fast the world can shift under our feet."[3] By as late as 1999 (a little less than a decade after the change in the structure of the economy began) some economists, such as Solow, were still not sure that anything had changed. The *Wall Street Journal* reported that those it called "renowned skeptics" on the subject of technology's contribution to the economy "are now having second thoughts."[4] The skeptics were looking through the dark glasses of conventional economics. Later that same year Greenspan said, "With trend growth in productivity now clearly in play, the weakness of a simple demand-side evaluation of economic forces has been brought into sharp focus. It may no longer be the case that an acceleration in demand presages an overheated and unstable economy."[5] Some well-known economists were sure that nothing was changing or would ever change.[6] And then early in 2000 he said that "it has become increasingly difficult to deny that something profoundly different from the typical postwar business cycle has emerged. . . . Analysts are struggling to create a credible conceptual framework to fit a pattern of interrelationships that have defied conventional wisdom based on our economy's history of the past half century. . . . It may take years before we fully understand the nature of the rapid changes currently confronting our economy."[7] They have not.

Curiously, in the same speech Greenspan said, "I do not say we are in a new era, because I have experienced too many alleged new eras in my lifetime that have come and gone. We are far more likely, instead, to be experiencing a structural shift similar to those that have visited our economy from time to time in the past. These shifts can have profound effects, often overriding conventional economic pattern for a number of years, before these patterns begin to show through again over the longer term."[8]

Because Greenspan thinks these shifts may not be permanent, he makes the need to understand their nature less of a priority. President Clinton's Council of Economic Advisers, for its part, asserted, "It will be a grave error to assume that the economy has been so transformed that the basic rules of economics no longer apply."[9] In his appearance before a Senate committee in September 2000, however, Greenspan admitted that the U.S. economy had exhibited features that had not been seen before. It is these new features that constitute what many people term the "New Economy." The *Economic Report of the President* defined what, in the view of Clinton's Council of Economic Advisers, constitutes the New Economy: "the extraordinary gains in performance —including rapid productivity growth, rising incomes, low unemployment and moderate inflation —that have resulted from this combination of mutually reinforcing advances in technology, business practices and economic policies."[10]

A *Wall Street Journal* article in January 2000 defined the New Economy in terms of three changes in the American economy. The first is that the most important source of wealth has changed, with wealth-creating innovations substituting knowledge for energy or materials. The article quoted Greenspan's statement that through the second half of the twentieth century, the real value of output has tripled with no increase in the weight of materials produced. In all cases, it argued that there was substitution of knowledge for mass and effort. In the long term, it claimed, wealth will continue to increase in a less and less materially based economy. Creativity is overtaking capital as the principal elixir of growth.

The second change the article points out is that the nature of value is different. In the past, supply and demand meant that increased supply caused lower value. Now, value tends to increase as supply increases. The article cites as an example what it called "knowledge-replete products" such as music: "Web pages and operating systems can be stamped out over and over. After making the first copy, the marginal cost of every other copy is virtually nil, even as its value to the user grows," it claimed.

The third change described in the article is a basic change in economic decision making. "At one time, if you had 50 or 100 giant companies [in the United States] doing the same thing in lockstep at the same time, you could destroy the economy. . . . But you don't have that anymore. . . . The economy is splintering into ever-smaller and more specialized pieces."[11]

Each of these three defining characteristics of the New Economy was an attack on the accepted norms of conventional economic thinking. So how does conventional economics explain the rapid productivity growth, rising income, low unemployment, and moderate inflation that characterized the U.S. economy in the 1990s? Greenspan points out that sharp increases in productivity are said to occur normally when the economy is recovering from recession. But since 1995, the U.S. economy has been following a steeper productivity trend, which started well after the 1990–91 recession was over. Statistics suggest that none of the acceleration in productivity after 1995 was cyclical.[12] The explanation for these unprecedented increases in labor productivity, he said, hinges on technological synergies that have developed, especially among microprocessor, laser, fiber-optic, and satellite technologies. These, Greenspan said, have dramatically raised the potential rates of return not only on new telecommunication investments but more broadly on many types of equipment that embody or utilize the newer technologies.[13]

These newer technologies, according to Greenspan, have begun to alter the manner in which Americans do business and create value—often in ways not readily foreseeable five years ago. He asserted that the defining characteristic of the current wave of technology is the role of information. Prior to the advent of the avalanche of information technology (IT) innovations, most business decisions were hampered by limited information. Because of this, businesses required "substantial programmed redundancies to function effectively." Doubling up on materials and people was an essential backup to the inevitable maladjustments of real-time activity in a company. He argued that information technology has therefore reduced the labor and cost involved in doing business. For example, information access in real time resulting from such processes as electronic data interface between the retail checkout and the factory or the satellite location of trucks is said to have led to reductions in delivery lead times and the related work-hours required for production and delivery of all sorts of goods, from books to capital equipment. Shortened lead times and reduced need for redundancy reduce the cost of capital. The rapid pace of innovation that has fostered shortened product cycles has also contributed to driving down the prices of high-tech equipment.

Greenspan's overall position is that because of developments such as information technology, "fewer goods and worker hours are caught up in activities that, while perceived as necessary insurance to sustain valued output, in the end produce nothing of value. . . . Those intermediate production and distribution activities, so essential when information and quality control were poor, are therefore being reduced in scale and, in some cases, eliminated."[14] Design time and costs have fallen

with computer modeling, for example, and medical diagnostics have become more accurate and faster with access to heretofore unavailable information. Greenspan concluded, "In short, information technology raises output per hour in the total economy principally by reducing hours worked on activities needed to guard productive processes against the unknown and the unanticipated. Narrowing the uncertainties reduces the number of hours required to maintain a given level of production readiness. . . . Employment of scarce resources to deal with heightened risk premiums has been reduced."[15] He also asserted that some new technologies have introduced products and services with more than average value added.

This analysis of the causes of increased productivity is essentially microeconomic. In order to make it macroeconomic, those promoting this explanation need to say something about the redundant factors released by the introduction of IT. They need to argue that new technologies have created new products and services that not only utilize the redundant factors but also ask for more factors. The innovating technologies are said to have spawned a ubiquity of start-up firms, many of which claim to offer the chance to revolutionize and dominate large shares of the U.S. production and distribution system.[16] Creative destruction—the process of moving into new technologies from older or failing ones—has been facilitated by a process of capital reallocation across the economy by "a significant unbundling of risks in capital markets made possible by the development of innovative financial products, many of which themselves owe their vitality to advances in IT."[17] It is often claimed by those in the financial market that the more evolved financial markets are in the New Economy and are better at nurturing new companies than traditional bankers, who were more likely to support large, established companies than start-ups. But nowhere are we told in all these analyses why the New

Economy brought unprecedented new employment levels. This is where the attempt to transfer the argument from the microeconomic level to the macroeconomic level has faltered.

In order to explain the low inflation associated with new economy, Greenspan's reasoning typically goes as follows. In a consolidated sense, he said, reduced cost is reflected mainly in reduced labor cost resulting from a rise in productivity—fewer hours worked per unit of output. There is, according to him, a kind of virtuous cycle at play: New investments raise productivity, which for a time raises profits and spurs further investment and consumption. But at the same time, greater productivity puts a lid on unit costs and prices. Firms hesitate to raise prices for fear that competitors will be able, with lower costs from new investments, to wrest market share from them. The result is strong growth as well as low inflation. The surge in investment not only restrains costs but also increases capacity more than the rise in factory output. The resultant slack puts greater competitive pressure on business to hold down prices despite tight labor markets.[18]

The argument here contains contradictory features. In a rapidly enlarging market, such as is seen in the New Economy, competition is not as keen as in a depressed one. It is in a booming market that traditionally prices go up as production tries to catch up with rising demands. Profits boom in a rising market. It therefore seems contradictory to argue that in a period of increasing demand, companies are afraid to increase prices. The companies were making very good profits. Indeed, the Federal Reserve Board stated in its report to Congress in July 2000 that profits of nonfinancial corporations posted another "solid increase" in the first quarter of that year, and profits earned from their domestic operations were 10 percent higher than a year before and lifted the share of profits in the sector's nominal output close to its 1997 peak.[19] The position Green-

span was describing is indeed typical of conditions in a depression, when companies are trying to hold on to their market share.

The process of price containment is said to be, according to his argument, self-reinforcing because lower inflation has altered expectations. Workers are said to no longer believe that large gains in nominal wages are needed to reap respectable increases in real wages. Incongruously, at the same time that the labor market becomes tighter, workers' fear of job skill obsolescence is said to rise, due apparently to rapid changes in technology that have induced an accelerated churning of the country's capital stock, with which the workforce must interact on a daily basis. As a result, job security is said to be more important than wage gains as a result. The argument is not sustainable. Because neither business firms nor their competitors can currently count any longer on general inflationary tendencies to validate decisions to raise their own prices, each company feels compelled to hold down costs. Again, this argument applies in part more to a depression than to a boom market.

It was also argued that the low inflation was in a sense "imported" through international trade. Technological developments in international trade together with a more competitive world trading order have broken down barriers to cross-border trade. It is claimed that enhanced global competition has enhanced world supply and exerted restraint on prices in all countries' markets. The U.S. economy in the 1990s was said to have benefited from persistently weak growth in Japan and continental Europe and more latterly from the Asian crisis. These delivered a powerful dollar, global excess capacity, and weak prices for commodities, including oil. With the dollar so strong and world prices so weak, Martin Wolf of the *Financial Times* asserted that the United States "imported disinflation."[20]

Despite his fairly detailed review of the causes of low inflation in the United States, Greenspan still admitted that "it is difficult to judge how much of our benign overall price behavior during the past half decade is attributable to these significant shifts in the environment in which firms function. Undoubtedly other factors have been at work.... There also may be other contributory forces lurking unseen in the wings that will become clear in time."[21]

Conventional reasoning attributes the rapid growth of the New Economy to high capital formation. It is said that capital deepening significantly increased after 1995 as capital became cheaper, enabling firms to substitute capital for labor and other inputs.[22] This acceleration of capital deepening after 1995 was said to be due to investments in computers and software as a response to robust economic growth, low real interest rates, a strong stock market, and rapidly falling computer prices. Investment in information technologies was said to have added slightly more than 0.6 percent to the increase in structural productivity.[23] Real investment in information technology rose at a 19 percent annual rate from 1990 to 1995 and at a 28 percent annual rate from 1995 to 1999. While investment in computers soared after 1995, investment in software also went up, from $11 billion in 1980 to $50 billion in 1990 to about $225 billion in 2000.[24]

Peter Hooper and Trevor Dinmore, economists at Deutsche Bank building on the work of two U.S. government economists, Stephen Oliner and Daniel Sichel, have attempted to extrapolate the contribution of various types of capital equipment to growth. They reckoned that since 1990 investment in general capital equipment grew in the single digits, while investment in computers has gone ahead at a 45 percent rate of increase annually, investment in software at around 25 percent, and communications (from a larger base) at 20 percent. According to them, the tremendous growth in IT-related investment in recent years raised the share of IT capital from 10 percent to nearly 15 percent of total business fixed capital. They esti-

mated that the contribution of the three IT components to economic output growth rose from around 1 percent in 1997 to 1.7 percent in 2000. That, they claimed, amounted to half of the United States' entire economic growth.

The relation between prices and real investment in computer and peripheral equipment is shown in Figure 9.1, as formulated by the President's Council of Economic Advisers (2001). The relationship between price and investment in software is also said to follow a somewhat similar relationship, though the price reductions have not been as dramatic. Conventional economists will normally credit the GDP growth generated by IT as coming from these high rates of investment. In this context, Greenspan's statement in 1999 that "the newer technologies obviously can increase outputs or reduce inputs only if they are embodied in capital investment" is significant, although he chose to define capital investment ambiguously by saying that capital investment in the broadest sense is "any outlay that enhances capital asset values or for that matter even enhances the value of an idea." He added, "In particular, technology synergies appear to be currently engendering an ever-widening array of prospective new capital investments that offer profitable cost displacement. ... It would be an exaggeration to imply that whenever a cost increase emerges on the horizon, there is a capital investment that is available to quell it. Yet the veritable explosion of equipment and software spending that has raised the growth of capital stock dramatically ... could hardly have occurred without a large increase in the pool of profitable projects becoming available to business planners. Had high prospective returns on these projects not materialized, the current capital investment boom—there is no better word—would have petered out long ago. Indeed, equipment and capitalized software outlays as percent of GDP in current dollars are at their highest point in post–World War II history."[25]

Figure 9.1 **Prices and real investment in computer and peripheral equipment.**

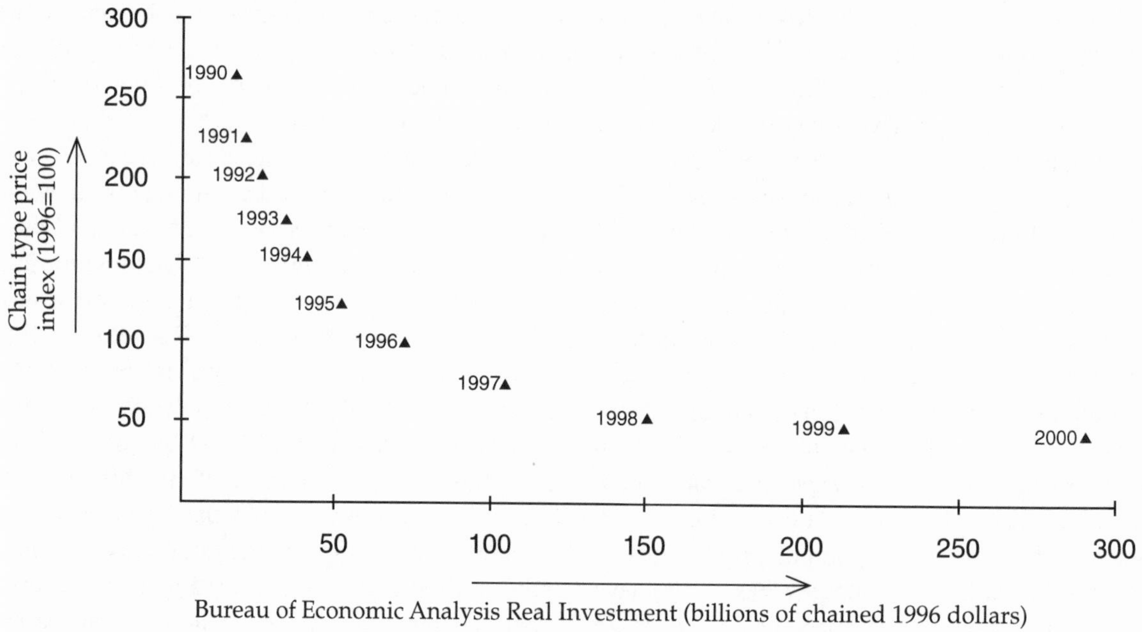

Bureau of Economic Analysis Real Investment (billions of chained 1996 dollars)

Source: Economic Report of the President (Washington, DC: U.S. Government Printing Office, 2001).

Conventional Economics' Difficulties in Analyzing the New Economy

The explanations just reviewed for the high productivity, high economic growth, and low inflation in the U.S. economy during the 1990s are inadequate. Policy makers in the United States clearly accepted that what happened to the U.S. economy took them by surprise and was in every way a new experience, one that they were not fully able to understand. They lacked the proper tools to understand what was happening in front of them and had to explain it in the language they knew best—that of conventional economics. Sometimes, as we have seen, they did so in the belief that these new phenomena would gradually give way to "normal" economics. Sometimes they were hoping that with time they would come to understand what forces are at play.

If we take the issue of productivity, conventional

economics believes that productivity drives economic growth in the new economy. In ascribing increases in productivity to changes in business methods—reduction in redundant business inventories and labor arising from better information—the analysis runs into a theoretical problem. Forgetting for a moment that we are dealing with IT, a shift of redundant resources away from existing businesses and using them elsewhere does not necessarily mean that output has increased. One must show that by transferring them to other purposes, they have contributed to a net increase in the economy's total output. If resources are transferred to new IT investments, as is claimed, it must be shown what it is in IT that yields the claimed higher overall output per hour in the economy. If it is claimed that it is the increased fixed investment in IT that is the cause of growth, then there is another analytical problem, because according to conventional economics, such increased productivity could have been achieved with increased investment in any activity, not just IT. Any explanation must be able to tell us what essential technical characteristics of IT have made such a growth pattern possible, and how they interact with other sectors of the economy.

There is a problem facing conventional analysts who proceed to analyze and quantify productivity on an industry-by-industry basis.[26] Conventional economics, lacking the tools to link micro- and macroeconomics, go on the basis that the arithmetical sum of the productivity for the parts equals the productivity of the whole. Certainly there is a strong body of opinion that links economic transformation in the New Economy only with the production and use of information technology. The *Economic Report of the President* asserted that information technology has "stimulated remarkable improvement in production processes and other business practices outside the information technology sector." The fact that businesses were able to carry out their operations in a cheaper way by applying IT and by laying off workers does not necessarily mean that the macro economy has grown. From a scientific economic structural point of view, it does matter in a macroeconomic context whether the "idle" factors are located on the premises of the new "efficient" companies or transferred elsewhere in the economy. The general use of IT businesses in the way it is being described by Greenspan was not a useful tool for determining the growth prospects of the macro economy.

Uchitelle disagreed with the idea that all sectors of the economy witnessed positive changes in productivity because of IT. He cites work to support the idea that the IT sector itself has high productivity but that the ripple effects across the broader economy are still small. Uchitelle concluded: "The biggest shot in the arm came from within the computer industry itself from the manufacture of ever faster, more powerful computers and semiconductors. . . . As a result, computer power plummeted in price and sales soared." Such is the controversy on the effects of IT on the New Economy, because conventional economics lacks the tools to understand the structural issues involved. It is, however, noteworthy that Uchitelle emphasized data suggesting that computers "lifted the economy"—but mainly through the manufacture of computers themselves and production of semiconductors, communications equipment, software, and other computer-related devices. In other words, the contribution to the economy was from manufacturing of computers, not in services using computers. Uchitelle correctly stated that the use of computers in a wide range of services is "simply a speeding up of what we were already doing." He added, "Computers ease or automate shopping, ticket buying, hotel reservations, information gathering, banking, data processing, manufacturing. But these activities always existed."[27]

There is a further weakness in the conventional economic explanation of the New Economy. As we have mentioned, it is claimed that availability of data on a real-time basis has improved business efficiency and empowered workers at lower levels with more decision-making responsibility. The resulting ability to better coordinate activities has flattened hierarchical structures and reduced inventory. This claim, however, is based on the assumption that the unprecedented growth of the New Economy was dominated by large companies with hierarchies. The claim ignores the fact that the economic structure of the United States has significantly changed with the New Economy. As the *Wall Street Journal* correctly observed early in 2000, the 1990s witnessed a massive outflow of decision making from a number of monolithic corporations to an untold number of small firms and individuals. "There is no doubt that the economy is splintering into ever-smaller and more specialized pieces. All job growth in the 1990s occurred in companies with fewer than

500 employees and the vast majority of that occurred in firms with head counts of 20 or less. Startups are growing at three times the rate of the national economy. Surveys of households reveal that businesses are formed at roughly three times the rate expressed in tax records."[28] In this context, the picture of large corporations using IT to level out decision making and reduce inventory and labor is not typical of the macro economy of the United States.

Our quarrel, however, is with the concept of productivity itself. The *Economic Report of the President* spoke of changes in IT this way: "The most impressive technological advances have come in terms of speed, storage capacity and data transmission capacity. Moore's law—the prediction by semiconductor pioneer Gordon Moore back in 1968 that transistor density on silicon wafers would continue to double every 18 months—has generally held true." It is difficult to see what this has to do with labor productivity. The scientists behind IT innovations simply discovered that microprocessor materials have the innate properties to store more and more information. It is analytically incorrect to equate such gains with productivity. If more was produced because of a microprocessor, the increase in output is due only to the nature of materials used. Productivity is a convenient financial-political yardstick needed to enable workers and owners of capital to establish a basis for sharing the financial rewards of business: the workers get the labor productivity and the owners of capital the profits. It is of no use in economic science.

Labor productivity grew by 1.39 percent annually between 1973 and 1995 but increased by 3.01 percent between 1995 to 2000. One might have thought this was due at least in part to the improved quality of labor, but the *Economic Report of the President* denies this: "Labor quality has risen as education and skills of the workforce have increased. Because that increase occurred at the same rate before and after 1995 . . . the contribution of labor

quality to the recent acceleration in productivity has been negligible."[29] Rather, it identified four factors that it claimed contributed either individually or in combination to what it called "structural productivity acceleration": (1) growth in the amount of capital per worker-hour (capital deepening) throughout the economy, (2) improvements in measurable skills of the workforce or labor quality, (3) total factor productivity (TFP) growth in computer-producing industries, and (4) TFP in other industries.[30]

This analysis gets bogged down in analytical problems on the TFP front. The report claimed that the decline in computer prices over the period, particularly from 1997 to 1999, indicated that computer manufacturing industries contributed to an 11 percent rise in TFP in the New Economy. But the report conveniently ignored the fact that in 1992, when the New Economy was born, the producer price index for computers was on the increase and started falling only in 1994, reaching its lowest level in 1998. It was again on the increase by late 1998. The remaining growth in TFP (accounting, according to the report, for 63 percent of the structural productivity increase) was supposed to have been from outside the computer sector, due to "improvements in the way capital and labor are used throughout the economy." This is a purely subjective assumption by the authors. Strangely, it is this "residual" that is supposed to have caused the bulk of the structural productivity gains over this period, but because it is a residual, we are ignorant of what actually caused those gains.

The *Economic Report of the President,* in line with those who advocate the TFP concept, gave a less prominent role to capital deepening in the claimed structural labor productivity explosion of the New Economy. The report pointed out that even though investments in IT soared over the period, investments in other capital goods slowed during the post-1995 acceleration of structural labor productivity gains. As a result, it argued, capital deepening accounted for only about 24 percent of the acceleration in these gains.

On the other hand, Greenspan awarded capital deepening the accolade for causing the accelerated productivity of the New Economy. According to him, economists have noted that capital has deepened significantly in the United States since 1995.[31]

Despite the attempts by conventional economists to explain the New Economy, they do not say in that context why there weren't the usual business-cycle-related slowdowns during this period. They only seem to imply that the growth in productivity has been so outstanding that it has continued to propel growth past the times when a downward swing should have occurred.

It is fair to conclude that conventional economics acknowledges that the jury is still out. As Greenspan correctly indicated, analysts are still struggling to create a credible conceptual framework to fit the emerging pattern of interrelationships, which so far has defied conventional wisdom. It is to this effort that we now turn.

Capital Deepening

The whole issue of claims about capital deepening in the New Economy—whether it was the major cause of structural productivity growth, as Greenspan held, or a minor player, which is what Clinton's economic advisers thought—is an important topic because all the claimants assert that productivity, which is supposed to be the engine of growth, depends on efficiently achieving higher capital/labor ratios. We need therefore to examine the issue of capital growth in this period in greater depth, to see what conventional economists call capital and contrast this with what in scientific economics is called capital. Within the science of economic development and growth, capital, as we had earlier stated, is a production factor operating in a three-cornered economic relationship with the other

factors of production of labor and material. Capital is largely man-made. It is a production aid required because of the many limitations of the human body. It is to assist man in converting basic material to his needs. Material conversion involves physical and/or chemical transformation of material.

Table 9.1 outlines U.S. private fixed investment by type from 1990 to 2000. According to this table, investment in software and equipment has remained strong since 1993, with an acceleration in information processing equipment and software since 1995. In 1999 and 2000, annual growth in investment in information processing and software was said to be roughly 25 percent. An important component of this growth is the replacement of the large but rapidly depreciating stock of equipment that has been built up in recent years. A primary motivation for this strong pace of investment is said to be the declining prices of computer equipment.[32]

Greenspan has argued that the replacement of labor by capital in an atmosphere of high profitable investment has helped to contain rises in labor costs. Strong stock market gains since 1994 have also been said to have made these investments easier to finance. Sharp decreases in computer prices have encouraged steep increases in investments in information technology by businesses in the wholesale and retail trade, financial services, and manufacturing sectors.[33] The table shows that real investment in information technology rose at a 19 percent annual rate from 1990 to 1995 and at a 28 percent annual rate from 1995 to 1999. Real investment in information technology (chained 1996 dollars) in 1999 was about $540 billion. The table shows that between 1990 and 2000 private fixed investment in industrial equipment only increased at an average annual rate of a little over 5 percent; transportation equipment fared better, at an average annual rate increase of about 20 percent. The private fixed investment (chained 1996 U.S. dollar) in 2000 was shown as almost double the 1990 value. On the basis of these figures,

Table 9.1

U.S. Real Private Fixed Investment by Type (billions of chained U.S. 1996 dollars)

Year	Private fixed investment	Total nonresidential	Nonresidential												Residential
			Structures					Equipment and software						
			Total	Nonresidential buildings incl. farms	Utilities	Mining exploration, shafts and wells	Others	Total	Information processing equipment and software			Ind. equipment	Trans. equipment	
									Computers & peripherals equipment	Software	Other			
1990	894.6	641.7	236.1	173.6	33.0	21.3	8.3	415.7	14.2	45.9	96.2	105.8	87.4	253.5
1991	832.5	610.1	210.1	142.7	38.9	20.8	7.8	407.2	15.4	51.4	83.6	99.0	87.7	221.1
1992	886.5	630.6	197.3	129.2	41.8	17.2	9.2	437.5	20.8	58.7	84.1	100.8	92.3	257.2
1993	958.4	683.6	198.9	131.7	38.4	20.5	8.5	487.1	26.4	66.8	93.3	109.6	103.4	276.0
1994	1,045.9	744.6	200.5	137.2	36.1	19.8	7.6	544.9	32.6	74.3	100.6	119.6	120.4	302.7
1995	1,109.2	817.5	210.1	147.6	36.8	18.2	7.5	607.6	49.2	82.0	121.3	131.3	128.2	291.7
1996	1,212.7	899.4	225.0	161.7	36.0	21.1	6.2	674.4	90.9	95.1	129.8	136.4	138.9	313.3
1997	1,328.6	1,009.3	245.4	177.0	35.3	26.2	6.8	764.2	102.9	119.0	140.7	140.0	150.5	319.7
1998	1,485.3	1,140.3	263.0	189.1	43.0	24.4	6.7	879.0	149.3	151.0	163.1	146.9	168.0	346.1
1999	1,621.4	1,255.3	259.2	187.4	43.5	21.5	7.3	1,003.1	217.3	188.0	163.1	147.8	191.8	368.3
2000	1,771.3	1,413.3	285.6	201.1	45.2	29.2	7.4	1,140.4	304.2	228.7	175.9	164.2	189.5	366.3

Source: U.S. Department of Commerce, Bureau of Economic Analysis.

Table 9.2

U.S. Capital Expenditures, 1998 ($ billions)

Capital expenditures	Capital expenditures for all companies	Capital expenditures for companies with employees	Capital expenditures for companies without employees
Total	973.6	879.0	94.5
Structures	328.1	290.4	37.8
New	283.5	250.8	32.7
Used	44.6	39.5	5.1
Equipment	645.4	588.7	56.8
New	609.9	564.8	45.1
Used	35.6	23.9	11.7

Source: U.S. Bureau of Census 2000.

Table 9.3

Revised U.S. Capital Expenditures, 1997 ($ billions)

Capital expenditures	Capital expenditures for all companies	Capital expenditures for companies with employees	Capital expenditures for companies without employees
Total	871.8	772.3	99.4
Structures	273.3	236.2	37.1
New	254.5	225.1	29.3
Used	18.8	11.1	7.8
Equipment	598.5	536.2	62.3
New	562.0	516.0	46.1
Used	36.4	20.2	16.2

Source: U.S. Bureau of Census 2000.

it looks as if conventional economists have unveiled the cause of the rapid growth of the New Economy.

These messages of high investment are very similar to those highlighted in the Annual Capital Expenditure Surveys (ACES) undertaken by the U.S. Bureau of Census. According to the bureau, these surveys are part of a comprehensive program designed to provide detailed and timely information on capital investment in buildings and other structures and equipment by nonfarm businesses in the United States. A five-year survey plan was developed in 1993. The five-year cycle is based on basic surveys that collect total capital expenditure for new and used structures and equipment annually from companies with five employees or more and biennially for those with fewer than five employees (including those with no employees). The 1998 survey (published in May 2000) was based on a sample of 34,000 companies with employees and 12,000 businesses without employees. For those companies with employees, total capital expenditures were published for 1997 industries, while total capital expenditures with no industry detail are shown for businesses without employees. In the new five-year survey beginning 1999, a major change involved the conversion to the North American Industrial Classification System (NAICS) in place of the old Standard Industrial Classification (SIC) system.

Table 9.2 is the 1998 U.S. capital expenditures for structures and equipment (billions of dollars); Table 9.3 is the revised capital expenditures for 1997 (billions of dollars); Table 9.4 is the breakdown of capital expenditures by business sector for businesses with employees.

In releasing the 1998 survey in May 2000, the Census Bureau announced that "U.S. businesses invested a record $974 billion in capital goods in 1998. . . . The total represents an increase of 12 percent from 1997 to 1998 and follows an increase of 8 percent in 1997 from 1996. Businesses with employees accounted for 90 percent of all 1998 capital investment, spending $879 billion. About two-thirds of this, or $565 billion, was spent on new machinery and equipment, an increase of 9 percent from 1997." This survey broke the new machinery and equipment down broadly into information-processing equipment (including computers and communications equipment), $184 billion; transportation equipment (primarily cars and light trucks), $157 billion; and industrial equipment, $143 billion. In regard to structures, businesses with em-

Table 9.4

Breakdown of U.S. Capital Expenditures
(business with employees)

Business sector	1998 Capital expenditures ($ billions)	1997 Capital expenditures ($ billions)	% Change
Manufacturing	207.3	192.3	7.8
Services	182.4	165.0	10.6
Finance	110.1	91.3	20.5
Communications	78.5	68.5	14.6
Retail trade	63.1	55.9	12.9
Transportation	51.8	45.0	15.1
Insurance and real estate	50.3	29.3	71.9
Utilities	42.3	38.7	9.3
Mining	40.3	39.0	N.S.
Wholesale trade	31.2	28.8	N.S.
Construction	18.3	15.5	17.8

Source: U.S. Bureau of Census 2000.

ployees spent $290 billion, of which $251 billion was for new buildings and structures, and the remainder for used structures. Eighteen percent of the amount spent by businesses with employees on construction of new facilities was for utility structures and facilities, 15 percent for industrial buildings, 14 percent for commercial buildings, including shopping malls, 13 percent for mine shafts and wells. It further clarified that manufacturing led all sectors in spending on capital goods, with $207 billion or nearly 24 percent of total expenditures. Investment by durable-goods manufacturers totaled $119 billion, or 57 percent of the manufacturing total. Most of their investment ($100 billion) was for equipment. Within the durable-goods sector, the communications equipment and electronic components industries spent the most on capital goods, $28 billion. Nondurable-goods manufacturers spent $88 billion on capital goods, with chemical products (excluding drugs) at $22 billion and food products (excluding beverages) at $13 billion together accounting for nearly 40 percent of that. Reporting to Congress in July 2000, the Federal Reserve Board indicated that real outlays for business equipment and software shot up at an annual rate of nearly 25 percent in the first quarter of 2000, with computers and peripheral equipment up by almost 40 percent from a year earlier. Real investment in private nonresidential structures jumped at an annual rate of more than 20 percent in the first quarter of 2000.[34] Based on these figures, conventional economists will be tempted to say that the New Economy was the direct result of massive investments in all significant sectors—that is, capital deepening.

The real private fixed investment data in Table 9.1 are not easily comparable with those in Tables 9.2, 9.3, and 9.4. The former has had a relatively long history, while the latter began in 1991, and its basic methodology is still changing. Charles Fonk, the current head of the ACES unit, differentiates between the two by describing the former as production-based data, adjusted for export and import, while the ACES is consumption-based. The private fixed investment data (sometimes called the National Income and Productivity Account, NIPA) then is analyzed to allocate U.S. investments between the nonresidential sector, including farms, and the residential sector. ACES concentrates on what has been purchased for use by different types of businesses in the nonfarm sector. In regard to what is capital, it is to be noted that up until 1999 ACES did not treat software as capital. Since 1999, selected items of software are now treated as capital. Many companies in the United States, however, establish a threshold dollar value below which any equipment purchases are not treated as capital. Such accounting simplification detracts from a correct capital evaluation because what is capital derives from use. The new changes in regard to software in ACES will no doubt show up in the 2003 survey report. Table 9.1 is adjusted for inflation. The nominal gross dollar equivalent of Table 9.1 can be compared with the ACES (which are also in nominal dollars) to notice the differences in the values described. NIPA (nonresidential) in 1998 was $1,107 billion (nominal) to $973.6 billion in the ACES survey. Such a large difference brings into question the accuracy of official evaluation of the scale of capital investment in the United States.

The definition of capital in these official statistical data is interesting. ACES 1998 defines as capital any item with an expected use period of more than one year. This covers structures such as offices, warehouses, commercial buildings, shopping malls, cars, trucks, mine shafts, wells, and utilities. In the case of the NIPA, this includes private residential buildings and other residential structures and residential equipment. For 1998 these categories—structures, transport equipment, and other equipment together with residential structures —accounted for around $956.6 billion out of the $1,472.9 billion in 1998 private fixed investment (about 65 percent). ACES 1998 (in Table 9.4) shows that, for businesses with employees, the bulk of the capital expenditures—about 65 percent of the total capital investment—was made by services (finance, communications, retail trade, transportation, insurance and real estate, wholesale trade). The bulk of investments in information processing equipment and software were made by the services sector.

Investment in the Services Sectors in the U.S. Economy

The high percentage of "financial" capital investment that went into services shows the increasingly dominant position of services in the U.S. economy. It is therefore important to examine the difference between this kind of investment and the investment in production represented, for example, by manufacturing. This difference arises from the economic distinction between services and production, a distinction established by nature.

Services are as old as man. In primal societies, the person who produced also provided himself with the services required to get value and satisfaction from what is produced. His labor was therefore divided between production and service provision for himself. With increasing specialization, which has reached its peak in the U.S. economy, labor is now divided between production and services. It follows that as more goods are produced per person in an economy, the percentage of people in services will increase as is presently the case in the United States.

Manufacturing (production) is a three-factor input activity (enabling man to) convert material (natural resources) into needed goods using production aid (capital). Services, on the other hand, involve only labor and manufactured goods as input. When the goods are to be useful for at least one year, they qualify as capital investment within the U.S. official definition. The manufactured computer and peripheral equipment purchased by a U.S. bank or insurance company in order to improve its services are finished production goods and financially are capital investments. They are not different from other finished manufactured goods that have an economic life of less than one year. They are, however, different from capital (production aid) in the economic science context, because they are not used in combination with material and labor to produce (new) products by chemical or physical change.

Production Aid (Capital) in the U.S. New Economy

Because it is in the services sector, the 65 percent of total investment claimed as investment cannot qualify as capital in the science of economic development and growth. The ACES 1998 breakdown of the remaining 35 percent shows that in manufacturing $167.5 billion went for capital equipment, in utilities $19.9 billion, in mining $14.0 billion, and in construction $17.0 billion. A sizable proportion of this investment in equipment is not for actual production, in view of the ACES definition of capital. For example, furniture and vehicles by definition are capital. At the most, capital used for production represented a total of $218.4 billion, or nearly 25 percent of what is claimed as capital investment in the United States.

We therefore arrive at the conclusion that in 1998, at least 75 percent of U.S. capital investment as reported in ACES 1998 for businesses with employees could not qualify as capital under the scientific definition of capital as production aids. The truth is that the broad definition of capital in all official U.S. statistics does not have production as its focus. It is essentially a financial definition needed to enable the business world and the tax authorities to define the allocation of money on an agreed-upon basis. The error of analysis arises when this financial capital volume is equated to economic production capital by economists. The impressive increase in "financial" capital investment (ACES: 8 percent from 1996 to 1997, 12 percent from 1997 to 1998; NIPA: 6 percent from 1995 to 1996, 9.3 percent from 1996 to 1997, 9.6 percent from 1997 to 1998, 11.8 percent from 1998 to 1999, 9.2 percent from 1999 to 2000— see Table 9.4), when added to a 20 percent rise in the first quarter of 2000 of real investment in private nonfinancial structures compared with a year before, will accord with Greenspan's observation that capital deepening in the United States has accelerated since 1995. As Greenspan said in his Monetary Policy Report to Congress in 2000, "Sustained high rates of investment spending have been a key factor shaping the current economic expansion."[35]

We now turn more specifically to investments in IT. The 2001 *Economic Report of the President* asserted that the total real fixed investment in information technology (based on its summation of computer and peripheral equipment software and communications equipment) was about $433 billion (NIPA data). Investment in computers soared after 1995, while investment in software tripled despite little reduction in prices. But these figures do not represent investments in production aids, in the scientific economic sense. They are financial purchases for items with an expected use period of more than one year.

In Table 9.5 we have attempted to assemble available data depicting yearly capital investments in IT product manufacturing industries from 1990 to 1997, the last year the latest ACES covers. The totals in this table give us an idea of the range in capital investment volume in the IT manufacturing sector. The completeness or otherwise of this list is complicated by the change from the SIC classification to the NAICS classification in which SIC industries have been split and reapportioned and new items brought in without full regard to their old links (if any). There are no reliable figures of IT equipment investment in other non-IT manufacturing. However, it is clear from this table that between 1990 and 1997 yearly investment in IT manufacturing probably grew by only 2 to 3 times. The figures (even allowing for IT equipment investment in other manufacturing) are very modest. Considering that according to the latest ACES, capital investment in manufacturing in 1997 was $193 billion, investment in IT manufacturing was less than 10 percent of the manufacturing investment.

We will next look at the trend in capital/labor ratio in manufacturing (which includes IT products manufacturing) to see whether the claim of capital deepening after 1995 is borne out.

In Table 9.6, we tabulate capital/labor ratios from 1963 to 1996.

Figure 9.2 is a trend graph worked out from the capital/labor ratio for the years indicated, that is, column C of Table 9.6.

It is clear from the graph that the rate of increase of the capital/labor ratio was lower in the 1990s than in the preceding decades. As a matter of fact, the drop in the rate of increase in capital/labor ratio started in the 1980s. The dynamic cumulative ef-

Table 9.5

U.S. Yearly Investment in IT Manufacturing Industries ($ millions)

Item of manufacture	1990	1991	1992	1993	1994	1995	1996	1997
Electron tubes	169.7	77.3	61.7	85.5	132.3	141.6	181.4	160.0
Computer storage devices	426.5	392.8	455.6	557.7	521.9	614.4	956.3	772.0
Electronic computer	1,222.3	1,153.5	1,242.0	1,042.9	932.7	907.2	854.9	1,053.4
Bare printed circuit	405.1	311.1	316.8	282.8	365.9	455.3	585.4	696.8
Electronic component	539.4	485.0	540.3	740.8	991.9	990.6	992.3	424.9
Electronic capacitor	52.1	57.1	64.0	63.9	78.5	156.6	212.3	124.1
Electronic resistor	53.3	33.6	21.3	25.7	53.0	40.6	42.1	55.4
Electronic (oil) trans- former and other inductors	25.3	21.1	20.1	21.9	31.8	28.9	21.8	43.2
Electronic connector	173.5	142.2	144.3	210.7	200.4	207.1	228.1	237.9
Computer terminals	45.4	42.4	44.4	29.3	41.7	54.0	26.0	34.7
Communication equipment	71.6	63.6	65..0	83.8	99.6	124.9	179.5	151.8
Computer peripheral equipment	299.1	223.8	393.0	415.1	410.8	360.2	855.5	980.4
Semiconductors	3,439.0	2,945.0	3,118.0	3,838.5	5,697.8	9,181.7	11,994.4	10,532.9
Total	6,992.3	5,948.2	6,486.7	7,398.6	9,558.3	13,263.1	17,118.6	15,643.4

Source: Manufacturing and Distribution (Farmington, MI: Dale Group, 1998, 1999).

fect of this reduction led to the New Economy. Two factors are at work here in the dynamic changes occurring in the U.S. economic structure. As the size of output of an economy increases, its threshold capital stock per capita must necessarily increase. This obtains for both advanced and primal society economies. This increase will work alongside other changes in factor proportions in economy, which will have the effect of increasing or reducing the economy's overall rate of increase of its capital/labor ratio. It is noteworthy, for example, that since World War II capital/labor ratios for traditionally labor-intensive activities in the United States have continued to show an upward trend. The rate of increase in capital/labor ratio in the New Economy will seem (as Figure 9.2 and the percentage rates in column D of Table 9.6 confirm) to be less than in previous decades.

Capital deepening in the United States has not accelerated since 1992. Capital deepening is not re-

sponsible for the high growth witnessed in the New Economy.

Our theory of factor proportions states that maximum growth is achieved if factor proportions of all economic production activities are dynamically equal and equal to the endowed factor proportions of the economy. This is a balanced economy. One feature of this is the absence of unemployment. We shall now examine what changes have taken place in the U.S. economy to see whether these approximate to the balanced economy conditions stipulated in our effort to determine the source of the New Economy.

One major change in the U.S. factor endowment is an increase in population. The U.S. population has increased almost four times since 1900. The country's natural resource endowment has not significantly changed; if anything, there has been a decrease due to exploitative use in the past. What matters with regard to factors is not the absolute

Table 9.6

Average Manufacturing Capital/Labor Ratios, 1963–1996

	A (total number of employees, thousands)	B (invested capital, $ millions)	C ($ thousands per employee)	D (% increase over the preceding year)
1963	17.00	11,400	670.50	—
1967	19.30	21,500	1,113.98	66.1
1972	19.00	24,100	1,268.42	13.8
1982	19.09	74,600	3,826.53	201.7
1987	18.90	78,600	4,158.73	8.7
1990	18.80	102,000	5,425.53	30.5
1991	18.10	99,000	5,469.61	44.1
1992	18.20	103,200	5,668.79	3.6
1994	18.30	112,000	6,111.20	7.8
1995	18.73	128,400	6,855.31	12.2
1996	18.76	139,300	7,462.36	8.2

Notes: Columns A and B: Bureau of the Census, Census of Manufactures 1963, 1967, 1972, 1982, 1987, and 1992 and Annual Survey of Manufactures.

quantities of factors but their proportions. It means immediately that material/population ratio has witnessed significant reductions over the twentieth century. It means that any technology that reduces the relative contribution of material in production will be in line with the conditions for accelerated economic growth.

The United States has since 1900 evolved an economy in which there is a wide range of capital intensiveness between sectors—say, between the textile sector (labor-intensive) and petrochemicals (capital-intensive). The trend in the United States up to 1980 has been greater and greater capital concentration in a large portion of its modern sector and, consequently, wider differences in this ratio between sectors.

Let us now look at the IT sector as a relatively new entrant into the U.S. economy. To do this we will take a factor proportions snapshot of a range of activities in the United States at the end of 1997, a date which is halfway in the life of the New Economy to date. (We say "snapshot" because we are dealing with a dynamic situation in which

changes are taking place all the time.) We have picked a range of production activities covering a broad spectrum of representative industrial sectors.

We needed to work out for each sector the capital/labor ratio. We therefore needed to quantify new capital in each of the industrial sectors in plant and machinery in 1997. We also needed to quantify for each sector net assets per employee to enable us to compare this with the whole manufacturing sector. We also needed to assess the relative material input compared to inputs of capital and labor. We wanted to estimate material input by comparing annual material costs and annual shipments. The difficulty we have is that of all the three factors, only labor is calculated in the same unit in scientific economic analysis as in conventional financial and economic analysis. For capital and material, we are faced with conventional published statistics which have these only in financial quantities. Published statistics for sectors do not state what the total inputs are even in financial terms. Published shipment figures—the output—are the only data to work with.

In a scientific inquiry into production, we are only

Figure 9.2 **U.S. industrial capital/labor ratio, 1960–1995.**

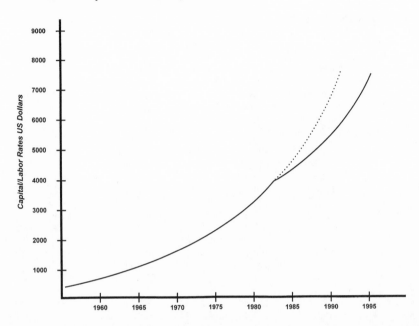

interested in the hard-core technology of the industry, namely, the investment in plant and equipment deployed directly for production and the material and labor deployed directly for production. Investments in structures have no direct bearing on the production techniques. The capital/labor ratio derived from investments in plant and machinery (in financial values) gives us only an idea of the relative physical quantities of factors in this ratio, approximating the scientific formula indicated in Chapter 3.

In dealing with the published figures for shipment in an attempt to gain an idea of the relative magnitude of material contribution, we have further problems. As we had indicated in earlier chapters, it is not possible to split output and determine the precise contribution to it of the three factors because the final output is the result of a sort of "chemical" interaction among the factors. The position is made more difficult because the financial values attached to the shipment, like all financial figures, distort the picture. The prices set by an industry for its shipments may be monopolistic. In industries such as aircraft and pharmaceuticals, a large component of their prices is the recovery of large prior outlays in R&D. For the computer industry and related activities, prices have been falling over a long time. While a good part of this fall in price is due to smaller quantities of materials used per unit of output, the technical gains achieved in performance sometimes involved extra materials.[36] The shipment value in these areas will therefore need to be adjusted in order to give us an idea of the real material consumption. Wages, which are a major component in shipment prices, vary from industry to industry, while the prices of material inputs reflect many factors. However, we are only dealing with each industry on its own in order to assess its material input. Therefore differences in wages and material pricing between industries will not affect the results. Material prices include transportation costs and are more likely to depend on the cost of producing the material and whether the material is in a raw state (for example, clinker for cement) or an intermediate material. We needed to

Table 9.7

U.S. Industrial Sector Factor Proportions, 1997

NAICS number [1]	Activity [2]	Production Workers W (in thousands) [3]	Material Cost M ($ millions) [4]	Capital Investment in plant/ machinery C ($ millions) [5]	Shipment S ($ million) [6]	C/W ($) [7]	M/S (%) [8]	Fixed Assets per Employee F/W₁ ($) [9]
313111	Yarn Spinning	53,370	5,163,237	380,824	8,162,644	8,207	63	94,313
325311	Nitrogenous Fertilizer	3,490	1,985,754	563,625	3,672,501	161,497	54	964,709
322110	Pulp Mills	7,849	2,439,672	426,203	4,067,328	58,122	60	721,524
325110	Petrochemicals	6,207	10,603,799	1,080,210	19,299,957	174,031	54	1,227,360
325412	Pharmaceuticals	62,741	14,274,912	1,548,520	29,637,201	24,681	48	172,442
336111	Automobile	7,979	65,593,492	3,088,860	94,685,883	31,525	69	198,883
324110	Petroleum Refining	42,227	119,108,330	3,825,161	154,316,441	90,586	80	1,049,351
327310	Cement Mfg.	12,524	3,269,136	470,730	6,335,469	37,586	52	437,086
325181	Alkalis & Chlorine Mfg.	3,348	948,960	273,318	2,201,981	81,636	43	551,900
334414	Elec. Capacitor Mfg.	13,097	746,777	106,992	2,107,956	8,169	35	53,003
334113	Computer Terminal	2,843	691,379	28,429	2,567,424	9,999	27	47,254
332510	Hardware Mfg.	56,958	3,847,236	329,630	10,303,314	5,787	37	49,375
334250	Communication Equipment Mfg.	12,149	1,198,417	118,641	3,647,314	9,765	32	34,287
334210	Telephone Apparatus Mfg.	41,936	11,243,985	908,672	35,992,678	21,668	31	67,388
334412	Bar Printed Board Mfg.	56,755	2,811,711	588,087	9,090,956	10,361	31	51,073
325188	Basic Inorganic Chemicals	27,259	6,135,373	719,309	12,319,047	26,388	50	230,083
325188	Basic Organic Chemicals	52,793	27,850,498	3,465,625	51,551,453	65,645	54	476,090
325212	Synthetic Rubber	7,667	2,878,365	362,932	5,901,377	47,337	49	321,888
325182	Carbon Black Mfg.	1.1	399,350	86,544	980,391	78,676	41	406,940
336312	Gasoline Engine Mfg.	65,971	15,859,324	1,556,618	24,467,675	23,595	65	138,986
313312	Textile & Fabric Finishing	24,751	2,208,330	196,253	4,192,008	7,929	68	53,549
325312	Phosphatic Fertilizer Mfg.	6,188	3,350,662	204,348	5,643,818	33,023	59	468,780
336322	Other Motor Vehicle Electronic & Electrical Equipment Mfg.	75,419	7,794,618	635,206	15,533,390	8,422	50	46,366
334111	Elec. Computer Mfg.	37,754	30,007,110	924,393	100,639,036	24,485	27	69,798
334611	Software Reproducing	8,027	438,293	140,935	1,258,435	17,556	25	—
334411	Electron Tube Mfg.	16,676	2,152,653	111,195	7,431,368	6,668	29	80,857
334112	Computer Storage Device Mfg.	19,355	4,852,415	1,066,399	20,169,532	55,096	24	105,041
334416	Electronic Coil & Transformer & Other Inductors Mfg.	15,283	435,356	35,493	1,514,631	2,322	29	17,752
334119	Computer Peripheral Mfg.	40,976	11,208,176	847,314	46,816,254	20,678	24	71,007
334417	Electronic Connector Mfg.	27,784	1,476,883	214,051	5,554,449	7,704	27	57,938
331111	Iron & Steel Mfg.	115,141	30,307,305	2,568,887	56,575,837	22,310	55	240,344
334418	Printed Circuit Assembly (Electronic) Mfg.	65,377	11,851,028	640,119	49,377,758	9,791	24	44,553
334419	Electronic Components Mfg.	60,676	3,125,132	374,788	9,654,474	6,177	32	36,580
334415	Electronic Resistor Mfg.	8,640	218,388	48,520	992,935	5,616	22	46,779
334413	Semiconductor and Related Device Mfg.	105,781	10,907,171	8,639,424	7,577,187	81,672	14	268,073

Source: Columns 1, 2, 3, 4, 5, 6, 9 from Bureau of the Census, Manufacturing-Industry Series, 1997 Economic Census, October 5, 1999.

identify only material costs that were directly used in production from the published figures. We have no interest in inventory.

The results are displayed in Table 9.7, showing capital investment per production worker (column 7) and percentage of the cost of material in the price of shipments M/S (column 8). M/S should be regarded merely as indicative, for reasons previously stated. It will be seen that capital/labor ratios (column 7) for investments for production of IT products are at the lowest end of the capital/labor spectrum of the industries analyzed. Indeed, a labor-intensive activity such as yarn spinning has a higher capital/labor ratio than some IT manufacturing.[37] In a dynamic sense, it means that IT manufacturing investments were adding to the growth of the economy by adding less than a proportionate capital/labor ratio to the economic structure of the United States. It is useful to put the position of IT technology in perspective, however crudely, in relation to their fixed investment position in the U.S. economy. Column 9 is the fixed investment per employee (all employees) for the industrial activities studied. The fixed investment in this column covers both production investments and nonproduction investments, as these have not been separated in the Bureau of Census figures. It will be seen that, except for electronic storage (NAIS 334112), IT-producing industries have fixed assets per employee less than the average fixed investment per employee for the total U.S. manufacturing sector, which is $82,088. What we have is a fundamental change in the U.S. economic structure in which new activities with low capital intensiveness were growing in size at the same time as old activities with high capital intensiveness were losing their share of the economy. An economic realignment creating a more balanced structure had started.

Even though they are commonly called high-tech industries, IT-producing industries are therefore not capital-intensive. In relative terms, they are instead, in conventional two-factor economics, labor-intensive. In conventional economic terms, it can be said that this is the first time since 1900 that a new production technique in the United States was preponderantly labor-intensive. IT has therefore introduced a new production paradigm, away from the well-beaten track of growing capital intensiveness characteristic of the past century in the United States. It is incorrect therefore to describe IT industry growth as being led by heavy capital investment or by the ability of the industry to replace labor with capital in an attempt to contain costs and reduce inflation.

A second significant finding from Table 9.7 is that the material component of most IT production is smaller than for all non-IT sectors. Most IT production had a material percentage of about 30 percent or less. Traditional labor-intensive activities such as textiles have a higher percentage material component than some IT activities. The high percentage of material content occurs in both traditional labor-intensive and capital-intensive activities. For example, pulp mill manufacturing, with a capital/labor ratio of $58,122 per production employee in 1997, has 60 percent material content; there is a similar percentage in automobile manufacturing (capital/labor ratio of $31,525 per production employee) and yarn spinning (with a capital/labor ratio of $8,207 per production employee). If there was a two-factor regime in economics, as conventional economics maintains, it would have followed that activities with similar capital/labor ratios will register similar material proportions. This is not the case because in a three-factor regime, the ratios obtained between any two factors are determined by the relative contribution of the third factor. It is not a simple substitution between labor and capital, as conventional economics maintains.

Figure 9.3 is a display of the percentage of material input as against capital/labor ratio of a number of activities taken from Table 9.7. Those for the IT-producing activities are shown as crosses and

Figure 9.3 **Investment in plant/machinery per production employee versus material content of production for some U.S. manufacturing activities.**

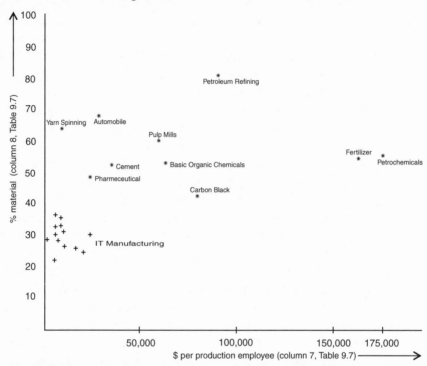

those for non-IT production are shown as stars. It will be seen that the IT crosses are in a cluster in the lower left-hand side of the figure, the low-material, low capital/labor part of the figure.

The fact that in IT the material input per unit is less than in other sectors is not new. Kelly wrote, "The US economy is already demassing, drifting towards . . . intangibles. The creation most in demand from the US (and those exported) lost 50 percent of their physical weight per dollar of value in only six years. The disembodied world of computers, entertainment and telecom is now an industry larger than the old giants such as construction, food products or automobile. This new information-based sector already occupies 15 percent of the total U.S. economy."[38] Mitchell claims that "information has become dematerialized and disembodied."[39]

Seltzer and Bentley labeled employment in the New Economy "weightless work," arguing that there are now more part-time, temporary, fixed-contract, and self-employed workers. In a more fluid and unstable organizational environment workers manage themselves. There is also what they called "knowledge and skills exclusion"—that increasing premium on new skills and qualification that is creating new patterns of marginalization among those who lack the means or motivation to acquire marketable knowledge. Developing new kinds of skills, they say, is now central to workers' future prospects.[40]

Greenspan's comment, referred to in Chapter 4, that "almost all the rise in value added relative to physical input has reflected the substitution of ideas —new insights—for brute human effort and material bulk . . . and that like labor inputs, material requirements per unit output also have fallen in many sectors of the economy" is significant.[41] Greenspan further elaborated: "The insights of metallurgy and architectural design, for example, enables construction of buildings that use far less physical material per unit of space, than say a half-century ago. The insight of central heating, as well as synthetic fiber, facilitated reduced clothing weight, while the development of the jet engine brought far greater annual passenger miles per unit of aircraft size." Greenspan's observations help to illustrate that reduction in material quantity input is not confined to IT.

But these observations by Kelly, Greenspan, and Seltzer and Bentley did not put the development they observed in its macroeconomic structural context. Neither ideas nor knowledge nor intangibles can substitute for material mass in a productive context. It is therefore misleading to call the New Economy a knowledge economy. All economies, primal or modern, derive, as we have emphasized in this book, from knowledge. Throughout history, whenever there is a change in production techniques, there is always its associated labor instability and abandonment of old facilities and practices—Greenspan's creative destruction.

It should now be clear from the data we have produced how the U.S. economy fundamentally changed through IT. The reduction in proportional material input is in consonance with the changing material/population ratio of the United States. The trend (i.e., less relative material consumption) led by IT-producing industries is being reflected in other sectors of the U.S. economy in part due to increasing science in material technology. Digital technology is being introduced in the production aid structure of non-IT production, reducing material input. The low capital/labor ratio of IT has for the first time had the effect of reducing the large imbalances in capital/labor ratio of production sectors, reversing a trend that had been a growing feature of the U.S. macro economy since the late 1800s. For example, Table 9.7 shows a range of capital/labor ratios of between $2,322 and $174,031 per production employee. But the share of the high capital/labor industries in GDP is decreasing. The altered fundamental characteris-

tics of the U.S. economy in the New Economy did not derive from the investments in IT by all business sectors, as conventional economics will claim. The fundamental change in the economic structure of the United States arose instead from the fact that, as some commentators (with a measure of exaggeration) have stated, communication *is* the economy, not just a sector of the economy. IT has fundamentally changed the way we communicate, which is increasingly affecting every facet of life in the United States. Prices of IT equipment have dropped so much, improving potential rates of return so much, that demand has skyrocketed. The result in the New Economy was the enlargement of the IT-producing sector, with its unique new factor proportions, to a scale that has created an economy fundamentally more structurally balanced than has been witnessed since the beginning of the twentieth century, with factor proportions more in tune with the natural factor endowments of the United States. This was occurring as the relative dominance of the capital-intensive sectors in the U.S. economy was on the wane. For the first time emerging technologies in the United States have moved in the direction of labor-intensive production regimes. It is a new production paradigm. This new paradigm may well herald what Piore and Sabel could have called the "success of mechanization along craft lines," in that the new IT production paradigm combined the mechanization of mass production with the capital/labor characteristics of craft production. Flexible manufacturing emerged as what Piore and Sabel described as the "second industrial divide." IT production techniques have heralded what we call a "third industrial divide," with emphasis on material saving and labor augmentation.

Structural economics, various aspects of which we have explored in depth in different chapters of this book, indicates that economic cycles are caused by structural economic imbalances. The booms and bursts follow a cycle in which when an economy is growing, people dive into heavy capital-intensive investments under the prevailing euphoria. The economy then plunges into recession and the investments cease, giving time for the economy to attain some measure of balance before it resumes growth, followed by another investment euphoria. In the euphoria of the 1990s the productive investment that followed was for the first time not in the capital-intensive direction. A more balanced economy in which factor proportions are moving in the direction of the natural factor proportions of the United States will tend to have near full employment, as the New Economy bears out.

Inflation and the New Economy

In the last years of the twentieth century, there was concern among economic leaders in the United States about the direction of the economy, as it seemed to be roaring away with increasing speed without inflation pressures. At the heart of their problem was the difficulty they had in interpreting the New Economy with conventional economic tools. At issue was the NAIRU. Conventional economics had it as an article of faith that rising economic demand leads to overheating of the economy, which necessarily causes inflation as employment increases in the economy's attempt to meet the rising demand. The fact that the ever-rising growth of the New Economy was accompanied by little or no inflation left conventional economists puzzled. Said the *Economic Report of the President,* "The acceleration of productivity after 1995 appears to have initiated a process that allows unemployment rate to fall lower temporarily, with less consequence for inflation than would have been possible otherwise. . . . The new, higher trend of productivity since 1995 has temporarily lowered the NAIRU."

In a 1999 paper for the Federal Reserve Bank of Boston titled "Is Inflation Dead?" Roger Brinner argued—rather unscientifically—that NAIRU was not dead but merely sleeping. He insisted that

NAIRU remained at 5.5 percent except when times were exceptionally favorable. He sought to explain that while the low unemployment at the time would normally raise inflation, weak import prices—especially with the collapse in the emerging economies of East Asia—would more than offset its effects after 1996.[42] Indeed, three economists had unsuccessfully sought to trace an empirical relationship between unemployment and real price of crude oil since the mid-1950s.[43] We know, for example, that oil price hikes in 2000 and 2004 did not increase U.S. inflation and had no direct effect on employment. The expectation of conventional economists that the New Economy's effects on NAIRU were temporary were increasingly being dented as NAIRU itself seemed to be increasingly fated for destruction. Greenspan saw danger in what he regarded as an imbalance in the economy between resources and the demand for resources during this period. At the height of the expansion of the New Economy, Greenspan many times argued that the rising demand in the United States, fueled by what he called the "wealth effect," was putting pressures on the economy that might in the end bring back inflation. He argued at one point that inflation was being avoided because the growth in demand was being met through the "safety valves" of increased net imports and through the demand for goods and services produced by the net increase in newly hired workers over and above the normal growth of the workforce, including a substantial net inflow of workers from abroad. He warned that if the objective of maximum sustainable growth is to be achieved, the pool of workers cannot shrink indefinitely. The worker pool depletion, he maintained, constituted a critical upside risk to the inflation outlook. However, he argued that the existence or nonexistence of an empirically identified NAIRU has no bearing on the existence of the venerable law of supply and demand.[44] He said he was doubtful about a Phillips curve and the associated NAIRU, yet he proceeded to reenunciate NAIRU in a more generalized form by saying that there has to be a limit to how far the pool of available labor can be drawn down without pressing wage levels beyond productivity.[45] Greenspan's attempt to explain the economic changes facing him in terms of the new concept of wealth struck some economists as rather strange.

Greenspan believed that the economy needed cooling through the use of interest rates so as to push employment back to its "natural level." Conventional economists believe that the limit to growth in gross domestic product cannot exceed the sum of growth in structural productivity and in the working-age population without risks. The theory of factor proportions holds that the concept of the natural rate of unemployment and its sister concept of an output gap have no scientific validity. Like the natural rate concept, the idea of an output gap posits that the degree of inflation is linked to how close the economy is to its potential output, which is calculated by extrapolating the economy's previously achieved levels of output—another statistical construct.

During congressional testimony in July 2000, Greenspan quite courageously sounded what the *New York Times* called an "epitaph" to NAIRU. He said, "My forecast is that NAIRU, which served as a very useful statistical procedure to evaluate how the economy was behaving over a number of years, like so many types of temporary models which worked, is probably going to fail in the years ahead as a useful indicator."[46] In an earlier chapter we had questioned the validity of statistical (empirical) constructs and statistical correlations as a useful instrument of economic theory. The *New York Times,* correctly commenting at the time on Greenspan's statement on NAIRU, said that it made the next interest rate increase by the Fed harder to justify. This is because if there is no connection between employment and inflation, the use of interest rate cuts in the belief that they slow investment, which is supposed to reduce demand, is pointless. Such a situation makes monetary control irrelevant.

According to Bootle, the prime difficulty facing macro policy makers since the mid-1970s has been the containment and reduction of inflation. He added, "The collapse of this enemy leaves them a bit like the West's defense establishment after the collapse of the Soviet Union and the end of the Cold War— still possessing the old equipment but not sure where to point it."[47] Bootle did not add that the Western defense establishment quickly discovered other "dangers" to the West's security that helped it to re-establish its relevance. The danger is that in the presence of developments seeming to eliminate the relevance of monetarism in economic development and growth management, monetarists will seek other ways to redefine their relevance as they have done before.

The collapse of NAIRU in the New Economy cuts at the very foundation of monetarism. There is no scientific link between money supply and aggregate demand or inflation. Across wide variations in the rate of unemployment, there is no systematic relation between the level of demand and the rate of inflation.[48] The monetarist foundation, which had virtually collapsed, received a reprieve when in late 2000 the U.S. economy went through what commentators called a slowdown and the year 2001 started with panicked pleas for interest rate cuts so as to increase aggregate demand. It looked as if the economy was returning to "normal economics," as Greenspan had expected. By the middle of 2001, Greenspan and every other economist had forgotten the unresolved issues of the New Economy, and "normalcy" returned via the wielding of the interest rate sword.

What Bootle called monetarism's enduring appeal is its simplicity, which provides solace both inside and outside the academic world. According to Bootle, monetarism's simplicity and certainty enable professional economists to get on with their own part of the subject, confident that when it comes to monetary aspect or to the integration of their specialist topic with the rest of economics, they can latch on to an edifice that itself has secure foundations. He pointed out that if they were instead to believe that the edifice of monetary economics is built on shifting sands, this would cause profound insecurity and not a little difficulty.[49]

Conventional Economics and New Economic Cycles

Since the late 1980s, long periods of steady growth in some advanced economies have given conventional economists the confidence to assert that business cycles are beginning to be a thing of the past. Weber observed, "For both empirical and theoretical reasons, in advanced economies the waves of business cycles may be becoming more like ripples." He asserted, "[A] growing body of evidence suggests [that] the world may indeed be witnessing important changes in how business cycles work."[50] He claimed, "[The] modern business-cycle is essentially a series of stories about cyclical responses to external shocks. . . . The real questions," he stated, "are where shocks come from and what turns a shock into a business cycle."[51] He claims that shocks come principally from the demand side. But if demand is an integral part of the economy, why, we ask, should it be regarded as a shock, meaning that it is external, and "irrational" or unpredictable or both. Weber also claimed that shocks can come from the supply side. He concluded that uncertainty and errors in responding to these shocks lead to "mistakes" that spread throughout the economy. He asserted that "complex psychological factors come into play as business planners look not only to the external world, with its confused signals about prices and demand, but also to other signals of optimism and pessimism."[52] Weber has really not told us anything. He is in effect saying that business cycles arise because of the difficulty businesses have in adjusting to unexpected changes in demand or

supply. That does not lead us anywhere. Conventional economists disagree as to what causes demand "shock." This has provided behavioral experts with a field day.

Weber is basically recycling the old theories of underconsumption and overproduction. These theories, as we noted in Chapter 8, were floated by economists and politicians in the 1930s when they did not know what hit them when the depression started. As we have shown, the theories do not stand up. They are simplistic.

Weber, despite these handicaps, went on to attempt to explain why waves of business cycles may have become ripples in advanced economies. He listed what he called six "facets" of the modern economy, which, he claimed, contribute to the dampening of business cycles: (a) globalization of production; (b) changes in finance; (c) changing employment patterns (i.e., an increase in part-time work), in particular increasing employment in services, which he claims are noncyclical; (d) government policies that tend to make government services anticyclical; (e) emerging markets, which he claims give advanced countries steady and increasing markets that enable these countries to counter cyclical trends; and (f) information technology.

Greenspan discussed the subdued-cycle phenomenon, which occurred during the downturn in the U.S. economy that started at the end of 1999 and the beginning of 2000, according to his testimony to the House Committee on Financial Services on February 27, 2000. It will be recalled that in the midst of the tremendous growth that the United States experienced in the 1990s, Greenspan drew our attention to what he regarded as a chief characteristic of the new economy, namely information management. He said then that the application of information technology (IT) had enabled companies more accurately and efficiently than ever before to control inventory and costs. According to him, "Thirty years ago, the timeliness of available information varied across companies and industries, often resulting in differences in the speed and magnitude of their response to changing business conditions." "In contrast to the situation that prevails today [during the boom of the 1990s]," he said, "businesses have real-time data systems that enable decision makers in different enterprises to work from essentially the same set of information. In those early years [that is, before IT], imbalances were inadvertently allowed to build up to such an extent that correction engendered significant economic stresses. That process of correction and economic and financial disruption too often led to deep and prolonged recessions."[53] This is basically the same theory of overproduction that Weber was discussing.

Greenspan told the House in February 2002 following the slowdown that started in 2001, ". . . [I]f the tentative indications that the contraction phase of this business cycle is drawing to a close are ultimately confirmed, we will have experienced a significantly milder downturn than the long history of business cycles would have led us to expect. Crucially, the imbalances that triggered the downturn and could have prolonged this difficult period did not fester. . . . The obvious questions," he said, "are what has changed in our economy in recent decades to provide such resilience and whether such changes will persist in future." He answered as follows: "Doubtless, the substantial improvement in the access of business decision makers to real-time information has played a key role."[54] He asserted, "The apparent increased flexibility of the American economy arguably, also reflects the extent of deregulation over the past quarter century."[55]

If that is the case, the question then is why did the contraction on which he was reporting happen in the first place if businesses had all these latest real-time data information to control it? He told the House, "Inventories, especially among producers and purchasers of high-tech, did run to excess over the past year [that is, during the slowdown] as sales

forecasts went badly astray; alas, technology has not allowed us to see into the future any more clearly than we could previously." He reported that the result was that there were "significant levels of excess capacity in a number of industries." He further reported, "Many firms were responding to the realization that significant overcapacity had developed. The demand for capital goods had dropped sharply, and inventories were uncomfortably high in many industries." Right up to the beginning of the economic contraction, Greenspan, it should not be forgotten, was worrying about "excess" demand in the economy, which he said was fueled by the "wealth effect"; this demand, he said, was outstripping the economy's production capacity. At the time that he complained of excess demand, there were unprecedented high levels of employment and inflation was low. Why then did this demand suddenly evaporate? Despite all these unanswered questions, Greenspan just talked of the weakening sales and buildup of inventories. He claimed that the same IT technology that made it possible for businesses to see the future clearly and helped precipitate the downturn was now what helped to "facilitate the quick recognition of the weakening sales and buildup of inventories. . . . This enabled producers," he claimed, "to respond forcefully, as evidenced by output adjustments, and has resulted in the extraordinary rate of inventory liquidation we experienced late last year." It was clear that Greenspan's testimony did not explain, but raised more fundamental economic questions about, what really happened to the economy.[56]

The implied assumption by Greenspan that IT can help forecast changes in demand is incorrect. While it is correct that IT can help detect changes in demand as they occur, it cannot help in determining their probable extent, nature, or duration. If this is the case, then the claim by Greenspan and Weber that the deregulation of a wide sector of the U.S. economy (and other related factors named by

Weber as contributing to the increasing flexibility of present advanced economies) has helped to reduce the number of business cycles is incorrect. Conventional economics, in short, has not yet provided us with a valid explanation either of business cycles or why there are fewer of them of late in advanced economies.

Inflation and the New Economy

How does the theory of factor proportions affect conventional concepts about inflation? Before the natural rate concept held sway, many economists argued that the inflationary character of the postwar world and the acute inflationary problems of the 1970s had their roots in real structural phenomena that acted directly on the price level.[57]

Bootle correctly argued that for a number of unsustainable reasons, including the monetarists' determination to push ahead with managing economic development through the money supply, the importance of structural factors was ignored by economic theorists. He observed that in recent years the assortment of structural factors that influence inflation have changed in a favorable direction, just as they deteriorated in the 1970s.[58] One will assume that he was saying this in the context of the New Economy. There is no doubt that the structural changes we have discussed as shaping the New Economy have killed off NAIRU. Bootle declared that "inflation is caused by the struggle between different groups within the society over their share of national income." He observed that in the primal economy small units of production made it impossible for persistent inflation to arise from producer groups. In effect, Bootle was saying that primal economies were balanced, with small units of production activities with equal factor proportions deriving directly from the surrounding natural factor proportions. Bootle remarked that industrialization changed all this: "Goods were highly differentiated

one from another. The nature of mass-production technology limited the number of firms which could viably operate in an industry, so that there was a tendency towards industrial concentration. . . . The conditions of mass production favored mass organization of labor into unionized groups, mirroring the cartelization of employers. . . . It can be described as the attempt by both labor and capital employed in manufacturing to bag all of the benefits of increased productivity. Inflation is the mechanism through which this cornering of the benefits was resisted by other groups and the real income gains spread throughout the society."[59] Bootle was not very precise as to what he meant by the struggles alleged to exist among different groups. He was in effect talking of imbalances in the economic structure. For example, industrial concentration created a contrast between a few activities with a very high capital/labor ratio and a multitude of activities with a much lower capital/labor ratio. The struggle between these economic activities to corner the factors of production for themselves, to the exclusion of others, is essentially what Bootle is saying is the cause of institutional inflation. It is a simple description of an unbalanced economic structure with transfer of factors between different capital-intensive sectors, which we detailed in Chapter 6.

It follows from this line of reasoning that an economy in which all production activities have equal factor proportions, in line with the theory of factor proportions, is inflation free, with full employment guaranteed. The reason the New Economy witnessed very high growth with little inflation pressures and the longest period of sustainable growth is therefore evident.

New Growth Heights

Despite the sustainable growth achieved in the New Economy, market and monetary authorities in the United States are locked in an unjustified state of pessimism about the long-run potential for economic growth. This pessimism arises from their long-held views about natural rates. The theory of factor proportions as the formulation for sustainable economic development and growth shows that the United States—and in fact all countries—can, through the right strategies, confidently aim for much higher growth rates without engendering inflation pressures.

It is clear that the New Economy changed basic economic structure of the United States. A new economy arrived whose basic characteristics were different from those of the preceding era. But this is not to say that the New Economy was balanced. What we are saying is that for the first time since the end of the nineteenth century, an unregulated U.S. economy significantly moved toward a balanced state.[60]

Capital concentration as a preeminent method of production receded as production that was less capital-intensive and less material-intensive took over in the New Economy. It is risky to forecast the future of the U.S. economy. We can, however, say that one result of this structural change is likely to be the muting of business cycles, if not their elimination if the IT production sector and similar activities grow. Unfortunately, long runs of growth usually induce U.S. businesses to engage in capital-intensive activities and economic concentration, and so interrupt sustained growth and induce the muted economic cycles.

The appearance of these muted business cycles superimposed over a rising growth base deriving from a New Economy may from time to time give the impression of a return to "normal" economics. There are still large areas of communication waiting for new IT initiatives in the United States—whether it is communication between humans and humans, or between machines and humans, or between machines and machines. Mitchell says, "We are a long way from running out of new ideas for miniaturizing, cranking up clock speeds, and increasing parallelism."[61] Production aid (capital) in the economy, in this context, will increasingly require less material content as it incorporates more IT components and as the material mass being converted into new finished goods drops per unit of input. As an example, the low capital/labor ratio and low fixed investment per employee in automobile parts production, noted in Table 9.7, was probably due to the use of IT equipment in production techniques. Beck summarized the changed economic structure in the United States best when she said that the New Economy consists of new industries that have not peaked structurally.[62]

The low-capital/labor-ratio, low-material production paradigm has come about not because production techniques are moving in the direction of more labor input per unit of input but because research and development in materials is evolving a growing galaxy of new and diverse material technical properties and characteristics that are being increasingly exploited in technology.

In the long term, the United States can still achieve higher levels of sustainable growth than it has to date, by pursuing a policy of balanced factor proportions. Lack of balance in U.S. factor utilization is an impediment to the country's attainment of fuller and better use of its endowed factors. The resulting structural economic problems have characteristically produced an economy that can "grow" without equivalent expansion in employment but with increasing inequality. In the end, it is the full utilization of production factors that determines an economy's full potential for economic growth.

10

Conclusion

The theory of factor proportions is an economic formulation at the heart of economic development and growth. We argued that economic development and economic growth are one and the same thing. The theory of factor proportions can therefore be said to be a formulation for economic growth, exogenous in character.

In this book we have attempted to take this theory through the major faces of conventional economics that deal with economic development and growth—technology, international trade, international factor mobility, globalization. This has enabled us to show how and where conventional framing of these major topics is defective and unscientific.

We have also sought through the theory of factor proportions to integrate microeconomics with macroeconomics, a departure from the present conventional economics, where the two economics live separate lives and economists on both sides believe quite wrongly that the arithmetic sum of the parts equals the whole. Despite its central role in conventional economic textbooks and in business research, a one-sector model does not provide a correct description of an economy.

We have examined the role of intellectualism and philosophizing in economics. The two have filled conventional economics with an abundance of theories. The theory of values, rational theory, and the theories of prices, welfare, governance, and so on may be very persuasive but they are not scientific. Many of these theories are culturally based, ethnocentric, and often partially true, but not true in their total content. Because they do not have a scientific basis, they impede the evolution of scientific economic principles and concepts.

In Chapters 3, 8, and 9 we took an in-depth look at the history and economy of countries at different stages of economic development. We established in these chapters that noncompliance or compliance with the theory of factor proportions was at the root of failure or success of these economies. We showed that those who succeeded did so because they developed in line with their economic personality based on their factor proportions. The failure of African economies to date, we suggested, is not due to reasons adduced by conventional development experts. It is due to consistent attempts to give African countries an economic personality that is out of line with their factor proportions. Africa has been through a history that destroyed Africa's basic personality. It will take a long psychological trauma for African countries to change track and move in the direction of their appropriate factor proportions.

We thought it necessary to undertake an in-depth study of American economic history in Chapter 8 and the New Economy in Chapter 9. The United States is to date the most successful economy in the world and the largest in size. However, it has had its successes and failures. Through our detailed analysis of U.S. economic history, we have sought to show that the periods of successes were the times when the economic structure was tilted in the direction of balance of factor proportions. Periods of recession arose from structural economic imbalances. We sought to show that in many ways conventional economists do not know how the United States came from nowhere in economic terms, to reach its present state of economic preeminence. This ignorance on the part of conventional economist been demonstrated by the appearance of the "New Economy," which, as we saw in Chapter 9, caught conventional economists by surprise. They were unable to explain what had fundamentally changed the U.S. economic structure in the context of a "New Economy." We sought to explain the factors that have caused these fundamental changes in Chapter 9.

There was another reason why the chapters on the American economy were important. In a world in which, up to now, there has been no scientific theoretical economic formulation for economic growth, the economic study has been dominated by empiricism and statistical theorizing. Because the United States has been so successful economically, there has developed the trend by which economic data and concepts that arise from the United States are passed out to other countries as the universal principles of economic development and growth. The growing dominance of economic texts worldwide that regard American "technology," and economic and financial organization as the way forward for all economies derive from American "success" with them.

We examined the increasing dominance of finance in conventional economics. Money and price have become the essence of conventional economics. In practical life, we all need a means of exchange and value. Price provides that means. But that does not mean that price is a scientific concept. Our means of exchange is at best an approximation for dealing with the availability and use of real things—materials, labor, and capital. The science of economics is about these real things, not money and finance. In a science of economics, we are interested in the use and supply of the natural (scientific) factor endowments of material, labor, and production aids (capital). These are the real substance, while finance is the shadow.

Price distorts the real picture. Most conventional international trade theories are misleading, as they valiantly try to compare the resource base of countries by comparing prices and productivity. The fact that in microeconomics a company reduced its financial costs and became more profitable does not mean that the macro economy has made better use of its factor endowments.

The financial convenience route that conventional economics has taken has come at a cost—that of imprecision. Most "natural" sciences tediously work away at physical quantities in their attempt to establish scientific precision and universal truths. Conventional economics increasingly does not, as it seeks mathematical precision and "science" from financial concepts that are not in themselves scientific.

In order that a science of economic development and growth can flourish, we therefore need a new regime of statistics and data gathering geared to meeting the needs of that science, in which monetary and financial statistics take a second place. Presently, almost all official economic statistics in all countries lack detailed data on the availability, quantity, volume, usage, and conversion of factors. It is difficult to find in published economic statistics the data needed to test out scientific economic theory. In the present state, the necessary statistical tools required to effect a change in economic growth management in accordance with the theory of factor proportions are not yet available. The application of the theory of factor proportions will herald the beginning of what we call "structural economics." Priority is needed in each country to pursue the path of high sustainable growth (which is achievable irrespective of a country's size, population, and resources) through widespread application of the theory of factor proportions.

The adoption of a formulation of economic growth involving factor proportions means that economic management of economies will need to be undertaken back stage and not front stage. Instead of monitoring and controlling a fire by checking the flue at the top of the chimney, factor proportions theory provides us the tools to manage the fire itself, inside the house. In conventional economic management, monetary and fiscal measures are like instruments and controls mounted at the top of the chimney so as to monitor and control the flue from the economic fire in the house. The U.S. economy is today monitored by such indirect and often contradictory financial and monetary data as wholesale price index, inventory values, housing starts, productivity, construction index, share value indices, and so on, that is after the event. Consumer confidence has slowly risen in importance as an index of economic activity. Each of these measures is an attempt to monitor the flue of the economic chimney.

Using this data, Michael Mandel at one time predicted impeding economic doom in the United States in his book *The Coming Internet Depression: Why the High Tech Boom Will Go Bust, Why the Crash Will Be Worse Than You Think and How to Prosper Afterward.*[1] Other economic commentators reached the opposite conclusion that the economy is set to prosper further. Christopher Farrell in a *Business Week* commentary said that Mandel's dark prediction rested on "a series of worst case assumptions."[2] Such is the guessing game that dominates a field that is supposed to be a science. Such controversy in economic journalism, in which some academics participate, helps to sell newspapers and magazines. Economics as a science is being bastardized.

In the course of this book, the issue of the best sociopolitical environment, and in particular the role of government, for achieving rapid economic growth cropped up many times. We argued that there were no clear answers. In theory, it should be easier for a government that has accepted our growth formulation to regulate the use of factors of production in the economy, whether directly or indirectly, to meet the needs for rapid sustainable growth with the cooperation of its citizens. After all, this, in effect, was what the United States tried to do with its World War II economy. In a free enterprise situation, the achievement of the required balance in factor proportions may be somewhat more difficult. Concentration of industry through mergers and takeovers —a continuing feature of the U.S. economy since the late nineteenth century, is not likely to go away easily. The tendency to industrial concentration negates the equal factor proportions requirement. On the other hand, there were periods such as the middle 1800s, when in a free market situation, the United States achieved near correct factor proportions management of its economy, as indicated in Chapter 8. The recent achievements of the New Economy, which we analyzed in Chapter 9, arose from new changes in production techniques in a free enterprise environment. It is our view that economic texts that want to say that one political framework or another is best suited for sustainable economic development are misleading. The Soviet Union failed not because it was socialist in its economic management but because its spending on capital-intensive development created a situation in which its factor proportions were completely out of step with its endowed factor resources. Being exogenous, our factor proportions economic formulation can operate in any political setting, everything else being equal. Democracy therefore has no distinctive economic dividends. It is our conclusion therefore that unless democracy and economic growth are separated, democracy may in the long run be rejected in poor countries when the hoped-for economic dividends of democracy are not attained. Societies that presently are experimenting with democracy and economic development in the conventional style may in the near future face social unrest and anarchy when poverty grows and human suffering increases. It was our view that the case for democracy ought to be made for its own sake and not for what it will bring economically.

Globalization has become a cornerstone of conventional economic development theory. Many of its promoters believe, as we have seen, that by sharing the benefits of "modern technology" and by promoting the international mobility of factors, all countries will benefit from an enlarged global economy. It is a belief, as we have shown, that has no scientific basis. The case for globalization does not rest on any analyzed scientific economic theory. Proponents of globalization often believe that the case for it is obvious. They therefore show a sense of frustration and impatience at the slow pace of globalization. They smirk at the apparent ignorance of their opponents. For example, in *Entering the 21st Century* the World Bank complained of the fragmentation of production processes across international boundaries. The report urged the "fusing of domestic firms into a global production network."[3] Greenspan himself in a January 2000 speech enthused that "the combination of a marked surge in mergers and acquisitions, especially the vast increase in strategic alliances, including across borders, is dramatically altering business structures to conform to the imperatives of newer technologies."[4] Such statements are based on the misplaced belief in the supremacy of a model of "best production techniques," which is supposed to link every country utilizing "modern technology" in the context of unrestrained mobility of resources around the globe. Apologists have argued that there is nothing wrong with the concept of globalization, only with how it is being practiced. There have been attempts to claim victories for globalization. For example, people claim that China's phenomenal growth is due to the country's entry to the global system.

Opponents of globalization have equally not advanced a scientific case against it. The case against globalization has regretfully been fought by its opponents on essentially emotive and political grounds. There therefore seems to be a political divide between proponents and opponents of globalization. The result is that arguments for and against globalization have to date not advanced the search for a viable economic development and growth theory. The chapter on globalization was an attempt to present a detailed economic and technical analysis of the issues involved. We came to the reluctant conclusion that despite the good intentions of people and governments promoting globalization, globalization was not the means to achieve sustainable global economic development and growth. It was also more likely to degrade the economy of poor countries further. We described the technical and economic contradictions in the globalization concept and observed that some of these are likely in the medium and long term to lead to the unsustainability of globalization. At best, globalization is premature, because of the present wide economic gaps separating the countries that are supposed to be part of it.

One of the biggest problems that we faced in writing this book was in regard to the word *technology*. Technology has recently moved into the center stage of economic theory, especially with the recent emergence of new growth theory. New growth theory picks technology as the source of economic growth. The theory is not quite sure what to make of the old man, capital. It is sadly true that to many conventional economists, technology is a black box—something goes in and something comes out. The residual—a "measure of our ignorance"—has also been equated nebulously by others with technology. Nowhere in our research on this book did we find any economist who gave a precise scientific definition of technology. It meant different things to different people. The position is not helped by the fact that the word is now as commonly used by the layperson as much as by the economist. Technology is now used to refer to things, to new ideas, to practices. The term *science* is losing out as people confuse science with technology because the term technology sounds more glamorous. On Wall Street, people talk of 'technology stocks.' In view of its economic importance, we did define *technology* in the book. But we found ourselves having sometimes to use the word in ways that went against our definition because that made it easier to convey meaning and achieve a quick mental connection with the reader. There are times in the book when we unguardedly fell into the same trap as other economists who use the word, because technology was the word that came out first in describing what we were trying to say. The reader therefore should not lose sight of our definition and regard instances where *technology* was not used in line with our definition in the light of this explanation. The true definition of technology is a vital part of our theory of factor proportions.

The mixture in the economic profession of those who think that economics is a science, or should be, with those who think that it is not a science, and should not be, has confused the profession on what its broad approach to the subject is. If economics is science, it will, like all sciences, evolve immutable laws and generalized principles. If it is not a science, then, like all nonscience subjects, it is subject to changes over time and space and bears the stamp of the individual expert dealing with the subject. But as we saw in Chapter 1, economic development theory in a nonscientific setting is moving round in circles. As we pointed out in that chapter, ideas have continued to be recycled and presented as new ideas. For example, new growth theory was presented—as its name implies—as a brand-new car the likes of which no one had ever seen before. It turned out that the theory was a careful repackaging of an old model with bits and pieces painted over in new colors.

Conventional theories of development and growth lack scientific permanence and are unable to explain new circumstances or discover the cause of changes it meets, as in the case of the New Economy, discussed in Chapter 9. The basic, humbling question that conventional economists need to answer is this: If nature has preordained all that now makes up the ingredients of discoveries in natural science—on the earth, below the earth, in the sea, and in the atmosphere—why couldn't nature preordain the economic order as to how humans can achieve maximum benefit from endowed factors? The theory of factor proportions is the best shot we have at an answer. Our effort may not be completely successful. Some of the ideas may not have been researched enough, and there may well be serious gaps in our analysis. It is, however, a beginning, an attempt to look at economic development and growth from an entirely new perspective. It is hoped others will come to build on our efforts.

We will conclude this book by putting the issue of resource (factor) availability and use and economic development and growth in one unifying context. The dynamic equilibrium, which we have in this book identified as being at the heart of economic development and growth, depends on nature's established cycles of resource supply and use. The production factors of human labor and materials are constantly depreciating from use and are constantly replenished through nature's cycles. The number of people in any society may in the process fluctuate, but the basic cycle of supply of people continues through deaths and births. Likewise, with the stock of natural resources there is a cycle of usage, depreciation, and replenishment by nature. In primal societies, the two cycles of labor and material supply and use usually were uninterrupted except in case of natural disasters. Nature largely kept the cycles going.

Production aids (capital) were manufactured in primal societies by man using materials to produce needed capital assets. Capital, too, like the human that produced it and the material from which it was produced, depreciates due to use and gets replenished by repairing or upgrading it or replacing it at the end of its useful life. Primal man changed a weak or broken piece of wood in his hand loom. He sharpened his blunt tools. He, as we pointed out, used parts of his body as production aids. In effect, labor, the material of the human body, was used sometimes as capital (production aid). Humans are able to provide labor because they have and are material. Labor, being material, also has the same qualities as some other materials. Materials in turn were also used as capital, especially in primal societies, where, for example, stone was a valuable production aid. Capital is basically transformed material. Original capital was just material.

Within the natural cycle of supply and use of each factor, there is a further related element—that of substitution. The constituents of each factor in any economy are economic substitutes for each other, either immediately or over time. In primal as well as modern economies, for example, training was one way of substituting one source of labor for another. One material can be substituted for another. Since material and labor are essential inputs in the production of capital, it follows that capital can be substituted for by different materials or different production techniques, either immediately or over time.

There is, in addition, an enveloping cycle—the outer cycle, as it may be called. This outer cycle links the three factors in a relationship of mutual substitution, as we described in Chapter 3. Each factor (labor, material, and capital) can be substituted with the other two factors within the context of a three-factor production system. The relationships described are shown in Figure 10.1.

The cycles and substitutions indicated in Figure 10.1 are a coordinated entity in the natural factor endowment of any socioeconomic unit. This natural relationship of endowed factors needed to

be in a changing dynamic equilibrium in order to rejuvenate and replenish itself. It is this dynamic equilibrium that is at the heart of the theory of factor proportions. Without this dynamic equilibrium, sustainable economic development and growth will be impossible.

Two basic issues can be settled from these considerations in the context of the economic management of resources. The first is that labor and material and capital are all materials. The natural origin of all economic systems is therefore material. The economic system revolves around the different qualities nature has given different materials. It is these qualities that assign to each material or combination of materials the economic function it performs—labor, material, capital. Human material has additionally been endowed, for lack of a better description, with intellect—a coordinating control system that is utilized in both economic and noneconomic matters. The theory of factor proportions derives from an inquiry into the nature of the different economic qualities and functions that nature has assigned to different materials.

Second, conventional economics wrongly asserts that the greatest bottleneck to economic development is capital.[5] It follows, according to it, that increased capital investment in any economy leads to economic growth. So conventional economics goes to great lengths to incorporate the concepts of capital depreciation and new capital investments into its economic models. But it is obvious that without material and labor, there will be no capital. Therefore, capital depreciation is a concept derived from the depreciation qualities of its constituents, labor and material. Modern man goes to great lengths to preserve mankind and assist in its continued natural regeneration. Much of what man is doing in this effort is incorporated into conventional economic texts: health care, welfare, education, and so on. Regrettably, conventional economics does not have the same interest in materials. Conventional eco-

Figure 10.1 **The natural factor cycles—outer and inner cycles.**

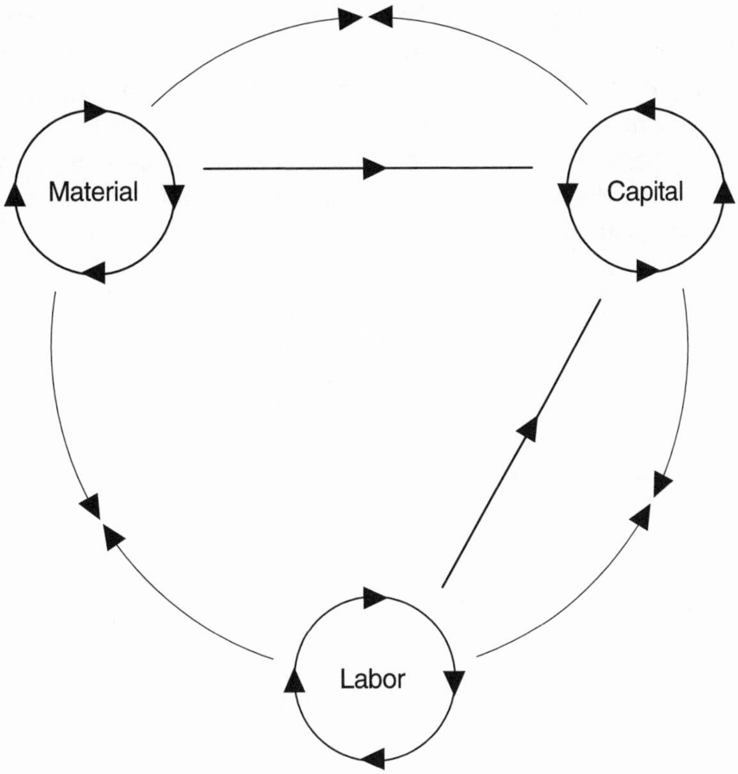

nomic texts assume the availability of materials. They assume that any difficulties in material availability are usually temporary and can be solved through the price mechanism or substitution. The theory of factor proportions says that the greatest bottleneck to economic development and growth is not capital but materials. It is from materials that capital is produced. The bulk of technology that propels economies forward depends on the dynamics of the science of materials.

The result of the misleading attitude of conventional economic wisdom toward material is that the issues of care of the environment, conservation of natural resources, and how to preserve and not interfere with nature's cycles of material supply and use are treated as lying outside conventional economic theory. Care of the environment

and conservation of natural resources, on the other hand, are an integral part of the theory of factor proportions if the dynamic balance on which the theory rests is to be preserved. To do otherwise will mean that the endowed supply will become unstable due to unpredictable fluctuations in natural resources availability.

It is in the context of the cycles described that this book will challenge the concept of an exhaustible stock of natural resources. Economists and conservationists alike have classified some natural resources as exhaustible. In the context of our analysis, it is inappropriate to classify any natural resource as exhaustible. In nature, replenishments for different natural resources have different cycle gestation periods. When people talk of exhaustible resources, they in fact mean either that there is a mismatch between man's rate of use of the resource and its natural replenishment cycle or that man had through aggressive destruction of the associated resources system interrupted the natural replenishment cycle of the particular resources. Conventional economic development seems to be at the forefront of this interruption. Exploitive use and destruction of the world's natural resource base, especially by multinational corporations, are the hallmarks of conventional economics, including the massive conversion of enormous quantities of natural resources into an exploding capital goods industry in the belief that capital growth is economic growth. No development/growth theory is worth its salt if it does not have conservation (green) at the center of its formulation.

Notes

Notes to Chapter 1

1. "Trends and Policies in the World Economy," *World Economic and Social Survey* (New York: United Nations, 1998).

2. Ibid.

3. S. Burke and S. Edwards, "Dismantling the Populist State—The Unfinished Revolution in Latin America and the Caribbean," World Bank, June 1996, 2.

4. T. N. Srinivasan, "Evolution of Development Theory and Strategy: Changing Perception of the Role of the Market, the State and Foreign Trade," in Waltraud Schelkle et al., eds., *Paradigms of Social Change: Modernization, Development, Transformation, Evolution* (New York: St. Martin's Press; Frankfurt: Campus Verlag, 2000).

5. For example, the London School of Economics has established an Institute of Development Studies concerned with "the process of social development and change . . . and oriented towards the less developed countries or the relationship between these countries and the advanced economies." Yale University's Economics Department has set up an Economic Growth Center with the object of "studying and promoting understanding of economic development process within the low income countries and how development is affected by trade and financial relations between these countries and those that developed earlier."

6. G. Meier, *Leading Issues in Economic Development,* 2nd ed. (New York: Oxford University Press, 1970), 86.

7. H. Myint, "Economic Theory and Development Policy," *Economica* 34, 134 (1967): 123–27.

8. W. W. Rostow, *The Stages of Economic Growth: A Non-Communist Manifest* (Cambridge: Cambridge University Press, 1961), 4. We do not agree with Rostow's detailed analysis of the stages.

9. R. Barro and X. Sala-i-Martin, *Economic Growth* (New York: McGraw-Hill, 1995), 12.

10. P. Krugman, *Development, Geography, and Economic Theory* (Cambridge, MA: MIT Press, 1995), 7.

11. C. Leys, *The Rise and Fall of Development Theory* (Bloomington: Indiana University Press, 1996).

12. Ibid., 8.

13. C. Leys, "The Rise and Fall of Development Theory," lecture to Royal African Society, London, February 15, 1996, 4.

14. D. Booth, "Marxism and Development Sociology: Interpreting the Impasse," *World Development* 13, 7 (1985); F. H. Buttell, P. Vendergeest, and F. Marx, "Weber and Development Sociology: Beyond the Impasse," *World Development* 16, 7 (1988); L. Sklair, "Transcending the Impasse: Metatheory, Theory and Empirical Research in Sociology of Underdevelopment," *World Development* 16, 6 (1988); J. Manor (ed.), *Rethinking the Third World* (New York: Crane Russak, 1992); J.-F. Bayart, *The State in Africa: The Politics of the Belly*, trans. E. Harrison et al. (London and New York: Longman, 1992); J. Crush, ed., *Power of Development* (New York: Routledge, 1995).

15. M. P. Todaro, *Economic Development*, 5th ed. (New York and London: Longman, 1994), 35.

16. K. Griffin, *Alternative Strategies for Economic Development* (London: Macmillan, 1989), 25.

17. D. Booth, "Development Research: From Impasse to a New Agenda," in *Beyond the Impasse: New Directions in Development Theory*, ed. F. J. Schuurman (London and Atlantic Highlands, NJ: Zed Books, 1993).

18. For a review of the classical Marxist school (not included here), see C. C. Onyemelukwe, *Underdevelopment: An Inside View* (London and New York: Longman, 1974).

19. W. A. Lewis, "Economic Development with Unlimited Supplies of Labour," *Manchester School of Economic and Social Studies* 22 (1954): 139–91.

20. C. K. Eicher and J. Staaz, *Agricultural Development in the Third World* (Baltimore: Johns Hopkins University Press, 1984).

21. See also J. C. H. Fei and G. Ranis, *Development of the Labor Surplus Economy: Theory and Policy* (Homewood, IL: Richard D. Irwin, 1964).

22. A. Hirschmann, *The Strategy of Economic Development* (New Haven, CT: Yale University Press, 1958).

23. P. N. Rosenstein-Rodan, "Notes on the Theory of Big Push," Center for International Studies, Massachusetts Institute of Technology, March 1957.

24. R. Nurske, "Some International Aspects of Economic Development," *American Economic Review* 43 (1953): 572.

25. H. Leibenstein, *The Collected Essays of Harvey Leibenstein*, ed. K. Button (Aldershot: Elgar, 1989).

26. R. Nelson, *Economic Growth and Poverty* (Santa Monica, California: Rand Corporation, 1965).

27. Nurske, "Some International Aspects of Economic Development."

28. H. Singer, "The Concepts of Balanced Growth and Economic Growth: Theory and Facts," in E. Nelson, ed., *Economic Growth, Rationale, Problems, Cases* (Austin: University of Texas Press, 1960), 77.

29. S. Enke, *Economics for Development* (Englewood Cliffs, NJ: Prentice-Hall, 1963), 315.

30. Hirschmann, *The Strategy of Economic Development*.

31. Ibid., 44.

32. T. W. Schultz, *Transforming Traditional Agriculture* (New Haven, CT: Yale University Press, 1964).

33. Myint, quoted in Meier, *Leading Issues in Economic Development*, 80.

34. Hirschmann, *The Strategy of Economic Development*.

35. P. Samuelson et al., *Economics* (New York: McGraw-Hill, 1989), 886. How does this tie up with the opposite view, that poor countries have low capital absorption ability?

36. K. Coman, *Industrial History of the United States* (New York: Macmillan, 1913).

37. D. S. Landes, *The Wealth and Poverty of Nations: Why Some Are So Rich and Some So Poor* (New York: W. W. Norton, 1998), 186.

38. H. Heaton, *Economic History of Europe* (New York and London: Harper and Brothers, 1936), 502.

39. Landes, *The Wealth and Poverty of Nations*, 191. Landes called the last third of the eighteenth century a period of "contagious novelty" in which all the previous gains and inventions came together. See also D. S. Landes, *The Unbound Prometheus: Technological Change and Industrial Development in Western Europe from 1750 to the Present* (Cambridge: Cambridge University Press, 1969), 724–25.

40. Heaton, *Economic History of Europe*, 343.

41. M. J. Daunton, *Progress and Poverty: An Economic and Social History of Britain, 1700–1850* (New York: Oxford University Press, 1995), 232.

42. J. Nef, "The Progress of Technology and Growth of Large Scale Industry in Great Britain 1540–1640," *Economic History Review* 245 (1934): 3–24.

43. Landes, *Wealth and Poverty of Nations*, 73.

44. A. Gerschenkron, *Economic Backwardness in Historical Perspective* (Cambridge, MA: Harvard University Press, 1962).

45. World Bank, *World Development Report: Knowledge for Development* (Washington, DC: World Bank, 1998–99), 16.

46. In the weary concepts of "capital absorption" and "capital deepening," poor societies are thought not to have the capacity to utilize the capital introduced.

47. D. Apter, "Changing African Perspectives," in D. Apter and C. Rosberg, eds., *Political Development and the New Realism in Sub-Saharan Africa* (Charlottesville: University Press of Virginia, 1994).

48. T. Oloko, "Some Socio-Cultural Factors Affecting Response To Innovation," *The Nigerian Journal of Economic and Social Studies*, June 1962.

49. I. Gendzier, *Managing Political Change: Social Scientists and the Third World* (Boulder, CO: Westview Press, 1985).

50. E. Hobsbawm, *Age of Extremes: The Short Twentieth Century, 1914–1991* (London: Michael Joseph, 1994).

51. P. Kennedy, *African Capitalism: The Struggle for Ascendancy* (Cambridge: Cambridge University Press, 1988).

52. E. Hagen, *On the Theory of Social Change: How Economic Growth Begins* (Homewood, IL: Dorsey, 1962).

53. D. McClelland, *The Achieving Society* (Princeton, NJ: Van Nostrand, 1961).

54. F. Riggs, *Administration in Developing Countries: The Theory of Prismatic Society* (Boston: Houghton Mifflin, 1964); F. Riggs, *Prismatic Society Reconsidered* (Morristown, NJ: General Learning Press, 1973); D. Lerner, *The Passing of Traditional Society: Modernizing the Middle East* (New York: Free Press, 1958).

55. D. North, *Structure and Change in Economic History* (New York: W. W. Norton, 1981).

56. R. Bates, *Markets and States in Tropical Africa* (Berkeley: University of California Press, 1981).

57. North, *Structure and Change in Economic History*.

58. World Bank, *World Development Report* (Washington, DC: World Bank, 1986, 1987, 1991, 1994).

59. The distinguished former British governor of Hong Kong, after synthesizing his close view of East Asia, concluded that "I find myself drawn to the conclusion that what we see when we compare West and East is a consequence most of time lags than of profound cultural differences." C. Patten, *East and West: The Last Governor of Hong Kong on Power, Freedom, and the Future* (London: Macmillan, 1998).

60. J. M. Roberts, *History of the World* (New York: Oxford University Press, 1993).

61. Landes, *Wealth and Poverty of Nations*, 4.

62. W. Tu, *Confucian Ethics Today: The Singapore Challenge* (Singapore: Federal Publications, 1984), 33.

63. C. Lingle, *The Rise and Decline of the Asian Century: False Starts on the Path to the Global Millennium* (Hong Kong: Asia 2000, 1997), 264.

64. S. Huntington, "The Clash of Civilization?" *Foreign Affairs* 72, 3 (1993). Huntington later expanded his view in a book, *The Clash of Civilizations and the Remaking of World Order* (New York: Simon and Schuster, 1996).

65. Patten, *East and West*, 154.

66. Landes, *Wealth and Poverty of Nations*, 219.

67. Ibid., 154.

68. P. Kennedy, *Preparing for the Twenty-first Century* (New York: Random House, 1993).

69. We are here concerned with how colonialists destroyed traditional industry and know-how.

70. S. Latouche, *The Westernization of the World*, trans. R. Morris (Cambridge: Polity, 1996), 76.

71. A. Ihle, *Das Alte Königreich Kongo* (Leipzig-Engelsdorf: C. und C. Vogel, 1929), 151.

72. Landes, *Wealth and Poverty of Nations*.

73. Onyemelukwe, *Underdevelopment: An Inside View*.

74. Leys, *Rise and Fall of Development Theory*, 70.

75. S. Berry, "Understanding Agricultural Policy in Africa: The Contributions of Robert Bates," *World Development* 22, 6 (1993): 1055–62. See also Berry, *No Condition Is Permanent: The Social Dynamics of Agrarian Change in Sub-Saharan Africa* (Madison: University of Wisconsin Press, 1992).

76. Leys, *The Rise and Fall of Development Theory*, 99; see also B. Gustafsson, "Some Theoretical Problems of Institutional Economic History," *Scandinavian Economic History Review* 46, 2 (1998): 20.

77. Leys, *The Rise and Fall of Development Theory*, 43.

78. Ibid., 151.

79. North, *Structure and Change in Economic History*, 57.

80. J. Wolfensohn, "People First," Paul G. Hoffman Lecture, 1997.

81. World Bank, *Assessing Aid: What Works, What Doesn't and Why*, World Bank Policy Research Report (Washington, DC: Oxford University Press, 1998).

82. S. Bondy, contribution to a conference at the Vienna Institute for Development and Cooperation, 1971.

83. P. Krugman, *The Accidental Theorist: And Other Dispatches from the Dismal Science* (New York: W. W. Norton, 1998).

84. Leys, *The Rise and Fall of Development Theory*, 86.

85. T. Dos Santos, "The Crisis of Development Theory and the Problems of Dependence in Latin America," in H Bernstein, ed., *Underdevelopment and Development: The Third World Today: Selected Readings* (Harmondsworth, UK: Penguin, 1973).

86. F. H. Cardoso, "Dependency and Development in Latin America," *New Left Review*, June 1972.

87. O. Sunkel, "National Development Policy and External Dependence in Latin America," *Journal of Development Studies* 65, 1 (1969).

88. Dos Santos, "The Crisis of Development Theory," 75.

89. P. J. O'Brien, "A Critique of Latin American Theories of Dependency," in I. Oxaal, T. Barnet, and D. Booth, eds., *Beyond the Sociology of Development: Economy and Society in Latin America and Africa* (London: Routledge and Paul, 1975).

90. Leys, *The Rise and Fall of Development Theory*, 113.

91. Sanjaya Lall, "Is Dependence a Useful Concept in Analyzing Underdevelopment," *World Development* 3, 11 (1975).

92. G. Kay, *Development and Underdevelopment: A Marxist Analysis* (London: Macmillan, 1975), 103.

93. J. Larraín, *Theories of Development: Capitalism, Colonialism and Dependency* (Cambridge: Polity, 1989), 178.

94. Leys, *The Rise and Fall of Development Theory*, 113.

95. Ibid., 149. Extreme examples of countries with large regional inequalities are Canada and Italy.

96. O. Sunkel, "National Development Policy."

97. Cardoso, "Dependency and Development in Latin America."

98. Leys, *The Rise and Fall of Development Theory*, 118.

99. It is also sometimes called redistribution with growth.

100. C. Colclough and J. Manor, *States or Markets? Neoliberalism and the Development Policy Debate* (Oxford: Clarendon Press, 1991).

101. M. Roemer and S. Radeler, "Macroeconomics Reforms in Development Countries," in D. H. Perkins and M. Roemer, eds., *Reforming Economic Systems in Developing Countries* (Cambridge, MA: Harvard Institute for International Development, Harvard University, 1991), 72.

102. World Bank, *World Development Report 1983* (New York: Oxford University Press, 1983), 52–56.

103. C. Colclough, "Are African Governments as Unproductive as the Accelerated Development Report Implies?" *IDS Bulletin* 14, 1 (1983): 249.

104. R. Ram, "Government Size and Economic Growth," *American Economic Review* 76, 1 (1986): 191–203; Barro and Sala-i-Martin, *Economic Growth*.

105. P. Aghion and P. Howitt, *Endogenous Growth Theory* (Cambridge, MA: MIT Press, 1998), 58.

106. Roemer and Radeler, "Macroeconomics Reforms in Development Countries," 79.

107. Aghion and Howitt, *Endogenous Growth Theory*, 389–90.

108. C. Colclough, "Are African Governments as Unproductive," 249.

109. A. Kruger, "Export-Led Growth Reconsidered," paper presented at the Eleventh PAFTA [Pacific Free Trade Area] Conference, Seoul, Korea, 1980.

110. Margaret Thatcher of the United Kingdom asserted in 1980 that there was no alternative to capitalist development.

111. J. Tobin, "Why We Need Sand in the Market's Gears," *Washington Post*, December 21, 1997.

112. Interview with Bhagwati in *Times of India*, December 31, 1997.

113. R. Wade and F. Veneroso, "The Asian Crisis: The High Debt Model Versus the Wall Street–Treasury–IMF Complex," *Foreign Affairs*, September 1998, 10–19.

114. P. Krugman, "Competitiveness: A Dangerous Obsession," in *Competitiveness: An International Economics Reader* (New York: Council on Foreign Relations, 1994), 30, 39.

115. Ibid., 35.

116. M. Porter and H. Takeuchi, "Fixing What Really Ails Japan," *Foreign Affairs*, May–June 1999, 74.

117. R. Kuttner, *Global Competitiveness and Human Development: Allies or Adversaries?* (New York: Office of Development Studies, United Nations Development Programme, 1996), 13–14.

118. Ibid., 12.

119. J. Sachs, "Global Capitalism: Making It Work," *The Economist*, February 12, 1998, 23.

120. Kuttner, *Global Competitiveness*, 10.

121. P. Krugman, *Peddling Prosperity: Economic Sense and Nonsense in the Age of Diminished Expectations* (New York: W. W. Norton, 1994), 125–26.

122. Kuttner, *Global Competitiveness*, 8.

123. Ibid., 10.

124. Kuttner in his book *The Economic Illusion: False Choices Between Prosperity and Social Justice* (Boston: Houghton Mifflin, 1984) rejects the notion that it is a choice between equality and efficiency.

125. L. Taylor and U. Pieper, *Reconciling Economic Reform and Sustainable Human Development: Social Consequences of Neo-Liberalism* (New York: Office of Development Studies, United Nations Development Programme, 1996); "Economic Organization, Information and Development," in H. Chenery and T. N. Srinivasan, eds., *Handbook of Development Economics* (Amsterdam: North-Holland, 1988), 1:98.

126. A. Maddison, *Monitoring the World Economy, 1920–1992* (Paris: Development Centre of the OECD, 1995), 16.

127. Kuttner, *Global Competitiveness*, 16.

128. Leys, *The Rise and Fall of Development Theory*, 119.

129. Kuttner, *Global Competitiveness*, 16.

130. D. Lal, *The Poverty of "Development Economics"* (Cambridge, MA: Harvard University Press, 1985), 4–5.

131. For details of the damaging results of IMF structural adjustment programs in some poor countries, see T. Killick, *The IMF and Stabilisation: Developing Country Experiences* (London: Heinemann, 1984).

132. Aghion and Howitt, *Endogenous Growth Theory*, 1.

133. D. North, *Institutions, Institutional Change, and Economic Performance* (Cambridge: Cambridge University Press, 1990), 7. See also M. K. Nabli and J. B. Nuget, "The New Institutional Economics and Its Applicability to Development," *World Development* 17, 9: 1333–47, written by two institutional economists with a similar characterization of the economic growth process.

134. Aghion and Howitt, *Endogenous Growth Theory*, 8.

135. Ibid., 1.

136. R. E. Lucas, "On the Mechanics of Economic Development," *Journal of Monetary Economics* 22 (1988).

137. Aghion and Howitt, *Endogenous Growth Theory*, 327.

138. Barro and Sala-i-Martin in *Economic Growth*, for example, regressed the average growth of several countries on several macroeconomic variables, including educational training and public spending on education as a fraction of GDP. They found, first, that educational attainment (i.e., average years of schooling) is significantly correlated with subsequent growth (a correlation of 0.05); second, that public spending on education has a significant positive effect on growth. A 1.5 percent increase of the ratio of public education spending to GDP over 1965 to 1975 should, according to them, have raised average growth over the same period by 0.3 percent per year.

139. Aghion and Howitt, *Endogenous Growth Theory*, 279.

140. J. Ventura, "Growth and Interdependence," *Quarterly Journal of Economics* 112, 1 (1997): 57–84.

141. C. Freeman and L. Soete, *The Economics of Industrial Innovation*, 3rd ed. (Cambridge, MA: MIT Press, 1997), 326–27.

142. Aghion and Howitt, *Endogenous Growth Theory*, 7.

143. Ibid., 25–26.

144. Ibid., 187.

145. R. E. Lucas, "Making a Miracle," *Econometrics* 61 (1993): 251–72.

146. Freeman and Soete, *The Economics of Industrial Innovation*, 328.

147. Aghion and Howitt, *Endogenous Growth Theory*, 2.

148. P. K. Ghosh, *Appropriate Technology in Third World Development* (Westport, CT: Greenwood Press, 1984).

149. Freeman and Soete, *The Economics of Industrial Innovation*, 15.

150. Ibid., 24.

151. OECD, *New Technologies in the 1990s: A Socio-Economic Strategy* (Paris and Washington, DC: OECD, 1998), 117.

152. D. C. North, "The Sources of Productivity Growth in Ocean Shipping, 1600–1850," in R. W. Fogel and S. L. Engerman, eds., *The Reinterpretation of American Economic History* (New York: Harper and Row, 1971).

153. Aghion and Howitt, *Endogenous Growth Theory*, 1.

154. D. C. North and R. P. Thomas, *The Rise of the Western World: A New Economic History* (Cambridge: Cambridge University Press, 1973), 2.

155. Barro and Sala-i-Martin, *Economic Growth*, 12.

156. For example, creative destruction is not a universal feature. In some societies there may be no vested interests.

157. Aghion and Howitt, *Endogenous Growth Theory*, 1.

158. Freeman and Soete, *The Economics of Industrial Innovation*, 319.

159. Leys, *The Rise and Fall of Development Theory*, 100.

160. R. Nelson, "What Has Been the Matter with Neoclassical Growth Theory," in G. Silverberg and L. Soete, eds., *The Economics of Growth and Technical Change: Technologies, Nations, Agents* (Aldershot: Edward Elgar, 1994).

161. P. Romer, "Endogenous Technological Change," *Journal of Political Economy* 98, 5, part 2 (1990): 71–102; G. Grossman and E. Helpman, *Innovation and Growth in the Global Economy* (Cambridge, MA: MIT Press, 1991).

162. Aghion and Howitt, *Endogenous Growth Theory*, 99.

163. Ibid., 66.

164. D. Jorgenson, *Productivity* (Cambridge, MA: MIT Press, 1995).

165. C. Jones, "R&D-Based Models of Economic Growth," *Journal of Political Economics* 103 (1995): 759–84.

166. Aghion and Howitt, *Endogenous Growth Theory*, 437.

167. Ibid., 436–37.

168. F. Fukuyama, *The End of History and the Last Man* (New York: Free Press, 1992), 456.

169. Aghion and Howitt, *Endogenous Growth Theory*, 435.

170. M. F. Scott, *A New View of Economic Growth* (Oxford: Clarendon Press, 1989), 77.

171. Freeman and Soete, *The Economics of Industrial Innovation*, 427.

Notes to Chapter 2

1. M. Godelier, *Rationality and Irrationality in Economics*, trans. B. Pearce (New York: Monthly Review Press, 1973), 72.

2. M. Weber, *The Methodology of the Social Sciences* (New York: Free Press, 1949), 81.

3. J. Buchanan, "Political Economy and Social Philosophy," in P. Koslowski, ed., *Economics and Philosophy* (Tübingen: J. C. B. Mohr, 1985), 19.

4. Ibid., 20.

5. L. Robbins, "An Essay on the Nature and Significance of Economic Science," in D. Hausman, ed., *The Philosophy of Economics: An Anthology* (Cambridge: Cambridge University Press, 1984), 113.

6. D. S. Landes, *The Wealth and Poverty of Nations: Why Some Are So Rich and Some So Poor* (New York: W. W. Norton, 1998), 194.

7. P. Samuelson and W. Nordhaus, *Economics*, 13th ed. (New York: McGraw-Hill, 1989), 20.

8. Hausman, ed., *The Philosophy of Economics*, 2–3.

9. B. Gower, *Scientific Method: A Historical and Philosophical Introduction* (London: Routledge, 1997), 4.

10. P. Davies, *Superforce* (London: Heinemann, 1984).

11. N. Hanson, *Patterns of Discovery: An Inquiry into the Conceptual Foundations of Science* (Cambridge: Cambridge University Press, 1958).

12. C. Van Doren, *A History of Knowledge: Past, Present and Future* (New York: Ballantine Books, 1992), 184.

13. A. O'Hear, *An Introduction to the Philosophy of Science* (Oxford: Clarendon Press, 1989), 7.

14. M. Friedman, *Essays in Positive Economics* (Chicago: University of Chicago Press, 1953), 4.

15. Hausman, ed., *The Philosophy of Economics*, 29.

16. P. Krugman, *The Accidental Theorist: And Other Dispatches from the Dismal Science* (New York: Norton, 1998), 113.

17. Ibid., 8.

18. Ibid., 19.

19. R. Solow, "A Contribution to the Theory of Economic Growth," *Quarterly Journal of Economics* 70 (1956): 65.

20. Samuelson and Nordhaus, *Economics*, 624.

21. Robbins, "An Essay on the Nature and Significance of Economic Science," 99.

22. Ibid.

23. Hausman, ed., *The Philosophy of Economics*, 24.

24. Friedman, *Essays in Positive Economics*, 7.

25. Hausman, ed., *The Philosophy of Economics*, 38.

26. "The Way It Was," *The Economist*, June 20, 1998, 5.

27. O'Hear, *An Introduction to the Philosophy of Science*, 7.

28. B. Ellis, "What Science Aims to Do," in D. Papineau, ed., *The Philosophy of Science* (London: Oxford University Press, 1996), 169.

29. P. Aghion and P. Howitt, *Endogenous Growth Theory* (Cambridge, MA: MIT Press, 1998), 66.

30. Van Doren, for example, claimed in his book *A History of Knowledge: Past, Present and Future* that "of all kinds of knowledge that the West has given to the world, the most valuable is a method of acquiring knowledge called scientific method" (184).

31. Van Doren also described the enormous social and economic changes money has brought by acting as incentives to endeavor, research, competition, etc. Ibid., 244.

32. The perception of life in primal societies as brutish has softened considerably since the 1960s. John Reader in his book *Africa: A Biography of the Continent* (New York: Knopf, 1998), 116, argued that this is because the West has been reassessing its social values as it faces the contradictions of material success.

33. On the other hand, John Reader argued that when anatomically modern man appeared, "the cognitive brain endowed humanity with a unique capacity to learn by experience and not to act according to a premeditated assessment of likely cause and effect, rather instinctively, on impulse. Nurture took its place along side nature" (ibid., 104).

34. M. Okediji, "The Mythic Mechanics: Art and Technology in Western Nigeria," in G. Thomas-Emeagwali, ed., *African Systems of Science, Technology, and Art: The Nigerian Experience* (London: Karnak House, 1993), 103–4.

35. C. Spring, *African Arms and Armour* (London: British Museum Press, 1993), 18.

36. B. Achi, "Engineering in Pre-colonial Nigeria: The Construction of Fortifications," in Thomas-Emeagwali, ed., *African Systems of Science, Technology and Art*, 118–9.

37. Okediji, "The Mythic Mechanics," 112.

38. Ibid., 99.

39. Ibid., 108–9.

40. Aghion and Howitt concluded that growth technology depends on economic (financial) decisions at least as much as capital accumulation (*Endogenous Growth Theory*, 23).

41. Okediji, "The Mythic Mechanics," 100–101.

42. A. Fisher, *Africa Adorned* (New York: Harry N. Abrams, 1984), 195.

43. Davidson, *Old Africa Rediscovered* (London: Victor Gollancz, 1964), 72.

44. Spring, *African Arms and Armour*, 17.

45. On the other hand, Spring observed that "contrary to popular belief, contact with imported technology in Africa has never by itself caused the demise of hand-crafted objects. Amongst the emergent forest kingdoms of West Africa," he noted, "the introduction of firearms was instrumental in determining the development of the ritual and ceremonial use of previously utilitarian weaponry and armour." This led, in his view, "to the production of a wide range of beautiful, crafted and intriguing objects" (ibid., 47). Spring got his facts wrong. First, imported firearms are not technology. They are an imported finished good. Second, if available indigenous firearms were demoted to ritual and ceremonial use, then it means that imported firearms displaced indigenous firearms. What little of firearms survived, as he admitted, was because of the ritual (religious) and ceremonial needs of the people. The truth is that thereafter Africans did not develop their firearms know-how. Spring contradicted himself when writing about fifteenth- and sixteenth-century Portuguese trading interests in West Africa who supplied European firearms widely in this area. He (correctly) stated that the various indigenous firearm objects that adorned the palaces of various kingdoms in West Africa then "depict arm and armour much of which either became obsolete and disappeared, or were developed cinctures almost out of recognition into ceremonial or ritual pieces" (ibid., 48).

46. F. Anozie, "Metal Technology in Pre-colonial Nigeria," in Thomas-Emeagwali, ed., *African Systems of Science, Technology, and Art*, 95.

47. J. Ohiare, "Textile in the Ebira-speaking Region: An Aspect of Its Technological Development Since the 19th Century," in Thomas-Emeagwali, ed., *African Systems of Science, Technology, and Art*, 35.

48. Contrast the fate of the blacksmith in Africa with that of the blacksmith in Canada. Given the "natural" industrial transition in that country, Wylie reported that "the [Canadian] blacksmith of the 19th Century was on the cusp between traditional and rural life and the forces of modernization." He concluded, "By a direct understanding of the processes of the blacksmith's work one can come to understand how it was that the blacksmith provided a pool of talent from which many early Canadian entrepreneurs emerged." W. N. T. Wylie, *The Blacksmith in Upper Canada, 1784–1850: A Study of Technology, Culture and Power* (Gananoque, Ontario: Longdale Press, 1990), 14.

49. Samuelson and Nordhaus, *Economics*, 886.

50. M. P. Todaro, *Economic Development*, 5th ed. (New York: Longman, 1994), 101.

51. Samuelson and Nordhaus, *Economics*, 886.

52. Ibid., 887.

53. Fisher, *Africa Adorned*, 7–8.

54. Samuelson and Nordhaus, *Economics*, 885.

55. Fisher, *Africa Adorned*, 42

56. Ibid., 48.

57. R. N. Okagbue, "The Scientific Basis of Traditional Food Processing in Nigerian Communities," in Thomas-Emeagwali, ed., *African Systems of Science, Technology, and Art*, 74–75.

58. Spring, *African Arms and Armour*, 29.

59. Aghion and Howitt, *Endogenous Growth Theory*, 23.

60. W. A. Lewis, "Economic Development with Unlimited Supplies of Labour," *The Manchester School of Economic and Social Studies* 22 (1954): 139–91.

61. I. Amato, *Stuff: The Materials the World Is Made Of* (New York: Basic Books, 1997), 5–6.

62. Ibid., 6.

63. Primal societies knew about economies of scale well before us.

64. C. L. Goucher, "Iron Is Iron 'Til It Is Rust: Trade and the Decline of West African Smelting," *Journal of African History* 22 (1981).

65. Todaro, *Economic Development*, 676.

66. E. Denison, *Trends in American Economic Growth, 1929–1982* (Washington, DC: Brookings Institute, 1985); and E. Denison, *Accounting for Slower Economic Growth: The United States in the 1970s* (Washington, DC: Brookings Institute, 1979).

67. H. McRae, *The World in 2020* (Boston: Harvard Business School Press, 1994), 19–20.

68. Not everyone agrees that China will be a superpower. For example, Chris Patten asserted that "China is not an economic superpower today and is a long way from becoming one" (C. Patten, *East and West: The Last Governor of Hong Kong on Power, Freedom, and the Future* [London: Macmillan, 1998], 292). In an article in *Foreign Affairs*, September–October 1991, titled "Does China Matter," Gerald Segard argued that "in truth China is a small market that matters relatively little in the world, especially outside Asia." But international power politics is not the concern here. China has achieved sustainable growth, a position different from all other non-Western societies (except of course Japan). All prophets of doom about the rising economy of China have been proved wrong. Many Western companies are still lining up, lured by what one commentator called "the prospects of a foot in the door of the economic powerhouse of tomorrow."

69. For example, C. Totman, *Japan Before Perry: A Short History* (Berkeley: University of California Press, 1981), from which these data are taken.

70. Ibid., 7.

71. Ibid.

72. J. M. Roberts, *History of the World* (New York: Oxford University Press, 1993), 373.

73. G. Sanson, *A History of Japan*, vol. 3, *1615–1867* (Stanford: Stanford University Press, 1963), 124.

74. T. Morris-Suzuki, *The Technological Transformation of Japan: From the Seventeenth to the Twenty-first Century* (Cambridge: Cambridge University Press, 1994).

75. Landes, *The Wealth and Poverty of Nations*, 378.

76. Ibid., 353.

77. Ibid., 355.

78. Roberts, *History of the World*, 378.

79. Ibid., 107.

80. Ibid., 112.

81. D. Li, *The Ageless Chinese: A History* (New York: Charles Scribner & Sons, 1965), 176–77.

82. A. Wright, *The Sui Dynasty* (New York: Alfred A. Knopf, 1978), 12.

83. Ibid., 82.

84. Li, *The Ageless Chinese*, 286.

85. Landes, *The Wealth and Poverty of Nations*, 94–95.

86. Ibid., 335.

87. Ibid., 53.

88. Roberts, *History of the World*, 667.

89. S. Mosher, *China Misperceived: American Illusions and Chinese Reality* (New York: Basic Books, 1990), 44.

90. Landes, *The Wealth and Poverty of Nations*, 342.

91. Ibid., 343.

92. Ibid., 336.

93. Ibid., 342.

94. Aghion and Howitt, *Endogenous Growth Theory*, 23, 84, 102.

95. Roberts, *The History of the World*, 363.

96. A. de Riencourt, *The Soul of China* (New York: Coward-McCann, 1958), 87.

97. Landes, *The Wealth and Poverty of Nations*, 341.

98. Ibid., 24.

99. Lucian Pye confirmed that animal power is more conspicuous in China than it is in Southeast Asia, India, and Africa. Even in modern times, the transport system in China depends a lot on roads for animal-drawn carts. See Pye, *China: An Introduction* (Boston: Little, Brown, 1972), 21.

100. M. Elvin, *The Pattern of the Chinese Past: A Social and Economic Interpretation* (Stanford: Stanford University Press, 1973), 297–98.

101. Landes, *The Wealth and Poverty of Nations*, 337–38.

102. Roberts, *History of the World*, 662, 667.

103. Spring, *African Arms and Armour*, 17.

104. Davidson, *Old Africa Rediscovered*, 73.

105. T. Pakenham, *The Scramble for Africa, 1876–1912* (London: Weidenfeld and Nicolson, 1991), 92.

106. Ibid.

107. Davidson, *Old Africa Rediscovered*, 121.

108. Spring, *African Arms and Armour*, 84.

109. Pakenham, *The Scramble for Africa*, 590, 599–600.

110. Ibid., 599–600.

Notes to Chapter 3

1. P. Samuelson and W. Nordhaus, *Economics*, 13th ed. (McGraw-Hill, 1989), 855.

2. M. P. Todaro, *Economic Development*, 5th ed. (New York: Longman, 1994), 101.

3. Samuelson and Nordhaus, *Economics*, 972.

4. R. Mikesell, *Economic Development and the Environment: A Comparison of Sustainable Development with Conventional Development Economics* (London and New York: Mansell, 1993), 67.

5. D. Hausman, ed., *The Philosophy of Economics: An Anthology* (Cambridge: Cambridge University Press, 1984), 344.

6. Ibid., 352.

7. Samuelson and Nordhaus, *Economics*, 751.

8. Hausman, ed., *The Philosophy of Economics*, 352.

9. H. Daly, "Environmentally Sustainable Economic Development," in R. Goodland, H. Daly, and S. El Sarafy, comps. and eds., *Environmentally Sustainable Economic Development: Building on Brundtland*, Environment Working Paper no. 46 (Washington, DC: World Bank, 1991), 20.

10. D. Lal and H. Myint, *The Political Economy of Poverty, Equity, and Growth: A Comparative Study* (Oxford: Clarendon Press, 1996), 179.

11. Ibid., 105.

12. E. Leamer, "Paths of Development in the Three-Factor, n-Good General Equilibrium Model," *Journal of Political Economy* 95, 5 (1987): 961–99.

13. E. Hagen, *The Economics of Development*, 3rd ed. (Homewood, IL: Richard D. Irwin, 1980), 365–68.

14. J. Timbergen, "Maximizing National Product by the Choice of Industries," discussion paper no. 60, Centre for Development Planning, Erasmus University, Rotterdam, 1981.

15. Lal and Myint, *Political Economy of Poverty, Equity and Growth*, 110. Conventional economics, which lays emphasis on capital accumulation, expects the pattern of development to be dependent on the size of the country.

16. Hausman, ed., *The Philosophy of Economics*, 34.

17. Samuelson and Nordhaus, *Economics*, 885.

18. C. Onyemelukwe, *Economic Underdevelopment: An Inside View* (London: Longmans Group, 1974), 20–21.

19. It is estimated that human beings presently extract about 15 billion tons of raw material from the earth each year. Amato, *Stuff*, 2.

20. Mikesell, *Economic Development and the Environment*, 141.

21. D. Pearce, A. Markandya, and E. Barbier, *Blueprint for a Green Economy* (London: Earthscan, 1990), 7.

22. H. Chenery, S. Robinson, and M. Syrquin, *Industrialization and Growth: A Comparative Study* (New York: Oxford University Press, 1986).

23. *The East Asian Miracle: Economic Growth and Public Policy*, World Bank Policy Research Report (New York: Oxford University Press, 1993), 55.

24. *World Development Report: Knowledge for Development* (New York: Oxford University Press, 1999), 21.

25. D. Ray, *Development Economics* (Princeton, NJ: Princeton University Press, 1998), 122.

26. C. Lingle, *The Rise and Decline of the Asian Century* (Hong Kong: Asia 2000, 1998), 77.

27. R. Solow, "Perspectives on Growth Theory," *Journal of Economic Perspectives* 8, 1 (1994): 51.

28. World Bank, *World Bank Development Report: Knowledge for Development* (New York: Oxford University Press, 1999), 19.

29. K. Basu, *Analytical Development Economics: The Less Developed Economy Revisited* (Cambridge, MA: MIT Press, 1997), 56.

30. OECD, *21st Century Technologies: Promises and Perils of a Dynamic Future* (Paris: OECD, 1998), 32.

31. World Bank, *World Development Report: Knowledge for Development*, 19.

32. R. Solow, *Growth Theory: An Exposition* (New York: Oxford University Press, 1987), xxii.

33. Ibid., xxiv.

34. R. Lipsey and K. A. Chrystal, *Principles of Economics*, 9th ed. (Oxford: Oxford University Press, 1999), 553–54. Lipsey and Chrystal have said that there are two types of technical change, embodied and disembodied, the second being merely changes in the organization of production.

35. Samuelson and Nordhaus, *Economics*, 657.

36. E. Denison, *Slower Economic Growth: The United States in the 1970s* (Washington, DC: Brookings Institution, 1979); *Accounting for United States Economic Growth, 1929–1969* (Washington, DC: Brookings Institution, 1974); *Sources of Economic Growth in the United States and the Alternatives Before Us* (New York: Committee for Economic Development, 1962).

37. C. Freeman and L. Soete, *The Economics of Industrial Innovation*, 3rd ed. (Cambridge, MA: MIT Press, 1997), 5.

38. J. Galbraith, *American Capitalism: The Concept of Countervailing Power* (Boston: Houghton Mifflin, 1952), 91.

39. For example, A. Young, "The Tyranny of Numbers: Confronting the Statistical Realities of the East Asian Growth Experience," *Quarterly Journal of Economics* 110, 3 (August 1995): 641–80.

40. World Bank, *World Development Report: Knowledge for Development*, 23.

41. M. Hobart and Z. Schiffman, *Information Ages: Literacy, Numeracy, and the Computer Revolution* (Baltimore: John Hopkins University Press, 1998), 1.

42. Ibid., 171–72.

43. I. Amato, *Stuff: The Materials the World Is Made Of* (New York: Basic Books, 1997), pp. 1–8.

44. Reverend Barbara Fast, Unitarian Church, Westport, Connecticut, March 17, 2002.

45. Samuelson and Nordhaus, *Economics*, Figure 21-3, 507.

46. Ibid., 855.

47. R. Solow, *Growth Theory*, 777.

48. D. S. Landes, *The Wealth and Poverty of Nations: Why Some Are So Rich and Some So Poor* (New York: W. W. Norton, 1998), 437.

49. R. Bean, *Comparative Industrial Relations: An Introduction to Cross-national Perspectives*, 2nd ed. (London and New York: Routledge, 1994), 10–11.

50. M. Porter, *The Competitive Advantage of Nations* (New York: Free Press, 1990), 74–77.

51. Samuelson and Nordhaus, *Economics*, 296–97, 155.

52. P. Krugman, *Peddling Prosperity: Economic Sense and Nonsense in the Age of Diminished Expectations* (New York: W. W. Norton, 1994), 25.

53. E. Denison, *Trends in American Economic Growth, 1929–1982* (Washington, DC: Brookings Institution, 1983), xxi.

54. *Economic Report of the President* (Washington, DC: GPO, 1979), 72.

55. *Economic Report of the President* (Washington, DC: GPO, 1977).

56. *Economic Report of the President* (Washington, DC: GPO, 1979), 52.

57. Krugman, *Peddling Prosperity*, 114.

58. Ibid., 125.

59. Ibid., 125–26.

60. R. Solow, *Growth Theory: An Exposition* (New York: Oxford University Press, 1969), 80.

61. Ibid., 59.

62. P. Krugman, *The Age of Diminished Expectations: U.S. Economic Policy in the 1990s*, 3rd ed. (Cambridge, MA: MIT Press, 1997), 20.

63. P. Romer and R. Nelson, "Economics of Science and Innovation II," in D. B. Audretsch and S. Klepper, eds., *Innovation, Evolution of Industry and Economic Growth* (Cheltenham: Elgar, 2000), 431.

64. J. Sloman with the collaboration of Mark Sutcliffe, *Economics* (New York: Prentice Hall, 1999), 789.

65. J. Rees and C. Smith, *Economic Development* (London: Macmillan, 1998), 104.

66. Krugman, *The Age of Diminished Expectations*, 11.

67. P. Krugman and M. Obstfeld, *International Economics: Theory and Policy*, 4th ed. (Reading, MA: Addison-Wesley, 1997), 227.

68. Krugman, *Peddling Prosperity*, 59–60.

69. "The Aircraft Industry Survey," *The Economist*, June 2, 1985.

70. K. Man, interviewed in *Air International* 58, 1 (January 2000).

71. E. Denison, *Accounting for Slower Growth: The United States in the 1970s* (Washington, DC: Brookings Institution, 1979), 44; E. Mansfield et al., *Technology Transfer, Productivity, and Economic Policy* (New York: W. W. Norton, 1982), 219–21.

72. Krugman, *The Age of Diminished Expectations*, 16.

73. Many believed that the energy crisis of 1973 was at the root of the U.S. productivity slowdown then.

74. F. Klemm, *A History of Western Technology*, trans. D. W. Singer (New York: Scribner, 1959), 293.

75. L. Mumford, *Technics and Civilization* (New York: Harcourt, Brace, 1934), 385.

76. S. Kuznets, *Modern Economic Growth: Rate, Structure and Spread* (New Haven, CT: Yale University Press, 1966), Table 5.2.

77. G. Becker, *Human Capital: A Theoretical and Empirical Analysis, with Special Reference to Education* (New York: National Bureau of Economic Research, 1964).

78. Ibid., 12.

79. M. Abramovitz, *Thinking About Growth and Other Essays on Economic Growth and Welfare* (Cambridge: Cambridge University Press, 1989), 174.

80. Lipsey and Chrystal, *Principles of Economics*, 552.

81. Samuelson and Nordhaus, *Economics*, 974.

82. Much of growth theory derives from actions and models based on financial incentives and investment.

83. R. Nelson and E. Phelps, "Investment in Humans, Technological Diffusion and Economic Growth," *American Economic Review* 61 (1966): 69–75.

84. P. Aghion and P. Howitt, *Endogenous Growth Theory* (Cambridge, MA: MIT Press, 1998), 179–80.

85. D. Price et al., "Is Technology Historically Independent of Science," *Technology and Culture* 6, 4 (1995): 533.

86. A. Musson and E. Robinson, *Science and Technology in the Industrial Revolution* (Manchester: Manchester

University Press, 1969); B. Hessen, "The Social and Economic Roots of Newton's *Principia*," in N. Bukharin et al., *Science at the Cross Roads* (London: Frank Cass, 1971); J. Jewkes, D. Sawers, and R. Stillerman, *The Sources of Invention* (London: Macmillan, 1969).

87. The 1987 *Standard Industrial Classification Manual* of the United States defines *factory* as an establishment engaged in mechanical or chemical transformation of materials into new products.

88. Hagen indirectly arrived at a similar definition of technology when he distinguished between what he called "the state of technology" and the "state of technique in use." By "the state of technology," he said, he was referring to "scientific or technical ideas in individuals' heads plus the state of managerial, engineering and other skills needed to put the technical knowledge into effect." This, he said, may differ from the state of techniques in use "if factors are present (such as shortage of capital, workers, natural resources or markets for the products) which prevent putting available technology into effect" (Hagen, *The Economics of Development*, 240). We will use the term *technique* to refer, almost like Hagen, to the actual factor combination used for each production.

89. It is accepted that one can talk of technology change to mean a change in the direction of the science of factor proportions. But science is supposed to be an ongoing activity. Those who talk of technology change do not really have this interpretation in mind.

90. A. Alesina and D. Rodrik, "Distributive Policies and Economic Growth," *Quarterly Journal of Economics* (1994): 465–90; T. Persson and G. Tabellini, "Is Inequality Harmful to Growth," *American Economic Review* 84 (1994): 600–621.

91. T. Gylfason, *Principles of Economic Growth* (Oxford: Oxford University Press, 1999).

92. A. Smith, *The Wealth of Nations* (New York: Alfred A. Knopf, 1991), 249.

93. Ibid., 248.

94. A. Smith, *An Inquiry into the Nature and Causes of the Wealth of Nations*, abridged with commentary and notes by L. Dickey (Indianapolis, IN: Hackett, 1993), 215.

95. L. Robbins, *A History of Economic Thought: The LSE Lectures*, ed. S. Medema and W. Samuels (Princeton, NJ: Princeton University Press, 1998), 129.

96. P. Chaudhuri, *Economic Theory of Growth* (Ames: Iowa State University Press, 1989), 69.

97. World Bank, *Entering the 21st Century: World Development Report 1999/2000* (New York: Oxford University Press, 2000), 2.

98. Gylfason, *Principles of Economic Growth*.

99. Ibid., 29, 135–36.

100. R. Barro and X. Sala-i-Martin, *Economic Growth* (New York: McGraw-Hill, 1995).

101. Gylfason, *Principles of Economic Growth*, 29.

Notes to Chapter 4

1. M. J. Piore and C. F. Sabel, *The Second Industrial Divide: Possibilities for Prosperity* (New York: Basic Books, 1984), 20–21, 37.

2. M. P. Todaro, *Economic Development*, 5th ed. (New York: Longman, 1994), 589.

3. J. Sloman with the collaboration of Mark Sutcliffe, *Economics* (New York: Prentice Hall, 1999), 789.

4. N. Kaldor, "A Model of Economic Growth," *Economic Journal* 67 (1957), 603.

5. Piore and Sabel, *The Second Industrial Divide*, 30.

6. A. Keyssar, "Men Out of Work: A Social History of Unemployment in Massachusetts, 1870–1916," Ph.D. dissertation, Harvard University, 1977.

7. Piore and Sabel, *The Second Industrial Divide*, 26.

8. Ibid., 27.

9. See, for example, R. Clark, *The Japanese Company* (New Haven, CT: Yale University Press, 1979).

10. J. H. Dyer, "How Chrysler Created an American Keiretsu," *Harvard Business Review*, July–August 1996, 42–61.

11. C. Freeman and L. Soete, *The Economics of Industrial Innovation*, 3rd ed. (Cambridge, MA: MIT Press, 1997), 281.

12. Piore and Sabel, *The Second Industrial Divide*, 39.

13. Ibid., 38–39.

14. Freeman and Soete, *The Economics of Industrial Innovation*, 139–40.

15. Ibid., 141.

16. Piore and Sabel, *The Second Industrial Divide*, 40.

17. Ibid., 44–46.

18. Ibid., 54.

19. Ibid., 56.

20. J. K. Gibson-Graham, *The End of Capitalism (As We Knew It): A Feminist Critique of Political Economy* (London: Blackwell, 1996), 151.

21. Ibid., 151.

22. Piore and Sabel, *The Second Industrial Divide*, 181.

23. J. Beddoes, A. H. Rahmani, and C. Onyemelukwe, "Acquisitions—The Synergy Question," *Acquisitions Monthly*, December 1987, 18–20. Happily, acquisitions and mergers based on hedging risks in unrelated markets are on the decline.

24. Piore and Sabel, *The Second Industrial Divide*, 166.

25. Ibid., 252. It is to be noted that Piore and Sabel regard craft production and flexible specialization as the same thing.

26. P. Abemawat and A. M. Spence, "Modeling Global Competition," in M. E. Porter, ed., *Competition in Global Industries* (Boston: Harvard Business School Press, 1986), 70, 72.

27. B. Coriat, "Globalization Variety and Mass Production: The Metamorphosis of Mass Production in the New Competitive Age," in J. R. Hollingsworth and R. Boyer, eds., *Contemporary Capitalism: The Embeddedness of Institutions* (Cambridge: Cambridge University Press, 1997), 260.

28. V. Bignell et al., eds., *Manufacturing Systems: Context, Applications and Techniques* (Oxford: Basil Blackwell, 1985), 99.

29. R. W. Hall, *Attaining Manufacturing Excellence* (Homewood, IL: Dow Jones-Irwin, 1987), 30.

30. J. Browne et al., "Classification of Flexible Manufacturing Systems," in Bignell et al., eds., *Manufacturing Systems*, 30.

31. Ibid., 113.

32. V. Allsopp, *Understanding Economics* (London: Routledge, 1995), 47.

33. P. Samuelson and W. Nordhaus, *Economics*, 13th ed. (New York: McGraw-Hill, 1989), 43.

34. P. Hirst and J. Zeitlin, "Flexible Specialization: Theory and Evidence in the Analysis of Industrial Change," in Hollingsworth and Boyer, eds., *Contemporary Capitalism*, 271–72.

35. Piore and Sabel, *The Second Industrial Divide*, 276–277.

36. See, for example, the account of Chinese rural industry in W. Byrd and Q. Lin, eds., *China's Rural Industry: Structure, Development and Reform* (Oxford: Oxford University Press, 1990).

37. J. R. Hollingsworth and R. Boyer, "Coordination of Economic Actors and Social Systems of Production," in Hollingsworth and Boyer, eds., *Contemporary Capitalism*, 20.

38. K. Suzaki, *The New Manufacturing Challenge: Techniques for Continuous Improvement* (New York: Free Press, 1987), 57–58.

39. P. J. O'Grady, *Putting the Just-in-Time Philosophy into Practice* (New York: Nichols, 1988), 89.

40. Hirst and Zeitlin, "Flexible Specialization," 233.

41. See M. Cusumano, *The Japanese Automobile Industry: Technology and Management at Nissan and Toyota* (Cambridge, MA: Council on East Asian Studies, Harvard University, 1985).

42. Freeman and Soete, *The Economics of Industrial Innovation*, 153.

43. Bignell et al., eds., *Manufacturing Systems*, 100.

44. J. Beardshaw et al., *Economics* (London and New York: Financial Times–Prentice Hall, 2001).

45. D. Begg, *Economics* (New York: McGraw-Hill, 1994).

46. R. G. Lipsey and K. A. Chrystal, *Principles of Economics*, 9th ed. (Oxford: Oxford University Press, 1999).

47. Boyle's law states that for gases $P_1 V_1 = P_2 V_2$. Charles' law states that $T_1/V_1 = T_2/V_2$. Combined $P_1 V_1/T_1 = P_2 V_2/T_2$ or $PV/T = k$ (constant) where P, V, T are pressures, volume, temperature.

48. D. Stinton, *The Anatomy of the Airplane* (Oxford: Blackwell Science, 1998), 57.

49. Based on the step count method. For example M_c for carbon steel is 1, 1.15 for low-grade steel, 1.2 for medium-grade steel, 1.3 for low-grade stainless steel, etc.

50. A. Myers and R. Manning, "The Shocks of a World of Cheap Oil," *Foreign Affairs*, January–February 2000, 19.

51. Todaro, *Economic Development*, 510.

52. R. Lipsey and C. Harbury, *First Principles of Economics* (Oxford: Oxford University Press, 1998), 148.

53. Samuelson and Nordhaus, *Economics*, 505.

54. *The Wall Street Journal*, February 1, 2000, A6.

55. T. Petzinger Jr., "So Long, Supply and Demand," *Wall Street Journal*, January 1, 2000, R31.

56. Freeman and Soete, *The Economics of Industrial Innovation*, 100.

57. P. Hawken, A. Lovins, and L. Lovins, *Natural Capitalism: Creating the Next Industrial Revolution* (London: Earthscan, 1999), 5.

58. N. Lieberman and E. Lieberman, *A Working Guide to Process Equipment: How Process Equipment Works* (New York: McGraw-Hill, 1997), xv.

59. J. Douglas, *Conceptual Design of Chemical Processes* (New York: McGraw-Hill, 1998), 104.

60. Ibid., 4.

61. Ibid., 104.

62. Freeman and Soete, *The Economics of Industrial Innovation*, 86.

63. R. Smith, *Chemical Process Design* (New York: McGraw-Hill, 1995).

64. T. F. Edgar and D. M. Himmelblau, *Optimization of Chemical Processes* (New York: McGraw-Hill, 1988), 481–82.

65. J. McCusker and R. Menard, *The Economy of British America, 1607–1789* (Chapel Hill: University of North Carolina Press, 1991), 310.

66. "Age of Superpower Is Here," *New York Times Magazine*, September 22, 1929.

67. M. Hobart and Z. Schiffman, *Information Ages: Lit-*

eracy, Numeracy, and the Computer Revolution (Baltimore: Johns Hopkins University Press, 1998), 205.

68. Ibid., 204.

69. Ibid., 209.

70. Remarks by Alan Greenspan to the Federal Reserve Board, Minneapolis, Minnesota, September 30, 1999.

71. Samuelson and Nordhaus, *Economics*, 506.

72. Remarks by Alan Greenspan to the Federal Reserve Board, Minneapolis, Minnesota, September 30, 1999.

73. Capital, as we earlier pointed out, is made up of material and labor.

74. Alan Greenspan, "Technology and the Economy," lecture to the Economic Club of New York, January 13, 2000.

75. *Wall Street Journal*, February 23, 2000.

76. W. J. Mitchell, *E-topia: "Urban Life, Jim, but Not as We Know It"* (Cambridge, MA: MIT Press, 1999), 5.

77. L. Thurow, *Building Wealth* (New York: HarperCollins, 1999), xv–xvi.

78. Even as of today, the economy of standardization, repetition, and mass production forms the core of many current economic texts.

79. E. Fingleton, *In Praise of Hard Industries: Why Manufacturing, Not the Information Economy, Is the Key to Future Prosperity* (Boston: Houghton Mifflin, 1999).

80. C. Dugger, "India's Unwired Villages Mired in Distant Past," *New York Times*, March 19, 2000, 1, 14.

81. B. Gates with C. Hemingway, *Business @ the Speed of Thought: Using a Digital Nervous System* (New York: Warner Books, 1999), 367.

82. Freeman and Soete, *The Economics of Industrial Innovation*, 362–63.

Notes to Chapter 5

1. P. Krugman and M. Obstfeld, *International Economics: Theory and Policy*, 4th ed. (Reading, MA: Addison-Wesley, 1997), 13.

2. M. Krauss, *How Nations Grow Rich: The Case for Free Trade* (New York: Oxford University Press, 1997), 5.

3. P. Samuelson and W. Nordhaus, *Economics*, 13th ed. (New York: McGraw-Hill, 1989), 904.

4. H. Bowen, A. Hollander, and J.-M. Viaene, *Applied International Trade Analysis* (Ann Arbor: University of Michigan Press, 1998), 109.

5. Krugman and Obstfeld, *International Economics*, Chapter 3.

6. Ibid., 41.

7. R. Lipsey and K. Chrystal, *Principles of Economics*, 9th ed. (Oxford: Oxford University Press, 1999), 581.

8. Krugman and Obstfeld, *International Economics*, 56.

9. Ibid., 51.

10. Ibid., 67.

11. Ibid.

12. Lipsey and Chrystal, *Principles of Economics*, 599.

13. Krugman and Obstfeld, *International Economics*, 68.

14. Ibid., 77.

15. Ibid., 78.

16. What they mean by superior and inferior technology is not clear. It is the prejudice in economic analysis.

17. Krugman and Obstfeld, *International Economics*, 79.

18. Ibid., 82.

19. M. Abramovitz and P. David, "Convergence and Deferred Catch-up," in R. Landau, T. Taylor, and G. Wright, eds., *The Mosaic of Economic Growth* (Stanford, CA: Stanford University Press, 1996).

20. B. Brindle, "Technology in Early America," in J. McGaw, ed., *Early American Technology: Making and Doing Things from the Colonial Era to 1850* (Chapel Hill: University of North Carolina Press, 1994), 52.

21. M. Porter, *The Competitive Advantage of Nations* (New York: Free Press, 1990), 284–86.

22. Bowen, Hollander, and Viaene, *Applied International Trade Analysis*, 5.

23. Ibid., 228.

24. Krugman and Obstfeld seem to recognize only "differences in the political context." *International Economics*, 159.

25. H. Bowen, E. Leamer, and L. Sveikauskas, "Multi-Country, Multi-factor Tests of the Factor Abundance Theory," *American Economic Review* 77 (1987): 791–809.

26. Bowen, Hollander, and Viaene, *Applied International Trade Analysis*, 321.

27. Krugman and Obstfeld, *International Economics*, 39.

28. Bowen, Hollander, and Viaene, *Applied International Trade Analysis*, 253.

29. Todaro, speaking of the static character of various neoclassical models of trade in regard to the relationship between the North and South, declared, "No country likes to think of itself as specializing in unskilled labor activities while letting foreigners reap the rewards of higher skills, technology and capital." We know what Todaro is trying to say, but unfortunately it has been put in a political context. There is nothing wrong with "specializing in unskilled labor activities" if that is the correct relevant stage of a country's economic development. But that does not mean that they have to import high-technology goods because they believe that that is the route to their economic development and growth. Todaro was, however,

right when he said that "by pursuing the theoretical dictates of their endowments . . . less developed countries may lock themselves into a domestic economic structure that reinforces such relatively poor endowments and is inimical to their long-run development aspirations." M. P. Todaro, *Economic Development*, 5th ed. (New York: Longman, 1994), 428.

30. Porter, *The Competitive Advantage of Nations*, 675.

31. T. Gylfason, *Principles of Economic Growth* (Oxford: Oxford University Press, 1999), 19.

32. A. Smith, *The Wealth of Nations* (New York: Alfred A. Knopf, 1991), 307.

33. Bowen, Hollander, and Viaene, *Applied International Trade Analysis*, 567.

34. Kofi Annan had this to say on the plight of poor countries: "All they ask is a fair chance to trade their way out of poverty." "Trade and Aid in a Changed World," *New York Times*, March 19, 2002.

35. M. Kreinin, *International Economics: A Policy Approach* (Ft. Worth, TX: Dryden Press, 1998), 64.

36. P. Krugman, "Is Free Trade Passé?" *Journal of Economic Perspectives* 1, 2 (1987): 131–41.

37. Krugman and Obstfeld, *International Economics*, 137.

38. Ibid., 128.

39. Porter, *The Competitive Advantage of Nations*, 38.

40. Ibid., 60.

41. "The Way It Was," *Economist*, June 20, 1998, 5.

42. R. Reich, *The Work of Nations* (New York: Alfred A. Knopf, 1991), 7–8.

43. A. Nevins and F. Hill, *Ford*, vol. 3: *Decline and Rebirth, 1933–1962* (New York: Charles Scribner's Sons, 1962), 79.

44. Ibid., 85.

45. Ibid., 390.

46. Porter, *The Competitive Advantage of Nations*, 56.

47. J. Womack, D. Jones, and D. Roos, *The Machine That Changed the World* (New York: Rawson Associates, 1990), 204.

48. Ibid., 207.

49. Lipsey and Chrystal, *Principles of Economics*, 582.

50. Todaro, *Economic Development*, 433.

51. D. Abodaher, *Iacocca* (New York: Macmillan, 1982), 55.

52. J. Rae, *The American Automobile Industry* (Boston: Twayne, 1984), 34.

53. Ibid., 35.

54. Ibid., 36.

55. Ibid., 37.

56. Womack, Jones, and Roos, *The Machine That Changed the World*, 227–28.

57. B. Yates, *The Decline and Fall of the American Automobile Industry* (New York: Empire Books, 1983), 185.

58. Nevins and Hill, *Ford*, 355.

59. Ibid., 356.

60. Porter, *The Competitive Advantage of Nations*, 60.

61. Womack, Jones, and Roos, *The Machine That Changed the World*, 201.

62. Ibid., 102.

63. Krugman and Obstfeld, *International Economics*, 142.

64. Womack, Jones, and Roos, *The Machine That Changed the World*, 98.

65. Ibid., 225.

66. Ibid., 205.

67. Ibid., 219.

68. Ibid., 270.

69. Ibid., 13.

70. U. Seiffert and P. Walzer, *Automobile Technology of the Future* (Warrendale: Society of Automotive Engineers, 1991), 13.

71. Womack, Jones, and Roos, *The Machine That Changed the World*, 205.

72. Ibid., 91, 278.

73. See N. Yoshimuga and P. Anderson, *Inside the Kaisha: Demystifying Japanese Business Behavior* (Boston: Harvard Business School Press, 1997); P. Smith, *Japan: A Reinterpretation* (New York: Pantheon Books, 1997); M. Porter and H. Takeuchi, "Fixing What Really Ails Japan," *Foreign Affairs*, May–June 1999, 67–81.

74. M. Piore and C. Sabel, *The Second Industrial Divide* (New York: Basic Books, 1984), 282.

75. Bowen, Hollander, and Viaene, *Applied International Trade Analysis*, 382.

76. Samuelson and Nordhaus, *Economics* (New York: McGraw Hill, 1989), 930.

77. Kreinin, *International Economics*, 108.

78. Todaro, *Economic Development*, 491.

79. Krugman and Obstfeld, *International Economics*, 254.

80. These five headings are summarized from Krugman and Obstfeld, *International Economics*, 255–59.

81. Krugman and Obstfeld, *International Economics*, 255–56.

82. Ibid., 259.

83. Lipsey and Chrystal, *Principles of Economics*, 575.

84. Krugman and Obstfeld, *International Economics*, 258.

Notes to Chapter 6

1. W. Ethier, *Modern International Economics*, 3rd ed. (New York: W. W. Norton, 1995), 292.

2. M. Todaro, *Economic Development*, 5th ed. (New York: Longman, 1994), 533.

3. C. Onyemelukwe, *Economic Underdevelopment: An Inside View* (London: Longman, 1974), 16.

4. K. Griffin and T. McKinley, *New Approaches to Development Cooperation* (New York: United Nations Development Programme, Office of Development Studies, 1996).

5. Todaro, *Economic Development*, 533–34.

6. Ibid., 535.

7. D. Appleyard and A. Field Jr., *International Economics* (New York: Irwin/McGraw-Hill, 1998), 236.

8. Ibid., 233.

9. Ibid.

10. P. Krugman and M. Obstfeld, *International Economics: Theory and Policy*, 4th ed. (Reading, MA: Addison-Wesley, 1997), 14.

11. Appleyard and Field, *International Economics*, 234.

12. World Bank, *Global Development Finance 1998* (Washington, DC: World Bank, 1998), 23.

13. World Bank, *Entering the 21st Century: World Bank Development Report 1999/2000* (New York: Oxford University Press, 2000), 81.

14. Conventional economics holds that the price profile of a product determines the use of resources and hence the amount of resources allocated to its production over time.

15. T. Killick, ed, *The Flexible Economy: Causes and Consequences of Adaptability of National Economics* (London and New York: Routledge, 1995).

16. H. Bowen, A. Hollander, and J. Viane, *Applied International Trade Analysis* (Ann Arbor: University of Michigan Press, 2001), 228.

17. C. Freeman and L. Soete, *The Economics of Industrial Innovation* (Cambridge, MA: MIT Press, 1997), 331.

18. Appleyard and Field, *International Economics,* 193.

19. Freeman and Soete, *The Economics of Industrial Innovation*, 344.

20. World Bank, *World Development Report 1999/2000: The Changing Development Landscape* (New York: Oxford University Press,1999), 72; although World Bank, *Global Development Finance 1998* claims that between 1991 and 1996, FDI outflows from developing counties increased three and half times to $11.1 billion.

21. World Bank, *Global Development Finance 1998,* 23. This surely is an exaggeration when the bulk of developing countries make no FDI and those that did are collapsing.

22. S. Linder, *An Essay on Trade and Transformation* (New York: Garland, 1983).

23. D. Ernst, T. Ganiatsos, and L. Mytelka, eds., *Technological Capabilities and Export Success in Asia* (London: Routledge, 1998), 108.

24. Ibid., 120.

25. Ibid., 134.

26. Ibid., 142.

27. Freeman and Soete, *The Economics of Industrial Innovation,* 317.

28. Ibid., 351.

29. Ibid., 352.

30. Ibid., 364.

31. Ibid., 364.

32. H. Selim, *Development Assistance Policies and the Performance of Aid Agencies* (New York: St. Martin's, 1983), 2.

33. O. Franks, "Lessons of the Marshall Plan Experience," in *From Marshall Plan to Global Interdependence: New Challenges for the Industrialized Nations* (Paris: OECD, 1978), 18.

34. A. Milward, *The Reconstruction of Western Europe, 1945–1951,* (London: Methuen, 1984), 3–4.

35. W. McWilliams and H. Piotrowski, *The World Since 1945,* 4th ed. (Boulder, CO: Lynne Rienner, 1997), 43.

36. Ibid.

37. Milward, *Reconstruction of Western Europe*, 91.

38. Ibid., 98.

39. T. Geiger, "Western Europe: Economic and Social Changes Since 1945," in C. Schultze, ed., *Other Times, Other Places: Macroeconomic Lessons from U.S. and European History* (Washington, DC: Brookings Institution, 1986), 14.

40. Milward, *Reconstruction of Western Europe,* 112.

41. R. Riddell, *Aid in the 21st Century* (New York: Office of Development Studies, United Nations Development Programme, 1996), 7.

42. World Bank, *Assessing Aid: What Works, What Doesn't, and Why* (Washington, DC: Oxford University Press, 1998), 7.

43. Riddell, *Aid in the 21st Century*, 9.

44. Ibid., 24.

45. World Bank, *World Bank Development Report 1990* (New York: Oxford University Press, 1990), 127.

46. S. Owen Vandersluis and P. Yeros, eds., *Poverty in World Politics: Whose Global Era?* (Houndsmills: Macmillan, 2000), 58.

47. For example, World Bank, *Assessing Aid,* 11.

48. Ibid., 39.

49. L. Demery and M. Walton, *Are Poverty Reduction*

and Other 21st Century Social Goals Attainable? (Washington, DC: World Bank, 1998).

50. Riddell, *Aid in the 21st Century*, 11.

51. D. Booth, ed., *Rethinking Social Development: Theory, Research, and Practice* (Harlow: Longman Scientific & Technical, 1994).

52. World Bank, *Assessing Aid,* 23.

53. Ibid., 13.

54. O. Törnquist, *Politics and Development: A Critical Introduction* (London: Sage, 1999), 99.

55. Vandersluis and Yeros, eds., *Poverty in World Politics,* 18.

56. Ibid., 18.

57. Ibid., 19.

58. World Bank, *Assessing Aid*, 116, 89.

59. Ibid., 11.

60. Ibid., 14.

61. Riddell, *Aid in the 21st Century,* 11–12.

62. Vandersluis and Yeros, eds., *Poverty in World Politics,* 15.

63. Ibid., 25.

64. Ibid., 159.

65. P. Gibbon, Y. Bangura, and A. Ofstad, eds., *Authoritarianism, Democracy and Adjustment: The Politics of Economic Reform in Africa* (Uppsala: Scandinavian Institute of African Studies, 1992), 52.

66. G. Arnold, *Aid and the Third World: The North/South Divide* (London: Robert Royce, 1985), 163–64.

67. For example, a 1999 report, *Can Africa Claim the 21st Century?* by the World Bank, the Africa Economic Research Consortium, ABD, Global Coalition on Africa, and UNECA, says that many African countries are worse off today than they were at independence in the 1960s. Africa barely accounts for 1 percent of global GDP and only 2 percent of world trade. Over the past thirty years, African countries have lost market share even in primary goods. Many of them have foreign debts accumulated through earlier foreign aid and borrowings. The report attempted (poorly) to end up with an optimistic note.

68. Gibbon, Bangura, and Ofstad, *Authoritarianism, Democracy and Adjustment,* 52.

69. World Bank, *Assessing Aid,* 3.

70. S. Gill, "Globalization, Market Civilization and Disciplinary Neo-liberalism," *Millennium Journal of International Studies* 24, 3 (1995): 393–423. Gill called the World Bank an agent of disciplinary neoliberalism.

71. J. Weiss, *Economic Policy in Developing Countries: The Reform Agenda* (London: Prentice Hall, 1995), 134.

72. Ibid., 132.

73. J. Mittelman and A. Tambe, "Global Poverty and Gen-

der," in J. Mittelman, *The Globalization Syndrome: Transformation and Resistance* (Princeton, NJ: Princeton University Press, 2000), 74.

74. L. Hogben, *Statistical Theory: The Relationship of Probability, Credibility and Error* (New York: W. W. Norton, 1968), 252–53.

75. P. Krugman, "Competitiveness: A Dangerous Obsession," *Foreign Affairs,* March-April 1994, 8.

76. World Bank, *Assessing Aid,* 60.

77. Ibid., 121.

78. B. Ingham, *Economics and Development*, (London: McGraw-Hill, 1995), 365–66.

79. K. Deininger et al., "Does Economic Analysis Improve Quality of Aid Assistance," *World Bank Economic Review* 12, no. 3 (1998): 2.

80. Ibid., 12.

81. Ibid., 13.

82. R. Cassen and associates, *Does Aid Work? Report to an Intergovernmental Task Force* (New York: Oxford University Press, 1986), 87.

83. Ibid., 87.

84. Ibid., 88.

85. M. Black, *Learning What Works: A 20 Year Retrospective View on International Water and Sanitation Cooperation, 1978–1998* (Washington, DC: UNDP–World Bank, Water and Sanitation Program, 1998).

86. Ibid., 4.

87. Ibid., 5.

88. Ibid., 11.

89. L. Masua and A. Makokha, *Legal and Institutional Options for Community Management of Water Supplies in Kenya* (Washington, DC: UNDP–World Bank Water and Sanitation Program, 1997), 4.

90. Black, *Learning What Works,* 24–25.

91. Ibid., 28.

92. Ibid., 27.

93. Ibid., 28.

94. Ibid., 55–56.

95. J. Sara, A. Gross, and C. Van Den Berg, *Rural Water Supply and Sanitation in Bolivia: From Pilot Project to National Program* (Washington, DC: UNDP-World Bank Water and Sanitation Program, 1996), 7.

96. Black, *Learning What Works,* 29, 22.

97. Black called it "a menu of options that in price, appeal and technology matched the potential market." *Learning What Works,* 57.

98. Ibid., 62.

99. Ibid., 52.

100. Vandersluis and Yeros, eds., *Poverty in World Politics,* 158.

Notes to Chapter 7

1. C. Patten, *East and West: The Last Governor of Hong Kong on Power, Freedom, and the Future* (London: Macmillan, 1998), 134–35.

2. T. Friedman, *The Lexus and Olive Tree* (New York: Anchor Books, 2000).

3. C. Henderson, *Asia Falling: Making Sense of the Asian Crisis and Its Aftermath* (New York: McGraw-Hill, 1998), 94–95.

4. Krugman, *The Return of Depression Economics* (New York: Norton, 1999), 87.

5. Ibid., 101.

6. Henderson, *Asia Falling*, 162, 211.

7. World Bank, *The East Asian Miracle: Economic Growth and Public Policy*, World Bank Policy Research Report 1020–0851 (New York: Oxford University Press, 1996), 213.

8. World Bank, *East Asia Recovery and Beyond* (Washington, DC: World Bank, 2000), 14.

9. *American Banker* (August 20, 1998), 5.

10. "Prudence Begins at Home," *Financial Times* editorial, September 26–27, 1998.

11. World Bank, *East Asia: The Road to Recovery* (Washington, DC: World Bank, 1998), 35–36.

12. Henderson, *Asia Falling*, 95.

13. Krugman, *The Return of Depression Economics*, 160.

14. World Bank, *East Asia Recovery and Beyond*, 15.

15. Interview in the *Times of India,* December 31, 1997.

16. Krugman, *The Return of Depression Economics*, 100–101.

17. Henderson, *Asia Falling*, 200.

18. D. Dwor-Frécaut, F. Colaço, and M. Hallward-Driemeir, eds., *Asian Corporate Recovery: Findings from Firm-Level Surveys in Five Countries* (Washington, DC: World Bank, 2000), 14.

19. BAPPENAS (national development planning agency), "Indonesia: The Impact of the Economic Crisis on Industry Performance," in Dwor-Frécaut, Colaço, and Hallward-Driemeir, eds., *Asian Corporate Recovery,* 143.

20. M. Kawai, H. Hahm, and G. Iarossi, "Corporate Foreign Debt in East Asia: Too Much or Too Little," in Dwor-Frécaut, Colaço, and Hallward-Driemeier, eds., *Asian Corporate Recovery,* 111.

21. M. Hallward-Driemeier, D. Dwor-Frécaut, and F. Colaço, "Asian Manufacturing Recovery: A Firm-Level Analysis," in Dwor-Frécaut, Colaço, and Hallward-Driemeier, eds., *Asian Corporate Recovery,* 14.

22. C. Morris, *Money, Greed, and Risk: Why Financial Crises and Crashes Happen* (New York: Times Business, 1999).

23. R. Wade and F. Veneroso, "The Asian Crisis: The High Debt Model Versus the Wall Street Treasury–IMF–Complex," *New Left Review* 228 (1998).

24. Henderson, *Asia Falling*, 216.

25. A. Amsden, *Asia's Next Giant: South Korea and Late Industrialization* (New York: Oxford University Press, 1989), 219.

26. Friedman, *The Lexus and the Olive Tree,* 59–67.

27. Patten, *East and West,* 146–72.

28. World Bank, *East Asia Recovery and Beyond,* 19.

29. J. Hoagland, "East Asia Takes a Time-Out for Globalization," *International Herald Tribune,* September 1, 1997.

30. World Bank, *The East Asian Miracle,* 1.

31. Amsden, *Asia's Next Giant,* 8.

32. S. Suh, "Economy in Historical Perspective," in V. Corbo and S. Suh, eds., *Structural Adjustment in a Newly Industrialized Country: The Korean Experience* (Baltimore: Johns Hopkins University Press, 1992), 7.

33. Ibid., 11.

34. Ibid., 15.

35. Ibid., 19.

36. Ibid., 20.

37. Ibid., 21.

38. Ibid., 24.

39. Wan-Soon Kim, "The Korean Economy in Distress: Major Challenges in the 1990s," in T. Kawagoe and S. Sekiguchi, *East Asian Economies: Transformation and Challenges* (Singapore: Institute of Southeast Asian Studies, 1995), 341.

40. A. Savada and W. Shaw, eds., *South Korea: A Country Study* (Washington, DC: Federal Research Division, Library of Congress, 1992), 156.

41. Kim, "The Korean Economy in Distress," 344.

42. Ibid., 342.

43. Ibid., 369.

44. World Bank, *Global Economic Prospects and the Developing Countries 1998/9: Beyond Financial Crisis* (Washington, DC: World Bank, 1999), 75.

45. I. Verchere, "A Tiger Economy Losing Its Stripes—Is the 'New Japan' Coming Full Circle?" *World Press Review,* July 1997, 10.

46. Economist Intelligence Unit Country Report, South Korea, 3rd Quarter, 1997.

47. World Bank, *Global Economic Prospects,* 73.

48. N. Choi and D. Kang, "A Study on the Crisis, Recovery, and Industrial Upgrading in the Republic of Korea," in Dwor-Frécaut, Colaço, and Hallward-Driemeier, eds., *Asian Corporate Recovery,* 162.

49. Ibid., 165.

50. BAPPENAS, "Indonesia," 150.

51. Ibid., 147.

52. Henderson, *Asia Falling*, 99.

53. J. Fallows, *Looking at the Sun: The Rise of the New East Asian Economic and Political System* (New York: Pantheon, 1994), 316.

54. Henderson, *Asia Falling*, 198.

55. R. Garnaut, "Economic Lessons," in R. McLeod and R. Garnaut, eds., *East Asia in Crisis: From Being a Miracle to Needing One?* (London: Routledge, 1998), 353.

56. R. Garran, *Tigers Tamed: The End of the Asian Miracle* (Honolulu: University of Hawaii Press, 1998), 159.

57. P. Hirst and G. Thompson, *Globalization in Question: The International Economy and the Possibilities of Governance*, 2d ed. (Cambridge: Polity Press, 1999), 138.

58. P. Aghion, P. Bacchetta, and A. Banerjee, "Capital Markets and the Instability of Open Economies," in P. Agénor et al., eds., *The Asian Financial Crisis: Causes, Contagion and Consequences* (Cambridge: Cambridge University Press, 1999), 168–79.

59. Fallows, *Looking at the Sun,* 399.

60. K. Lee, S. Urata, and I. Choi, "Industrial Organization: Issues and Recent Developments," in Corbo and Suh, eds., *Structural Adjustment in a Newly Industrialized Country,* 206.

61. J. Jacobs, *Cities and the Wealth of Nations: Principles of Economic Life* (New York: Random House, 1984), 154.

62. A. Tanzer, "Silicon Valley—East," *Forbes,* June 1, 1998, 127.

63. Fallows, *Looking at the Sun,* 398.

64. S. Meyanathan and I. Salleh, "Malaysia," in S. Meyanathan, ed., *Industrial Structures and the Development of Small and Medium Enterprise Linkages: Examples from East Asia* (Washington, DC: World Bank, 1994), 23.

65. K. Wie, "Indonesia," in Meyanathan, ed., *Industrial Structures,* 115.

66. "Taiwan Semiconductors: Nice Market, We'll Take It," *The Economist,* July 4, 1998, 92.

67. Fallows, *Looking at the Sun,* 387.

68. S. Kuo, G. Ranis, and J. Fei, *The Taiwan Success Story: Rapid Growth with Improved Distribution in the Republic of China, 1952–1979* (Boulder, CO: Westview Press, 1981), 143.

69. Friedman, *The Lexus and the Olive Tree*, 47–51.

70. M. Obstfeld and K. Rogoff, *Foundations of International Macroeconomics* (Cambridge: MIT Press, 1999), 456.

71. Friedman, *The Lexus and the Olive Tree*, 67.

72. G. Easterbrook, "Who's Afraid of Globalization," *Wall Street Journal,* April 14, 2000.

73. J. Garten, "Lessons for the Next Financial Crisis," *Foreign Affairs,* March/April 1999.

74. W. Tabb, "Progressing Globalism: Challenging the Audacity of Capital," *Monthly Review* 50, 9 (February 1999).

75. Wade and Veneroso, "The Asian Crisis," 20.

76. Friedman, *The Lexus and the Olive Tree*, 464.

77. P. Marber, *From Third World to World Class: The Future of Emerging Markets in the Global Economy* (Reading, MA: Perseus Books, 1998), 36.

78. Friedman, *The Lexus and the Olive Tree*, 342–43.

79. Friedman says that "globalization is the international system that has replaced the Cold War system." Ibid., 29.

80. Easterbrook, "Who's Afraid of Globalization."

81. Garten, "Lessons for the Next Financial Crisis," 77.

82. D. Macintyre, "Korea Thinks Small," *Time*, April 19, 1999.

83. Hirst and Thompson, *Globalization in Question,* 69.

84. Garten, "Lessons for the Next Financial Crisis."

85. Krugman, *The Return of Depression Economics*, 158.

86. P. Krugman, "Recovery? Don't Bet on It," *Time,* June 21, 1999.

87. World Bank, *Global Economic Prospects and the Developing Countries 2000,* 47.

88. Ibid., 3, 17.

89. Obstfeld and Rogoff, *Foundations of International Macroeconomics,* 454.

90. W. Sengenberger and F. Wilkinson, "Globalization and Labour Standards," in J. Michie and J. Smith, *Managing the Global Economy* (New York: Oxford University Press, 1995), 113.

91. D. Appleyard and A. Field Jr., *International Economics* (New York: Irwin/McGraw-Hill, 1998), 195.

92. There is, therefore, the suggestion that national economies should be managed simply as part of a global system. Global considerations should be accorded priority.

93. A. Singh and A. Zammit, "Employment and Unemployment, North and South," in J. Michie and J. Smith, eds., *Managing the Global Economy* (New York: Oxford University Press, 1995), 113.

94. J. Chamberlain, *The Roots of Capitalism* (Indianapolis: Liberty Press, 1976), 207.

95. Hirst and Thompson, *Globalization in Question*, 95, 69.

96. G. Rist, *The History of Development: From Western Origins to Global Faith,* trans. P. Camiller (London: Zed Books, 1997), 138–69.

97. Henderson, *Asia Falling*, 63.

98. "Is the Mexico Model Worth the Pain?" *Wall Street Journal*, March 8, 1999.

99. The U.S. rescue and the cushion provided to Mexico may have contributed to the failure to see the East Asian crisis coming.

100. Henderson, *Asia Falling*, 79.

101. J. Mittelman, *Globalization Syndrome* (Princeton: Princeton University Press, 2000), 75.

102. World Bank, *Global Economic Prospects and the Developing Countries 1998/99,* xix.

103. Friedman, *The Lexus and the Olive Tree*, 438–39.

104. World Bank, *East Asia Recovery and Beyond,* 113–37.

105. World Bank, *Global Economic Prospects and the Developing Countries 1998/99,* xix, 107.

106. Krugman, *The Return of Depression Economics*, 151–53.

107. *Wall Street Journal,* March 2, 2000.

108. D. Roberts, "In China It Is a Black Hole," *Business Week,* June 22, 1998.

109. D. Perkins, "Industrial and Financial Policy in China and Vietnam: A New Model or Replay of the East Asian Experience?" in J. Stiglitz and S. Yusuf, eds., *Rethinking the East Asian Miracle* (Washington, DC: World Bank; New York: Oxford University Press, 2001), 247.

110. J. Lin and Y. Yao, "Chinese Rural Industrialization in the Context of the East Asian Miracle," in Stiglitz and Yusuf, eds., *Rethinking the East Asian Miracle,* 144. The authors' emphasis on rural industry was, however, wrong. As we showed, the factor proportions of the rural and state industries in China are not too different.

111. N. Hughes, "Smashing the Iron Rice Bowl," *Foreign Affairs,* July/August 1998, 73.

112. Ibid.

113. Lin and Yao, "Chinese Rural Industrization in the Context of the East Asian Miracle."

114. P. Bowring, "China: Gradual Economic Reform Presupposes Growth," *International Herald Tribune,* April 28, 1998, 8.

115. Perkins, "Industrial and Financial Policy in China and Vietnam," 253.

116. Ibid.

117. F. Li and J. Li, *Foreign Investment in China* (New York: St. Martin's Press, 1999), 203.

118. Lin and Yao, "Chinese Rural Industrialization," 155.

119. Y. Wang, "FDI and Industrial Development in China," Working Paper 1997–013, China Center for Economic Research, Beijing University.

120. Lin and Yao, "Chinese Rural Industrialization," 155.

121. Perkins, "Industrial and Financial Policy in China and Vietnam," 251.

122. Lin and Yao, "Chinese Rural Industrialization."

123. Ibid.

124. J. Studwell, *The China Dream* (New York: Atlantic Monthly Press, 2002), 192.

125. G. Chang, *The Coming Collapse of China* (New York: Random House, 2001), 191.

126. S. Panitchpadki and M. Clifford, *China and the WTO* (Singapore: John Wiley & Sons [Asia], Pte. Ltd., 2002), 32.

127. Studwell, *The China Dream,* 192–93.

128. Ibid., 194.

129. Ibid., 194–95.

130. James Kynge, "China: Economic Transition Fails to Inspire Foreign Confidence," *Financial Times* (April 11, 2002); "Burned Once," *Wall Street Journal*, March 10, 2004; "A Billion Three, But Not for Me," *Economist*, March 20, 2004.

131. Studwell, *The China Dream,* 196.

132. Panitchpadki and Clifford, *China and the WTO,* 22.

133. Studwell, *The China Dream,* 199.

134. Ibid., 263, 264.

135. This is not dissimilar to measurements that have been carried out over the years by some development economists regarding telephone usage. It was claimed that the number of telephones connected per thousand population correlated with economic growth.

136. Friedman, *The Lexus and the Olive Tree,* 372.

137. Ibid., 372–73.

138. Ibid., 47.

139. B. Crossette, "Making Room for the Poor in a Global Economy," *New York Times,* April 16, 2000.

140. Peter Landes, "G8 Creates 'Dot-Force' to Help Poor Countries Tap Technology," *Wall Street Journal,* July 24, 2000.

141. For example, Morris claimed that the financial sector is an economy's plumbing system. He argues that a company failure—even by a company like IBM—is like a broken sink, but that the failure of the financial sector threatens the entire water system. Morris, *Money, Greed and Risk,* 233.

142. D. Ranson and P. Russell, "Has Globalization Built a House of Cards? No, a Beehive," *Wall Street Journal,* December 2, 1998.

143. Marber, *From Third World to World Class,* 35.

144. B. Eichengreen, *Toward a New International Financial Architecture: A Practical Post-Asia Agenda* (Washington, DC: Institute of International Economics, 1999), 1.

145. M. Feldstein, "Refocusing the IMF," *Foreign Affairs,* March/April 1998, 20–33.

146. M. Porter and H. Takeuchi, "Fixing What Really Ails Japan," *Foreign Affairs,* May/June 1999.

147. D. Emmerson, "Americanizing Asia," *Foreign Affairs,* May–June 1998.

148. P. Krugman, "Depression Economics Returns," *Foreign Affairs,* January–February 1999, 74.

149. Ibid.

150. *Safeguarding Prosperity in a Global Financial System: The Future International Financial Architecture: Report of an Independent Task Force Sponsored by the Council on Foreign Relations* (Washington, DC: Institute for International Economics, 1999).

151. H. Soesastro, "Long-Term Implications for Developing Countries," in McLeod and Garnaut, eds., *East Asia in Crisis*, 317.

152. Morris, *Money, Greed and Risk*, 221.

153. J. Stiglitz, "Financial Markets and Development," *Oxford Review of Economic Policy* 5, 4 (1989): 59–68; and "Boats, Planes and Capital Flows," *Financial Times,* March 25, 1998.

154. *Safeguarding Prosperity in a Global Financial System,* 4–7.

155. Garten, "Lessons for the Next Financial Crisis," 90.

156. M. Feldstein, "A Self-Help Guide for Emerging Markets," *Foreign Affairs,* March/April 1999, 93.

157. J. Tobin, "Why We Need Sand in the Market's Gears," *Washington Post,* December 21, 1997, A23.

158. Interview in *Times of India,* December 31, 1997.

159. Wade and Veneroso, "The Asian Crisis," 20–21.

160. J. Micklethwart and A. Woodbridge, *A Future Perfect: The Challenges and Hidden Promise of Globalization* (London: Heinemann, 2000), xxii.

161. J. Garten, "Lessons for the Next Financial Crisis," 88.

Notes to Chapter 8

1. T. Cochran and W. Miller, *The Age of Enterprise: A Social History of Industrial America* (New York: Macmillan, 1942), 2.

2. J. Chamberlain, *The Enterprising Americans: A Business History of the United States*, new ed. (New York: Harper and Row, 1974), 1–2.

3. S. Ratner, J. Soltow, and R. Sylla, *The Evolution of the American Economy: Growth, Welfare, and Decision Making* (New York: Basic Books, 1979), 184.

4. G. Walton and H. Rockoff, *History of the American Economy*, 8th ed. (Fort Worth: Dryden Press, 1998), 52.

5. Ibid., 52.

6. D. Landes, *The Wealth and Poverty of Nations: Why Some Are So Rich and Some So Poor* (New York: W. W. Norton, 1998), 297.

7. Ratner, Soltow, and Sylla, *The Evolution of the American Economy,* 185.

8. Chamberlain, *The Enterprising Americans*, 82.

9. R. Fogel (*Railroads and American Economic Growth: Essays in Econometric History* [Baltimore: Johns Hopkins University Press, 1964]) and A. Fishlow (*American Railroads and the Transformation of the Antebellum Economy* [Cambridge, MA: Harvard University Press, 1965]) have sought to show that the railway was not indispensable to the economic growth of America. Economic growth arises only when capital, labor, and material interact. Transport is not economic growth.

10. Walton and Rockoff, *History of the American Economy*, 120.

11. Ibid., 140.

12. Ibid., 155.

13. A. Chandler Jr., "Anthracite Coal and the Beginnings of the Industrial Revolution in the United States," *Business History Review* 46 (1972): 141–81.

14. Chamberlain, *The Enterprising Americans*, 12.

15. Ibid., 112–13.

16. J. L. Bishop, "British Imperial Policy and the Economic Interpretation of the American Revolution," *Journal of Economic History* 28 (1968): 438.

17. L. Hunter, "Influence of the Market upon Technique in the Iron Industry in Western Pennsylvania up to 1860," *The Journal of Economic and Business History* 1 (1928–29): 244.

18. Ibid., 88.

19. Ibid., 245.

20. *Pittsburgh Gazette,* December 10, 1852.

21. F. Overman, *The Manufacture of Iron* (Philadelphia: H.C. Baird, 1850).

22. J. Swank, *History of the Manufacture of Iron in All Ages* (Philadelphia: 1892), 366.

23. Hunter, "Influence of the Market," 251.

24. Ibid., 250.

25. R. Gordon, "Custom and Consequence: Early Nineteenth-Century Origins of the Environmental and Social Costs of Mining Anthracite," in J. McGaw, ed., *Early American Technology: Making and Doing Things from the Colonial Era to 1850* (Chapel Hill: University of North Carolina Press, 1994), 248.

26. Ibid.

27. Hunter, "Influence of the Market," 256.

28. Ibid.

29. H. Faulkner, *American Economic History,* 7th ed. (New York: Harper and Row, 1954), 70–71.

30. Walton and Rockoff, *History of the American Economy*, 216.

31. Ibid.

32. Ratner, Soltow, and Sylla, *The Evolution of the American Economy*, 282.

33. R. Cameron, *A Concise Economic History of the World: From Paleolithic Times to the Present,* 2nd ed. (New York: Oxford University Press, 1993), 231.

34. P. Uselding, "Studies in the Technological Development of the American Economy During the First Half of the Nineteenth Century," *Journal of Economic History* 31, 1 (1971): 264–65.

35. P. Uselding, "Factor Substitution and Labor Productivity Growth in American Manufacturing 1839–1899," *Journal of Economic History* 32, 3 (September 1972): 80–81.

36. Ibid.

37. Walton and Rockoff, *History of the American Economy*, 216.

38. W. Sundstrom, "Internal Labor Markets Before World War I: On-the-Job Training and Employee Promotion," *Explorations in Economic History* 25, 4 (1988): 425–45.

39. M. Abramovitz and P. David, "Convergence and Deferred Catch-up: Productivity Leadership and the Waning of American Exceptionalism," in R. Landau, T. Taylor, and G. Wright, eds., *The Mosaic of Economic Growth* (Stanford: Stanford University Press, 1996), 22–23.

40. Y. Brenner, *A Short History of Economic Progress: A Course in Economic History* (London: Cass, 1969), 171.

41. Ibid.

42. Cameron, *A Concise Economic History of the World*, 229.

43. Ratner, Soltow, and Sylla, *The Evolution of the American Economy*, 197.

44. L. Davis et al., *American Economic Growth: An Economist's History of the United States* (New York: Harper and Row, 1972), 288.

45. Walton and Rockoff, *History of the American Economy*, 227.

46. H. Habakkuk, *American and British Technology in the Nineteenth Century: The Search for Labour-Saving Inventions* (Cambridge: Cambridge University Press, 1962), 33.

47. Ibid., 25, 34.

48. Ibid., 99.

49. *New York Industrial Exhibition: Special Report of M. G. Wallis and J. Whitworth* (UK parliamentary paper, 1854), xxxvi.

50. Habbakuk, *American and British Technology*, 104.

51. Ibid., 28.

52. This point was one of the central principles of technology that we sought to enunciate in Chapter 3. It is clear that the fixed or near-fixed coefficients of factors that dominate conventional economics of technology are only a late-twentieth-century idea with no theoretical support.

53. Habakkuk, *American and British Technology*, 29.

54. Ibid., 30–31.

55. G. Cole, *Introduction to Economic History, 1750–1950* (London: Macmillan, 1952), 55.

56. Habakkuk, *American and British Technology*, 34.

57. Ibid.

58. Ibid.

59. *Report of Committee on Machinery* (UK parliamentary paper, 1854), 360.

60. Habakkuk, *American and British Technology*, 107.

61. D. Burn, "The Genesis of American Engineering Competition 1850–1870," *Economic History* (supplement to the *Economic Journal*) 55 (1935): 161.

62. Brenner, *A Short History of Economic Progress*, 171.

63. Walton and Rockoff, *History of the American Economy*.

64. Ratner, Soltow, and Sylla, *The Evolution of the American Economy*, 167.

65. Cochran and Miller, *The Age of Enterprise*, 14, 76, 53, 189, 298.

66. Davis et al., *American Economic Growth*, 288.

67. Burn, "The Genesis of American Engineering Competition," 161.

68. Ratner, Soltow, and Sylla, *The Evolution of the American Economy*, 196.

69. Habakkuk, *American and British Technology*, 123–24.

70. Ibid., 204.

71. G. Gunderson, *A New Economic History of America* (New York: McGraw-Hill, 1976), 156.

72. L. Cain and D. Paterson, "Factor Biases and Technical Change in Manufacturing: The American System, 1850–1919," *Journal of Economic History* 41, 2 (June 1981): 342–43.

73. Gunderson, *A New Economic History of America*, 157.

74. The widening horizon in technology may have modified this finding because substitutability between capital and material is now very high in many sectors as we noticed in Chapter 5.

75. Cain and Paterson, "Factor Biases and Technical Change," 349.

76. Though Cain and Paterson started their study with a four-factor model (the fourth factor was called "residual"), they seem to have abandoned the fourth factor in their conclusion. They admitted that the exact components of the residual were not well known to them. They introduced this fourth factor because, dealing with financial aspects, they felt compelled to allow for costs that are incidental to technical production but not part of it, e.g., salaries. The authors also felt impelled to introduce TFP into their analysis. But they seem to have forgotten that TFP only recognizes two physical factors—capital and labor. They were incorrect to claim that the source of TFP arose from rearrangement of factors over time.

77. J. Williamson, "Did English Factor Markets Fail During the Industrial Revolution?" in N. Crafts et al., eds., *Quantitative Economic History* (Oxford: Clarendon Press, 1991), 75–76.

78. Cole, *Introduction to Economic History, 1750–1950,* 59.

79. T. Marshall, "The Population Problems During the Industrial Revolution," *Economic History,* no. 4 (1929): 438.

80. R. Floud and D. McCloskey, eds., *The Economic History of Britain Since 1700,* 2nd ed. (Cambridge: Cambridge University Press, 1994), 1:290–91.

81. W. Smith, *An Historical Introduction to the Economic Geography of Great Britain* (London: G. Bell & Sons, 1968), 144–45.

82. Habakkuk, *American and British Technology,* 139.

83. Ibid., 143.

84. Floud and McCloskey, *Economic History of Britain Since 1700,* 1: 290.

85. M. Dobb, *Studies in the Development of Capitalism* (London: George Routledge & Sons, 1947), 317.

86. Floud and McCloskey, *Economic History of Britain Since 1700,* 1: 295.

87. Smith, *An Historical Introduction to the Economic Geography of Great Britain,* 147, 149, 160.

88. Habakkuk, *American and British Technology,* 205.

89. Cole, *Introduction to Economic History,* 24.

90. Habakkuk, *American and British Technology,* 157.

91. Cameron, *A Concise Economic History of the World,* 226.

92. Habakkuk, *American and British Technology,* 158.

93. Ibid., 159.

94. Ibid.

95. Ibid., 200.

96. Burn, "The Genesis of American Engineering Competition, 1850–1870."

97. *Artisans Report, Exhibitions of 1867* (UK parliamentary paper), 200.

98. W. Langer, *Political and Social Upheaval, 1832–1852* (New York: Harper and Row, 1969), 32–33.

99. Habakkuk, *American and British Technology,* 190–91.

100. J. Fraser, *Report to School Inquiry Commission* (UK parliamentary paper, 1867), 496.

101. J. Anderson, R. Burn, and T. Warlow, *Report of the Commission on the Machinery of the United States* (UK parliamentary paper), 1854–55), 77.

102. W. Lewis, *Growth and Fluctuations, 1870–1913* (London: George Allen and Unwin, 1978), 129.

103. N. Rosenberg, *Technology and American Economic Growth* (New York: Harper and Row, 1972), 75.

104. L. Lau, "The Sources of Long-Term Economic Growth: Observations from the Experience of Developed and Developing Countries," in R. Landau, T. Taylor, and G. Wright, eds., *The Mosaic of Economic Growth* (Stanford: Stanford University Press, 1996), 89.

105. "End of the Road," *Iron Age,* March 31, 1931, 3.

106. H. McCracken, "Technological Change, Monopolistic Competition, and Unemployment," in Edward Chamberlain, *The Theory of Monopolistic Competition* (1931); reprinted in R. Himmelberg, ed., *The Great Depression and American Capitalism* (Boston: Heath, 1968), 37, 38.

107. Franklin D. Roosevelt, *The Public Papers and Addresses of Franklin D. Roosevelt,* comp. S. Rosenman (New York: Random House, 1938), 163–65.

108. Cochran and Miller, *The Age of Enterprise,* 139.

109. Walton and Rockoff, *History of the American Economy,* 392.

110. "Problems of Industrial Maturity," *Iron Age,* March 12, 1931, 880.

111. A. Adams, "Monopoly of Power," in R. Himmelberg, ed., *The Great Depression and American Capitalism* (Boston: Heath, 1968), 19.

112. E. Erickson, "The Great Crash of October 1929," in H. van der Wee, ed., *The Great Depression Revisited: Essays on the Economics of the Thirties* (The Hague Nijhoff, 1972), 6.

113. "Oil Industry's Ills Laid on Price Cuts," *New York Times,* September 21, 1929, 31.

114. "Rationing Outputs Urged in Industry," *New York Times,* September 22, 1929, 20.

115. Cochran and Miller, *The Age of Enterprise,* 141.

116. A. O'Brien, "Factory Size, Economies of Scale, and the Great Merger Wave of 1898–1902," *Journal of Economic History* 48 (1988): 639–49.

117. McCracken, "Technological Change, Monopolistic Competition, and Unemployment," 39.

118. Davis et al., *American Economic Growth,* 288.

119. R. McElvaine, *The Great Depression: America, 1929–1941* (New York: Times Books, 1984), 37.

120. Ibid.

121. Ibid.

122. Roosevelt, *Public Papers,* 163–65.

123. McElvaine, *The Great Depression,* 37.

124. R. Gordon, "Exhaustion of Industrial Opportunities," in R. Himmelberg, ed., *The Great Depression and American Capitalism* (Boston: Heath, 1968).

125. Walton and Rockoff, *History of the American Economy.*

126. J. Atack and P. Passell, *A New Economic View of American History: From Colonial Times to 1940,* 2nd ed. (New York: W. W. Norton, 1994).

127. "Men or Machines," interview in *Sunday New York Post,* February 4, 1934, 15.

128. "Organize for Curb on Unemployment," *New York Times,* August 23, 1929, 16.

129. Ibid.

130. "Hazelwood Warns Banks on Credit," *New York Times,* October 2, 1929, 5.

131. "Bank Sees Benefit in Slackened Trade," *New York Times,* October 1, 1929, 46.

132. "Financial Market," *New York Times,* September 22, 1929, N9.

133. "The Merchant's Point of View," *New York Times,* September 29, 1929.

134. P. Temin, "The Great Depression: Real and Imagined Causes," in S. Engerman and R. Gallman, eds., *The Cambridge Economic History of the United States* (Cambridge: Cambridge University Press, 2000), 3:304–5.

135. Ibid., 304.

136. M. Friedman and A. Schwartz, *Monetary Trends in the United States and the United Kingdom, Their Relation to Income, Prices, and Interest Rates, 1867–1975* (Chicago: University of Chicago Press, 1982), 122.

137. P. Temin, *Did Monetary Forces Cause the Great Depression?* (New York: W. W. Norton, 1976), 172.

138. R. Szostak, *Technological Innovation and the Great Depression* (Boulder, CO: Westview Press, 1995), 13.

139. P. Krugman, "The Return of Depression Economics," *Foreign Affairs,* January/February 1999, 58.

140. M. Skousen, *Economics on Trial: Lies, Myths, and Realities* (Homewood, IL: Business One Irwin, 1991), 110–11.

141. Ibid.

142. Krugman, "The Return of Depression Economics."

143. J. C. R. Dow, *Major Recessions: Britain and the World, 1920–1995* (New York: Oxford University Press, 1998), 440.

144. Ibid.

145. E. Phelps, *Structural Slumps: The Modern Equilibrium Theory of Unemployment, Interest, and Assets* (Cambridge, MA: Harvard University Press, 1994), 162.

146. Atack and Passell, *A New Economic View of American History,* 592.

147. Roosevelt, *Public Papers,* 163–65.

148. Adams, "Monopoly of Power," 18–20.

149. McElvaine, *The Great Depression.*

150. Ibid., 38.

151. Ibid., 38–39.

152. Ibid., 40.

153. P. Sylos-Labini, *The Forces of Economic Growth and Decline* (Cambridge, MA: MIT Press, 1984), 236–37.

154. U.S. Department of Labor, *Economic Forces in the United States in Facts and Figures* (Washington, DC: US Government Printing Office, 1956).

155. D. Shannon, ed., *The Great Depression* (Englewood Cliffs, NJ: Prentice-Hall, 1960), 8–9.

156. "Rationing Outputs Urged in Industry," 20.

157. "Merchant's Point of View," *New York Times,* August 29, 1929, 20.

158. "Rationing Outputs Urged in Industry," 20.

159. M. Blackford, *The Rise of Modern Business in Great Britain, the United States, and Japan,* 2nd ed. (Chapel Hill: University of North Carolina Press, 1998), 95.

160. L. Corey, *The Decline of American Capitalism* (New York: Covici, Friede, 1935), 124.

161. Ibid., 80.

162. G. Smiley, "Did Incomes for Most of the Population Fall from 1923 Through 1929?" *Journal of Economic History* 42 (1983): 209–16.

163. Walton and Rockoff, *History of the American Economy,* 504.

164. C. Philips, T. McManus, and R. Nelson, *Banking and the Business Cycle: A Study of the Great Depression in the United States* (New York: Macmillan, 1937), 58.

165. Corey, *The Decline of American Capitalism.*

166. C. Snyder, "Overproduction and Business Cycles," *Proceedings of the Academy of Political Science* 14, 3 (June 1931): 358.

167. Temin, "The Great Depression. Real and Imagined Causes," 303–4.

168. J.-O. Hairault, P.-Y. Hénin, and F. Portier, eds., *Business Cycles and Macroeconomic Stability: Should We Rebuild Built-in Stabilizers?* (Boston: Kluwer Academic, 1997), 197.

169. J. Morgan, "Manic-Depressive Psychoses of Business," in R. Himmelberg, ed., *The Great Depression and American Capitalism* (Boston: Heath, 1968), 9–15.

170. Between 1927 and 1929, for example, net new domestic corporate financing by common stock increased by 42 percent.

171. Subject to the substitution effect between labor and material in the economy.

172. Corey, *The Decline of American Capitalism,* 124.

173. "Final Markets," *New York Times,* September 22, 1929.

174. Walton and Rockoff, *History of the American Economy,* 490.

175. Ibid., 531–32.

176. C. Brown, "Fiscal Policy in the Thirties: A Reappraisal," *American Economic Review* 46 (December 1956): 879.

177. Walton and Rockoff, *History of the American Economy,* 534.

178. Ibid.

179. Bureau of the Census, U.S. Department of Commerce, "Capital in Manufacturing Industries 1863–1970 in the Historical Statistics of the United States," *Colonial Times to 1970, Part 2* (Washington, DC: GPO).

180. Walton and Rockoff, *History of the American Economy*, 535.

181. Indeed, by 1939 many U.S. companies invested to profit from supplying European countries that were at war.

182. H. Vatter, *The U.S. Economy in World War II* (New York: Columbia University Press, 1985), 14.

183. B. Jones, "The Role of Keynesians in Wartime Policy and Postwar Planning, 1940–1946," *American Economic Review* 62, 2 (May 1972): 125–34.

184. R. Higgs, "Wartime Prosperity? A Reassessment of the U.S. Economy in the 1940s," *Journal of Economic History* 52 (1992): 56.

185. Ibid., 43.

186. S. Kuznet, *National Product in War Time* (New York: National Bureau of Economic Research, 1945).

187. Ibid., 7.

188. J. Cape, ed., *The American Century—People, Power and Politics: An Illustrated History* (London: Pimlico, 1998), 346.

189. D. Novick, M. Anshen, and W. Truppner, *Wartime Production Controls* (New York: Columbia University Press, 1949), 15.

190. Vatter, *The U.S. Economy in World War II*, 14.

191. Walton and Rockoff, *History of the American Economy*, 504.

192. E. Janeway, *The Struggle for Survival: A Chronicle of Economic Mobilization in World War II* (New Haven: Yale University Press, 1951), 195.

193. Vatter, *The U.S. Economy in World War II*, 18–19.

194. U.S. Secretary of the Treasury, *Final Report of the Reconstruction Finance Corporation* (Washington, DC: GPO, 1959), 135.

195. E. Shapiro and M. Mendelson, "A Decade of Corporate Capital Investment, 1946–1955," in R. Freeman, ed., *Postwar Economic Trends in the United States* (New York: Harper, 1960), 312.

196. Bureau of the Census, *Historical Statistics of the United States Colonial Times to 1970: Part 2* (New York: Basic Books, 1976); D. Wilson, "Wartime Construction and Expansion," *Survey of Current Business,* October 18, 1944 (reprinted in G. Hooks, *Forging the Military-Industrial Complex: World War II's Battle of the Potomac* [Urbana: University of Illinois Press, 1991]), puts the total cost of manufacturing plant and machinery in the United States from July 1940 to December 1943 as $20.5 billion ($13.7 billion public and $6.8 billion private).

197. Vatter, *The U.S. Economy in World War II*, 14–16.

198. Ibid., 20.

199. Walton and Rockoff, *History of the American Economy*, 566.

200. Hooks, *Forging the Military-Industrial Complex,* 129, 159.

201. Janeway, *The Struggle for Survival*, 195.

202. "War Council Set Up by Auto Industry," *New York Times,* January 1, 1942, 21.

203. Janeway, *The Struggle for Survival*, 193–94.

204. *New York Times,* November 2, 1943.

205. Novick, Anshen, and Truppner, *Wartime Production Controls,* 15.

206. Janeway, *The Struggle for Survival*, 176.

207. *New York Times,* January 11, 1943.

208. Vatter, *The U.S. Economy in World War II*, 28–29.

209. Hooks, *Forging the Military-Industrial Complex*, 239.

210. "Half a Century of Progress 1894 to 1944. Facts and Figures About Growth of Economic Life in the United States," *Investor Syndicate of Minneapolis* (1945).

211. Walton and Rockoff, for example, commented, "America's decision to mass-produce the weapons of war turned out to be a brilliant success. . . . Not only were supplies such as small arms and ammunitions mass-produced but also planes and even ships to carry the arms to the theatres of war." *History of the American Economy,* 521.

212. Vatter, *The U.S. Economy in World War II*, 60.

213. Ibid., 61.

214. Ibid.

215. H. Zinn, *A People's History of the United States* (New York: Harper Colophon, 1980), 416.

216. Vatter, *The U.S. Economy in World War II*, 158.

217. Shapiro and Mendelson, "A Decade of Corporate Capital Investment," 315.

218. E. Mandel, *The Second Slump: A Marxist Analysis of Recession in the Seventies*, trans. J. Rothschild (London: NLB, 1978), 31.

219. "Keynes Attacks Fund Plan Critics," *New York Times,* July 7, 1944, 9.

Notes to Chapter 9

1. A. Greenspan, "Is There a New Economy," speech at the Haas Annual Business Faculty Research Dialogue, University of California, Berkeley, California, September 4, 1998.

2. *Economic Report of the President* (Washington, DC: U.S. Government Printing Office, 2001), 21.

3. A. Greenspan, "The American Economy in a World Context," 35th Annual Conference on Bank Structure and Competition, Chicago, May 6, 1999.

4. S. Lohr, "Computer Age Gains Respect of Economists," *Wall Street Journal,* April 14, 1999, A1.

5. A. Greenspan, "Information, Productivity, and Capital Investment," speech to the Business Council, Boca Raton, Florida, October 28, 1999.

6. Raul Romer of Stanford, known for his theories on growth, was quoted as saying, "Visionaries will exaggerate and overstate and disdain. And in the end, the economy of the next century will not be dramatically different from the economy of this century." *Washington Post,* January 18, 2000.

7. A. Greenspan, "Technology and the Economy," speech to the Economic Club of New York, January 13, 2000.

8. Greenspan, "Information, Productivity, and Capital Investment."

9. Ibid., 24.

10. Ibid., 23.

11. P. Petzinger Jr., "There's a New Economy Out There—and It Looks Nothing Like the Old One," *Wall Street Journal,* January 1, 2000, 21.

12. Ibid., 27.

13. Greenspan, "The American Economy in a World Context."

14. Greenspan, "Technology and the Economy," 3.

15. Ibid., 3.

16. Ibid., 1.

17. Ibid., 2.

18. Ibid., 4.

19. Federal Reserve Board, *Monetary Report to Congress, Part II,* July 20, 2000, 8.

20. *Financial Times,* October 9, 2000.

21. Greenspan, "The American Economy in a World Context," 5.

22. Ibid.

23. *Economic Report of the President,* 29.

24. Ibid., 98.

25. Greenspan, "Information, Productivity and Capital Investment," 3.

26. For example, the Council of Economic Advisers has constructed a table of labor productivity growth under twenty-six broad industry headings by percentage points from 1989 to 1995 and 1995 to 1999. Yet the council warned that their results should not be taken as definitive (*Economic Report of the President,* 32).

27. L. Uchitelle, "In a Productivity Surge, No Proof of a 'New Economy,'" *New York Times,* October 8, 2000.

28. Petzinger, "There's a New Economy Out There," 21.

29. *Economic Report of the President,* 29.

30. Ibid., 29.

31. Greenspan, "The American Economy in a World Context," 5.

32. *Economic Report of the President,* 62.

33. Ibid., 95.

34. Federal Reserve Board, *8th Annual Report to Congress,* July 2000, 68–69.

35. Ibid., 68.

36. For example, extra insulation materials have sometimes been used to reduce heat emission and thus increase output.

37. Semiconductors, even though they are loosely regarded as IT, do not have the electronic digital origins of the other IT activities displayed in the table.

38. K. Kelly, *New Rules for the New Economy: Ten Radical Strategies for a Connected World* (New York: Viking, 1998).

39. W. Mitchell, *E-topia* (Cambridge, Mass.: MIT Press, 1999), 13.

40. K. Seltzer and T. Bentley, *The Creative Age: Knowledge and Skills for the New Economy* (London: Demos, 1999), 13.

41. A. Greenspan, "Trade and Technology," speech to the Federal Reserve Board, Minneapolis, September 30, 1999.

42. R. Brinner, "Is Inflation Dead?" Federal Reserve Bank of Boston, January 1999.

43. A. Carruth, M. Hooker, and A. Oswald, "Input Prices and Unemployment Equilibria: Theory and Evidence for the United States," *Review of Economics and Statistics* 80 (November 1998).

44. Greenspan, "Technology and the Economy."

45. Ibid., 6.

46. L. Uchitelle, "Epitaph for a Rule That Just Won't Die," *New York Times,* July 30, 2000, 4BU.

47. R. Bootle, *The Death of Inflation: Surviving and Thriving in the Zero Era,* new ed. (London: Nicholas Brealey, 1997), 216.

48. Ibid., 211.

49. Ibid., 197.

50. S. Weber, "The End of the Business Cycle?" *Foreign Affairs* 76, 4 (July/Aug. 1997).

51. Ibid., 68.

52. Ibid., 69.

53. A. Greenspan, Testimony: Monetary Policy Report to the Congress U.S. House, Federal Reserve Board, Feb. 2002, 6.

54. Ibid., 6

55. Ibid., 7.

56. Ibid., 8.

57. Bootle, *The Death of Inflation: Surviving and Thriving in the Zero Era*, 209.

58. Ibid., 205.

59. Ibid., 209.

60. World War II was a period when the U.S. economy moved toward a balanced economy, as we saw in Chapter 8. Not only was the economy coming out of a recession, when major concentration investments did not take place, but the period was one in which the economy was highly regulated—a command economy. There was no time in the war emergency to plan and implement large capital-intensive projects. The private sector was reluctant to invest its resources in the war projects.

61. Mitchell, *E-topia,* 13.

62. N. Beck, *Excelerate: Growing in the New Economy* (London: HarperCollins, 1996), 47.

Notes to Chapter 10

1. M. Mandel, *The Coming Internet Depression: Why the High-Tech Boom Will Go Bust, Why the Crash Will Be Worse than You Think, and How to Prosper Afterward* (New York: Basic Books, 2000).

2. C. Farrell, "The Case for Optimism," *Business Week,* October 9, 2000, 183.

3. World Bank, *Entering the 21st Century: World Development Report 1999/2000* (New York: Oxford University Press, 2000), 65.

4. A. Greenspan, "Technology and the Economy," speech to the Economic Club of New York, January 13, 2000, 5.

5. S.J. Stiglitz, *Globalization and Its Discontents* (New York: Norton, 2002).

6. In recent times, some conventional economists have begun to say that the bottleneck is human capital, others say it is knowledge and information, and yet others say it is technology.

Index

Clement Onyemelukwe is the Chairman and founder of Colechurch International Ltd., an international project promotion and management company. Mr. Onyemelukwe is an engineer and economist. The author of three previous books on management and economic development, he has published many articles in technical and economic journals. He now lives in the United States with his American wife.